Analyzing Digital Discourse and Human Behavior in Modern Virtual Environments

Bobbe Gaines Baggio
American University, USA

A volume in the Advances in Human and Social
Aspects of Technology (AHSAT) Book Series

Information Science
REFERENCE
An Imprint of IGI Global

Published in the United States of America by
Information Science Reference (an imprint of IGI Global)
701 E. Chocolate Avenue
Hershey PA, USA 17033
Tel: 717-533-8845
Fax: 717-533-8661
E-mail: cust@igi-global.com
Web site: http://www.igi-global.com

Library of Congress Cataloging-in-Publication Data

Names: Baggio, Bobbe, editor.
Title: Analyzing digital discourse and human behavior in modern virtual
  environments / Bobbe Baggio, editor.
Description: Hershey, PA : Information Science Reference, [2016] | Includes
  bibliographical references and index.
Identifiers: LCCN 2015047367| ISBN 9781466698994 (hardcover) | ISBN
  9781466699007 (ebook)
Subjects: LCSH: Virtual reality--Social aspects. | Information
  technology--Social aspects. | Communication and technology. | Digital
  communications.
Classification: LCC HM851 .A623 2016 | DDC 302.23--dc23 LC record available at http://lccn.loc.gov/2015047367

This book is published in the IGI Global book series Advances in Human and Social Aspects of Technology (AHSAT)
(ISSN: 2328-1316; eISSN: 2328-1324)

British Cataloguing in Publication Data
A Cataloguing in Publication record for this book is available from the British Library.

For electronic access to this publication, please contact: eresources@igi-global.com.

Advances in Human and Social Aspects of Technology (AHSAT) Book Series

Ashish Dwivedi
The University of Hull, UK

ISSN: 2328-1316
EISSN: 2328-1324

MISSION

In recent years, the societal impact of technology has been noted as we become increasingly more connected and are presented with more digital tools and devices. With the popularity of digital devices such as cell phones and tablets, it is crucial to consider the implications of our digital dependence and the presence of technology in our everyday lives.

The **Advances in Human and Social Aspects of Technology (AHSAT) Book Series** seeks to explore the ways in which society and human beings have been affected by technology and how the technological revolution has changed the way we conduct our lives as well as our behavior. The AHSAT book series aims to publish the most cutting-edge research on human behavior and interaction with technology and the ways in which the digital age is changing society.

COVERAGE

- ICTs and human empowerment
- Cultural Influence of ICTs
- Technoself
- Public Access to ICTs
- Gender and Technology
- Computer-Mediated Communication
- Technology Adoption
- Cyber Bullying
- Technology Dependence
- Human Rights and Digitization

IGI Global is currently accepting manuscripts for publication within this series. To submit a proposal for a volume in this series, please contact our Acquisition Editors at Acquisitions@igi-global.com or visit: http://www.igi-global.com/publish/.

Titles in this Series

For a list of additional titles in this series, please visit: www.igi-global.com

Cultural, Behavioral, and Social Considerations in Electronic Collaboration
Ayse Kok (Bogazici University, Turkey) and Hyunkyung Lee (Yonsei University, South Korea)
Business Science Reference • copyright 2016 • 374pp • H/C (ISBN: 9781466695566) • US $205.00 (our price)

Handbook of Research on Cultural and Economic Impacts of the Information Society
P.E. Thomas (Bharathiar University, India) M. Srihari (Bharathiar University, India) and Sandeep Kaur (Bharathiar University, India)
Information Science Reference • copyright 2015 • 618pp • H/C (ISBN: 9781466685987) • US $325.00 (our price)

Human Behavior, Psychology, and Social Interaction in the Digital Era
Anabela Mesquita (CICE – ISCAP/Polytechnic of Porto, Portugal & Algoritmi Centre, Minho University, Portugal) and Chia-Wen Tsai (Ming Chuan University, Taiwan)
Information Science Reference • copyright 2015 • 372pp • H/C (ISBN: 9781466684508) • US $200.00 (our price)

Rethinking Machine Ethics in the Age of Ubiquitous Technology
Jeffrey White (Korean Advanced Institute of Science and Technology, KAIST, South Korea) and Rick Searle (IEET, USA)
Information Science Reference • copyright 2015 • 331pp • H/C (ISBN: 9781466685925) • US $205.00 (our price)

Contemporary Approaches to Activity Theory Interdisciplinary Perspectives on Human Behavior
Thomas Hansson (Blekinge Institute of Technology, School of Management (MAM), Sweden)
Information Science Reference • copyright 2015 • 404pp • H/C (ISBN: 9781466666030) • US $195.00 (our price)

Evolving Issues Surrounding Technoethics and Society in the Digital Age
Rocci Luppicini (University of Ottawa, Canada)
Information Science Reference • copyright 2014 • 317pp • H/C (ISBN: 9781466661226) • US $215.00 (our price)

Technological Advancements and the Impact of Actor-Network Theory
Arthur Tatnall (Victoria University, Australia)
Information Science Reference • copyright 2014 • 331pp • H/C (ISBN: 9781466661264) • US $195.00 (our price)

Gender Considerations and Influence in the Digital Media and Gaming Industry
Julie Prescott (University of Bolton, UK) and Julie Elizabeth McGurren (Codemasters, UK)
Information Science Reference • copyright 2014 • 357pp • H/C (ISBN: 9781466661424) • US $195.00 (our price)

DISSEMINATOR of KNOWLEDGE

www.igi-global.com

701 E. Chocolate Ave., Hershey, PA 17033
Order online at www.igi-global.com or call 717-533-8845 x100
To place a standing order for titles released in this series, contact: cust@igi-global.com
Mon-Fri 8:00 am - 5:00 pm (est) or fax 24 hours a day 717-533-8661

Table of Contents

Section 1
Working and Learning in Virtual Environments

Section 2
Human Behaviors and Discourse in Modern Virtual Environments

Detailed Table of Contents

Section 1
Working and Learning in Virtual Environments

This section explores the challenges of humans who work and learn in modern virtual environments and what makes them unique, perplexing, and different.

Chapter 1

Jamie S. Switzer, Colorado State University, USA
Ralph V. Switzer, Colorado State University, USA

As the use of virtual teams becomes increasingly more common in all types of organizations, those involved must have the knowledge to operate efficiently and collaboratively and communicate effectively, particularly the virtual team leaders. Virtual teams will not succeed without strong leadership. Many traditional leadership principles apply to virtual teams, but virtual team leaders have additional challenges. This chapter examines the role of virtual team leaders and determines what characteristics and behaviors are exemplified by those leaders, using an instrument developed by Jim Kouzes and Barry Posner. The Leadership Practices Inventory (LPI) identifies five practices and behaviors of successful leaders. Additionally, embedded in the "Five Practices of Exemplary Leadership" model are behaviors that serve as the basis for learning to lead, called "The Ten Commitments of Leadership."

Chapter 2

Latonia M. Ayscue, La Salle University, USA

Perception research helps to understand how stimuli (gist) interacts with learners' sensory systems (visual, auditory, tactile). Communication in virtual learning environments is significant because when the laws of perception are manifested, the strategy should include discovering how the relationships between the instructional design process (analyze, design, develop, implement and evaluate) synthesizes learning theories and learners' experience to create effective communication in virtual instructional events, learning objectives and goals.

Chapter 3

Susanne Ingle, Kuprevich Consulting, USA
Carol L. Kuprevich, Kuprevich Consulting, USA

The authors present anecdotal and peer reviewed information relative to the increase in use of technology within behavioral healthcare. Emphasis is on education, training, professional community development, and networking aspects of the field. The use of email discussion lists, blogs, conferences, and online training management tools are discussed. The authors define the use of technology in workforce development, build out examples of use, explore different methods of digital discourse, and discuss the challenges of technology implementation in a clinical setting. The authors attempt to provide both sides of the debate as to whether the increased use of technology in workforce development within behavioral healthcare is working while addressing the overall expectation to reduce costs, provide positive outcomes, and increase the skills and knowledge of a diverse workforce. This chapter provides an overall picture of types of technology are offered and a general overview of the benefits and opportunities for improvement specific to the development of the healthcare workforce.

Chapter 4

Pete B. Rive, Auckland University of Technology, New Zealand

Design innovation increasingly requires cross-functional virtual teams and is becoming plural, collaborative and distributed. In order for global companies to compete they must be able to sync with the rapidly increasing pace of change and be able to tap the international talent that may, in the future, only connect via virtual worlds and virtual reality. It is important to recognise how design innovation and knowledge flow are regulated and how the virtual ecosystem can either inhibit or excite collaboration and the creation of new ideas, and the design of useful prototypes. This chapter presents a theoretical framework using three models, with examples, to explain and understand how virtual design teams can identify the regulation of knowledge flow and collaboration in the virtual world, Second Life.

Chapter 5

Petros Chamakiotis, University of Sussex, UK
Niki Panteli, Royal Holloway University of London, UK

Despite the increasing adoption of global virtual teams in industry, and their implications for traditional management practices, creativity within this context has been under-researched, with most studies focusing on students partaking in contrived virtual team projects in educational environments. This chapter focuses on a global virtual organization, Omega (a pseudonym), with the aim of exploring creativity in an organizational virtual team context. Using a qualitative case study approach in a single organization, the study makes the following contributions: (a) it identifies the personal values that motivate creativity; and (b) it explains how individuals, technology, task and organization influence creativity, drawing on the participants' perceptions. Discussed also in the chapter are implications for practice and future research.

Section 2
Human Behaviors and Discourse in Modern Virtual Environments

This section explores human interactions and behaviors in a variety of modern virtual environments.

Whether they are checking out at the grocery store, watching a sporting event or eating out in a restaurant; people are texting. Text messaging has become very popular form of contact. Texting is increasingly a part of the overall communications strategy not only for teens but for everyone. Privacy is the number one reason for sending and receiving text messages. The ability to communicate anytime and anywhere but to do so with privacy makes texting attractive and popular. Although some research has been done on the impact of personality, identity and anonymity on texting messaging, very little definitive conclusions have been established either for usage or preferences. Some research indicates that introverts act more like extroverts and extroverts act more like introvert when they communicate using text messages. More research needs to be done to establish the influence of personality and identity on texting and texting on personality and identity.

This descriptive case study considers a tech-savvy and geographically distributed group of librarians and information professionals, led by an initiative of the Alliance Library System of Illinois, who gathered together to brainstorm and organize ways to provide online users with real library services. Through document analysis of written conversations in their online discussion group, the researcher has explored the development process of these librarians as they began to provide information services to users in the virtual online world of Second Life®.

The wisdom society is the latest iteration of the idea of collective intelligence, which has accelerated due to social media and other online collaborative tools. This chapter offers a background on information, collective intelligence and its elements, virtual environments, and theories that relate to collective intelligence. Benefits and issues related to collective intelligence are detailed, and conditions for optimum collective intelligence, including its transformation through virtual environments, are explained. Individual and group dynamics, and group models are also discussed in terms of their impact on collective intelligence in virtual environments.

Chapter 9

QQ has been a leading force of China's social media revolution both in terms of its user reach and its socio-cultural impact. This chapter offers an analysis of QQ groups based on semi-structured in-depth interviews of 33 users with a particular emphasis on participants' rationales, motivations, and communicative behaviors as displayed in different types of groups. This is accomplished through interrogating a multiple set of individual, collective, social, and contextual factors that shape group dynamics and individual participation. It also discusses the implications of the findings for the scholarship on online communities in general, and the understanding of Chinese online groups in particular.

This chapter discusses the implications of giving and receiving social support in virtual communities and online groups. The chapter first offers a literature review about social support in general, and then delves into specific details about online social support. More specifically, this chapter focuses on informational and socio-emotional support, especially as they pertain to online groups and virtual communities. Three specific examples of online groups and virtual communities studied by the authors are offered, along with research findings and hypotheses. Finally, best practices are outlined for those who are interested in starting and maintaining an online group with the purpose of offering informational and/or socio-emotional support to potential users.

Chapter 11

Mobile communication and devices have raised a series of challenges concerning the delimitation of public and private, intimate and personal spheres. Specifically, and because of its close connection to the nervous system and emotions, these devices allow a wide variety of affordances while, and in accordance to the broad scope of previous dimensions, a series of worrying risks – because of the same relationship and interdependence between users' rational and sensorial sides. Thus, an international state of the art review will be discussed and the results and conclusions of the 'Public and Private in Mobile Communications' European FEDER will be offered. A range of quantitative and qualitative methodologies were applied: surveys about general use and habits, personal data and images; focus groups; interviews in person and by telephone; content analysis with a special focus on social media and an observation ethnography and digital ethnography.

Chapter 12
Yowei Kang, Kainan University, Taiwan
Kenneth C. C. Yang, The University of Texas at El Paso, USA

The digital game industry has contributed disproportionally to the overall U.S. economy and GDP in spite of recent economic recession. The rapid ascent of MMORPGs as an increasingly popular digital game genre has affected the manners that gamers interact with each other to generate a new type of digital discourses and human experiences that are multimodal, synchronous, interactive, and engaging. Despite the existence of ample digital game research in user experience (UX) in the human-computer interaction (HCI) literature, there is a lack of programmatic exploration from a rhetorical perspective to examine the process and outcome of these digital interactions and co-generated discourses. Derived from the concept of "the rhetoric of experience," this book chapter analyzed a representative gaming session captured in real time to study digital discourses that represent various aspects of gameplay experiences in World of Warcraft. The chapter discusses the methodological and theoretical implications of this approach to analyze and study MMORPGs and other digital game genres.

Preface

Virtual communications impact all aspects of our lives. Communications that are mediated with technologies connect people in different ways not only physically but mentally and emotionally. Exploring the theories and models of virtual communications expands our understanding and allow us to compare the past, present and future of communications for the individual, organization and society. Although humans have been communicating virtually since the invention of the telephone, new and emerging technologies continue to expand the reach and the extent of our ability to connect virtually. New ways of communicating virtually have changed how we live life in the workplace, classroom and home. Smart phone technologies and the applications associated with these technologies have enhanced the immediacy of our messages. Compression technologies and increased bandwidth have enabled multiple interactive media delivery in real-time. Open source and cloud-based technologies have provided platforms for creative innovation in our communication methods. Communicating virtually has impacted where we work, when we work and with whom we work. It has changed learning from a classroom experience to an anytime, anywhere individualized and adaptive process. Virtual communications have allowed us to stay in contact with our families and colleagues more often and over greater distances. These ever evolving technologies allow us to share everything and keep a digital record. They influence what we see of the world as much as how we see it. This book addresses and examines the challenges and opportunities of living in a virtual world, globally dispersed but connected by ever changing technologies, rules, norms and mores. It explores digital discourse and human behavior in the virtual workplace, the virtual classroom and with the virtual individual including issues of trust, anonymity, relationships, and connections in virtual worlds. Most importantly it asks important questions and presents opportunities to take the conversation much further because so little is known about the relationship between virtual connectivity and human behaviors (Chorley, Roger& Allen, 2015).

The objective of this reference book is to examine the implications of virtual communications, explore current research and methodologies and provide a foundation for further developing models of human behaviors in environments supported totally by virtual technologies. The book discusses and addresses the differences and challenges that develop when humans communicate virtually and how this impacts working, learning and living. It is written for an audience of government officials, academicians, researchers, students, technology developers, human resource departments, and corporate, institutional and organization leaders but anyone with an interest in the impact of technologies on human behaviors will find this text enlightening and relevant. It will provide researchers with the latest research in virtual communication theories, findings, best practices, and emerging trends and support decisions, and the creation of best practices. Although virtual environments and communications has been studies for more than a decade, along with mobility and human behaviors, our knowledge and understanding of the effects of being "always on" and "perpetually connected" is still in an embryonic stage (Sagerstad & Weilnmann, 2013). Technologies have changed and are continuing to change the conditions of communications, information access, socialization and human behaviors.

THE CHALLENGES AND OPPORTUNITES

The end of the 20th century has produced changes in technologies and new ways of thinking about how people communicate and interact. Early attempts at virtual environments traded the inclusion of technologies for the efficacy of human interaction. Technologies, however, have changed and continue to evolve. The continuing development of these new technologies support the new ways of connecting. The days of faceless interactions are not yet gone, but they are numbered. Video and voice are common place and everywhere. Faceless was then and this is now. Over two decades has passed since individuals began using the internet for all most everything. Technological innovation now successfully connects people to each other and to information and knowledge from almost everywhere on the planet. Today many people have expertise and make decisions and shape perceptions without ever having come in contact because they can freely exchange data and ideas on social platforms of all varieties. Social networks, messaging, blogs, vlogs and other forms of synchronous online communications are being used by everyone. Social media, big data and web and search engine analytics are providing us with more ways to draw strategic meaning and channel this information to corporations, organizations and individuals than ever before. Whether we want it or need it we have "social intelligence" that is looking forward, looking global and capable of changing our lives as it plays out in real time (Harrysson, Metayer & Sarrazin, 2012).

Traditional communications formed people into groups and fostered a top down approach to communications. Social networks take a grassroots and bottom up approach. Some experts in online adaption attribute the surge of internet connectivity to the adaption of social software. Others contend that it is the restructuring of corporations, because of a change in business climate that is making the difference in the way humans communicate. Still another adaption theory says that people are searching for a sense of belonging and community over the internet. Social software is providing a way of making this connection. It is highly probable that each of these theories holds some truth regarding the high adaption rate and ever increasing popularity of social software. Social software undoubtedly adds another way to establish human connections in virtual environments and may help to support collaboration (Kaplan-Leiserson, 2003).

The Millennial Generation has had access to the Internet throughout most of their lives. They are as comfortable communicating digitally as they are face to face. Many may feel more comfortable doing this. They are used to mobility and they are used to interacting in virtual environments. Connecting with friends and coworkers through text messaging may not only be more comfortable for these young people, it may also be a way of connecting differently. Increasingly, those working in virtual environments are coming from nontraditional venues and often have jobs and families. These workers are remote and are often in diverse geographical locations, busy with families and work responsibilities. Fields like mobile healthcare (mHealth) are emerging at astonishing rates, with the ability to serve virtually new populations and populations that were not successfully served before. mHealth is a virtual connection to populations who were unreachable, had limited access to a healthcare workforce or limited financial resources. From affecting behavior change to disseminating vital information, health care is only one example of an industry moving rapidly into virtual environments (Corrnick, Kim, Rodgers, Gibbons, Buekens, Belizan & Althabe, 2012).

Collective contributions have also found their way into the world of the workforce. Social software of all varieties have invaded the virtual workplace. Virtual environments with remote access and inter connectivity has influenced everything including job titles like Web Master and Blog Master to virtual meetings some in virtual worlds. Corporate connectivity is driving company culture and strategy. A global workforce is being connected by technology and an ever changing workplace. Aligning company needs and capitalizing on collective intelligence companies are solving problems and developing strategies to position themselves for the new century, much of which will take place in the virtual workplaces, mobile environments and with global teams.

There is an underbelly to the online virtual world that that grapples with deceit, dishonestly, cheating, authenticity, identity, privacy, and the dark side of just about everything. It also struggles with the reliability of identity, sources, deception and trust. The anonymity present in virtual environments and issues of trust are interrelated. Facial recognition and finger print applications have helped and yet in online virtual environment very few people feel totally relaxed and truly safe or at least not for long. The secrecy and obscurity of faceless communications digitally mediated provides a sense of inscrutability, mystery and ambiguity. Anonymity may affect trust and a person's abilities to discern deception but it may also affect qualitative patterns of communications and conversations in virtual communities (Burgoon, Stoner, Bonito, & Dunbar, 2003). Anonymity is directly tied into privacy and identity. Cultures and countries have different histories and values concerning and an individual's right to privacy. These cultural mores are impacted significantly when the globe is connected and has instant access to almost everything. There is also a dichotomy in virtual communications that suggests the safety of privacy by allowing you to be in your own environment but records in ones and zeros by nature of the technology, every bit of information. Different cultures have chosen different approaches to regulating an individual right to privacy. Some of these are compatible and some are contrasting. The definition of privacy and "time off" has also changed. A community that operates 24/7, 365 has little time off. Virtual workers and teams are faced with a world that is always on and with a day that never ends.

The internet records everything and forgets nothing. It is just the way it currently is on the digital frontier. Little attention has been given so far to ethics, privacy and life in virtual environments. This is true for the length of the employment day and is especially true for personal data. People who have passed on and organizations that are no longer viable can still be up and online and thriving in cyberspace. It has become a really big problem. One of the biggest issues is lack of awareness of what content is out there in digital form and how quickly things can travel in virtual environments. Once something goes viral it is literally everywhere. The reality of cyberspace is that digital finger prints and footprints are being tracked and watched literally online and off. The digital fingerprints and footprints are stored forever. People have been fired from office jobs for complaining of boredom and from NFL position for declaring derogatory opinions of the management. Every NCAA student athlete is warned not to post anything on Facebook you don't want in front of the Commissioner. Human resource professionals are being asked by their companies to do online "research". Anything is fair game from online gaming sites, to Twitter, Instagram, LinkedIn, Facebook or You Tube.

Social networks and connections are blooming like bunnies in the spring time. New video chats and anonymous sex chats, and of course your personal gamer channel are all available. New sites that support intentional anonymity exemplified by sites like Whisper and Secret and YikYak are hosting millions of users who chose to communicate, load and exchange content with the intent of anonymity. These allow people to further hide, post as they please and better protect their offline identities. (Correa, Silva, Mondal, Benevenuto & Gummadi, 2015) In addition to present new threats to privacy, this also presents new threats to psychological health. It is difficult to forget, forgive and move on when the information is permanently archived in the Library of Congress, which by the way bought the files of Twitter since 2006 and has decided to permanently store them. Surely all this chatting and collecting will soon lead to even more analyzing. Now instead of being defined by ancestry, village, class, occupation or job individuals are defined by posts. Social mobility once founded on individualism and achievements may now be limited by social media. The idea of controlling your own identity for different segments of life maybe flawed. Influenced by friends, family, coworkers and neighbors, the idea of the segmented self has become unrealistic. Open or public data is being stored, sold and messaged in ways none of us are aware and new industries are springing up to take care of our reputations online and wipe out what is stored in cyberspace but we can't get our hands on. Digital discourse in virtual environments will only continue to grow as the Internet of Things (IoT) adds to the data explosion and the analytics.

In analyzing digital discourse in virtual environments much that was taken for granted proved to be in need of investigation and this will continue for decades to come. As long as technologies continue to evolve, the way that humans behave and interact with them and each other will continue change also. Simple things that were taken for granted like privacy and protection have vanished in less than a few decades. Large and growing larger, amounts of data are transmitted via networks and the ability to connect and protect both the senders and receivers is a dynamic evolutionary responsibility (Ye, Xiong, Wu, 2013). Yet there is a glimpse into a collective consciousness in virtual environment that supports the best in human behaviors. Often a great deal is made of the dark side of the virtual world but in the worst of times, times of crisis and devastation, there is a great deal of evidence that the information shared is credible and for the common good. A variety of behavioral outcomes ranging from personal responsibility to concern and increased openness give indications that trust and truth are not something that are lost in virtual environments but something that may be evolved and may need to be further explored. This book establishes the need for additional research, and lots of it, as human kind embarks down the road of digital discourse in modern virtual environments (Thomson, Suda, Lin, Liu, Hayasaka, Isochi & Wang, 2012).

ORGANZATION OF THE BOOK

This book is organized into twelve chapters. A brief description of the chapters follows:

Chapter 1, "Virtual Teams: Profiles of Successful Leaders," addresses an aspect of the workforce that is becoming common place in all types of organizations. Virtual teams require new knowledge to operate efficiently and collaboratively and communicate effectively, particularly the virtual team leaders. Virtual teams will not succeed without strong leadership. Many traditional leadership principles apply to virtual teams, but virtual team leaders have additional challenges. Geography, borders, and time zones are rapidly becoming irrelevant in the way today's business and people's personal lives are conducted in virtual environments. A new paradigm for leadership is emerging; the modern virtual environment is changing leadership roles. This chapter will examine the role of virtual team leaders and determine what characteristics and behaviors are exemplified by those leaders.

Chapter 2 looks at the "Perception of Communication in Virtual Learning Environments: What's In It for Them?" Learners' perception of written communication in virtual learning environments can be complex, if there is often no strategy to support the communication or learning process. For practitioners who design communication in virtual learning environments, there is the tendency to focus on the task and activities to deliver the content that impacts learners' educational experiences. Even though there are still controversies over the quality of virtual learning environments, organizations that tried to hold onto the traditional are realizing that learners are departing quickly to venues that affords them the opportunity to choose an environment that best suites them and they are opting to select a virtual learning environment because of the benefits it affords.

Chapter 3 examines the relationship between technology and behavioral healthcare workforce development in the mid twenty-first century. "Workforce Development in Behavioral Healthcare and the Increased Use of Technology: Is it Working or Not? Are We Asking the Right Questions?" assumes the relationship is an ongoing and developing process with pockets of significant use and pockets of slow adapters and evidence of just about every degree of separation between the two. It explores some research on effective dissemination methods of clinical treatment best practices, and how technology plays a role in the acceptance of new practices, but concludes there is a lack of comprehensive studies with actionable items. The objective of this chapter is to provide a broad scope discussion, using multiple types of data sources, regarding the status of the use of technology to advance behavioral healthcare workforce development. Material is presented to encourage further conversation that will lead to specific research studies to support the needs of the workforce in a manner that leads to optimum outcomes for both the workforce and for the recipients of services.

Chapter 4, "Virtual Design Teams in Virtual Worlds: A Theoretical Framework Using Second Life," examines the pervasive discipline of design and the early lessons to be gained from design practice and design education in the virtual world SL (Second Life). Three case studies that were conducted in SL are used to explain examples of how virtual teams collaborate and connect on design projects within that virtual world. The primary research question posed was: how to design a virtual innovation ecology in SL? There were two important sub-questions related to this: what enables knowledge creation during design innovation in SL? What enables creative collaboration amongst designers in SL? The objective of this chapter is to describe a theoretical framework that could provide a useful means of examining how design teams interact in a virtual world when they are sharing a design innovation goal.

Chapter 5, "The World is Your Office: Being Creative in a Global Virtual Organization," aims to improve understanding of creativity within a global virtual organizational context in order to both bridge a theoretical gap and also to inform the practitioner community. An exploratory case study was conducted with a global virtual organization in the sales industry, involving observations and interviews with 15 employees who are members of intra-organizational GVTs, with the aim of advancing understanding of creativity within an organizational, virtual context. The study contributes to theory by (a) identifying the personal values that motivate creativity; and (b) explaining how individuals, technology, task and organization influence creativity, drawing on the participants' perceptions. In what follows, background information on GVTs and creativity is provided drawing on relevant literature.

Chapter 6, "Why We'd Rather Text than Talk: Personality, Identity, and Anonymity in Modern Virtual Environments," explores some explanations why texting is increasingly a part of the overall communications strategy not only for teens but for everyone. Privacy is the number one reason for sending and receiving text messages. The ability to communicate anytime and anywhere but to do so with privacy makes texting attractive and popular. Although some research has been done on the impact of personality, identity and anonymity on texting messaging, very little definitive conclusions have been established either for usage or preferences. The growing popularity of text messaging as a preferred method of communication tells can tell human beings something about not only the characteristics of our virtual environments but about ourselves. Text is a communication form that puts everyone on the same page and within reach. More research is needed to determine the effects texting has on our personalities and how we express ourselves in virtual environments. Also, research is needed to determine how virtual environments support our sense of identity and why we would rather text than meet face to face. Research in this field is in its infancy and many opportunities exist to help us understand the influence virtual environments have on our lives and the influence we have in virtual environments.

Chapter 7, "Analysis of Initial Involvement of Librarians in the Online Virtual World of Second Life," examines how users of the online virtual environment known as Second Life®, are able to contribute their own content, such as topography, buildings, interactive features and objects, to the simulated space they share with others. Development in a virtual world goes through a variety of stages as it takes shape, especially when the development process is negotiated by a diverse group of users with various goals. The librarians of Second Life® have thus discovered and shared many lessons and practices, as well as suggested and improved several system modifications, during the first year of their multi-year development process. The librarians of the Alliance Library System, and their national and international partners, eventually revised key elements to support improved social dynamics about and within the virtual space, and to utilize a virtual world successfully in the provision of library and information services.

Chapter 8, "Using Virtual Environments to Transform Collective Intelligence," defines the wisdom society as the latest iteration of the idea of collective intelligence, which has accelerated due to social media and other online collaborative tools. This chapter offers a broad perspective on information, collective intelligence and its elements, virtual environments, and theories that relate to collective intelligence. Benefits and issues related to collective intelligence are detailed, and conditions for optimum collective intelligence, including its transformation through virtual environments, are explained. Individual and group dynamics, and group models are also discussed in terms of their impact on collective intelligence in virtual environments.

Chapter 9, "Virtual Ties, Perceptible Reciprocity, and Real-Life Gratifications in Online Community Networks: A Study of QQ User Groups in China," examines how the Internet has been a leading force of sociocultural transformation in the past two decades in China, a variety of blossoming platforms of social media have been pushing grassroots-led user-generated communication to ever-new territories. Although Social Networking Service (SNS) sites modeled after Facebook, Twitter and YouTube in China are as earth-shattering as found anywhere in the world (albeit not without significant twists and turns in their processes of adapting to the Chinese soil), one particularly notable hotspot that has defined China's new media culture is the popularization of QQ, an Instant Messaging (IM) service developed by Tencent.

Chapter 10 first reviews the current literature on informational and socio-emotional support broadly, especially as it relates to health outcomes. Then, "Impacts on Society: Informational and Socio-Emotional Support in Virtual Communities and Online Groups" focuses on informational and socio-emotional support as they relate to online interactions. For example, online support can be viewed by everyone in the community, not just the people who are exchanging it. Thus, online informational and socio-emotional support may have a larger effect than face-to-face support. Finally, the authors use data and examples derived from their research program to discuss how online forums have been used by members as a place to find and offer knowledge and comfort to fellow members who are experiencing similar challenges or seeking answers to similar questions. Suggestions for suture research are then discussed.

Chapter 11, "Liquid Communication in Mobile Devices: Affordances and Risks," explores a range of both quantitative and qualitative methodologies to discover user attitudes, behaviors and performances. The intention is to offer a step forward in Portuguese research because few initiatives have been carried so far. This chapter looks at with the different approaches and concepts that framed and continue to attempt to explain the dichotomies between the public and private spheres in virtual communication.

Chapter 12, "Analyzing Multi-Modal Digital Discourses during MMORPG Gameplay through an Experiential Rhetorical Approach," addresses an industry which in the past was often ignored by academics but one that has grown into a market that supports billions dollars. The computer and video game industry has continued to contribute exponentially to the overall U.S. economy and total sales of the industry have grown consistently. Computer and video games impact many other facets of our society and although digital game research has often been marginalized and ignored in the last decade that has changed. Role-playing and interactions with other gamers in the virtual space have generated new research topics to examine, such as notions of self, identity, representation, collaboration, and social interaction.

Bobbe Gaines Baggio
American University, USA

REFERENCES

Burgoon, J., Stoner, G., Bomito, J., & Dunbar, N. (2003). Trust and deception in mediated communications. In *Proceedings of the 36th Hawaii International Conference on System Sciences*. IEEE.

Chorley, M., Whitaker, R., & Allen, S. (2015). Personality and location-based social networks. *Computers in Human Behavior, 46*, 45–56.

Correa, D., Silva, L., Mondal, M., Benevenuto, F., & Gummadi, K. (2015). *The many shades of anonymity: Characterizing anonymous social media content*. Retrieved January 3, 2016 from www.aaai.org/ocs/index.php/ICWSM/ICWSM15/paper/viewFile/10596/10490

Corrnick, G., Kim, N., Rodgers, A., Gibbons, L., Buekens, P., Belizan, J., & Althabe, F. (2012). Interest of pregnant women in the use of SMS (short message service) text messages for the improvement of perinatal and postnatal care. *Reproductive Health, 9*(9).

Harrysson, M., Metayer, E., & Sarrazin, H. (2012, November). How 'social intelligence' can guide decisions. *The McKinsey Quarterly*.

Kaplan-Leiserson, E. (2003, December 15). We learning: Social software and e-learning. *Learning Circuits*. Retrieved January 3, 2016 from learningcircuits.org/2003/dec2003/Kaplan.htm

Segerstad, Y., & Weilenmann, A. (2013). Methodological challenges for studying cross-platform conversations. *Selected Papers of Internet Research, 14*.

Thomson, R., Ito, N., Suda, H., Lin, F., Liu, Y., & Hayasaka, R., … Wang, Z. (2012). *Trusting tweets: The Fukushima disaster and information source credibility on Twitter*. Paper presented at the International ISCRAM Conference, Vancouver, Canada.

Ye, J., Xiong, X., & Wu, S. (2013). Dynamic model for anonymity measurement based on information entropy. *Journal of Internet Services and Information Security, 4*, 27–37.

Section 1
Working and Learning in Virtual Environments

This section explores the challenges of humans who work and learn in modern virtual environments and what makes them unique, perplexing, and different.

Chapter 1
Virtual Teams:
Profiles of Successful Leaders

Jamie S. Switzer
Colorado State University, USA

Ralph V. Switzer
Colorado State University, USA

ABSTRACT

As the use of virtual teams becomes increasingly more common in all types of organizations, those involved must have the knowledge to operate efficiently and collaboratively and communicate effectively, particularly the virtual team leaders. Virtual teams will not succeed without strong leadership. Many traditional leadership principles apply to virtual teams, but virtual team leaders have additional challenges. This chapter examines the role of virtual team leaders and determines what characteristics and behaviors are exemplified by those leaders, using an instrument developed by Jim Kouzes and Barry Posner. The Leadership Practices Inventory (LPI) identifies five practices and behaviors of successful leaders. Additionally, embedded in the "Five Practices of Exemplary Leadership" model are behaviors that serve as the basis for learning to lead, called "The Ten Commitments of Leadership."

INTRODUCTION

The modern world now lives and works in cyberspace. Geography, borders, and time zones are rapidly becoming irrelevant in the way today's business and people's personal lives are conducted. As the use of virtual teams becomes increasingly more common in organizations, those involved must have the knowledge to operate efficiently and collaboratively and communicate effectively, particularly the virtual team leaders. Virtual teams will not succeed without strong leadership. A new paradigm for leadership is emerging; the modern virtual environment is changing leadership roles. Many traditional leadership principles apply to virtual teams, but virtual team leaders have additional challenges. This chapter will examine the role of virtual team leaders and determine what characteristics and behaviors are exemplified by those leaders.

DOI: 10.4018/978-1-4666-9899-4.ch001

Problem Statement

As the use of virtual teams becomes more prevalent in both business and education, those involved must have the knowledge to operate efficiently and effectively, particularly the virtual team leaders. Virtual teams will not succeed without strong leadership. There are still some constants in good leadership regardless of the environment, but a new paradigm for leadership is emerging. The virtual environment, defined by Merriam-Webster (2015) as "existing or occurring on computers or on the Internet," is changing leadership roles. Just because a particular leadership style is effective in a face-to-face environment does not mean it will work in a virtual setting. Many traditional leadership principles apply to virtual teams, but virtual team leaders have additional challenges.

What characteristics are demonstrated by a virtual team leader? What behaviors contribute to the successful leadership of a virtual team? Do leaders in a traditional face-to-face environment demonstrate similar leadership traits in a virtual environment? These are questions that need to be answered as the use of virtual teams becomes more and more prevalent in the modern way of doing business.

Purpose Statement

The purpose of this chapter is to examine if people identified as leaders in a traditional (face-to-face) environment and in a virtual environment (an online MBA) demonstrate leadership characteristics as originally developed by Jim Kouzes and Barry Posner (1995, 2002, 2012) using their instrument, The Leadership Practices Inventory (LPI). Based on their research, the "Five Practices of Exemplary Leadership" model was developed, which identifies five practices and behaviors of successful leaders: Model the Way, Inspire a Shared Vision, Challenge the Process, Enable Others to Act, and Encourage the Heart. Kouzes and Posner also identify behaviors, the "Ten Commitments of Leadership," embedded in the five leadership practices that serve as the basis for learning to become an outstanding leader.

Research Questions

Specifically, this chapter answers the following research questions:

1. Are there similarities or differences in the leadership profiles of identified leaders based upon whether the interaction occurs in a traditional environment or a class-based virtual environment?
2. Are there similarities or differences in the leadership profiles of identified leaders based upon whether the interaction occurs in a traditional environment or a project-based virtual environment while performing a specific task?
3. Are the same people identified as team leaders regardless of the virtual environment (class-based or project-based)?
4. Do people identified as virtual team leaders (class-based or project-based) share any common leadership characteristics? If so, what are those characteristics?

BACKGROUND

To understand the concepts inherent in leading a virtual team, several disciplines must be examined. This literature review explores the topics of leadership, virtual teams, virtual team leadership, and leadership as defined by Kouzes and Posner.

Leadership

Research conducted on the topic of "leadership" has spanned over a century (Day, 2014; Sohmen, 2015). There is still no consensus on what exactly constitutes leadership, despite thousands of empirical studies yielding hundreds of definitions of the term (Evans, 1996; Tobin, 2015). "Leadership in the real world rarely fits exactly into neat theories" (Higson & Sturgess, 2014, p. 1). One thing is certain, however. In today's information-rich, technology-driven society, the traditional concept of leadership must be redefined. The old paradigm of a hierarchical pyramid-shaped organization no longer produces effective results. Machiavellian management styles do not inspire the modern workforce. A new paradigm is necessary – leadership today demands "people who think critically and reflectively with the head of a strategist who make decisions with a moral and ethical heart and who execute strategy with the hand of a collaborative leader" (Kucia & Gravett, 2014, p. 149).

The leader of the future will be one "who creates a culture or a value system centered upon principles... who has the vision, courage, and humility to constantly learn and grow" (Covey, 1996, p. 149). According to Cutler, the challenges facing leaders in the 21st century are innovation, talent management, communications (especially social media), and globalization (2014, p. 225). Successful leadership depends upon the ability to effectively respond to and proactively drive positive change (Puccio, Murdock, and Mance, 2011) and involves a complex web of relationships, practices, and structures (Chreim, 2015).

Leadership is crucial to collective success (in Zaccaro, 2014). In this 21st century global society where traditional roles and job functions are becoming increasingly blurry, the need for strong visionary leadership is all the more critical (Anantatmula & Thomas, 2010; Burke & Barron, 2014; Nanus, 1992). To survive, organizations need to identify and nurture people's potential. The success of these new leaders depends upon understanding and practicing the power of appreciation, reminding people of what is important, generating and sustaining trust, and having the ability to ally with the led (Bennis & Sample, 2015). According to leadership guru Peter Drucker (1995), effective leaders need to know just four simple things:

1. A leader is someone who has followers.
2. An effective leader is not someone who is loved or admired. She or he is someone whose followers do the right things. Popularity is not leadership. Results are.
3. Leaders are highly visible. They therefore set examples.
4. Leadership is not rank, privileges, titles, or money. It is responsibility.

Virtual Teams

Technology and globalization have driven the increasing use of virtual teams (Brake, 2008; Cramton & Webber, 2005). "A virtual team – whether across the street or across the world – is a team whose members simultaneously work together to a common purpose, while physically apart" (Zofi, 2012, p.

7). As Scott states, virtual team members "work interdependently, but are located far from each other, not just across the country, but around the world" (2013, p. 302). Virtual teams address the needs of the new work environment – the office is where the worker is, not the other way around. Organizations utilizing virtual teams can maximize resources and hire the best people for the job regardless of where they live (Lepsinger & DeRosa, 2010). Virtual team members communicate using a variety of information and communication technologies (ICTs), such as email, text messaging, wikis, groupware tools, teleconferencing tools, and even the good old-fashioned telephone.

Virtual teams are geographically dispersed, culturally diverse, and often do not have constant membership. Virtual teams can be difficult to design, costly and complex to implement, a challenge to manage, and far less productive than collocated teams (Klitmoller & Lauring, 2013; Melymuka, 1997). Yet their use continues to expand (Haines, 2014) because there are also opportunities in using virtual teams. Virtual teams must address a variety of challenges, such as cultural differences, technology, communication, time zones, and resources. To be successful, a virtual team requires a strong leader to address those challenges.

Leadership in Virtual Teams

There is a consensus among scholars that leading a virtual team is more challenging than leading a co-located team (in Hoch & Kozlowski, 2014). Most virtual teams exist in environments that are adaptive where the situation is constantly changing, yet traditional styles of leadership do not work well in adaptive situations (Duarte & Snyder, 2006). "The role of leading virtual teams is riddled with complexity" (Zander, Mockaitis, & Butler, 2012, p. 593). Some of the challenges for virtual team leaders include maintaining communication, establishing relationships, and managing conflict (Jonsen, Maznevski, & Davison, 2012). Many of these challenges can be addressed through effective leadership (Avolio, Kahai, & Dodge, 2001). Yet virtual environments require leaders to have different personal skill sets, leadership strategies, and communication techniques than traditional leaders (Neufeld, Wan, & Fang, 2008). Virtual team leaders must have excellent communication skills, be technologically savvy, and be engaging, culturally sensitive, and approachable (in Zander et al., 2012).

Duarte and Snyder (2006) have identified four leadership behaviors that support successful virtual teams. The first is communicating about the business and benefits of virtual teams; that virtual teamwork is respected by everyone involved. Establishing expectations about procedures, goals, and standards for performance is the second behavior. The third leadership behavior is allocating resources for the virtual team; providing time and money for training travel for face-to-face meetings, and resources for technology. The final behavior is modeling – working together across geographic and cultural boundaries as well as soliciting input. Leading a team in an adaptive environment requires leaders to work from a different perspective. Heifetz and Laurie (1997) identified eight principles for leaders in adaptive settings: get on the balcony (look at the big picture), identify the adaptive challenge, regulate distress, maintain disciplined attention, rely on distributed intelligence, encourage leadership by all members of the team, encourage robust communication, and create a learning obligation.

Leaders of virtual teams must possess certain individual competencies above and beyond traditional team leaders. According to a study by Joshi and Lazarova (2005), virtual team leaders must be proficient in direction and goal setting, communication, facilitating teamwork, and motivating and inspiring. Duarte and Snyder (2006) have identified seven competencies necessary for leading a virtual team effectively: coaching and managing performance without traditional forms of feedback; selecting and appropriately using electronic communication and collaboration technologies; leading in a cross-cultural environment; managing the performance, development, and career development of team members; building and maintaining trust; networking across hierarchical and organizational boundaries; and developing and adapting organizational processes to meet the demands of the team.

Leadership as Defined by Kouzes and Posner

Kouzes and Posner (1995, 2012) also believe that the world today is in a state of constant chaos and change. Knowledge is the key. Everyone is linked electronically, yet society has never been more fragmented. Organizations have flattened their hierarchies; the power base has shifted. People are cynics, yet search for meaning in their lives. Kouzes and Posner have developed a leadership model for today's environment, a set of leadership practices based on the real-world experiences of ordinary people who have accomplished extraordinary things – and "how leaders mobilize others to want to make extraordinary things happen in organizations" (2012, p. 2).

"Leadership is everybody's business" (Kouzes & Posner, 1995, p. xxv), yet people increasingly feel there is a serious lack of leadership today. Kouzes and Posner believe this is because of outdated notions about leadership. Traditional teachings state organizations are stable and orderly, lead by emotionless leaders with an eye on the bottom line. It was thought these leaders occupied a superior position because they possessed a special gift reserved for a select few. Yet Kouzes and Posner believe that "we need more exemplary leaders...leaders who can unite us and ignite us" (2012, p. 7).

While almost all leaders do at some time demonstrate similar behaviors, Kouzes and Posner believe leadership is an "observable, learnable set of practices" (Kouzes & Posner, 1995, p. 16), and there are "clearly identifiable behaviors and actions that make a difference" (2012, p. 15). In the new world reality, leaders tend to shake up organizations. They have a long-term vision. They care deeply about others, and support and nurture their organizations. In short, effective leaders have "heart."

Kouzes and Posner define leadership as "the art of mobilizing others to want to struggle for shared aspirations" (1995, p. 30). Fundamentally, leadership is a relationship (2012). There is a reciprocal process between those who choose to lead and those who choose to follow. The majority of people admire and will willingly follow leaders who are honest, forward-looking, inspiring, and competent (2012).

The Five Practices of Exemplary Leadership

From their research, Kouzes and Posner (2012, p. 15) have identified five fundamental practices exhibited by leaders performing at their personal best:

1. Model the way;
2. Inspire a shared vision;
3. Challenge the process;
4. Enable others to act;
5. Encourage the heart.

Kouzes and Posner also identify behaviors, the "Ten Commitments of Leadership," embedded in the five leadership practices that serve as the basis for learning to become an outstanding leader (2012, p. 29).

Model the Way

"Leaders model the way through personal example and dedicated execution" setting examples through simple, daily acts that earn the respect of their constituents (Kouzes & Posner, 1995, p. 13). Leaders articulate their guiding principles and stand up for their beliefs. They base their actions on a collective set of aims and aspirations. They "DWWSWWD: Do What We Say We Will Do" (Kouzes & Posner, 2012, p. 40).

The first commitment for leaders is to set an example by behaving in ways that are consistent with shared values (Kouzes & Posner, 2012). They first reflect upon and identify their own personal values, then write a leadership credo to clarify the principles by which they will lead others. Effective leaders open a dialogue about personal and shared values with their constituents, often swapping jobs with their employees to get and receive feedback. Most importantly, they practice what they preach.

Commitment two calls for leaders to achieve small wins that promote consistent progress and build commitment. They set the example by aligning actions with shared values (Kouzes & Posner, 2012). Leaders always keep the vision in mind, then act and adapt one step at a time. They take everything personally. They make a plan for the organization, creating a model to move forward incrementally and not attempt to accomplish too much at once. Leaders who model the way make certain their constituents are aware of all decisions and progress to stay dedicated. This can be accomplished by simple acts such as taking people out for lunch or dinner.

Inspire a Shared Vision

"Leaders have a desire to make something happen, to change the way things are, to create something that no one else has ever created before" (Kouzes & Posner, 1995, p. 11). They have visions and dreams of the future of the organization, and they clearly communicate them to inspire their constituents. As Kouzes and Posner state, "leaders are expressive, and they attract followers through their energy, optimism, and hope" (2012, p. 100). A vision is an ideal and unique image of the future for the common good.

The third commitment for leaders is to envision the future by imagining exciting and ennobling possibilities (Kouzes & Posner, 2012). Leaders who inspire a shared vision think first about their past. They then build on that foundation to determine what they really want and write a short vision statement. From this statement leaders can test the assumptions underlying the vision as well as clarifying and affirming the vision. To keep the vision current, leaders study the future to look for trends, and often act on their own intuition to further the vision.

Leaders who inspire a shared vision do so by enlisting others to invest in the vision by appealing to their values, interests, hopes, and dreams. The fourth commitment calls for leaders to identify their constituents and find a common ground among people from diverse backgrounds and interests – to enlist others by appealing to shared aspirations (Kouzes & Posner, 2012). Leaders breathe life into the vision by speaking positively, from the heart, and making the intangible tangible. And they listen. Kouzes and Posner (1995, 2012) found that listening is one of the key characteristics of exemplary leaders.

Challenge the Process

"Leaders venture out" (Kouzes & Posner, 1995, p. 9). They challenge the process and strive to change the status quo. Sometimes leaders are the ones who initiate the action; other times they merely recognize and support the new ideas and innovations. Leaders seek and accept challenging opportunities to "test their abilities…(and) motivate others …to exceed their self-perceived limits" (Kouzes & Posner, 2012, p. 157).

"Challenge calls forth leadership" (Kouzes & Posner, 1995, p. 55). The fifth commitment for leaders is to search out challenging opportunities to change, grow, innovate, and improve. To do this, leaders treat every job as an adventure, every new assignment as a new beginning, and begin to do things differently. They shake up the status quo and eliminate practices that are not critical to the organization but merely matters of tradition. They "search for opportunities by seizing the initiative and looking outward for innovative ways to improve" (Kouzes & Posner, 2012, p. 156).

Leaders who challenge the process send people shopping for ideas while at the same time personally gathering new ideas. They collect suggestions and innovations that may identify something within the organization that needs attention. These leaders assign people to investigate possible opportunities for the organization, not just the problems.

Teams that have been together for a while can fall into a rut. Leaders who challenge the process refresh and renew their teams by providing professional development opportunities or rotating the group membership, as well as by taking a class or learning a new skill themselves. These leaders add adventure and fun to everyone's work to keep them motivated.

The sixth commitment for leaders who challenge the process is to experiment and take risks, generating small wins yet learning from the mistakes (Kouzes & Posner, 2012). They set up experiments to determine the effect of a new idea, and create a safe environment for others to experiment. They strive to bring people out of their comfort zones and work with all new ideas, even if they sound a little strange initially. This means taking some risks personally as well as acknowledging the other risk takers.

There will be failure when challenging the process. Leaders debrief every failure as well as every success. This encourages everyone to think positively about challenges and to recognize potential. They provide people with alternative choices when implementing innovative changes. Lastly, when challenging the process, leaders allow the organization to break out of the traditional organizational culture by doing things like making formal clothing and titles optional.

Enable Others to Act

"Leadership is a team effort" (Kouzes & Posner, 1995, p. 11); leaders "know that they can't do it alone… (and) need partners to make extraordinary things happen" (Kouzes & Posner, 2012, p. 215). Effective leaders enable others to act by giving their constituents more authority and information to produce positive results. Particularly in a virtual organization, everyone who has a stake in the vision – peers, managers, customers, suppliers – must function as a team founded on trust and confidence to make the organization successful.

The seventh commitment is for leaders to foster collaboration by promoting cooperative goals, building trust and facilitating relationships (Kouzes & Posner, 2012). This can be accomplished by increasing interaction among people, forming planning and problem-solving partnerships and focusing on gains and not losses. Leaders who enable others to act use the word "we" and create a collaborative organization.

Effective leaders strengthen people by giving power away, providing choices, developing competence, assigning critical tasks, and offering visible support. The eighth commitment calls for leaders to strengthen others by increasing self-determination and developing competence (Kouzes & Posner, 2012, p. 243). Leaders should avoid symbols of power such as staying inside a large, plush office with the door closed. Instead, leaders are connecting with their constituents and other people important to the organization by networking and forming strategic relationships, sharing information and keeping everyone informed. Leaders who enable others give people the training and professional development needed to act with more latitude and authority within the organization, making sure the tasks are relevant and substantive.

Encourage the Heart

"Leaders encourage the heart of their constituents to carry on," uplifting their spirits with genuine acts of caring (Kouzes & Posner, 1995, p. 14). People often become frustrated and disenchanted. It is the leader's job to show people that they can succeed, that the task can be accomplished. Leaders encourage the heart by "visibly recognizing people's contributions to the common vision" (Kouzes & Posner, 2012, p. 272). One way to accomplish this is to celebrate milestones, either with dramatic gestures or simple actions. "When leaders give gifts of the heart, it's the thought that counts the most" (Kouzes & Posner, 1995, p. 308).

Leaders that encourage the heart recognize individual contributions to the success of every project and show appreciation for individual excellence (Kouzes & Posner, 2012). Commitment nine calls for leaders to be creative about rewards and recognition, giving them personally and publicly. By designing the reward system participatively and soliciting feedback, leaders can determine who is deserving of the recognition.

Leaders also celebrate team accomplishments regularly. The tenth commitment for leaders is to celebrate the values and victories of the team by creating a spirit of community (Kouzes & Posner, 2012), scheduling celebrations within the organization and encouraging members of the organization to simply have fun. Leaders who encourage the heart cheer individuals and teams on. They have "their heart in the business and the business in their heart" (Kouzes & Posner, 1995, p. 312).

METHODOLOGY

Operational Definitions of Terms and Descriptions of Concepts/Procedures

There are several terms, concepts, and procedures that will be used and referred to throughout the rest of this chapter that must first be defined.

Online Plus

Online Plus is the university's distance education initiative. Offering its first class using videotape technology in 1968, Online Plus now offers 23 graduate-level degrees that can be earned without a residency requirement. The first distance learner to earn a Masters of Business Administration graduated in 1975. To date, students from all 50 states and 46 foreign countries have earned an AACSB-accredited MBA without setting foot on campus.

Course content is delivered using a variety of technologies. The on-campus MBA class meetings are streamed to distance learners. Class activities streamed are usually professor lectures, group discussions, and student presentations. Exercises and discussions requiring interaction among distance learners are done electronically using a proprietary course-management system utilized by the university.

BUS620

A course titled "BUS620: Leadership and Teams" is a class in the MBA curriculum offered on-campus and via Online Plus. It is a graduate seminar in which advanced topics of leadership and effective teams are explored. Specific topics include: management and leadership activities, the roles of leaders in a dynamic work environment, the relationship of leadership and successful teams, the elements of intra-team and inter-team relationships, diversity in the work environment and how it impacts team processes and performance, and ethical considerations and dilemmas.

In the BUS620 Online Plus syllabus, there are four course objectives: to understand the major concepts of leadership, based on the Kouzes and Posner leadership model and other models of leadership; to understand one's own leadership strengths and weaknesses, based upon insights provided by the LPI model; to experience team decision-making and participation in high-performance teams; and to practice leadership and team skills inside and outside the classroom.

Traditional Environment

Online Plus students never meet in person. There may be very rare exceptions, such as when a group of students at a corporate site elect to enroll in a class together. But for the most part all interaction between Online Plus classmates occurs electronically.

Obviously, each student has contact with people outside of the MBA program: managers, constituents, workplace and/or social peers, and others such as family members. These people are able to learn and know more about each student because of the simple fact they can see each other and observe subtle cues like body language and facial expressions that are not apparent online. A student's personal, physical face-to-face interaction with other people outside of the MBA program constitutes a traditional environment.

Class-Based Virtual Environment

Each distance education student in the BUS620 course is a member of a randomly assigned team that stays together for the duration of the eight-week term. There are 10-12 people per team. Students work in this team on various assignments and tasks throughout the semester. Team interactions occur electronically. This team assignment constitutes the class-based virtual environment.

Project-Based Virtual Environment

Additionally, each virtual team is required to participate in a one-time-only exercise. The team members are the same as in the class-based virtual team, but the interaction is very different. In this project-based virtual environment, team members come together electronically for only three hours and perform a specific task known as "Summit."

Summit

The Summit exercise defines the project-based virtual team environment. Summit explores the interactions between two groups of people and is a complex exercise meant to illustrate the many nuances involved in team interactions. It is conducted for the Online Plus students synchronously and electronically. The purpose of the exercise is to experience first-hand the dynamics of team behavior. Specifically highlighted are issues relating to trust, communication, conflict resolution, and leadership.

The objective of the exercise is to earn points based on decisions made in a war-themed situation. At the beginning of the exercise, each team receives 20 electronic "cards" that represent weapons. The cards are used to symbolically "disarm" the team for the good of all involved, or to "arm" and "attack" the other team. The two teams can work together for their mutual benefit, or each team can chose a path that may benefit the team at the expense of the competing team.

Each team identifies two people as negotiators to work with the other team's two negotiators to determine if they can cooperate and disarm. Another possibility is at the end of the negotiations each team can decide to arm themselves to attack or protect themselves from attack by the other team. The status of the weapons (armed, disarmed, attacking) determines the amount of points earned by the team.

LPI

The Leadership Practices Inventory was developed by Jim Kouzes, Dean's Executive Fellow of Leadership at the Leavey School of Business at Santa Clara University, and Barry Posner, the Accolti Endowed Professor of Leadership at the Leavey School of Business at Santa Clara University (Kouzes & Posner, 2015). In 1982, Kouzes and Posner began a research project to determine patterns of leadership success, and to determine how ordinary people set their own personal leadership standards. They conducted hundreds of interviews and reviewed hundreds of case studies and survey questionnaires. What emerged were the five fundamental practices common to extraordinary leadership achievements discussed earlier.

The LPI is based on a 12-page survey called the Personal-Best Leadership Experience Questionnaire. Respondents took one to two hours to answer 38 open-ended questions such as: Who initiated the project? What did you learn most from this experience? What key lessons would you share with another person about leadership from this experience? Kouzes and Posner collected more than 4000 of the personal-best surveys, and more than 7500 additional responses to a shorter version of the survey.

Additionally, in-depth interviews were conducted with middle- to senior-level managers in a variety of public and private sector companies around the world. The number of collected interviews, ranging in length from 45 minutes to five hours, is well over 500. From the surveys and the interviews, Kouzes and Posner developed their conceptual framework consisting of the five key leadership practices (challenging the process, inspiring a shared vision, enabling others to act, modeling the way, and encouraging the heart).

Kouzes and Posner, with assistance from other experts, wrote statements describing each of the above leadership behaviors and applied them to a five-point Likert scale representing the use of the specific leadership behavior. Following discussion and feedback sessions with respondents and experts in the field as well as empirical analyses, the statements were modified, discarded, or included in the final product.

The LPI consists of 30 statements representing the five different leadership practices; responses are on Likert-type scale from 1 to 10, ranging from "almost never" to "almost always." Raters are asked to be realistic about the extent to which the leader actually behaves, not how they think the leader should behave. From these responses a score ranging from 5 to 60 on each of the five criteria is derived.

There is no one single "leadership score" attained from the LPI, but five separate scores on each leadership practice. For example, a person scoring a high score of 58 on the "modeling the way" behavior is a leader that sets examples and builds commitment through his/her own behavior. A low score of 10 on the "challenging the process" trait indicates that person does not venture out and confront the status quo with radical new ideas.

The LPI is continually being refined and analyzed by the authors and other scholars. To date Kouzes and Posner's database contains over 100,000 respondents (Kouzes & Posner, 2002), information from people who have used the LPI to determine leadership characteristics. The LPI offers a set of leadership behaviors developed by examining the real-world experiences of many people, not just a few famous charismatic men and women. The purpose of the instrument is to assist people in "furthering their abilities to lead others to get extraordinary things done" (Kouzes & Posner, 1995, p. xx).

- **Reliability:** The LPI has been administered in studies of many diverse groups, including high school principals, bank managers, hospital managers, college vice-presidents, business leaders, church leaders, and community college presidents. Based on these and other studies using the LPI, internal reliabilities (Chronbach alphas) range between .77 and .93 (Kouzes & Posner, 2002).

Comparing LPI scores from participants in The Leadership Challenge Workshop every two years since 1987, there is consistency across the five leadership practices, indicating the scores have been relatively stable over time as well as across different countries (Kouzes & Posner, 2012). LPI scores are also generally not related to various demographic factors (such as age or educational level) or organizational characteristics (such as size or functional area).

- **Validity:** The relationship between leader effectiveness as defined by Kouzes and Posner and leadership practices as measured by the LPI is well established. A regression analysis, with leader effectiveness as the dependent variable and the five leadership practices as the independent variables, yields a highly significant regression equation with R-square at .756 and $p<.0001$ (Kouzes & Posner, 2002).

Using discriminant analysis as a classification technique, the LPI has been shown to consistently group managers into various performance-based categories. The LPI correctly classified over 92 percent of managers in low- and high-performing categories, with $p<.001$ (Kouzes & Posner, 2002).

Research Design

This study examined the leadership profiles of peer-identified leaders in three different environments: traditional, class-based virtual, and project-based virtual.

Data Sources

The data was collected from students enrolled in BUS620 virtually via Online Plus; n=207.

Distance students were divided into sections of approximately 40, based as closely as possible on their resident time zone, with a total of 20 sections. Within each section, students were randomly assigned to one team that engaged in two distinct tasks. One of the activities lasted for the entire 8-week duration of BUS620 (the class-based virtual environment) and consisted of team members working together on various assignments and tasks throughout the semester. The other activity was the specific class exercise titled "Summit" that occurred over a period of three hours (the project-based virtual environment).

Completing the LPI was mandatory for all BUS620 distance students. While completing the LPI was a mandatory course requirement, participation in this study was entirely voluntary.

Data Collection Strategies

The data was collected using the LPI survey, and a short demographic survey. LPI surveys were submitted in both paper form and in electronic. In the traditional environment, the LPI was hardcopy because face-to-face interaction was possible. The class-based virtual teams and the project-based virtual teams submitted the demographic survey and the LPI electronically.

Traditional

To determine an LPI score for each student in a traditional environment, students gave a paper version of the LPI to at least three different people. These could be managers, constituents, peers (workplace or social), or others such as family members with whom the student interacted personally and physically face-to-face outside of the MBA program.

Class-Based Virtual

At the end of the semester, team members were asked to identify the person they perceived was the leader of their BUS620 class-based virtual team and electronically submit an LPI for that particular person. If there were multiple LPIs for the same person, those scores were averaged so each student had just one score per each of the five leadership practices.

Project-Based Virtual

At the conclusion of the Summit exercise, team members were asked to identify who they felt was the team leader during the interaction. The project-based virtual team members completed an LPI for the perceived leader and returned the instrument electronically. Multiple LPI scores were averaged and each student had only one score per each of the five leadership practices.

Data Analysis

Research Questions One and Two

Similar methods were used to answer the first two research questions: Are there similarities or differences in the leadership profiles of identified leaders based upon whether the interaction occurs in a traditional environment or a class-based virtual environment; and are there similarities or differences in the leadership profiles of identified leaders based upon whether the interaction occurs in a traditional environment or a project-based virtual environment while performing a specific task.

In the three different environments (traditional, class-based virtual, and project-based virtual), each identified leader had five scores that corresponded to the five characteristics of a leader as identified by Kouzes and Posner (1995, 2012). Descriptive statistical analyses were used to determine if there were similarities or differences in the leadership behaviors of people based upon the environment in which the team interaction occurred as a whole, and if the distinct leadership traits differed according to the environment in which they occurred.

Research Question Three

To determine if the people identified as leaders in the class-based virtual team environment were the same people identified as leaders in the project-based virtual environment, a list of the leaders in each situation was compiled and alphabetized. A simple comparison of lists was done to see if the same names were on each list. If an individual's name appeared on both lists, that person was thereby identified as a virtual team leader regardless of the type of team interaction.

Research Question Four

To determine if those people identified as virtual team leaders in a class-based or project-based environment shared any common leadership traits as defined by Kouzes and Posner (1995, 2012), descriptive statistical analyses were used. Analysis of the results determined if people identified as team leaders in both virtual environments shared any common leadership characteristics.

Descriptive analysis also identified which (if any) common leadership characteristics as defined by Kouzes and Posner were shared by the perceived virtual team leaders. For example, if Student A was identified as a class-based virtual team leader, and Student B was identified as a project-based virtual team leader, did they both score highly on "encouraging the heart"?

Kouzes and Posner's (1997) studies indicate a "high" score is one at the 70th percentile of the thousands of people ranked in their LPI database. The most any one person can possibly score per each of the five leadership criteria is 60. As identified by Kouzes and Posner (1997), a high score in "challenging" is 49 and above; a high score for "inspiring" is 48 and above; a high score for "enabling" is 52 and above; a high score for "modeling" is 51 and above; and a high score for "encouraging" is 50 and above.

RESULTS

Response Rates

There were a little over 200 students on the BUS620 Online Plus roster. Table 1 shows the response rates.

The response rate in the traditional environment is lower because many of the returned LPIs were invalid. Of a possible 621 total LPIs from the three environments, 235 were returned, a response rate of just under 38%.

Table 1. Response rates

Item Returned	n = 207	%
Traditional LPI	38	18
Class-Based LPI	88	43
Project-Based LPI	109	53

Average LPI Profiles

Average LPI profiles for each of the three environments (traditional, class-based virtual, and project-based virtual) were derived from the data collected.

Traditional Environment

Table 2 shows the average LPI profile for students in the traditional environment. Almost 58% of students were taking their first Online Plus class. All but one of the BUS620 teams was represented. Men were 68.4% of the leaders in the traditional environment, but women scored higher than men in all five LPI categories, sometimes by as much as four points (6.7%). The mean age was 35.9, with the majority of students listing their occupations as managers or engineers. There were no significant differences in LPI scores based on team, age, occupation, and the number of Online Plus classes taken.

Class-Based Virtual Environment

Table 3 shows the average LPI profile of the identified leaders in the class-based virtual environment. There were 41 individual leaders selected, with 11 people (26.8%) identifying themselves as the leader.

The mean age of the class-based virtual environment leaders was 36, with just over 70% men. Management, engineering, and finance were once again the majority of the occupations of the students. All but one of the BUS620 teams was represented, with 68.3% of the identified leaders taking their first Online Plus class. Thirty-nine of the class-based virtual environment leaders were also selected by their team members to act as the negotiators during the Summit exercise.

The team scoring the lowest in the project-based virtual environment scored high on all categories but "challenging" in the class-based virtual environment. An additional two teams scored high on everything but "encouraging." Negotiators for the Summit exercise scored higher by two points (3.3%) or less in "challenging," "modeling," and "encouraging." Women scored higher than men in all but "inspiring," but only by two (3.3%) points or less. There were no significant differences in LPI scores based on age, occupation, and the number of Online Plus classes taken.

Table 2. Average LPI profile in the traditional environment

LPI Characteristic	Range	Mean	Median	SD
Challenging	31.5 - 56	46.4	47.3	5.1
Inspiring	31 - 55.7	43.9	44.5	5.7
Enabling	40.5 - 58	49.6	49.5	4.5
Modeling	34 - 56.5	48.2	47.9	4.8
Encouraging	36.5 - 56.5	46.4	46.8	5.5

Table 3. Average LPI profile in the class-based virtual environment

LPI Characteristic	Range	Mean	Median	SD
Challenging	33 - 60	46.6	45.7	5.4
Inspiring	34 - 56	47.3	47	5.1
Enabling	40 - 58	50.7	51	4.3
Modeling	42 - 60	50.7	51	3.8
Encouraging	35 - 58.5	47.4	47.8	5.4

Project-Based Virtual Environment

Forty-five individuals were identified as leaders in the project-based virtual environment. Their average LPI scores are shown in Table 4. Nine people (20%) identified themselves as the leader.

Demographically, the majority of the identified leaders in the project-based virtual environment were again male (75.6%). The mean age was 35.6, with the primary occupations being managers, engineers, and finance. Just over 60% were taking their first Online Plus class, and all teams were represented.

Just over 33% of the people identified as leaders in the project-based virtual environment were chosen by their team members as negotiators in the Summit exercise. One team had the lowest scores for each of the five LPI categories in this environment. Another team scored the highest in all five categories, while another team scored second highest in all but one category.

Men scored slightly higher in "challenging," but women scored higher in the remaining four categories, though only by one two point (1.7%). Summit negotiators scored barely higher in "challenging" and "modeling," with the non-negotiators scoring less than a point higher in the rest of the categories. There were no significant differences in LPI scores based on age, occupation, and the number of Online Plus classes taken.

LPI Scores

None of the mean LPI scores in any of the three environments were high, as shown in Table 5. As defined by Kouzes and Posner, a high score in "challenging" is 49 and above; a high score for "inspiring" is 48 and above; a high score for "enabling" is 52 and above; a high score for "modeling" is 51 and above; and a high score for "encouraging" is 50 and above.

There were identified leaders in each environment that individually scored high on the LPI. Table 6 shows the percentage of students with high scores.

Table 4. Average LPI profile in the project-based virtual environment

LPI Characteristic	Range	Mean	Median	SD
Challenging	38 - 58	46.3	45.5	4.3
Inspiring	34.1 - 58	45.9	45	4.9
Enabling	34.5 - 59	48.7	49	4.8
Modeling	36.5 - 59	48.7	49	3.9
Encouraging	36 - 56	46.9	48	5.2

Table 5. Mean LPI scores in the three environments

LPI Characteristic	Traditional	Class-Based	Project-Based
Challenging (49)	46.4	46.6	46.3
Inspiring (48)	43.9	47.3	45.9
Enabling (52)	49.6	50.7	48.7
Modeling (51)	48.2	50.7	48.7
Encouraging (50)	46.4	47.4	46.9

Table 6. Percentage of leaders with high scores

LPI Characteristic	Traditional	Class-Based	Project-Based
Challenging	24.5	26.5	26.5
Inspiring	12.5	39.6	31.3
Enabling	17.3	32.7	26.9
Modeling	19.6	41.2	31.4
Encouraging	18	30	28

Table 7. Average LPI scores for the traditional environment and the class-based virtual environment

LPI Characteristic	Traditional	Class-Based	Differential
Challenging	46.4	46.6	0.2 (0.3%)
Inspiring	43.9	47.3	3.4 (5.7%)
Enabling	49.6	50.7	1.1 (1.8%)
Modeling	48.2	50.7	2.5 (4.7%)
Encouraging	46.4	47.4	1 (1.7%)

The Research Questions

Research Question One

The first research question asked if there were similarities or differences in the leadership profiles of identified leaders based upon whether the interaction occurred in a traditional environment or a class-based virtual environment. Table 7 shows the average LPI scores for those two environments.

None of the scores in either environment were high (as defined by Kouzes and Posner). The scores in the class-based virtual environment were slightly higher than those in the traditional environment, yet only varied at the most by a little over three points (5.7%). This leads to the conclusion that leadership characteristics as identified by the LPI in a traditional environment and in a class-based virtual environment are similar.

Research Question Two

The second research question asked if there were similarities or differences in the leadership profiles of identified leaders based upon whether the interaction occurred in a traditional environment or a project-based virtual environment. The average LPI scores for those two environments are shown in Table 8.

As was also true with the data from the first research question, none of the average LPI scores were high. Identified leaders in the traditional environment scored just one-tenth of a point (0.8%) higher in "challenging" and less than a point (1.7%) higher on "enabling." The scores for the remaining three leadership characteristics were just slightly higher in the project-based environment, varying at the most

Table 8. Average LPI scores for the traditional environment and project-based virtual environment

LPI Characteristic	Traditional	Project-Based	Differential
Challenging	46.4	46.3	0.1 (1.7%)
Inspiring	43.9	45.9	2 (3.3%)
Enabling	49.6	48.7	1.9 (3.2%)
Modeling	48.2	48.7	0.5 (0.8%)
Encouraging	46.4	46.9	0.5 (0.8%)

by just two points (3.3%). Therefore, the leadership characteristics of students in a traditional environment and in a project-based environment are similar.

Research Question Three

The third research question asked if the same people were identified as team leaders regardless of the virtual environment (class-based or project-based). Of the 62 individual leaders in the two environments, 38.7% were identified as leaders in both the class-based and project-based virtual environments. Table 9 shows their average LPI scores. None of the mean scores were high.

The mean age was 35.1, and three-quarters of the leaders were men. The students had taken an average of only 1.5 Online Plus classes. Almost half (45.8%) of those identified as leaders in both virtual environments were selected by their team members to be the negotiators during the Summit exercise.

Table 10 shows the number of people whose LPI scores all increased or all decreased from the project-based virtual environment (which was administered first) to the class-based virtual environment.

Research Question Four

The final research question asked if people identified as virtual team leaders (class-based or project-based) shared any common leadership characteristics and if so, what were those characteristics. Table 11 shows the mean LPI scores for both those environments.

None of the average scores were high. The class-based virtual LPI scores were slightly higher than the project-based virtual scores, but the mean scores between the two environments varied at most by only two points (3.3%).

Table 12 shows the LPI score averages of the people in the two virtual environments who did score high on each characteristic. Again, the class-based scores were just slightly higher than the project-based scores, and vary only up to 1.1 points (1.8%)

Because there were no real differences in the LPI scores of students in both the class-based virtual and the project-based virtual environments, people identified as team leaders did share common leadership characteristics for each of the five LPI categories. The data indicated, regardless of the virtual environment, the students scored almost exactly the same on each leadership characteristic.

Table 9. Average LPI scores for leaders in both the project-based and class-based virtual environments

LPI Characteristic	Range	Mean	Median	SD
Challenging	35 - 37	47.2	47	4.3
Inspiring	40 - 56	47	46.4	3.9
Enabling	40 - 56	49.1	50	4.2
Modeling	43 - 57	50	50.2	3.2
Encouraging	39 - 58.5	47.7	48	4.6

Table 10. LPI Score total increase or decrease

Direction	n = 24	%	Range
Increase	8	33.3	0.5 - 12
Decrease	2	8.3	0.3 - 18

Table 11. Mean LPI scores for the class-based leaders and the project-based leaders

LPI Characteristic	Class-Based	Project-Based	Differential
Challenging	46.6	46.3	0.3 (0.5%)
Inspiring	47.3	45.9	1.4 (2.3%)
Enabling	50.7	48.7	2 (3.3%)
Modeling	50.7	48.7	2 (3.3%)
Encouraging	47.4	46.9	0.5 (0.8%)

Table 12. Mean high LPI scores for the class-based leaders and the project-based leaders

LPI Characteristic	Class-Based	Project-Based	Differential
Challenging	52.5	51.8	0.7 (1.2%)
Inspiring	51.6	51.4	0.2 (0.3%)
Enabling	54.8	53.7	1.1 (1.8%)
Modeling	53.6	52.6	1 (1.7%)
Encouraging	53	52.5	0.5 (0.8%)

Summary

None of the mean LPI scores in each of the three environments were high (as defined by Kouzes and Posner). Scores in the class-based virtual environment were slightly higher than the project-based virtual environment and the traditional environment, by as little as 0.5% up to only 5.7%. The sex, age, and occupations of the identified leaders were consistent with the makeup of the MBA program and the overall study population, with no single variable having an impact on overall LPI scores. This is consistent with Kouzes and Posner's findings that LPI scores are unrelated to demographic characteristics or organizational features (Kouzes & Posner, 2002, 2012).

There were no differences in the leadership profiles of the identified leaders based upon whether the interaction occurred in a traditional environment and a class-based virtual environment, or in a traditional environment and a project-based virtual environment. Almost 39% of the students were identified as leaders in both of the virtual environments. A little over 33% of the students' LPI scores increased from the project-based virtual environment to the class-based virtual environment, while just over 8% of the students' LPI scores actually decreased. Finally, those identified as leaders in each of the virtual environments shared almost identical leadership profiles; no one leadership characteristic was clearly more evident than any of the others.

SOLUTIONS AND RECOMMENDATIONS

Discussion of LPI Scores

Kouzes and Posner (1995) found, based upon mean scores, enabling others to act is perceived to be the leadership practice most frequently used. As shown in Table 13, all of the environments in the study identified "enabling" as the most-demonstrated leadership practice. While each of the three environments were in almost unanimous agreement on the order of the rest of the LPI characteristics, they did deviate somewhat from those means derived from Kouzes and Posner's research.

Table 13. Most frequently used leadership practices

Kouzes/Posner Most Demonstrated Leadership Practices (Ranked from Most to Least)	Traditional Most Demonstrated Leadership Practices (Ranked from Most to Least)	Class-Based Most Demonstrated Leadership Practices (Ranked from Most to Least)	Project-Based Most Demonstrated Leadership Practices (Ranked from Most to Least)
Enabling	Enabling	Enabling	Enabling
Modeling	Modeling	Modeling	Modeling
Encouraging	Encouraging	Encouraging	Encouraging
Challenging	Challenging	Inspiring	Challenging
Inspiring	Inspiring	Challenging	Inspiring

Physical vs. Synchronous vs. Asynchronous Interaction

"Any group of people will become a team (even if they do not know each other) if there is an urgent reason to do so" according to Jude-York, Davis, and Wise (2000, p. 23). Obviously, being in the same course and needing to complete assignments is a good reason to form a team. Yet the teams in the project-based virtual environment and in the class-based virtual environment never once met face-to-face in a more traditional setting.

The virtual teams literature states some physical face-to-face interaction is desirable when forming a virtual team. That is often not possible, however, depending upon the circumstances. According to the LPI results from this study, there was no significant difference in the profiles of identified leaders regardless of the environment. Leaders in face-to-face (traditional) interactions scored almost the same as those whose interactions with their team members occurred in a synchronous (project-based) manner or in an asynchronous (class-based) way. This would indicate identified leaders were successful team leaders regardless of the type of interaction: face-to-face, synchronous virtual, or asynchronous virtual.

The Role of the Negotiator

There were a disproportionate number of identified leaders who were chosen by their team members to act as the Summit negotiators. With the number of students in BUS620, a total of 19.3% of the class would have been able to be negotiators. But the results of this study show that a significantly higher proportion of identified leaders acted as the negotiators. Table 14 shows the percentages in each envi-

Table 14. Identified leaders who acted as Summit negotiators

Environment	%
Class Average	19.3
Traditional	31.6
Class-Based	39
Project-Based	33.3
Both Project- and Class-Based	45.8

ronment, as well as the percentages of people who were identified as leaders in both the project-based and class-based environments.

Because the role of the negotiator is so critical in Summit, it is logical that those who were chosen by their team members to be the negotiators assumed a leadership role during the exercise. What is interesting about this data is those who were identified as leaders in the other environments were also disproportionately negotiators. While there were no significant differences in the LPI scores of the identified leaders in the different environments, this data seems to indicate students who acted as negotiators in the Summit exercise were more apt to be identified as leaders of their teams, regardless of the environment.

Effect of the Leadership Class

Kouzes and Posner believe leadership is based on an observable, learnable set of practices, that leadership is within the grasp of everyone, and that the "opportunities for leadership are boundless and boundary-less" (Kouzes & Posner, 2012, p. 3). "Leadership is, after all, a set of skills" (Kouzes & Posner, 1995, p. 323). The students participating in this study were all members of the BUS620: Leadership and Teams class. The three separate LPI scores were derived at different times during the term. The LPI scores from the traditional environment were collected during the second week of the class. The LPI data for the project-based virtual environment was collected during the sixth week of the course, and during the eighth (and final) week of class for the class-based virtual environment.

Because of the nature of the course, students' leadership profiles could have changed throughout the progress of the term as they learned more and more about leadership skills. In fact, just over 33% of the students' LPI scores did increase from the project-based virtual environment to the class-based virtual environment, from as little as 0.8% to as much as 20%. But a little over 8% of the students actually recorded total decreases in LPI scores, ranging from 0.5% to 30%.

This data suggests that while the leadership class may have been of benefit to some because their LPI scores increased, other students did not appear to develop their leadership abilities as evidenced by their LPI scores. Additionally, the LPI is an extremely reliable instrument. This fact may impact the inter-rater reliability of the study, because knowledge the students received from the class may not be reflected in the LPI scores because of the LPIs reliability.

Limitations

1. There is absolutely no face-to-face interaction between the distance learning students. Much of the virtual team literature says at least some face-to-face is critical for the success of a virtual team.
2. In the traditional environment, the LPI survey was filled out in the physical environment of the students studied, most probably the students' workplace. In the class-based virtual and the project-based virtual environments, the LPI surveys were completed in a strictly educational setting with the same group of students.
3. Some people may have already had experience working in virtual teams. If students have prior Online Plus experience then they will have had additional exposure to using the communications technology and working in a virtual team, which may make them more comfortable with the environment and therefore more apt to take on a leadership role.

4. Team dynamics certainly play a significant role in the functioning of virtual teams. That topic was not explored in this study.
5. Factors such as keyboarding skills or the lack of broadband can impact the effectiveness of synchronous communication via the Internet, thus affecting a person's perceived leadership abilities.
6. People who are disciplined enough to earn a graduate degree via distance education tend to be strong, high-energy personalities. Those personality types also tend to exhibit more leadership qualities.

FUTURE RESEARCH DIRECTIONS

Because this study was limited to using one particular instrument in a unique educational setting, it is not generalizable to the whole of the virtual team leadership research. It is, however, a start to future research efforts. There are no cases in the literature with which to compare the results of this particular study. Consequently, there is a great need for further research in the area of leadership and virtual teams.

Some recommendations for further study include:

1. Create a research design that can be more generalizable to the overall virtual teams literature.
2. Use the LPI to determine leadership profiles in corporate virtual teams.
3. Use the LPI to compare leadership profiles of team members who never meet face-to-face and those where there is some physical interaction with others on the virtual team.
4. Study the literature and research conducted on team dynamics to determine the impact dynamics has on leadership profiles of people in virtual teams.

CONCLUSION

The results of this study indicate the leadership profiles of the online students are similar to those as defined by Kouzes and Posner, regardless of whether the interaction occurred in a traditional, class-based virtual, or project-based virtual environment. Over one-third of the students were identified as leaders in both of the virtual environments. In this study, leaders performed consistently regardless of the environment. If further research finds this fact to be generalizable throughout the virtual team leadership research, it would have major implications. It may encourage more organizations to put their leaders in charge and use virtual teams without fear of failure. As Kouzes and Posner state, "although the *context* of leadership has changed dramatically…the *content* of leadership has not changed much at all" (2012, p. 15).

In responding to the request to identify and complete an LPI for the team leaders, one student wrote, "I do not believe leadership can truly be developed or appreciated when team members only know one another and interact in a virtual world." Indeed, this is probably the attitude of many people. But the virtual world is a reality, and more and more people will be interacting at all levels (conducting business, socially, educationally, etc.) solely in a virtual environment. New paradigms for leadership are required, because the old paradigms don't fit the current circumstances. For teams to be successful in modern virtual environments, strong, effective leadership will be required.

REFERENCES

Anantatmula, V., & Thomas, M. (2010). Managing global projects: A structured approach for better performance. *Project Management Journal*, *41*(2), 60–72. doi:10.1002/pmj.20168

Avolio, B. J., Kahai, S., & Dodge, G. E. (2001). E-leadership: Implications for theory, research, and practice. *The Leadership Quarterly*, *11*(4), 615–668. doi:10.1016/S1048-9843(00)00062-X

Bennis, W., & Sample, S. B. (2015). *The art and adventure of leadership: Understanding failure, resilience, and success*. Hoboken, NJ: John Wiley & Sons.

Brake, T. (2008). *Where in the world is my team? Making a success of your virtual global workplace*. John Wiley & Sons.

Burke, R., & Barron, S. (2014). *Project management leadership: Building creative teams*. Wiley.

Chreim, S. (2015). The (non)distribution of leadership roles: Considering leadership practices and configurations. *Human Relations*, *68*(4), 517–543. doi:10.1177/0018726714532148

Covey, S. R. (1996). Three roles of the leader in the new paradigm. In F. Hesselbein, M. Goldsmith, & R. Beckhard (Eds.), *The leader of the future* (pp. 149–159). San Francisco: Jossey-Bass.

Cramton, C. D., & Webber, S. S. (2005). Relationships among geographic dispersion, team processes, and effectiveness in software development work teams. *Journal of Business Research*, *58*(6), 758–765. doi:10.1016/j.jbusres.2003.10.006

Cutler, A. (2014). *Leadership psychology: How the best leaders inspire their people*. London: Kogan Page.

Day, D. V. (2014). The future of leadership: Challenges and prospects. In D. V. Day (Ed.), *The Oxford handbook of leadership and organizations* (pp. 859–869). doi:10.1093/oxfordhb/9780199755615.013.041

Drucker, P. F. (1995). Not enough generals were killed. In F. Hesselbein, M. Goldsmith, & R. Beckhard (Eds.), *The leader of the future* (pp. xi–xv). San Francisco: Jossey-Bass.

Duarte, D. L., & Snyder, N. T. (2006). *Mastering virtual teams: Strategies, tools, and techniques that succeed*. San Francisco: Jossey-Bass.

Evans, R. (1996). *The human side of school change: Reform, resistance, and the real-life problems of innovation*. San Francisco: Jossey-Bass.

Haines, R. (2014). Group development in virtual teams: An experimental reexamination. *Computers in Human Behavior*, *39*, 213–222. doi:10.1016/j.chb.2014.07.019

Heifetz, R. A., & Laurie, D. L. (1997). The work of leadership. *Harvard Business Review*, *75*(1), 124. PMID:10174450

Higson, P., & Sturgess, A. (2014). *Uncommon leadership: How to build competitive advantage by thinking differently*. London: Kogan Page.

Hoch, J. E., & Kozlowski, S. W. J. (2014). Leading virtual teams: Hierarchical leadership, structural supports, and shared team leadership. *The Journal of Applied Psychology, 99*(3), 390–403. doi:10.1037/a0030264 PMID:23205494

Jonsen, K., Maznevski, M., & Davison, S. C. (2012). Global virtual team dynamics and effectiveness. In G. K. Stahl, I. Bjorkman, & S. Morris (Eds.), *Handbook of research in international human resource management* (pp. 363–392). London: Edward Elgar Publishing.

Joshi, A., & Lazarova, M. B. (2005). Do global teams need global leaders? Identifying leadership competencies in multinational teams. In D. L. Shapiro (Ed.), *Managing multinational teams: Global perspectives* (pp. 281–301). Amsterdam: Elsevier. doi:10.1016/S0747-7929(05)18011-1

Jude-York, D., Davis, L. D., & Wise, S. L. (2000). *Virtual teaming: Breaking the boundaries of time and place*. Menlo Park, CA: Crisp Publications, Inc.

Kitmoller, A., & Lauring, J. (2013). When global virtual teams share knowledge: Media richness, cultural difference, and language commonality. *Journal of World Business, 48*(3), 398–406. doi:10.1016/j.jwb.2012.07.023

Kouzes, J., & Posner, B. (1995). *The leadership challenge*. San Francisco: Jossey-Bass.

Kouzes, J., & Posner, B. (1997). *The leadership practices inventory facilitator's guide*. San Francisco: Jossey-Bass.

Kouzes, J., & Posner, B. (2002). *The leadership practices inventory: theory and evidence behind the five practices of exemplary leaders*. Retrieved from http://www.leadershipchallenge.com/UserFiles/lc_jb_appendix.pdf

Kouzes, J., & Posner, B. (2012). *The leadership challenge*. San Francisco: Jossey-Bass.

Kouzes, J., & Posner, B. (2015). *The leadership challenge: Achieve the extraordinary*. Retrieved from http://www.leadershipchallenge.com/about-section-our-authors.aspx

Kucia, J. F., & Gravett, L. S. (2014). *Leadership in balance: New habits of the mind*. Palgrave Macmillan. doi:10.1057/9781137393449

Lepsinger, R., & DeRosa, D. (2010). *Virtual team success: A practical guide for working and leading from a distance*. Hoboken, NJ: John Wiley & Sons.

Melymuka, K. (1997). Virtual realities. *Computerworld, 31*(17), 70–72.

Merriam-Webster. (2015). *Definition of the word "virtual"*. Retrieved from http://www.merriam-webster.com/dictionary/virtual

Nanus, B. (1992). *Visionary leadership: Creating a compelling sense of direction for your organization*. San Francisco: Jossey-Bass.

Neufeld, D., Wan, Z., & Fang, Y. (2008). Remote leadership, communication effectiveness, and leader performance. *Journal of Group Decision and Negotiation, 19*(3), 227–246. doi:10.1007/s10726-008-9142-x

Puccio, G., Murdock, M., & Mance, M. (2011). *Creative leadership: Skills that drive change*. Thousand Oaks, CA: Sage Publications.

Scott, M. E. (2013). Communicate through the roof: A case study analysis of the communicative rules and resources of an effective global virtual team. *Communication Quarterly*, *61*(3), 301–318. doi:10.1 080/01463373.2013.776987

Sohmen, V. S. (2015). Reflections on creative leadership. *International Journal of Global Business*, *8*(1), 1–14.

Tobin, T. J. (2015). *Your leadership story: Use your story to energize, inspire, and motivate*. Oakland, CA: Berrett-Koehler.

Zaccaro, S. J. (2014). Leadership memes: From ancient history and literature to twenty-first century theory and research. In D. V. Day (Ed.), *The Oxford handbook of leadership and organizations* (pp. 13–39). doi:10.1093/oxfordhb/9780199755615.013.001

Zander, L., Mockaitis, A. I., & Butler, C. L. (2012). Leading global teams. *Journal of World Business*, *47*(4), 592–603. doi:10.1016/j.jwb.2012.01.012

Zofi, Y. (2012). *A manager's guide to virtual teams*. Amacom.

KEY TERMS AND DEFINITIONS

Challenge: To arouse or stimulate especially if presented with difficulties.

Cyberspace: The environment in which communication occurs using information and communication technologies (ICTs), particularly associated with the Internet and Internet culture.

Enable: Provide the tools necessary to get the job done.

Encourage: Provide support and advice to someone so that they can be successful.

ICTs: Information and communication technologies, such as email, instant messaging, and video-conferencing.

Inspire: To make someone want to do something; the cause something to happen or to be created.

Leadership: Showing people in an organization a course of action and causing them to follow by ideas and deed. The functions or processes of establishing direction, aligning people and resources, and energizing people to accomplish results.

Model: Setting a standard of example for imitation or comparison.

Virtual Team: A geographically dispersed group of people that works together using a variety of communication technologies.

Chapter 2

Perception of Communication in Virtual Learning Environments:
What's in It for Them?

Latonia M. Ayscue
La Salle University, USA

ABSTRACT

Perception research helps to understand how stimuli (gist) interacts with learners' sensory systems (visual, auditory, tactile). Communication in virtual learning environments is significant because when the laws of perception are manifested, the strategy should include discovering how the relationships between the instructional design process (analyze, design, develop, implement and evaluate) synthesizes learning theories and learners' experience to create effective communication in virtual instructional events, learning objectives and goals.

INTRODUCTION

United States National Center for Educational Statistics, Digest of Educational Statistics (2011) reported that by the year 2020, eighty-million, nine-hundred and fifty-five thousand learners are predicted to be enrolled in technology-based virtual learning education and training programs. According to these statistics, each day learners will either enroll themselves or be involuntarily enrolled, in virtual learning environments, for the specific purpose of learning something new. Learners' perception of written communication in virtual learning environments can be complex, if there is no strategy to support the gist of the communication or support the learning process. For practitioners who design communication in virtual learning environments, there is the tendency to focus on the task and activities to deliver the content that impacts learners' educational experiences. Even though there are still controversies over the quality of virtual learning environments, organizations that tries to hold onto the traditional class ball on the educational court are realizing that learners are departing quickly to venues that affords them the opportunity to choose the learning environment that is best for them. As more and more learners realize that promotional opportunities are tied to higher education, learners are opting to select virtual

DOI: 10.4018/978-1-4666-9899-4.ch002

learning environments because of the benefits it provides. The frequent movement to virtual learning environments provides the ripe opportunity for instructional designers to, as Kahn (1997) stated, provide innovative approaches to remote audiences.

Conclusions can be drawn from the staggering numbers that learners have endorsed the idea behind the benefits of virtual learning environments, some of which are mentioned in a higher-order thinking study conducted by McLoughlin & Mynard (2009):

1. Non-intimating environment;
2. Offers flexibility to reach career and educational goals without disrupting work or personal life;
3. Equal participating in discussion forums where learners can interact with instruction and other learners on a regular basis;
4. Environment is not dominated by instructor; and,
5. Offers the opportunity to collaborate with learners who have different perspectives.

Whether the leaner initiated the process, which means their endorsement had been tendered, or the learner enters the learning environment with skepticism, communication is important for the learner to understand the purpose of the learning environment. With their endorsement comes the perception that the virtual learning environment would:

1. Be what the advertisement said it will be;
2. Be just as effective as other learning environments they perceived they were successful (many times traditional); and,
3. Allow the improved skill(s) and knowledge to be utilized immediately or towards a specific goal.

In these scenario, instructional designers, who design instruction for adult learners, will design instruction for learners who are willing, skeptical, impassive and cynical. Rather than being focused *only* on task and measurable goals, in the design phase, practitioners focus must also consider how the learning environment will be communicated to instigate and ignite the learners' thirst for learning so that the desired behavior will be achieved and engagement will not be terminated by the learner, either withdrawing physically or checking out mentally.

Perception research helps to understand how stimuli (gist) interacts with learners' sensory systems (visual, auditory, tactile). Communication in virtual learning environments is significant because when the laws of perception are manifested, the strategy should include discovering how the relationships between the instructional design process (analyze, design, develop, implement and evaluate) synthesizes learning theories and learners' experience to create effective communication in virtual instructional events, objectives and goals.

Communication influences the learners' conception of what they expect, see, hear and interpret. Communication designed to motivate learners to sign up or to change behavior should not encompass contorted syntax, in the advertisement (to draw the learners), the introduction, learning goals, objectives, discussion forums or even the Syllabus. Communication should be clear so that the learners' expectations are not met with disappointment and the learning environment does not produce dysfunctional learners.

This chapter utilizes a combination of approaches: the importance of learning theories and the instructional design process; focus on the significance of designing communication that could be influential on reshaping perceptual learning; and, how that communication can trigger adult learners' interactions and engagements in areas that allow the opportunity to communicate to in virtual learning environments (learners-to-content; learner-to-instructor/facilitator; and, learner-to-learner). The chapter also emphasizes:

1. What is perception and what does it have to do with communication;
2. Adult learners and how they learn;
3. Content that produces learning and performance;
4. The importance of incorporating artistic, scientific and practical communication tactics to deconstruct instructional content that is problematic and produces conflicts between what was meant and what was perceived; and,
5. Practical application of communication in virtual learning environments.

WHAT IS PERCEPTION AND WHAT DOES IT HAVE TO DO WITH COMMUNICATION?

Perceptions are an individual's reality. Written communication provides the documentation that describes what that learner will expect in the virtual learning experience. The communication maneuvers the learner's perception of what he/she will be experiencing in the learning environment - therefore the substance of the communication should not be misleading. Freiermuth (2002) stated that asynchronous material must be carefully constructed. Reigeluth (1999) advised that educational systems are powerful in that learning is influenced by the climate in which it occurs.

When learners study virtual learning advertisements, content in courses, learning/knowledge objects and any curriculum material, it starts an internal process that sifts through their past knowledge and their biases to perceive some benefit and form some understanding of what will be expected of them, in the learning experience, how they would navigate through the instructional events and how the process could benefit them in the future. This shift to virtual learning environment requires a shift in mental processes. Learning theories shed light to explain observed behavior by making inferences about the kinds of behavioral and cognitive processes that underlie learner's behavior (Morris & Maisto, 2008).

Learning theories, according to Smith & Ragan (2005) are organized statements that have allowed instructional designers to explain what should happen, predicted what would happen and optimistically controlled what could happen. Behavioral learning theories explain the concept of learning by concentrating on external occurrences as the root of change in observable behaviors (Morris & Maisto, 2008; Woolfolk, 2011). Research in other fields began to shed new light on behaviorism and focused on the workings of the mind. Cognitive theorist viewed learning as an active mental process of acquired, remembered and used knowledge (Morris & Maisto, 2008; Woolfolk, 2011).

Cognitive learning theories explained learning through mental processes and reflection of the knowledge communicated to explain behavior change (Laurillard, 2008). Behavioral and Cognitive Learning Theories, and others like Information-Processing theories, continue to evolve in this popular culture of technology (Smith & Ragan, 2005). Virtual learning exposes learners to an abundance of information versus information that was previously only possible with traditional classrooms (Laurillard, 2008). The theoretical approach to virtual learning also shifted the way instructional theories approached the phenomena of the knowledge age and explained behavior change through instruction.

Cognitive processes that lead to learning, under certain circumstances, are what instructional design stands for (Smith & Ragan, 2005). Technology enhanced learning environments contributed to the solution of reaching learners that traditional classrooms cannot (Laurillard, 2008). Linking instructional theories to instructional objectives, in virtual, computer-based and other diverse learning environments, provides the foundation which users can adapt the design process to fit unique learning needs, in diverse context (Reigeluth, 1999; Smith & Ragan, 2005).

This internal data processing systematically starts a paradigm that would determine the integrity of the design especially when the learners and the instructor are distance apart. Reading the communication allows the learner to see the content, perceive the expectations, make distinctions, identify through their imagination how to make sense of the data, formulate ideas consider how to perform and then actually perform. Kanuka & Garrison, as cited in McLoughlin & Mynard (2009), recommended that pose is crucial in encouraging actual knowledge construction.

If virtual communication includes specific characteristics, the instruction can result in particular types and amounts of learning (Reigeluth, 1999; Smith & Ragan, 2005). For example, virtual learning environments changes the way learners learn through observation because learners are in separate places, at separate times. Because learners are in different places at different times, instructional designers have to be knowledgeable of theories that describe, explain and predict learning, in multiple learning environments. Changing human disposition or capabilities that continue to persist or scaffold over time, in planned learning, is not only ascribable to process of growth but to design, structure, systems, learning theories and instructional design theories that all worked together for a common goal (Gagné, as cited in Smith & Ragan, 2005).

How communication is designed in virtual learning environments is crucial because, for the learner, there is a head-to-head tie between perception and action. Understanding how the brain translates written communication into action and learners' perception can be the solution to why many designs did not work, especially when the instructional design discipline universal position is that designing instruction should be a holistic process. Understanding there is a relationship between instructional strategies that should determine how information is communicated in virtual learning environments coupled with learners' perception will guide in making decisions about the gist of information in virtual learning environments. Since the learning environment should be designed for adults learners as *the* core element, practitioners must consider, what's in it for them (WIFT).

ADULT LEARNERS AND HOW THEY LEARN

Learning is not simplistic but rather a sophisticated and innate life-long pursuit that occurs both deliberately and inadvertently (Driscoll, 2005). WIFT? More and more adult learners are enrolling in virtual learning environments. Adult learners are intelligent and bring with them multiple learnt experiences, either:

1. Formally or informally;
2. Through observation;
3. Performing and accomplishing;
4. Creating;
5. Through social interactions; and,
6. Through trial and error.

These multiple learnt experiences allows them to interpret and reinterpret the virtual communication, the planned instructional experience and what's in it for them as a result of the virtual learning.

Rosenberg (2001) definition of learning was a "means to an end" (p. 5). The challenge for instructional designers to be valuable contributors rests in being privy to applicable learning theories, instructional methodologies, delivery systems and learning environments. In addition, engagement, problem solving, higher order thinking, relevancy and motivation must be included in the mix (Ertmer et al, 2008; Lauril-lard, 2008; Williams, 2002). The philosophies of learning is the composition of concepts, paradigms and philosophies that link observed changes in behavior with hypotheses believed to be precipitated by the predicted changes in various situation(s) (Driscoll, 2005). For this reason, the engine that drives the focus of organizing the plan on 'how to guide learning' means shifting and synchronizing the virtual communication strategies to deliver planned content, engage learners with the content, the facilitator and each other and meet the learning expectations. This means converting energy towards time spent with traditional dynamism to pedagogy that supports effective and efficient designed virtual communication and instruction. The dividend is examining the way information is communicated in various approaches, in instruction, in order to shape learning in a specific direction (Rosenberg, 2001).

For example, the postmodern approach meant that instructional designers must take the five societal factors for learning into account:

1. Learners had access to multiple sources other than the textbook and teacher;
2. Learners were diverse, which meant the instruction should be appropriate for all learners;
3. Innovations from the World-Wide Web;
4. Sources outside of the learning environment; and
5. How learners interpreted truth (Brown & Green, 2011).

These factors permit deviations from linear instructional models and algorithms to models that allow individuals a greater degree of freedom to create virtual communication that helps learners interpret how their learning can occur (Brown & Green, 2011). Learners interpret truth differently and can change behavior depending on the context, content, facilitator and other learners involved. For this reason, the designer has to also consider how the learner interprets information they read virtually from conscious and/or unconscious level based on experiences, practices and interactions with the world (Ayscue, 2015; Driscoll, 2005; Schunk, 2012; Smith & Ragan, 2005).

Instructional designers distinguish the potential, theory and practice of this complex phenomenon and recognize that learning is the nucleus to the eight distinct categories of learning:

1. "Domain-specific";
2. Problem solving;
3. Cognitive strategies;
4. Attitude change and motivation;
5. Declarative knowledge;
6. Concepts;
7. Procedures; and
8. "Psychomotor skills" (Driscoll, 2005, p, 1; Smith & Ragan, 2005).

This distinction translates to how to utilize learning theories to structure instruction that

1. Facilitates learning;
2. Promotes creativity (from a constructivist point-of-view);
3. Is problem-, inquiry-, and goal-oriented;
4. Encourages performance that is practical;
5. Provides feedback;
6. Is engaging; and
7. Applies what is known about learning theories (Laurillard, 2008).

Virtual learning is defined by Anderson (2008) as the use of technology to access learning materials to interact with the content, instructor and other learners and to obtain support during the learning process, to acquire knowledge, to construct personal meaning, and to grow from the learning experience. Virtual learning environments is defined as the learner and the instructor being in separate places at separate times. Since the learning environment encompasses the virtual structure, virtual communication is key. Learners need a strong knowledge foundation that not only involves the strategic process of instruction and learning but also involves a reflective process where the essence of the communication will equip the learner in a way that facilitates, represents obtainment of knowledge and sparks their understanding of how they can renew themselves in a particular learning engagement. That engagement period spans from the time the learner is enrolled to the completion of the course. The span of time should involve and incorporate multiple transitions where learning is scaffold in a way that meets learners' perceptions so discord is tamed and learning can occur, as planned. Bruner (1996a), as cited in Driscoll (2005), stated that education is more than curriculum and instructional strategies and there should be consideration on how the learners construct their world and conceptions.

Incorporating instructional strategies, with learning theories, principles, methodologies and procedures will allow the learners' perceptual systems to be re-shaped through perceptual learning. Strategies routed in instructional design theories encourage effective and appropriate interaction with the content with the ability to utilize practice in performing specific sensory tasks. As an Adjunct Professor, this practitioner has a golden rule for designing instruction whose gist borrowed from the five rights of nursing - which was changed for instructional design purposes:

1. Right assessment for the right learners;
2. Right developmental process to build the right plan;
3. Right design that incorporates the right learning 'es' (methodologies, practices, policies, principles, observes, and prepares);
4. Right implementation for the right learning environment; and,
5. Right evaluation methods to determine if the design was appropriate for the right situation. Virtual communication has to be Right!

Reflecting and strategizing on how to utilize the 'right' way to improve virtual communication, that has motivational appeal, is decisive for the instructional designer. For example, John Keller (1988) - ARCS (Attention, Relevance, Confidence, Satisfaction) Model of Motivational Design use of perceptual arousal to use surprise and incitement to gain learners' interest and change negative perception. Keller's ARCS model of Motivational Learning model suggests that learning occurs most effectively when learners are engaged throughout the entire learning process, and that strategies can be put in place to ensure that this engagement carries forward through to the completion.

Unfortunately and unholistically, many times learners' perceptions sit outside of the globally recognized Analysis, Design, Development, Implementation and Evaluation (ADDIE) framework invisibly orbiting like the rings of Saturn. Unfortunate because perception, dating back to ancient times, is one of the oldest and most fundamental disciplines within Psychology. Unholistically because if learner perception is understood as the process from which learner experiences is obtained, why isn't it considered in virtual communication? Learners' purposes are not always clear, learners' perceptions are not always considered and WIFT are not always factored into the analysis by the instructional designer or any practitioner who is designing the instruction. McKeachie (2002) stated that when learners are motivated to learn they will opt for activities they believe will enhance their learning and not only will they choose the task but will be diligent and persistent to achieve the goal in spite of any difficulties they might face.

The practitioner's arrow is aimed at a target (goals and learning objectives) that is motivated by information gleamed from the needs analysis. The needs analysis is largely based on the gaps that have been identified in the scrutiny of who didn't it work for, what didn't work, why it didn't work, where did it go wrong and what can be done to make this better, or, in some cases make this go away. Instructional design is such an amazing and outstanding science that supports constructing knowledge methodologically and identifying gaps in any stage of the ADDIE process to reach desired performance that training, instruction, pushing out and receiving information, communication and conduct (or performance) failed to facilitate. Virtual learning environments provide the opportunity to create multifaceted situations utilizing virtual communication to individually and collectively create instructional programs that address learners' perception to learn, practice and repurpose their lives resulting in long-lasting, continuing regeneration transformations.

CONTENT THAT PRODUCES LEARNING AND PERFORMANCE

While theoretical perceptions provide a useful framework for understanding the basic nature of interactive communication (how learning materials are accessed and how learners interact with the materials and another learners), understanding what learning is and the learner's perception would better explain the interactive process. When communication in virtual learning is created, the goal is to persistently change performance or performance potential by strategically linking the right learning theories with a cycle of instructional schemes in a didactic situation where results can be seen and measured, the catalyst that will be responsible for the learning is identified and the resources and real-life experiences that trigger learning, through instructional objectives, will be precise.

Instructional Objectives

Robert Mager's (1975) system for developed behavioral instructional objectives described what learners would be doing and allowed learners to demonstrate their achievement so that the initiator (user) would know they are doing it (Woolfolk, 2011). Gronlund's (2009) cognitive instructional objectives were generalized, which allowed the initiator (user) to support learners through understanding, solving, appreciating, etc. The instructional objectives, coupled with sample behaviors, provided evidence that the learner had obtained the targeted objective in real-work situations (Woolfolk, 2011).

In real-world situations, even workplace demands involved foundational knowledge, independent learning, critical thinking, communication, creativity, problem resolutions, managing, transferring and distributing knowledge (Laurillard, 2008). Instructional objectives purposes organized learning situations and assembles content into diverse context for learning to promote and accomplish an intended goal (Baggio, 2005; Driscoll, 2005; Harvey, 2005a; Laurillard, 2008; Richey & Klein, 2007; Smith & Ragan, 2005). Instructional designers' intent is to draw emphasis to features within the learning and make the learner an active participant in reaching the intended goal (Smith & Ragan, 2005).

Previously the author mentioned that Driscoll (2005) stated that learning is lifelong, is intentional and can be obtained either formally or informally. Learning in formal settings, one element of the constructivist theoretical approach, is to create communication that transforms the learning environment where learners can develop meaning from task and activities through dialogues, discussions and debates with other learners, the instructor or the facilitator. Tools, such as learning objects, for example, can be effective utilized for design flexibility and as a coping mechanism for struggling learners when used supplemental with other learning materials or as a stand-alone when learners are required to morph and change behavior from learning situations that are preset, inflexible or constant.

The benefits of flexible instructional tools is that, when used in virtual communication, they can be adaptive for diverse learners who have multiple learning needs and deficiencies. Suggestions from Morgan & Tam (1999) and Ozga & Sukhnanden (1998) is that epistemological factors such as impediments in communication and the learner's perceived difficulty with content are significant factors leading to continuity. Smith & Ragan (2005) stated that communication should not be unplanned or incidental. For instructional designers, it is important to recognize that factors such as: learning styles, which explains how individuals learn; instructional strategies, which explains how individuals process new knowledge and represent information; and, perception, how learners interact and react to content, must be factored into the design process, especially in the evolution of social media and social collaboration.

Social Media

Social Collaboration

Gibson (1992) maintained that a theory of perceptual learning must answer basic questions: What is learned and what is the function? What instigates learning and what terminates the process? Table 1 lists learning instigators to trigger knowledge, engagement, retention and creativity coupled with characteristics for each instigator that provides a link in behavioral foundations to understand how stimuli and perception is directed at discovering the relations between learning and subjective experience.

Utilizing Table 1, identifying a well-defined task is the proponent of situated cognition learning experience because: knowledge incorporates a discovery process that is intimate to that learner; engagement allows the opportunity to experience the situation personally and sift through the learner's innermost psyche; retaining keeps the learnt information close and allows for in-depth processing; and, creating and constructing the learning experience in the learner's mind opens up opportunities to fashion detailed accounts that enable the learner to share first-hand information, to engage with other learners in the discussion forums and to create narratives that show how the learning experience was individually interpreted, based on the learner's perception of the task at hand.

Without even a basic useful knowledge of how perception drives virtual communication framework and theory, imprecise virtual communication can hit the learners' sensory systems much like water

Table 1. Virtual communication

Learning Instigators	Characteristics			
	Knowledge	**Engagement**	**Retaining**	**Creating**
Well defined task	Discovering	Experience	Comprehension	Narrate
Information	Instructional Tools	Facts	Knowledge	Intellect
Access	Contact	Approach	Recalling	Retention
Autonomy	Absorbing	Communication	Describe	Testimonies
Distractors	Fragmented	Hold Back	Cramming	Frustration
Well Defined Activities	Information	Illustrate	Characterize	Personify
Well Defined Deliverables	Evidence	Data	Knowledge	Intelligence
Engagement	Relate	Arrive	Recount	Express

hits dirty hands and splatters the bowl with the dirt everywhere – asymmetrically with no point and no reason. Transitioning from traditional classroom to virtual learning environments means that learners must adapt from the recursive manner in which they received knowledge (which may create some barriers), put aside their biases about virtual learning (which may create some preconceptions) and subscribe to a new way of receiving communication (which may create change issues). This means that unless the virtual learning environment is Hybrid or Blended, the learners will only receive communication electronically via an unhuman technology produced entity that displays virtual learning materials for the programme on discussion boards, blogs, wikis, Skype, IPads, social networks and any other virtual learning delivery system geared to move the learner through the didactic and enlightening process. Virtual communication is even more significant, in these situations, because learners don't have physical cues from body language to supplement their understanding of the gist virtual and technological-based E-Learning education programs generate.

ARTISTIC, SCIENTIFIC, AND PRACTICAL COMMUNICATION TACTICS

The importance of incorporating artistic, scientific and practical communication tactics to deconstruct instructional content, that is problematic and produces conflicts between what is meant and what was perceived, is important to recognize before it impacts the ability to successfully build effective written communication. Scientifically, which is not the author's forte, perception research helps practitioners understand how stimuli (content) interacts with learners sensory systems (visual, auditory, tactile, olfactory, and gustatory). Practitioners who design instruction can use to their advantage of understanding that the individuals' perception causes them to form mental representations of the world that results in how they build relationships between environmental events and subjective experience. The mental representations are massive because the learner has experienced a wide range of challenges and situations by the time they have reached adulthood that extends from:

1. The structured formal and informal learning;
2. The multiple ways they have learned to process information;

3.   The nature of idiosyncratic experiences; and,

4.   The process and approach of perfect (or imperfect) chronicles of how the adult obtained the experience. As such, all these things brings to bear on how learners will perceive and understand all current events.

Instructional design provides detailed strategies that facilitates the learning of subject matter at all levels from simplistic to complex (Brown & Green, 2006). Because it is reflective, because it is systematic, because it is methodical and because the entire process starts anywhere in the cycle, from analysis to implementation, there is no contention that an instructional designer could start anywhere in the design process (Brown & Green, 2006; Reigeluth, 1999; Smith & Ragan, 2005).

The nature of designer thinking and decision making is critical in the design process where virtual communication is important to create information strategically. Whether the virtual communication is used to advertise, for the content in the course or for task/activities for participation, care must be taken to hypothesize instructional/pedagogical concerns and approached human learning in the instructional system design process (Smith & Ragan, 2005). The ADDIE methodology (Analyze, Design, Develop, Implement and Evaluate) phases facilitated how the process could be advantageous in virtual learning environments. For example: *Analyze* learning needs, learners' needs, purpose, decisions about theories, methodologies, principles, potential and structure of the virtual learning environment; make *Design* decisions around communication that directly impact the message, in virtual, computer-generated learning environments; *Develop* and assemble announcements, interactions, engagements, responses and exchanges into content for diverse learners; *Implement* how the content would be available to learners through various delivery systems; and, *Evaluate* throughout the instructional design process (Ertmer et al, 2008).

When learners sign up, they imagine that their specific purposes will be attained. Behind the scenes, the practitioner injects the content structure and sequences utilizing a strategy intertwined with learning theories and instructional strategies to influence learning goals, learning objectives, tasks and information the learner needs to get out of the learning experience. Their imagination is constructed by their perception of what they anticipate they will get out of the learning experience. Instructional designers and other practitioner, who design instruction, must recognize that perceptions are an individual's actuality. It is important, during the analysis stage, that instructional designers and other creators of instruction understand that success of the strategy must also consider learners' past knowledge and their biases on how they perceive and understand what they want to get out of the learning experience.

PRACTICAL APPLICATION OF COMMUNICATION IN VIRTUAL LEARNING ENVIRONMENTS

Perceptual development can be achieved with the appropriate communication to facilitate learning, deconstruct negative experiences and biases and allow learners to generate and control their learning from the interactions with the content, their experiences and their ideas (so that they can transfer what they have learned for their own purposes). This challenge to design instruction, that allows learners to perform, change behavior (as predicted) and realize an experience they would enjoy, means more and more instructional designers would be faced with designing instruction that would be delivered on tablets, Smartphones, virtual, computer, web-based and other diverse learning environments (Ayscue, 2015)

This knowledge about human learning provides the proficiency and connects the precise learning theory (behaviorism, cognitivism, or constructivism) to tailor instruction based on the needs of learners, design content and create appropriate tasks, using instructional communication and tools, that will trigger optimal instructional actions to spark a behavior change (Ertmer & Newby, 2013). Eclectic instructional design models, too, address the design process in the virtual learning environments. The wide-ranging designs blends the ideas from multiple learning theories and theoretical influences, much like transforming reusable learning objects that are applied in different ways by different instructional designers based on different learning needs (Ertmer & Newby, 2013; Honebein & Sink, 2012; Kabel, de Hoog & Wielinga, 2003).

Virtual learning environments allow many adults to continue and pursue their educational goals. They come because of what they believe is in it for them. For example: the classes are accessible – 24 hours a day; learners can pace themselves, with some restrictions tied to mandatory deadlines; learners can continue their education without disrupting individual necessities and not worry about work schedules, babysitters, holidays/vacations, life; learners recognize the need and desire for career and life changes when jobs become repetitious; learners want to advance in their current career or future career when work has become unchallenging; and, the individual list goes on and on.

Because virtual learning environments are a *reality* instructional designers and other, who design instructional communication to equip learners to meet their individualized educational goals, designers have to consider factoring WIFT in order to incorporate the multiple individualized differences in learning and performance. For example creating content in the initial post from the learner's perspective.

Picture this – a well-known judge queries the plaintiffs and the defendants. Cameras are situated and cued to display the demonstrative emotions, giving viewers the advantage of not only hearing the exchange of communication but also seeing the reactions on the face of the judge, the plaintiffs and the defendants. The faces exhibited variations of: imprudence, prudence, confusion, indifference, comprehension, anger, frustration, emotional breakthroughs, laughter and pain. Individuals in the courtroom, who were behind the plaintiffs and the defendants, may not see the emotions that television viewers are seeing. This perception came from the observation of some of the individuals who were shifting around in their seats in an attempt to adapt their diminished visual capabilities and utilize other sensory systems that would allow them to feel the exchange, grasp some meaning, remember what was being said, think about the exchange, analyze, learn from the judges' ruling and carry on – all simultaneously. One perception could be that if participants could only see the plaintiffs' and the defendants' backs, does this impede the information heard, does it change how the information is representation (in their minds), and does it hinder the rich processing of new knowledge that could affect their perception of the individuals, the judge ruling and even their interest in the case?

Virtual learning environments does not allow facilitators see sensory interactions when the learners sees, hears and performs the task. This is why the communication in virtual learning environments have to be dead-on: the content, the structure, the strategy, the delivery systems have to be intertwined and in synch so that information not only gain learners attention but holds their attention, their interests so that the environment influences what needs to be learned, what function this new revelation can benefit the doer, what ignites the learning and what concludes the process so that the sequence can move up to the next level of learning to a more complex platform. Communication involves message-designed principles that guide how the message is transmitted, what it should say (and to whom), what it should look like, how the learner should perform (where and with whom), the benefits (objectives) and why learners want to be motivated and want to engage and perform. Practitioners who design, train and facilitate instruction, in multiple virtual learning environments to impart information to learners, must shift knowledge and content in ways that will exemplify specific information in a manner that allows the learner an awareness of the learning situation in order to comprehend the information, learn, process the new knowledge and perform some task.

What does perception have to do with communication? It is suggested that current research literature in the area of learning styles and strategies can provide instructional designers with insights into individual differences in learning and performance that should be factored into the design process. Much like the previous scenario, content from the learner's perspective means, if the learner is a visual thinker and a visual learner, lack of knowledge about what motivates a visual learner would result in creating a design the learner perceives as a blank slate (or the person's back) and having to call the instructor, email the instructor (sometimes the school), rely on other learners they hope get it, adapt their diminished visual capabilities and utilize other sensory systems that would allow them to feel the exchange, grasp some meaning, remember what was being said, think about the exchange, analyze, learn from their cohorts and instructor's ruling (grades) and carry on – again, all simultaneously. In many cases, the learner will check out either physically, mentally or emotionally.

What does this scenario have to do with perception? The next virtual class the learner enrolls in, the facilitator will have the cross to bear. Entering the classroom will be the learner who has actively processed the negative event and will bring past knowledge and their biases to present - this will affect how information is perceived because they have formed concepts which can influence any notion of perceptive exploration. Multiple learners affirm I will not or I cannot take classes on-line. In many cases, this is not an option. As one colleague has stated, they are voluntoldily enrolled in classes. There are many opinions about communication that is appropriate in virtual learning environments. Certainly communication should allow for:

1. Interactions that encourage a participatory tango between learner-to-learner, learner-to-content and learner-to-instructor;
2. The scaffolding of information that encourages a growing interest in the content that gives them an appreciation for learning information that will equip the learner to pursue educational goals;
3. Non-ambiguous but clear and robust content that is appropriate to the learning situation, problem and task; and,
4. Breadth learning theories that are inclusive of the manner in which adults learn.

SUMMARY

This chapter is not about the character of the mind, personalities, and the nature of reasoning or the mysteries of knowing if something is as it appears. This chapter is about understanding that the learner's perception is the learner's reality. The question that will drive the emphasis is how practitioners devise strategies where learners perceive that the content they interact with and engage with, in discussion boards or any virtual forum will support their learning and their understanding in ways they can retain and utilize the information learnt in real-life situations. For those individual experiencing virtual learning for the first time or who have had prejudicial experiences with virtual learning, an added bonus would be the expectation that virtual learning will look, feel and be like traditional learning to ease learners through the change process and eliminate lack of control.

Diverse and virtual learning environments have sprouted from computer technology. Technology provides the delivery mechanism for users to reach learners through multiple settings. For example, delivery mechanisms such as Smartphones, social media, podcast, webinars, and the Internet to deliver knowledge in this virtual age (Rosenberg, 2001). Instructional designers transforming ideologies of learning and standards of instructional theories into plans for instructional virtual communication is important. The emphasis is comprised of comprehensive and exhaustive thinking that thoughtfully and analytically assesses, identifies, translates, and evaluates the most operative way the communicates to learners what they will expect when they enter a virtual classroom or training event. This thought process involves the competency that matches and balanced principles of learning with principles of instruction to stimulate learners and support the gist of the communication or support the learning process (Brown & Green, 2006; Driscoll, 2005; Harvey, 2005a; Harvey, 2005b; Reigeluth, 1999; Richey & Klein, 2007; Schunk, 2012; Smith & Ragan, 2005).

REFERENCES

Baggio, B. (2005). *What impact are the main issues/concerns associated with learning objects having on training and education.* Unpublished manuscript, Department of Education, Capella University.

Bennett, S., Agostinho, S., Lockyer, L., Harper, B., & Lukasiak, J. (2006). Support university teachers create pedagogically sound learning environment using learning designs and learning objects. *IADIS International Journal, 4*(1), 16-26. Retrieved from http://ro.uow.edu.au/cgi/viewcontent.cgi?article=2 511&context=edupapers

Bichelmeyer, B., Boling, E., & Gibbons, A. (2006). Reflections on instructional design and technology models: Their impact on research, practice and teaching in IDT. In M. Orey, J. McLendon, & R. Branch (Eds.), *Educational media and technology yearbook 2006* (pp. 33–50). Westport, CT: Libraries Unlimited.

Brown, A., & Green, T. A. (2006). *The essentials of instructional design.* Boston, MA: Pearson Education, Inc.

Brown, A., & Green, T. A. (2011). *The essentials of instructional design* (2nd ed.). Boston, MA: Pearson Education, Inc.

Davenport, T. H. (2011). Rethinking knowledge work: A strategic approach. *McKinsey Quarterly.* Retrieved from http://www.mckinsey.com/insights/organization/rethinking_knowledge_work_a_strategic_approach

Dodds, P., & Fletcher, J. D. (2003, June). *Opportunities for new "smart" learning environments enabled by next generation web capabilities.* In Ed-Media World Conference on Educational Multimedia, Hypermedia & Telecommunications Symposium conducted at meeting of the Association for the Advancement of Computing in Education, Honolulu, HI.

Driscoll, M. P. (2005). *Psychology of learning for instruction* (3rd ed.). Boston, MA: Pearson Education, Inc.

Ertmer, P. A., & Newby, T. J. (2013). Behaviorism, cognitivism, and constructivism: Comparing critical features from an instructional design perspective. *Performance Improvement Quarterly*, 26(2), 43–71. doi:10.1002/piq.21143

Freeman, R. E. (1994). *Instructional design: Capturing the classroom for distance learning*. Chicago, IL: The Association of Christian Continuing Education Schools and Seminaries (ACCESS). Retrieved from http://p4mriunimed.files.wordpress.com/2009/09/instructional-design.pdf

Freiermuth, M. R. (2002). Internet chat: Collaborating and learning via e-conversations. *TESOL Journal, 11*(3), 36–40.

Gibbons, A. S., Merrill, P. F., Swan, R., Campbell, J. O., Christensen, E., Insalaco, M., & Wilken, W. (2008). Reexamining the implied role of the designer. *The Quarterly Review of Distance Education, 9*(2), 127–137.

Gronlund, N. E. (2009). *Writing Instructional Objectives* (8th ed.). Upper Saddle River, NJ: Peason Education, Inc.

Harvey, B. (2005a). *Learning objects and instructional design* [Report R49/0503]. Retrieved from Athabasca University website: http://cde.athabascau.ca/softeval/reports/R490503.pdf

Honebein, P. C., & Sink, D. L. (2012). The practice of eclectic instructional design. *Performance Improvement, 51*(10), 26–31. doi:10.1002/pfi.21312

Laurillard, D. (2008). Technology enhanced learning as a tool for pedagogical innovation. *Journal of Philosophy of Education, 42*(3-4), 521–533. Retrieved from http://onlinelibrary.wiley.com/doi/10.1111/j.1467-9752.2008.00658.x/abstract

Levenberg, A., & Caspi, A. (2010). Comparing perceived formal and informal learning in face-to-face versus online environments. *Interdisciplinary Journal of E-Learning and Learning Objects, 6*. Retrieved from http://www.ijello.org/Volume6?IJELLOv6p323-333Levenburg706.pdf

McLoughlin, D., & Mynard, J. (2009, May). An analysis of higher order thinking in online discussions. *Innovations in Education and Teaching International, 46*(2), 147–160. doi:10.1080/14703290902843778

Moore, M., & Kearsley, G. (2005). *Distance education: A systems view* (2nd ed.). Belmont, CA: Wadsworth.

Morris, C. G., & Maisto, A. A. (2008). *Understanding Psychology* (8th ed.). Saddle River, NJ: Pearson.

Mowat, J. (2007, July). The instructional design of learning objects. *Learning Solutions Magazine*. Retrieved from https://www.learningsolutionsmag.com/articles/176/the-instructional-design-of-learning-objects

Muzio, J. A., Heins, T., & Mundell, R. (2002). Experiences with reusable e-learning objects: From theory to practice. *The Internet and Higher Education, 5*(1), 21–34. doi:10.1016/S1096-7516(01)00078-1

O'Leary, R. (n.d.). Virtual Learning Environment. *ALT/LTSN Generic Centre Leaflet 2*. Retrieved from https://www.alt.ac.uk/sites/default/files/assets_editor_uploads/documents/eln002.pdf

Pawlowski, J. M. (2002). Reusable models of pedagogical concepts - a framework for pedagogical and content design. In Proceedings of World Conference on Educational Multimedia, Hypermedia and Telecommunications. Chesapeake, VA: AACE. Retrieved from http://www.editlib.org/p/10229

Reigeluth, C. M. (1999). *Instructional-design theories and models: A new paradigm of instructional theory* (Vol. 2). Mahwah, NJ: Lawrence Erlbaum Associates.

Richey, R. C., & Klein, J. D. (2007). *Design and development research.* New York, NY: Routledge.

Rosenberg, M. J. (2001). e-Learning: Strategies for delivering knowledge in the digital age. New York, NY: McGraw-Hill.

Rothwell, W. J., & Kazanas, H. C. (2008). *Mastering the instructional design process: A systematic approach* (4th ed.). San Francisco, CA: Pfeiffer.

Ryder, M. (2010). *Instructional design models & theories.* Retrieved from http://www.instructionaldesign-central.com/htm/IDC_instructionaldesignmodels.htm

Smith, E. (n.d.). *Learning to learn online.* Retrieved from http://www.ascilite.org.au/conferences/brisbane99/papers/smith.pdf

Smith, P. L., & Ragan, T. J. (2005). *Instructional design* (3rd ed.). Hoboken, NJ: John Wiley & Sons, Inc.

U.S. National Center for Educational Statistics. (2011). Programs and Plans of the National Center for Education Statistics 2005 Edition. *Education Statistics Quarterly, 7*(1), 1-11. Retrieved from http://nces.ed.gov/pubs2006/2006614_1.pdf

U.S. National Center for Educational Statistics Digest of Educational Statistics. (2011). *School enrollment with projections* (Table 219). Retrieved from http://www.census.gov/compendia/statab/cats/education.html

Williams, D. D. (2002). The instructional use of learning objects. In D. Wiley (Ed.), *Evaluation of learning objects and instruction using learning objects* (pp. 173–199). Bloomington, IN: Agency for Instructional Technology and Association for Education Communications & Technology.

Woolfolk, A. (2011). *Educational psychology: Active learning edition* (11th ed.). Boston, MA: Pearson.

Chapter 3
Workforce Development in Behavioral Healthcare and the Increased Use of Technology:
Is It Working or Not? Are We Asking the Right Questions?

Susanne Ingle
Kuprevich Consulting, USA

Carol L. Kuprevich
Kuprevich Consulting, USA

ABSTRACT

The authors present anecdotal and peer reviewed information relative to the increase in use of technology within behavioral healthcare. Emphasis is on education, training, professional community development, and networking aspects of the field. The use of email discussion lists, blogs, conferences, and online training management tools are discussed. The authors define the use of technology in workforce development, build out examples of use, explore different methods of digital discourse, and discuss the challenges of technology implementation in a clinical setting. The authors attempt to provide both sides of the debate as to whether the increased use of technology in workforce development within behavioral healthcare is working while addressing the overall expectation to reduce costs, provide positive outcomes, and increase the skills and knowledge of a diverse workforce. This chapter provides an overall picture of types of technology are offered and a general overview of the benefits and opportunities for improvement specific to the development of the healthcare workforce.

INTRODUCTION

Implementation and integration of technology in behavioral healthcare workforce development is an ongoing and developing process with pockets of significant use and pockets of slow adapters with evidence of just about every degree of separation between the two. In an age of ever-diminishing resources,

DOI: 10.4018/978-1-4666-9899-4.ch003

organizations want the largest return on investment when training their staff and significant time and money are invested in training the workforce: the current average dollars spent on training and development is estimated to be USD\$1,208 per employee, and there are 31.5 average number of learning hours used per employee (Association for Talent Development, 2014). In this age of diminishing resources, the evident prioritization of workforce development supports the imperative that organizations maintain their investment in their workforce. One method to track this investment would be to establish and document a 'gold standard' for connecting technology and workforce development with optimal outcomes for each employee, and also, in the case of behavioral health, connect service recipient outcomes (SAMHSA, 2014; Sipek, 2015). There are several barriers, however, to measuring desired outcomes for increase of use of technology in workforce development; some are specific to the behavioral healthcare workforce and others are generalized to the economy and current workforce composition.

As evidenced by pilot studies and funded research initiatives, there is a great need and interest to establish working protocols for the implementation of technology support in behavioral healthcare. However, the nature of the field is that it is an ever changing one: the client population changes over time; there is a high rate of staff turnover; new regulations and mandates emerge; new technology presents itself in novel and interesting applications. Measuring consistent desirable outcomes presents a challenge in the face of the necessarily fluid and responsive nature of behavioral healthcare. The fluidity of the field, in both staff and service recipients as well as outside influences, presents a major challenge to produce repeatable and consistent data-driven protocols, with so many of the underpinnings of infrastructure shifting in sometimes unpredictable ways.

It is now necessary that staff be both proficient in service provision and with the use of technology in their clinical work, neither skill being optional. In one survey conducted by AMN Healthcare Services, Inc. 86% of the 300 clinical leaders and human resource (HR) survey respondents described the need for new types of health care workers in both technology and service provision (Sipek, 2015). In previous decades, staff needed only to be skilled at providing services and technology use was not a priority. However, it is relatively clear and universally accepted within behavioral healthcare that re-training of the workforce is of paramount importance given the explosion of medically related knowledge, processes of integrating care, and the resulting implications for decision making. Necessarily, in most clinical settings, the primary focus of professionals is on the service recipient and in actively engaging in hands-on treatment. Unfortunately, this may lead to staff avoiding or under using technology. Whether they lack the interest, knowledge, or simply time to pursue these avenues, this puts the entire field at a disadvantage because staff may not necessarily be getting up-to-date information and may not be practicing fully within the standards of care to which their respective professions subscribe.

Diversity of service delivery choices, or different methods to provide treatment, within integrated behavioral health teams are another area that is growing or changing across the field and are presenting their own set of unique challenges with regard to technology acceptance. According to Dr. Chantelle Thomas, Ph.D., a Behavioral Health Consultant from Access Community Health Center in Madison, Wisconsin, more service choices are needed for a multitude of reasons. Some of these include the following: treatment options in the community are limited by insurance coverage disparities; there are high levels of psychosocial stress and increased severity of symptoms; and, population based care requires more sophisticated outlets for case management. Technology is at the core of many of the service delivery options that behavioral health is considering (Masys, 2002). This proposal diverges from the existing, more hands-on, treatment practice and staff would not only need to receive education on how to effectively deliver these types of services, but they would also require additional skills training in order to support service recipients who may be using technology in a do-it-yourself type model. As services continue to evolve, so must the skills of the staff providing them – technology provides a path to do this efficiently.

In addition to technology adoption barriers, there are other aspects of behavioral workforce development to consider; specifically, appropriate and relevant learning materials, a content management system (CMS) and/or a learning management system (LMS), and how these two elements correlate for service delivery. According to Workforce Management Magazine and the American Society for Training and Development (2008), now known as the Association for Talent Development, over 30% of workforce development hours (employee time spent on training skill development) use technology-based delivery systems similar to a CMS or LMS. An inherent challenge to using these supportive technologies is that there are so many choices for online education-related resources surrounding behavioral healthcare that it can be overwhelming to perform necessary due diligence regarding quality, content, appropriateness, cost, time, and outcome on the options. Too often, a program purchases an LMS, or a CMS, and stays with that choice because it is in place and easier to remain with the status quo than to do ongoing quality control. It becomes a challenge to stay relevant and agile with new technologies for many of the same reasons that there is a challenge to perform due diligence. There is the added complexity of a growing demand for technology including mobile applications and other web-based tools that were initially not in the scope of most LMS or CMS purchase requirements for new project implementations.

In an attempt to resolve the barriers and challenges of user adoption and system selection, there is emerging research on effective dissemination methods of clinical treatment best practices and how technology may play a role in the acceptance of new practices. Implementation science focuses on this emerging field of research, but it is just that – an emerging field and there is a lack of comprehensive studies with actionable items.

Technology is defined, for purposes of this chapter, as the use of tools for education and behavioral health service delivery that may include hardware (e.g., laptops, tablets, smartphones), applications/software (social networking platforms, email discussion lists, blogs), and infrastructure (network connections, security, and support). The referenced technologies can be used in a classroom, in virtual settings, and in a myriad of devices, including televisions, computers, and telephones. Clearly, the use of the word technology, for these purposes, is intended to be broad spectrum and inclusive. While telehealth and electronic health records fall within this broad concept of technology, these two specific arenas are large enough, in terms of impact in behavioral health, that they deserve their own concentration. When mentioned in this chapter, these two terms are used with the intent to add emphasis to the broadest concept of technology within behavioral health.

The objective of this chapter is to provide a broad scope discussion, using multiple types of data sources, regarding the status of the use of technology to advance behavioral healthcare workforce development. Material is presented to encourage further conversation that will lead to specific research studies to support the needs of the workforce in a manner that leads to optimum outcomes for both the workforce and for the recipients of services.

BACKGROUND

"There's a learning crisis in the marketplace" according to John Ambrose, a Skillsoft senior vice president in a special report on learning providers in the know, in the now (Everson, 2014). Ambrose describes the need for creating new global footprints for learning and that it needs to be considered a core function in order to fix deficits in skilled employees. Jackie Funk, Senior Vice President of Global Marketing for SumTotal Systems, a technology-based LMS, writes about the need for business to make learning a core function of their work in order to address the well-documented deficits in skilled employees. "Historically, people have seen learning as a nice-to-have rather than a must-have. We have to make sure the business leaders in the organizations understand that this isn't an optional exercise anymore." (Everson, 2014). This is especially applicable to the behavioral healthcare workforce. Not only are mental health and substance abuse service systems not meeting expectations, as reported by the media; they are also understaffed, under-supported, unprepared to treat the volume and intensity of the situations.

There is a noted disconnect between the knowledge and skills of the behavioral healthcare workforce and employer expectations; ever increasing and shifting on-the-job requirements for staff present a challenge. In recognition of this disconnect, in a 2001 report, the American Hospital Association (AHA) emphasized the need for health systems to improve their capacity for developing skills among their staff. Recommendations from the report included: provide continuing education through the web, provide education to teach new skills, and partner with all education to ensure that students are taking the essential courses needed to provide the services the system needs in urban, suburban, and rural settings. It should be noted that, while the AHA recommends web-based continuing education, the evidence to support the effectiveness of online learning approaches appears quite broad across different content and learner types and needs continued research to establish best practices (Means, Toyama, Murphy, Bakia, & Jones, 2010).

Recommendations for skill development extend beyond existing and seasoned employees. There is a growing body of research that shows that schools are not teaching students the realistic picture of today's clinical environment and new graduates may have unrealistic expectations as a result (Delaware Department of Health and Social Services, 2014; California, 2009; Illinois Public Health Institute, 2006; Ohio Department of Health, 2012; Pennsylvania Department of Health, 2004; Jeffreys, 2012, 2004, et al.; AHA Strategic Policy Planning Committee, 2015; CSI Solutions, LLC, 2013).

Data released in 2008 by the American Society for Training and Development (ASTD) indicated that one in three hours of training is delivered by technology and the expectation was that the ratio was expected to grow with time. The ASTD, in its many publications, repeatedly mentions the high cost of instructor led classes, reluctance or inability for staff to have release time from their duties to attend training, book-bound workers retiring, and an increase in a younger workforce who are increasingly using technology as part of all aspects of their everyday life. The 2014 Association for Talent Development (ATD) data release indicated that of 340 participating and vastly diverse organizations 38% of them deliver training using technology. Given the significant percentage, there is an inherent challenge of producing consistent and reproducible measurement of return on investment and also developing reproducible desired outcomes across diverse populations.

In the 2010 U.S. Department of Education meta-analysis of over 1,000 online, face-to-face, and blended instructional method studies (blended instruction is the combination of face-to-face learning and technology-assisted education such as offered through an LMS or another e-learning experience), the study types and study designs reviewed were reputed to be strong; notably, they included experimental or controlled and quasi-experimental designs. However, while large in scope, this body of research is fraught with weaknesses such as small sample sizes, failure to report retention rates within the conditions of the studies, and bias. Thus, the studies that contrast blends of online and face-to-face instruction with solely face-to-face instruction do not demonstrate that online learning is superior. Additionally, earlier work (Bernard, Abrami, Lou, Borokhovski, Wade, Wozney, Wallet, Fiset, & Huang, 2004) and other reviews of using distance learning technology (Cavanaugh, 2001; Moore, 1994) found no significant differences in effectiveness between education using technology and education in face-to-face classrooms. While not all of these earlier studies addressed adult populations they, again, found tremendous variability in effect sizes. These study findings cannot necessarily be generalized, but they do further encourage the ongoing support for the need of specific studies involving workforce development and outcomes using technology within behavioral healthcare.

At a higher level, in the United States, States have developed systemic identified needs and action plans to meet common health needs of their residents. Among those needs are the requirement for education, workforce development, and technology-related progress. Markedly, these common needs are often included in more than one State Health Improvement Plan (SHIP); this includes the District of Columbia). There is a majority participation in these action planning steps: as of 2010, 25 states have a SHIP completed or in progress; 15 states (29%) had no SHIP but had a Healthy People plan; and 10 states (20%) had no SHIP or Healthy People plan. No information was available for one state. Findings for each SHIP or Healthy People plan were reviewed, evaluated, and incorporated into the individual state SHIP guidance and recommendations (Marshall, Pyron, Jimenez, Coffman, Pearsol, & Koester, 2014).

SHIPs and Healthy People plans and related documents (Delaware Department of Health and Social Services, 2014; California, 2009; Illinois Public Health Institute, 2006; Ohio Department of Health, 2012; Pennsylvania Department of Health, 2004; Jeffreys, 2012, 2004; Texas Department of State Health Service, 2014) can be defined as comprehensive approaches to assessing individual State health. Each State has developed action plans based on identified needs to improve the State's health through community engagement. Common examples, throughout the 40 developed plans, that are education, workforce development, and technology related within the behavioral healthcare arena include the following concepts: continue efforts to work with educational institutions to train people for the jobs necessary to meet growing healthcare needs; partner with professional health schools; strengthen undergraduate health workforce training; improve health education services to lay population; need for appropriate implementation of and support for new technologies; meet the workforce capacity which is currently outpaced by demands; train workforce to address diversity in population; design education and continuing education to integrate learning into job requirements; and, ensure that there is an investment in the education of the workforce.

The SHIP and Healthy People plans are action-oriented and provide a detailed roadmap to better increase the health of each individual State that has participated. How to accomplish the suggested approaches toward improved workforce skill sets involves a significant increase in the use and integration of technology. It is clear that technology has a part to play in workforce development, most especially in behavioral health, but it is not clear which technologies are the most cost effective, provide the largest return on investment, and can apply in various circumstances.

States involved in the Western Interstate Commission for Higher Education (WICHE) (Alaska, Arizona, California, Colorado, Hawaii, Idaho, Montana, Nevada, New Mexico, North Dakota, Oregon, South Dakota, Utah, Washington, and Wyoming) have provided additional focus on workforce development and technology integration to improve rural behavioral health. Due to the rural nature of the WICHE regional geography, they have a significant incentive to incorporate effective technology-based solutions and have been early adapters to online meeting solutions for ease of sharing and for decreasing costs (Western Interstate Commission for Higher Education, n.d.). Fiber optics have made it possible to network with other groups and funding to make these options affordable may be available through the federal government, universities, mental health trust authorities, and state departments of health and social services. There is renewed focus on using technology to link with behavioral health components of academic institutions for the behavioral health providers and for primary care providers who need additional education in behavioral health related topics in order to better serve their population (Lake, 2014; Raney, 2015). As integrated care becomes more de rigueur, this need will be magnified and the role of technology will be ever more important. The WICHE States are paving the way to establish best practices with technology use in workforce development and behavioral health.

There are also inherently conflicting elements of modern day training: multiple generations of staff with different learning expectations and desired outcomes; the balance between staff development and maintaining a safe environment for clients; and the selection of relevant and cost-effective training modules. Specific to behavioral health, there are additional challenges, including the relevancy and feasibility of calculating a return-on-investment for training, if possible. There is also the dimension of different generations of clients – a previously low-impact data point, but now with the adaptation of technology and the active engagement of clients with technologically savvy treatment it is a significant data point that needs further measurement and research.

It should also be noted that barriers to technology use in clinical settings, not just limited to behavioral healthcare, have been well documented, especially with regard to implementing Electronic Medical Records (EMRs) (Ajami & Arab-Chadegani, 2013; Ajami, Ketabi, Isfahani, & Heidari, 2011). When EMRs were first proposed several decades ago, there were very clear technological and cultural limitations to their potential application and, as a result, there is a developing body of research that provides an evolving view on how to practically implement an EMR system. One aspect of this research that is recognized consistently is the failure of hardware and infrastructure to support a new and constantly evolving technology-heavy process.

Keeping this in mind, as this chapter focuses more on education, training, and professional community development, not on the implementation of EMRs, at its core, technology can present a barrier to already-reluctant communities to adopt new technology-based processes. The adoption challenge is twofold: first, the individual clinician or behavior workforce employee has to have an interest/desire in expanding their knowledge about their field (to include learning evidence-based treatments, developing supportive professional networks, etc.); second, technology must support the desire for personal development and not hinder it. There is a great, and recognizable, need for workforce development in behavioral healthcare, but the effort to use technology to build effective and long term solutions is not without its inherent challenges.

KNOWLEDGE DISSEMINATION AND TECHNOLOGY APPLICATION IN BEHAVIORAL HEALTHCARE

In the increasingly expansive behavioral healthcare business environment, there is a growing need to utilize information technology to achieve efficiencies, coordination, and communication (Laudon & Laudon, 2006; Porter & Miller, 1985). It has been well established that individuals are conditioned by their culture, which, in recent decades, has been extended into a new application of study as it applies to the influence of culture towards the use of technology. While adoption and usage of technology theories abound, they are often rooted in earlier research literature that references cultural theories. Among the more common examples of cultural theories in which technology theories are based are individualism/collectivism, masculinity/femininity, and uncertainty/avoidance (Hofstede, 1997); conservatism, mastery, and harmony (Schwartz & Bilsky, 1990); and persons relationship to other people, primary mode of activity and nature of people (Kluckhohn, & Strodtbeck, 1991).

A selection of technology acceptance models that have aspects of the more general cultural theories within them include the Technology Acceptance Model (Davis, 1989) which essentially says that if the cultural norm is to use technology, then individuals will likely use it. The Unified Theory of Acceptance and Use of Technology model, refers to social influence representing societal pressure on the users to use technology (Bandyopadhyay, & Fraccastoro, 2007). The Theory of Reasoned Action (Ajzen & Fishbein, 1980) emphasizes that the individual believes that most people who are important to them think that they should or should not perform the behavior.

A novel idea for behavioral health settings to consider is to conduct an internal survey to determine how the cultural constructs, as perceived by their unique staff, are spread across the existing research. This could easily be modeled and adjusted to be site specific by items used in a multi-national research study (Srite, 2006). Among the items to be considered are the following:

- **Perceived Usefulness:**
  - Using computers enhances my productivity in college.
  - I find computers useful in my college activities.
  - Using computers enhances my effectiveness in college.
  - Using computers improves my performance in college.
- **Perceived Ease of Use:**
  - It is easy for me to become skillful in using computers.
  - I find computers easy to use.
  - I find it easy to get a computer to do what I want it to do.
  - Learning to operate a computer is easy for me.
- **Behavioral Intention to Use:**
  - I intend to use a PC during my studies.
  - I intend to use a PC frequently during my studies.
- **Subjective Norms:**
  - I believe that my relatives think I should use a computer. Their opinions are important to me.
  - I believe that my friends think I should use a computer. Their opinions are important to me.
  - I believe that my classmates (co-workers) think I should use a computer. Their opinions are important to me.
- **Masculinity/Femininity:**
  - There are some jobs in which a man can always do better than a woman.
  - It is more important for men to have a professional career than it is for women to have a professional career.
- **Individualism/Collectivism:**
  - Being accepted as a member of a group is more important than having autonomy and independence.
  - Being accepted as a member of a group is more important than being independent.
- **Power Distance:**
  - Employees should not question their manager's decisions.
- **Uncertainty Avoidance:**
  - Rules and regulations are important because they inform workers what the organization expects of them.

Cultural aspects of technology acceptance must be taken into consideration when planning, designing, introducing, and implementing new technologies. The support of peers who are early adapters and the reactions from subordinates may influence, in a positive or negative manner, the transition of others. For example, it may be helpful for behavioral healthcare environments to consider group-based training in technology for team-based settings (collectivistic type culture) and on-line training may work better for more solo practitioner based environs (individualistic culture).

Behavioral healthcare (which includes mental health and substance abuse treatment, as well as integrated care (Lushniak, 2014)) has additional cultural acceptance barriers that need to be considered: clinical research barriers and *in vivo* treatment protocols. There is a challenge of managing 'sharing lived experiences' between treatment and research communities. Sharing experiences enhances the acceptance of new treatments and encourages staff to take an active role in skill-based training. Often, behavioral health staff want to "provide feedback to researchers on the barriers they encounter in implementing some suggested treatments, but lack an effective feedback mechanism with the research community" (Wolf & Goldfried, 2014).

A barrier contributed by the research community is the inconsistent use of terminology across studies and various authoritative sources that may present conflicting findings. In an already taxed workforce, there is little time or inclination to interpret findings if they are not clear. In the behavioral health field, a central repository for research and treatment communications that are verified and confirmed and present information in a timely fashion does not exist at present; it should also be kept in mind that there are several authoritative bodies and many clinical research centers that contribute to this body of information – APA, AHA, SAMHSA, NIDA, etc.

Staff acceptance of technology use in treatment methods may be an adoption barrier, regardless of the level of training or preparedness. As service recipients respond and embrace treatment that allows them a more active role in their recovery, treatment that often includes a technology component, staff must also master these systems and programs in order to support individuals in treatment. In addition to using technology for the development of their own personal knowledge, skills, and abilities, staff needs to keep pace with the treatments that involve technology in behavioral health.

Also of note, historically general medical healthcare and behavioral healthcare have operated in different spheres but often with overlapping client bases. Evidence Based Treatment (EBT) protocols are emerging on issues of co-morbidity: not just substance use disorders and mental health, but also general medical health issues and behavioral health. As this is a newer practice and experienced clinical staff may not have been exposed to these ideas in their initial training, this can be a significant barrier to adoption of new protocols (Shafran, et al., 2009). This is just one example of a treatment advancement that there is a great need to implement, but is slower on the uptake as staff gradually acclimate to new requirements.

It is of paramount importance, then, that knowledge (e.g., evidence-based treatments to clinical staff) is disseminated effectively and efficiently; it is not something likely to happen easily on its own, no matter how promising the developments in the clinical procedures (Beidas, Koerner, Weingardt, & Kendall, 2011). There are inherent challenges to disseminating new treatments, among them the cultural challenges of staff: fidelity to current treatments, concerns about client outcomes, changes compatible to existing protocols. Another challenge, often outside the control of behavioral health staff, is information technology infrastructure to support new methods of knowledge dissemination: network availability for web based trainings; appropriately sized firewalls to allow for clinical research and searching for best practices; and the selection and application support for a LMS.

One method to disseminate knowledge would be leveraging developed frameworks and heuristics. These systems have the potential to effectively and efficiently distribute knowledge within large networks, e.g., the Consolidated Framework for Implementation Research (CFIR), however they have not yet garnered complete empirical support. Components within these proposed systems are designed and proven using evidence-based theories; there are several well-formed case studies where their application has been successful. For example, the Veterans Administration (VA), a government supported system, was an early adopter of the CFIR and has provided leadership in the use of technology-enhanced treatment. The Mayo Clinic system of care, a non-profit medical practice and medical research group, is another successful adopter of the CFIR. Several state and county government systems have developed small pockets of technology use for their workforce development initiatives and some have developed systems that are more robust; it is not clear if these systems have used a proposed framework for implementation of technology-supported training initiatives and service delivery as the VA and Mayo Clinic have done. It is also possible that larger programs and programs with direct connection to academic institutions, may have a resource advantage with regard to testing new technological processes for both treatment and training – these partnerships may make failure easier to learn from and support a longer learning curve with room for needed fiscal adjustments.

Much research has been done to understand the best practice to implement a new technology or, in the case of health care, a new treatment (Fixsen, Naoom, Blase, Friedman & Wallace, 2005; Gotham, 2004; Chorpita & Regan, 2009; Corrigan, Steiner, McCracken, Blaser, & Barr, 2001), keeping in mind the necessary behavioral adaptations of staff. Rogers (2003) is highly cited for his Diffusion of Innovation Theory. At its core, the theory speaks to how individuals are more receptive to new ideas when people that are like themselves propose them and when the idea can be adaptable to their current process. This concept is generally supported by the adult learning phenomena.

Multiple approaches can be undertaken to assist slow technology adapters to learn. Academia teaches the Socratic method of problem solving as a means to assist students to learn critical thinking. The ARCS model is another problem solving approach to address the motivational aspects of learning environments that stimulate and sustain individuals' motivation to learn (Keller, 1983, 1984, 1987, 1988, 1999, 2010). This two-part model includes four categories of human motivation and a design process that utilizes the individuals' motivational characteristics. While perhaps over-simplified for purposes of this chapter, the actual ARCS Model is relatively easy to understand and to apply. Using four main motivational categories of attention, relevance, confidence, and satisfaction, an instructor can easily adapt content and style to each learner's needs. Keller (1999, 2010) provides a complete list of questions to self-analyze one's approach and design materials accordingly. This problem-solving approach has been used extensively around the world in schools, workplace settings, and in government, military, and nonprofit organizations (Keller, 2010).

One needs to consider motivation and instructional influences on learners as well as their capabilities, external and cultural influences, and environmental factors when introducing new technology to the workforce. When combined, this becomes a complex process that the ARC Model may help to systematically improve and may lead to more positive outcomes as behavioral health services transition to the use of technology. Moreover, instruction on new technology should be connected to available resources and procedures to meet the goals of learners and to create levels of challenge that are individually unique with the overarching goal of having learners feel successful goal accomplishment as they become technology adapters.

Taking into account theories such as this one and supported by knowledge of adult learning, concerns from staff need to be addressed before implementing a new practice – in this example, the implementation of web-based training for improving treatment outcomes. A clinician needs to be able to see the applicability of a new treatment to their existing procedures or cases. Several studies have documented the fidelity that clinicians can have towards specific service provision and treatments, even to the disregard of evidence-based procedures with a higher rate of efficacy. This is not to say that their fidelity is unfounded; they require specific examples that apply to their own settings, opportunity to discuss and contribute to proposed changes, and acknowledgement of the influence of their first-hand knowledge of the system in which they are immersed.

A common technology framework to systematically manage and track workforce development would be the implementation of a learning management system (LMS). From the perspective of management of training, to include courses, webinars, continuing education units (CEUs) or continuing education contact hours, often managed in house by a training department, LMSs have the capacity to manage multiple desired functions seamlessly: provide online training, webinars, self-studies, tests; manage scheduling of participants, rooms, equipment; map staff to specific competency development plans; provide statistics; ensure compliance with federal and state regulations with training courses; and host education related videos. These systems typically offer the end user learner the opportunity to manage their own learning and provide immediate access to their personal training. Robust LMSs have become a 'must have' within the realm of workforce development to help justify training return on investment (ROI) and to keep organizations in compliance with federal and other regulations. The persistent challenge is in the personnel cost to manage, develop content, and maintain the systems, as well as to teach the learners how to use them. A robust LMS requires an agile and supportive information technology infrastructure that may not be available in all behavioral healthcare venues.

Alternatively, the corporate arena and higher education have led this implementation of LMS and have well documented descriptions of the value of using these systems within their scopes of influence. They, equally, are researching the cost benefit ratios of using LMS technology as well as the outcomes. In general, it appears from this emerging body of research that blended learning may result in the most positive learning findings.

In a less formal, but perhaps not less effective fashion, new methods for knowledge sharing via technology have emerged: email discussion lists, Really Simple Syndication (RSS) feeds, blogging, and other social media. These technologies are most commonly used in informal settings, but can also be applicable to work settings – particularly in developing the workforce and in disseminating knowledge.

Email discussion lists are a form of communication that can be used to bridge the gap between research and treatment communities. These lists may have fallen out of practice – many new entrants to the field are not familiar with the practice and process of these discussion lists, but they may very well benefit from their use. LISTSERV software, or the original backend application to manage email lists, was created in the 1980s to automatically manage said lists and has continued to technologically evolve to keep pace with virus protection and spam filters. Culturally, professionals are so overloaded with information that it is a challenge to just keep up with email or Rich Site Summary or Really Simple Syndication (RSS) feeds, much less monitor professional communications. However, it is in email that those in the field are more likely to keep informed. Information provided in the existing context of a tool used daily is more likely to be well received than necessitating use or development of a new non-integrated tool or source.

A case study using an email discussion list to support dialog in forensic occupational therapy (Dieleman & Duncan, 2013) suggests that health professionals in specialized and often isolated areas of practice are keen to connect with colleagues and learn from each other's experiences. The main purposes for which online discussion groups are used can be summarized as communication, information sharing, and networking. It was found, however, that although participation was active at the start, activity within the group declined significantly during the last three years of the data collection period. This raises questions about the sustainability of online discussion groups within the rapidly developing social media environment. Typical to most new technology, there is often a quick uptick of interest when a service starts, but interest wanes over time if the tool is not integrated into everyday practice. This begs the question: how sustainable do these services need to be if they can provide necessary point of care interaction in the short term?

There are a few persistent issues with using email discussion lists, however. The quality of information provided is only as good as the persons providing it; and, there is often very little peer review or verification of the content. That being said, for a forum-type interaction, asking questions via an email list and receiving a fair amount of answers, is handled well with this technology. The volume of responses can be overwhelming and, as a result, high impact emails can be overlooked or, on the reverse side, a person asking a question can be overwhelmed with the responses by the group. (Adams, Kaplan, Soboko, Kuziemsky & Koppel, 2015)

There is a significant body of research on the effective use of journaling and, by extension, blogging, for client care. Blogging, or writing for a web log, is a form of rapid, real-time communication. For healthcare staff, it is suggested that blogging can help to increase compliance with quality measures, update staff on need to know information such as changes in policies and procedures, and provide up-to-date educational resources at any time, from anywhere (Curry, 2012). However, by the nature of services provided, blogging is not always an appropriate communication method for staff or workforce development. Personal blogs by those in the field can chronicle an individual's feelings or thoughts about a situation, but may not have an authoritative response or a 'teachable moment' attached to them. Blogs work very well for one way communication and sharing procedural information, but lack the ability to allow for a dialog, which is a necessary component of workforce development. There are also potential Health Insurance Portability and Accountability Act (HIPAA) confidentiality concerns as well as liability issues that a health care institution may face if a personal blogger's written content is not carefully vetted and screened with regard to client care. Institutions are using blogs to share authoritative updates as well as to stand as a repository of communications, which, again, provides a one way level of communication and lacks the capability for those in the field to ask questions or for their concerns to be heard.

Some well renowned medical journals (e.g., New England Journal of Medicine) provide a blog in addition to their publishing cycle in order to provide the community with more timely research findings and updates. In addition, specific to the field of psychology, there are many blogs written by researchers and practitioners who describe current findings, latest interpretations, and general insight to the field – all very useful pieces of information, especially to clinicians. The challenge, as noted previously, is that this presents just one-way communication with some challenges for how to implement proposed strategies effectively and how to provide and receive feedback. For the most part, these blogs present interesting reading and 'food for thought', but the next step – the critical element for workforce development – is how to implement these proposed changes in a practical fashion (if applicable or relevant).

Conferences provide the added benefit of face-to-face interaction, professional networking, and reinforcement of knowledge and skills. It is unclear how to measure the efficacy of the conference teachings, if the knowledge is not applied to the attendees' work within a period. There is a lack of research on this topic in the scholarly literature, but there are some anecdotal pieces of evidence presented by training organizations for using technology to reinforce training concepts. Lori Freifeld (2013), author for train-ingmag.com states, "Technology provides a cost-effective, fun way to stay in front of your (conference) participants with key content reminders after the training is over...whether you're reinforcing a strategic skill change such as sales, or simply changing the way employees complete their expense accounts, technology can help you ensure behavior change sticks." She goes on to describe how email, video, and other technology can be used to strengthen concepts and enact behavioral change following a conference or training event. It is reasonable to translate this use of technology to behavioral healthcare workforce development, but more research needs to be done, especially with regard to clinical skills and client care.

Mather and Cummings (2014) conducted a relatively small sample-size trial with clinical supervisors around the receptiveness and willingness to engage in an online social community for clinical practices. Overall, supervisors would be willing to work within the network as passive participants, e.g., receive clinical treatment updates and monitor changing guidelines, but were not necessarily strong supporters of being active contributors or members. This may be because they were not as confident about their clinical skills to share knowledge, but would have value for knowledge sharing from others, specifically more experienced staff. Engaging in a community such as this will likely increase the understanding of staff in new treatment methods and case studies for their applicability. The challenge is getting to the tipping point of adoption – something that would require time and dedication of an already taxed staff. This brief example is also reinforced by the large body of adult learning whose basic tenants include joining adults by acknowledging what they already know and giving credence to adult's experiences that influence new learning.

Several emerging treatment models for service recipients are now integrating technology at the onset and staff are meeting the challenge through new skill development. These models are attempting to keep pace with the evolving technology-integrated culture, all while continuing to provide the same high level of quality of care to their client base.

The Therapeutic Education System (TES) is an example of an evolving model for behavioral health staff to teach clients about a self-directed, web-based service provision. The model is designed to ad-dress behaviors that help persons in treatment for substance use disorders to stop their use of substances, learn life skills, and develop new, healthy, and adaptive behaviors. TES is available on multiple plat-forms including web-based desktop computers, smartphones, tablets, etc. The National Institute of Drug Abuse (NIDA) funded a research trial using a partial replacement model of TES and demonstrated that the system enhances abstinence rates in outpatient addiction treatment when TES substitutes for part of standard counseling (Institute for Healthcare Improvement, 2014). A similar effect was observed in a Clinical Trial Network (CTN) Trial. Additionally, data showed that technology-based interventions may be useful in minimizing the impact of specific risk factors on treatment outcomes (Acosta, Marsch et al., 2012; Kim et al., Under Review).

Pat Deegan, Ph.D., is a well-respected researcher and psychologist with lived experience. Dr. Deegan is an adjunct faculty member at Dartmouth College Medical School, Department of Community and Family Medicine and the Boston University, Sargent College of Health and Rehabilitation Sciences. She first implemented the web-based software program, CommonGround, in 2006 in conjunction with the Kansas Department of Social and Rehabilitation Services. CommonGround helps mental health clients identify treatment preferences and effectively communicate them to their service providers. This is an example of using software to make shared decisions between the service provider and the client, and the process can be completed online prior to an appointment. Data shows that using this collaborative software can lead to increased satisfaction among clients (Agency for Healthcare Research and Quality, 2012; Dartmouth-Hitchcock Medical Center, n.d.; Deegan, Rapp, Holter & Riefer, 2008).

As another example of this approach, the University of Wisconsin, School of Engineering, Center for Health Enhancement Studies has created innovative technology in the form of a smartphone application designed to help persons in treatment for substance use disorders. Persons in residential treatment are able to access a virtual online recovery community and receive psycho-education relative to relapse prevention and harm reduction. Additional examples of the use of technology are tracking tools for persons with high risk factors and individualized data information that is collected and reviewed prior to appointments. Behavioral health staffs are responsible for learning to use these approaches and for teaching others to use them.

The Center for Integrated Health Solutions project (CSI Solutions, 2013) is focused on integration and technology research and sponsored by the Substance Abuse and Mental Health Services Administration (SAMHSA) and Health Resources and Services Administration (HRSA). The interventions, TES and smartphone applications, are being piloted and data collection is ongoing (Cacciola, Alterman, DePhilippis, Drapkin, Valadex, Fala, Oslin, & McKay, 2012). There are supports for the development of these technologies that are consistent with those described earlier by Dr. Thomas of Wisconsin. They include: transitioning to population based care that requires more sophisticated case management; there are limited community treatment options; there is a high severity of mental health symptoms in populations being served; and, treatment options require the client base to follow through on treatment recommendations. Technology and technology-based treatment are considered an aid to meet these needs and behavioral healthcare staffs require training in their own use of the technology as well as training to assist clients to use the technologies.

The Center for Technology and Behavioral Health is a national Center of Excellence supported by NIDA and includes research and development focused on technologies used to deliver behavioral health treatment services. Lisa A. Marsch, Ph.D., Director, Center for Technology and Behavioral Health, Director, Dartmouth Psychiatric Research Center, Department of Psychiatry, Geisel School of Medicine at Dartmouth College applauds the promise of applying technology to health through on-demand access, prevention of costly escalation of unnecessary healthcare utilization, reduction of stigma and barriers, and increasing service capacity of systems of care. Dr. Marsch references the extraordinary rates of growth for access to internet and mobile devises by referencing the statistic revealing that over 90% of individuals worldwide have access to mobile phone services totaling about 6.8 billion mobile phone subscriptions worldwide (Felipe, Feit, & Thomas, 2014).

Likewise, there are over 1.4 billion smartphones in the world, and smartphone access is expected to triple globally to 5.6 billion by 2019. A demonstrated researched response to these facts has established that when developed well and in collaboration with the target audience, technology-based behavioral health tools can be useful, acceptable, and have an impact on health outcomes that are comparable to or better than clinicians. They increase quality, reach, and personalization of care by allowing the client to have a non-confrontational voice in their treatment whereas they may not be comfortable verbalizing out loud. Because of the relatively low overhead personnel costs associated with technology-based or supported care they can be most cost effective than traditional care and can, ultimately, be more responsive to individual needs (Felipe, Feit, & Thomas, 2014).

Researchers are beginning to gather adequate data to answer some of the questions that have been raised, but additional data and further research are necessary to answer others.

SOLUTIONS, RECOMMENDATIONS, AND CONCLUSION

A multi-faceted response approach that is based on specific assessment of need at the highest level of influence is likely the most reasonable approach to managing workforce development in behavioral healthcare over the next few years. Based on the incredibly quick advances in technology and the increasingly researched approaches to effective service delivery, there is an urgency to learn quickly, to learn effectively, and to learn the 'right thing'. In order to stay nimble, provide quality up to date information, and be constantly 'future ready' it is critical to place an emphasis on adequately resourcing the training and education providers. Those providers, in turn, need to partner with other training and education specialists in order to maximize knowledge resources and to assure the ability to make adjustments as technology and information evolves.

Prognostication about the future use of technologies within behavioral healthcare should be made with careful consideration and should use modest timeframes. The longer timeframes to try to foretell what it will look like the more likely the forecast will not hit the mark. For example, a ten year forecast in the use of technology to train in behavioral healthcare is nothing more than a combination of wishful and possibility thinking, all of it is based solely on what is known about technology today, and it is likely not even close to accurate. If the last five years of cell phone changes and the use of smart phones relative to service delivery, e.g. smart phone applications to assist recovery, are even remotely indicative of the speed and volume of one small piece of technology, behavioral healthcare's general use of technology will be even more profound.

Rather, the emphasis needs to be on strategic learning and finding measures to support which type of learning structure achieves the outcome whereby behavioral health service providers can garner information leading to changes in their service delivery that are connected to the defined individual client outcomes. The continued vast growth of information available to everyone will need to be culled, by trusted and informed educators, to manageable and usable amounts. The delivery methods will need to be updated, adjusted, and re-designed iteratively based upon constant quality initiatives and data collection that is connected to both workforce (on an individual level) development and to individual client outcomes. Technology, when adjusted for use by these criteria, is more likely to be embraced by all.

As the discussion for integrating primary care and behavioral health becomes the norm in practice, rather than the first layers of trial and error occurring now in the mid part of the twenty-first century, workforce development and the use of technology becomes of paramount importance (U.S. Department of HHS, grant). The Institute for Healthcare Improvement in its 90-Day research reported that new technologies for self-care are a solution for some persons; they discussed the need for full spectrum integration for behavioral health and the need to leverage technologies to provide the services (Institute for Healthcare Improvement, 2014). Training and education of the workforce, as well as the service recipients, is vital to achieve positive outcomes. The workforce deserves adequate training so they can provide services with expected outcomes and so they can train the service recipients.

"Our work has repeatedly shown that you can increase the quality of service delivery, improve client outcomes and maintain cost effectiveness when you embed technology systems as part of service delivery models…combining an in-person approach with mobile technologies can extend the scope and reach of mental health providers. That could be particularly beneficial in places where community health centers are overburdened…." (Marsch, Center for Technology and Behavioral Health at Dartmouth College, 2014). While the technology for clients is well-researched and documented, there is a dearth of research on the preliminary and seemingly, fundamental, question: what technologies work most effectively and create positive outcomes for learners in the behavioral health workforce? To obtain maximum client outcomes using technology critical step may have been overlooked, but it is not too late. There is a generally growing sentiment that suggests that the use of technology for workforce development in the 21st century may outperform earlier usage of technology in terms of effects on learning (Zhao, et al., 2005).

When computers were first introduced to the general workforce in the 1970s and 1980s there was a steep learning curve because the technology was brand new – most staff did not have a frame of reference or experience with such technology. Staff are now more comfortable with technology and associated applications and can better take their at-home knowledge and experience and apply it to their work. Vendors can support this knowledge dissemination by integrating the products with existing tools – e.g., provide a Learning Management System module to work on a mobile device so that clinical staff can leverage point-of-care skills drills.

Alternatively, the more time that is taken to re-train the workforce the non-adapters to technology and the slow-to-adapt will age out of the workforce. The emerging workforce in behavioral healthcare will likely not need the same level of training using technology; however, they may, need skill-based learning on relationship building and one-to-one in-person therapeutic interactions, as this is a well-documented and fundamental component to individual and successful client outcomes. The importance of the relationship may very well be lost, diminished, or less emphasized as clinical practice leans toward the increased use of technology and neglect to balance online training with in person interaction.

On April 27, 2015, in a media release from the United States Social Security Administration, Acting Commissioner Carolyn W. Colvin provided comments about Social Security's vision for 2025 that are a hundred percent applicable to preparing the behavioral healthcare workforce. She said, "We must be prepared to adapt as technology and society changes at an unprecedented rate,…. making sure we keep up with these changes, and how we position ourselves to best serve the public in the future. When employees, customers, and partners are given the right tools to help them work better together, wonderful things happen." As Daniel R. Masys (2002) aptly stated, "in health care as much as or more than in other human endeavors, knowledge is power, and the redistribution of access to knowledge will mean an inevitable redistribution of power over the decisions that affect the delivery of health care and the makeup of the health care workforce."

In conclusion, technology is working much of the time. The right questions are being asked most of the time. Specific short term research projects to direct and support clinical choices and to direct treatment efforts need to be continued and developed. These types of quality research projects need to be done with regularity and with specific venues in order to stay current with the constant changes. There remains much to do and it is not too late to do it.

REFERENCES

Adams, M. B., Kaplan, B., Sobko, H. J., Kuziemsky, C., Ravvaz, K., & Koppel, R. (2015). Learning from colleagues about healthcare IT implementation and optimization: Lessons from a medical informatics listserv. *Journal of Medical Systems*, *39*(1), 157. doi:10.1007/s10916-014-0157-3 PMID:25486893

Agency for Healthcare Research and Quality. (2013) Using Decision Aids in Shared Decisionmaking. *AHRQ Health Care Innovations Exchange*. Retrieved April, 29 2015 from https://innovations.ahrq.gov/issues/2013/08/28/using-decision-aids-shared-decisionmaking

AHA Strategic Policy Planning Committee. (2001). *Workforce Supply for Hospitals and Health Systems: Issues and recommendations*. Retrieved on March 17, 2015 from http://www.aha.org/advocacy-issues/workforce/workforceB0123.shtml

Ajami, S., & Arab-Chadegani, R. (2013). Barriers to implement Electronic Health Records (EHRs). *Materia Socio-Medica, 25*(3), 213–215. doi:10.5455/msm.2013.25.213-215 PMID:24167440

Ajami, S., Ketabi, S., Isfahani, S. S., & Heidari, A. (2011). Readiness Assessment of Electronic Health Records Implementation. *Acta Informatica Medica, 19*(4), 224–227. doi:10.5455/aim.2011.19.224-227 PMID:23407861

Ajzen, I., & Fishbein, M. (1980). *Understanding Attitudes and Predicting Social Behavior*. Englewood Cliffs, NJ: Prentice Hall.

American Society for Training & Development Research. (2008). *State of the Industry*. ASTD Research: Connecting Research to Performance. Retrieved March 15, 2015 from https://www.td.org/Publications/Research-Reports/2008/2008-State-Of-The-Industry?mktcops=c.learning-and-development~c.lt~c.sr-leader

Association for Training Development. (2014). *State of the Industry*. ATD Research: Connecting Research to Performance. Retrieved March 19, 2015 from https://www.td.org/Publications/Research-Reports/2014/2014-State-of-the-Industry?mktcops=c.learning-and-development%7ec.lt%7ec.sr-leader%7ec.learning-and-development

Bandyopadhyay, K., & Fraccastoro, K. A. (2007). The Effect of culture on user acceptance of information technology. *Communications of the Association for Information Systems, 19*, 23. Available at http://aisel.aisnet.org/cais/vol19/iss1/23

Beidas, R. S., Koerner, K., Weingardt, K. R., & Kendall, P. C. (2011). Training Research: Practical recommendations for maximum impact. *Administration and Policy in Mental Health, 38*(4), 223–237. doi:10.1007/s10488-011-0338-z PMID:21380792

Bernard, R. M., Abrami, P. C., Lou, Y., Borokhovski, E., Wade, A., Wozney, L., & Huang, B. et al. (2004). How does distance education compare with classroom instruction? A meta-analysis of the empirical literature. *Review of Educational Research, 74*(3), 379–439. doi:10.3102/00346543074003379

California. (2009). *State Health Care Workforce Development Planning Grant*. Retrieved March 17, 2015 from http://www.cwib.ca.gov/res/docs/special_committees/hwdc/meeting_materials/2013/California%20State%20Healthcare%20Workforce%20Development%20Planning%20Grant%20-%202012.pdf

Cavanaugh, C. (2001). The effectiveness of interactive distance education technologies in K-12 learning: A meta-analysis. *International Journal of Educational Telecommunications, 7*(1), 73–78.

Chorpita, B. F., & Regan, J. (2009). Dissemination of effective mental health treatment procedures: Maximizing the return on a significant investment. *Behaviour Research and Therapy, 47*(11), 990–993. doi:10.1016/j.brat.2009.07.002 PMID:19632669

Corrigan, R. W., Steiner, L., McCracken, S. G., Blaser, B., & Barr, M. (2001). Strategies for disseminating evidence-based practices to staff who treat people with serious mental illness. *Psychiatric Services (Washington, D.C.)*, *52*(12), 1598–1606. doi:10.1176/appi.ps.52.12.1598 PMID:11726749

CSI Solutions LLC. (2013). *The business case for behavioral health care*. Retrieved March 19, 2015 from http://www.integration.samhsa.gov/integrated-care-models/The_Business_Case_for_Behavioral_Health_Care_Monograph.pdf

Curry, K. (2012). Increasing communication in the intensive care unit: Is blogging the answer? *Critical Care Nursing Quarterly*, *35*(4), 328–334. doi:10.1097/CNQ.0b013e318266c010 PMID:22948365

Dartmouth-Hitchcock Medical Center. (n.d.). *Center for Shared Decision Making - About Shared Decision Making*. Retrieved April 29, 2015 from http://www.dartmouth-hitchcock.org/medical-information/decision_making_help.html

Davis, F. D. (1989). Perceived usefulness, perceived ease of use, and user acceptance of information technology. *Management Information Systems Quarterly*, *13*(3), 319. doi:10.2307/249008

Deegan, P. E., Rapp, C., Holter, M., & Riefer, M. (2008). Best Practices: A Program to Support Shared Decision Making in an Outpatient Psychiatric Medication Clinic. *Psychiatric Services Journal*, *59*(6), 603–605. doi:10.1176/ps.2008.59.6.603 PMID:18511580

Delaware Health and Social Services, Division of Public Health. (2014). *The First Delaware State Health Improvement Plan, Assessing and Improving Community Health in Delaware*. Retrieved March 17, 2015 from http://dhss.delaware.gov/dhss/dph/files/shaship.pdf

Dieleman, C. & Duncan, E. A. (2013). Investigating the purpose of an online discussion group for health professionals: a case example from forensic occupational therapy. *BMC Health Services Research Journal, 13*, 253. doi: .10.1186/1472-6963-13-253

Everson, K. (2014). *Special report: learning providers in the know, in the now*. Workforce®. Retrieved on February 26, 2015 from http://www.workforce.com/articles/print/21006-special-report-learning-providers-in-the-know

Felipe, R., Feit, B., & Thomas, C. (2014, August 21). *Making Apps and Web-based Tools Part of Your Integrated Behavioral Health Team* [Webinar]. Retrieved from www.integration.samhsa.gov

Fixsen, D. L., Naoom, S. F., Blase, K. A., Friedman, R. M., & Wallace, F. (2005). Implementation research: A synthesis of the literature. Tampa, FL: University of South Florida, Louis de la Parte Florida Mental Health Institute, National Implementation Research Network. (FMHI Publication No. 231).

Freifeld, L. (2013, October). How-to: Use technology to reinforce training. *Training: The source for professional development*. Retrieved January 23, 2015, from http://www.trainingmag.com/content/how-use-technology-reinforce-training

Gotham, H. J. (2004). Diffusion of Mental Health and Substance Abuse Treatments: Development, Dissemination, and Implementation. *Clinical Psychology: Science and Practice*, *11*(2), 160–176. doi:10.1093/clipsy.bph067

Hofstede, B. (1997). *Cultures and organizations: software of the mind*. London: McGraw Hill.

Illinois Public Health Institute. (2006). *State Health Improvement Plan, forces of change assessment*. Retrieved March 17, 2015 from http://www.idph.state.il.us/ship/Assessments/ForcesofChangeExecutiveSummary.pdf

Institute for Healthcare Improvement. (2014). *IHI 90-day R&D Project Final Summary Report: Integrating behavioral health and primary care*. Retrieved March 19, 2015 from http://www.ihi.org/resources/Pages/Publications/BehavioralHealthIntegrationIHI90DayRDProject.aspx

Jeffreys, M. R. (2004). *Nursing student retention. Understanding the process and making a difference*. New York, NY: Springer Publishing Company.

Jeffreys, M. R. (2012). *Nursing student retention. Understanding the process and making a difference*. New York, NY: Springer Publishing Company.

Keller, J. M. (1983). Motivational design of instruction. In C. M. Reigeluth (Ed.), *Instructional-design theories and models: An overview of their current status*. Hillsdale, NJ: Lawrence Erlbaum Associates.

Keller, J. M. (1984). The use of the ARCS model of motivation in teacher training. In K. Shaw & A. J. Trott (Eds.), Aspects of Educational Technology Volume XVII: Staff Development and Career Updating. London: Kogan Page.

Keller, J. M. (1987). Development and use of the ARCS model of motivational design. *Journal of Instructional Development*, *10*(3), 2–10. doi:10.1007/BF02905780

Keller, J. M. (1988). Motivational design. In Encyclopaedia of Education Media Communications and Technology (2nd ed.; pp. 406-409). Westport, CT. Greenwood Press.

Keller, J. M. (1999). Motivation in cyber learning environments. *Educational Technology International*, *1*(1), 7–30.

Keller, J. M. (2010). *Motivational design for learning and performance: The ARCS model approach*. New York: Springer. doi:10.1007/978-1-4419-1250-3

Kluckhohn, F. R., & Strodtbeck, F. L. (1961). *Variations in value orientations*. Evanston, IL: Row, Peterson.

Lake, J. (2014). *Integrative mental health care: A therapist's handbook*. New York, NY: W. W. Norton & Company, Inc.

Laudon, K. C., & Laudon, J. P. (2006). *Management Information Systems: Managing the Digital Firm*. Upper Saddle River, NJ: Pearson/Prentice Hall.

Lushniak, B. D. (2014). *Why should you care about mental health*. Mentalhealth.gov. Retrieved March 18, 2015 from http://www.mentalhealth.gov/blog/2014/10/why-you-should-care-about-mental-health.html

Marshall, D., Pyron, T., Jimenez, J., Coffman, J., Pearsol, J., & Koester, D. (2014). Improving public health through state health improvement planning: A framework for action. *Journal of Public Health Management and Practice*, *20*(1), 23–28. doi:10.1097/PHH.0b013e3182a5a4b8 PMID:24322682

Masys, D. (2002). Effects of current and future information technologies on the health care workforce. *Health Affairs*, *21*(5), 33–41. doi:10.1377/hlthaff.21.5.33 PMID:12224907

Mather, C., & Cummings, E. (2014). Usability of a virtual community of practice for workforce development of clinical supervisors. In H. Grain, F. Martin-Sanchez, & L. Schaper (Eds.), Investing in E-Health: People, Knowledge and Technology for a Healthy Future (pp. 104-109). IOS Press.

Means, B., Toyama, Y., Murphy, R., Bakia, M., & Jones, K. (2010). *Evaluation of Evidence-Based Practices in Online Learning: A Meta-Analysis and Review of Online Learning Studies*. U. S. Department of Education. Retrieved February 24, 2015 from http://eric.ed.gov/?id=ED505824

Moore, M. (1994). Administrative barriers to adoption of distance education. *American Journal of Distance Education, 8*(3), 1–4. doi:10.1080/08923649409526862

Ohio Department of Health. (2012). *Ohio 2012 – 2014 State Health Improvement Plan*. Retrieved March 17, 2015 from http://www.odh.ohio.gov/~/media/ODH/ASSETS/Files/lhd/Ohio%202012-14%20SHIP.ashx

Pennsylvania Department of Health. (2004). *State Health Improvement Plan: White Paper: The nurse workforce in Pennsylvania*. Retrieved March 19, 2015 from http://www.dsf.health.state.pa.us/health/lib/health/ship/nursewhitepaper.pdf

Porter, M., & Miller, V. (1985). How information gives you a competitive Advantage. *Harvard Business Review*, (July-August), 149–160.

Raney, L. (Ed.). (2015). *Integrated care: Working at the interface of primary care and behavioral health*. Arlington, VA: American Psychiatric Publishing.

Rogers, E. M. (2003). *Diffusion of Innovations* (5th ed.). Free Press.

SAMHSA. (2014, Fall). Building the behavioral health workforce. *SAMHSA News, 22*(4). Retrieved April 12, 2015 from http://www.samhsa.gov/samhsaNewsLetter/Volume_22_Number_4/building_the_behavioral_health_workforce/

Schwartz, S. H., & Bilsky, W. (1990). Toward a Theory of the Universal Content and Structure of Values: Extensions and Cross-Cultural Replications. *Journal of Personality and Social Psychology, 58*(5), 878–891. doi:10.1037/0022-3514.58.5.878

Shafran, R., Clark, D. M., Fairburn, C. G., Arntz, A., Barlow, D. H., Ehlers, A., & Wilson, G. T. (2009). Mind the gap: Improving the dissemination of CBT. *Behaviour Research and Therapy, 47*, 902–909. doi:10.1016/j.brat.2009.07.003 PMID:19664756

Sipek, S. (2015). *Health care reform creates problems, and jobs to solve them*. Workforce®. Retrieved February 18, 2015 from http://www.workforce.com/articles/21035

Social Security Administration. (2015). *Social Security Announces Vision 2025, a Long-Range Service Delivery Vision* [News release]. Retrieved from http://www.ssa.gov/news/press/releases.html#!/post/4-2015-8

Srite, M. (2006). Culture as an explanation of technology acceptance differences: An empirical investigation of Chinese and US users. *Australasian Journal of Information Systems, 14*(1), 5–23. doi:10.3127/ajis.v14i1.4

Texas Department of State Health Service. (2014). *The mental health work shortage in Texas*. Retrieved March 19, 2015 from http://www.dshs.state.tx.us/legislative/2014/Attachment1-HB1023-MH-Workforce-Report-HHSC.pdf

U.S. Census Bureau. (2013). *Computer and Internet Use Main*. Retrieved March 31, 2015 from http://www.census.gov/hhes/computer/

Western Interstate Commission for Higher Education. (n.d.). *Behavioral Health Workforce Development*. Retrieved February 26, 2015 from http://www.wiche.edu/mentalHealth/10926

Wolf, A. W., & Goldfried, M. R. (2014). Clinical Experiences in Using Cognitive-Behavior Therapy to Treat Panic Disorder. *Behavior Therapy*, *45*(1), 36–46. doi:10.1016/j.beth.2013.10.002 PMID:24411112

Zhao, Y., Lei, J., Yan, B., Lai, C., & Tan, H. S. (2005). What Makes the Difference? A Practical Analysis of Research on the Effectiveness of Distance Education. *Teachers College Record*, *107*(8), 1836–1884. doi:10.1111/j.1467-9620.2005.00544.x

Chapter 4
Virtual Design Teams in Virtual Worlds:
A Theoretical Framework using Second Life

Pete B. Rive
Auckland University of Technology, New Zealand

ABSTRACT

Design innovation increasingly requires cross-functional virtual teams and is becoming plural, collaborative and distributed. In order for global companies to compete they must be able to sync with the rapidly increasing pace of change and be able to tap the international talent that may, in the future, only connect via virtual worlds and virtual reality. It is important to recognise how design innovation and knowledge flow are regulated and how the virtual ecosystem can either inhibit or excite collaboration and the creation of new ideas, and the design of useful prototypes. This chapter presents a theoretical framework using three models, with examples, to explain and understand how virtual design teams can identify the regulation of knowledge flow and collaboration in the virtual world, Second Life.

INTRODUCTION

This chapter will examine the pervasive discipline of design and the early lessons to be gained from design practice and design education in the virtual world SL (Second Life). Three case studies, that were conducted in SL, will be used to illustrate examples of how virtual teams collaborate and connect on design projects within that virtual world. The primary research question posed was: how to design a virtual innovation ecology in SL? There were two important sub-questions related to this: what enables knowledge creation during design innovation in SL? What enables creative collaboration amongst designers in SL?

Three models were used to assist with the interpretation of the ethnographic data collected during the research in SL. They were:

1. The spectrum of fidelity that was used to interpret perceptions of presence (Rive, 2012);
2. Lessig's model of cybernetic regulators, and the four modes of knowledge flow (Lessig, 2004, 2006, 2008); and
3. The indosymbiotic knowledge life cycle (Rive, 2012). These models will be discussed in greater detail.

DOI: 10.4018/978-1-4666-9899-4.ch004

Design is a discipline that has become pervasive in almost all areas of human endeavor and goes far beyond aesthetics to shape products, processes, society, and even the foundations of life (Mau, Leonard, & Institute without Boundaries, 2004). By its very nature design is virtual and while it is becoming increasing hidden through the miniaturization of products, and the implicit design of process and organization, teams of designers are working together in the virtual space to determine the future of technological evolution (Kurzweil, 2005; Taylor, 1997). Design is no longer about one designer, one client, and one location, it is now becoming plural, collaborative and distributed (Mau et al., 2004). In order for global companies to compete they must be able to sync with the rapidly increasing pace of change with agile tools and be able to tap the international talent that may, in the future, only connect via virtual worlds and VR. It is important to recognize how design innovation and knowledge flow are regulated and how the virtual ecosystem can either inhibit or excite collaboration and the creation of new ideas, and the design of useful prototypes. Three models will be introduced that can help to explain and understand how virtual teams can identify the regulation of knowledge flow and collaboration with examples from the three case studies.

Following negative reports in the media, and the collapse of media interest, many technologies continue to evolve and improve only to eventually be part of another future hype cycle. The technology consultancy the Gartner Group describes a hype cycle as one in which the media enthusiastically reports a new technology that over-sells the features and attracts new users only to collapse once those features are not fulfilled. Both virtual reality and virtual worlds have participated in a number of hype cycles and it appears a new wave of these technologies are about to be hyped again (Gartner, 2007). The long history of interest in virtual experiences suggests these technologies will continue to evolve and are not simply fads, (Grau, 2003; Wertheim, 1999). There have been many organizations around the world that have experimented with, and used virtual worlds, such as SL for collaboration within virtual teams. Despite enthusiastic experimentation many have now abandoned their virtual islands, and had their virtual property returned to them. SL has just passed its tenth year anniversary, and while 400,000 new users still sign up every month, many do not last longer than that first month (Au, 2014). However, according to Wagner Au, the first embedded journalist in SL, believes virtual worlds are set to once again take off (2014). There has also been a recent resurgence of interest in VR, and the acquisition of Oculus Rift by Facebook for USD$2 billion, and the release of other virtual reality products from Samsung and Microsoft, to name a few, suggests that there could be more developments to come in virtual reality, virtual worlds and social media.

The objective of this chapter is to describe a theoretical framework that could provide a useful means of examining how design teams interact in a virtual world when they are sharing a design innovation goal. Three case studies; six years of cyber-ethnographic observation of *residents* (as they are known by the users) in SL; and a literature review provided the basis for this theoretical framework.

THEORETICAL ISSUES

The case study research attempted to build on the existing literature and to extend cybernetic theory in the application of knowledge life cycles, control and regulation, in order to understand how virtual design teams work to achieve innovation in a virtual design innovation ecology in SL. The case study research was the basis for a thesis that formulated the following proposition:

In order to design a virtual design innovation ecology, cybernetic regulators must provide feedback, and will either enable or inhibit design collaboration, and knowledge creation in SL.

Within the limited space available it is only possible to present a summary of the findings of the research, and the theoretical framework that underpins them. By conducting a cyber-ethnographic study of how design teams collaborate it was hoped that this research would identify the current limitations and advantages of this virtual world ecology, as well as the potential opportunities for future research into virtual teams and design studios. In order to interpret the cyber-ethnographic culture of design teams in SL this study includes instrumental case studies to focus on knowledge creation and creative collaboration as part of the design innovation process in the virtual world. This research applies the cybernetic epistemological linkage between knowledge creation and regulation, and the design innovation process in SL. It applied a second-order cybernetics approach to the virtual innovation ecology within SL using multidisciplinary techniques that have strong roots with the anthropology of Gregory Bateson, known for his concept of *the ecology of mind* (Bateson & Donaldson, 1991), and the biological epistemology of Maturana and Varela (1992).

It is the author's intention to briefly discuss the nature of the *virtual* and the *real* to provide a brief argument for why these concepts should not be considered dichotomous and to lay the foundation for a new understanding of how virtual teams interacting in a virtual world are experiencing something more like an alternative reality, with as much validity as any other shared reality. This theoretical framework must first address the confusion over the meaning of the word *virtual*, especially in the context of technology. This confusion probably stems back to the 1980s when William Gibson published *Neuromancer* (1984), and when Jaron Lanier coined the phrase 'virtual reality' (1989). Many now believe that the word *virtual*, and the immersive technology associated with it, are the anthesis of the *real* or reality based on an implicit logical positivism and a hegemonic empirical reality. Virtual worlds and virtual technology, such as SL, have suffered as a result of this misconception (Boellstorff, 2008; Shields, 2003). Simply stated it is thought by some that something is either real, or it is virtual — to them this relationship is unquestionably dichotomous. This paper will briefly discuss why this is not the case, and why this belief holds important implications for the theoretical framework of this research because, while this false dichotomy is widely accepted, it is founded on some fundamentally misleading philosophical assumptions. An objective *reality* was once considered empirically obvious, and uncontroversial, and even today many consider that it is a concept that is self-evident. It was widely regarded as something that was provable, and materially existed as a physical truth unaffected by human thought or senses; it was *common sense*, and while many still believe that to be true, there have been significant shifts in the philosophy of science that have brought this into contention. Regarded by some to be the most successful scientific theory in the history of science, quantum mechanics, has shown that it is impossible for the observer not to influence, or be affected by the subject. Reality is no longer thought by physicists to be something that is immutable, objective and solid but rather something that is relative; explained by probability; and materialized by observation and measurement. What was once held to be a common sense view of reality has been proven to be wrong at both the very small and very large scales and can be shown to be an incorrect explanation of our day-to day-reality (Greene, 2005, 2011). There is not sufficient space here to fully explore either the *virtual* or the *real*, however, this theoretical framework will touch briefly on why this apparently semantic argument is important to the topic of virtual teams, and creative collaboration in design.

Etymology is instructive about the origins of ideas and cultures that are embedded in word assumptions. It gives a reader the provenance, and evolution of that word and teaches us how a culture has shaped, and been shaped by its use (Malkiel, 1975).

The Oxford English Dictionary defines *virtual* in the earliest recorded use of the word as:

1. *Possessed of certain physical virtues or capacities; effective in respect of inherent natural qualities or powers; capable of exerting influence by means of such qualities. Now rare.(as used in the 14th century)*
2. *Morally virtuous. (archaic)*
3. *That is so in essence or effect, although not formally or actually; admitting of being called by the names so far as the effect or result concerned* (The Compact edition of the Oxford English dictionary: complete text reproduced micrographically, 1971).

These definitions briefly highlights three important aspects of virtual worlds, and immersive technology with reference to our research and this theoretical framework. They are:

1. First, what is interesting about this past use of the word is that there is a hint of a strong interest in the *virtual*; and that it is both primordial and deeply engrained, and not some neologism invented by techno-journalists at the end of the 20th century. Researchers such as Grau (2003) and Wertheim (1999) have illustrated how there was an ancient spiritual and mystical fascination with virtual immersive art. Its original goal was of psychological transcendence dating back as far as the Pompeii frescos of 60 BCE.
2. The relationship between the two concepts of the *virtual* and the *real* implies a deep connection. The *virtual* is the essence of the real and is connected, and not in opposition to it. The meaning of the *virtual* within the ancient philosophical and religious writings was more real than the real; it was virtuous if not transcendent. The essence of something actual was not something ersatz, inferior or faux but something to be highly regarded and worthy of deeper understanding. The modern conception of the *virtual* has been perverted to mean something *not real,* but *fake*, and this pejorative connotation often undermines the virtual experience for both the users and the commentators of virtual worlds and the relationships between avatars in those worlds (Boellstorff, 2008; Shields, 2003). For those that have not spent time in a virtual world this alternative reality can be threatening, as friends and family can keenly feel the competition for attention because some *residents* of SL were spending over 20 hours per week in-world (Castronova, 2005, 2007; de Nood & Attema, 2006). A common phrase of derision relating to SL is: *You are into Second Life, what's wrong with your first one?*
3. For some readers these sketchy historical and philosophical discussions may remain unconvincing; the argument of false dichotomy is better described in detail by others (Grau, 2003; Heim, 1993, 1998; Shields, 2003; Taylor, 1997; Wertheim, 1999). What may be more compelling is a summary of the scientific foundation of this theoretical framework. According to the theoretical physicist, Greene: *The overarching lesson that has emerged from scientific inquiry over the last century is that human experience is often a misleading guide to the true nature of reality* (Greene, 2005). Epistemological evolutionists have pointed out that our perception is mediated by our nervous system and is almost indistinguishable from a hallucination (Maturana & Varela, 1980, 1992); cybernetic

anthropologists have explained how reality is a social construct (Bateson & Donaldson, 1991); and psychologists describe how our senses mediate our subjective reality (Riva & Ijsselsteijn, 2003).

Scientific theories have come to dominate the discussion around reality and are regarded by many to be the most persuasive description of reality. Unfortunately, despite the outstanding predictive successes of theories such as quantum mechanics and relativity these descriptions of reality appear to be more virtual than physical. Einstein's two theories of relativity brought about a revolution overthrowing Newton's ruling physical theory of reality. However, because Einstein's theories are only apparent at the extremes of speed and gravity most of us still assume a Newtonian reality that ignores relativity and defaults to some so-called 'objective' physical reality (Greene, 2005). One individual's experience of time and space can be hugely different to another's if they travel close to the speed of light, or they are located near a black hole. This concept was clearly illustrated in the popular movie, Interstellar. Einstein thought that the raw material underlying all reality was spacetime which has proven to be much stranger than even he had believed possible (Greene, 2005). Einstein's relativity has challenged the concept of absolute objectivity. *Observers moving relative to each other have different conceptions of what exists at a given moment, and hence they have a different conception of reality* (Greene, 2005).

These theories of multiple realities present the universe, or universes, like a game of chance, where all possible realities exist in a virtual state of probability only to become actual when they are observed or measured (Greene, 2005, 2011; Mee, 2012). Quantum mechanics questions what might be an intuitive sense of reality in that it says that reality is *non-local*, and that two objects can be far apart in space but remain a single entity. According to the frontrunners of scientific theories, superstring theory, and M theory, the tinniest components of the universe could be made of sub-atomic particles, or superstrings known as membranes. Everything is connected by energy fields and the only thing that differentiates the building blocks of the universe are identical strings that vibrate at different energies. According to M theory our reality is not composed of just three spatial and one time dimension, but of ten spatial dimensions and one time dimension, *superstring theory is telling us that we've so far glimpsed but a meagre slice of reality* (Greene, 2005, p. 18). Invisible to our senses, there could be an infinite number of universes with infinite copies of ourselves, and therefore, an infinite number of realities. *We are forced to concede that our view of reality is but one among many — an infinite number, in fact — which all fit together within the seamless whole of spacetime* (Greene, 2005, p. 78).

Computer simulations can even be regarded as real. The Oxford philosopher Bostrom assumes that realistic computer simulations of our universe are possible and goes on to say if our descendants were to create an immense number of simulated universes filled with self-aware inhabitants then digital universes may even outnumber physical universes. Bostrom believes that it is highly probable that we are living in a computer simulation right now (Bostrom, 2003). While Greene doubts that we might be unwittingly instantiated in a computer simulation he believes that *if* a high fidelity simulation was possible that it would be more likely that simulated inhabitants would be able to *migrate into the real world or be joined in the simulated world by their real biological counterparts. In time, the distinction between real and simulated beings might become anachronistic* (Greene, 2011). Interestingly, the findings of this research show that to be already the case as SL *residents*, and AI (artificial intelligence) avatars have begun to share a co-presence in virtual worlds. The liminal blurring of these realities, that has been observed in the case studies, could be the first signs that the virtual and the actual will eventually share a co-presence.

As the fidelity of virtual worlds increases the discussion of a virtual/real dichotomy will become less relevant. Empirical reality, that once appeared to be the objective truth, is being challenged by scientific theories, virtual worlds, and mediated realities. As psychologists, Riva & Ijsselsteijn, have observed all reality is mediated by our senses and perceptions, so mediation can no longer be a defining criteria that differentiates the virtual and the real (Riva & Ijsselsteijn, 2003). This approach supports the theoretical framework that others have also used with respect to research in virtual worlds (Boellstorff, 2008; Malaby, 2009; Riva, Davide, & Ijsselsteijn, 2003; Taylor, 1997).

The search for a grand unified theory that will unite the theories of relativity with quantum mechanics has led to the Standard Model of particle physics. The recent discovery of the Higgs Boson particle in 2012 has been described as one of the greatest discoveries of science and strongly confirms the predictive power of superstring theory and the Higgs field. The presence of this unifying invisible field gives everything in the universe mass, and in affect provides the universe with the essence of reality (Mee, 2012). The Higgs field is something that cannot be seen, but that can exert a force beyond the physical, much the same as an electromagnetic field.

This theoretical framework introduces three models to assist in understanding the epistemological context using an ecological systems approach: The *spectrum of fidelity*; Lessig's cybernetic regulatory modality; and the *indosymbiotic knowledge life cycle*. The theoretical frameworks of Von Krogh, (2000) and Lessig (2004) were adapted and modified to help address the research question. A summary of the three models follows:

- **The Spectrum of Fidelity (Rive, 2012):** This model was devised to account for the perception of presence in a virtual world. It was designed to fit the theoretical framework illustrating and describing a new theory of presence based on earlier work by Lombard and Ditton, and also Riva's simplified co-presence (Riva & Waterworth, 2003).
- **Lessig's Cybernetic Regulators:** This model is an adaptation of Lessig's four modes applied to SL. It explains how the four modes can inhibit or encourage creative collaboration, knowledge creation and innovation in SL based on cybernetic feedback and regulation (Lessig, 2004, 2006, 2008).
- **The Indosymbiotic Knowledge Life Cycle (Rive, 2012):** This model was designed to explain the life cycle of a design innovation in the SL context. It is partly based on the epistemological biology of Maturana and Varela (1992); the evolutionary microbiology and endosymbiosis of Margulis (1970); Bateson's *ecology of mind* (Bateson & Donaldson, 1991); and the models of Von Krogh et al., (2000) and Hussi, (2003).

The Spectrum of Fidelity

Much of the literature around virtual reality and virtual worlds touches on reality, however, the virtual and the real are not dichotomous with regard to either the word's etymology, or the philosophy of science (Boellstorff, 2008; Greene, 2005, 2011; Shields, 2003). In SL it is common to hear *residents* refer to the offline world as RL or *real life*. This dichotomous concept of SL vs. RL has been imported into the virtual world and is even mentioned by the development company of SL, Linden Lab. However, it is also common for avatars or cyborgs to discuss a liminal blurring between these psychological states or realms (Boellstorff, 2008; Heider, 2009; Loke, 2009). Virtual teams in SL experience a knowledge creation ecology as a cyborg, a cybernetic organism, and are therefore likely to also experience this liminal blurring as observed during the case studies.

Figure 1. Spectrum of fidelity
(Rive, 2009).

Spectrum of Fidelity

Low fidelity model   High fidelity model

The spectrum of fidelity was a model devised by the researcher to explain how the subjects of the case studies perceive their virtual experience without arguing about whether it is real or not, or indeed questioning SL's validity. Figure 1 illustrates how a virtual experience; a cyborg; an avatar; a virtual space or a virtual object perceives, or can be perceived, and where it sits along this spectrum. At one extreme there are low-fidelity models, and these are the simplest informational units, that the subject recognizes as a simulation or model of the actual object; at the other extreme is a high-fidelity copy of the physical object which is indistinguishable from the actual.

Fidelity is used here to mean *the exact degree to which something is copied or reproduced* (The Compact edition of the Oxford English dictionary: complete text reproduced micrographically, 1971). The purpose of this model is to assist in determining to what extent a simulation can represent the actual, and to assess how a simulation may approach the same informational density as the actual when it is observed or communicated.

Face-to-Face Simulation

Face-to-face meetings have been shown to be the most effective means of tacit knowledge exchange and breakthrough innovation in design teams, (Dixon, 2000; Von Krogh, 2007; Pentland, 2010, 2014). Therefore, in order to enable design innovation within virtual teams face-to-face meetings must be simulated. Virtual worlds provide various channels of communication within virtual teams to enable knowledge flow and creation (Thomassen & Rive, 2010). It is important to make a distinction between tacit and explicit knowledge creation; tacit knowledge is difficult to codify and relies heavily on face-to-face communication, and yet it is a driver of breakthrough design innovation, while explicit knowledge can be written down or easily codified and communicated, but is more suited to incremental innovation (Dixon, 2000; Hussi, 2003; Leonard & Swap, 2004; Pentland, 2010, 2014; Von Krogh, Nonaka, & Ichijo, 2000). Von Krogh et al. wrote: *Individual face-to-face interaction is the only way to capture the full range of physical sensations and emotional reactions that are necessary for transferring tacit knowledge.* (2000). However, Von Krogh did acknowledge that virtual context or *cyber ba* could enable tacit knowledge exchange, (2000).

The challenge is to communicate tacit knowledge in a simulated environment during a virtual face-to-face exchange. Tacit knowledge or *deep knowledge* requires communication of emotions via a rich spectrum of the senses and extended conversations within an understood context (Leonard & Swap, 2004; Nonaka & Takeuchi, 1995; Polanyi, 1967). It is tacit knowledge exchange that is most valuable and contributes the most to innovative knowledge creation and learning within virtual teams, and the higher the fidelity of the simulated face-to-face experience the higher the tacit knowledge exchange (Rive & Thomassen, 2012; Rive, Thomassen, Lyons, & Billinghurst, 2008). Within the context of a virtual world participants in a virtual team must have a sense of presence in order to successfully convey tacit knowledge (Rive et al., 2008). The perception of presence is influenced by the spectrum of fidelity, both in terms of the virtual spatial context; sensory fidelity; and avatar appearance and interaction (Rive, 2012; Rive & Thomassen, 2012). SL as a design innovation ecology should not only be assessed according to its ability to simulate how virtual teams interact face-to-face, but based on other advantages over actual interactions due to the augmentation of the virtual space (Rive & Thomassen, 2012). According to Lombard and Ditton there are six criteria of presence: realism, immersion, transportation, social richness, social actor within medium, and medium as social actor (Lombard & Ditton, 1997). Riva further simplified the theory of presence to describe physical and social presence, with co-presence intersecting the two. They wrote: *Physical presence refers to the sense of being physically located in mediated space, whereas social presence refers to the feeling of being together, of social interaction with a virtual or remotely located communication partner* (Riva et al., 2003). Co-presence, at the intersection of physical and social presence, according to Riva, is being together in a shared virtual space, and virtual worlds and virtual teams sit at this intersection (2003). Research has shown that cyborgs will maintain similar interpersonal distance between their avatars and subconsciously obey social norms in simulated face-to-face situations (Bailenson, Beall, Loomis, Blascovich, & Turk, 2004; Bailenson, Blascovich, Beall, & Loomis, 2003; Beall, Bailenson, Loomis, Blascovich, & Rex, 2008).

Lessig's Cybernetic Regulators

The Stanford law professor, Lawrence Lessig, was asked to consult to Linden Lab in 2003 after a shaky start with declining numbers in SL. Lessig recommended that SL adopt a radical approach to the IP (intellectual property) created by the users in SL and allow them to own their own creations. This approach has been credited with the subsequent success of SL and the dramatic growth in user numbers (Boellstorff, 2008; Lessig, 2001, 2004, 2008; Ondrejka, 2006; Turner, 2006). Lessig (1999, 2007) argues that there are four modalities that inhibit or excite the free flow of ideas and knowledge rights which are based on the cybernetic principles of feedback and control. This provides us with a cybernetic framework to consider both barriers and enablers of idea flow and how we can improve knowledge creation and creative collaboration within a virtual innovation ecology by addressing what these modes are and how they are regulated.

Lessig's modes are: market; architecture; law; norms. The barriers and enablers of knowledge creation can be examined as knowledge regulation and flow (Lessig, 1999; Thomassen, 2003; Von Krogh et al., 2000). Combining Lessig's model with second-order cybernetics provides an additional method of describing the symbiotic regulators that influences the feedback to the system and knowledge creators in SL (Maturana & Varela, 1992; Wiener, 1954, 1961). Lessig's (2006, 2008) regulators are applied to the specific context of the design innovation ecology in SL. The inception of a creative idea is recognized as an individual act and yet design innovation and knowledge transactions are seen as collaborative activities (Hamel, 2007; Hippel, 2005; Hunter, 2008; Prahalad & Ramaswamy, 2004; Von Krogh et al., 2000). Thus, knowledge creation and creative collaboration in the virtual innovation ecology are seen within the social context of SL. In figure 2 Lessig's four modes can be seen to interact in a dynamic ecology. Lessig (2004) explained that, *At the center of this picture is a regulated dot: the individual or group that is the target of regulation, or the holder of a right* (p. 121).

*Figure 2. The four modes of regulation
(Lessig, 2004).*

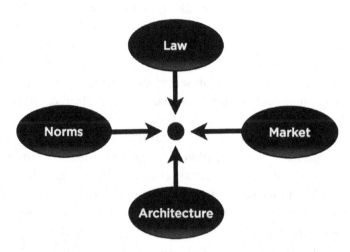

Indosymbiosis: The Life Cycle of Knowledge Creation in SL

Indosymbiosis is based on the cybernetic work of epistemological evolution by biologists, such as Margulis (1970), and Maturana and Varela (1992). The evolutionary biological theory of epistemology is a massive field of research that goes beyond the scope of this chapter (see Rive, 2012). This field underpins the very foundations of creative constructivism and predicates the sociological and ideological beliefs or paradigms about what enables design innovation and its models. Indosymbiosis is a neologism meaning a knowledge life cycle in a virtual world. This research defines *indosymbiosis* as:

An emergent innovation process driven by self-replicating ideas or inogisms that evolve in a cybernetic virtual ecosystem, supported by micro-communities and an intelligent network of users, designers and leaders known as a hive or colony (Rive, 2009).

An *inogism* is a cybernetic design innovation organism or cyborg; a self-replicating innovative idea with a life cycle determined by a knowledge vision and final maturation described by a successful user ecosystem. (Rive, 2009)

The benefit of the *indosymbiotic model* is that it provides a number of features that are consistent with the common goals of the agile innovation design process (Highsmith, 2004).

Following Highsmith's (2004) recommendations, the features of indosymbiosis are that it is: creative; agile; emergent; informal; self-replicating; self-organizing; lean and resourceful; distributed; plural; and symbiotic, collaborative, collective intelligence. It is a non-linear, recursive model that incorporates Lessig's four modes, and borrows from biological metaphors and theories to help to understand the evolutionary epistemology of knowledge creation and the learning process in a virtual world. It posits a symbiotic social approach to knowledge creation and learning based on a rejection of the neo-Darwinist theory of the *selfish gene* (Dawkins, 1976) and the simplistic epistemological view of *natural selection* that views the individual survival of an idea as a violent competition, *red in tooth and claw*.

In the Knowledge Economy it is intangible assets that have become the focus of business, (Stewart, 2001; Teece, 2000) politics, (Lessig, 2004) design (Hippel, 2005; Leadbetter & Demos (Organization),

2002; Mau et al., 2004) and education (Thomassen & Rive, 2010; Tiffin, 1995; Tiffin & Rajasingham, 2003). Design innovation carried out by virtual teams is, therefore, inexorably tied to the economics of intellectual capital, and SL provides us with, not only a lens to view how the tensions play out between tangible and intangible property, but is an important environment to understand as virtual worlds develop and grow. The dynamics of the network society, (Castells, 2000), and the essential quality of sensory experience and emotions are prevalent in SL, as people strive for connections and a *presence* to improve their communication channels in order to collaborate, share ideas, and share deeply personal experiences, (Pine & Gilmore, 1999; Roberts, 2004). SL in the knowledge economy is a highly networked, experiential, and emotionally charged virtual environment in which social networks have come to dominate. The network effects of the community assist in a positive feedback loop which in turn attracts more residents to SL (Shapiro & Varian, 1999). SL, like most of the MMORPGs, (massively multiplayer online role playing games), such as World of Warcraft, is first and foremost a social experience, (Bartle, 2004; Book, 2004). Von Krogh et al. (2000) argue that the ideal micro-community for innovation would consist of five to seven people from across diverse disciplinary areas. Johansson (2004) supports this in *The Medici Effect*, which argues that cultural diversity generates more innovation.

Biologists have recognized the close biological connection between innovation, knowledge creation and evolution and refer to evolutionary novelty and variety, in primitive bacteria, as innovation, (Margulis, 1970). Evolutionary theory has been applied to knowledge generation, and the analogy of biological diversity; viral ideas on the Internet; *memes*; natural selection and mutation, (Blackmore, 1999; Brand, 1988; Dawkins, 1976; Kurzweil, 2005; Laszlo & Loye, 1998). Co-operation and symbiosis in evolutionary design has effectively been going on for approximately three and a half billion years, as long as the first microbial communities started cannibalizing each other, and sharing RNA through a process of endosymbiosis, (Margulis, 1970; Margulis & Sagan, 1991, 1997; Skoyles & Sagan, 2002). Margulis has convincingly proven that the powerhouse of the human cell, mitochondria, evolved and survived from the earliest prokaryote cell through a symbiotic sharing of information (1970). Knowledge creation, is a homeothetic process and implies a directed, purposeful approach to modelling the world, and this is just what cybernetic scientists have shown to be the case, even in simple cell organisms such as E. Coli bacteria, ever since life could move, (Bateson & Donaldson, 1991; Margulis & Sagan, 1991; Maturana & Varela, 1992; Montague, 2007). The deep laws of cosmic evolution are at work in epistemology through the aggregation of information and knowledge in complex adaptive systems, and are in turn counter balanced by the second law of thermodynamics which dissipates information through entropy, (Capra, 1983a, 1983b; Gell-Mann, 1994; Kurzweil, 2005; Laszlo, 1987, 2007). According to Kurzweil epistemological evolution began with the physics of the universe, then chemistry, then evolved into biology, neurology, then the story, ideas, knowledge, technology, computers, and the Internet (Kurzweil, 2012). Kurzweil, and others, recognized that biology exhibits distinct traits and is capable of self-creation and reproduction moving beyond a mechanistic epistemological evolution.

Indosymbiosis is an initial attempt to provide a biological metaphor to help to understand learning and epistemology in a virtual world by virtual design teams and requires further research and detailed analysis. The phases or stages of the knowledge life cycle are not necessarily linear, are recursive and can be regulated at any point by Lessig's four modalities; they are:

- **Infection:** The host is infected by an inogism is similar to Dawkins' *meme* (Blackmore, 1999; Dawkins, 1976) and can take place anywhere, either in SL or outside the virtual world, prior to the creation of their cyborg. A cyborg is created when a human logs in to SL. The idea that begins the indosymbiotic cycle may be either well developed or barely formed prior to the cyborg's infection.

- **Recombination:** As in endosymbiosis, one inogism engulfs another, or as Kelly wrote (1994), *the membraned cells incorporated the bacteria and their informational assets as wholly owned subsidiaries working for the cells. They kidnapped the innovations* (Kelly, 1994, p. 371). The cyborg will then recombine the inogism with other inogisms in SL and will also draw upon ideas from outside SL. The membrane is semi-permeable; the virtual and the actual continually shift states.

- **Incubation:** The phase when the cyborg thinks about and even plays with other inogisms that may contribute to the innovative design. SL is not a closed system but like a biosphere or another ecosystem it has a semi-permeable membrane, with ideas flowing back and forth with the outside environment.

- **Hive:** According to Kelly (1994), a hive mind is distributed but thinks as one, as if it was a super-organism. This self-organizing emergent state would be the optimum state for a distributed design team but is more likely to occur in larger numbers. A hive can occur at a point when the cyborg feels ready to include others and may need help to progress the inogism; they can move on to build a hive of five to seven other cyborgs.

- **Migration:** The group or hive feeds the inogism with their own inogisms and their DNA is swapped as ideas quickly evolve, mutate and co-create. This is an important phase in an innovation's life cycle as a hive or team must find support from the wider ecosystem and their self-organization and direction will shape the survival rate of the inogism. An inogism is unlikely to continue to evolve as a discrete innovation without care, resources and constant feeding with other ideas (Von Krogh et al., 2000). The infant inogism will continue to adapt and evolve according to its ecology and this will eventually expand to include a migration to a larger ecosystem which could include others outside the hive, such as other groups, suppliers and customers.

- **Colonization:** In this phase a hive of inogisms may expand to consume other hives, becoming a hive mind or *collective intelligence*, and even engulf colonies of hives that freely share DNA and knowledge between each other in a swarm *out of control* (Kelly, 1994). This can expand and evolve to such an extent that it defines an entirely new ecosystem or paradigm that is almost self-contained. This is equivalent to a paradigm shift; examples include electric power or personal computing and are said to be breakthrough or radical innovations (Highsmith, 2004; Hippel, 2005; Marinova & Phillimore, 2003; Teece, 2000). More modest innovations are defined by smaller colonies and less self-containment, and are said to be incremental or modest innovations.

- **Globalization:** This step follows on from a runaway colonization by a breakthrough innovation and is a hive mind *out of control*; the self-organizing and expansionary phase of an inogism moves to globalization. At this point the innovation attempts to spread throughout all possible areas of human endeavor. This phase is much like the behavior of a pan-global virus and could even have disturbing implications for unbounded general AI and nanobot swarms (Garreau, 2005).

- **Universalization:** The original inogism is consumed, redesigned and adapted by the market. The original DNA of the inogism can be subsumed or remixed by others to become part of new inogisms which can adapt and evolve into unrecognizable descendants with only passing resemblance to their parents. Thus evolutionary innovations are irreversible (Chesbrough, 2003; Hippel, 2005; Rogers, 2003). The original idea may end up in a new industry, school of thought or embodiment through the demands of lead users in a novel design requirement.

Mitosis is the phase where a continually evolving inogism replicates itself by division. The new inogism may mutate, be consumed, or procreate with another inogism, or it might wither and die due to lack of resources in a new ecosystem. The copying of one inogism gives an opportunity for evolution through random influences, serendipity or simply informational entropy. The adaptability of any descendant inogism is dependent on how easily it can be reduced to bits and bytes and remodelled into a new species.

Population limits of any organism are determined by the 'S' curve of innovation and population growth, which predicts its diffusion into the larger ecosystem. Thus, the take up and evolution of an inogism by lead users can be followed by a rapid take-up by the early majority, followed by a tailing off and eventual decline, as the laggards are infected by elderly inogisms (Hippel, 2005; Rogers, 2003). Meanwhile, in the final days of an innovation's life, when many would regard it as no longer novel, some will only just be discovering it. Meanwhile new inogisms spawned by the life cycle of previous generations will be infecting willing hosts in a new evolutionary cycle. (Rive, 2012)

The dearth of research into the effects in SL of reward, incentive and motivation influencing knowledge creation and sharing suggested this model of a cybernetic knowledge life cycle. According to Pink there are three major areas of personal motivation: autonomy; mastery; and purpose (Pink, 2010). Each of these were seen to provide motivation to the cyborgs in the case studies during the knowledge life cycle and relate to the outpouring of design innovation related to self-directed mastery and purpose when cyborgs created and collaborated on design projects in SL. Because SL has a digital rights management (DRM) engine that provides cyborgs with considerable flexibility, means that it is an excellent virtual ecology to see how the various tensions play out in a knowledge economy that allows many different approaches to IP, knowledge sharing and knowledge creation (Bainbridge, 2007; Rive, 2008). Therefore, if knowledge creation and innovation are social activities, the question remains: How do design managers stimulate collective knowledge sharing and motivate an individual to give up private claims for the collective good, and how will they be fairly assessed? Could individual designers be motivated by self-interest with the creation of knowledge markets, as suggested by Hamel (2007) and Bryan and Joyce (2007)?

Figure 3 illustrates the synthesis of Indosymbiosis and Lessig's four modes in an attempt to show how throughout the life cycle of an innovative idea, or *inogism*, knowledge flow can be regulated and we can understand how motives can support creativity in SL. Throughout the inogism's life cycle Lessig's regulators will either inhibit or provide a catalyst for its future growth. For example during the first stage of an inogism's life a *norm* could motivate the cyborg by supporting and encouraging knowledge sharing; a *market* can stimulate growth through profit incentives and financial returns; the *architecture* can regulate sharing through peer-to-peer collaborative projects providing, or denying access to files; and the *law* can be a catalyst or inhibitor of knowledge creation through the reward or punishment based on the limited monopoly provided by copyright and patents. Indosymbiosis is a model that provides an overview of the ecosystem and how social actors, cyborgs, and regulators all provide feedback in a complex adaptive system.

DATA AND METHODOLOGY

The data was collected using a bricolage of techniques informed by cyber-ethnography; also known as virtual ethnography; online ethnography; and netnography (Boellstorff, 2008; Hine, 2000; Kozinets, 2002; Rybas & Gajjala, 2007). This approach assumes that reality is a subjective and relative world view (Denzin, 1997; Guimaraes, 2005; Hine, 2000, 2005). Cyber-ethnography provided the theoretical

Figure 3. Revised indosymbiosis life cycle with cybernetic regulators (Lessig, 2004; Rive, 2012).

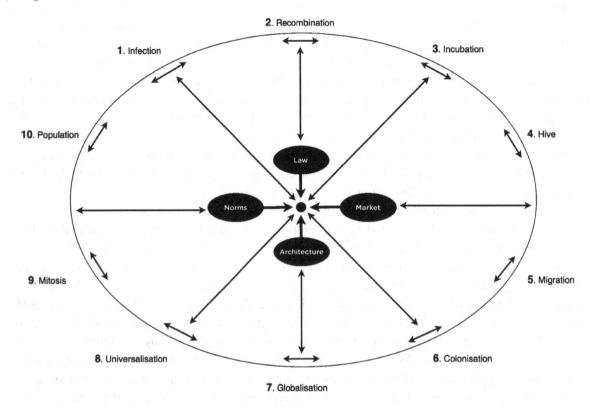

framework that supported the research of the three case studies in SL. The anthropologist Boellstorff in his introduction to a book on SL wrote that many writers on virtual worlds have emphasized a very close relationship with cybernetics (Boellstorff, 2008; Markley, 1996; Turner, 2006). Participants and collaborators in a virtual world can be seen as merging with the machine to become a cyborg, a cybernetic organism, and as an avatar: part human; part machine; part network; to become a resident cyborg in a virtual world (Garreau, 2005; Grau, 2003; Haraway, 1992, 1993).

The original cybernetics, conceived by the likes of Wierner (1954, 1961) evolved into second order cybernetics, which took a more biological systems approach to epistemology, and was sensitive to the theories of ethnographic anthropologists and quantum physics (Bateson & Donaldson, 1991; Chown, 2007; Greene, 2005, 2011; Maturana & Varela, 1980, 1992).

Rybas and Gajjala argue that cyber-ethnography should be based on the *epistemology of doing* in order for the researcher to appreciate the subtleties of the online space (Rybas & Gajjala, 2007). This cyber-ethnographic approach also accords with constructivist pedagogical theory as SL affords the *epistemology of doing*. Boellstorff defends an ethnographic methodology in his research into SL, and he explains that although there are many subcultures and groups to be found in the SL community that SL can still be viewed as one culture, (Boellstorff, 2008). Cyber-ethnography gives us a qualitative understanding of how a virtual world, such as SL, can be used as an innovative ecosystem, and reveals the benefits and current limitations of the technology. The three case studies will show that virtual worlds are regulated in their ability to communicate tacit knowledge, that is still best served by actual face-to-face meetings, but that future advances in theory and technology will see on-going improvements that will help virtual teams connect and collaborate more effectively.

The researchers spent six years from 2006 to 2012 in SL observing design collaboration and knowledge creation in SL using a cyber-ethnographic approach to understand virtual teams within the three case studies and the wider SL environment. The researcher is currently exploring the alpha release of the virtual world, High Fidelity. Previous models of knowledge creation supported the design of a new prototype for explaining knowledge flow; design innovation; knowledge creation; and learning that are all closely connected, (Dixon, 2000; Leonard & Swap, 2004; May, 2007; Thomassen, 2003; Weick, 1991).

CASE STUDY OVERVIEW

The case studies can only be presented here at a high level of abstraction; the detailed analysis of surveys, interviews, and observations are available in the full dissertation cited (Rive, 2012). In each of the case studies only a few selected examples of how Lessig's modalities regulated knowledge flow and creation are provided.

An Overview of the Sloodlers Case Study

- **Group Title:** Sloodlers.
- **No. of Members in SL:** 1485.
- **Group Charter:** The community group for anyone interested in the integration of virtual worlds and Learning Management Systems.
- **Website:** www.sloodle.org.

Sloodle, is an acronym for, Simulation Linked Object Oriented Dynamic Learning Environment (see http://www.sloodle.org/moodle/), and is a tool designed to extend the reach and capability of the web based Moodle education tool set. Moodle is an open source, web based, learning management toolset that is internationally popular with a large educational base.

The Sloodle case study and community provided insight into the difficulties faced by the other case study, *Design 2029* and how the Sloodle normative values regulated it. One leader of the Sloodle development team described how important it was to build a community, and the difficulty of maintaining engagement and dialogue within a virtual community. Von Krogh (2000) identified the need for *knowledge activists* who dedicated time and resources to promoting the knowledge vision and community collaboration. In a virtual learning ecology the requirements for knowledge activism will be dictated by the context and necessary objectives of the knowledge facilitators, albeit virtual team leaders, or self-directed learning by a self organizing group. While many virtual teams who spent a lot of time in SL willingly suspended disbelief, and achieved co-presence by participating in what Gibson called a *consensual hallucination* (Gibson, 1984), many SL informants, in their own words, reported that the spectrum of fidelity was insufficient to build sustainable trust and community purpose (Rive, 2012). It should also be noted that this is not unique to virtual worlds and that the concept of community is itself virtual, and the ability of knowledge activists to sustain a compelling knowledge vision is a challenge for many organizations that may enjoy actual face-to-face meetings (Guimaraes, 2005; Pentland, 2010). Without high fidelity facial expressions and communication channels that supported rich sensory experiences the Sloodlers and the other case studies found it difficult to maintain unity within the wider community and within their virtual teams. Some members of the Sloodlers had physically met face-to-face and that assisted the normative knowledge vision; the levels of trust; and reputations of the cyborgs. Like other professional groups in SL the Sloodlers encouraged members to provide their actual identity that could be viewed in the SL profiles. The Studio Wikitecture leaders did not insist on this disclosure as the wider normative expectation in SL was that it was considered impolite to ask, however, *Theory Shaw* one of the founders of Studio Wikitecture did provide his legal name and background to encourage trust. The Sloodle teacher's toolkit provided identity and security measures to verify students on the related Moodle websites to allow student assessment and entry into courses. It was observed that even though all three case studies published a normative vision that was *open source*, that in the wider context of SL many relied on the DRM (digital rights management) to prevent copying and maintain value through the artificial scarcity of virtual objects.

An Overview of the Studio Wikitecture Case Study

- **Group Title:** Studio Wikitecture.
- **No. of Members:** 380.
- **Group Charter:** Studio Wikitecture is a group composed of a diverse spectrum of individuals interested in exploring the potential of applying an Open Source paradigm to the design and production of both real and virtual architecture and urban planning. We have over the 3 years been conducting *Wikitecture* projects within SL to tease out the procedures and protocols necessary to harness the w*isdom of crowds* in designing architecture.
- **Website:** www.studiowikitecture.com.
- **kw:** architect architects wikitects.

From 2007 until 2009 the WikiTree software development was funded by Studio Wikitecture and originally developed by i3D Inc. In 2009 it became an open source project that released the source code, and began a supporting group in SL called, Open Wikitree. According to their website the objective of the Studio Wikitecture projects is:

Improving Architecture and City Planning by Harnessing the Ideas behind: Web 2.0, Open Source, Mass Collaboration, Social Networking, Crowd Sourcing, Crowd Wisdom, Social Production, Open Platforms, Open Innovation, Collective Intelligence, Decentralized Collaboration, Participatory Culture and the like (from the website Studio Wikitecture: Opening Architecture http://studiowikitecture. wordpress.com/).

While the Studio Wikitecture website publicized the *open architecture* knowledge vision that informed the teams normative behavior, and this was built into the software architecture and code that enabled the Wikitree, the *law* or copyright licensing was not readily available. This lead to one of the virtual team members of the *Safe Trestle* project to express their concern that others could take their textures and virtual objects (Rive, 2012). The terms of the design competition did explicitly state that all designs must be licensed under one of the Creative Commons copyright licenses, however, as the Wikitree could only work with *full perms* or full permissions, meant that team members could feel exposed without explicit information of the *law*. Further research is required to understand to what extent all of the case studies were inhibited because of the lack of clear copyright licensing according to Lessig's theory using the cybernetic regulator, the *law*. The Sloodlers and Studio Wikitree both regulated knowledge flow using open source licensing, but they did not explicitly employ Creative Commons licensing that Lessig has advocated to encourage greater innovation and sharing within and between virtual teams. Design 2029 attempted to incorporate explicit Creative Commons licensing into the *architecture* of its software, however, two other cybernetic regulators, *norms* and *markets* inhibited the completion of this part of the project (Rive, 2012).

An Overview of the Design 2029 Case Study

The Sloodlers and Studio Wikitecture case studies went some way towards answering the research questions. However, it was determined that an action based ethnographic case study could strategically pinpoint some of the issues not easily illustrated in the existing SL groups. The case study unit of research included the game developers, and competition entrants of *Design 2029*, Sloodle designers and users, and participants of Studio Wikitecture, with the design teams, and individuals as sub units of the research and analysis.

- **Group Title:** Design 2029 – The End Game.
- **No. of Members:** 18.
- **Location:** MediaZone.
- **Group Charter:** Design 2029 - The End Game is open to all in SL who believe we can build the foundations for the future based on openness and knowledge sharing. It is a thought experiment to build tools to assist creative collaboration.

Design 2029: The Interaction of the Case Studies

The Sloodlers and Studio Wikitecture were two groups that had already been established before the researcher began to investigate them as case studies. *Design 2029* was designed because no other case study offered the opportunity to consider what has been called the *fuzzy front end of innovation*, known here as infection, or the first phase of indosymbiosis. The *Design 2029* case study incorporated the activities and virtual teams from both the Sloodlers and the Studio Wikitecture groups. It focused on the primary research question concerned with design innovation in a virtual ecology, and was a game that was conceived to provide design teams with a cybernetic feedback response to knowledge creation and collaboration with other designers. *Design 2029* also provides pedagogical examples of how to encourage or inhibit learning and knowledge creation in SL.

Design 2029 – The End Game was designed to be an SL game *in-world* that would attract teams of five to seven designers who would creatively collaborate to create a self-replicating design innovation organism, or inogism based on the model of indosymbiosis. This cybernetic approach to self-directed design and organization were also intended to appeal to what Pink described as the motivation of autonomy (Pink, 2010). The inogism would include the Sloodle award system, and the Studio Wikitecture WikiTree that would be integrated into a design tool that would provide the cyborgs with cybernetic feedback and rewards for design innovation and knowledge creation. The Creative Commons rights machine was to be integrated in the *Design 2029* inogism in order to provide a clear description of copyright ownership. The game's objective was for the design teams to achieve the highest score as awarded by the *wisdom of the crowd*, awarded by those who appreciated the team's design innovation and used it. The top team would receive 100,000 Linden dollars. The first group, *Design 2029 – The End Game*, was open to anyone in

SL, and the other two *Design 2029* groups were intended for the developers and through invitation only. *Design 2029* illustrated the shortcomings of an ambitious research plan within an academic context and how cybernetic regulators can impact on virtual teams and design innovation in a virtual world.

CYBERNETIC REGULATORS OF KNOWLEDGE CREATION

Of the four modes identified by Lessig (2004), it could be argued that while all modes interact, the other modalities are subservient to the *norms* of the design innovation ecology. Norms are the precursor to the formalization of the *law* (Schultz, 2006); the assumptions and rules of the *markets* (Reeves & Read, 2009; Tapscott & Williams, 2006); and the design of technological *architecture*, and code (Lessig, 2006). Following the data collection of the three case studies they were all analyzed according to the theoretical frameworks of Von Krogh, Riva, and Lessig, with assistance from the spectrum of fidelity and the indosymbiotic life cycle of design innovation. In addition to the three case studies the research included a wide data collection taken from a broad range of virtual events, experiences and relationships; using a bricolage of observations to support triangulation of findings. It is difficult to determine which of Lessig's four modalities was the most important and all four interact with each other in SL. The first regulator or enabler may be *norms*, and these could take many forms, from peer group interest in virtual worlds, to fascination with media hype, or an interest in VR and IP. Schultz argues for the primacy of *norms* over the *law* as he shows that normative pressure, can be more powerful than legal regulation (Schultz, 2006). Malaby agrees that in SL the strongest protection against IP violation was not the law but community opinion: *Far more stringent is the community of content creators who watch over each other and report on instances of theft or more vaguely defined "copying"* (Malaby, 2009, p. 138). When an individual decides to join up they are very quickly made aware of the most explicit regulator, the *law*. The Terms of Service is the first legal document that is encountered when signing up to SL. It is also underpinned by a semi-legal Code of Conduct or Community Standards document but this is not readily available when they sign up and they have to go searching to find it. The law is the last gate they must pass through before they can enter SL and if they do not click the button that says *I Agree to the Terms of Service,* they can go no further, and will never get to experience this virtual world. Lessig has also described the code as law, by which he means that software code will either enable or limit entry and behavior in SL. The first obvious example of that is the user name and password that authenticates and either enables entry or prevents access to SL. Other examples include End User License Agreements, the Linden Scripting Language, and server software.

Closely related to the code is *architecture*, which Mitch Kapor also described as the law (Lessig, 2006). The architecture regulates your access to SL by means of Internet protocols and access speeds; it also includes server and client connections that in turn are negotiated via software and hardware. One of the biggest architectural limitations and regulators for users in SL is the GUI (Graphic User Interface) and the time and effort required to master even the basics. When the voice chat architecture was introduced in 2007 some cyborgs resisted it as they felt a loss of anonymity but students who were remotely taught a machinima class found voice an essential component for knowledge exchange within their teams, and this finding was supported by all three case studies (Rive, 2012; Thomassen & Rive, 2010). Network lag, or latency was also a significant inhibitor of knowledge flow between cyborgs. Researchers found that unless first time users were to spend a minimum of 2 hours initially in SL they were unlikely to return. The benefit of this architecture was that because of the complexity of the GUI it enabled more customization and creative expression. Another important mode that regulates entry into SL is the *market*. The case studies were all affected by the market regulation of the wider SL ecology. This was despite the facts that they were all open source projects and the tools were all licensed under open source licenses. When a design team sets out to form a strong knowledge vision that can support a virtual design innovation ecology, there is often competition for the survival of an idea or inogism, just as in nature. The non-linear model of indosymbiosis attempts to describe the knowledge cycle of that inogism. Without this mechanism and *creative capitalism* it is unlikely that SL would have been the big success it was (Boellstorff, 2008; Lessig, 2008; Malaby, 2009; Ondrejka, 2006). The inogism's or cybernetic design innovation organism's life cycle provides a model to help extract meaning from activities that are regulated by the intersection of the four modes.

The difficulty of drawing together self-organising teams of geographically dispersed designers under a normative unifying knowledge vision has been highlighted in all three of the case studies: *Design 2029*; Studio Wikitecture; and Sloodlers. The most successful community, Sloodlers, emphasized that *community-building* was the most important challenge that they faced. A powerful knowledge vision that is shared can unite a community and give it purpose and goal objectives that can enable knowledge creation and design innovation (Von Krogh et al., 2000). The knowledge vision *Creationist capitalism*, or the buying and selling of virtual objects and services even within a learning environment that is non-price based, and reciprocal, has been credited with kick starting SL (Au, W. J., 2008; Boellstorff, 2008; Lessig, 2008; Malaby, 2009; Ondrejka, 2008).

In early exploratory research carried out, prior to the case studies, it was observed that student design teams remained unified by the common objective of academic assessment, and that would often gloss-over team differences missing from a shared knowledge vision (Thomassen & Rive, 2010). In virtual design praxis a knowledge vision may hold less community bond for a design team than the clear goal of completing the design objective of the design team, however, a knowledge vision is an important support to a more pragmatic approach. As it has been emphasized in the Von Krogh et al. (2000) and Hussi (2003) models, it first requires a knowledge vision to unite a team in a common purpose to carry a project forward.

There are four norms that are important to knowledge creation and virtual teamwork within the SL design innovation ecology. They are: trust; reputation; reciprocity; value systems. These four important norms work together to provide cybernetic feedback to the cyborgs in SL. Trust is often built on reputation and reciprocity, and a cyborg's reputation is contingent on whether they comply with the normative value system expected of their community. The Sloodle Awards System and game show were two attempts to build a value system that provide cybernetic feedback and used reputation and reward to motivate knowledge creation and learning in SL. Educational tools such as the Sloodle Awards System and interactive virtual quiz chairs provide teachers with valuable tools for monitoring student response and engagement. Virtual currency and point systems can help to evaluate and motivate innovative learning solutions (Reeves & Read, 2009). In order for *Design 2029* to be a compelling game and a potentially rewarding project it needed a means of providing feedback to the game participants and a scoring system to make it fun and engaging (Reeves & Read, 2009). If there is no trust between cyborgs, or no trust in the architecture, laws, or markets that enforce expected behavior between cyborgs, then there is unlikely to be a free flow of knowledge, knowledge creation, and creative collaboration.

There is an on going tension, both inside and outside SL, based on the normative assumptions of what is the essence of the knowledge economy; what drives it; and what is the determinant of value? Is value determined by the embodiment of a product or service, or is it the intangible ideas baked into the design? This tension is played out daily in SL as cyborgs in virtual teams negotiate, trade, sell and give away virtual objects, code and notecards. There is an unresolved normative paradox that is common amongst cyborgs in SL that relates to attitudes towards virtual objects, and IP in SL.

According to Yochai Benkler (2005), peer production, also known as co-design, and open innovation are important areas of research that have been neglected with respect to norms, the role of technology, and the interaction between incentives and volunteers (2005). In the literature there has been little detailed analysis of what is regulating design innovation in the SL ecology, and most writers have tended to only consider the enablers and not the inhibitors limiting knowledge creation and creative collaboration. Lessig, who is enthusiastic about how SL enables design innovation and user-generated content does not closely question the assumptions around the permissions system built into the SL client (Lessig, 2006, 2008).

In an innovative design ecology it is important to set the normative context for knowledge creation. For virtual team this will be very much contingent on the circumstance and formality of their collaborative experience. With respect to the interaction between the norm of trust and Lessig's mode of *architecture* the complexity of the SL permissions system often encouraged cyborgs to grant other cyborgs they trust with almost unfettered control over their virtual property. In some cases this went as far as giving access to their avatar by sharing their user name and password. This implies the ultimate trust of one designer cyborg in another in order to overcome some of the architectural limitations of the DRM permissions system. The *law* is a mode also influencing the norm of trust, and in contravention of the Terms of Service, some cyborgs have given trusted cyborgs their passwords to their Linden Lab account. In SL this is the ultimate trust as this exposes the cyborg to the potential of identity theft and monetary loss regulated by the law or Linden Lab rules. Copyright and patents are other legal regulators that are influenced by the norms of the community.

Design 2029 used two knowledge activists to actively talk to SL residents about Design 2029. However, the launch of Design 2029 never took place because the requisite inogism, or seed to begin the project was not complete, this was largely due to limited commitment to the knowledge vision from the stakeholders and those that allocated the necessary resources of time and money. The Design 2029 project required resources to complete the development of code to enable a scoring feature for the game that combined the Wikitree, and Sloodle Awards System. Design 2029 project was proposed as a University research grant application and the application was successful, however, the terms of the grant were that work was to be carried out by University research assistants, and a senior research technician, in order that the University should own and retain the knowledge created during the Design 2029 research project. At that juncture there were at least two normative constraints that limited the cybernetic knowledge flow and ability of the virtual team to work together on the Design 2029 project. They were: 1) Lack of a shared knowledge vision (Von Krogh, et al., 2000). 2) A closed innovation paradigm that believed in *owned* knowledge as a competitive advantage. Lessig's market modality (Lessig, 2006).

All the case studies shared an open source knowledge vision and commitment to open source projects and the tools were all licensed under open source licenses. The case studies all exhibited tensions with market regulators, for example Studio Wikitecture projects were regulated in a less direct way through a non-price-based knowledge market and a non-commercial talent market. The knowledge market can be seen as an example of the gift economy commonly referred to in the open source community (Ghosh, 2005a, 2005b).

The Studio Wikitecture project had experimented with various ways to assess the quality of designs and to engage the wisdom of the crowd and the collective intelligence of the community. The experiments played with the interdependence of three of Lessig's four modes regulating the design of a technical architecture, legal considerations of copyright and open source, and the normative values of participants. The market modality was not fully considered, as the open source philosophy negated a commercial approach. A number of commentators on peer production have identified the ability of knowledge markets to assist in quality assessment of ideas, that helped to overcome the limitations of a voting system that had no cost (Bryan & Joyce, 2007; Hamel, 2007; Reeves & Read, 2009; Sunstein, 2006). The Studio Wikitecture WikiTree, unlike a scoring system with a limited number of points that could be added and subtracted, has the limitation that every voter could simply add another point or subtract it without proper consideration and without benefit or cost. The market modality and attention to economics were two considerations that *Design 2029* attempted to improve.

The ability to successfully allocate resources of time, money and personnel (Hunter, 2008) is dependent on the various modalities that regulate knowledge creation and creative collaboration within an academic ecology. Research design policy in academia can also be enabled or inhibited by Lessig's modalities and can either encourage or discourage experimentation and innovative research design.

CONCLUSION

The original research questions were: how to design a virtual innovation ecology in SL? Also, there were two important sub-questions related to this: what enables knowledge creation during design innovation in SL? And, what enables creative collaboration amongst designers in SL? The findings of the case studies showed that virtual worlds provide a unique opportunity for virtual teams to creatively collaborate together and provided a conducive ecosystem for design innovation. SL does provide cyborgs with tools only found in-world that can augment tacit knowledge sharing, communications and knowledge creation, such as 3D objects, shared web experiences, artificial intelligence, and aural, visual and spatial abstractions (Rive, 2012). It is argued here that a shared knowledge vision should be the first priority to engage virtual teams and that will support co-creation and knowledge sharing. A commitment to open knowledge and collaboration are seen as enabling regulators despite tensions with the market mode. This normative mode will interact with the other three modes including the markets, law, and architecture. SL's complex GUI and issues that contributed to lag and latency, imposed inhibiting factors via the architectural regulators. The spectrum of fidelity indicated that cyborgs in SL suffered from low fidelity and the architecture inhibited the flow of tacit knowledge and communication, and therefore knowledge creation. Virtual worlds must have low latency and high bandwidth to allow the maximum fidelity to achieve high tacit knowledge flow and design innovation. The GUI should be intuitive, quick to learn, and also allow a great deal of customization and flexibility for creativity and expression. Improvements to these features in a virtual world such as SL will help to encourage knowledge flow. The founder of SL, Philip Rosedale in his next venture, High Fidelity, (still in alpha at the time of writing this) is looking to achieve improvements to these features as well as sensors that capture head, eye, and body movements of the actual user represented by the cyborg avatar. Architecturally, SL had a limited ability to interface with external applications and due to SL's shortcomings with respect to data storage the researcher experimented with other means of screen sharing, web on a prim, and wikis within the Design 2029 virtual office space.

This brief summary of the three case studies provides a few examples of how the spectrum of fidelity and the regulation of knowledge flow interact to both inhibit and enable knowledge creation and learning in SL. Improvements in the fidelity of virtual worlds and attention to the four modes effecting that flow would help to increase the design innovation ecology for virtual teams within those virtual worlds.

REFERENCES

Au, W. J. (2014, March 9). *Second Life turns 10: what it did wrong, and why it may have its own second life — Tech News and Analysis*. Retrieved from http://gigaom.com/2013/06/23/second-life-turns-10-what-it-did-wrong-and-why-it-will-have-its-own-second-life/

Bailenson, J. N., Beall, A. C., Loomis, J., Blascovich, J., & Turk, M. (2004). Transformed Social Interaction: Decoupling Representation from Behavior and Form in Collaborative Virtual Environments. *Presence (Cambridge, Mass.)*, *13*(4), 428–441. doi:10.1162/1054746041944803

Bailenson, J. N., Blascovich, J., Beall, A. C., & Loomis, J. M. (2003). Interpersonal Distance in Immersive Virtual Environments. *Personality and Social Psychology Bulletin*, *29*(7), 819–833. doi:10.1177/0146167203029007002 PMID:15018671

Bainbridge, W. S. (2007). The Scientific Research Potential of Virtual Worlds. *Science, 5837*(27), 472–476.

Bartle, R. A. (2004). *Designing virtual worlds*. Indianapolis, IN: New Riders.

Bateson, G., & Donaldson, R. E. (1991). *A sacred unity : further steps to an ecology of mind* (1st ed.). New York: Cornelia & Michael Bessie Book.

Beall, A. C., Bailenson, J. N., Loomis, J., Blascovich, J., & Rex, C. S. (2008). *Non-Zero-Sum Gaze in Immersive Virtual Environments*. Retrieved from vhil.stanford.edu/pubs/2003/beall-non-zero.pdf

Benkler, Y. (2005). Coase's Penguin, or, Linux and the Nature of the Firm. In R. A. Ghosh (Ed.), *CODE : collaborative ownership and the digital economy* (pp. 169–206). Cambridge, MA: MIT.

Blackmore, S. J. (1999). *The meme machine*. New York: Oxford University Press.

Boellstorff, T. (2008). *Coming of age in Second Life: An anthropologist explores the virtually human*. Princeton Univ Pr.

Boellstorff, T. (2008). *Coming of age in second life: an anthropologist explores the virtually human*. Princeton, NJ: Princeton University Press.

Book, B. (2004). *Moving Beyond the Game: Social Virtual Worlds*. Academic Press.

Bostrom, N. (2003). Are We Living in a Computer Simulation? *The Philosophical Quarterly*, *53*(211), 243–255. doi:10.1111/1467-9213.00309

Brand, S. (1988). *The Media Lab : inventing the future at MIT*. New York: Penguin Books.

Bryan, L. L., & Joyce, C. I. (2007). *Mobilizing minds : creating wealth from talent in the 21st-century organization*. New York: McGraw-Hill.

Capra, F. (1983a). The Tao of physics: an exploration of the parallels between modern physics and Eastern mysticism (2nd ed.). Boulder, CO: Shambhala.

Capra, F. (1983b). *The turning point : science, society, and the rising culture*. Toronto: Bantam Books.

Castells, M. (2000). *The rise of the network society* (2nd ed.). Malden, MA: Blackwell Publishers.

Castronova, E. (2005). Synthetic worlds : the business and culture of online games. Chicago: University of Chicago Press. Retrieved from http://www.loc.gov/catdir/toc/ecip059/2005007796.html

Castronova, E. (2007). *Exodus to the virtual world : how online fun is changing reality*. New York: Palgrave Macmillan. Retrieved from http://www.loc.gov/catdir/enhancements/fy0711/2007014272-b. html http://www.loc.gov/catdir/enhancements/fy0714/2007014272-d.html http://www.loc.gov/catdir/enhancements/fy0714/2007014272-t.html

Chown, M. (2007). The never-ending days of being dead : dispatches from the frontline of science. London: Faber and Faber. Retrieved from http://www.loc.gov/catdir/toc/fy0712/2007390061.html

Dawkins, R. (1976). *The selfish gene*. Oxford, UK: Oxford University Press.

De Nood, D., & Attema, J. (2006). *The Second Life of Virtual Reality*. Retrieved January 1, 2007, from http://www.epn.net

Denzin, N. K. (1997). *Interpretive ethnography: ethnographic practices for the 21st century*. Thousand Oaks, CA: Sage Publications. doi:10.4135/9781452243672

Dixon, N. M. (2000). Common knowledge: how companies thrive by sharing what they know. Boston: Harvard Business School.

Garreau, J. (2005). *Radical evolution: the promise and peril of enhancing our minds, our bodies--and what it means to be human* (1st ed.). New York: Doubleday.

Gartner. (2007). *Gartner Says 80 Percent of Active Internet Users Will Have A "Second Life" in the Virtual World by the End of 2011*. Retrieved April 24, 2007, from http://www.gartner.com/it/page.jsp?id=503861

Gell-Mann, M. (1994). *The quark and the jaguar: adventures in the simple and the complex*. London: Little, Brown.

Ghosh, R. A. (Ed.). (2005a). *CODE: collaborative ownership and the digital economy*. Cambridge, MA: MIT.

Ghosh, R. A. (2005b). Cooking-Pot Markets and Balanced Value Flows. In R. A. Ghosh (Ed.), *CODE: collaborative ownership and the digital economy* (pp. 153–168). Cambridge, MA: MIT.

Gibson, W. (1984). *Neuromancer*. New York: Ace Books.

Grau, O. (2003). *Virtual art: From illusion to immersion (Rev. and expanded)*. Cambridge, MA: MIT Press.

Greene, B. (2005). The Fabric of the Cosmos: Space, Time and the Texture of Reality (New Ed.). Penguin.

Greene, B. (2011). *The Hidden Reality: Parallel Universes and the Deep Laws of the Cosmos*. Penguin.

Guimaraes, M. J. L. J. (2005). Doing anthropology in cyberspace: fieldwork boundaries and social environments. In C. Hine (Ed.), Virtual methods: issues in social research on the Internet (pp. 141–156). Oxford, UK: Berg. Retrieved from http://www.loc.gov/catdir/toc/ecip056/2005001815.html

Hamel, G. (2007). *The future of management*. Boston: Harvard Business School Press.

Haraway, D. (1992). The Promises of Monsters. In L. Grossberg, C. Nelson, & P. A. Treichler (Eds.), *Cultural studies* (pp. 295–337). New York: Routledge.

Haraway, D. (1993). A cyborg manifesto. In S. During (Ed.), *The Cultural studies reader* (pp. 271–291). London: Routledge.

Heider, D. (2009). Identity and reality: What does it mean to live virtually? In *Living Virtually: Researching New Worlds* (pp. 131–143). New York: Peter Lang.

Heim, M. (1993). *The metaphysics of virtual reality*. New York: Oxford University Press.

Heim, M. (1998). *Virtual realism*. New York: Oxford University Press.

Highsmith, J. A. (2004). *Agile project management : creating innovative products*. Boston: Addison-Wesley.

Hine, C. (2000). Virtual ethnography. London: SAGE. Retrieved from http://www.loc.gov/catdir/enhancements/fy0656/00269452-d.htmlhttp://www.loc.gov/catdir/enhancements/fy0656/00269452-t.html

Hine, C. (2005). *Virtual methods: issues in social research on the Internet*. Oxford, UK: Berg. Retrieved from http://www.loc.gov/catdir/toc/ecip056/2005001815.html

Hunter, I. (2008). *Imagine: what Wedgwood, Da Vinci, Mozart, Eiffel, Disney (and many others) can teach us about innovation*. North Shore, New Zealand: Penguin.

Hussi, T. (2003). *Reconfiguring knowledge management: Combining Intellectual Capital, Intangible Assets and Knowledge Creation*. The Research Institute of the Finnish Economy.

Johansson, F. (2004). The Medici effect: breakthrough insights at the intersection of ideas, concepts, and cultures. Boston: Harvard Business School Press. Retrieved from http://www.loc.gov/catdir/toc/ecip0415/2004003850.html

Kelly, K. (1994). *Out of control: the rise of neo-biological civilization*. Reading, MA: Addison-Wesley.

Koch, R., & Leitner, K.-H. (2008). The Dynamics and Functions of Self-Organization in the Fuzzy Front End: Empirical Evidence from the Austrian Semiconductor Industry. *Creativity and Innovation Management*, *17*(3), 216–226. doi:10.1111/j.1467-8691.2008.00488.x

Kozinets, R. V. (2002). The Field behind the Screen: Using Netnography for Marketing Research in Online Communities. *JMR, Journal of Marketing Research*, *39*(1), 61–72. doi:10.1509/jmkr.39.1.61.18935

Kurzweil, R. (2005). *The singularity is near: when humans transcend biology*. New York: Viking.

Kurzweil, R. (2012). *How to create a mind: the secret of human thought revealed*. New York: Viking.

Laszlo, E. (1987). *Evolution: the grand synthesis*. Boston: New Science Library.

Laszlo, E. (2007). Science and the akashic field: an integral theory of everything (2nd ed.). Rochester, VT: Inner Traditions. Retrieved from http://www.loc.gov/catdir/toc/ecip078/2007000623.htmlhttp://www.loc.gov/catdir/enhancements/fy0705/2007000623-b.htmlhttp://www.loc.gov/catdir/enhancements/fy0705/2007000623-d.htmlhttp://www.loc.gov/catdir/enhancements/fy0705/2007000623-s.html

Laszlo, E., & Loye, D. (1998). *The evolutionary outrider : the impact of the human agent on evolution: essays honoring Ervin Laszlo*. Westport, CT: Praeger.

Leadbetter, C., & Demos (Organization). (2002). *Innovate from within: An open letter to the new Cabinet Secretary*. London. *Demos (Mexico City, Mexico)*.

Leonard, D., & Swap, W. (2004). Deep Smarts. *Harvard Business Review*, 13.

Lessig, L. (2004). *Free culture: how big media uses technology and the law to lock down culture and control creativity*. New York: Penguin Press.

Lessig, L. (2006). Code: Version 2.0 (2nd ed.). New York: Academic Press.

Lessig, L. (2008). Remix: making art and commerce thrive in the hybrid economy. New York: Penguin Press. Retrieved from http://www.loc.gov/catdir/enhancements/fy0906/2008032392-d.html doi:10.5040/9781849662505

Loke, J. (2009). Identity and Gender in Second Life. In *Living virtually: researching new worlds* (pp. 145–161). New York: Peter Lang.

Lombard, M., & Ditton, T. (1997). At the heart of it all: The concept of presence. *Journal of Computer-Mediated Communication*, *3*(2). Retrieved from http://jcmc.indiana.edu/vol3/issue2/lombard.html

Malaby, T. M. (2009). *Making virtual worlds: Linden Lab and Second Life*. Ithaca, NY: Cornell University Press.

Malkiel, Y. (1975). Etymology and modern linguistics. *Lingua*, *36*(2–3), 101–120. doi:10.1016/0024-3841(75)90009-1

Margulis, L. (1970). *Origin of eukaryotic cells; evidence and research implications for a theory of the origin and evolution of microbial, plant, and animal cells on the Precambrian earth*. New Haven, CT: Yale University Press.

Margulis, L., & Sagan, D. (1991). *Mystery dance: on the evolution of human sexuality*. New York: Summit Books.

Margulis, L., & Sagan, D. (1997). *Slanted truths: essays on Gaia, symbiosis, and evolution*. New York: Copernicus. doi:10.1007/978-1-4612-2284-2

Marinova, D., & Phillimore, J. (2003). Models of Innovation. In L. V. Shavinina (Ed.), *The international handbook on innovation* (pp. 44–53). Amsterdam: Elsevier. doi:10.1016/B978-008044198-6/50005-X

Markley, R. (1996). *Virtual realities and their discontents*. Baltimore, MD: Johns Hopkins University Press.

Maturana, H. R., & Varela, F. J. (1980). *Autopoiesis and cognition: the realization of the living*. Springer. doi:10.1007/978-94-009-8947-4

Maturana, H. R., & Varela, F. J. (1992). The tree of knowledge: the biological roots of human understanding (Rev.). Boston: Shambhala.

Mau, B., Leonard, J., & Institute without Boundaries. (2004). *Massive change*. London: Phaidon.

May, M. E. (2007). The elegant solution: Toyota's formula for mastering innovation. New York: Free Press. Retrieved from http://www.loc.gov/catdir/enhancements/fy0665/2006048411-d.htmlhttp://www.loc.gov/catdir/enhancements/fy0666/2006048411-s.htmlhttp://www.loc.gov/catdir/enhancements/fy0666/2006048411-t.html

Mee, N. (2012). *Higgs Force: Cosmic Symmetry Shattered* (2nd ed.). Quantum Wave Publishing.

Montague, R. (2007). Your brain is (almost) perfect: how we make decisions. New York: Plume.

Murray, J. A. H., & Philological Society (Great Britain). (1971). *The compact edition of the Oxford English Dictionary: Complete text reproduced micrographically* (Vols. 1–2). Oxford, UK: Oxford University Press.

Ondrejka, C. R. (n.d.). *Escaping the Gilded Cage: User Created Content and Building the Metaverse*. SSRN. Retrieved from http://ssrn.com/paper=538362

Page, S. E. (2007). The difference: how the power of diversity creates better groups, firms, schools, and societies. Princeton, NJ: Princeton University Press. Retrieved from http://www.loc.gov/catdir/enhancements/fy0704/2006044678-d.htmlhttp://www.loc.gov/catdir/enhancements/fy0704/2006044678-t.htmlhttp://www.loc.gov/catdir/enhancements/fy0734/2006044678-b.html

Pentland, A. (2010). *Honest Signals: How They Shape Our World*. The MIT Press.

Pentland, A. (2014). *Social Physics: how good ideas spread - the lessons from a new science*. Scribe.

Peters, T. J. (1997). *The circle of innovation: you can't shrink your way to greatness* (1st ed.). New York: Knopf.

Peters, T. J. (2003). *Re-imagine!* [business excellence in a disruptive age]. London: Dorling Kindersley.

Pine, B. J., & Gilmore, J. H. (1999). *The experience economy: work is theatre & every business a stage*. Boston: Harvard Business School Press.

Pink, D. H. (2010). *Drive: The Surprising Truth About What Motivates Us*. Edinburgh, UK: Canongate Books.

Prahalad, C. K., & Ramaswamy, V. (2004). *The Future of Competition: Co-Creating Unique Value With Customers*. Boston: Harvard Business Review Press.

Reeves, B., & Read, J. L. (2009). *Total engagement: using games and virtual worlds to change the way people work and businesses compete*. Boston: Harvard Business Press.

Riva, G., Davide, F., & Ijsselsteijn, W. A. (2003). Being there: concepts, effects and measurements of user presence in synthetic environments. Amsterdam: IOS Press.

Riva, G., & Ijsselsteijn, W. A. (2003). Being There: The experience of presence in mediated environments. In Being there: Concepts, effects and measurements of user presence in synthetic environments (pp. 4–16). Amsterdam: IOS Press.

Riva, G., & Waterworth, J. (2003). *Presence and the Self: a cognitive neuroscience approach*. Retrieved January 1, 2007, from http://presence.cs.ucl.ac.uk/presenceconnect/articles/Apr2003/jwworthApr72003114532/jwworthApr72003114532.html

Rive, P. B. (2008). Knowledge Transfer and Marketing in Second Life. In P. Zemliansky & K. St. Amant (Eds.), *Handbook of research on virtual workplaces and the new nature of business practices* (pp. 424–438). Hershey, PA: Information Science Reference. doi:10.4018/978-1-59904-893-2.ch030

Rive, P. B. (2012). Design in a Virtual Innovation Ecology: A Cybernetic Systems Approach to Knowledge Creation and Design Collaboration in Second Life. Wellington, New Zealand: Victoria University of Wellington. Retrieved from http://researcharchive.vuw.ac.nz/handle/10063/2747

Rive, P. B., & Thomassen, A. (2012). International Collaboration and Design Innovation in Virtual Worlds: Lessons from Second Life. In *Computer-Mediated Communication Across Cultures: International Interactions in Online Environments* (pp. 429–448). Hershey, PA: Information Science Reference - IGI Global.

Rive, P. B., Thomassen, A., Lyons, M., & Billinghurst, M. (2008). *Face to Face with the White Rabbit: Sharing Ideas in Second Life*. Presented at the IEEE International Professional Communications Conference. doi:10.1109/IPCC.2008.4610236

Roberts, K. (2004). *Lovemarks: the future beyond brands*. Auckland, New Zealand: Reed.

Rybas, N., & Gajjala, R. (2007). Developing Cyberethnographic Research Methods for Understanding Digitally Mediated Identities. *Forum Qualitative Sozial Forschung*, *8*(3). Retrieved from http://www.qualitative-research.net/index.php/fqs/article/viewArticle/282/619

Schultz, M. F. (2006). Fear and norms and rock & roll: What jambands can teach us about persuading people to obey copyright law. *Berkeley Technology Law Journal*, *21*(651), 651–728.

Shields, R. (2003). *The virtual*. London: Routledge.

Skoyles, J. R., & Sagan, D. (2002). Up from dragons: the evolution of human intelligence. New York: McGraw-Hill. Retrieved from http://www.loc.gov/catdir/bios/mh041/2001007857.htmlhttp://www.loc.gov/catdir/description/mh021/2001007857.html

Stewart, T. A. (2001). *The wealth of knowledge: intellectual capital and the twenty-first century organization* (1st ed.). New York: Currency.

Sunstein, C. R. (2006). Infotopia: how many minds produce knowledge. Oxford, UK: Oxford University Press. Retrieved from http://ezproxy.aut.ac.nz/login?url=http://www.loc.gov/catdir/toc/ecip065/2005036052.htmlhttp://ezproxy.aut.ac.nz/login?url=http://www.loc.gov/catdir/enhancements/fy0635/2005036052-d.html

Tapscott, D., & Williams, A. D. (2006). *Wikinomics: how mass collaboration changes everything*. New York: Portfolio.

Taylor, M. C. (1997). *Hiding*. Chicago: University of Chicago Press.

Teece, D. J. (2000). *Managing intellectual capital: organizational, strategic, and policy dimensions*. Oxford, UK: Oxford University Press.

The Compact edition of the Oxford English dictionary: complete text reproduced micrographically. (1971). Oxford, UK: Clarendon Press.

Thomassen, A. (2003). *In Control: Engendering a continuum of flow of a cyclic process within the context of potentially disruptive GUI interactions for web based applications*. Utrecht, The Netherlands: Hogeschool Voor De Kunsten Utrecht.

Thomassen, A., & Rive, P. (2010). How to enable knowledge exchange in Second Life in design education? *Learning, Media and Technology, 35*(2), 155–169. doi:10.1080/17439884.2010.494427

Tiffin, J. (1995). *In Search of the Virtual Class: Education in an Information Society*. London: RoutledgeFalmer. doi:10.4324/9780203291184

Tiffin, J., & Rajasingham, L. (2003). *The Global Virtual University*. London: RoutledgeFalmer. doi:10.4324/9780203464670

Turner, F. (2006). *From counterculture to cyberculture: Stewart Brand, the Whole Earth Network, and the rise of digital utopianism*. Chicago: University of Chicago Press. doi:10.7208/chicago/9780226817439.001.0001

von Hippel, E. (2005). Democratizing innovation. Cambridge, MA: MIT Press. Retrieved from http://mit.edu/evhippel/www/books.htm

Von Krogh, G., Nonaka, I., & Ichijo, K. (2000). *Enabling knowledge creation: how to unlock the mystery of tacit knowledge and release the power of innovation*. Oxford, UK: Oxford University Press. doi:10.1093/acprof:oso/9780195126167.001.0001

Weick, K. E. (1991). The nontraditional quality of organizational learning. *Organization Science, 2*(1), 116–124. [REMOVED HYPERLINK FIELD] doi:10.1287/orsc.2.1.116

Wertheim, M. (1999). *The pearly gates of cyberspace: a history of space from Dante to the Internet*. New York: W.W. Norton.

Wiener, N. (1954). *The human use of human beings: cybernetics and society* (2nd ed.). New York: Doubleday.

Wiener, N. (1961). *Cybernetics: or control and communication in the animal and the machine* (2nd ed.). Cambridge, MA: M.I.T. Press. doi:10.1037/13140-000

Chapter 5
The World is your Office:
Being Creative in a Global Virtual Organization

Petros Chamakiotis
University of Sussex, UK

Niki Panteli
Royal Holloway University of London, UK

ABSTRACT

Despite the increasing adoption of global virtual teams in industry, and their implications for traditional management practices, creativity within this context has been under-researched, with most studies focusing on students partaking in contrived virtual team projects in educational environments. This chapter focuses on a global virtual organization, Omega (a pseudonym), with the aim of exploring creativity in an organizational virtual team context. Using a qualitative case study approach in a single organization, the study makes the following contributions: (a) it identifies the personal values that motivate creativity; and (b) it explains how individuals, technology, task and organization influence creativity, drawing on the participants' perceptions. Discussed also in the chapter are implications for practice and future research.

INTRODUCTION

Global virtual teams (GVTs) have become commonplace in most industries, while few teams operate completely *face-to-face (F2F)* (Dixon & Panteli, 2010). The literature agrees that GVTs have emerged as a response to pressures of globalization (e.g. Bell & Kozlowski, 2002; Berry, 2011; Cascio, 2000; Lipnack & Stamps, 2000; Malhotra, Majchrzak, & Rosen, 2007; Powell, Piccoli, & Ives, 2004; Schweitzer & Duxbury, 2010) and offers useful accounts around their implications for management (e.g. Algesheimer, Dholakia, & Gurău, 2011; Berry, 2011; Brake, 2006; Kayworth & Leidner, 2000; Maynard, Mathieu, Rapp, & Gilson, 2012). However, *creativity*—a significant and topical issue (Andriopoulos & Dawson, 2009; Gilson, Maynard, Jones Young, Vartiainen, & Hakonen, 2015)—has been under-researched within the context of GVTs. In fact, there are only a handful of studies that have looked into creativity in GVTs, which we review in detail later (Chamakiotis, Dekoninck, & Panteli, 2013; Chang, 2011; Letaief, Favier, & Coat, 2006; Martins & Shalley, 2011; Nemiro, 2007; Ocker, 2005). However, they carry important

DOI: 10.4018/978-1-4666-9899-4.ch005

limitations. For example, none of them have looked into creativity within an organizational context, as most have taken the case of students within university settings. This chapter aims to improve understanding of creativity within a global virtual organizational context, which the extant literature has neglected, in order to both bridge a theoretical gap and also to inform the practitioner community.

In view of the above, an exploratory case study was conducted with a global virtual organization in the sales industry, involving observations and interviews with 15 employees who are members of intra-organizational GVTs, with the aim of advancing understanding of creativity within an organizational, virtual context. The interviews were semi-structured in nature and the ensuing data were analyzed using thematic analysis as well as the laddering technique (Bourne & Jenkins, 2005; Reynolds & Gutman, 1988). The study contributes to theory by (a) identifying the personal values that motivate creativity; and (b) explaining how individuals, technology, task and organization influence creativity, drawing on the participants' perceptions. In what follows, background information on GVTs and creativity is provided drawing on relevant literature. Presented next are the research approach, methods, site and procedure, and lastly, the findings and contributions of the study, as well as its implications for practice and future research.

BACKGROUND

GVTs—also known as globally distributed or dispersed teams—are teams whose members are geo-temporally and/or organizationally dispersed and interactions largely computer-mediated (e.g. Lipnack & Stamps, 2000; Townsend, DeMarie, & Hendrickson, 1998). They are mostly known for their unprecedented benefits, such as their ability to transcend the boundaries of the traditional organization and capitalize on flexible team compositions, cross-cultural collaboration, and time differences (Ebrahim, Ahmed, & Taha, 2009). However, there is also an acknowledgement that not all GVTs are the same. They vary in terms of: purpose (Tong, Yang, & Teo, 2013); degree of geographical dispersion and continuity (Panteli, 2004); degree of virtuality (Griffith, Sawyer, & Neale, 2003); and level of synchronicity (De-Luca & Valacich, 2006); among others. What is more, scholars posit a number of challenges encountered by GVT members, including their ability to develop trust (Bierly III, Stark, & Kessler, 2009; Crisp & Jarvenpaa, 2013; Nandhakumar & Baskerville, 2006), exercise leadership pertinently (Avolio, Kahai, & Dodge, 2000; Carte, Chidambaram, & Becker, 2006; Cascio & Shurygailo, 2003; Chamakiotis & Panteli, 2010), and resolve conflict at a distance (Ayoko, Konrad, & Boyle, 2011). These studies show that the unique characteristics of virtuality, such as geo-temporal dispersion, technology mediation, and the heterogeneity characterizing them, require different management practices to the ones found in the traditional literature on collocated teams. For instance, it has been argued that a different type of leadership may be more suitable in the virtual organizational environment (Avolio et al., 2000).

Creativity has been recognized as an important issue within GVTs (Gilson et al., 2015), and some scholars have begun to explain what are the factors influencing creativity in the virtual environment. For example, Ocker (2005) identifies a set of enhancers of (e.g. stimulating members, collaborative climate) and inhibitors to (e.g. dominance, technical problems) creativity. In a recent study, Chamakiotis et al. (2013) unpacked a number of individual, team, and technology-related factors influencing creativity in their study of a GVT project in the engineering domain. They found, for example, that subgroups, i.e. collocated individuals within GVTs, may have to play both an enhancing and an inhibiting role in different situations. Building on media richness theory, which argues that the more synchronous (real-time) a communication medium is, the richer the level of information (Dennis, Fuller, & Valacich, 2008),

Chamakiotis et al. (2013) argue that both synchronous and asynchronous media have the potential to enhance creativity. Nemiro (2007) identifies five building blocks which need to be in place when an organization wishes to attain high levels of creativity in their virtual teams. They are: design, climate, resources, norms and protocols, and continual assessment and learning. She also argues that task- and interpersonal-connection are necessary in virtual teams for creativity to flourish, with task-connection being dependent on the level of dedication/commitment and goal clarity, and interpersonal-connection on information sharing, personal bond, and trust (Nemiro, 2001). Lastly, Martins and Shalley (2011) suggest that some demographic differences (e.g. nationality) influence creativity in virtual teams, and others (e.g. gender) do not.

The study of creativity in organizations is important in that it may lead to organizational innovation and has therefore constituted a widely explored area in the extant literature (e.g. Amabile, 1997; Andriopoulos & Dawson, 2009). Initially, scholars focused on the individual level of creativity and explored characteristics that make the creative person (i.e. cognitive factors, personality traits, relevant knowledge, and motivation) (Andriopoulos & Dawson, 2009; Mumford, Hunter, Eubanks, Bedell, & Murphy, 2007). Amabile (1998) emphasizes motivation and discusses the relationship between extrinsic/intrinsic motivation and creativity. There exists a view that employees are after intrinsic rewards, such as a sense of meaningfulness, choice, competence, and progress to engage in their work with success (Thomas, 2009). Further, Amabile (1998) advocates that intrinsic motivation is far more important for creativity to flourish, since it stems from one's inner passions. Extrinsic motivation, in contrast, is dependent on outer factors and often managers attempt to build it up by offering their employees financial rewards, though this might not always prove effective. It is external to the work itself and was paramount in older eras, when work used to be heavily routinized, and interpersonal issues did not matter in the workplace (Thomas, 2009). Amabile (1985) also considers that intrinsic motivation is conducive to creativity, contrary to extrinsic motivation which can be detrimental.

Increasingly, there is a view that creativity is not necessarily an individual characteristic, but it can be seen through the lens of the team and the organization. In fact, the individual-team-organizational framework has a dominant position within this literature, arguing that the three levels are intertwined (e.g. Chen, 2006; Thatcher & Brown, 2010). The factors associated with creativity at the team level are: team composition, heterogeneity, and group characteristics and processes (Woodman, Sawyer, & Griffin, 1993); and at the organizational level: organizational climate, culture, systems and resources (Andriopoulos, 2001). Moreover, creativity has been discussed in relationship with leadership and business strategy, and is seen as the precursor of innovation, or applied creativity, and improvement, or routine creativity (van Gelder, 2005). For example, democratic and collaborative leadership styles are seen as positively associated with creativity (Woodman et al., 1993), whilst leadership also plays a connecting role between creativity and environment (Mumford et al., 2007).

It follows that despite these important accounts of creativity within the traditional literature, little is known about it in the GVT context. For example, scholars have not explored the importance of the individual-team-organizational framework in GVTs. Moreover, existing studies looking into creativity in GVTs have neglected the organizational and global character of GVTs, as they have mostly focused on teams (a) operating within the same country; and (b) comprising students instead of professionals. Thus, this study addresses the following research questions:

What influences creativity and what motivates individuals to be creative within the context of a global virtual organization?

Presented next is the methodology adopted for this study.

METHODOLOGY

Research Approach and Methods

The study adopted an exploratory case study approach involving observations and interviews within an organization. One of the strengths of the case study approach is that it allows for the use of multiple data collection methods (Cavaye, 1996). Observations were conducted by the lead author who was employed by Omega, and provided rich contextual information. Per Halberstam (2003), it is possible for researchers to coexist with their participants within the same context, acting as co-conspirators. Semi-structured interviews can provide the fuel for the interviewee to disclose rich information that cannot be otherwise measured (Yin, 2008). Semi-structured interviews were selected as a means of gaining insight into the selected organization through the participants' experiences and perceptions. A narrative style was adopted, encouraging participants to share their stories and experiences of working virtually, emphasizing issues of creativity within their GVTs. The laddering technique was also adopted, whose use in organization studies has been hitherto limited. Laddering is generally used to identify the consequences actors believe that their performed actions result in, while the personal values behind each action performed are disclosed (Reynolds & Gutman, 1988). This technique constitutes a form of cognitive mapping (Baker, 1996) which has been principally used in action research (Easterby-Smith, Thorpe, & Lowe, 2002) in marketing and psychology. Bourne and Jenkins (2005) highlight the strength of the laddering method in terms of providing the researcher with access to the interviewee's personal system of values. In this study, it was selected because it can help to disclose some of the values that motivate Omega's staff to be creative; values which may be closely affiliated to intrinsic motivation—one that has been seen as supportive of creativity and that has not received attention in the virtual context.

Research Site

The selected organization—one that is globally dispersed and which is herein referred to as Omega (a pseudonym) for confidentiality—defines itself as an international press and communication company, a group holding organization, leader in its industry, with eleven agencies under its name, and forty-five years of history. These agencies have exclusive distribution agreements with leading newspapers and magazines worldwide. They specifically produce country reports (with principally economic and political focus), by forming and retaining teams in various countries simultaneously, whose task is to sell as much advertising space as possible to political and business leaders. So far, they have produced country reports on more than 180 countries worldwide (Omega's website). Before the sale has been made, the journalist of each team conducts the interviews and the journalistic department takes over and finalizes the report. The report, or *advertorial* since it embodies advertising and editorial content, is published within the newspapers and magazines as an advertorial supplement. What makes Omega a pertinent research site for this study is the fact that it holds three different physical offices spread across two continents, while it also hosts a large number of dispersed (virtual) offices in various countries across the globe (namely the teams whose aim is to sell advertising space and conduct the interviews). These offices are temporarily set up as they usually have a lifecycle of between four and nine months. In other words, Omega is an organization which systematically deploys GVTs comprising different individuals. Creativity features in the company's philosophy:

Creativity—We thrive on innovation and originality, encouraging radical moves to get things done. (Omega's website)

Omega's headquarters (HQ) is in a European city which also hosts the majority of the departments. The company also has permanent offices in another European city and in a North American metropolis. This composition enables Omega to initiate new as well as to sustain existing agreements with its associates (European and American media) and partner-companies. Omega is committed to continuous recruitment because: (a) it has an expanding business plan; and (b) the nature of this job demands that employees travel for eleven months a year, which is not sustainable over time. Hence, Omega employs young staff that are regularly rotated (between different offices) and quickly promoted. Per their website,

At [Omega], the world is your office. [Omega] provides individuals unique opportunity to develop a truly international career consisting of travelling and working around the world ...

The use of computer-mediated communication (CMC) essentially commences from day one when an employee is assigned a project. Following the first briefing, which is a F2F daylong session in the HQ, field-employees fly to their destination and join a team of three people in total. From that point on, each three-person team has to maintain frequent contact principally with the company's Commercial Department, though contact with the Journalistic, the Human Resources and other departments is also frequent. Moreover, the HQ is situated in two different buildings, compelling the HQ' employees to use CMC extensively.

Research Procedure

This chapter draws on the experiences of 15 employees from different divisions and locations, attempting to look at different perceptions and thus identify what is it that influences creativity within Omega. Observations aimed at providing an improved understanding of the context within which the participants operated, and took place in the HQ only, given the difficulty entailed in research involving virtual, dispersed settings (Schultze & Orlikowski, 2010). The interview participants differed from each other in terms of age, gender, seniority, locality, background, skillset and responsibilities. Gender balance was aimed when recruiting participants, and participant recruitment stopped when it was felt by the authors that saturation had been reached. For analytical purposes and in order to maintain interviewees' anonymity, the sample was categorized based on the dual criterion seniority-locality (where seniority is either senior or junior, and locality is either HQ or field work), thus falling into the following categories:

1. Senior-office;
2. Junior-office;
3. Senior-field; and
4. Junior-field (Table 1).

While recruiting participants, the authors also aimed to interview a relatively equal number of employees from each category. All participants in the study, regardless of category, experience difference degrees of virtuality or dispersion. For example, staff members belonging in the first category (senior-office) are engaged in frequent traveling between, for example, the HQ and the field, thus sharing their time between multiple locations. Thus, though all participants form part of Omega's GVTs, their level of dispersion varies. For presentation purposes, and to protect the participants' anonymity, random names have been selected for each interviewee, highlighting Omega's global character, as they all vary in origin.

Table 1. Presentation of research participants

Name	Gender	Seniority – Locality
Penelope	Female	Senior – Office
Elizabeth	Female	Senior – Office
Hans	Male	Senior – Office
Bernat	Male	Senior – Office
Antonio	Male	Senior – Office
Astrid	Female	Junior – Office
Ivi	Female	Junior – Office
Dimitra	Female	Junior – Office
Brad	Male	Junior – Office
Henry	Male	Junior – Office
Victoire	Female	Senior – Field
Carlos	Male	Senior – Field
Giovanna	Female	Junior – Field
Lina	Female	Junior – Field
Sofia	Female	Junior – Field

The semi-structured interviews aimed at disclosing employees' experiences and opinions, preferably via specific examples, with regard to creativity enhancement and/or inhibition throughout their virtual interactions. At first, each interviewee described the framework within which they work (media used, project duration, etc.), and then they were asked to elaborate on their unique stories of creativity. They were asked to share brief stories where one had a creative idea, or at least willingness to exhibit creative behavior, and virtuality either contributed to or prevented them from communicating said idea (or behavior) effectively. Each interviewee provided up to three stories. The last part of each interview was focused on extracting the values that motivate each individual to be creative in their workplace, which was achieved via the laddering technique, following Bourne and Jenkins' (2005) suggestion that the laddering technique can be incorporated into a wider qualitative interview. Employees were asked to associate creativity, based on their personal perception of creativity, as a term and within the virtual context, with its direct and indirect consequences. Again, implementing the laddering technique aimed at unpacking each participant's individual perception of creativity and its consequences in an attempt to unveil each participant's personal value(s) which act as a lever in exhibiting creativity when working virtually. Through this part, which is also known as *laddering up*, the *why* probe continued, divulging indirect consequences of exhibiting creative behavior, until the value-level was reached. Subsequently, at the interview transcription phase, a unique ladder for each interview was developed. An interviewee's ladder has been cited in the Figure 1, as an example.

Interviews were conducted in person, lasted around 50 minutes each and were conducted in Omega's HQ during working hours. Those with time limitations and heavy workload were asked to share their stories by email, as they requested time to think and come up with apt stories first. Hand-written notes were taken throughout each interview (some interviewees would not feel comfortable if voice-recorded), and the notes were transcribed straight after so that no important elements were missed. Manual coding

Figure 1. Ladder example

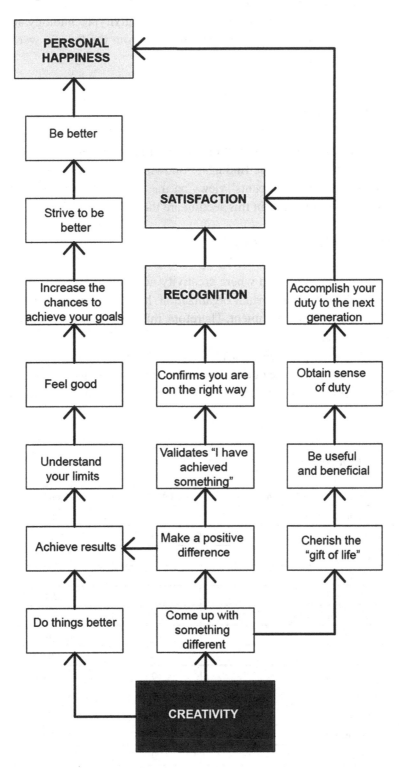

was thereafter performed following the principles of thematic analysis (Braun & Clarke, 2006), leading to the identification of themes that were found to influence creativity: technology, individual, task and organization-related. The consequences/values that emerged from the ladders were grouped together into broader categories (Tables 3, 4).

ANALYSIS AND FINDINGS

This section begins by explaining how information and communication technologies (ICTs) are used at Omega as a means for contextualizing the findings. Following, the values that were found to motivate creativity are discussed, and the participants' views on the importance and state of creativity within their GVTs are presented. Explored last in this section are the factors influencing creativity at Omega.

Technology-Mediated Nature of Work

Omega presents itself as an organization where creativity not only matters but it is embedded within its organizational culture. As a global virtual organization, however, it is expected that creativity will develop in a technology-mediated environment. Therefore, this section focuses on the use of ICTs within Omega and their role for creativity.

Table 2 shows interviewees' preferences with regard to the ICTs they use the most in their interactions. Not all employees share the same duties, nor do they participate in comparable projects; they are based in very different countries, are members of different teams, have different objectives, and all these

Table 2. ICT choice at Omega

Name	ICTs Used	CMC %	Telephone %	F2F %
Penelope	Email	70	15	15
Elizabeth	Email	65	35	(1 visit)
Hans	Email	50	35	15
Bernat	Email	50	25	25
Antonio	Email, text	50	50	-
Astrid	Skype, email, database	40, 40, 5	15	-
Ivi	Email, server	80	20	-
Dimitra	Email	80	20	-
Brad	Email	60	30	10
Henry	Skype, email	50	20	30
Victoire	Email	60	20	20
Carlos	Skype, email	20, 50	30	-
Giovanna	Email	40	30	30
Lina	Email	50	20	30
Sofia	Email, BlackBerry Messenger (BBM)	70	20	10

factors prescribe the selection of specific ICTs. Email, though it does not always transmit move, lies, optimism and sentiments (Antonio, Carlos, Sofia), plays a dominant role in Omega's communications.

Further, Table 2 also shows that CMC at Omega is relatively constrained. The ICTs used between both the office-based and dispersed staff members who are constantly on the move, are primarily telephone and email, and less often Skype and other servers. As a participant put it,

The use of Skype in my work decreases creativity. This is mainly due to the fact that Skype as a technology medium is not completely reliable. Often I would make calls using Skype, be in the middle of a conversation with a client, only to have the conversation cut off because of a bad connection. This hinders the confidence the client has in me while I am trying to sell the product, and also decreases my credibility. (Astrid)

But even with regard to this relatively constrained availability and selection of ICTs, participants are not trained or proficient enough to make the most out of them:

A lot of the features like file sharing, people don't know how to use them; they haven't been trained, and are not using them to the maximum. (Antonio)

Limited ICTs, however, had a positive impact on creativity on certain occasions:

… being able to creatively lie to clients and even colleagues, I think the virtual created a sense of distance and protection between the liar and the person being lied to [...] I had to pretend that one of the people had left the company so as to stall even more, which could only be done in the virtual world, since otherwise they would know my voice/face/etc. (Ivi)

Most participants agreed that Omega is not as technologically developed as it should be, and thereby "… a lot is left to chance" (Antonio).

The word FAX (fax of the day) says it all. People don't have time to spend to fill out a 10-page document for the office to evaluate their work. This should be done via an advanced online system, as most sales-force companies have, where field employees effortlessly upload the info needed, and the HQ can access it filtering out what they don't want for example. (Sofia)

Though voice-over-IP technologies on the one hand are found to be constraining (e.g. Skype example), email on the other was found not only to enhance communication but also creativity:

The use of email in my work increases creativity. This is because email is the primary way that I send examples, or mock-ups, of our product to the client so they can visualize how the final product will appear. It is important that the email be concise and contains just enough information so that the client isn't overwhelmed, but so that they are interested to buy the product. Email also allows communication between myself and the client to be constant and on-going. Once a client purchases the product email is used to communicate, ultimately increasing the confidence the client has in the product and in me. The success of a telephone sale depends a lot upon the quality and success of how email is used because it allows me to build rapport with the client, and allows the client to communicate any concerns or problems they may have. (Astrid)

Most of the interviewees believe that, with CMC one can "… have the certainty that it [your message] will arrive, it speaks up" (Bernat), "… inform a large number of people with one click" (Dimitra, Penelope), "… you have more time to think and re-read your text [when using email]" (Lina), "… have everyone within easy reach, no matter in which part of the globe they are" (Hans), and also that "… if you write an email and I'm reading it, I can hear your voice. But not knowing the person I'm talking to, and reading his or her email and 'voice', I can be easily offended" (Ivi). People also "often hide behind this tool" (Bernat), "… you are never a 100% sure if your email has been actually read" (Penelope), "… there is a tone of voice which hasn't been recorded" (Lina), "… when you send an email to many people you may receive so many different answers which leads to miss-communication" (Elizabeth), while "… it can also be very difficult at times to deal with servers and information systems for which you have received no training at all" (Astrid).

The language differences were found to intensify distances within Omega:

Phone lines are so bad in the countries we are in, so we tend to use email. When I send an artwork request my English is very good. Communication with the client is again good, because it has been mostly F2F. But when I get a response from the office, I get a response that has nothing to do with my initial request. This is because not everyone is native in English. (Sofia)

During the interviews, employees expressed their views and expectations regarding virtuality and dispersion at Omega. "In a global organization with various offices worldwide, such as Omega, virtual technologies are essential" (Carlos). "It's true that we don't use IT as much as we could here, but this happens for a number of reasons. Only when you travel to the field you see the whole picture" says Hans, being a senior-office employee, in an effort to demonstrate that it is not always possible to work 100% virtually and that F2F communication matters. Furthermore, Antonio commented that the use of ICTs very much depends on the country your project is: "In Africa […] you'd want to do everything in person. In other countries however, the business culture is more technology-oriented".

Some staff members considered loyalty an important facet of dispersion within Omega. Most are loyal to the team more than to the organization (e.g. Antonio, Carlos):

… loyalty from the field employees to the company is very high compared to the company's loyalty to its employees. Personally, I'm loyal to the team; teams from within are very loyal to each other. (Sofia)

Victoire argued that Omega needs to upgrade its "virtual hardware and software", thus its IT infrastructure, as this is the principal channel of communication. Elizabeth claimed that "communication between field employees and the HQ is not too bad; but virtual communication is very bad among office employees. People […] write full page emails, instead of picking up the phone." Many also expressed the need for an intranet which could be useful among the field employees: "it would be beneficial to have an intranet for us, because people in the field must know what's going on; at present, in order to contact a person who belongs to another team, you need to call the office" (Victoire). Ivi found it difficult to work without leadership or direction when physically collocated, let alone when working from a distance. "Omega simply doesn't have the tools: money-wise, infrastructure-wise, development-wise" (Bernat).

In the main, senior staff viewed the organization as supportive of creativity. Few exceptions (e.g. Antonio) report insufficient training or that Omega is not technologically competent. On the other hand, junior staff believed that the company does not offer the tools necessary for creativity, yet they have learned to utilize limited ICTs to the organization's advantage (e.g. Ivi).

Creativity: Significance, Perceptions, and Motivations

"Creativity is the talent, the skill to find solutions to matters difficult to understand" says Bernat, while other common perceptions of creativity include: "… thinking out of the box" (Antonio, Hans, Penelope), "… being innovative and achieving your goals" (Hans), it is "… an avenue to sarcasm, a non-verbal cue, a secondary cue which you cannot get through virtual means" (Victoire), or for others creativity simply means "… looking for alternatives" (Giovanna). Carlos also argued he has seen examples where "... creativity has made a difference in our job". Despite the positive perceptions of creativity, it was also purported that "creativity might also lead to wrong solutions" (Hans), or that "… is the opposite for 'analytical', so it's not necessarily always good" (Elizabeth).

Communicating almost entirely by email to coordinate complex visa processes engaging parties across the world was an interesting experience. I developed my communication skills extensively and my ability to work under pressure and to strict deadlines. Using email allowed me to work effectively and efficiently by developing creatively the way I work and to better my administrative/communication practice. (Brad)

"[Creativity] gives you the edge against the competition" (Bernat), "… is directly related to productivity" (Astrid), and at the organizational level, "Omega manages and develops creativity through its senior management, managers with experience, who bring ideas and suggestions and who also support the juniors" (Penelope). Work dispersion at Omega does not inhibit the promotion of creative solutions (Hans, Penelope), yet lack of vicinity (Hans), the fact that employees in different locations do not have the same level of input/information (Antonio, Hans, Sofia), that language is not properly used through ICTs (Ivi, Sofia), that Omega has not invested properly in information technology (IT) infrastructure (Elizabeth), that "the same things are written and exchanged again and again" (Lina), that "…there is a strict top-down management, where you are told not to question things" (Bernat, Victoire), and lastly the slowness of ICTs alongside the lack of training (Astrid) and overall direction (Ivi) are significant inhibitors to successfully communicating an idea in a virtual environment.

One participant also noted that at Omega "… you are not encouraged to have your own input in what you do, there are templates you have to follow" (Lina) and therefore it is not uncommon to "… get shut down and not praised for your creativity. Also, you don't propose anything because you know the answer will be NO" (Ivi). "… You are obliged to follow a very structured working method, a 'tried and tested' method which is the way we do it" (Bernat). Thus, the organizational culture does not encourage the development of creativity, although creativity was generally seen as positive. However, senior staff consider that creativity is greatly enhanced and encouraged through Omega's practices, in line with the company's philosophy, since a lot of autonomy and flexibility is given to the field employees. Nonetheless, creativity is encouraged only in terms of networking and not in terms of developing your own working practices: "… you have various ways how to develop strategies to get to the clients, this is totally up to you to decide" (Lina).

The use of the laddering technique revealed a set of values associated with the participants' motivation and creativity. Table 3 summarizes the consequences of creativity as per the interviewees' perceptions, while Table 4 cites the inner values which ultimately motivate each employee to be creative when working in a virtual setting. Learning and development was seen as the most popular consequence of being creative. This was also expressed as 'personal growth' and 'personal development'. Second most frequent consequence was 'coming up with something different', or 'discovering new avenues'. Less frequent consequences include 'contributing', 'being liked', 'achieving goals', and perhaps surprisingly an extrinsic consequence, that of 'making money' constituted a motivating force for creativity. Further, 'satisfaction'—the most common value (phrased also as 'personal satisfaction' or 'fulfillment')—was considered the outcome of finding the right solution (e.g. Elizabeth), taking the most out of your life (Giovanna), or accomplishing your duty towards the next generation (Henry, Penelope). Likewise, 'recognition', (phrased also as 'reward' or 'financial reward/security') constituted a confirmation of being on the right way (Penelope), whilst associated with a sense of achievement (Astrid). 'Social acceptance' (also put forth as 'personal validation' and 're-assurance') was linked to being accepted by your society (Hans, Lina). 'Personal happiness' was strongly associated with achieving your goals (Brad, Penelope), making things better (Brad, Dimitra, Elizabeth), and increasing your self-confidence (Bernat, Henry), while 'personal development' or 'personal growth' was related to moving forward (Ivi) and teaching others (Astrid).

It follows that creativity is valued by both senior and junior staff within Omega, though the interviewees gave an inconsistent image of whether it is supported in practice. Further, the data also present a picture of what motivates individuals to be creative in a virtual environment. Explored next are the factors influencing creativity at Omega.

Factors Influencing Creativity in GVTs

The findings revealed that technology-, individual-, task- and organization-related factors influence creativity at Omega.

Table 3. Hierarchical classification of consequences

Consequences	Frequency
Learning and development	10
Discovering something new	9
Achieving goals	7
Contributing	6
Being liked or recognized	4
Make money	2

Table 4. Hierarchical classification of values

Values	Frequency
Satisfaction / Pride	8
Recognition / Achievement / Security	7
Personal Happiness	7
Personal Development	5
Social Acceptance	4

Technology-Related

Although limited ICTs were used by the participants in this study, CMC was in some cases found to enhance creativity within the virtual environment:

… one can have a very simple, basic idea, and with this concise idea one can find/spark searches for much greater ideas… kind of like a domino effect/snowball effect where something small can lead to much greater things—ideas that may never have been reached if one didn't have the mass amount of information at one's fingertips. Ideas can bounce from person to person, it's kind of like the phenomena of when multiple-way calling came into being—people could learn to multi-task very easily, which saves a lot of time in most cases. (Ivi)

… take Googling as an example, the same happens with emailing, it gives inspiration, new ideas, access to more ideas, and in the end it makes the whole process very creative. (Hans)

My boss was very restrictive with approaching creative ideas, and on some occasions, he would present his ideas to his superiors as his. Thanks to technology, I took the initiative and put in BCC his immediate superior when I decided to express a creative idea I had, and this way, although he again presented it as his idea, his superior popped by my desk and congratulated me. (Henry)

Though technology was earlier presented as an enabling factor for enhancing creativity, it was also found to act as an inhibitor.

… since we are so virtual and have very little contact with our 'people' in the field, a lot of the professional business aspect of a company is lost…business becomes casual in a virtual world…we can hide behind our computers and our spell checks and it's acceptable to write words incorrectly and to use words that might not even really exist and it's considered OK—not only because for many people our chosen language of English is not native, but because Omega accepts 'good enough' as OK… I have not seen a lot of change and/or growth in my experience in Omega—where in other companies where there is less of this virtual world, people learn a lot more from each other and can grow as people both professionally and personally. (Ivi)

We were trying to come up with a name for a new agency, so everyone had a meeting with Person X and she then streamlined the forum over email. This gave us the opportunity to pitch in without meeting F2F with everyone again and again; it was simply accomplished through CMC, so it was very efficient. However, brainstorming proved limited in the end, ideas could not evolve naturally. (Bernat)

Further to the above, technology may have a different constraining impact on creativity—that by not being available:

An intranet for example, which we do not have, or a new section on the server that we already have, could be a forum for new ideas, a medium for us to know what's going on among the other teams in the field. I recall many times when I had to get in contact with someone from a different team and creativity was lost on the way. (Victoire)

Unexpected technology-related events seemed to inhibit creativity:

Towards the end of a negotiated agreement, it was very important that a phone call was made for con-firmation purposes. However, my mobile broke and it could only function using the speakerphone. The rest of the people in the room would hear what my boss from the office would say, so this resulted in me not making the phone call, which could have been extremely useful. (Henry)

Individual-Related

In addition to the availability of technology, the role that individual members play in encouraging cre-ativity seemed to matter. Through the interviewees' narratives, it became apparent that initiatives were taken by individuals to generate ideas:

I once started an initiative through Facebook in order to build up a solid relationship among us; I put a picture of a colleague of ours who is very well known by all of the people in the field, and this triggered comments and questions, so everybody felt suddenly closer to us. There was no quantitative feedback, but still it was an initiative outside the job, which had a positive impact on the job. (Bernat)

… 'A small world' and Facebook have been really helpful with communication, enabling me to get in touch with previous colleagues and also finding newly made friends, colleagues I met at Omega's annual party… I now know I can get in touch with any of these, whether this be for work or personal reasons. (Giovanna)

Task-Related

The project-based, temporary and global nature of the tasks involved within Omega had both an enabling and constraining role for creativity. On the one hand, the high level of flexibility and autonomy embed-ded in individuals' jobs were seen as key enhancers of creativity:

Using my initiative, I worked to centralize all visa processes. Having total autonomy in running the project, I designed a new way of displaying data using Excel which was then sent to the whole company by email. At this moment, creativity was enhanced in my work as I had the freedom to design and execute my own administrative processes. The virtual […] allowed me to gain rapid feedback on the processes I had created so I could improve them and change them accordingly. (Brad)

It's been quite good that technology has enabled us to work individually when it comes to preparing presentations. This is a core task in our sales activities and we can modify everything easily, without having to send everything back and forth to the office, which would slow down the whole process. (Sofia)

On the other, however, the sales-oriented nature of Omega tasks appeared to be an inhibitor to cre-ativity. Omega is a sales-oriented company and money is all that matters (Bernat, Giovanna, Henry, Ivi). Therefore limited attention is given to issues other than money generation:

From a complete business side, managers here have been successful and thus promoted to upper-management level because they made money. Their view is based on numbers and the basic idea behind their minds is 'commissions'. That's why they have the power to say NO to creative ideas; it's not as important. (Ivi)

My creativity was inhibited when managing high level stakeholder communication—working to obtaining interview agenda on behalf of my line managers. I would usually communicate effectively by telephone and email in my own manner—however, my communication with clients was micro-managed by my boss and I was forced to follow my manager's agenda, rather than working more independently and working to my own. (Brad)

Although the company seems to follow, like the interviewees said *'tried and tested practices'*, the findings demonstrated that the company does not exploit the potentials offered by technology to accomplish these relatively standardized tasks:

Proposals are given to us in PPT or Word format. But they are too generic and do not apply to every client. I remember once in Nigeria the director of the project spent a month into customizing a generic proposal, which could be perhaps shared in a common intra-company server so that other teams benefit from it. But people don't have time for sloppy things, proposals or anything really, and the international makes it even more difficult to communicate a creative idea. (Antonio)

Organization-Related

Several organizational factors were found to influence creativity. The main inhibitors were lack of infrastructure, training, intranet, F2F communication, strict *'tried and tested'* practices. Moreover, the culture of the organization, and the absence of definitive hierarchies, inhibited creativity:

Our Website was very poorly constructed, contains grammatical errors and is not easy to navigate. Also the programming of the site is not professional as there are often broken links. Instead of directing clients to our Website, which is what I would have liked to have done, I would have to send PDFs of the mock-ups that we wanted the client to see. Because of the unprofessional execution of the Website, my production and overall ability to sell the product was decreased. The Website also made it difficult for me to be proud of the product that I was selling. (Astrid)

... the servers we use to sell our product to the clients are very slow. They serve in nothing more than preventing you from informing the client and selling the actual product. (Elizabeth)

Obviously, though it was recognized that technology offers potentials for the organization to project itself in an appealing manner, the findings show that the business focus is elsewhere; and therefore, the organization itself presents a constraint in supporting and enhancing employee creativity:

The webpages in the marketplace have become very sophisticated. Ours are unattractive, very basic. Omega has been forced that has to improve in that respect, as the cyberspace in general is a good calling card. There have been cases where everything has worked very well in a F2F meeting with a client, but you can often tell that the client has gone our website and this first negative impression has been decisive. (Antonio)

DISCUSSION

Overall, it was found that despite Omega's philosophy for creativity and innovation, the participants expressed concerns about the state of creativity in the organization. On the one hand, *senior-office* staff perceived that creativity is demanded and not just encouraged, but field-employees felt unable to communicate their ideas creatively. They have flexibility and autonomy, yet the company's tools and culture were not found to be supportive of their decisions (no factual encouragement, no infrastructure). A critical inhibitor therefore in creativity within GVTs is found within the organization itself. In categorizing the study participants as senior and junior, it was realized that the two perceive creativity differently. The former consider support for creativity is in place, while the latter reported a number of inhibitors to creativity.

Technology, individual, task and organization-related factors were found to influence creativity at Omega. These factors exert an influence in their own right on one's creativity, but are also best understood and studied in relationship to each other. For instance, though technology may be available, its use may be problematic if discouraged by the systems and practices of the organization (e.g. due to preference for F2F communication).

The study shows that, as per traditional creativity literature (e.g. Chen, 2006; Thatcher & Brown, 2010), the roles of the individual and the organization are significant in a global virtual work environment; and is the first to start presenting a picture of how these influence creativity within the wider context of globally dispersed work environments. It furthermore supports existing literature which argues that creativity depends not only on personal, but also on contextual and organizational factors (Andriopoulos, 2001; Tierney, Farmer, & Graen, 1999). Though this study has shown that technology and its usage may have a significant impact on creativity within this context, these factors alone are not sufficient for creativity to flourish in an organization. Instead, the nature of the task undertaken and the organizational systems and wider context that surround GVTs also have a vital role to play. These factors have been neglected in earlier studies which have used student-based virtual teams (Chamakiotis et al., 2013; Chang, 2011; Ocker, 2005). These studies were initiated with artificially created, well-articulated tasks for the teams to complete, which, in effect, did not allow the researchers to show how tasks and context may influence creativity. Therefore, whilst existing studies are useful, they have limitations when attempting to apply their findings in an organizational context. This is a limitation that has been overcome with the study of Omega in this chapter.

Reduced organizational loyalty was highlighted in the literature as one of the disadvantages of distributed work (DeSanctis & Monge, 1999), and this is also corroborated here. Interviewees signaled that not only they themselves were more loyal to their teams than the organization, but also that Omega's HQ follows a similar tactic, projecting a disloyal profile to field employees. This can be looked at from an additional angle. Nemiro (2001) stressed the importance of establishing task- and interpersonal-connection in accomplishing creativity in VTs. In the study presented here, the staff's attempts to develop personal bonds with their teams and thereby establish higher levels of trust were witnessed (e.g. Bernat and Giovanna, individual-related factors). Such initiatives can be considered 'stimulating' and this corroborates the positive influence of the presence of stimulating members in such environments

(Ocker, 2005). These initiatives occurred among individuals and not the entire organization. Hence, this might explain why Omega's staff are more loyal to their teams than to Omega. On the other hand, establishing task-connection was not always feasible, as inadequate CMC selection prevented the teams from attaining goal clarity.

This study also initiated a significant exploration of the personal values that motivate employees to be creative, and corroborated the argument that intrinsic motivation is far more imperative than extrinsic motivation, when attempting to unveil creative ideas in the workplace (Amabile, 1998). In particular, some participants referred to extrinsic motives, such as *'money'* (Table 3), which although not a popular motive, was for this reason included in Table 3. *'Security'* (Table 4), which was rated high, was also somehow associated with extrinsic motives. This exploration of motivation adds to the literature in that it was carried out in a virtual context, which to the authors' knowledge no other study has achieved. Lastly, these findings corroborate that flexibility and autonomy enhance creativity in a global virtual organization (e.g. Brad).

FUTURE RESEARCH DIRECTIONS

The study has limitations that generate suggestions for future research. First, given that the participants belonged to different GVT, the study did not look into factors influencing creativity at the team level, whose importance has been recognized in the literature (e.g. Thatcher & Brown, 2010). Future research should therefore consider focusing on specific GVTs within organizations in order to explain how team-related factors influence creativity in virtual environments. Second, this study is largely based on the participants' perceptions of creativity, as observations were only used for familiarization purposes. Scholars could adopt methods that will allow them to study creativity as it happens. Third, the qualitative character of the study does not allow for statistical generalization. As such, scholars should seek to conduct larger studies of quantitative character in order to assess these findings' relevance in other contexts and identify values that motivate GVT members to be creative, which may have not been unpacked in this chapter.

CONCLUSION

This study aimed to improve understanding of the importance of creativity in a global virtual organization. By focusing on a single organization, the study succeeded in looking into organizational aspects of creativity, by presenting the views of organizational members at different levels. The findings suggest that there exist factors relating to technology, the individual, the task and the organization, and these have an enabling or an inhibiting role for creativity to play, or both under unlike circumstances. At the individual level, it expands current knowledge by identifying what motivates individuals to be creative in an organizational GVT setting. At the organizational level, the study contributes to knowledge by explaining how the organization and its characteristics influence creativity—for example, though technology may be in place, organizational culture and priorities may render its use troublesome for the dispersed members. The study offers implications for future research (as outlined in the earlier section) and for practice. For example, in order for managers to support and enhance creativity in a virtual organizational environment, systems, processes and context need to be supportive. Finally, managers should also be aware of the values that are likely to motivate GVT members to be creative.

ACKNOWLEDGMENT

The authors wish to thank the research participants and Omega, as well as all those who provided feedback on earlier versions of the study.

REFERENCES

Algesheimer, R., Dholakia, U. M., & Gurău, C. (2011). Virtual Team Performance in a Highly Competitive Environment. *Group & Organization Management*, *36*(2), 161–190. doi:10.1177/1059601110391251

Amabile, T. M. (1985). Motivation and creativity: Effects of motivational orientation on creative writers. *Journal of Personality and Social Psychology*, *48*(2), 393–399. doi:10.1037/0022-3514.48.2.393

Amabile, T. M. (1997). Motivating creativity in organizations: On doing what you love and loving what you do. *California Management Review*, *40*(1), 39–58. doi:10.2307/41165921

Amabile, T. M. (1998). How to kill creativity. *Harvard Business Review*, *76*(5), 77–87. PMID:10185433

Andriopoulos, C. (2001). Determinants of organisational creativity: A literature review. *Management Decision*, *39*(10), 834–841. doi:10.1108/00251740110402328

Andriopoulos, C., & Dawson, P. (2009). *Managing Change, Creativity and Innovation*. London, UK: Sage Publications Ltd.

Avolio, B. J., Kahai, S., & Dodge, G. E. (2000). E-leadership: Implications for theory, research, and practice. *The Leadership Quarterly*, *11*(4), 615–668. doi:10.1016/S1048-9843(00)00062-X

Ayoko, O. B., Konrad, A. M., & Boyle, M. V. (2011). Online work: Managing conflict and emotions for performance in virtual teams. *European Management Journal*, *30*(2), 156–174. doi:10.1016/j.emj.2011.10.001

Baker, S. (1996). *Consumer cognitions: mapping personal benefits relating to perfume purchase in the UK and Germany* Paper presented at the 207th ESOMAR Seminar: Capturing the Elusive Appeal of Fragrance: Techniques, Experiences, Challenges, Amsterdam, The Netherlands.

Bell, B. S., & Kozlowski, S. W. J. (2002). A typology of virtual teams: Implications for effective leadership. *Group & Organization Management*, *27*(1), 14–49. doi:10.1177/1059601102027001003

Berry, G. R. (2011). Enhancing Effectiveness on Virtual Teams. *Journal of Business Communication*, *48*(2), 186–206. doi:10.1177/0021943610397270

Bierly, P. E. III, Stark, E. M., & Kessler, E. H. (2009). The moderating effects of virtuality on the antecedents and outcome of NPD team trust. *Journal of Product Innovation Management*, *26*(5), 551–565. doi:10.1111/j.1540-5885.2009.00680.x

Bourne, H., & Jenkins, M. (2005). Eliciting managers' personal values: An adaptation of the laddering interview method. *Organizational Research Methods*, *8*(4), 410–428. doi:10.1177/1094428105280118

Brake, T. (2006). Leading global virtual teams. *Industrial and Commercial Training, 38*(3), 116-121.

Braun, V., & Clarke, V. (2006). Using thematic analysis in psychology. *Qualitative Research in Psychology*, *3*(2), 77–101. doi:10.1191/1478088706qp063oa

Carte, T. A., Chidambaram, L., & Becker, A. (2006). Emergent leadership in self-managed virtual teams. *Group Decision and Negotiation*, *15*(4), 323–343. doi:10.1007/s10726-006-9045-7

Cascio, W. F. (2000). Managing a virtual workplace. *The Academy of Management Executive, 14*(3), 81-90.

Cascio, W. F., & Shurygailo, S. (2003). E-leadership and virtual teams. *Organizational Dynamics*, *31*(4), 362–376. doi:10.1016/S0090-2616(02)00130-4

Cavaye, A. L. M. (1996). Case Study Research: A Multi-Faceted Research Approach for IS. *Information Systems Journal*, *6*(3), 227–242. doi:10.1111/j.1365-2575.1996.tb00015.x

Chamakiotis, P., Dekoninck, E. A., & Panteli, N. (2013). Factors Influencing Creativity in Virtual Design Teams: An Interplay between Technology, Teams and Individuals. *Creativity and Innovation Management*, *22*(3), 265–279. doi:10.1111/caim.12039

Chamakiotis, P., & Panteli, N. (2010). E-Leadership Styles for Global Virtual Teams. In P. Yoong (Ed.), *Leadership in the Digital Enterprise: Issues and Challenges* (pp. 143–161). Hershey, PA: IGI Global. doi:10.4018/978-1-60566-958-8.ch011

Chang, C. M. (2011). New organizational designs for promoting creativity: A case study of virtual teams with anonymity and structured interactions. *Journal of Engineering and Technology Management*, *28*(4), 268–282. doi:10.1016/j.jengtecman.2011.06.004

Chen, M. H. (2006). Understanding the benefits and detriments of conflict on team creativity process. *Creativity and Innovation Management*, *15*(1), 105–116. doi:10.1111/j.1467-8691.2006.00373.x

Crisp, C. B., & Jarvenpaa, S. L. (2013). Swift Trust in Global Virtual Teams. *Journal of Personnel Psychology*, *12*(1), 45–56. doi:10.1027/1866-5888/a000075

DeLuca, D., & Valacich, J. S. (2006). Virtual teams in and out of synchronicity. *Information Technology & People*, *19*(4), 323–344. doi:10.1108/09593840610718027

Dennis, A. R., Fuller, R. M., & Valacich, J. S. (2008). Media, tasks, and communication processes: A theory of media synchronicity. *Management Information Systems Quarterly*, *32*(3), 575–600.

DeSanctis, G., & Monge, P. (1999). Introduction to the special issue: Communication processes for virtual organizations. *Organization Science*, *10*(6), 693–703. doi:10.1287/orsc.10.6.693

Dixon, K. R., & Panteli, N. (2010). From virtual teams to virtuality in teams. *Human Relations*, *63*(8), 1177–1197. doi:10.1177/0018726709354784

Easterby-Smith, M., Thorpe, R., & Lowe, A. (2002). *Management research: An introduction*. London, UK: Sage Publications Ltd.

Ebrahim, N. A., Ahmed, S., & Taha, Z. (2009). Virtual Teams: A Literature Review. *Australian Journal of Basic and Applied Sciences*, *3*(3), 2653–2669.

Gilson, L. L., Maynard, M. T., Jones Young, N. C., Vartiainen, M., & Hakonen, M. (2015). Virtual Teams Research: 10 Years, 10 Themes, and 10 Opportunities. *Journal of Management*, *41*(3), 1313–1337. doi:10.1177/0149206314559946

Griffith, T. L., Sawyer, J. E., & Neale, M. A. (2003). Virtualness and knowledge in teams: Managing the love triangle of organizations, individuals, and information technology. *Management Information Systems Quarterly*, *27*(2), 265–287.

Halberstam, J. (2003). What's that smell? Queer temporalities and subcultural lives. *International Journal of Cultural Studies*, *6*(3), 313–333. doi:10.1177/13678779030063005

Kayworth, T. R., & Leidner, D. E. (2000). The global virtual manager: A prescription for success. *European Management Journal*, *18*(2), 183–194. doi:10.1016/S0263-2373(99)00090-0

Letaief, R., Favier, M., & Coat, F. (2006). Creativity and the Creation Process in Global Virtual Teams: Case Study of the Intercultural Virtual Project. In F. Feltz, B. Otajacques, A. Oberweis, & N. Poussing (Eds.), *Information Systems and Collaboration: State of the Art and Perspective* (Vol. P-92, pp. 242–258). Bonn, Germany: GI-Edition.

Lipnack, J., & Stamps, J. (2000). *Virtual Teams: People working across boundaries with technology*. New York, NY: John Wiley & Sons.

Malhotra, A., Majchrzak, A., & Rosen, B. (2007). Leading virtual teams. *The Academy of Management Perspectives*, *21*(1), 60–69. doi:10.5465/AMP.2007.24286164

Martins, L. L., & Shalley, C. E. (2011). Creativity in Virtual Work: Effects of Demographic Differences. *Small Group Research*, *42*(5), 536–561. doi:10.1177/1046496410397382

Maynard, M. T., Mathieu, J. E., Rapp, T. L., & Gilson, L. L. (2012). Something(s) old and something(s) new: Modeling drivers of global virtual team effectiveness. *Journal of Organizational Behavior*, *33*, 342–365. doi:10.1002/job.1772

Mumford, M. D., Hunter, S. T., Eubanks, D. L., Bedell, K. E., & Murphy, S. T. (2007). Developing leaders for creative efforts: A domain-based approach to leadership development. *Human Resource Management Review*, *17*(4), 402–417. doi:10.1016/j.hrmr.2007.08.002

Nandhakumar, J., & Baskerville, R. (2006). Durability of online teamworking: Patterns of trust. *Information Technology & People*, *19*(4), 371–389. doi:10.1108/09593840610718045

Nemiro, J. E. (2001). Connection in creative virtual teams. *Journal of Behavioral and Applied Management*, *2*(2), 92–112.

Nemiro, J. E. (2007). The Building Blocks for Creativity in Virtual Teams. In S. P. MacGregor & T. Torres-Coronas (Eds.), *Higher creativity for virtual teams: developing platforms for co-creation* (pp. 98–121). Hershey, PA: IGI Global. doi:10.4018/978-1-59904-129-2.ch005

Ocker, R. J. (2005). Influences on creativity in asynchronous virtual teams: A qualitative analysis of experimental teams. *IEEE Transactions on Professional Communication, 48*(1), 22–39. doi:10.1109/TPC.2004.843294

Panteli, N. (2004). Situating Trust within Virtual Teams. In S. Reddy (Ed.), *Virtual Teams: Contemporary Insights* (pp. 20–40). Hyderabad, India: ICFAI University Press.

Powell, A., Piccoli, G., & Ives, B. (2004). Virtual teams: A review of current literature and directions for future research. *ACM SIGMIS Database, 35*(1), 6–36. doi:10.1145/968464.968467

Reynolds, T. J., & Gutman, J. (1988). Laddering theory, method, analysis, and interpretation. *Journal of Advertising Research, 28*(1), 11–31.

Schultze, U., & Orlikowski, W. J. (2010). Research Commentary---Virtual Worlds: A Performative Perspective on Globally Distributed, Immersive Work. *Information Systems Research, 21*(4), 810–821. doi:10.1287/isre.1100.0321

Schweitzer, L., & Duxbury, L. (2010). Conceptualizing and measuring the virtuality of teams. *Information Systems Journal, 20*(3), 267–295. doi:10.1111/j.1365-2575.2009.00326.x

Thatcher, S., & Brown, S. A. (2010). Individual creativity in teams: The importance of communication media mix. *Decision Support Systems, 49*(3), 290–300. doi:10.1016/j.dss.2010.03.004

Thomas, K. (2009, November/December). The four intrinsic rewards that drive employee engagement. *Ivey Business Journal: Improving the Practice of Management The Workplace.*

Tierney, P., Farmer, S. M., & Graen, G. B. (1999). An examination of leadership and employee creativity: The relevance of traits and relationships. *Personnel Psychology, 52*(3), 591–620. doi:10.1111/j.1744-6570.1999.tb00173.x

Tong, Y., Yang, X., & Teo, H. H. (2013). Spontaneous virtual teams: Improving organizational performance through information and communication technology. *Business Horizons, 56*(3), 361–375. doi:10.1016/j.bushor.2013.01.003

Townsend, A. M., DeMarie, S. M., & Hendrickson, A. R. (1998). Virtual teams: Technology and the workplace of the future. *The Academy of Management Executive, 12*(3), 17-29.

van Gelder, S. (2005). The new imperatives for global branding: Strategy, creativity and leadership. *The Journal of Brand Management, 12*(5), 395–404. doi:10.1057/palgrave.bm.2540234

Woodman, R. W., Sawyer, J. E., & Griffin, R. W. (1993). Toward a theory of organizational creativity. *Academy of Management Review, 18*(2), 293–321.

Yin, R. K. (2008). *Case study research: Design and methods.* Thousand Oaks, CA: Sage Publications, Inc.

KEY TERMS AND DEFINITIONS

Creativity: The ability or process through which one can generate a new idea.

Face-to-Face (F2F): Communication and/or collaboration that takes place in a physically collocated (as opposed to virtual or dispersed) environment.

Global Virtual Team (GVT): A team whose members: (a) are geo-temporally and/or organizationally dispersed; and (b) communicate and collaborate mostly through technology.

Section 2
Human Behaviors and Discourse in Modern Virtual Environments

This section explores human interactions and behaviors in a variety of modern virtual environments.

Chapter 6
Why We Would Rather Text than Talk:
Personality, Identity, and Anonymity in Modern Virtual Environments

Bobbe Gaines Baggio
American University, USA

ABSTRACT

Whether they are checking out at the grocery store, watching a sporting event or eating out in a restaurant; people are texting. Text messaging has become very popular form of contact. Texting is increasingly a part of the overall communications strategy not only for teens but for everyone. Privacy is the number one reason for sending and receiving text messages. The ability to communicate anytime and anywhere but to do so with privacy makes texting attractive and popular. Although some research has been done on the impact of personality, identity and anonymity on texting messaging, very little definitive conclusions have been established either for usage or preferences. Some research indicates that introverts act more like extroverts and extroverts act more like introvert when they communicate using text messages. More research needs to be done to establish the influence of personality and identity on texting and texting on personality and identity.

INTRODUCTION

Online personality and identity can be seen as a continuation of a person's everyday life. A sense of identity is defined by innate characteristics and the environment a people are operating in at the time. Personality and a sense of self or an identity, with boundaries, limits and norms, creates an online persona that then interacts with others. What people do and talk about when texting is very close to what they do and discuss in a face to face environment. The concept of identity that comes into play with virtual environments is linked to one important construct, anonymity. Anonymity plays out through interacting with others online. Texting is done either in a one on one environment or one on many environment like on social media sites. Aspects of our personalities when we are texting are either the same or different

DOI: 10.4018/978-1-4666-9899-4.ch006

than when we communicate face to face. Identity online is concerned with the ability to gain attention, create social engagement, explore boundaries and develop a following. Texting environments offer a place for the instantaneous and free exchanges of ideas, thoughts and information. Text has become a strategic communication tool based on the rapid exchange of messages and the viral aspects of the media. Text gives us the freedom to express our personalities like we really want to, not constrained by the expectations in strong environments but free to act more like who we really are. Texting environments are two dimensional environments and are missing very important nonverbal cues. This makes the environment weaker and this has advantages and disadvantages that influence how people express themselves, through personalities and identities.

Our identity, our sense of who we are, comes from social and cultural context. Identity and the self are intricately connected. Identity, personality and behaviors are integrated into relationships with others and eventually this helps us to define our sense of "self". The self today, is acknowledged by some of the characteristics that are found in modern virtual environments (Hansson, 2012). In modern online virtual environments, it is common for a person to have more than one profile or identity, on more than one social media site. Discovering multiple profiles for the same individual is not uncommon. This allows researchers and data analysts to merge profiles or identities based on IP addresses, common attributes, usage profiles and social linkages. Social relationships then define not only who people say they are online but who they really are online (Bartunov, Korshunov, Park, Ryu & Lee, 2012).

BACKGROUND

Since the beginning the Internet has been about communications, connections and alternatives. Before the Internet became a reality only a few decade ago, the last big communications innovation was the telephone. Social media sites and text messaging proved to be evidence that humans will embrace new ways of communicating almost overnight. These new technologies allowed us to interact easily and instantly. There is a growing concern that since technologies are used to communicate, communications skills are being lost. Even though people can stay connected 24 hours a day, 365 days a year, the quality of our connections is changing. There are more devices to stay connected with; including laptops, mobile phones, tablets and more social networks and social media sites to deliver that connectivity. What was once used primarily for business and education, is now an integral party of a global social structure. The global village is connected and regulated by the connections to mobile devices. This is transforming communication patterns. Verbal and written communications skills are an important part of life. If text messaging is here to stay, and it certainly looks like it is, what impact will this have on personalities, a sense of identity and interactions in virtual environments.

Communications skills in some ways define who we are and the position in society. Voice communications was often about breaking down hurtles. Properly addressing people, speaking clearly, using appropriate body language, listening and a firm handshake are all missing from text based communication. Voice communication involves dealing with hurtles as they arise, where text communications is created to sidestep and pre-empt those hurtles in the first place (Stokoe, 2014). Whether this new and preferred method of communicating is actually superior depends on how a person embraces anonymity than on the affordances of the technologies. Text based communications is a distant relative to more traditional face to face communicating. Being connected by texting may require disconnection from community life and ourselves.

Emails, texts, messages, voice and video and a variety of other functions like eBook reader, music player and Internet browser make their mobile devices the most important communication device most people own. This all in one functionality, creates a bond that is so addictive, research has supported people would rather give up caffeine than smart phones. Checking out at the grocery store, watching a sporting event, eating out in a restaurant people are texting. Text messaging has become our most popular form of contact. This ability to create short burst of communication rather than formulated thoughts and conversation extends the level of informality. Text messaging allows for push or asynchronous communications. It gets straight to the point and eliminates the small talk usually necessary in voice, face to face or email conversations. It allows people to speak in a concise way that eliminates the variable of time. Often people respond to a text message days after the sender has sent it and long after the thoughts contained in the message had any meaning to any of the parties involved (Pinchot, Douglas, Paulett & Rota, 2011). Since time is also missing, it is much easier to have miscommunication in a texting environment.

This chapter seeks to answer the questions:

- Why is texting increasingly preferred over voice communications?
- How do personality, identity and anonymity influence communications choices in virtual environments?

MAIN FOCUS OF THE CHAPTER

The use of texting as a way of knowledge sharing is growing. Social media platforms have changed the paradigm of how knowledge is created and disseminated. By posting on social media, messaging platforms and social networks knowledge is shared with a much broader audience. Technologies also change the way individuals are engaged in the conversation. Whether in one on one sharing or publically visible postings, texting allows for more freedom in interpretation, modification and use of information (Majchrzak, Faraj, Kane & Azad, 2013).

Text messaging and mobile technologies have impacted communication habits and preferences. This medium allows a person to engage in short bursts of communication and extends the level of informality. Text puts everyone on the same page. Text gets straight to the point. Texting, email and social networking communications are increasingly replacing the phone call or face to face meetings. The numbers of text messages are staggering particularly with young people. The typical teen sends over 1,500 texts a month (Pichot, et. al., 2011). Texting is increasing part of the overall communications strategy not only for teens but for everyone. Privacy is the number one reason for sending and receiving text messages. The ability to communicate anytime and anywhere but to do so with privacy. Texting has increased because the communication is asynchronous and allows for privacy and allows people to avoid face to face communications. Several studies support not only the increase in text communications but the reasons people chose to communicate using text: privacy, asynchronously and instantly.

Research conducted in 2011 (Pinchot, et all, 2011) found that when participants were asked if they used text messaging to avoid face to face contact or voice to voice communication nearly 67% said they did use text in that way. When they were asked whether they preferred text over making a phone call 66% in the Millennial (18-33) age group said they did, 40% of Generation X (34-45) and 18% of Baby Boomers (46-64) said they preferred text. Amazingly, 96% of the participants received the majority of their communications on a mobile phone. On average the participants sent 49 text messages a day and received 57 text messages a day. The study indicated that text messaging is unmistakably on the increase.

Mobile technologies are increasing how we interact with each other and the world around us. These technologies are connective and social in nature and allows humans to be always on and always connected. This constant connection affects verbal and interaction patterns and provides new ways of expressing and defining ourselves. For over a decade mobile connectivity has been studies usually from a perspective of large scale quantitative studies rather than the content of actual conversations. These support that texting is used by the majority of people that have mobile devices and that most texting is done for private purposes. To get a more complete picture of how texting affects human interaction which has evolved into a continuous conversation which many engage in daily and often crosses platforms, devices and channels, it may be helpful to look at what motivates people to share experiences in the manner they do. (Segerstad & Weilenmann, 2013).

Mobile devices are altering the way we communicate and the speed of these communications is astounding. Each generation is attached to communication patterns that are ingrained in the core of who we are. Technologies have become a part of our lives. They help us to fulfill our need to connect and make decisions. Constantly connected, people can obtain information without ever speaking to a person. The allure of constant connectivity is irresistible but the impact on behavior patterns, cognition and emotions will require more research.

People use to share information by gathering together and sharing conversation. In a sense they still do but they gather together using technologies that are ever evolving and always changing. These technologies allow for continuous texting conversations and this affects how people interact. There is no question that these new technologies allow friends and family to communicate more easily and strangers to become familiar with each other almost instantly. Conversations can be interpreted, re-used, and dynamically shared. This can have a very positive affect on moving conversations forward and a very confrontational effect when miscommunications lead to unintended consequences. How individuals engage in these texting conversations depends on who they are, how they see themselves and how much they are willing to step beyond those limits.

There is no question texting is a low cost and convenient tool for communications. Text messages can include pictures, video and text. A broader picture of text messaging must look beyond tools and platforms to the ethics and decision making that support behaviors in modern virtual environments. Often texting is blamed for behaviors that are sited as unethical and compromise confidentiality and trust. The sigma of confrontation is lessened because of the anonymity of text only interactions. This same anonymity can help people process emotions, feeling and thoughts before they react. Texting can take place both synchronously and asynchronously which allows for making meaning of messages and formulating responses. It is easier when texting to set boundaries with interactions and yet in some ways it is more difficult in other ways.

Familiarity with the technologies doesn't mean people understand how to effectively use them to communicate. Anonymity and identity in an asynchronous environment can be deceiving. Messages can be interpreted in different ways than they were intended and modified with additional text, graphics or punctuation. Privacy, security and the implications of the actions are inexplicably mixed with boundary issues including professional and private lives. Particular attention needs to be paid to tone and language. Just because it is possible to say anything in text messaging doesn't mean it is appropriate. Boundaries and an integral part of human identity and being able to set these limits both four yourself and others with text communication is essential for success (Sude, 2013).

Since the beginning of the Internet, in the early 1990's, communication have been about influencing others and contributing to a collective consciousness. Information is disseminated and consumed both vicariously and socially. Whether it is ecommerce or eLearning, the pattern is one of contribution, collaboration and collective information. People can observe and they can contribute. They can vicariously seek and consume information and knowledge and they can also create it. Communications both positive and negative are shared by individuals and can be made available to a multitude of people very quickly and very easily. Sharing the information with others usually depends on the quality, quantity, credibility, usefulness and adoptability of the information. Other elements such as satisfaction, pleasure, joy, or sadness also motivate sharing experiences and opinions with others. Because influence and control are such an integral part of the human psychological state, both in business and personal relations, the anonymity of the communicators can create new dynamics. Both intentionally and unintentionally, messages can be interpreted out of context. In addition, the interpretation of text messages are subject to the geographical, cultural and social influences each individual brings to the conversation (Jililvand, Esfahani & Samiei, 2010). Online and especially in text, opinions are exchanged and trust is either established or dissolved.

By curating perspectives both by individuals and organizations texting helps to establish a kind of internal and external check and balances system. On the Internet, everyone can be an expert. Expertise is established by sharing information and wide exposure through multimedia and networks. People with expert knowledge can post it in many forms and exchange data, viewpoints and messages. Strategic significance is established by drawing meaning from the data, its application and impact and developing a social intelligence. This social intelligence applies to individuals or organizations and plays out in real time. Analytic techniques analyze topics like "buzz volume", "discussion topics" and "consumer sentiment" aggregating texts, posts and likes to make meaning out of conversations. This land of knowing is not like the published and proprietary sources that were guarded and trusted. This land is open to gun slingers, dance hall girl and sheriffs on horseback (Harrysson, Metayer & Sarrazin, 2012).

The power of texting really comes from the ability to interact with others with a degree of concealment and a sense of control. Texting allows for targeting and exchanging information in ways that voice and face to face just do not support. When used effectively and with deliberate intent texting can at its best provide positive support, active communication and a chance to optimize contributions both from individuals and the collective by giving the communicators the opportunity to reflect upon and formulate thoughts (Kim, 2011). It also gives a voice to many who might otherwise experience limits. Text messaging can reach people in remote areas, isolated conditions and hard to reach areas. Texting has the potential to change behaviors in people and because it reaches people where they are, it allows people to ask questions through the vail of anonymity and provides a low cost and efficient way of disseminating information (Cormick, 2009).

Personality, identity and anonymity play an interesting role in determining behaviors in virtual environments. Defining how people behave and in particular patterns of behavior in a variety of situations is termed personality. Personality has been under debate both biologically and psychologically for some time. Discussions on what aspects of a person's personality are attributable to a genetics rather than the effects of one's environment is still under consideration. Generally though, both aspects are considered to be important in determining a person's personality. Personality is often measured by personality tests or type indicators. A wide variety of such instruments exist and are used regularly to measure how others see us behaving such as extroverted (acting talkative, assertive, adventurous) or introverted (more reserved and solitary behavior). For the purposes of this chapter, personality is the lens others see us through and identity is the lens we use to see ourselves.

Identity is the unique characteristic belonging to any individual, or shared by all members of group or society. Identity can be defined in terms of how people relate to themselves or others and has been part of psychology, philosophy and sociology for quite some time. Personal identity is process of the development of the distinct individual and social or cultural identity is concerned with development of those traits that make us part of the larger group. It is what defines a person and what makes them unique and individual. The term individuation was used by Carl Jung and others to indicate how we set ourselves apart. Jung said "In general, it is the process by which individual beings are formed and differentiated (from other human being); in particular, it is the development of the psychological individual as a being distinct from the general, collective psychology" (Jung, 1975, ¶ 757). Identify affects conversations and interactions between individual and groups.

Anonymity, which is a unique characteristic in virtual environments also impacts communications and interactions. The anonymity afforded by technologies provides a refuge for our true identities or intentions, and is not always used for the common good; it is often used for distorting truth. Anonymity is embedded in every facet of communication with technologies and includes trust itself. Anonymity may be defined as the absence of identity and the ability to act impersonally. Technologies often give the individual the feeling of being anonymous. Because of this physically detached and isolated environment, anonymity in virtual communications gives the feeling of safety and undetecability while actually providing the opposite. Often there is a false sense of safety and privacy that is both misleading and illusive. This allows people to "deindividuate" or lose a sense of personal identity or responsibility. Deindividuation allows a person to step beyond or out of their identity and take on new roles and norms.

The anonymity inherent in mobile communications impacts how texting supports the emergence of new identities. The definition of identity in virtual environments is multidimensional. Texting with mobile technologies may simultaneously restrict free interactions and facilitate new ways of capturing and tracking data. It can support freedom of expression and alter egos and deception. The implications reveal how the issues of anonymity, authenticity, identity, and trust are at the center of communications in virtual environments (Baggio & Beldarrain, 2011). Anonymity allow us to step beyond where we are, who we are and take on new attributes of personalities, identities and selves.

Personality

Personality research in virtual environments is in its infancy. Partly because the technological revolution has happen so quickly and partly because the field is evolving. Examining the relationship between personality and choice, usage, impact and interactions online has just begun. Research has mostly focused on the "Big Five" factors. The Big Five defines personality traits or a branch of personality psychology that tries to describe personality in terms of openness, conscientiousness, extraversion, agreeableness, and neuroticism. Trait research often examines the relationship between the personality traits and behaviors in virtual environments. Personality traits are usually defined as independent of situations and represent consistent aspects of behavior across conditions. Many studies have reported a systematic change of behaviors in virtual environments, so the question arises "How and why are personalities expressed differently in virtual environments?" (Blumer, T & Doring, N, 2012).

Personality traits have been shown to influence a wide range human behaviors. Debatably, personality traits are deep and natural characteristics of human behavior that capture how a person approaches and responds to a wide range of situations and interactions in their lives. Personality trait have been linked to influences in behavior in consumer marketing, performance at work, student behaviors, musical taste, leadership of change, travel decision, residential choices and smoking. Concerning technologies personality has been correlated with self-efficacy, mobile phone use, activity on social networks, and media consumption (Chorley, Whitaker & Allen, 2015).

- **The Big Five:** Neuroticism, Extraversion, Openness to experience, Agreeableness, and Conscientiousness, currently constitute the most excepted model used to explain and research personality. It is considered both broad and efficient in explaining differences in behavior. The research in this area which includes online education and computer mediated communication, has led to diverse findings. There are studies that look at the influence of the five traits on the choices people make in online communications and there are studies that look at the effect computer mediated communications have on the five factors. Either way the results are mixed. This is especially true when it comes to the frequency and intensity of usage and the medium. Currently no coherent results exist that link usage to personality.

Interactionalism takes into account multiple aspects including: situations, personality traits and interactions in trying to understand human behavior. Today research looks more at the situational influences on interactions in trying to determine and disrobe the effects on human behaviors. Mischel, 1977, (Blumer & Doring 2012, p. 12) differentiated between weak, strong and powerful situations. The term weak situations indicates a condition where there are few social constraints or behavioral guidelines. In strong situations the personality of the persona has less influence than in weak situations. In strong situations the behavioral options are usually very limited by the situation itself. In weak situations this is not the case. In comparison to face to face communications, texting is usually considered a weak situation because there is little social control and behavioral instructions are voluntary and rare. The perceived anonymity and detachment of the virtual environment offer an immense amount of individual freedom. Therefore behaviors are more likely to be unvarying in virtual environments and personality is more likely to play a role. Expression of personality in general is weaker with technology mediated communications. All five factor express less intently in virtual environments than in face to face situations. The influence of personality is reduced because of the two-dimensionality of the environment and the absence of contextual cues. For example, studies show a lower expression of shyness in online and computer mediated environments. The only exceptions to this with the trait of narcissism where and additional effect occurs. With narcissism, the emotional stability tends to increase with digitally mediated communications and can likely be attributed to the typical features of this environment. The expression of personality here seems to be higher here and there is still a definitive difference between personality expressions in face to face and virtual environments (Blumer & Doring, 2012).

Personal characteristics are more easily examined now through the use of smartphones with GPS tracking. Data is available from location based social networking that puts an individual in a physical location. It may be possible in the future to do more research that examines the relationships between physical presence and personality traits and dispositions. Little is known know about the relationships between human mobility and personality. More research is need to determine the relationship between personality and mobile connectivity. Personality traits have also been shown to not influence the perceived usefulness of communication tools such as apps and applications. Cognitive traits seem to be the dominant force in the perceived usefulness of online tools and usage (Saade, Kira, Nebebe, 2012).

There are mixed findings on the Big Five personality traits and communications styles and preferences (Chorley et. all, 2015). Many of the characteristic of online environments have inherent characteristics that relate to the traits in the Big Five. Openness for example is inherent in social networks. Autonomy, freedom of structures, self-expression, expectations and support for relationships with others are a few scenarios in which personal activity is corresponding to personality traits. Although openness was not correlated with a higher use of digitally mediated communication, it did correlate to of wider range of discussion topics and a wider use of the features. Similarly narcissism was correlated with a larger number of Facebook friends and self-centric tweets. Extroversion has been dominate trait related to online social network posting and usage and activity. Introversion has been associated with benefiting from online social network postings because this requires less interaction and therefore less interpersonal skills. Agreeable people expressed more regret when inappropriate content was shared and generally made more postings about themselves than less agreeable people. Neuroticism alone scored higher for use to eliminate loneliness and facilitate inclusion.

Other studies look at readiness to participate, actual participation and quality of participation to determine if personality traits have an influence. Some determinants such as discussion topic sensitivity, gender, or media characteristics are used to further quality the research. A greater interest in discussing sensitive over non sensitive topics can explain an increase in participation rates. Overall text chat seems to be a preferred medium for discussion. One research study shows that participant s preferred text because they felt more comfortable discussing sensitive topics. This same study indicated that extroverts preferred more revealing communication media and introverts preferred text chat.

Studies that deal with individual compared to group chat sessions are equally indecisive on the effects of personality. Sensitivity of topic and medium characteristics, such as media richness, where face to face environments are thought to be the riches and therefore the best for sensitive and complex messages still produce mixed findings. Empirical research on media richness has discovered that some evidence supports it, while others indicate that the distractors inherent in the medium draw attention away from the message. In general text chat is a "leaner" form of communication both for sensitive and non-sensitive topics smaller amounts of actual participation is revealed in text chat. Participants are more likely to use text for sensitive topics but contributed less than in a face to face or voice conversation. This may allow for more emotional processing and reflection on the topic. Text based group discussions are less structured than face to face and may result in information overload. This well-known phenomena may account for the lower degrees of participation. Text chatters need a higher degree of concentration to express their opinions and unlike face to face of voice, where responses are made by taking turns, text responses are often made simultaneously. Text may be preferred because the quality of the communication is perceived as the same or better and the length of the contributions are shorter. Participants clearly prefer to discuss non sensitive to sensitive topics regardless of the medium but actual participation on sensitive topics was almost twice as high in text. Participant showed an increased readiness to participate in texting over both voice and face to face communications (Blau & Barak, 2012).

Text has been shown to have a "hyper-personal" effect, where text based interactions equal or exceed relational effects derived from similar face to face interactions. The equalization effect is supported by many studies that indicate online group text chat diminishes internal and external real and fictitious status cues. It seems that voice and face to face communications transmits cues and therefore disables the occurrence of the equalization effect in spoken interactions both online and off. Text chat then might have the effect of empowering marginalized people such as women, minorities and other groups. (Blau & Barak, 2012).

Personality continues to be an area of research in education, performance development. Since more and more jobs are moving into the virtual environment, the influence of personality traits on virtual job performance is worth examination. Generally it is agreed that broad personality traits have more influence than narrow ones. Broad traits include those found in the Big Five: Agreeableness, consciousness, extroversion, narcissism (emotional stability) and openness. Narrow personality traits can include adaptability, self-efficacy, tough mindedness and work drive. Emotional stability and agreeableness were found to be the most significant and positive correlated with job performance (Holmes, Kirwan, Bova, & Belcher, 2015).

Social presence is established differently in a texting environments than with voice or face to face interactions. Bao, 2013 argues that online social behaviors reflect a "discrepant personality" and that behaviors online are more agreeable, consciences and emotionally stable than face to face behaviors. This supports the concept that introverts act more like extraverts and extrovers act more like introverts online. An investigation into word counts and word usage supported this based on the use of first person pronouns, positive emotion and negative emotion and swear words. In four of the Big Five (extraversion, emotional stability, agreeableness and conscientiousness) personality traits there appears to be convergence. The actual personality or how the personality is played out in transactions like texting, is in respects different than the idealized personality. Discrepant personality is the difference in the four traits that play out differently online than in a face to face environment. Bao postulates that people find relief in the social pressures of offline life by create a social presence online that balances. Online virtual interactions then balance out traits like introversion, where an overly introverted person may become much more active online, and where an overly extraverted person may become less active online. The study reveals that the more extraverted behavior appeared offline the less it appeared in social life online (Bao, 2013).

Another suggestion is that a person's sense of presence in the online environment affects their attitudes and behaviors. The presence of digital symbols that make a person feel comfortable or uncomfortable may influence and of the Big Five personality traits and online behaviors. This proposes that humans confront their environments by perceiving and interpreting symbols and define the nature of situations by orienting themselves to social and physical objects. In virtual environments, many of the cues like smells and touch are missing so social cues become more important. Humans interact online by taking the role of the other and anticipating their response based on symbols in any given social situation. Prior interactive episodes are internalized and remember and entails cognitive rehearsal. Taking the role of the other includes objects as well as others and imagination. By rehearsing ones behavior cognitively, taking the role of another allows for positioning ones thoughts prior to reacting to people or objects. This maybe one of the reasons for an increase in social presence and acceptance in online texting environments. The degree of perceived presence does seem to affect attitudes online (Bellamy & Becker, 2015).

Social networking is playing an important role in building relationships and establishing collaborative working relationships. Personality traits have been shown to affect the evolution of network topography overtime. The personality traits of individual can influence their social presence and engagement in the group. This in turn influences their ability to build relationships and the likelihood of being placed in key positions to further facilitate network engagement. Alignment of similar lifestyles and acceptances may have as much influence as personality on affecting the resulting social network dynamics (Chinowsky, Robinson, B. & Robinson, S. (2013).

Online social presence and online identity go hand in hand. Dialogue is how we construct relationships and how we define what it is to be human. A great deal of research is dedicated to how social abilities relate to personal drive and how they build social systems. Activity in sharing collective goals, systems of thing and transformation define others and self. Using activity to define identity can be traced back at least to Leontev's 1978 version of activity theory (Hansson, 2012). A plausible theory of identity construction, this version of activity theory begins with the emergence of a social self that is then placed in context or structure with agency and then activities, consciousness and personality. The need for recognition through consciousness emerges then from how humans socialize with others, shared situations and with shared activities. This transforms both the individual's identity and the shared culture where the activities take place.

Identity and Anonymity

What determines Identity? Identity it seems depends on where people are and who people ask. Although identity is a term commonly used in our vocabulary, the actual meaning of identity is difficult to pin point. Identity can be defined by your relationship with self and relationship with others. Most definitions of identity though are comprised of two parts: personal identity and social identity.

Personal identity is used to describe the self-appraised characteristics of an individual. "I'm short, I'm tall, I'm smart, I'm dumb, I'm shy, I'm talkative, I'm cool, I'm a geek" are all terms individuals use to differentiate themselves. As Individuals we label ourselves and other people give us labels. Over time we integrate some of these into our personality. Different aspects, components and experiences of a person's life become integrated into what is now the whole person. Individuation is the term Carl Jung used to describe the development of the self and is equivalent to identity. Individuation is the way we form the concept of ourselves and differentiate who we are from everyone else. It includes our dos and our don'ts, our wills and our won't, our personal guide posts and defining limits.

The idea of our personal identity can also be traced back to work by Milton Erickson in 1968. Erickson wrote about the identity crisis and that one's feelings about the self are reflected in our character, goals and origins. Personal identity then, is an individual's self-appraisal of their physical and cognitive abilities, personal traits, motives and a variety of other attributes. Personal identity affects everything an individual thinks, feels and does (Baggio, 2010).

Social identity on the other hand, is derived from membership in a group. Social identity attaches values and emotions to membership the group. This encompasses the interpersonal self-concept derived from connections and role relationships with others as well as identity with the collective whole. Social identity includes the expected behaviors, alleged characteristics and distinguishing features that an individual takes pride in or views as unchangeable but socially consequential as part of member ship in a group (Meng, 2005).

Identity and the self are intricately connected. The social self has evolved to not only include a reflection of the physical world but also, to include a reflection of the online world as well. Our original sense of identity, which included reflective thinking usually about ourselves has a different and broader dimension and includes the social dimension we share others. This social construction comes before the individual construction and helps to define our individual identity. Identity, personality and activity are then integrated into relationships and natural contradictions. A lot of our sense of identity comes from comes from social and cultural context. The modern self is identified by some of the characteristics that are found in modern virtual environments (Hansson, 2012).

In modern online virtual environments, those connected by technologies, it is common for a person to more than one profile or identity on more than one social network. Discovering multiple profiles for the same individual is not uncommon. This allows researchers and data analysts to merge profiles or identities based on IP addresses, common attributes, usage profiles and social linkages. Social relationships then define not only who we say we are online but who we really are online (Bartunov, Korshunov, Park, Ryu & Lee, 2012).

Certainly the challenges of identity and technologies is moving into social spaces and tied to morals and ethics. The old rules no longer apply or at least not in the same way. Privacy is also frequently linked to identity and these lines have been undeniably blurred. The new rules involving privacy and identify are often buried in the small print. Often in comprehensible or inaccessible terms define how to set up your profile or define user licenses. Posting or texting that identifies a person as an ethnic, gender, racial, sexual or other marginalized group may also have effects on identity. Often our identities are negotiated through language construction and online spaces often do not lead to positive participation or fail to account for particular community practices (Dich, McKee, & Porter, 2013).

Online identities can be seen as a continuation of a person's everyday life. This is especially true of young people who construct, co-construct and reconstruct their identities through interactions on social media sites. Identify in online environments is not defined as a stable, which is traditionally the psycho-dynamic view but rather as socially constructed. A number of theories have indicated that the ability to construct and reconstruct through role playing, fragmented text discussions and an online social context is making identity in you ng people more fragmented. Because of the anonymity afforded online, the ability to cheat and change things like age, gender and therefore define who the person wants to be in the moment creates a kind of jigsaw puzzle identity. Interest many studies have found that what people do and talk about online is very close to what they do and discuss in a face to face environment.

Lemke, 2003, (Larsen, 2007) presented two concepts of identity come into play with online environments: identity-in-the moment" and "Identity-across-timescales". "Identity-in-the-moment" is concerned with "who I am right now" and is the aspect that plays out differently in different situations and could assume the characteristics of role playing. "Identity-across-timescales" is concerned with institutional values and lifespan development. Both these concepts of identity are linked to one construct which plays out through interactions online. Anonymity and social constructs play a role in identity performances and are linked to long term and short term identity.

Predictability, which is the ability to predict a person's behaviors based on what they have previously done online plays a large role in identity construction. Individuals are more predictable when acting alone than when acting in small groups or online communities. Interacting with other in online groups though, can be predicted by observing past interactions (Wang & Huberman, 2012). In online forum or discussion threads conversations are represented by a sequence of text posts and replies to one or more earlier posts. The thread length and activity are not related to the accuracy of the post (Aumayr, Chan & Hayes, 2011). Interactions are predictable, however, based on the history of interactions between the participants. Substantiating that identity is defined by interacting with others online.

Online social presence and online identity go hand in hand. How we interact with others is our social presence. Social presence theory has been around for nearly three decades and it has been over a decade since it was identified as a key element in online communications. Social presence is a dynamic and the roles we assume are related to a variety of factors including the online context. In an online environment many of the clues to identity and social presence that we take for granted in face-to-face environments are missing. Dialogue is how we construct relationships and how we define what it is to be human.

A great deal of research is dedicated to how social abilities relate to personal drive and how they build social systems. Activity in sharing collective goals, systems of thing and transformation define others and self. Using activity to define identity can be traced back at least to Leontev's 1978 version of activity theory (Hansson, 2012). A plausible theory of identity construction, this version of activity theory begins with the emergence of a social self that is then placed in context or structure with agency and then activities, consciousness and personality. He need for recognition through consciousness emerges then from how we socialize with other is shared situations and with shared activities. This transforms both the individual's identity and the shared culture where the activities take place.

Identity is also expressed in online social environments in collective ways; through text contributions like metavoicing, triggered attending, network informed associating and generative role-taking. Because of the affordances of these environments which included anonymity and the opportunity to voice ones opinion not only in a one to one or one to many manor but as a collective or to become part of the voice of the group. So that one is not just voicing an opinion but joining voices with many. This can be done by metavoicing like retweeting, voting, liking, commenting etc. Where individuals not only share their ideas with others but also share their reactions to the ideas of others, the contributions to ongoing knowledge conversations contributes to their personal identity and the identity of the group. Triggered attending is the ability to be notified or triggered to respond to the conversation of the group. It allows the individual to not be involved in the conversation deliberately unless there is an activating event. Similarly, network informed attending is the ability to join the conversation by relationship or content ties.

Texting and contributing in social media environments allows for connections to the content, others and content that is connected to the content. It informs identity because it allows for viewing connection that other possess, using this to make decisions and the developing associations. This creates a social capital where identity is associated with popularity and where people connect or associate with others not because there is a real or valued connection but because they have a lot of other associations. Finally, generative role-taking is keeping the dialogue going. Participants in these conversation share, complain, argue and participate in general not because they identify with anything but because the conversation is visible and they feel the need to keep it going. Others identify with the champion role and step in to support other's ideas. Identity then, is defined in these online texting environments through the individual, the group and the technologies.

Identity online is defined beyond reputation, connection strategy, social capital and image. High levels of engagement on social media is a balance between anonymity and identity. Online conversations give the individual the opportunity to exercise the prerogative to explore aspects of attention, social engagement, exploring boundaries and developing. The lack of deep ties and the sense of anonymity provided in texting online environments is free of deep roots, emotional ties and supports the emergent nature of interaction and the reformulation of identity both for the individual and the group. Identity online is linked at the individual level, group level and integrated with the technology and this provides a valuable lens for examining the relationship between the individual and technology artifact (Majchrzak, Faraj, Kane & Azad, 2013). Analyzing patterns of behavior in texting and discussion boards have revealed consumption patterns that help to affiliate subculture identities. The consumption of commodities and the discussion around them is central to the social capital used to identify a person with a subculture grouping. The online world provides a fertile field to create or substantiate alternative subcultures (Strubel, Pookulangara & Murray, 2013). By displaying their unity in consuming clothing or music, those that identify with a subculture are defining their identity by communicating these preferences in modern virtual environments.

Online text conversation have changed aspects of the English language. Grammar and spelling convention were not given preference and communication transpired that was aimed solely at send the message. Messages are sent to institutions like newspapers, television stations, networks and newsrooms using text. Text has become a strategic communication tool based on instantaneous exchange and the viral aspects of the media. The ability to get your message out as quickly as possible is often realized by truncating, abbreviating and omitting letters. Approximately 79% of all text messages use abbreviations. The adoption of this informal language structure and the implementation of it speaks to the identity of the sender. There are no guide books or few for text language. Yet the adaption and consistency of the texting language is wide spread (Joseph, Muthusamy, Michael, Telajan, 2013).

Identity online is developed through a curtain of anonymity. Anonymity is the capacity to act anonymously. Anonymity affects our interactions with others and ourselves. Anonymity or at least a perceived degree of anonymity, in online presents both ethical concerns as well as benefits. The protection of anonymity and privacy of electronic messages is under scrutiny. Although texting, emails and posting are common forms of communication the problem of privacy invasion has become more serious. Large amounts of digital data are transmitted via networks. Many technical schemas are used to protect identifiable information whether it is in a text message or an online payment. Anonymity has always been a double edged sword on the Internet. On one hand it can shield the privacy of users and on the other hand because everything is digital, things are not as transparent as they seem (Ye, Xiong, & Wu, 2013).

Anonymity provides the cover of invisibility. It provides us with opportunities that are not possible in a traditional environment. Texting provides a unique opportunity to engage in unobserved interaction. It can also provide the opportunity to take on a new identity. Using pseudonyms allows for a sense of anonymity and the chance to adopt new identities and create new perspectives. Online there is also an opportunity for identity deception. Identity deception in online communities is foundationally unethical and misinformation can be costly. There are many reasons why people do it ranging from the complex to the very simple…because they can.

Dialog through online text messages can lead to the developing strong relationships. Online relationships are developed between two individuals and between individuals and the group. Trust is earned over time. The group determines worth by an individual's contributions, conversations and relationships. Social presence and hierarchies can and do evolve and individual accrue social capital based on the validity of the ideas they contribute and trust.

Text can occur on a one to one basis or one to many in asynchronous discussion boards or real time synchronous chats. These discussion thrive because they provide a forum for the exchange of ideas and interests. Although they may be geographically dispersed and dislocated in time, the participants share common interests. Acceptance requires participation and reciprocation. In order to become an accepted part of the community, active participations is a requirement. Associated interests, brand identification, product involvement or any other related issue that captures people's attention can serve as a unifying agent. This can be linked back to the origins of the internet as a collective consciousness and in a sense democratic. This is a key contradiction in contributing to online chat communities. Anonymity allows participants to hide their identities. It also allows them to invent new ones. Impressionists believe that as human being we are always managing our impressions by revealing some attributes and concealing others and therefore always presenting multiple personalities with a variety of roleplaying being everyday life, it is undeniable that the faceless interaction of texting attracts some more than others.

In general anonymity and trust are at the heart of credibility in text based communications. With the planet nearing ubiquitous mobile connectivity, texting is more wide spread than ever. New social media sites and social networking applications are springing up everywhere. Participants create original texts, combine texts to make new ones and re-text text sent by others. This has given rise to the phenomena of going viral and the concerns that some of this information is unsubstantiated and unconfirmed but still travels very quickly. More importantly, the anonymity in text based commination has been shown to elicit a variety of behaviors ranging from increased openness to a decrease in personal responsibility and truthfulness.

Anonymity requires evaluating the creditability of information and information sources. Credibility is can be assess in a logical way by looking at the claims of the content or in a more peripheral way by looking at the reliability of the source doing the communication. The sources ability to provide the information and the intention in doing that are figured into the trustworthiness. Generally, high volume sources are thought to be less trusted than lower ones and ironically, however, those sending more text messages were generally able to discern high credibility better (Thomson, Ito, Suda, Lin, Liu, Hayasaka, Isochi & Wang, 2012).

FUTURE RESEARCH DIRECTIONS

The growing popularity of text messaging as a preferred method of communication tells can tell human beings something about not only the characteristics of our virtual environments but about ourselves. Text is a communication form that puts everyone on the same page and within reach. More research is needed to determine the effects texting has on our personalities and how we express ourselves in virtual environments. Also, research is needed to determine how virtual environments support our sense of identity and why we would rather text than meet face to face. Research in this field is in its infancy and many opportunities exist to help us understand the influence virtual environments have on our lives and the influence we have in virtual environments.

Many opportunities exist to explore the influence of modern virtual environments and methods of communicating like texting on the individual, community and society. Human communications are being reshaped by the technologies embrace and this in turn is causing us to rethink who we are and how we express ourselves. Opportunities exist to explore not only personalities and interactions in online virtual environments but the influences these environments have on us as individuals our personalities, interactions, social presence, and identity. Many more opportunities are available to explore our preferences in terms of usage, interaction and interface. Because this is happening so fast and has such a wide impact on our world, it is imperative we explore through solid empirical research the transformative aspects of technologies on our environment, society and ourselves.

In the online world, anonymity acts like a veil that permits the redefinition of self. Online identity is a bit paradoxical. On one hand we are free to define ourselves without the restrictions of visual cues and social inequalities. On the other hand our interactions with others provide a digital testimony to who we are, who we speak to and what we say. Research is needed into the part anonymity plays not only in our virtual environments but in our communications patterns overall. Anonymity is the capacity to act in private. Anonymity affects our interactions with others. Anonymity or at least a perceived degree of anonymity, in virtual environments presents both ethical concerns as well as benefits. How humans interact with others is our social presence. Again, much more research is needed to determine how our personalities determine these preferences and how environments influence out communication patterns and personalities.

REFERENCES

Baggio, B. (2012). *You, You Online, You When Nobody Knows It Is You Online. Michaels Allen's eLearning Annual 2012.* San Francisco, CA: John Wiley & Sons.

Baggio, B., & Beldarrain, Y. (2011). Anonymity and Learning in Digitally Mediated Communications: Authenticity and Trust in Cyber Education. Academic Press.

Bao, J. (2013). *Online social behavior reflects discrepant personality.* Retrieved October 13, 2015 from http://poseidon01.ssrn.com/

Bartunov, S., Korshunov, A., Park, S., Ryu, W., & Lee, H. (2012). *Joint link-attribute user identity resolution in online social networks.* The 6th SNA-KDD Workshop' 12, Beijing, China.

Bellamy, A., & Becker, J. (2015). *An exploratory analysis of the relationship between personality characteristics and the perceptions of virtual merchandising.* Retrieved October 13, 2015 from http://www.scirp.org/journal/PaperInformation.aspx?PaperID=54664

Blau, I., & Barak, A. (2012). How do personality synchronous media, and discussion topic affect participation? *Journal of Educational Technology & Society, 15*(2), 12–24.

Blumer, T., & Doering, N. (2012). Are we the same online? The expression of the five factor personality traits on the computer and the Internet. *Cyberpsychology: Journal of Psychosocial Research on Cyberspace, 6*(3), article 1. Retrieved October 11, 2015 from http://www.cyberpsychology.eu/view.php?cisloclanku=2012121201

Chinowsky, P., Robinson, B., & Robinson, S. (2013). *The use of personality assessment measures in social network analysis.* Presented at Engineering Project Organization Conference, Devil's Thumb Ranch, CO.

Chorley, M., Whitaker, R., & Allen, S. (2015). Personality and location-based social networks. *Computers in Human Behavior, 46*, 45–56. doi:10.1016/j.chb.2014.12.038

Cormick, G., Kim, N., Rodgers, A., Gibbons, L., Buekens, P., Belizán, J., & Althabe, F. (2012). *Interest of pregnant women in the use of SMS (short message service) text messages for the improvement of perinatal and postnatal care.* Retrieved from http://www.reproductive-health-journal.com/content/9/1/9

Dich, L., McKee, H., & Porter, J. (2013). *Ethical issues in online course design: negotiating identity, privacy, and ownership.* Retrieved October 13, 2015 from http://spir.aoir.org/index.php/spir/article/view/866/pdf

Harrysson, M., Metayer, E., & Sarrazin, H. (2012). How "social intelligence" can guide decisions. *The McKinsey Quarterly*, (November), 2012.

Holmes, C., Kirwan, J., Bova, M., & Belcher, T. (2015, Spring). An investigation of personality traits in relation to job performance of online instructors. *Online Journal of Distance Learning Administration, XVIII*, 1.

Jalilvand, M., Esfahani, S., & Samiei, N. (2011). Electronic word-of-mouth: Challenges and opportunities. *Procedia Computer Science, 3*, 42–46. doi:10.1016/j.procs.2010.12.008

Joseph, C., Muthusamy, C., Michael, A., & Telajan, D. (2013). strategies applied in SMS: An analysis of SMS column in star newspaper. *Asian Social Science*, *9*(15), 8–13. doi:10.5539/ass.v9n15p8

Jung, C.G. (1976). Psychological Types. *Collected Works, 6*, ¶ 757

Kim, H. (2011). *Effects of SMS Text messaging on vocabulary learning*. Received October 10, 2015 from http://kmjournal.bada.cc/wp-content/uploads/2013/05/14-2-7HSKim.pdf

Larson, M. (2007). *Understanding social networking: Online young people's construction and co-construction of identity online*. Retrieved October 11, 2015 from https://www.academia.edu/635848/Understanding_social_networking_On_young_peoples_construction_and_co-construction_of_identity_online

Majchrzak, A., Faraj, S., Kane, G., & Azad, B. (2013). The contradictory influence of social media affordances on online communal knowledge sharing. *Journal of Computer-Mediated Communication*, *19*(1), 38–55. doi:10.1111/jcc4.12030

Meng, M. (2005). *IT Design for sustaining virtual communities and identity based approach*. (Dissertation). University of Maryland, College Park, MD.

Penz, E. (2007). Paradoxical effects of the internet from a consumer behavior perspective. *Emerald Business*, *3*(4), 364–380.

Pinchot, J., Douglas, D., Paulette, K., & Rota, D. (2011). Talk to text: Changing communication patterns. *Consair Proceedings, V41830, Conference for Information Systems Applied Research*.

Saade, R., Kira, D., & Nebeb, F. (2012). *Understanding the role of personality traits on beliefs in online learning*. Retrieved October 11, 2015 from http://proceedings.informingscience.org/InSITE2012/InSITE12p613-624Saade0155.pdf

Segerstad, Y., & Weilenmann, A. (2013). Methodological challenges for studying cross-platform conversations. Selected Papers of Internet Research, 14.

Stokoe, E. (2014). From talk to text-Using the "Conversation analytic role play method" to engage (potential) mediation clients in spoken and written communications. *Research on Language and Social Interaction*, *47*(3).

Strubel, J., Pookulangara, S., & Murray, A. (2013). Musical identity online. *International Jouranl of Costume and Fashion*, *13*(2), 15–29.

Sude, M. (2013). Text messaging and private practice: Ethical Challenges and guidelines for developing personal best practices. *Journal of Mental Health Counseling*, *3*(3), 211–227. doi:10.17744/mehc.35.3.q37l2236up62l713

Thomson, R., Ito, N., Suda, H., Lin, F., Liu, Y., Hayasaka, R., . . . Wang, Z. (2012). *Trusting tweets: The Fukushima disaster and information source credibility on Twitter*. Presented at the 9th International ISCRAM Conference, Vancouver, Canada.

Ye, J., Xiong, X., & Wu, S. (2013). Dynamic model for anonymity measurement based on information entropy. *Journal of Internet Services and Information Security*, *4*(2), 27–37.

Chapter 7
Analysis of Initial Involvement of Librarians in the Online Virtual World of Second Life

Michelle Kowalsky
Rowan University, USA

ABSTRACT

This descriptive case study considers a tech-savvy and geographically distributed group of librarians and information professionals, led by an initiative of the Alliance Library System of Illinois, who gathered together to brainstorm and organize ways to provide online users with real library services. Through document analysis of written conversations in their online discussion group, the researcher has explored the development process of these librarians as they began to provide information services to users in the virtual online world of Second Life®.

DEVELOPING A PRESENCE IN A VIRTUAL WORLD

A new age of participatory culture around virtual environments has apparently evolved, as users flock to whichever online platforms give them the kinds of immersive, interactive environments they desire (Jenkins, 2006, p. 2). Users of the online virtual environment known as *Second Life®*, are able to contribute their own content, such as topography, buildings, interactive features and objects, to the simulated space they share with others. Linden Research, Inc., founder of Linden Lab and the provider of these online scripting tools for creating objects, did contribute much actual content of this kind to their virtual world at all. The company preferred to provide the mechanics of a grid of potential design space, and then to let the users decide what the world would look like and how they would interact with other users.

Several major decisions about virtual world design, then, need to be made by users of *Second Life®*, either individually or as a group. Academic librarians along with their education and technology colleagues decided to test the merits of this type of interactive environment for use in providing library services in a variety of library types. These decisions about areas of the world, known as islands, include various management, leadership, and design aspects such as the world's scope, ethos and culture, ap-

DOI: 10.4018/978-1-4666-9899-4.ch007

proach to management of participant interaction, alignment of roles, scale, and the like (Bartle, 2004). Librarians thus aimed to develop a presence in this online world and to undertake a variety of tasks from visioning to daily operations. A thorough analysis of the archived conversations of the *Second Life®* librarians, as documented through their online discussion group, has enabled the field to review these aspects of development in terms of frequency, context and motion over the course of the first year of their planning process.

Development in a virtual world may go through a variety of stages as it takes shape, especially when the development process is negotiated by a diverse group of users with various goals. The librarians of *Second Life®* have thus discovered and shared many lessons and practices, as well as suggested and improved several system modifications, during the first year of their multi-year development process. The librarians of the Alliance Library System, and their national and international partners, eventually revised key elements to support improved social dynamics about and within the virtual space, and to utilize a virtual world successfully in the provision of library and information services. As they have learned, "the support of multi-user, real-time interactions, persistent places and people, and the ability for end users to author and contribute to dynamic, expressive interactions has proven valuable for developing sustainable virtual environments" (Cheng, Farnham & Stone, 2002, p. 109). This personalization, opportunity to learn and experiment, and cooperative work on an international scale is an important contribution to the fields of both librarianship and information communication technologies.

As Bartle (2004) explains, during the pre-production stage of an online world effort, which can last up to six months, a vision document and design ideas may be created and discussed. The librarians of *Second Life®* have documented their thoughts on pre-production, testing and roll-out over time via their electronic discussion list, an online Google™ discussion group with open enrollment. The group's development, from visioning to building to opening of their *Second Life®* library and its many attendant islands and features, has been experienced from a variety of viewpoints among virtual participants from all over the United States and the world. This global conversation led to a rich discussion about the viability of new virtual services for providing information and assistance to library users and online patrons of many types.

Bartle's roll-out stage is "the most critical phases of development, when all the technologies and assets created are brought together to form a virtual world experience" (2004, p. 90). A culminating event of the group's first year of work -- the grand opening of the *Second Life®* librarians' Information Island to the public, as well as its aftermath of publicity and critique -- was captured via this discussion group and marks a boundary of the case. The grand opening party for Information Island, which was so well attended at certain times of day that it helped to crash the *Second Life®* servers, is an example of the group's self-reflective and analytical critique of their own work. Thus, the core team of librarians who led this initiative has experienced a variety of constructive and not-so constructive criticism about their initial foray into library services in *Second Life®*.

Lankes, Silverstein and Nicholson (2007) describe the potential for libraries as participatory conversations, and that "the library, as facilitator, needs to be varied in its modes and access points. In many cases, it is better to either create a personal space in which users may converse, or, increasingly, to be part of someone else's space" (p. 31). The librarians in this group migrated toward *Second Life®* as a platform which would reach many of their users at their preferred point of connection and exploration, which is so often online. Thus, this initial analysis of the group's strategy development, interaction processes, and decision-making sequences not only help us understand how they arrived at their present condition over the course of the initiative's first year, but also may help others who are considering pursuit of a similar large-scale distributed project and who will likely do research on prior efforts in order to inform their decisions as well.

DESIGNING LIBRARY SERVICES IN SECOND LIFE

If "the purpose of the *Second Life*® Library 2.0 is to provide real library services to *Second Life*® Residents" (Abram, 2007, p. 36), then the move by librarians toward virtual worlds as venues for their services seems logical. Since "most U.S. youth are not familiar with library electronic resources, but are very familiar with search engines, e-mail and chat" (OCLC, 2005, p. 5), a move toward digital library services by librarians seems to be a reasonable and appropriate response to a changing and increasingly technological society. Since patrons' "familiarity with more and different types of digital content is likely to increase" regardless of their age (OCLC, 2005, p. 5), virtual experiences are indeed one of the growing types of interactive online activities of this growing population. "Rather than setting up thousands of separated experiments, however, the library community should create a participatory network of its own" where they "can also directly experience life as a connected conversation" (Lankes, Silverstein & Nicholson, 2007, p. 31).

One of the original leaders of the *Second Life*® librarians' project, Lori Bell, works as the Director of Innovation at a regional library cooperative in the Midwest. Following her lead, and in partnership with several other information professionals such as Tom Peters from TAP Information Services in Missouri, the librarians of *Second Life*® organized themselves and began documenting their journey. Details of this journey, with its trials and tribulations, are documented in their electronic conversations using the Google Groups™ discussion forum, which has been open to librarians and interested people around the country and around the world. An important condition of the development is the ability of Bell to work on the *Second Life*® library initiative as part of her job as a professional librarian.

Abram (2007) explained that over 400 librarians in *Second Life*® working on virtual library services on a variety of islands, such as Info Island, the main portal for library services which attracted over 4,000 daily visitors early in the project's development. Cybrary City, where the Australian Libraries *Second Life*® building is located, had as many as 1,000 unique visits per day. The idea of visiting a library in a virtual world seems to have caught on for some users, if not solely the librarians themselves, then for a variety of hyper-connected library patrons as well. Library employers have dedicated staff to work on a *Second Life*® initiative; library consultants have donated expertise and resources to build environments in-world; and library users have spent time and energy on visiting these online locations. Something about this initiative had clearly caught people's attention and time, allowing it to flourish for more than five years as of this writing; similarly, the project's attractiveness to a profession with a never-ending search for modernization has motivated a large number of volunteers to continue its efforts.

The *Second Life*® development process experienced by academic, public and special collections librarians from all types of libraries may indeed be at the same time both unique and predictable. It is quite amazing that many different types of libraries -- everything from a medical library to a 19th Century library to a library for teens -- have come together in this space around a common purpose, providing information and reference services to all who enter. In real life, a collaboration of this magnitude might not have happened at all, and logistics of cooperation among governmental organizations, corporate centers, and academics certainly would have been more problematic. In addition, coordination of the efforts of librarians from many different parts of the country and the world would have been difficult if not impossible without the broadband Internet access, graphics-friendly computer hardware and user-driven software platform that formed the basis of these relationships in an online virtual environment. Collaboration and sincere efforts in investigating new ideas can thus be seen as a true sign of progress for the profession, and a commitment to innovation by the many stewards of librarianship.

Many real-life library functions, such as exhibiting special collections, arranging programs with guest speakers, and providing answers to questions at public service information desks began to be hosted in virtual worlds as well. An interesting aspect of this development process includes not only how these services are evolving in this new massively multiplayer online environment, but how new services are conceived and put into place. Similarly, the ways in which the job descriptions of some of those librarians is changing provides an interesting look at how professions as a whole embrace new technologies, especially after previously revolving around the printing industry.

New online environments have certainly presented new issues to librarians. Some of the challenges that the librarians are experiencing on Info Island, for example, include getting the profession's national organization on board (which the *Second Life*® Library founders have done successfully at some levels, although others are not ready to deal with this new medium); dealing with online griefers and vandals, along with randomly negative press from certain factions; finding the time to meet customer demand for faster development while managing growth; coordinating efforts of dozens of volunteers, which approaches the size of a multinational company at times; and developing in-world methods of teaching information literacy skills such as evaluating the quality of web site information.

How and when these types of services were discussed, developed and decided upon creates an interesting case study which provides us much information about these types of implementations for the future. The profession of librarianship, as well as other professions interested in developing an online presence, can learn much about online interaction, collaboration and innovation from these virtual pioneers.

RESEARCH DESIGN

The present research aims to understand this case through document analysis of the electronic discussions about the project. These investigations reveal, and are a documentary record of, the development processes of the librarians of *Second Life*® as they initially brainstormed together and built library services in an online virtual world. The researcher was simply one of the many interested librarians who joined and followed discussions in the early online discussion group, but did not work on the project itself.

For the purposes of this study, the "librarians" will refer to all of those who worked on the project and communicated in the online Google Group™, whether they were traditional librarians, information technology specialists, or other interested persons who were accepted by the group as participants. For clarity, the term "participants" is often used to describe the entire group of online interlocutors, essentially those who "build library services in-world and find

out what virtual world residents want in a Twenty-first Century library" (Bell, Peters, & Pope, 2008, p. 11). At its inception, the project/initiative was based on the idea that "libraries need to provide services and build a presence where the users are. In real life, libraries are an important and valuable part of their communities;" the initial group of librarians who became interested in this development believes this is true of virtual worlds as well (Bell, Peters, & Pope, 2008, p. 5).

A generally qualitative approach was used to study the development processes of the librarians of *Second Life®*. In order to capture the complexity of human behavior in this effort, qualitative methods are both appropriate and desirable. A main goal here was to understand the librarians' collaborative efforts as they design library services in the online virtual environment. A record of their ongoing progress has been archived via their group electronic discussion list; analysis of the content of these ongoing posts to the group's electronic discussion list revealed many features of their development of this online library initiative. Descriptive statistics were utilized to gain an overall understanding of the numbers and scope of participation throughout the group's first year of existence and operation.

Use of the *Second Life®* librarians' Google Groups™ online discussion forum as a primary source of information is paramount as an ongoing public record which aids in the understanding of their activity. As a case study, the current investigation attempted to be "noninterventive and empathetic," and the researcher tried "not to disturb the ordinary activity of the case" (Stake, 1995, p. 12), by obtaining information via discrete observation and examination of records only after online posts had been offered and aged, and calling attention to individual posts with care and discretion. The researcher's background as a professional librarian, and her experience teaching new librarians in and about *Second Life®*, as well as her legitimate peripheral participation in the online group, was a benefit to the current study and to an understanding of how the *Second Life®* librarians see and do things in this case.

The purpose of this descriptive study is to understand the development processes and to characterize the early communication among librarians working in *Second Life®*. These questions and others which resulted from the descriptive case at hand are important to the profession of librarianship since the *Second Life®* librarians' project represents an early and multifaceted foray into the digital world. By examining the ways they began the project, discussed ideas, involved new members, and by reporting these patterns and results from their first year of this endeavor, we stand to inherit a wealth of information about the ways in which a traditional profession learns to adapt to new technologies and advanced communication practices in a modern, computerized world. Essentially, this study set out to describe and characterize the efforts of this group by using systematic analyses and descriptive third-party reporting.

The *Second Life®* librarians have a complex and developing online culture, and thus an initial step in understanding their history and group process was an examination of some of their documentation and peer recognition of their efforts. The present method for studying this convergence included analysis of the early stages of their working group communications, which total several thousand ongoing electronic discussion list messages from the project's inception to the present. Of particular interest are the first third of the discussion, or roughly the initial 5,000 messages, which document the librarians' efforts to begin and sustain momentum for the *Second Life®* library project; these communications in particular help to enhance our understanding of this new and significant effort toward application of a new technology.

The researcher has protected both the real-life names and the online avatar names of participants as they so desired, and as monitored by an Institutional Review Board. The final analysis of the electronic discussion group herein was presented to participants in a spirit of transparency, and in order to obtain their views of its accuracy and completeness before publication. Participants requested only minor cosmetic changes to both the analysis and the interpretation of their work as provided in this manuscript, and only to improve its clarity. The researcher feels this is an important testament to the sincerity and reflective nature of all of those involved in the *Second Life®* library initiative; they were content to have significant portions of their efforts objectively analyzed by a third party and reported out as such.

DATA SOURCES AND SCOPE

Data for the present study focused on documentation of the development process as provided by the participants themselves via their electronic group discussion list, the Google Group™ of the Alliance *Second Life®* librarian participants. The group's archives of their conversations, negotiations and brainstorming provide an ongoing record of their development and achievements since the project's inception in 2005, through its first anniversary, and continuing to the present day. As of this writing, the group has continued to grow and innovate over the past several years; these artifacts possess "a longevity that permits their delivery to successive generations, thereby contributing to social continuity" (Thomas, 1994, p. 686).

While other measures of participation in this effort exist -- such as the Librarians of *Second Life®* in-world group, which was comprised of 791 members as of January, 2008, ("*Second Life®* librarians," 2008), or the *Second Life®* Library 2.0 in-world group, which was comprised of 1,463 members as of the same date ("*Second Life®* library," 2008) -- the main Alliance mailing list which used Google Groups™ was selected as the source from which to draw data. The Alliance *Second Life®* librarians' main Google Groups™ discussion forum was comprised of 640 members as of January, 2008 ("Alliance *Second Life®*," 2008), roughly two years after the inception of the SL project and the start of the online discussion.

Initial permission to utilize data from the Librarians of *Second Life®* electronic discussion lists in aggregate for purposes of research was procured from the *Second Life®* librarians' group electronic mailing list owner, Lori Bell. The group leader had collected some but not all information about members' real names, *Second Life®* names and institutional affiliations upon initial addition of any new member to the group, thus providing assistance in member identification and verification for this study as needed. Real names, institutional affiliations, and other identifying data was often withheld from the researcher by the leader as participants requested; similarly, individuals whose words or ideas appear in detail and other than in aggregate form were able to conceal either their real or online identities for this report as they wished. Therefore, readers who are familiar with this group will easily notice pseudonyms provided by the researcher to uphold individual participants' wishes during the process of informed consent.

DATA COLLECTION AND ANALYSIS PROCEDURES

A corpus of messages from the first year of the librarians' communication was assembled from the group's online Google archive. The researcher stripped the data of identifying personal information as requested by participants. As Creswell (2007) maintains, "an important step in the [case study] process is to gain access to and establish rapport with participants so that they will provide good data" (p. 118). The researcher had basic ongoing communication and participation with several members and leaders of this group, both online and in-person, over the course of the year during which this research was conducted. Aggregate data was agreed upon to be the primary method of reporting the case, with subsequent permissions obtained for particularly identifiable information such as quotes or screen names.

Evaluations presented in aggregate form were also provided to members via e-mail for final evaluation before publication. Effort was also made to contact individuals who had since left the list, so that their permission may be procured in the same manner if their messages or replies are deemed important to quote or highlight in the final manuscript. Many of these participants were ultimately contacted, and although not directly quoted if they so chose, their confidential exchanges with the researcher helped to provide a fuller understanding of the case.

The Google Groups™ discussion archive of the Alliance *Second Life®* participants – in other words, the text submitted online in group discussion of a topic of common interest -- comprised the data analyzed for this study. Analysis of this data was performed without preconceived notions of what would be found there, save the researcher's own experience of being a member on the *Second Life®* librarians' group discussion list in the year prior to analysis. The researcher spent significant time with the original raw data, alternately examining individual messages closely and analyzing them within the bigger picture and sequence of the year as a whole.

An important and unique aspect of this study is that no part of the analysis could have been completed purely via technological means. First, the corpus of messages as displayed via Google Groups™ was not easily downloaded in its entirety by several programs meant to perform this action. Second, the topics, or message threads, listed by Google do not combine messages when a participant's particular group reader or email system adds prefixes to the subject heading to a message upon reply. Instead, the message topic is listed as new, which necessitates aggregation of the topics for a true corpus.

Although disaggregation of group headers and footers and error messages resulting from temporary cut-and-paste functions performed on the original display were easier to parse, these were tasks less critical to the analysis and easily identified. Even simple descriptive statistics needed to be calculated by hand, since dates attached to message topics listed by Google Groups™ indicated only the most recent date a topic was discussed, rather than its beginning dates or duration of the discussions. The librarians' discussion list messages were thus "broadly studied not only for their formal or narrative characteristics but also for their appearance and placement over time" (Thomas, 1994, p. 686). Results below are grouped thematically, indicating an interesting and

SYNOPSIS OF RESULTS: OVERALL DEVELOPMENT PROCESS

Progression of the librarians' virtual world work can be seen in the many features of their posts over the course of the first year. Early messages within the first six to eight weeks contained general observations of their new *Second Life®* library and island, and their delight with the project's beginnings:

- "I had a reference question tonight!" (acknowledgement of users)
- "We now have a garden with a gazebo, lots of flowers, trees, and a water fountain" (report on new builds)
- "I found a cow!" (discovery of SL capabilities, in this case the sharing of inventory)
- "We're front page news in the metaverse!" (concern about outside perceptions)

By the end of the first three months of the initiative, group messages report on giving tours of Info Island, book clubs, and meetings. They include discussions of ideas for making health information available in-world, advertising for more volunteers, and tracking news of the initiative in blogs and other outlets. In addition, there is talk of splitting the librarians and/or libraries into groups -- reference, science fiction, medical, 19th Century, teen -- to better handle organizing and sharing of the workload. Analysis will include aspects of start-up, management, and marketing, for example, as each of these stages were negotiated by the participants in an ongoing discourse over time.

As the group approached its first six months of online existence, more advanced activities were discussed and organized. Automating the design of objects and spaces for new users, 3-D object interactivity, mashups and library database trials in *Second Life®*, and the possibility of mixed realities for live events (in-person, audiocast and in-world) become topics of conversation. Planning for a grand opening is also suggested.

After a half-year of work on delivering library services in *Second Life®*, the group begins to deconstruct themselves. They present at conferences and write articles in professional journals and websites with titles such as "Virtual Worlds and Alternate Realities -- Where Do Libraries Fit In?" In a spirit of representing alternate viewpoints, the participants publicly discuss, in their Google Groups™ and report on similar in-person conversations in their respective peer communities, including addressing the concerns of naysayers who sometimes angrily protest their initiative. It becomes clear that not every participant in the group is a professionally degreed librarian; in fact, the confluence of technologists, archivists, information consultants and managers help to create a diverse online conversation in which participants report that their particular skills, ideas and contributions are helping the overall cause.

At the close of their first year of discussion, large-group live events such as speakers, performances and art shows in-world are the norm. The participants in the Alliance *Second Life®* effort have already formed a solid partnership with their national professional organization, the American Library Association (ALA). They are reporting successful attempts at procuring funding from vendors and in holding online training and parties in *Second Life®*. They begin to have pubic discussions of trust, identity and intellectual property which impact their work. In the sequence of development, their growing pains mimic those encountered in real life, as well as provide unique new challenges in a multi-national, multi-organizational and multiple-time-zone project.

The researcher's interest in this case remains to understand the discourse of the *Second Life®* library participants, and to specifically find and analyze features of their online discussion archive which point to aspects of their development and collaboration. Naturally, the privilege of the researcher in case study is to assert what she finds meaningful as a result of her inquiries (Stake, 1995, p. 12). Since the role of the researcher cannot be disambiguated in case study, this presents a natural invitation for others to further examine this complex phenomenon -- perhaps through additional methods as well as through varied lenses -- for a continually evolving picture of phenomenon of the work of librarians and their peers in *Second Life®*.

FEATURES OF THE FIRST YEAR OF COLLABORATION AND DISCUSSION

Details of participation levels in the online group are important aspects of the development process which help us to understand the work of librarians and their peers in in initiating a presence in *Second Life®*. The corpus of online discussion messages of the Alliance *Second Life®* Library group was found to include 5,753 messages in 1,604 unique discussion topics during the roughly one-year time period bounded by the initial establishment of the Alliance *Second Life®* Google discussion group on April 12, 2006, and conclusion of the month in which they celebrated their first anniversary of services in-world in *Second Life®*, May 30, 2006. As mentioned earlier, use of the term "first year" in describing the data implies this 13 ½-month time period throughout the discussion. The timeline in Figure 1 provides an overview of the nature of the participants' messages with respect to their reported progress on the project.

Figure 1. Pattern of unique messages initiated in the Alliance Second Life® Google Group™ over time (by number of participants)

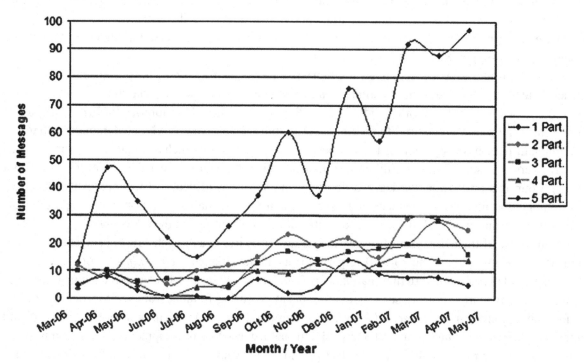

Original text was thus typed online and sent electronically to the group, often by the most active members of the 300 participants who signed up for the Alliance *Second Life*® Google Group™ in its first year, considered here to be April 2006 through May, 2007. Since data on individual members' activity is not easily disaggregated from the archive, and is not part of the requests for this study's human subject considerations, aggregate data about the messages themselves will remain the priority for this study. An individual message posted to the online group -- either initial or reply -- remains the unit of analysis.

While only 12% of the topics, or 695 messages, represented "announcement"-type activities in which a member experienced no feedback from the group, a total of 351 topics, or 22% of the total number of topics, were discussed by five or more participants. This group discussion aspect of the *Second Life*® participants' online discourse represents an exchange of 3,503 messages over the course of a year, or 61% of the total number of messages in the corpus. These calculations represent interesting and important aspects of the analysis with regard to development of computer-mediated communication of librarians over time.

Over half of the messages contained a back-and-forth exchange between two or more members in the public forum. This represents a shift in the way that online discussion groups are being used, which perhaps mimics the development of society's online communication processes as a whole. However, librarians discussing this *Second Life*® initiative spent less time sharing resources and answering traditional reference questions from patrons. Instead, members of this group engaged each other in topics of discussion more frequently and in larger groups, rather than focusing on transactions between individual members as was previously discovered in studies of librarian electronic discussion group interaction.

However, readers' differing definitions of what constitutes a "group" may affect further interpretation of this data. For example, consider the differences in analysis if a group did not consist of five or more people, but of a minimum of three; this would make the 504 topics discussed become only 30% of the total number of possible topics entertained by a "group." Similarly, 51 message topics attracted 10 or more participants in discussion during the year; this would indicate to some that only 3% of the topics could be categorized as "heavily" discussed. The same varieties in interpretation would be true as well if additional requirements were placed on what constituted "discussion" of the information or intent of the original post.

The particular number of messages initiated over time by individual participants shows a clear upward trend. While messages of an announcement nature grew with the most vigor in the last half of the first year of operation, messages of a conversational or multi-directional nature grew steadily as well, showing an increase in numbers for messages involving two, three or four participants. This may, in part, appear in tandem to the formation of smaller groups with similar interests, which is later documented in the group's first annual report.

Nevertheless, more of the information posted to this discussion group is shown to be more multidirectional than unidirectional; the participants' online offerings of ideas garnered responses by more than one other member in an increasing number over time. Figure 1 displays the trend lines of 83% of the messages in the total archive of the first year's discussions which, when taken together, show a slow but steady increase over time when compared with the steeper slope of single-participant, announcement-type messages.

A similar trend occurred in the first three months, albeit with fewer conversations and more announcements in its start-up phase, after which activity decreased markedly. Activity then decreased from 221 posts over the first three months to 136 posts within the subsequent three-month period. This may be due to the initial interest in and excitement about the librarians' *Second Life®* project, and then the general attrition which is known to occur after a new tool or conversation is investigated. Yet, midway through the first year, the number of multiple participants per message gently increases over time; taken together the slope of this line is clearly positive.

Of the total number of messages represented in Figure 1, 99% of the messages can be accounted for when considering all messages with 22 or fewer respondents. Nevertheless, the sheer number of participants and communicative events must be considered significant in this case. If performing a simple average -- using either a given membership of the *Second Life®* librarians' Google group™ in January, 2008, or an estimate of 500 members at the conclusion of the group's first year, based on estimates from the corpus and information from the group's first annual report -- an average 3 messages posted per member per year is the norm.

Membership and Participation

A review of the participants' roles in their home organizations, as offered directly by them in the first-year corpus, reveals that a large number of participants indeed follow an academic calendar in their real life occupations. An analysis of the participants shows that academic librarians at all levels make up roughly a third of the described prolific participants in the first year of discussion. Of the 74 participants who offered their real life roles in conversation with members of the whole group, academic librarian roles were listed more than any other librarian type or any other non-librarian role. At least 23 of the self-described roles of discussion group participants were that of "academic librarian," or a degreed library professional working in a college or university with a librarian title, even if that role is heavily technology-oriented, such as a systems librarian.

The second most indicated role among participants was that of "consultant," a professional who performs library or technology work independent of a library, or as a self-employed business owner; 15 such roles were identified among first year participants. The next significant role group was comprised of eight participants who self-identified as information technologists or webmasters, who did not possess library degrees or job titles which included the term "librarian." Some, but not all of these technology-focused participants worked for colleges or universities. Many other diverse roles were reported among first-year participants, including university professors, regional consortia staff, library managers and administrators, medical and public librarians, law librarians, government librarians, corporate librarians, archivists, art librarians and webmasters. When some participants changed jobs during this time period, their initial role was considered during this analysis.

From creation on April 11, 2006 by the group owner Lori Bell and her associate, Tom Peters, who both joined on the first day, membership in the discussion group increased steadily. As such, the number of participants and the date on which they joined the conversation may help to further determine participation levels. Upon a check of member "join dates" within the Google group™, it has been further determined that 416 of the current 736 members (as of October 12, 2008) of the Alliance *Second Life®* discussion group joined prior to May 31, 2007.

The peaks and valleys in participation levels from Figure 1 appear to be repeated in the pattern of new memberships. Months where numbers of messages with multiple participants increased were preceded by or concurrent with increased numbers of new participants. Upon a cursory review, join date did not appear to affect degree of participation; librarians who joined early, midway through the first year, and late into the first year of operation appear to all have participants who would be considered very active, those who posted messages infrequently or sporadically, and those who did not offer their own comments to the group but simply joined and/or read the discussion. A more detailed investigation of this phenomenon may be undertaken at a later date for other purposes; however, the development process in this case appears to be fueled by a steady influx of new members over time, as well as an increase in the number of messages shared with the group.

Numbers of "lurkers" on any electronic discussion list -- participants who join and read but do not author messages -- are known to be a large portion of any online group's membership. "When lurking was defined as 'no messages during a three month period', 48% and 84% of community members in 77 online health and 21 online technical support communities respectively, were found to be lurkers" (Nonnecke, Preece, & Andrews, 2004). While specific data is unavailable at this time for the particular number of lurkers to the librarians' Google Group™ for the time period of March 2006 to May 2007, estimates of participation averages may be calculated.

If at least half of the members of the group are, for purposes of argument, assumed to be lurkers, or even if two-thirds of the members are assumed to be lurkers, estimates still show this average level of participation to be indicative of continuing interest, at either 4 messages or 8 messages per person per year, respectively. Therefore, even if only 20% of the online group participants are considered "active" in this way, then those 83 members would average 20 posts per year. Specific data which refine these estimations may be acquired only by a "human" hand-count, due to the known issues with the Google software reporting methods and aggregate corpus keyword limitations of this type of investigation. An exact determination of the number of lurkers may be conducted at a later date via analysis of members who do not appear as authors in the corpus, and then verified by secondary sources, if this specific data is determined to have a possible impact on the study's conclusions. For the researcher's purposes here, participants who willingly contributed to the discussion, rather than those who did not, remain the focus of the analysis.

Sample Vignette: "What Are We Doing Here?"

The following vignette, taken from the most popular topic thread during the group's first year of online discussion, provides "a briefly described episode to illustrate an aspect of the case, perhaps one of the issues" (Stake, 1995, p. 128) which pervades the participants' experiences during development of their initiative. In the following exchange, participants trade messages in answer to an oft-asked question about their decision to work on library services in *Second Life®*.

"What are we doing here?" a participant asks the Second Life® (SL) librarians' online discussion group in March, 2007, as it approaches its one-year anniversary of existence. "We have terrific resources, but if we simply duplicate real-life (RL) buildings full of links back to the web, what do we achieve? Familiarity is comforting to some users, and an impressive duplication of a RL facility might grab the attention of a non-SL-using administrator, but does that help our patrons? What makes patrons return? Do we know the busiest sites and the reasons?"

A flurry of messages ensued. "These are really good questions," most participants reply, alternately offering their own answers and supplying more questions.

"Instead of using SL to try to provide/duplicate services to our human patrons who are in the real world, let's think about providing reference services to the avatar itself. What do they need?" asks one participant. The group pauses to consider.

"Some of the advantages of SL as I see it are as SL and SL-type interfaces become more common, many students will (and already do) find the current web interface flat and boring and are looking to be engaged," explains another. The topic appears to be one for which participants have much to say, averaging 50 or more words per post.

The group then decides to host two synchronous chats the following week to "talk through" this nagging issue in real time in an "informal brainstorming session." In the

meantime, several subsequent Google Groups™ discussions focus on procedural aspects of the upcoming real-time online discussion, including time zone accommodations and locations to post the archived chat transcripts.

"I'll try to be there, but being new and still learning the ropes, I'll probably learn more than contribute," a member muses.

"Don't worry. I'm new myself and just feel that the more meetings I can attend, the less new I will feel," another participant replies to the group.

Two chat times are set up to accommodate participants in different time zones, and negotiations are held on where in Second Life® to meet. The librarians decide to meet in the Reader's Garden, "a royal yet casual seating location on the waterfront" in CybraryCity II.

The participant who asked the original question was then invited by other members to lead one of the discussions. "I've been doing some thinking on this lately, and it seems we've got some questions that we can't quite figure out ourselves," the initiating member offers at the start of the first group's chat. "Discussion is totally open for everyone and every idea." Thus begins a typical online conversation in the Google Groups™ of the librarians of Second Life®.

In this sample exchange, the librarians of *Second Life®* discussed their own ideas and entertained the views of others in a flurry of posts -- from the nearly synchronous to the time-zone dependent asynchronous -- which proved to be one of the most sustained and significant reflective exchanges in their first-year discourse. The librarian participants proffer ideas, politely yet critically; responses to those ideas -- both positive and negative -- are offered with detail and explanation, often accompanied by a humbling phrase, and in a general spirit of negotiation. Direct and indirect requests for advice or information are extended, plans are made for action, and volunteers identify themselves. Forward movement is almost always the result.

As such, it is important to recall that the case focuses on the researcher's observations of the written discourse of the librarians in their online discussion group, as reasonably objective toward and independent of additional details provided by the participants outside of the corpus or otherwise after the analysis. Similarly, potentially significant information from outside of the discussion corpus, such as links to group and individual blogs, articles by or about the participants and their efforts, was not consulted during this study.

Prolific Authors and New Contributors

To recap, Figure 1 shows the development of the *Second Life®* librarians' process of computer-mediated communication over the first year of the project's existence. Low levels of participation in large group discussions were evident around the end of the summer of 2006, perhaps due to vacations or a lull in interest after a project's initial growth spurt. However, a clear upward trend, almost exponential toward the end of the first year, shows that small-group (subgroup) and large-group participation are on the rise as the project moves forward. For topics which interest all types of subgroups, it appears that more and more participants are involved in the discussions, especially around the project's first anniversary.

However, since sheer numbers of mentions in message posts cannot clearly or necessarily indicate significant contributions, other measures needed to be determined for a participant's selection as an important participant during year one. Second coders assisted in providing additional names of participants whose contributions appear significant during the first year and reasons for their choices. Sheer numbers of posts were not the sole decisive factors, but amount of participation evoked in others by the author, and length of discussion over time were now considered. However, slight disagreement among coders resulted in exploration of another method to follow the themes of the librarians' development; 85% of the unique author names in Table 1 were agreed upon via independent coding, and another three authors were added to the mutual list after calculation rationales were discussed and agreed upon.

Table 1. Most prolific authors' posting activity in the first year [some screen names have been changed upon request of individual participants]

Unique Author Name	Number of Messages	Percentage of Total Messages
Lori	744	12.975
Fleet	330	5.7551
Angel	289	5.0401
Abbey	256	4.4646
Smith	227	3.9588
Spike	226	3.9414
Lilac	141	2.4590
Krystal	124	2.1625
Brielle	116	2.0230
Christian	115	2.0056
Techno	114	1.9881
Roman	110	1.9184
Bill	106	1.8486
Donna	105	1.8312
Margaret	96	1.6742
Jilliana	88	1.5347
Shelley	85	1.4824
Beth	76	1.3254
Rebekah	75	1.3080
Esther	73	1.2731
Cheri	70	1.2208
Salma	63	1.0987
Rain Noonan	61	1.0638

Prolific authors who contributed the most to the online discussion of the Second Life librarians were contacted for their validation of the conclusions in this report, as well as for their informed consent to be mentioned by name and/or quoted in this manuscript. As such, those described in detail here should not be viewed as a list of *all of the participants* who made significant contributions to the project or as *the only participants* whose conversations about the project were considered meaningful by the calculations mentioned thus far. The most prolific authors' activity is described in Table 1.

Since email systems are not comparable, and email addresses, signatures and members names of participants can be either their real life names or their *Second Life®* avatar names -- or a combination of both with the intent to reveal neither their real identity nor workplace -- any master list of participants does not and will not exist. Again, the list above should not be construed as such for any purpose. Nevertheless, several leaders of the project have emerged and become associated in the popular press with their work on the Alliance *Second Life®* initiative, as well as many of the projects which resulted from the group's initial division of labor within the first month of online conversation. These participants can provide further details about the case via interview or public authorship about their work.

The inclusion of original messages in replies, and discussion *about* certain members in the text of a message, had initially indicated that Lori, Smith and Abbey were the most prolific authors. One reason these particular users' participation levels may have been ranked initially higher via software tool analysis could have been due to the use of their names in communication from multiple email addresses and/or inconsistency in choice or use of either real first name or avatar name across all communication with the group. Use of emergent coding by hand in addition to use of software tools during this study has helped to uncover this fallacy and has allowed the descriptive statistics to represent the purest form of the data.

The authors above represent authorship of 1% or greater percentage of the total messages exchanged in the group during its first year. A longer list of contributors who participated in the first year's discussion, via a simple average of one message per month, appears in Appendix H. Participants who did not wish to be acknowledged by name have been given a pseudonym in these lists by the researcher. At least 237 unique authors were identified in the first year of conversation; that would make the earlier estimate of 50% of participants as lurkers roughly accurate. Lori Bell, the group's leader, used a second avatar and persona in the discussion group to separate her transparent work relationship and personal relationships to the project; Rain Noonan, then, is the only avatar in the manuscript's tables who represents a duplicate human participant in the list.

The number of authors whose contributions averaged one per month was 94. This also dispels the notion that the group leader did most of the talking; her contributions were only 14% of the total conversation, including both her main and secondary aliases. Since the average percentage of contribution per member is so small, this indicates that discussion was spread among many members as well as spread out over time. In fact, even contributing 50 or 60 messages over the course of a year was not enough to dominate the conversation; those who averaged one message per week could not account for much more than one percent each of the total discourse conducted.

A difference in the number of messages from either male or female authors does not appear to be significant. Among the prolific contributors mentioned in this manuscript, 48 female and 24 male authors can be identified by participants' self-revelation in the corpus. A mix of male and female authors can be seen in an almost equivalent ratio in the table rankings of volume of messages contributed as in the composition of the group, with a two-to one female-to-male ratio. Contrary to common assumptions about the library profession, this particular convergence of participants was not heavily dominated by women.

Lastly, all of the librarians' Google Group™ discussions were conducted in English, although this was not necessarily the first language of all participants. A majority of the online discussion contributors were replying from the United States, as evidenced by their self-revelation in message text or message signatures. Participants were also noted to hail from the Netherlands, Canada, Ireland, the United Kingdom, and Australia. Clearly, facility with the English language was a common trait among participants in this group; it is unclear if this was a barrier to participation for those who may have left the group during the first year. A further limitation is the lack of country or language information for most or all of the participants. Some authors preferred to have details of their identity remain anonymous, and where requested, their identifying information including name, location, or role has been masked by the researcher via pseudonym, aggregation, or omission.

Patterns of Development

The sequence and repetition of certain features of the librarians' discourse about their initiative help provide preliminary information regarding the ways that the *Second Life*® librarians examine new ideas, and vision about their projects and their progress. Previously tagged sections of the discussion revealed representative instances of the content and sequence of the participant exchanges which demonstrate examples of cooperation, collaboration, and communication.

For example, an idea about the *Second Life®* library's building design is introduced by a member, with attachments of images of the "old design" and proposed "new design" generated just prior to initiation of the discussion group. The participant encourages comments on them, and quickly garners two replies of light critique and mild agreement with the poster's general initial assessment of the two ideas. Next, another poster expressed disagreement and lengthier critique of both the old and new designs, with an accompanying statement of what she liked about them, thus displaying positive critique (agreement with the negative comments of the two posters) sandwiched in between disagreement and explanation.

Yet another participant then compliments the prolific critic and also rejects both offered ideas and raises critical questions about the purpose of the activity and the users' needs in-world. The original poster replies with several indirect requests for help, a gentle backpedal and some self-deprecation, indicating that everyone is new at the tasks at hand. The original poster proceeds to make further statements of inclusion of many ideas, directly and indirectly compliments the other posters and their ideas, and suggests a temporary decision by the discussants to move the project forward, indicating that revisions can be made at any time. Thus, a representative discussion pattern shows that early talk is centered around purpose, goals, users, and direction, and is immediately followed by organization of communications and personnel. This may be in contrast to some rumors and criticism of the project where participants were accused of not having these conversations early in the project's development.

An additional pattern is seen in an idea offered for discussion about creating a blog to list events. The blog needed a description and tagline, so a participant offered ideas of how to do the former, then asked an open-ended "what do we want to say about this?" question. He elicited a number of new ideas in addition to comments on the original method of setting up the blog. This showed a quick evolution from the previous "introduction of choices, this-or-that vote" of earlier topics; in fact, more of the subsequent discussions utilized indirect requests for information and comments, using phrases such as "we could use this…" and direct requests for comments such as "how about this?" and offerings of ideas with preambles such as "I think it would be helpful to have…" In this manner, requests for consideration of ideas were offered frequently.

If an idea or post was rejected by others, it tended to include apology and humbling or self-deprecation, and sometimes was followed by introduction of another new idea.

This follows the lead of the previous respondents' patterns. A new idea was also introduced by "have you considered?" and followed by "great idea" phrases when directed at individuals as well as proposed to the group. Since participation which includes agreement and dissent seemed comfortable in the opening exchanges, this may be one reason why open exchanges of ideas helped move the discussion and process forward.

Also, new ideas were introduced almost every time with elaborations of two kinds, either a) reasons why the new idea might help, add to, change, or otherwise benefit the original idea or discussion, or b) facts that helped detail the proposed idea. Greetings were absent and perhaps implied when offerings were for general discussion, but when offerings were directed at a particular participant, greetings were included in the conversation and clearly used the target member's name, which resulted in generally civil exchanges.

Thus, upon attempting to introduce a new idea or influence the direction of the project, librarian discourse sequences appear to follow similar patterns. Participants compliment or thank others, then offer their own ideas often in great detail (discussing things they tried or want to develop based on their experiences or observations), then inform the group of their future actions, tempering these with an indirect request for advice, information or help, and a note of intent to collaborate further. This sequence puts forth the poster's ideas in a strong manner, but mitigates the delivery of the ideas by acknowledging the work of others and appearing to have concern for their expertise.

Where single messages were posted without answer by any participant, a further analysis revealed that, indeed, ideas both good and bad were not simply ignored. Most of the unanswered topics consisted of meeting announcements, websites or press mentions to share, a call for volunteers which directed replies to the author's individual email address, thank you messages, updates performed, and reports on events or activities which had taken place in-world or outside of the larger group.

Only seven of the four hundred participants had 15 or more messages ignored during the first year: Lori, the group leader, posted mostly informational messages about meeting dates, websites, and updates of activities; Krystal mostly posted thank-you's to the group for helping her, and 39 of these types of messages went unanswered; Fleet and Techno posted work updates and meeting times from their respective sub-groups, which included invitations to join as part of their 39 and 33 respectively unanswered messages; and three others posted information of interest to the group and remained those topics' only participant. One additional participant, a non-core member of the list who was obviously not a participant in any of their working groups, posted advertisements of happenings outside the group or in similar groups in *Second Life*®; this is the only participant deemed by the researcher to be often "ignored." Needless to say, all but the latter were core members of the group during year one.

A random sampling of the content of roughly half of the 63 other participants' one-person-only topics -- in other words, a view of those who had at least one thread unanswered during the first year -- appears to follow the same general trend. Specifically, 29 of those participants were found to have offered five or fewer messages each and received a response less than half of the time. While this may appear to indicate that their questions went unanswered and possibly contributing to their desertion the group, this cannot be assumed. At least 21 of those 29 non-core participants with at least one unanswered thread actually engaged with others in a discussion topic other than their own, and many joined in discussion topics more than a dozen other times. Further investigation of the "lurkers" or "deserters" via interview may help to determine the exact reasons participation by these members did not continue beyond year one.

Similarly, participants will use linguistic structures which imply tentativeness or reluctance to act without approval of the group. "I'm considering X" or "I'd love to set up X" are examples of attempts to indirectly gain acceptance of the new idea being offered, or to blunt the impact of sharing a prior decision on action, and one which the poster already believes is a good one. Quickly, the researcher's label of "inform of own ideas" as a node appeared frequently or concurrently with "indirect request for agreement." Often, without subsequent discussion or agreement, a participant reports on following through with their original idea for the group, and this is often not challenged. While this general method revealed the most popular methods for introducing and garnering support for a new idea among the *Second Life*® librarians, further research will need to be performed in the future to accurately understand the nuances of these transactions and how they may have helped or harmed the development of specific aspects of the project.

CONCLUSION AND IMPLICATIONS

Conclusions drawn from the results of this descriptive study of the participants in the Alliance *Second Life®* library online discussion group include:

- Online interactions were sustained over time by a core group of participants
- New participants were welcomed, and their contributions were valued
- Topics were not merely announcements, but also reflections and large-group discussions
- A diversity of professional roles was apparent in major discussions
- Librarians, technologists, information consultants and others reported respect for each others' skills, perspectives and contributions
- Views of libraries and virtual worlds were rarely black-and-white but open to discussion at any time
- Significant exchanges about services, not simply technology, focused their work
- Collaboration in the discussion group transcended time zones, geography, and levels of institutional support
- Online conversation served as an effective professional development tool
- Participants self organized into working groups or subgroups
- Many-to-many interactions yielded eventually to shared leadership

Since the librarians of *Second Life®* are a self-selected group, it would be difficult to generalize the points in this discussion to all librarians who use or are interested in *Second Life®* Specifically, since the online discourse was begun and sustained by a relatively small number of members who joined the discussion group of their own volition and then further actively posted of their own volition, the members and their conversations naturally may not be representative of interested or practicing *Second Life®* librarians or the profession as a whole. However, groups such as this not only represent change, they may also cause change, often leading the profession to explore new avenues for library service.

"The library has been a place that facilitates conversations, though often implicitly. Facilitation not only enriches conversations with diverse and deep information, it also serves as a memory keeper, documenting agreements and outcomes to facilitate future conversations" (Lankes, Silverstein, Nicholson & Marshall, 2007, p. 3). That the librarians themselves have enriched their own conversations with diversity, kept an archived record of these discussions and perhaps intended to utilize them at some future point in development is certain from this case. In addition, librarianship is a helping profession, so it is not unusual for the librarians of *Second Life®* to sustain a generally helpful position towards their colleagues in this effort, and towards the *Second Life®* users they aim to help.

At this time, it is unknown if this open, collaborative, energetic spirit is just a social phase that any new emigrant group experiences (and will eventually fade and develop into a different group spirit), or if there is something about the underlying social support structure of Second Life that will make it enduringly conducive to collaborative efforts. Either way, in the real world librarians are famous for their collaborative efforts. In Second Life, they have taken collaboration to a new level. (Peters, 2007, p. 16)

Organization of a massive effort such as the initiative presented in this case necessitates that some participants step up to take leadership roles along the way. As subgroups developed among the hundreds of participants in year one, some were able to manage and lead smaller teams in order to perform certain tasks or services which contributed to the whole group. Leadership of an online virtual initiative is a professional development opportunity that is not lost on the participants. Shared leadership, and the ability to influence the direction of the work of libraries in *Second Life®*, was certainly an outcome of this initiative and perhaps an unintended benefit to the participants who volunteered.

"As of 2007, we were at a stage with virtual worlds similar to where we were in 1995 with the graphical Web. Libraries were there to help their communities and patrons get online with the Web, teach them how to find and evaluate information, and provide access to those who could not access the Web for lack of a computer or ISP. Libraries need to be early adopters of technology" (Trueman, Peters, & Bell, 2007, p. 164), explain a team of Second Life library participants. Similarly,

It is essential that libraries look ahead and prepare for the future, since the Gartner Report (2007) suggests that by 2010, 80% of those online will have an avatar. Many believe that virtual worlds are the next step in the development of the Internet and it is essential that libraries be prepared for that possibility. This includes the provision of services in these new 3D virtual environments. (Buckland & Godfrey, 2008, p. 9)

Indeed, much of the librarians' literature is supporting this type of exploration and conversation.

Talbot (2008) concurs, explaining that *Second Life®* "is only one booming virtual world among many, including Entropia Universe and There.com; massively multiplayer online role-playing games like World of Warcraft; and more controlled and narrowly focused sites like the child-oriented Webkinz and Club Penguin, which is owned by Disney" (p. 60). The *Second Life®* librarians' estimation of their progress, then, is similar to that of IBM virtual business director Sandy Kearney, who explains that many corporations are similarly using virtual worlds for collaborative and training purposes and that 'if you look at all the platforms coming, it feels like 1994, when all of a sudden everybody was building a website" (Talbot, p.60).

The librarians themselves agree. In their own publications about the project, they continue to consider the big questions of librarianship in new virtual environments… They muse about the future of the project, in ponderings such as,

Books or no books? That is the question. In a twenty-first century virtual library, do we want books? What format do books and reading take in Second Life? Do people want to read while in Second Life or should the library function more as a gathering place to promote reading and use of real life libraries?" (Bell, Peters, & Pope, 2008, p. 6)

Similarly, they consider their own role in building the future, in comments such as,

Many naysayers wonder why librarians should explore technologies and applications that affect only about five percent of the general population. As can be seen from numerous examples – consider the migration of audiobooks from cassette, to CD, to downloadable audio – all technology applications begin with a small group of early adopters, with costs of entry that initially can be quite high. At the rate things are changing and growing, it will not be long before virtual worlds impact a significant percentage of people worldwide. (Trueman, Peters, & Bell, 2007, p. 164)

Nevertheless, at every turn, the librarians involved in the project seem to have been both a reflective and an analytical group.

SUMMARY

As librarians are increasingly designated as important partners in the learning process, their early skill with virtual worlds will benefit their organizations as new technologies are implemented to increase student learning. Savvy librarians can help to ease the transition for faculty as well as students, who may need coaching on how to utilize advanced technologies for learning in addition to entertainment. Much in the same way that librarians subsumed technologies in their own field -- such as with the introduction of personal and organizational web page design, which in technological terms may seem like ages ago -- these information professionals may certainly be in the process of ushering in a new era in which learning occurs through real-time embodied virtual interaction.

One of the significant features of the case of the *Second Life®* librarians is that most members of the group were not co-located geographically. In fact, most of the librarians contributing to this online virtual world project, and discussing it in the electronic discussion group, live in various cities across the U. S. and abroad. In their "Report on the First Year of Operation of the Alliance Second Life Library 2.0 Project, Also Known as the Alliance Information Archipelago (AIA)," the leaders state that "AIA has been a largely volunteer effort to date involving a wide variety of librarians and information technology professionals from different organizations and organizational cultures situated around the globe," (Peters, 2007, p. 38). The conversations about this world, which occurred in the project's online discussion groups, helped to garner volunteers from varied organizations and countries with similar interests in exploration. "When you build cooperation into the infrastructure . . . you arrange the coordination within the group and you get the same outcome without the institutional difficulties" (Shirky, 2005). Subsequently, good ideas often surfaced from new participants as well as veteran contributors.

Most librarians and library staff are, at any given time, members of multiple local, state, and national committees and working groups. In libraries, we love committees, and everything from holiday parties to presidential initiatives has its very own group of people slaving away to make it great. Efficiently tracking the work of each of the teams of which a person is a member can require a large amount of that person's time. When a work group uses technology to track time lines, documents, discussions, and work products, however, the technology does the tracking. Team members can check in and contribute as needed. No more lost e-mails. No more searching for the contact information for a committee member. The support provided by the technology reduces the frustration felt by all. (Boule, 2008, p. 7)

Similarly, "In the 3D virtual world, the reference desk is not associated with any particular library and the reference staff serves the reference desk on a voluntary basis" (Luo, 2008, p. 297). This previous research finding is also an accurate description of the current case. "Second Life reference librarians are geographically dispersed, and volunteering at the reference desk not only provides them an opportunity to extend the professional information assistance to the virtual world," the researcher explains, "but also establishes a platform for them to mingle and network with each other . . . and functions as a social place for both librarians and users, and hence creates a sense of community in the reference area" (Luo, p. 297). The participants in this study reported experiencing this type of networking and camaraderie on the online discussion list as well.

The results of this study can be used to promote understanding of the initiatives of the librarians of Second Life, as well as to provide advice and strategy to other professionals contemplating large-scale collaborative and virtual world projects. "The connections and tensions that develop among avatars speak volumes about the behavior of people and organizations in real life, which is intriguing" to social scientists (Foster, 2005, p. A35) and which will benefit the development of the profession of librarianship.

The participants in the Alliance *Second Life*® online discussion group both worked together and divided their labor, shared information and visions yet argued dissenting sides of many issues, then joined and lost members in a dynamic, large-scale conversation about the possibilities of library services in virtual worlds. Participants came and left; ideas both flourished and flopped; and the communications of the larger, multi-national distributed group continue -- even now, years later -- as the librarians and their tech-savvy peers carry on the task of exploring the affordances of persistent online environments.

Regardless of the particular medium, software, or circumstances, a new paradigm in librarianship is upon us -- one in which the librarian comes to the users, wherever they may be. As information professionals of all types work to identify their technological roles during this Information Age, adjustments to the public's traditional understanding of libraries are taking shape. No longer are librarians solely the gatekeepers of print volumes, the staff members who "shhhh" patrons in hallowed halls, or the quiet and introverted intellectuals who toil in isolation.

As the profession of librarianship evolves into a more public participatory and collaborative profession, we are able to truly view the many talents of library workers who are able to meet users' information needs in new online environments in addition to the expected and traditional physical environments. The participants in this *Second Life*® initiative have worked to create a bridge between these two worlds through their pioneering spirit and shared efforts; their model of dialogue and inclusiveness has informed the profession and firmly established librarianship as a viable and technological career for the 21st Century.

REFERENCES

Abram, S. (2007). At Second Life, info pros will find much to see, do, learn, play with, try out. *Information Outlook, 11*(4), 34–36.

Alliance Library System. (2008). Retrieved March 11, 2008 from http://www. alliancelibrarysystem. com/about/mission.cfm

Alliance Second Life Google Group Members. (2008). Retrieved January 28, 2008, from http://groups. google.com/group/alliancesecondlife/members

Bartle, R. A. (2004). *Designing virtual worlds.* New York: New Riders.

Bell, L., Lindbloom, M.-C., Peters, T., & Pope, K. (2008). Virtual libraries and education in virtual worlds: Twenty-first century library services. *Policy Futures in Education, 6*(1), 49–58. doi:10.2304/ pfie.2008.6.1.49

Bell, L., Peters, T., & Pope, K. (2008). *Enjoying your first life? Why not add a second? Developing library services in Second Life.* Retrieved August 25, 2008, from http://seriousgamessource.com/features/ feature_063006_second_life_library.php

Boule, M. (2008). Changing the way we work. *Library Technology Reports, 44*(1), 6–9.

Buckland, A., & Godfrey, K. (2008, August). Gimmick or groundbreaking? Canadian academic libraries using chat reference in multi-user virtual environments. *Proceedings of the World Library and Information Congress, 74th IFLA General Council and Meeting*. Retrieved October 31, 2008, from http://www. ifla.org/IV/ ifla74/papers/158-Buckland_Godfrey-en.pdf

Castronova, E. (2005). *Synthetic worlds: The business and culture of online games*. Chicago: University of Chicago Press.

Cheng, L., Farnham, S., & Stone, L. (2002). Lessons learned: Building and deploying shared virtual environments. In R. Schroeder (Ed.), *The social life of avatars: Presence and interaction in shared virtual environments* (pp. 90–111). New York: Springer-Verlag. doi:10.1007/978-1-4471-0277-9_6

Creswell, J. W. (2007). *Qualitative inquiry and research design: Choosing among five approaches* (2nd ed.). Thousand Oaks, CA: Sage.

Foster, A. L. (2005). The avatars of research. *The Chronicle of Higher Education, 52*(6), A35.

Grassian, E., & Trueman, R. B. (2006). Stumbling, bumbling, teleporting and flying . . . Librarian avatars in Second Life. *RSR. Reference Services Review, 35*(1), 84–89. doi:10.1108/00907320710729373

Jenkins, H. (2006). *Convergence culture: Where old and new media collide*. New York: New York University Press.

Lankes, R. D., Silverstein, J., & Nicholson, S. (2007). Participatory networks: The library as conversation. *Information Technology & Libraries, 26*(4), 17–33.

Lankes, R. D., Silverstein, J., Nicholson, S., & Marshall, T. (2007). Participatory networks: The library as conversation. Proceedings of the Sixth International Conference on Conceptions of Library and Information Science. *Information Research, 12*(4). Retrieved October 28, 2008, from http://informationr. net/ir/12-4/colis/colis05.html

Linden Lab. (2008). *About us*. Retrieved January 2, 2008, from http://lindenlab.com/about

Luo, L. (2008). Reference service in Second Life: An overview. *RSR. Reference Services Review, 36*(3), 289–300. doi:10.1108/00907320810895378

Nonnecke, B., Preece, J., & Andrews, D. (2004). What lurkers and posters think of each other. *Proceedings of the 37th Annual Hawaii International Conference on System Sciences* (HICSS'04). Retrieved September 30, 2008, from http://www2.computer.org/portal/web/ csdl/abs/proceedings/hicss/2004/20 56/07/205670195aabs.htm

Online Computer Library Center, Inc. (OCLC). (2005). *Perceptions of libraries and information resources*. Dublin, OH: OCLC Online Computer Library Center, Inc. Retrieved March 27, 2008 from http://www. oclc.org/reports/pdfs/ Percept_all.pdf

Peters, T. (2007). *A report on the first year of operation of the Alliance Second Life Library 2.0 Project also known as the Alliance Information Archipelago*. Unpublished report. TAP Information Services. Retrieved January 2, 2008, from http://www.alliancelibrarysystem.com/pdf/07sllreport.pdf

Second Life Librarians: Community Search. (2008). Retrieved January 2, 2008, from http://secondlife.com/community/search.php?search_terms=second+life+librarians&search_type=all&commit=Search&all_mature=n&events_mature=n&events_date_from=&events_date_to=&parcels_mature=n&parcels_max_price=&classifieds_mature=n&groups_mature=n

Shirky, C. (2005, July). *Institutions vs. collaboration.* [Video file]. Retrieved October 31, 2008, from http://www.ted.com/index.php/talks/clay_shirky_on_institutions_ versus_collaboration.html

Stake, R. E. (1995). *The art of case study research.* Thousand Oaks, CA: Sage.

Talbot, D. (2008). The fleecing of the avatars. *Technology Review, 111*(1), 58–62.

Thomas, S. (1994). Artifactual study in the analysis of culture: A defense of content analysis in a post-modern age. *Communication Research, 21*(6), 683–697. doi:10.1177/009365094021006002

Trueman, R. B., Peters, T., & Bell, L. (2007). Get a Second Life! Libraries in virtual worlds. In R. S. Gordon (Ed.), *Information tomorrow: Reflections on technology and the future of public and academic libraries* (pp. 159–171). Medford, NJ: Information Today.

Chapter 8
Using Virtual Environments to Transform Collective Intelligence

Lesley S. J. Farmer
California State University Long Beach, USA

ABSTRACT

The wisdom society is the latest iteration of the idea of collective intelligence, which has accelerated due to social media and other online collaborative tools. This chapter offers a background on information, collective intelligence and its elements, virtual environments, and theories that relate to collective intelligence. Benefits and issues related to collective intelligence are detailed, and conditions for optimum collective intelligence, including its transformation through virtual environments, are explained. Individual and group dynamics, and group models are also discussed in terms of their impact on collective intelligence in virtual environments.

INTRODUCTION

The adage "Two heads are better than one" was never more true than now. The world is changing faster than ever because of social and economic factors, which have been significantly impacted by technology. Today's wisdom society depends on intellectual capital, that is, collective knowledge and informational assets. Increasingly, the global scene reflects a more interactive mode relative to information, particularly because of social media.

As heterogeneous groups bring different expertise and perspectives, their gathered and organized knowledge can lead to more informed decisions and resultant actions. This collective intelligence has been transformed with the advent of easily accessible interactive technologies. This chapter explains collective intelligence, the conditions for its optimum use, and its transformation in virtual environments.

DOI: 10.4018/978-1-4666-9899-4.ch008

BACKGROUND

Information and Its Transformation

The 21st century has marked the democratization of information. Particularly with the advent of social media and low-cost Internet-connected equipment such as mobile devices, a substantial percentage of the population can not only access digital information, but can also comment on, and create, information. Such ease of content generation can also lead to a loss of quality control; information is more readily available but might not be accurate, legitimate, or objective. Individuals need to draw upon past knowledge and experience to determine the validity, relevance and significance of information accessed.

The nature of information itself has been affected by digital technology. Besides the obvious combination of text, image, and sound, technology facilitates the repurposing and transformation of information to address different objectives or different audiences. Indeed, content has been decoupled from its "container" such that concepts may be represented as a podcast, book, or email, each format of which may impact how the audience understands the content therein.

Moreover, applications such as Google docs and wikis enable participants to literally change documents on the fly, thereby putting at risk the concept of a permanent recorded document (Iacono, 2010). That dynamic nature of information can also endanger common understanding as individuals may be drawing upon different versions of a document, each of which differ in the content and its interpretation.

Defining and Contextualizing Collective Intelligence

Collective intelligence may be defined as the capacity of a group to think, learn, and create collectively. The adage of "the whole is greater than its parts" intuits the power of collective intelligence. Surowiecki (2004) asserted that collective intelligence combines cognition, cooperation, and coordination. Tapscott and Williams (2006) identified four underlying principles: openness, lateral collaboration, sharing, and global action. Malone, Laubacher and Dellarocas (2010) identified four collective intelligence "genes": what (the goal), who (the participants), how (the structure and processes), and why (incentives).

Educator John Dewey variously discussed the importance of social and collective intelligence as means of the communities having the opportunity to draw upon experiences and individual minds to achieve economic and cultural advancement together, transcending the limitations of any one person (Dewey, 1937). "While what we call intelligence be distributed in unequal amounts, it is the democratic faith that it is sufficiently general so that each individual has something to contribute, whose value can be assessed only as it enters into the final pooled intelligence constituted by the contributions of all" (p. 276).

The underlying concept of collective intelligence builds on the idea of social learning. Vygotsky and Luria (1994) asserted that learning exists first between people and then is internalized. The most common way to learn socially is through collaboration: typically, small groups working together towards a common goal or solution. Other features of collaboration include group and individual accountability, interdependence, distributed leadership, and group autonomy. Collective intelligence is distinguished from collaboration in that a specific goal is identified, processes of interaction are aligned with that goal, and decisions are made as a unified group.

Collective intelligence is witnessed in many sectors of society: politics, business, science, health, and education. Moreover, several forms of collective intelligence exist (Atlee, 2008). Wikipedia is probably the best known example of communications-based informational collective intelligence through gathering, organizing and monitoring expert knowledge from around the world. Genome projects exemplify the impact of collective intelligence as top scientists each contribute their expertise to sequence chromosomes. The SETI Institute searches for extraterrestrial intelligence, leveraging the collective efforts of private members throughout the world as citizen scientists; in this case, the emphasis is on crowdsourced statistical input. The open-source movement in computer programming, exemplified by Linux, makes the assumption that when source code is made available for peers to use and modify, improvements will occur more quickly and efficiently. The Delphi method of structuring expert consensus is used in prediction markets, while an alternative marketing strategy makes use of fans and trend setters in newer iterations of collective intelligence.

Virtual Worlds and Collective Intelligence

While a case may be made that collective intelligence has existed for centuries in the form of projects and repositories in knowledge such as libraries, collective intelligence has been transformed, similarly to information, by technology, as noted in the above examples. Before the advent of digital technology, collective intelligence was limited by the number of participants and by space. As the number of people grows, the complexity of group dynamics grows, often splintering into factions. When distances become large, regular interaction becomes problematic. However, digital technology has lowered the barriers of time and space. Advances such as cheaper hardware and Internet connectivity, open source resources and freeware, and web-based platform interoperability have greatly expanded access, and sped up processing. Social media, in particular, facilitates real-time effective generation of ideas and instant feedback that can be looped back into the discussion so that much larger groups can participate. Furthermore, automated agents can classify and filter participants' input, thus facilitating expert validation and organizing of results to offer new collective intelligence.

Rheingold (2003) pointed out, "Connected and communicating in the right ways, populations of humans can exhibit a kind of collective intelligence made possible by the Internet" (p. 179). Social theorist Pierre Levy (1997) took collective intelligence philosophy into the realm of cyberspace and virtual worlds. He envisioned knowledge as a dynamic and interactive multidimensional representational space (p. ix) in which "we think" (cogitamus) would replace "I think" (Descartes' cognitos). He had the premonition, now grounded in social media and the Creative Commons practices, that "the processing of information can be universally distributed and coordinated, no longer the privilege of separate social organisms but naturally integrated into all human activities, our common property" (p. xxvii). These perspectives transform collective intelligence from group-situated entity to an ever-evolving and enhanced universal flow. The result resembles more of an integrated global brain than a compendium of ideas.

Technically, virtual worlds consist of interactive computer-generated image displays that give the illusion of another location, as exemplified by Second Life. While such virtual spaces serve as a parallel university to face-to-face encounters, even the use of social media and cloud technologies offer aspects of shared digital environments in which to interact and generate collective intelligence, be it in the representation, conveyance processing, or management of information. Information can be represented textually, numerically, visually, graphically (such as mind maps and GPS systems), and aurally (such as interviews and storytelling). Technology can then organize, store and retrieve resources. Contributors can input, archive and retrieve data and documents (e.g., images, videos, research, assessments) on the Internet in social networks, collaborative applications such as Google Docs, databases, and remote servers ("the cloud"). Technological tools can organize and link documents in meaningful ways as defined by the participant group. Webinars expand opportunities to develop and share documents in real time and asynchronously.

Transformative Aspects of Collective Intelligence

Collective intelligence has greatest impact with solving problems and making complex decisions; these situations are change-making. Major change can be transformative, transcending factual knowledge gains to encounter and deal with whole new ways of thinking. A leader in transformative learning theory, Mezirow (1991) focused on strategies to help adults deepen their critical thinking questioning assumptions and re-evaluating long held premises, such as guided inquiry and the posing of disorienting dilemmas that help people become more accepting of new ideas. He posited three central factors in transformative learning, which align with collective intelligence: centrality of experience, critical thinking, and rational discourse.

Virtual worlds impact and facilitate transformative collective intelligence, not just because of technical advances but more fundamentally because of its impact on global and cyberspace. Globalization has resulted in international education and workforces. As people of varying experiences and expectations learn and work together by necessity, they will encounter change more often and more quickly, and will need to exhibit more cognitive – and affective – flexibility. Online networking sites serve as environments for democratic forms of collective intelligence as they support interaction and exchange of ideas. Knowledge management systems enable learning communities to pool their knowledge and generate new ideas for the improvement of the entire enterprise. These elements together enhance collective intelligence, and can lead to transformative changes on a global scale.

Applicable Theories

Transformative collective intelligence in virtual environments reflects a cluster of social, informational, and educational theories. These theories build on self-perceptions and self-worth, which are often developed in light of social interactions. Several of the theories also reflect a belief in the dynamic and situational meanings that collectives create.

Social cognitive theory acknowledges the role that observation of social experiences has on learning. As people are rewarded or punished for their behaviors, the learner models that way of thinking. Bandura (1997) expanded this theory, asserting that "perceived self-efficacy is concerned with judgments of how well one can execute courses of action required to deal with prospective situations" (p. 122). Individuals with high self-efficacy are likely to contribute more to collective intelligence than individuals with low self-efficacy. Similarly high expectations of the outcomes from participating (both in terms of the community and oneself) also impacts sharing; in fact, social good can outweigh personal gain in terms of contributing to collective intelligence.

Social capital theory addresses the collective benefits of "social capital" assets such as family background, norms of reciprocity, community ties, shared vision, social networks, and status in a social space. Individuals with high social capital tend to contribute more to collective intelligence (Bourdieu, 1977; Chiu, Hsu, & Wang, 2006).

Social phenomenology studies how people construct meaning cognitively and perceptually, particularly within the context of a problematic situation. It also explores common understandings. The theory further studies reciprocal interactions between human action and situational structuring. Schutz (1946) identified three types of people based on their informational assumptions and systems of relevance: man on the street with "recipe knowledge," "well-informed" citizen, and expert. Each of these types are likely to play different roles in collective intelligence.

Activity theory posits a relationship between a subject (person) and an object, with mediational means. Tools also mediate between the individual and the larger culture. Vygotsky and Luria (1994) focused on analyzing tasks that required the use of a goal-directed, mediated/cultural process. Engestrom (1987) expanded this model to acknowledge the collective nature of human activity. Good collective intelligence processes follow Vygotsky's zone of proximal development: providing a challenge (not just routine operations) that can feasibly be met; and leveraging community-established conditions such that the participants need to work with the group effectively in order for the outcome to be achieved.

MAIN FOCUS OF THE CHAPTER

Benefits and Issues of Collective Intelligence

Potentially, collective intelligence results in deeper engagement, growing expertise, knowledge retention, improved communication and collaboration, improved social skills, strengthened networking, greater flexibility, greater variety of interpretations, quicker and better decisions, and greater influence. Additionally, collective intelligence is less subject to political forces, especially when input is provided independently (Surowiecki, 2004). In studying crowdsourcing (e.g., eliciting contributions online from a crowd of people) as a way to enhance learning outcomes, Way, Ottenbacher, and Harrington (2011) found that a greater number of ideas were generated, ideas were high quality, and more information was available for decision-making. The greatest benefits included cross-functional team experience enhancement, general peer learning outcomes, a greater understanding of the concept refinement process, and increased learning based on greater diversity of ideas and backgrounds of the networked participants" (p. 261). At the minimum, collective intelligence can foster active involvement and generate much information (Alamantarioutou et al., 2014); at its optimum, collective intelligence can result in transformative change.

Not all group tasks lend themselves well to collective intelligence; The following list is representative of situations that benefit from collective intelligence.

- Decision-making for complex issues,
- Research projects,
- Annotated texts,
- Grants,
- Peer reviewing,
- Lists,
- Databases and repositories,
- Knowledge management,
- Marketing.

Groups do not always arrive at good solutions. One of the first hurdles is group consensus. A common goal and mutual understanding of the issues are key. Different cultures and norms may lead to unexpected behaviors. Individuals may come with different agendas, or may want to sabotage the group's agenda. In addition, groups need to establish norms – or social contract about their participation, processing, terms of use, responsibilities, and sanctions. "Group think," in which narrow social norms discourage independent opinion, can lead to mediocre conformity. The majority might be believed more than an expert few. On the other hand, experts themselves may harbor biases. Leaders and initial opinion makers can unduly influence subsequent opinions (sometimes referred to as a cascade effect), sometimes because they do not want to disperse control. Groups can become polarized, especially when like-mined people drive their opinions to extremes. Groups sometimes reach consensus or adopt a solution prematurely before giving alternative ideas sufficient consideration. Groups can amplify errors, once inaccurate decisions are made; this situation happens especially when there is general ignorance about the issue (Bonabeau, 2009; Buecheler, et al., 2010; Sunstein, 2006).

Fortunately, Sunstein also noted effective ways to deal with this negative aspects. Input can be structured so that valuable information emerges; it is a useful practice for each person to record individual ideas before sharing them in order to ensure that good information is captured. Likewise, groups should permit anonymous polling before deciding. Groups can develop norms that favor critical thinking and reward new competing ideas. Groups should encourage reasons more than conclusions before decisions are made.

Hesse et al. (2011), Gross and Convertino (2012), and Surowiecki (2004) identified other issues that may arise when dealing with collective intelligence tasks.

- Apathy and lack of willingness to contribute,
- Too much, or ineffective, communication, especially if multiple communication channels are used,
- Too much emotionality,
- Boundary problems of negotiating internal and external contributions,
- Concern about privacy and consumer protection,
- Intellectual property ethics,
- Lack of trust across specialization,
- Managing complexity,
- Managing inter-relationships where multiple ongoing collaborations exist,
- Inadequate data monitoring and evaluation.

SOLUTIONS AND RECOMMENDATIONS

Conditions for Transformative Collective Intelligence

Several elements need to be in place for effective, transformative collective intelligence to occur. Albors, Romas, and Hervas (2008) listed six variables that need to be considered when facilitating collective intelligence: information, intellectual property, knowledge access, communication, social interaction, and values. Gregg (2010) proposed seven principles for collective intelligence application: task-specific representations, user-added value, data centrality, facilitated data aggregation, facilitated data access, facilitated access for all devices, mentality of continuous change and improvement. Adding to this list, Boder (2006) mentioned the obvious factor of knowing the clientele or target audience.

Collective intelligence works most effectively when a diverse group of knowledgeable people with different areas of expertise work together to achieve a common goal or solve a problem that affects the group. One strategy posits that each expert draws upon a model to approach the task, with each model remaining independent. The different models provide diversity, and lead to better decisions if those individual models themselves are not modified in the process (Hong & Page, 2008).

In groups represented by a broad spectrum of expertise, initial independent input is key so that individuals are not intimidated by other opinions. Individual input is particularly useful for classifying or clustering information, and for estimation tasks (Hong & Page, 2008). Introne et al. (2013) suggested that ideas may be posed by anyone; thereafter, domain experts can evaluate those ideas in terms of novelty, feasibility and impact, and then give the contributers feedback so that ideas can be improved and resubmitted for further consideration.

Collective intelligence tasks also need to consider spacial factors. For instance, virtual reality environments should provide virtual entryways, teaching e-spaces, social e-spaces, areas for individual documentation, online public spaces for collaborative work, communication "surfaces" such as web-based whiteboards, and groupware and interfaces such as wikis to generate knowledge collectively. Gaming spaces reflect similar situated learning needs; participants think strategically and in social ways about the system as it ties to relationships and action, drawing upon their experiences in similar activity domains (DeVane, Durga, & Squire, 2010). While these examples illustrate systematic space allocation, such pre-determined places are not required for collective intelligence. The term "affinity space" refers to a place where groups of people gather because of a strong common interest of goal. Affinity spaces are often informal and group-defined, which works well for many collective intelligence initiatives because it frees the group from having to depend on a pre-designated space established by an outside or supervisory group. Indeed, group-defined affinity spaces can strengthen cognitive socialization (Chiu, Hsu, & Wang, 2006). Virtual environments significantly expand affinity space possibilities.

What makes collective intelligence transformative? Generally speaking, collective intelligence is better at generating ideas than evaluating them, and even less effective in assessing the underlying process itself. Adamic (2012) identified four factors leading to collective intelligence impact: individual interests and expertise, strong social ties, effective social network structure, and the properties of the information itself. Kim et al., (2001) emphasized the need for group reflection in order to identify deficiencies in knowledge and the task structures, as well as examine peer roles and workloads. Surowiecki (2004) contended that collective intelligence is most effective and transformative when decisions are the product of disagreement and contest, so measuring the amount of differing ideas, their justification, and deep negotiation of meaning and impact can reveal the group's commitment and seriousness in developing the best outcomes. New ways of thinking and action can emerge, leading to transformative change.

Conditions for Collective Intelligence in Virtual Environment

To situate collective intelligence within virtual environments, several conditions have to be met (Kamssu, Siekpe, & Ellzy, 2004): available and affordable IT (information technology) equipment and telecommunications service, convenient access to Internet-connected computers (or equivalent), technology competence of participants, and group culture that supports technology. In focusing on cyberspace contexts, Levy (1997) asserted that collective intelligence needs to involve effective mobilization of skills, real-time coordination of intelligence, and continuous enhancement. Andriessen, Baker and Suthers (2003) identified three conditions for technology to enhance collaboration: individual access and choice of tools, a good match between the tool and the task, and effective structure design and implementation. Specifically in choosing technology tools, Albors, Ramos and Hervas (2008) used the dimensions of social and information connectivity; databases are appropriate in low connectivity situations, online conferencing works when information needs to be highly connected but social needs are low, and knowledge networks are appropriate when both dimensions are important.

It should be noted that even before members engage in virtual environments, they must be able to physically access the relevant technology. For that reason, group leaders should survey participants' access to technologies (hardware, software, connectivity), and frontload the conditions for shared technologies. Additionally, all members need to have technical and intellectual expertise to use the technologies effectively. Skills include basic operations, productivity, Internet navigation and use, and communication. Particularly since virtual environments often lack social cues, learners have to make special effort to create structures that build a community of practice through group discussions and collaborative learning activities. Threaded discussion forums, wikis, Tweets, textual and visual sharing, and online conferencing are a few of the tools available. These community-based structures have to be supported through the online training of these tools.

As a vehicle for documenting information, knowledge management has gained attention in collective intelligence. Knowledge management refers to the process of systematically gathering organizational wisdom, organizing those ideas, archiving them, and providing for their easy retrieval and dissemination. Knowledge management typically uses a decentralized model where information could be stored in several physical and virtual spaces. Centralization occurs in the identification, description and classification of the information; a portal is usually developed as a means to link and relate the various informational sources to facilitate collective intelligence. Additionally, knowledge management provides a mechanism to sustain and transform collective intelligence because the shared documentation can outlast an individual's presence within the organization. (McElroy, 2006).

In addition, computer algorithms are now able to serve as expert agent systems to simulate how groups self-organize and work (Wong & Looi, 2012). This "swarm intelligence" captures the actions of adaptive systems, and analyzes the data in order to guide the groups and help predict and transform outcomes. Swarm intelligence methods are particularly useful to analyze interaction data generated by large-scale online learning communities. Diziol, Walker, Rummel, and Koedinger (2010) suggested a less automized solution for group analysis and support. They proposed to leverage intelligent tutoring technology that can provide adaptive support based on the individual's online actions. This system can also analyze discourse in order to improve collaborative efforts. Huang and Shiu (2012) took a collective intelligence step in using adaptive learning systems in that they employed a collaborative voting approach to estimate learners' abilities for recommending adaptive materials; the results were comparable to expert-design learning, and learners were more satisfied with the results. In both strategies, people can regular their actions, and make adaptions as needed. Software programs such as argumentation systems, can provide simple systematic structures to clarify issues and possible solutions, with arguments for and against each option; these system reduce redundancy and reveal conceptual gaps (Klein, 2012).

While adaptive systems can facilitate collective intelligence in virtual environments, leadership and facilitative roles are imperative for success and transformation (Kim, Hong, Bonk, & Lim, 2011). As they design structures for a collective intelligence task, leaders need to employ a user-centric approach, and tailor the environment to seed collective intelligence and help the group evolve. Leaders should also express expectation of divergent thinking and facilitate user participation. Leaders need to provide opportunities for self and community reflection on collective intelligence efforts. Even more than the level of activity in online contributions, collective reflective process leads to better performance because it enables the whole community to identify best practice and areas for improvement, thus acting as a system for continued, regulated change. Maier and Warren (2000) listed several technology-enhanced instructional design strategies that support collective intelligence:

- Flexible learning through ubiquitous access to resources, including the instructor.
- Resource-centered learning provided within a virtual environment, which enables learners to use tools to manipulate resources according to individual needs and interests.
- Self-paced learning, unhampered by class time or one-shot lectures.
- collaborative work using web-based tools to compare information and to generate knowledge together.

Individuals and Groups

For individuals to work together as a group effectively, all members need to share information, listen, follow directions, keep on track, clarify and check for information, share leadership and decision-making, and show respect (Dishon & O'Leary, 1994). As such, they need to communicate and interact with others, and determine what roles they will play in collective intelligence processes. First they have to decide whether to join in the group. Parvanta, Roth, and Keller (2013) focused on motivations behind collective intelligence: self-fulfillment, fortune, public recognition, and enjoyment. Brabham (2010) asserted that individuals participate in collective intelligence efforts to develop skills, gain fortune, enjoy the community, and relish the collective experience.

As individuals share their thoughts, they are reinforced when others acknowledge and reinforce those ideas. However, when perspectives conflict, then the individual has to weigh the negative feedback with the positives of staying in the group either for its social benefits or the ultimate collective informational outcome. As mentioned above in Bandura's social cognitive theory, self-efficacy impacts participation in group interaction. Interestingly, though, when an individual believes in the group's efficacy, that person is likely to adapt their behavior to the collective knowledge and strengthen his own knowledge base (Crses, Held, & Kimmerle, 2013).

It should be noted that the group's efficacy is a better predictor of the resultant decisions and actions than the efficacy of any one individual (Kellett, Humphrey, & Sleeth, 2009). The following group structures facilitate collective intelligence, and integrate social features: a coordinator or leader, a moderator of input, expert advisory board, broader-based expert council, and participants (Introne et al., 2013). McGrath (1991) noted how groups function over time. All groups go through a beginning stage as they establish their goals and processes, and all implement their plan. Some groups also have to solve technical problems and resolve group conflicts. McGrath asserted that the group functions of production, well-being, and member support drive the group's activities.

Technology impacts group efforts of collective intelligence. People can communicate and interact anytime, anywhere. The current wave of ubiquitous computing and social software tools enable an expanded repertoire of group interaction, distributed collaboration, and communication, and their transformative effects on society, learning, and networking are becoming increasingly visible. The online environment, in particular, can also provide a more level playing field for contributing ideas because it lowers barriers for English language learners who can use translation tools, and provides a safer environment for people who are uncomfortable or culturally discouraged from speaking out (Hau, 2010).

It should be noted collective intelligence in virtual environments is not inherently better than face-to-face collective intelligence, and no single factor about the group predicts success; rather the task itself informs group interaction (Barlow & Dennis, 2014). Nevertheless, relational links are critical for virtual teams, especially in light of reduced social cues within virtual worlds. Beranek and Clairborne (2012) identified five criteria for successful online relationships: cohesiveness, perceptions of the process, satisfaction with outcomes over time, group communication, and trust. The researchers found that when virtual team leaders were trained on relational links, their groups could set rules more efficiently, and then focus on doing the task. The training emphasized the following practices: pro-active communication, having a positive attitude, interacting frequently, responding to prior messages, being empathetic, providing clear goals, sharing socio-emotional information, establishing communication protocols, and practicing netiquette. The goal is for goals to have a shared goal and mutual knowledge building within a natural work process.

Group Models

- **Crowdsourcing:** Businesses and communications enterprises increasingly use crowdsourcing to gather information to supplement or complement internal data-gathering; the enterprise then reviews, sorts, and organizes the crowdsourced content. Parvanta, Roth, and Keller (2013) defined crowdsourcing as a "problem-solving approach that tapes the knowledge, energy, and creativity of a global, online community" (p. 163). Way, Ottenbacher, and Harrington (2011) found that crowdsourcing resulted in a greater number of ideas generated, more high quality ideas, and more information available for decision-making. The greatest benefits included cross-functional team experience enhancement, general peer learning outcomes, a greater understanding of the concept refinement process, and increased learning based on greater diversity of ideas and backgrounds of the networked participants" (p. 261). For the crowd, benefits include: opportunities to be commercially published, a venue for people to see and comment on content, and incentives for the best contributors. In collective intelligence, crowdsourcing can be used to get stakeholder opinion in much the same way that focus groups operate. These crowds can be incorporated throughout the collective intelligence process: from assessing the crowd's perceived needs to generating ideas to testing tentative collective intelligence products. It should be noted that crowdsourcing communication largely occurs between the contributor and the enterprise; however, crowds can build community, such as fandoms, that foster peer relationships and serve as an independent group for collective intelligence.
- **The Learning Organization**: With the advent of the information society has come the concept of the learning society and more specifically the learning organization; groups may collect informally for a single effort or longer-term learning goal. The explicit focus on a learning organization transcends informal and arbitrary practices to provide a predictable and sustainable system of knowledge sharing that undergirds collective intelligence. Senge (1990) defined learning organizations as:

... organizations where people continually expand their capacity to create the results they truly desire, where new and expansive patterns of thinking are nurtured, where collective aspiration is set free, and where people are continually learning to see the whole together (p. 3).

This approach to collective intelligence is particularly important in an information age where both internal and external change is constant. Learning communities enjoy several benefits (Buchanan, 2008).

- New members are trained more efficiently because they can get help from mentors and other experts.
- Institutional knowledge is shared so that operations can function successfully if members are absent or leave.
- Members can keep current in their fields by sharing their learning experiences, such as conferences and professional reading.
- Individual learning and group learning inform each other.
- Camaraderie and interdependence are facilitated through joint, meaningful actions.
- Members can analyze and reflect on their practice with the aim of improving individual and organizational efforts.

On the other hand, learning communities may face obstacles as they aim for collective intelligence. Groups may favor harmony over achievement, resulting in little learning or organizational improvement. Groups may push for action, forgetting about the need for reflection. Strong individuals may overpower the group, minimizing independent thought. Individual factors that contribute to the success of learning communities include learner expertise, learning history, attitude toward the learning activity, social skills, and volition.

A less formal version of a learning community is a community of practice (CoP), which consists of a group of people with common values and goals. Unlike a learning organization, CoPs are generally self-defined and self-established. In most cases a CoP has a social dimension that fosters interdependence, but the chief goal is organizational improvement through individual and group professional development and deployment. These arenas are ripe territory for collective intelligence. In online CoP environments individuals are largely self-motivated, and likely to connect at their convenience rather than at a set time and place. Therefore, online CoPs need to provide professional contact, modeling and coaching for participants, and a repository of objects and artifacts to support collective intelligence (Lave & Wenger, 1991).

CONCLUSION

The advent of digital technology has transformed aspects of collective intelligence because of the need to learn how to use technology tools, the opportunity for expanded access to resources, the expanded opportunities to engage with these resources and with other people, and the means to bring about significant change quickly. The logical extension of such technology-enhanced collective intelligence can lead to Levy's idea of a cosmopedia. In his 1964 seminal work, *Understanding Media,* McLuhan asserted that each medium is an extension of humankind; the medium rebalances the sense, so that it impacts individual perception. In turn, the organization of society changes as people connect through media. Even though his main works predated the Internet or the current trend of globalization, McLuhan envisioned a computer as a research and communication device, and asserted that technology would connect people together into a new form of global village, which would be made possible because technology can collapse space and time. McLuhan asserted that technological communication shapes society. Thus, content, virtual worlds, and human intelligence have a symbiotic relationship that can optimize collective intelligence and transform society.

REFERENCES

Adamic, L. (2012). Information propagation and filtering over social networks. *Collective Intelligence Proceedings*.

Alamantarioutou, K. (2014). Collective intelligence for knowledge building and research in community of practice and virtual learning environments. *International Journal of Health Research and Innovation*, *2*(1), 51–64.

Albors, J., Ramos, J., & Hervas, J. (2008). New learning network paradigms: Communications of objectives, crowdsourcing, wikis and open source. *International Journal of Information Management*, *28*(3), 194–202. doi:10.1016/j.ijinfomgt.2007.09.006

Andriessen, J., Baker, M., & Suthers, D. (2003). Argumentation, computer support, and the educational context of confronting cognitions. In J. Andriessen, M. Baker, & D. Suthers (Eds.), *Arguing to learn: Confronting cognitions in computer-supported collaborative learning environments* (pp. 1–25). Dordrecht, Germany: Kluwer. doi:10.1007/978-94-017-0781-7_1

Bandura, A. (1997). *Self-efficacy*. New York: Freeman.

Barlow, J., & Dennis, A. (2014). Not as smart as we think. *Collective Intelligence*, *1*, 1–5.

Beranek, P., & Clairborne, M. (2012). The impact of training on virtual project teams: A TIP investigation. *International Journal of Information Technology Project Management*, *3*(1), 36–48. doi:10.4018/jitpm.2012010103

Boder, A. (2006). Collective intelligence: A keystone in knowledge management. *Journal of Knowledge Management*, *10*(1), 81–93. doi:10.1108/13673270610650120

Bonabeau, E. (2009). Decisions 2.0: The power of collective intelligence. *Sloan Management Review*, *50*(2), 45–52.

Bourdieu, P. (1977). *Outline of a theory of practice*. Cambridge, UK: Cambridge University Press. doi:10.1017/CBO9780511812507

Brabham, D. (2010). Moving the crowd at threadless. *Information Communication and Society*, *13*(8), 1122–1145. doi:10.1080/13691181003624090

Buchanan, J. (2008). Developing leadership capacity through organizational learning. *Journal Of College Teaching & Learning*, *5*(3), 17–24.

Buecheler, T., Sieg, J., Fuchslin, R., & Pfeifer, R. (2010). Crowdsourcing, open innovation and collective intelligence in the scientific method. *Proceedings of the ALIFE XII Conference*.

Chiu, C., Hsu, M., & Wang, E. (2006). Understanding knowledge sharing in virtual communities: An integration of social capital and social cognitive theories. *Decision Support Systems*, *42*(3), 1872–1888. doi:10.1016/j.dss.2006.04.001

DeVane, B., Durga, S., & Squire, K. (2010). Economists who think like ecologists: Reframing systems thinking in games for learning. *E-Learning and Digital Media*, *7*(1), 3–20. doi:10.2304/elea.2010.7.1.3

Dewey, J. (1937). *Democracy and education: An introduction to the philosophy of education.* New York, NY: Macmillan.

Dishon, D., & O'Leary, P. (1994). *Guidebook of cooperative learning: A techniques for creting more effective schools.* Holmes Beach, FL: Learning Publications.

Diziol, D., Walker, E., Rummel, N., & Koedinger, K. (2010). Using intelligent tutor technology to implement adaptive support for student collaboration. *Educational Psychology Review, 22*(1), 89–102. doi:10.1007/s10648-009-9116-9

Engeström, Y. (1987). *Learning by expanding: An activity-theoretical approach to developmental research.* Helsinki, Finland: Orienta-Konsultit.

Grasso, A., & Convertino, G. (2012). Collective intelligence in organizations: Tools and studies. *Computer Supported Cooperative Work, 21*(4-5), 357–369. doi:10.1007/s10606-012-9165-3

Greenberg, J., & Baron, R. (2002). *Behavior in organizations* (10th ed.). Englewood Cliffs, NJ: Prentice Hall.

Gregg, D. (2010). Designing for collective intelligence. *Communications of the ACM, 53*(4), 134–138. doi:10.1145/1721654.1721691

Hao, C. (2010). A comparative study of collaborative learning in "paper scribbles" and "group scribbles". *Australasian Journal of Educational Technology, 26*(5), 659–674.

Hesse, B., O'Connell, M., Augustson, E., Chou, W., Shaikh, A., & Rutten, L. (2011). Realizing the promise of Web 2.0: Engaging community intelligence. *Journal of Health Communication, 16*(sup1), 10–31. doi:10.1080/10810730.2011.589882 PMID:21843093

Hong, L., & Page, S. (2008). Some microfoundations of collective wisdom. *Collective Wisdom,* 56-71.

Huang, S., & Shiu, S. (2012). A user-centric adaptive learning system for e-learning 2.0. *Journal of Educational Technology & Society, 15*(3), 214–225.

Iacono, A. (2010). OPAC, users, web. Future developments for online library catalogues. *Bollettino AIB, 50*(1/2), 69–88.

Kamssu, A., Siekpe, J., & Ellzy, J. (2004). Shortcomings to globalization: Using Internet technology and electronic commerce in developing countries. *Journal of Developing Areas, 38*(1), 151–169. doi:10.1353/jda.2005.0010

Kellett, J., Humphrey, R., & Sleeth, R. (2009). Career development, collective efficacy, and individual task performance. *Career Development International, 14*(6), 534–546. doi:10.1108/13620430910997286

Kim, P., Hong, J., Bonk, C., & Lim, G. (2011). Effects of group reflection variations in project-based learning integrated in a Web 2.0 learning space. *Interactive Learning Environments, 19*(4), 333–349. doi:10.1080/10494820903210782

Klein, M. (2012). Enabling large-scale deliberation using attention-mediation metrics. *Computer Supported Cooperative Work, 21*(4-5), 449–473. doi:10.1007/s10606-012-9156-4

Lave, J., & Wenger, E. (1991). *Situated learning*. Cambridge, UK: Cambridge University Press. doi:10.1017/CBO9780511815355

Levy, P. (1997). *Collective intelligence: Mankind's emerging world in cyberspace*. New York: Plenum Trade.

Maier, P., & Warren, A. (2000). *Integrating technology in learning and teaching* (2nd ed.). New York, NY: Routledge.

Malone, T. W., Laubacher, R., & Dellarocas, C. (2010). The collective intelligence genome. *Sloan Management Review, 51*(3), 21–31.

McElroy, M. (2006). *The new knowledge management: Complexity, learning and sustainable innovation*. Boston, MA: Elsevier Science.

McGrath, J. (1991). Time, interaction, and performance (TIP): A theory of groups. *Small Group Research, 22*(2), 147–174. doi:10.1177/1046496491222001

McLuhan, M. (1964). *Understanding media: The extensions of man*. New York: McGraw Hill.

Mezirow, J. (1991). *Transformative dimensions of adult learning*. San Francisco, CA: Jossey-Bass.

Parvanta, C., Roth, Y., & Keller, H. (2013). Crowdsourcing 101: A few basics to make you the leader of the pack. *Health Promotion Practice, 14*(2), 163–167. doi:10.1177/1524839912470654 PMID:23299912

Schutz, A. (1946). The well informed citizen: An essay on the social distribution of knowledge. *Social Research, 1*(3), 463–478. PMID:20285192

Senge, P. (1990). *The fifth discipline: The art and practice of the learning organization*. New York, NY: Doubleday.

Sunstein, C. (2006). *Infotopia: How many minds produce knowledge*. London: Oxford University Press.

Surowiecki, J. (2004). *The wisdom of crowds*. New York, NY: Doubleday.

Tapscott, D., & Williams, A. (2006). *Wikinomics: How mass collaboration changes everying*. New York: Portfolio.

Vygotsky, L., & Luria, A. (1994). Tool and symbol in child development. In R. van der Veer & J. Valsiner (Eds.), *The Vygotsky reader* (pp. 99–174). Oxford, UK: Oxford University Press.

Way, K., Ottenbacher, M., & Harrington, R. (2011). Is crowdsourcing useful for enhancing innovation and learning outcomes in culinary and hospitality education? *Journal of Culinary Science & Technology, 9*(4), 261–281. doi:10.1080/15428052.2011.627259

Wong, L., & Looi, C. (2012). Swarm intelligence: New techniques for adaptive systems to provide learning support. *Interactive Learning Environments, 20*(1), 19–40. doi:10.1080/10494821003714681

KEY TERMS AND DEFINITIONS

Affinity Space: A place where groups of people gather because of a strong common interest or goal.

Collaborative Intelligence: The capacity of a group to think, learn, and create collectively.

Collaborative Learning: Learning that involves the process of sharing resources and responsibilities to create shared meaning.

Community of Practice: A group of individuals participating in communal activity, with a shared identity and goal, who collectively contribute to the practices of their communities.

Crowdsourcing: A process for getting contributions (work or material), usually online, from a crowd of people, typically from outside the organization or company.

Intellectual Capital: Collective knowledge and informational assets.

Knowledge Management: The process of systematically gathering organizational wisdom, organizing those ideas, archiving them, and providing for their easy retrieval and dissemination.

Learning Community: A place where student learners are made to feel that their prior knowledge, the knowledge that they are acquiring, and the skills that they are learning to acquire future knowledge are all tied together.

Situated Learning: Learning that takes place in the same context in which it is applied, or at least simulates that setting.

Social Capital: Connections that exist between people, and their shared values and norms of behavior that facilities action.

Social Phenomenology: The study of how people construct meaning cognitively and perceptually, particularly within the context of a problematic situation.

Social Media: Web 2.0; interactive Internet technology and applications including blogs, wikis, social bookmarking, and social networks.

Swarm Intelligence: The collective behaviour of decentralized, self-organized systems.

Virtual Environments: Most narrowly, interactive computer-generated image displays that give the illusion of another location; more generally, online environments such as online conferencing, text-based virtual realities, multi-user chat systems, and virtual worlds.

Chapter 9

Virtual Ties, Perceptible Reciprocity, and Real–Life Gratifications in Online Community Networks:
A Study of QQ User Groups in China

Zixue Tai
University of Kentucky, USA

Xiaolong Liu
Guangdong Pharmaceutical University, China

ABSTRACT

QQ has been a leading force of China's social media revolution both in terms of its user reach and its socio-cultural impact. This chapter offers an analysis of QQ groups based on semi-structured in-depth interviews of 33 users with a particular emphasis on participants' rationales, motivations, and communicative behaviors as displayed in different types of groups. This is accomplished through interrogating a multiple set of individual, collective, social, and contextual factors that shape group dynamics and individual participation. It also discusses the implications of the findings for the scholarship on online communities in general, and the understanding of Chinese online groups in particular.

INTRODUCTION

While the Internet has been a leading force of sociocultural transformation in the past two decades in China, a variety of blossoming platforms of social media have been pushing grassroots-led user-generated communication to ever-new territories. Although Social Networking Service (SNS) sites modeled after Facebook, Twitter and YouTube in China are as earth-shattering as found anywhere in the world (albeit not without significant twists and turns in their processes of adapting to the Chinese soil), one particularly notable hotspot that has defined China's new media culture is the popularization of QQ, an Instant

DOI: 10.4018/978-1-4666-9899-4.ch009

Messaging (IM) service developed by Tencent. By far the leading IM service provider in China, QQ allows users to chat, email, file-share and engage in activities resembling conventional online forums or bulletin-board systems (BBS) and more via not only the conventional Internet but mobile phones, PDAs, and other emerging platforms of communication as well.

Contextualized in current strands of theoretical deliberations on virtual communities, this chapter scrutinizes one particularly popular aspect of QQ applications known as QQ Groups. The QQ Groups service allows users to create tiered levels of user groups catering to specific interests, purposes or needs of communication, and the size of QQ groups varies from 200 to 2,000. QQ groups can engage in members-only communicative tasks, and have effectively created an exclusive virtual communal space. Lately, more and more groups in China have utilized this QQ capability to organize contentious action or other public events.

The chapter starts with a brief overview of the historical development of QQ and its role in China's Internet industry, and then goes on to examine the dynamics of QQ user groups against the overall backdrop of Chinese cyber culture. This is followed by an analysis of our own qualitative data based on semi-structured in-depth interviews of QQ group members on the rationales, motivations, and communicative behaviors as displayed in different types of groups. Special emphasis is placed on the individual, collective, social, and contextual factors that shape group dynamics. It ends with a discussion on the implications of our findings for the research of online communities in general, and the understanding of Chinese online groups in particular.

REVIEW OF THE LITERATURE: SOCIAL SUPPORT AND COLLABORATIVE ACTION THROUGH VIRTUAL COMMUNITIES

The human desire for social bonds and interpersonal relationships has been of perennial interest to various disciplines in the social science tradition. In their seminal article aptly titled "The Need to Belong," Baumeister and Leary (1995) suggest that "human beings have a pervasive drive to form and maintain at least a minimum quantity of lasting, positive, and significant interpersonal relationships" (p. 497). As Baumeister and Leary point out, this basic drive can be met by two criteria: first, we need "frequent personal contacts or interactions" with others; second, the relationship or personal bond must be marked by "stability, affective concern, and continuation into the foreseeable future" (p. 500).

Besides primordial networks (e.g., family), the basic need for social connections manifests itself in the human hunger for variegated groups and community-oriented affiliations in social life. It is no surprise that the role of community for fulfilling human values and development has garnered considerable interest in social theories from classic writers such as Marx, Durkheim, Weber, Simmel to present-day intellectual thinkers. Traditionally, community sentiment has been conceptualized in terms of attachment to place (Hummon, 1992). Our sense of community, however, does not need to be locale-bound. Gusfield (1975) noted two prevalent usages of the term "community": one is territorial in nature and is rooted in "location, physical territory, and geographical continuity" (p. xv), and the other is relational in essence, focusing on "the quality or character of human relationships, without reference to location" (p. xvi). People grouped together based on spiritual orientations, professional followings, and personal interests, therefore, can be understood as particular types of relational communities. Indeed, as Durkheim (1984) and Parsons (1951) observed, more communities develop based on professional skills and personal interests than on geographic boundaries in modern societies. As will be highlighted later, this point is of particular relevance in scholarly contemplations on online communities.

McMillan and Chavis (1986) pinpoint four elements in defining the experience of sense of community: "the feeling of belonging or of sharing a sense of personal relatedness" (*membership*); "a sense of mattering, of making a difference to a group and of the group mattering to its members" (*influence*); "the feeling that members' needs will be met by the resources received through their membership in the group" (*integration and fulfillment of needs);* "the commitment and belief that members have shared and will share history, common places, time together, and similar experiences" (*shared emotional connection)* (p. 9). Relatedly, in what has become a well-trodden line of social inquiries, it is widely believed that participation in the community life leads to the accumulation of social capital (Gittell & Vidal, 1998; Putnam, 2001), which is generally defined as "the ability of actors to secure benefits by virtue of membership in social networks or other social structures" (Portes, 1998, p. 6).

From the perspective of communication, the most nutrient fodder for a healthy community life is unfettered and vibrant conversation. In this regard, central to any vital community is an inviting third place, which, as a "public place that hosts the regular, voluntary, informal, and happily anticipated gatherings of individuals beyond the realms of home and work" (Oldenburg, 1999, p.16), provides the locus of routine activities, casual encounters and sustained conversations for its members. Based on the premises of social exchange theory (Cook & Rice, 2003; Cropanzano & Mitchell, 2005), mutually rewarding sociocultural transactions over time will evolve into trusting, loyal and committed communal relations.

The historical rise of the Internet parallels an era in which many have noted a steady decline in public involvement in community life (e.g., Gittell & Vidal, 1998; Norris, 2011; Putnam, 2001). It is only natural, then, that the research community from different disciplines and perspectives jumped to the question of whether intimate, supportive groups are possible online, and whether virtual communities can offer the possibilities of reversing the longtime trend of the gradual loss of community life in the brick-and-mortal world (Ellis, Oldridge & Vasconcelos, 2004; Wellman & Gulia, 1999). Toward that end, Norris (2004) found that online community groups produce the effect of both widening and deepening people's social relationships; moreover, online communities have the potential to crosscut traditional barriers mainly based on territorial, ethnic, and socio-economic terms. Wellman et al. (2001) explored patterns of Internet use and identified multiple effects on social capital: "At a time of declining organizational participation, the Internet provides tools for those already involved to increase their participation. Yet, at a time when networked individualism reduces group social cohesion, extensive involvement with the Internet apparently exposes participants to situations that weaken their sense of community online" (p. 451). In other words, the Internet may intensify involvement in certain community groups but can also turn individuals away from all-encompassing communities. As we argue later, this is where social media groups may differ dramatically from previous online groups thanks to their highly focused and intimate nature.

Sharing is a pivotal hallmark of any type of community. While online communities obviously thrive on information distributing, they go beyond simply exchanging hard information and create a social space that can accomplish more among participants – sharing of knowledge, experience, wisdom, encouraging debates, generating new knowledge, problem solving, and so on (Ellis et al., 2004). A number of factors, such as the motivation to form social bonds and to maintain relationships (Ma & Yuen, 2011), community trust and altruism (desire to help others) (Chen, Fan & Tsai, 2014), moderate individual behaviors in this process. Bateman, Gray and Butler (2011) suggest that three types of community commitment – continuance community commitment (CC) (the belief that participation derives benefits to the individual), affective CC (emotional attachment to the community), and normative CC (sense of obligation to the community) – determine member willingness to engage in particular activities (e.g., reading, posting, replying) in online communities.

The routinization of online networks in everyday life has dramatically redefined the contours of collective action and social movements (McCaughey & Ayers, 2003). As Bennett and Segeberg (2012) point out, in the network era, digital technologies have become indispensable to the organization and staging of collective action, and consequently, we are witnessing a dramatic shift from the conventional logic of collective action rooted in the organization-centered and leader-driven mode of resource mobilization to the emerging model of the *logic of connective action* in which "taking public action or contributing to a common good becomes an act of personal expression and recognition or self-validation achieved by sharing ideas and actions in trusted relationships" (pp. 752-753). This logic of connective action enables fragmented and individualized populations, which are hard to be reached by formal organizations, to mobilize protest networks and coordinate contentious activities via co-production and co-distribution through pervasive social networks. It bears mentioning that dynamics of connective action are especially liberating for individuals in an authoritarian polity like China in which formal organizations and institutional establishments tend to align with state power and government interests, and cannot be expected to serve as reliable mobilizing channels of contentious actions.

Scholarly contemplations on virtual groups have been closely following the footprint of technological breakthroughs. Early discussions have revolved around email and discussion lists, Usenet, BBS, text chat, MUDs, and various forms of Web forums (Kollock & Smith, 1999). Social media networks and groups, however, mark a dramatic departure from prior formations in both structure and content, and open up brand-new possibilities for user participation and collaboration (Kane, Alavi, Labianca & Borgatti, 2014). As a matter of fact, Bennett and Segeberg's (2012) logic of connective action essentially hinges on the enabling dynamics of social media. Similar themes are echoed in Gerbaudo's (2012) "choreography of assembly" in his discussion of social media practices in contemporary movements such as the mass uprisings against Mubarak in Egypt, the Indignados protest in Spain, and the occupy Wall Street movement in the U.S.

SOCIAL MEDIA AND QQ GROUPS IN CHINA

The quick rise of social media in China is as earth-shattering and far-reaching as anywhere else. The first point to underscore about China's social media is its enormous size. According to the recent report by the China Internet Network Information Center (CNNIC) on Internet development in China, as of December 2014, China's Internet users reached 649 million, 557 million of which (86%) surfed the mobile Net via their smart phones (CNNIC, 2015). Three types of applications dominate social media use: instant messaging, social networking sites, and microblogging. By a large margin, leading all online applications are Instant Messaging (IM) and Mobile Instant Messaging services, with the former (QQ, wired & Internet-based) being regularly used by 90.6% and the latter (QQ & WeChat, smart phone-based) 91.2% of Chinese netizens. The next most-adopted social media service is social networking sites (e.g., QQZone, Pengyou, Renren), regularly accessed by 61.7% of the online population. Microblogging service (e.g., Sina Weibo), which used to lead the social media landscape, has shown signs of gradual decline in recent years and now penetrates to 38.4% of Internet users. Consistent with patterns of social media use elsewhere, Chinese individuals build their social media networks by relying heavily on existing relationships and with people they already know, with over 70% of their social media friends originating from real-life connections (CNNIC, 2015).

The second notability about China's social media is its obvious deviation from popular global points of congregation. China is reputed to have installed one of the most sophisticated online surveillance systems in the world as part of the state's multi-layered efforts to keep proscribed content out of Chinese cyber territory (Tai, 2010). As a result, most top social media sites from outside such as Facebook, Twitter, and YouTube are blacklisted and rendered inaccessible in China due to their refusal to cleanse what the Chinese regime considers sensitive information. This national policy has in turn facilitated the birth of Chinese home-grown counerparts (e.g., Renren vs. Facebook, Sina Weibo vs. Twitter, and Youku vs. YouTube) for major global social media applications to cater to the needs of Chinese users while complying with state mandate of content censoring.

Tencent is the undisputed leader in chartering the frontlines of the Chinese social media revolution. Two (i.e., QQ and WeChat) of the Big Three Behemoths of China's social media platforms are owned by Tencent, with the remaining one (Weibo) developed by Sina Corp. Of direct relevance to this research, QQ was debuted in February 1999, initially closely modelled after AOL's ICQ (I Seek You) at the time, under the name OICQ (Open I Seek You). Trademark litigation concerns prompted a subsequent name change to QQ, which has been since then leading China's IM service. QQ offers cross-platform instant messaging service via text, audio, video as well as P2P file-sharing, file transfer, storage and email functionalities. Currently, QQ owns an active user base of 500 million, and averages a daily log-in of over 200 million unique users.[1]

QQ Group implements a many-to-many chat feature to interconnect communities of QQ users via its instant messaging service, and it allows users to create BBS-like forums and file-sharing space accessible only to members. There are four tiers of groups: basic groups (maximum of 200 members) can be created by any QQ user; privileges to create groups capped at 500, 1,000, and 2,000 respectively are offered to members based on a fee structure plus years of QQ use. QQ groups dedicated to all sorts of topics and interests are numbered in the millions.[2] All four tiers of groups have designated account managers, with the exact allowable numbers ranging from five for the first two types to 12 for groups exceeding 500 numbers. Group creators can admit new members or terminate current memberships, and appoint account managers. Among the many features that make QQ groups different from conventional online communities, participation is confined to members, which allows more intimate relationships to develop over time; the networked space provides multiple modes of communicating from real-time chatting to message boards to group albums to archives; discussion threads can be initiated by any member, and the profile of each participant is subject to scrutiny by all others.

RESEARCH QUESTIONS, METHOD, AND PROCEDURE

As a special formation of social media communities from one of the most popular social networking platforms, QQ groups have rarely been studied by the research community. The purpose of this research is to interrogate the dynamics of QQ group use against the backdrop of a variety of motivational factors and behavioral outcomes as a platform of maintaining relations and coordinating collective action. Specifically, with regard to QQ group creators, we wanted to investigate what motivated them to initiate groups and spearhead discussions, and their personal reflections on the experience of nurturing these groups and fostering interactions; as for regular members, we were interested in gaining insight on the level/extent of their participation in group discussions and activities, the rationale, motivational factors, and their subsequent evaluations on benefits and barriers in participating.

Based on our understanding of the dynamics and culture of QQ groups, we decided to focus on three broad categories in our study:

1.   Groups that are tied to professional and geographic affiliations;
2.   Groups that primarily aim to organize contentious actions;
3.   Groups that are aligned along personal hobbies and interests.

Because QQ does not publish a comprehensive list of existing groups, it is hard to get an exact assessment on what types of groups are the most active for the time being. But we believe our long-time involvement in and extensive attention to QQ groups over the years affords us a vantage point in classifying these types of groups among the commonest in the field.

We resorted to a semi-structured in-depth interview approach in collecting data in addressing the aforementioned questions. A two-stage sampling process was adopted in identifying interviewees: stage one was the selection of groups, followed by the sampling of individuals in each group. We recruited five to seven members from each group for the interview, with an overview of the purpose of the study and the types of questions to be asked. Interviewees were assured of their confidentiality, and they were allowed to terminate the interview at any point in the process. This whole recruiting process took place via QQ, among the respective QQ groups, in all of which the junior researcher owns an active membership.

Individuals who agreed to participate were asked to indicate a preferred time slot, and choose either to complete the interview via QQ text or audio chatting. Each participant was asked similar, but not exactly identical, questions, often with follow-up prompts where necessary. The interviews took place in the months of March and April of 2015, and interviewing time differed quite a bit, ranging from about half an hour to well over two hours, with the majority of interviews taking about an hour. Altogether, thirty-four subjects agreed to participate in the interviews, with one withdrawal half-way through, resulting in a total of 33 completed, usable interviews. Thirty-one interviewees opted for text, and two used audio chatting in the process.

GROUP ADMINISTRATION AND DYNAMICS

We observed interesting dynamics in the management and administration of memberships and group activities in the context of their missions and stated goals that warrant detailed discussion here. Norms, expectations, patterns of interactions among group members testify to the identity and cultural formations of each group. As was previously mentioned, our initial group selection extended to three categories of groups, and each category included two groups. In order to alleviate privacy concerns from interviewees, we have anonymized identifying information of each of the groups in the data we report here.

There is a notable variation in how groups are formed and how members are recruited. For profession/geography-bounded groups, we had one group whose members are solely made up of faculty affiliated with ten universities living in the college district in a southern metropolis (coded Group A), the other group (hence Group B) caters to a particular body of visiting scholars from institutions of higher learning across China at a southern U.S. public research university. Group A, with an active list of 1,276 (as of May 2015), was started in March 2013 to rally support and coordinate participation in negotiating with local government for the construction of a new elementary and a new middle school in the district to meet rising demands of a fast-growing population. Intense demand from the local residents forced officials to respond in opening up two schools at the end of 2013, and fulfillment of its initial goal has now shifted this group into focusing on discussions of children-related topics and organization of youth-centered activities. Requests to join this group are only honored through a verification process for those who enjoy faculty status from one of the ten university campuses. For group B (with 347 current members), individuals are asked to clearly mark their employer in China (which must be a university) and reveal their real name in their QQ profiles in order to be granted member status. It functions as a social support platform through which individuals can exchange information, help one another, place items on sale, and plan events.

Break-neck socio-economic transformations for over three decades in China have created differing yet often contradicting stakes among social groups and local entities. As a result, a hotbed of popular contention lately has been environmental protection. We therefore picked two groups that set their main goal on contentious action in direct relation to expressed environmental concerns in their localities. One group (hereby Group C) specifically takes on the goal of protesting government effort to build a refuse incinerator in their vicinity in Guangzhou, with 388 members and the expressed motto "The Responsibility Rests with Everyone in Order to Make Our Habitat Livable." Requests must be made with an acknowledgement which apartment unit and which building they are from in order to gain membership status. The main activities promoted by the group include updating latest developments, sharing knowledge about how incinerating affects air quality, and coordinating protest events and activities. Noticeably, threshold of admission for this group stands the highest among all groups under investigation.

The second group (of 597 members) chosen in this category is dedicated to combating water pollution in a rural district in a central eastern city. Although one of the researchers was successful in being granted admission to the group by using a local residential unit as recommended by a close connection (the required procedure in member recruitment), numerous attempts for interviewing individual members fell short. Interview requests sent to two members were totally ignored, and the third individual indicated that he would not talk one-on-one but could answer questions in the group's public BBS space. Request to one account manager was met with suspicion, and he demanded the researcher to show proof of participation in the recent "sit-ins" and "walk-ins" (a popular type of silent gathering in protest of government actions). Eventually, failure to gain trust of group members aborted our interview efforts, and also led to the discontinuation of the researcher's short membership in the group. This is in sharp contrast to Group C – of which one of the researchers has been a long-time active member – whose participants showed no qualms in talking to the interviewer. This shows that trust is essential in obtaining individual cooperation in highly contentious groups, which is understandable considering the widespread belief among QQ users that government informants and undercover agents target and patrol QQ space as part of the state effort in monitoring contentious activities. This point is echoed in the interviews, as reported in the findings.

In the hobby/interest category, both groups take traveling as their main thread albeit in different approaches. One group (Group D in our coding) is called the "W City Backpackers," meaning it is oriented for people who are interested in pack-and-go light-weight traveling. With a member list of 457, this group is the most open-ended in membership make-ups, enforcing no real-name identity or background check. The majority of participants in this group are from W city, but many hail from other parts of the country, with a few residing overseas. Interestingly, as the group with the most diverse members, its topics are also the most widespread among all groups, ranging from travel tips to event organizing to other issues that are only marginally related to traveling. The other group in this category, the "Happy Outdoor Travel Group" (coded as Group E), has 321 active members and is heavily focused on a local neighborhood where the founder resides (in a southern city). Memberships are granted to local residents who are interested in outdoor travel, and the group managers work with local travel agencies in regularly organizing tours to various close-by destinations, including Hong Kong and Macau. Many events that take place in the vicinity of the city are free, and cater especially to families with young children; its paid tours in collaboration with local travel agencies offer a much more competitive rate than market listing. Group interactions focus heavily on organizing events and soliciting member input, and the latter as a strategy works well to boost participation.

DATA ANALYSIS

All text-based interviews were saved, and audio files were recorded and transcribed for further analysis. Our analytical procedure was inspired by the synthesized strategies as suggested by Charmaz (2006) in grounded theory coding of interview data as an effort to "understand participants' views and actions from their perspectives" (p. 47). Our initial coding (open coding) was conducted with about one-third of the interview data in crystalizing meanings and actions into major emerging categories. We then moved on to the stage of focused coding in which we applied, and modified where necessary, these coding schemes in sifting through the complete data corpus. At the completion of coding all the data, we reexamined the codes following the logic and logistics of axial coding, which "relates categories to subcategories, specifies the properties and dimensions of a category, and reassembles the data ... to give coherence to the emerging analysis" (Charmaz, 2006, p. 60).

We followed the systematic thematic analysis approach as developed by Joffe (2011) and Braun and Clark (2006) in pinpointing prominent and recurring themes and patterns of meaning as well as their prevalence in our interview data. This process started with developing initial codes, looking for thematic threads, and reviewing thematic extracts and it resulted in finding what we deem the most appropriate descriptive terms for the themes and integrating them into a coherent, analytic narrative in the context of our research questions. Because we believe that QQ group creators and managers may have different perspectives than the ordinary users, we have therefore separated these two types of interviewees in our analysis.

RESULTS AND FINDINGS

Group Creators and Managers

We obtained interview data from two QQ group creators (A & E) and four account managers (two from B and C each). A persistent thematic thread we have ascertained in the interviews is to use QQ groups as a platform for collective action and coordinated activities. The group creators had been both activists in the respective areas of actions, and hoped to use QQ groups as a venue to help like-minded individuals into deliberating and participating in meaningful acts. They both indicated expectations they pinned on the groups to "raise public awareness and identify companions," and to use their personal enthusiasm to create some type of "contagion" effects on group members in rallying public participation in events.

Take the example of the creator of Group A (coded A1), one that originated in organizing individuals to petition the district government to open more grade schools to local residents, this is what motivated her to leading the effort in this process through a newspaper interview: "As the college district expanded, and more and more young families moved in, we had an urgent need to build local schools for their children. Through a survey of local residents, we found over 170 school-age children from families of young faculty living in this district. So we mobilized a petition to the government, which led to the opening of schools in 2013. Although my own child is not school age yet, I will face similar problems in the near future. So I am pleased to promote such a cause that benefits all young faculty in the neighborhood."[3]

A1 expressed similar sentiments in her interview with us. She said that she was proud to be a leader and organizer of this movement. The use of QQ group as a platform was motivated by both expediency and efficiency, because "it is easy to reach everyone and it works well to organize activities." Moreover, QQ works the best in "circulating information and getting feedback." A1's outspokenness and prominent role in this effort antagonized local officials, who pressured administrators from her university to issue her warnings and demanded restraint. A1 published an angry post on the group BBS in 2014 bemoaning the pressure on her in June 2014, and she has relegated management responsibilities of this group to others, and diminished his role since then. In a different context, E1 told us that he decided to found the travel group because

I have a few friends with a lot of expertise and resources in organizing group tours, and I have had a lot of pleasant experience through my past contact with them. So I wanted to find a venue to share this with residents in my own neighborhood. This is the best I can do to improve relations with my neighbors while at the same time enjoying excursions and getting exercises in the outdoor. (E1, group creator)

A key theme that has been shared by account managers is the utility of QQ groups as a viable space of information sharing and interaction. For example, in regard to Group C, one manager remarked:

Users shared a lot of information on what causes stinking odor in the air, how to solve these problems, the role of incinerators in this process, and what we each can do to help protect our environment. They also posted constructive ideas on how we can work together to stop the incinerators from being built in our area. Much of the information was new to me, and it helped us to plan related events. (C2, account manager)

A great ethos of voluntarism and dedication is a must on the part of account managers, as echoed in all the interviews. Managers have to check QQ communications at least weekly, but often daily, typically through a combination of devices ranging from PCs to iPads to smart phones in order to moderate discussions and plan events. This is a substantial commitment of time and extra work for these individuals who at the same time keep a full-time job. But these interviewees also exhibit a palpable sense of reward and achievement in seeing success in staging events and getting to know people on a personal level. This finds testimonial in the following interview:

Originally, our QQ group had no plan for any event for this year's Qingming Festival,[4] because we expected most people to go back to their hometown to engage in family rituals. At the last moment (on Thursday), a few individuals in the neighborhood implored me to organize a group excursion for the holiday weekend. So I rushed into contact with a tourist guide on the same day, and we worked out a route specifically tailored to the demographics and likes of our community. Because this was designed as a family outing including a large number of children, we made substantial cuts in the distance covered during the trip, and we also made on-the-spot adjustments to the physical conditions of the group. Throughout the trip, people showed a high level of team spirit and comradery, with each trying to help the other in different ways. I am extremely gratified in this experience, and will definitely plan more similar events in the future. (E1, group creator)

Group creators and managers all put themselves at the frontline in protecting the collective interest of the group and maintaining a safe and worry-free environment in the group forums. As mentioned before, all groups enforced a varying degree of identity verification for member entrance, and managers were not hesitant to terminating member status for those who were found to engage in patterns of spreading deceptive or unwanted (mostly purely commercial) information. Most cited the potential loss of trust in the group and possible dilution of group focus if irrelevant messages are allowed to disseminate. In particular, group creator for Group A and manager for Group C mentioned external threats as a result of their leading roles in these groups: for the former, warning from her supervisor eventually forced her to loosen her detachment from the group; and the latter cited multiple concerns as barriers for the group to realize its full potential – among them constant eavesdropping on group communication and activities, citizens' rights are often violated, certain activists in the group were harassed offline for their involvement.

Finally, prevalent in all creators and managers is the belief in the principle of "equality of all members, freedom of participation, and will of the majority." They perceive their role as a facilitator, not an influencer, in group discussions and activity planning.

Regular Members

Analysis of the 27 interviews in the regular-member category was organized thus: we first look at salient commonalities across all groups in their thematic patterns and orientations, followed with a scrutiny of group-by-group variances. In the discussions that follow, thematic extracts are presented in the order of their relative prevalence.

First of all, consistent with typical communal practices, sharing of information, knowledge, and resources is a noticeable draw for all QQ groups. Specifically, the statistical distribution of interviewees indicating this is an important motivator for their participation in the groups stands as follows: 83.3% (Group A), 100% (Group B), 75% (Group C), 71.4% (Group D), and 66.7% (Group E). Although there are now a growing number of online resources that users can search for similar information, many admitted that the type of contextualized information obtained from fellow QQ group members – that is, information attached to personal experiences and individual perspectives in an environment they can relate to – has unique appeal to them. The human dimensions of soft information make a distinct currency that holds a community together. The various add-ons to the informational aspects of these online communications include: insiders' views, backchannel updates, veterans' wisdom, eye-opening angles. A common revelation from interviewees is their urge to hear from people who are like them (e.g., residents in the same neighborhood, families with children in the same age range, hikers who have similar interests and physical conditions, faculty from the same school). So even if the informational aspect of a particular message may stay the same, repackaging of the same information in a new delivery context may still add enlightenment.

Sharing, of course, must originate with the contributing side. This spirit of altruism is typical among those with an urge to share (concerning cures for certain children-prone illness):

Whenever I can, I always answer questions on how to care for sick children. Warm-hearted in nature, I hate to see any kid suffer. So I always respond to these questions with my personal experiences on what to do under these circumstances. I would feel uncomfortable if I knew something and did not respond. (A2, member of Group A)

Oversharing, however, may turn away members. The most common complaints we heard from the interviewees are information overload (too much irrelevant information) and junk information (commercial messages and sales pitches). This attitude is echoed by many:

Can you imagine that I get hundreds of messages when I log on to the group? After I scan the first few posts, if I don't see anything interesting, I will just ignore all of them. (A5, member of Group A)

I subscribe to many QQ groups. So my smart phone beeps constantly. I get annoyed when I find nothing interesting after I skim the screen. So I often block all of them. (E5, member of Group E)

The second motivating factor that gravitates users to QQ groups is the opportunity to expand one's social networks and personal relations. Many suggested that their longing to network is enhanced by proximity (e.g., living close to one another, working in the same university). These are typical responses:

Because I also live the college district, I thought this might give me the chance to make some new friends. (A3, member of Group A)

Through intense discussions in the group, I could relate well to the styles of doing things and their viewpoints, and I felt that I got to know them very well, and considered them to be close friends. Then I would try to find time to meet with them offline. However, there are also others that I will stay away from, because I know they are not my type from their communications in the group. (A5, member of Group A)

Sometimes I posted questions on the group forum, and a certain individual responded with enthusiasm repeatedly. Then I told myself: "This is the person I want to chat with more face-to-face!" (B2, member of Group B)

Some people live in the same neighborhood with me. We often saw each other on the street, but never struck up a conversation. After traveling together, we got to know each other better, and then a good friendship develops. (E4, a member of Group E)

The third drive to participate in groups is community events and collective action. This is the most noticeable from interviewees in Groups A and C, although similar sentiments can be found (less prominently) in other groups as well. Individual decisions on whether to be part of a group activity or not often rest with geographic proximity, timing, and how many people (especially those that one relates well to) show interest.

The fourth motivator, which was cited by slightly less than 30% of the interviewees, is to kill time. This is especially salient in hobby/interest-based groups (D & E), in which members indicated that the groups help them to stay away from boredom.

In the next section, we discuss differences in dynamics across the different groups. With regard to the two groups (Groups A and C) that focus on collective action, QQ groups are the most cited as a much-needed platform to "plan, mobilize, and organize" events. The ease of communication via QQ groups is also credited to be an enabler. Two particular phrases that are mentioned only in association with these two groups are "unity is power" (Group A) and "holding together to keep warm" (Group C). Regarding Group C, which engages in the most contentious activity, there is a notable "contagion" effect, as demonstrated in this statement from an interviewee:

I think that many members are like me in feeling powerless in front of the cruel reality. But if we can share the risk of contentious protest among the group, then the risk becomes minimized. Prior to join-ing this group, I thought the misfortune was just affecting me personally. After interacting with fellow members, I found out that this feeling was shared by most. (C4, member of Group C)

Of all the groups, participation is the most lop-sided in Group C, whose activity is the most contentious, with a small number of activists leading the discussions and organizing events. This led to complaints by half of the interviewees on most people being "free-riders" and largely detached from group activities. On the other hand, content of communication in Group C stays the most focused than all other groups.

Group B, which caters to a special group of scholars residing in a foreign country, is perceived to be the most effective in addressing personal questions and solving personal problems; it is called by inter-viewees the "all-capable" and "all-in-one" group (any question you can think of, somebody knows the answer). Mutual support is the key line throughout interviewee input, and many talked about the "helped-helping" role of group members (i.e., the experience of being helped triggers the urge to help others).

As for the two travel-oriented groups, these were the only groups that creators/managers mentioned the need to openly advertise for member recruiting. The range of content in these groups is the most diversified, with entertainment and time-killing cited as some of the reasons of participating.

CONCLUSION AND FUTURE DIRECTIONS

Internet-based network technologies and applications continue to charter into new territories. Social media has been no doubt at the frontline of change lately. Like the rest of the world, social networking technologies have introduced new dynamics into China's cyber world. Leading China's social media landscape is QQ, an instant messaging service that penetrates to more than 90% of China's Internet population. This study reports results from semi-structured in-depth interviews of 33 QQ Group users, and its findings shed light on our understanding of a number of dimensions of QQ groups as a particular type of online communities.

As Tai (2006) observes, Chinese Internet users display a higher propensity than most of their coun-terparts in other countries in contributing to, and in consuming, user-generated content (UGC). Content propagated on social media is produced exclusively by users themselves, and drives user participation to new levels. QQ groups, which are created, managed, and populated by users themselves, cater to variegated needs and purposes of diverse user bodies. Unlike any type of virtual communities we have seen thus far, QQ groups combine BBS, listserv, audio-video-text chat and instant messaging into one unified space that is supported by multiple platforms. These technical affordances consolidate QQ's pervasive presence in everyday life.

Our findings point to the prominent role proximity plays in the formations of QQ groups. All of the groups we studied are connected by a varying degree of geographic adjacency. Four groups (A, C, D and E) are mainly oriented toward participants in the same cities. For the remaining group (B), although members hail from diverse regions of China, they all converge on one campus in a foreign country. This certainly does not suggest that this is the case for all QQ groups. But it does show that existing ties (e.g., living close to one another, or being in the same profession in the same area), even if they are non-active (meaning most members did not know each other before joining the groups), are important enablers in QQ group formations. As our findings reveal, these pre-existing links create the added urge for individuals to join a particular QQ group, if the mission of the group fits what they are looking for (e.g., collective action toward a shared goal, same hobby, same status as visiting scholars). As Wellman and Gulia (1999) noted over a decade ago, virtual communities often build off on existing "real-life" communities. This certainly rings true in these QQ groups. On the other hand, it should also be obvious that online communities like these QQ groups activate and revitalize offline communal relationships. Most of the individuals that got to build personal relationships with their neighbors and colleagues in the groups we studied would probably not have been able to develop these connections without QQ group interactions.

Like in other communities, sharing is a key hallmark of QQ groups. Most group activities – be them travel, collective action or weekend excursion – start with members sharing information. But this typically goes beyond just "hard information" the like of which can be obtained from online searches; it is often "soft information" with personal touches and human perspectives (Ellis et al., 2004). That it comes from somebody they can relate to matters to the users.

QQ groups also provide empowering platforms for contentious action. In this regard, we notice a clear pattern of dynamics from deliberation to mobilization to action:

1. Sharing information to raise public awareness about pros/cons of action/inaction;
2. Deliberating on a rational course of action that the majority of members agree on;
3. Issuing a call on action to all members (signing a petition for A and staging walk-ins and sit-ins for C);
4. Engaging in planned actions.

Both group creators/managers and average users have noted a certain "contagion" effect in group interactions: consciousness and the urge to take action can spread among users under certain circumstances.

The logic of connective action as elaborated by Bennett and Segeberg (2012) is of particular relevance to collective action in China. Formal organizations and established institutions mostly align with state interests, and will most likely stay away from contentious politics. Resource-poor individuals, then, have to seek help from alternative channels in engaging in collective action that falls outside of state-prescribed boundaries. User participation via social media platforms such as QQ groups then opens up new possibilities for contentious action.

Because QQ groups create a member-only participatory space, they are thus conducive to more steady and more intimate relationships than conventional virtual communities. Trust is then the important currency for coordination of individual collaborations. As is common in field research, we had to gain the trust of the interviewees before they would agree to speak to us in many groups. As a matter of fact, all members we sampled in one group focusing on water protection refused to participate in the interviews because they did not place trust on us. This is usefully understood in the context of China's online surveillance apparatus. Like all networked space, there is a formidable presence of state monitoring of QQ group communications and activities, and netizens in China have responded with their own bottom-up counter-monitoring mechanism of collaboration.

Finally, our findings have to be evaluated in the context of their limitations: we could only ask interviewees questions that focused on a small number of topics; our choice of groups was not as broad as we would like; and interviewee sample could be more diversified. But we believe this study has made an important first step in understanding QQ groups, and we call for more efforts in this line of research to cover multiplicity of issues and user groups. There is precious much we can gain therein to expand our knowledge base of online communities as well as the evolving landscape of China's social media.

REFERENCES

Bateman, P. J., Gray, P. H., & Butler, B. S. (2011). The impact of community commitment on participation in online communities. *Information Systems Research*, *22*(4), 841–854. doi:10.1287/isre.1090.0265

Baumeister, R. F., & Leary, M. R. (1995). The need to belong: Desire for interpersonal attachments as a fundamental human motivation. *Psychological Bulletin*, *117*(3), 497–529. doi:10.1037/0033-2909.117.3.497 PMID:7777651

Bennett, W. L., & Segerberg, A. (2012). The logic of connective action: Digital media and the personalization of contentious politics. *Information Communication and Society*, *15*(5), 739–768. doi:10.1080/1369118X.2012.670661

Braun, V., & Clarke, V. (2006). Using thematic analysis in psychology. *Qualitative Research in Psychology*, *3*(2), 77–101. doi:10.1191/1478088706qp063oa

Charmaz, K. (2006). *Constructing grounded theory: A practical guide through qualitative analysis*. London: Sage.

Chen, H. L., Fan, H. L., & Tsai, C. C. (2014). The role of community trust and altruism in knowledge sharing: An investigation of a virtual community of teacher professionals. *Journal of Educational Technology & Society*, *17*(3), 168–179.

China Internet Network Information Center (CNNIC). (2015). *35th Statistical Report on China's Internet Development*. Retrieved on June 2, 2015, at http://www.cnnic.com.cn/hlwfzyj/hlwxzbg/hlwtjbg/201502/t20150203_51634.htm

Cook, K. S., & Rice, E. (2003). Social exchange theory. In J. Delamater (Ed.), *Handbook of social psychology* (pp. 53–76). New York: Kluwer Academic/Plenum Publishers.

Cropanzano, R., & Mitchell, M. S. (2005). Social exchange theory: An interdisciplinary review. *Journal of Management*, *31*(6), 874–900. doi:10.1177/0149206305279602

Durkheim, E. (1984). *The division of labor in society* (W. D. Halls, Trans.). New York: Free Press. (Originally published in German in 1893) doi:10.1007/978-1-349-17729-5

Ellis, D., Oldridge, R., & Vasconcelos, A. (2004). Community and virtual community. *Annual Review of Information Science & Technology*, *38*(1), 145–186. doi:10.1002/aris.1440380104

Gerbaudo, P. (2012). *Tweets and the streets: Social media and contemporary activism*. New York: Pluto Press.

Gittell, R., & Vidal, A. (1998). *Community organizing: Building social capital as a development strategy*. Thousand Oaks, CA: Sage Publications.

Gusfield, J. R. (1975). *Community: A critical response*. New York: Harper & Row.

Hummon, D. M. (1992). Community attachment: Local sentiment and sense of place. In I. Altman & S. M. Low (Eds.), *Place attachment* (pp. 253–278). New York: Plenum. doi:10.1007/978-1-4684-8753-4_12

Joffe, H. (2011). Thematic analysis. In D. Harper & A. R. Thompson (Eds.), *Qualitative research methods in mental health and psychotherapy: A guide for students and practitioners* (pp. 209–223). Malden, MA: Wiley & Blackwell. doi:10.1002/9781119973249.ch15

Kane, G. C., Alavi, M., Labianca, G. J., & Borgatti, S. P. (2014). What's different about social media networks? A framework and research agenda. *Management Information Systems Quarterly*, *38*(1), 274–304.

Kollock, P., & Smith, M. A. (1999). Communities in cyberspace. In M. A. Smith & P. Kollock (Eds.), *Communities in cyberspace* (pp. 3–25). New York: Routledge.

Ma, W. W., & Yuen, A. H. (2011). Understanding online knowledge sharing: An interpersonal relationship perspective. *Computers & Education*, *56*(1), 210–219. doi:10.1016/j.compedu.2010.08.004

McCaughey, M., & Ayers, M. D. (Eds.). (2003). *Cyberactivism: Online activism in theory and practice*. New York: Routledge.

McMillan, D. W., & Chavis, D. M. (1986). Sense of community: A definition and theory. *Journal of Community Psychology*, *14*(1), 6–23. doi:10.1002/1520-6629(198601)14:1<6::AID-JCOP2290140103>3.0.CO;2-I

Norris, P. (2004). The bridging and bonding role of online communities. In P. N. Howard & S. Jones (Eds.), *Society online: The Internet in context* (pp. 31–41). Thousand Oaks, CA: Sage. doi:10.4135/9781452229560.n2

Norris, P. (2011). *Democratic deficit: Critical citizens revisited*. New York: Cambridge University Press. doi:10.1017/CBO9780511973383

Oldenburg, R. (1999). *The great good place: Cafes, coffee shops, bookstores, bars, hair salons, and other hangouts at the heart of a community*. New York: Marlowe.

Parsons, T. (1951). *The social system*. New York, NY: Free Press.

Portes, A. (1998). Social capital: Its origins and applications in modern sociology. *Annual Review of Sociology*, *24*(1), 1–24. doi:10.1146/annurev.soc.24.1.1

Putnam, R. D. (2000). *Bowling alone: The collapse and revival of American community*. New York: Simon & Schuster. doi:10.1145/358916.361990

Tai, Z. (2006). *The Internet in China: Cyberspace and civil society*. New York: Routledge.

Tai, Z. (2010). Casting the ubiquitous net of information control: Internet surveillance in China from Golden Shield to Green Dam. *International Journal of Advanced Pervasive and Ubiquitous Computing*, 2(1), 53–70. doi:10.4018/japuc.2010010104

Wellman, B., & Gulia, M. (1999). Virtual communities as communities: Net surfers don't ride alone. In M. A. Smith & P. Kollock (Eds.), *Communities in cyberspace* (pp. 167–194). New York: Routledge.

Wellman, B., Haase, A. Q., Witte, J., & Hampton, K. (2001). Does the Internet increase, decrease, or supplement social capital? Social networks, participation, and community commitment. *The American Behavioral Scientist*, 45(3), 436–455. doi:10.1177/00027640121957286

KEY TERMS AND DEFINITIONS

China Internet Network Information Center (CNNIC): Founded in July 1997, CNNIC is a non-profit, semi-state agency responsible for the administration and overseeing of the Internet sector in China; it manages the China's domain name registry and represents China in the global governance of the Internet.

Contentious Action: Activities citizens organize that are often disruptive and protestive in nature, without approval from the government or agents of power from above.

QQ Groups: A special type of chatting service offered by QQ for communicating in a group context. Each QQ group is a member-only space that allows for text/audio/video chatting, online forums, digital albums, and file-sharing. There are four tiers of QQ groups: basic groups have a maximum of 200 members, and each QQ user is entitled to create up to five group accounts for free; other groups enforce a cap of 500, 1000, and 2000 members respectively, and can be created/owned by users based on a scheme of combining monthly fee and longevity of membership.

QQ: An instant messaging service that was debuted in February 1999; its initial name was OICQ (Open I Seek You), in apparent reference to the ICQ service owned by America Online (AOL) at the time. Under the threat of trademark litigation from AOL, the name was changed to QQ in 2000. QQ offers a variety of services, including instant messaging (via text, audio, and video), peer-to-peer file sharing, online storage, and electronic mail across multiple platforms.

Social Networking Service (SNS): A Web-based platform that allows users to create individual profiles and share them with others through building networks of friendships or connections based on social relations, interests, or other pursuits. Different SNS sites typically have their own add-on features to enable interactions among chosen nodes of interaction.

Tencent: Called 腾讯 in Chinese, it is a public company listed in Hong Kong Stock Exchange (SEHK: 700). With business interests encompassing media, entertainment, mobile services, and the Internet, it is a leading high-tech innovator in China and one of the largest Internet companies in the world. Among Its most popular offerings are QQ and WeChat (a smartphone-based mobile text and video messaging service).

ENDNOTES

[1]   See the Chinese wiki page for QQ at http://zh.wikipedia.org/wiki/腾讯QQ#QQ.E7.BE.A4

[2]   Detailed explanations can be found at the official QQ site via http://qun.qq.com

[3]   Tang Xueliang, "This Place is Full of Flavors of Nature and Energy of Upward Movement." *Southern Metropolitan News*, May 20, 2014, A1.

[4]   Qingming Festival is a traditional Chinese festival featuring the ritual of people paying respects to their ancestors at the graveside. It falls on April 5 of the lunar calendar.

Chapter 10

Impacts on Society:
Informational and Socio–Emotional Support in Virtual Communities and Online Groups

Shahar Gur
University of North Carolina at Charlotte, USA

Anita Lynn Blanchard
University of North Carolina at Charlotte, USA

Lisa Slattery Walker
University of North Carolina at Charlotte, USA

ABSTRACT

This chapter discusses the implications of giving and receiving social support in virtual communities and online groups. The chapter first offers a literature review about social support in general, and then delves into specific details about online social support. More specifically, this chapter focuses on informational and socio-emotional support, especially as they pertain to online groups and virtual communities. Three specific examples of online groups and virtual communities studied by the authors are offered, along with research findings and hypotheses. Finally, best practices are outlined for those who are interested in starting and maintaining an online group with the purpose of offering informational and/or socio-emotional support to potential users.

INTRODUCTION

Much of the early research on virtual communities in the 1990s examined if and how virtual communities affected face-to-face communities (Blanchard & Horan, 1998; Rheingold, 1993; Wellman & Gulia, 1997). Researchers were not interested in the virtual environment per se, but rather were focused on its effect on the "real world." From this research, the general consensus was that virtual communities were not going to destroy society, but they were also not an automatic solution to society's problems. None-

DOI: 10.4018/978-1-4666-9899-4.ch010

theless, as information and communication technologies (ICT) and virtual communities have become ubiquitous and adopted by more mainstream society, questions remain. As evident from the media, some discourse in virtual spaces may have detrimental face-to-face consequences. Trolls, anonymous ICT users who taunt group members, have been an issue for decades. The "fappening," when celebrities' private pictures were leaked online, made national news. Cyberbullies have become a real issue for high school students. Indeed, a survey conducted by Pew Research Center has found that 88% of teenagers who use social media have seen cruel or mean posts by other people (Lenhart et al., 2011).

But many times online communication can serve as a source of comfort and support, especially for people who are undergoing a stressful event. For example, research has shown that social support can aid with the psychological adjustment of cancer patients (Helgeson & Cohen, 1996). In addition, when people in need of social support receive it from their networks, they reported having higher levels of vitality, social functioning, and mental health (Melrose et al., 2015). On other hand, firefighters with low social support levels had higher levels of suicidal ideation when they reported experiencing a lot of stress at their jobs (Carpenter et al., 2015). Thus, supportive online communication can reduce stress and improve mental and physical health outcomes for users. The purpose of this chapter is to review the current literature on virtual informational and socio-emotional support in order to understand one of the positive effects of virtual communications on "real world" outcomes. Therefore, the chapter will discuss virtual communities' effects on society by focusing on literature and the authors' research on informational and socio-emotional support in online groups and virtual communities.

This chapter will first review the current literature on informational and socio-emotional support broadly, especially as it relates to health outcomes. Then, it will focus on informational and socio-emotional support as they relate to online interactions. For example, online support can be viewed by everyone in the community, not just the people who are exchanging it. Thus, online informational and socio-emotional support may have a larger effect than face-to-face support. Finally, the authors use data and examples derived from their research program to discuss how online forums have been used by members as a place to find and offer knowledge and comfort to fellow members who are experiencing similar challenges or seeking answers to similar questions. Future research directions are discussed.

BACKGROUND

Social support can come in many forms, but all forms are ultimately aimed at comforting and uplifting others (Finfgeld-Connett, 2005; Langford et al., 1997). People need social support especially when they are under stress (Cohen & Wills, 1985). Traditionally, social support has been studied within the health care and psychological research fields due to its direct relationship to the outcome of improving one's mental and physical health. In fact, studies find empirical support for the direct relationship between psychological adjustment and social support of cancer patients (for a review see Helgeson & Cohen, 1996). Lance Armstrong is a popular example of a patient who overcame the stress of his cancer diagnosis with the help of his family and friends. His website, Livestrong, originally was a support system for other cancer survivors. Moreover, on top of aiding in recovery from disease, having a supportive social network can positively affect a person's overall quality of life (Helgeson, 2003) and well-being (Lee, Noh, & Koo, 2013).

The study of social support crosses disciplines because it has important implications, especially within the context of organizations. One topic that spans across multiple disciplines, for example, is perceived organizational support, which is a type of social support that pertains to how much employees believe that their organizations create a positive, work-conducive environment (Eisenberger et al., 1986).

This chapter focuses on two specific types of social support: informational and socio-emotional. Informational support is when individuals share ideas or offer suggestions related to specific needs or problems (House, 1981; Krause, 1986). An example of an informational-supportive gesture is giving someone practical tips or advice, such as telling a person about a unique grocery store that sells inexpensive healthy food products. Socio-emotional support, on the other hand, is when people offer comforting words and gestures to those who are going through physical, mental, or emotional hardships (Shirai et al., 2009; Whalen & Lachman, 2000). The term "socio-emotional" is derived from the fact that the related emotions are elicited from social interactions. Hence, socio-emotional support stands for the notion that the receiver is cared for, esteemed, valued, and loved by the giver of the support (Cobb, 1976).

It is common for people to use ICT in order to seek and receive support (LaRose, Eastin, & Gregg, 2001) and regulate their negative emotions (Weiser, 2001). Further, processes of social support can occur in all types of ICT. In social media sites such as Facebook, for example, teens seek support from their peers by posting status updates in order to find ways to ameliorate their stress (Frison & Eggermont, 2015), and positive feedback from peers leads to higher levels of self-esteem (Valkenburg, Peter, & Schouten, 2006). Seeking and offering social support can also occur on Twitter by sending tweets (Shepherd et al., 2015). Social support is exchanged even while engaging in online chatting and playing video games (Leung, 2006).In addition to social media sites, user reviews on online shopping sites can serve as a mechanism by which users offer social support to contemplative consumers who are trying to evaluate products online (Lee & Hahn, 2015). Researchers have found that receiving online support increased members' global feelings of connectedness (Park, 2012; Welbourne, Blanchard, & Wadsworth, 2013). These examples show that online support can be broadly sought after in ICT, and the ease of not having to target it at a specific individual allows users to reach a wider range of audience as opposed to face-to-face support-seeking methods.

There are many more examples of the ways in which people can seek and offer support in virtual spaces, but this chapter deals specifically with informational and socio-emotional support within virtual communities and online groups. To provide some background, the first well-known online group was "The WELL" which developed in 1992 (Rheingold, 1993). Since then, online groups have become ubiquitous in society. Consequently, virtual communities have also became commonplace. Even though the two terms are used interchangeably (Faraj, Jarvenpaa, & Majchrzak, 2011; Ren et al., 2012; Walther & Bunz, 2005), the difference between online groups and virtual communities is that virtual communities exist as entities on their own, and virtual community members generally focus on their attachment to and membership with the virtual community. There are clear membership boundaries in virtual communities. The members likely feel a sense of community with the virtual entity (cf., Blanchard, 2008). Online groups, on the other hand, exist as a supplement for communities that already exist and interact with each other in the "real world." Participants of online groups may or may not have a sense of community with other members of the group (Blanchard, Askay, & Callas, 2010). Members may participate in online groups to exchange informational support. But when members are engaged in both informational and socio-emotional support, they are likely participating in a virtual community (Blanchard, 2008).

Even though informational support is usually the factor that drives members to join and engage with a virtual community, they often end up receiving socio-emotional support in the process of virtually interacting with other members (Lampe et al., 2010). Therefore, this chapter discusses both informational and socio-emotional support. The next section is about specific findings related to these two types of support as they come about in online groups and virtual communities.

FOCUS OF CHAPTER: SUPPORT IN ONLINE GROUPS AND VIRTUAL COMMUNITIES

Research supports the notion that online communication is just as good as face-to-face communication in terms of achieving social goals (Panzarasa, Opsahl, & Carley, 2009). This section discusses how informational support and socio-emotional support operate within the context of online groups and virtual communities to provide comfort for their members. After outlining the reasons why people choose to join certain communities over others, this section will go over the attributes of virtual support as they compare to face-to-face support.

Choosing the Right Supportive Community

With hundreds if not thousands of options available for online support (Ren, Kraut, & Kiesler, 2007), why people choose some virtual communities over others is an important issue. First, the design of the community can determine the extent to which members participate willingly (Ma & Argarwal, 2007). Community design can encompass many attributes, such as the user interface, features of the site, and policies of the organization (Ren et al., 2007). Different choices about the design can have varying levels of effect on how members interact (or expect to interact) with each other. For example, online communities that have the feature of showing when the last reply was made allows others to determine the rate by which other members check, read, and reply to posts; this feature can in turn help members decide whether they believe they will be able to receive support in a timely fashion from other members.

Design attributes may also include whether members of the community can control how to present their own avatar or choose from a prescribed list of options. Research on avatar choices has shown that detailed, user-created avatars enrich the process by which members communicate with one another (Williams, 2007). The same goes for user photos. Online communities that allow members to upload their own pictures can foster an intimate environment by highlighting the human contact component (Zimmer & Alexander, 1996). Thus, the perceived warmness (which can influence perceived social support) of other members of the community can be determined by design features that have nothing to do with members' actual behavior.

The specificity of the virtual community topic also plays a role in determining whether members choose to join it. People seek social support when experiencing difficult experiences (Cohen & Wills, 1985). However, it is erroneous to assume everyone experiencing hardship wants the same support. To illustrate this point, breast cancer patients require different social support than lung cancer patients (Ell et al., 1992). Therefore, people who are seeking social support for a specific type of challenge may spend a long time looking for the appropriate content in potential online communities.

Retention in Supportive Virtual Communities

The way in which members interact with each other also affects whether people choose to join, participate, and stay committed to the virtual group (Preece & Maloney-Krichmar, 2003). Members should feel like they have something important to add to or receive from the group. Ling and colleagues (2005) have found that members are more likely to contribute in online communities if they feel like they have something unique to add.

In addition, perceived similarity can play a large role in whether the members feel like a group (Crump et al., 2010; Rutchick, Hamilton, & Sack, 2008). Previous virtual community researchers have found that similarity and identification with similar others affects members' willingness to stay in the group (Ren et al, 2012). Further, sharing support with similar others may be an absolute need for some virtual communities. For example, in an infertility support group, women who have already given birth and "graduated" to motherhood are not welcome (Welbourne et al, 2012).

Finally, the exchange of support may affect their decision to stay in the virtual community and to become active. Support is positively related to identification, trust, and a sense of virtual community (Ren et al., 2012; Blanchard, 2008; Welbourne et al., 2013). In particular, a sense of community—which is a common outcome of exchanging support in a virtual community—can increase members' prosocial behavior and long-term retention (cf., McMillan & Chavis, 1986). Therefore, the exchange of support in virtual communities is important in creating successful virtual communities.

Benefits of Virtual Support

There are certain characteristics of virtual support that make it preferable to face-to-face support. For example, asynchronous communication allows for members to participate at their convenience without regard to time or location. Thus, members can be located in different parts of the world, but the fact that they are going through similar hardships enables them to seek and provide support for one another. Further, the longevity of posts in a virtual community allows for members to read about and share in the support well after the original discussion. Even though informational support (e.g., piece of advice) may become outdated, socio-emotional support hardly ever does.

Moreover, even though the members do not actually participate in directly giving or receiving support (which is similar to a dyadic face-to-face interaction that involves giving and providing support), the mere fact that members of a virtual community have access to the community and can see previous posts helps them know more about the topic and feel better about overcoming their personal challenges (Wellman & Gulia, 1997). Because most members of virtual communities are lurkers (Preece & Maloney-Krichmar, 2003), the active members' exchange of support can help many more group members than the few people who actually participate in exchanging it. Therefore, support multiplies online in ways that are simply not possible in face-to-face groups.

Another benefit of virtual support is that online spaces enable users to choose to be anonymous (Armstrong & Hagel, 1996). Although some people may use anonymity as a tool through which to cause damage to others without being held accountable, the benefit of being anonymous in virtual communities is that users can freely talk about their challenges without feeling as though their hardships can be traced back to them. For example, Cullen (1995) has found that some people who take part of online addiction therapy sessions are more comfortable revealing personal information if they know that they can do so anonymously. Thus, anonymity can aid in the process of social support via online communications.

Online Informational Support Processes and Findings

Informational support is needed in situations when someone is experiencing a hardship that requires knowledge on specific topics. At times, it may be hard to seek informational support face-to-face, especially if the topic is taboo. For example, Ellington (2014) studied African American women's struggle with acceptance of their natural hair. Due to a culture that does not seem to validate African American women who choose to wear natural hair, these women are less knowledgeable on how to care for their hair in effective ways. Women in Ellington's sample were not able to seek help in the form of informational support from those in their immediate physical environment, and so they turned to virtual communities in which the topic of natural hair is not only discussed, but also celebrated. Thus, through the process of disseminating useful information of how to care for African American women's natural hair, these virtual communities uplift the spirits of those who were originally shamed by society for being proud of their natural physical form.

Welbourne and her colleagues (2012) examined an infertility virtual community, another health problem that is also difficult to observe and is also stigmatized. In their researcher, they found that the more members provided informational support, the more support they believed they received. Further, the support they provided was related to their sense of community with other members of the group and the connectedness they felt to people in general. Thus, these two studies show that both giving and receiving informational support is beneficial to the members of supportive virtual communities.

Another type of virtual community that emphasizes informational support processes are online communities of practice (Johnson, 2001). In online communities of practice, knowledge transfer is crucial and having a diverse group of contributors allows the community to share as much knowledge as possible about the field of interest. However, the diversity of the group members may lead to differences in norms about communication (Amin & Roberts, 2008), which has the potential to hinder the development of trust and consequently socio-emotional support if the members feel that they cannot confide in others due to cultural barriers.

Online Socio-Emotional Support Processes and Findings

Previous research supports that while many members of virtual communities choose virtual communities based on the exchange of informational support, it is the socio-emotional support that is the glue that keeps members attached to the community (Blanchard & Markus, 2004; Welbourne et al. 2012; Ren et al., 2012). For some people, however, the socio-emotional support is the driver of why they choose a virtual community. For example, people who lost a family member unexpectedly (e.g., suicide, murder) seek the emotional support of others who have gone through similar experiences. Hence, people join the new community not necessarily seeking knowledge, but more for the purpose of seeking validation for their feelings and comfort in knowing that they are not alone. The anonymity of the support seeker on online communities is something that may lack in face-to-face interactions (Mesch, 2006), and therefore online communities may be a more attractive source of emotional support than offline networks.

Welbourne and her colleagues (2012) also examined the desire for socio-emotional support in the study of infertility virtual communities. They found that the desire for socio-emotional support had a very strong relationship to providing support to other members of the virtual community. Further, providing support to other virtual community members had a strong relationship to receiving support from others, increased feelings of sense of community and connectedness, and to decreased feelings of support. Their research determined that the outcomes of interest in their study (sense of community, connectedness and stress reduction) all started from the members' desire to connect with others through socio-emotional support. Therefore, socio-emotional support may not be the main driver of why people search out virtual communities, but it has a strong effect on member retention and activity and positive outcomes.

EXAMPLES OF ONLINE GROUPS AND VIRTUAL COMMUNITIES

In this section, the authors will present three examples from online groups and virtual communities related to their research program. The first example, ProfessionalMed (a pseudonym), is an occupational-based forum for healthcare providers that has existed for over 20 years. This site provides over 175,000 medical professionals with informational and socio-emotional support on a daily basis. This site will be used as a naturalistic example of a virtual community. GradNet, the second example, is similar to ProfessionalMed but targets graduate students at one institution. The authors have created this forum and have studied its use among graduate students. GradNet is an example of a virtual community that was created in order to provide a venue through which graduate students can support one another. The third and last example, Sportsforum, is an experimental research forum that was created explicitly for the purposes of collecting data. The authors have complete control over the forum, and research participants react to their perceptions of the members' exchange of support, similarity, and other important issues. Purported members on Sportsforum offer both informational and socio-emotional support to each other. Sportsforum is an example of how researchers can experimentally examine the effects of perceived support of users from an outsider's perspective.

Example 1: ProfessionalMed

ProfessioanlMed is a virtual community that was founded in the1990s with the goal of connecting health professionals. ProfessionalMed offers a substantial amount of informational support. It provides cutting-edge medical research, first-hand accounts of medical issues in blogs, and a variety of forums in which healthcare professionals ask specific questions and provide detailed information about a topic. In our research, members have reported valuing the quality and quantity of informational support provided by ProfessionalMed a great deal. One senior medical professional, who was the only professional at her level, reported sharing organizational forms and policies that made her work easier and more efficient. Nearly all of the medical professionals reported that discussions of cutting-edge medical reports were extremely useful for their work. Even very mundane information such as specialized clothing that worked well was very helpful to the community members.

ProfessionalMed also provides members with socio-emotional support. However, as reported by our interview participants, it is not as valued as the informational support it provides. Nonetheless, our participants reported that ProfessionalMed provided unique socio-emotional support that they were unable to receive in their face-to-face lives. For example, due to the need to hide emotional responses or self-doubt while working, the healthcare professionals could not seek some informational and most socio-emotional support from their work colleagues. One participant described concerns about doing specific procedures on the job for the first time and was relieved that others shared in her anxiety and validated it as normal when starting a new job.

Further, the specialized nature of their work experience means that most of their friends and family cannot provide informational nor appropriate socio-emotional support neither. Some members had to deal with problems and issues that the general public would consider "gory." While they could not share this at the dinner table with family, they could share it on ProfessionalMed and not only find support, but dark humor to relieve tension in these events. Therefore, ProfessionalMed fills a great gap in the need for support for these employees.

Further, the authors found this research that the medical professionals perceived that the informational and socio-emotional support moved from online to offline and had positive effects on their performance at work. They learned information useful for their jobs that was not available from their contacts offline. They could complain about work situations outside of work and resolve them without damaging work relationships. ProfessionalMed is a great example of how a virtual community can positively affect organizations and employees by sharing important support among likeminded, highly-skilled, and specialized professionals.

Example 2: GradNet

GradNet is an online group for graduate students at a large Southeastern university. GradNet was developed to provide informational and socio-emotional support for roughly 4,000 masters- and doctoral-level graduate students by the Graduate School of the university. It functions as a support forum for the students and the authors' ongoing data on how participating in the group affects students' attachment to and identity with their graduate programs and the larger university community. GradNet is considered an online group because it supplements the larger offline graduate student community under the supervision of the Center for Graduate Life.

When it first started, about 100 students joined GradNet and were active participants on the site. They shared tips with each other about ways to survive graduate school. The users also posted about campus and local events with the goal of showing students where they can go to have fun and relax from the stress of graduate school. Unfortunately, the active participation of the users attracted unwanted attention and GradNet got hacked. The founders of the site were forced to shut it down for six months while making repairs from the attack. After it reopened, about 100 more students joined GradNet, but the initial excitement was gone and the participation became less active and interactive. The users on the site are currently inactive, but it is still available for the public view.

Even though it is no longer used by graduate students, it is evident from previous posts that the site provided a space through which users can seek and offer informational and socio-emotional support to each other. As examples of informational support, students posted and responded to questions about good restaurants in the area, dog sitting options, and parking issues.

Socio-emotional support was much less frequent on this site. One post that contained socio-emotional support was titled "Class Struggles." A user initiated a discussion by asking for advice on how other users handle tough courses on top of other responsibilities. Other users responded by validating the concerns of the post's initiator (socio-emotional support) and offering advice on how to get through a hard class (informational support). However, this was one of the few, if not the only thread, in which we could identify direct socio-emotional support.

Surveys were sent to GradNet users to assess their thoughts and feelings about the online group and its users. Unfortunately, less than 15 percent of users responded to the surveys. The majority of user who did respond agreed that they obtain credible and reliable information on GradNet to some degree.

Additionally, most respondents thought that GradNet was a group and a community. While it is unclear to what degree GradNet has provided socio-emotional and informational support to its users, it is safe to assume that the online group was beneficial to those who used it.

While the users of GradNet wanted and needed informational support from their peers on this online community, the success of the community depended on socio-emotional support which was not being exchanged among the group members. The disruption from the outside attack certainly stopped momentum, but GradNet's lack of socio-emotional support was a bigger factor in the hindrance of the re-start of the community. Socio-emotional support seems to add "stickiness" to the group. Further, informational support provides answers to one-time questions that everyone can benefit from (e.g., a good restaurant nearby), but socio-emotional support helps individuals (e.g., "I need help"). Observing the exchange of socio-emotional support (e.g., "that person was helped") also means that each individual member could receive specialized help too (e.g., "I could get help for my unique concern, too").

Example 3: Sportsforum

Sportsforum is an online group the authors have created in order to conduct research. The purpose of this online group is to allow users to talk about issues related to the Football team at their University. Topics in the group range from acquiring tickets to best places for tailgating before games. The users of Sportsforum are all created by the researchers, and their profiles vary based on different experimental conditions. For examples, one condition, which is hypothesized to have the highest ratings of perceived entitativity, has pictures of the actual users as their avatars and contains members' signature lines in their posts. The users in this condition also respond to each other's posts. After browsing through one of the conditions, participants in the research study are asked to answer questions about the Sportsforum users' entitativity, history, interactivity, similarity, boundaries, and other group-related constructs. The authors believe that by altering avatars, signatures lines, and the extent to which the users reply or talk about each other's posts will influence participants' perceptions of the study variables.

Support will affect how research participants feel that Sportsforum is a successful group. Building on lessons from GradNet, the authors manipulate whether the participants see just informational support (e.g., "where is a good place to tailgate before a football game") or informational and socio-emotional support (e.g., "WOW! You are going to have so much fun tailgating!!"). Preliminary results indicate that observing socio-emotional support increases participants' feelings of how successful the group is and how much they would like to participate in the Sportsforum.

BEST PRACTICES

Research studies have examined the factors that lead to a thriving online community (Kairam, Wang, & Leskovec, 2012; Lin & Lee, 2007; Plant, 2004). Based on these research findings, along with the authors' anecdotal experiences, the authors would like to suggest evidence-based best practices to encourage and foster the support provided by members of online groups and virtual communities. Some of these best practices are effective before the group or community is even created. Others pertain to the maintenance of the group members' activities.

When starting the group, populating the group with a large number of new members is essential. This can be done by choosing a central topic that is easily shareable among the target population. For example, if targeting college students, university sports can be a topic that most undergraduate students share in common. Additionally, start with a small group from potential population and enforce active sharing on a small scale, then open it up and invite new members who are eager to join in on the already-existing conversations. The new members might be more encouraged to actively participate if there are discussion boards that are hot and active. However, all members should be encouraged to develop topics from the bottom-up, meaning that they should be allowed to start new discussion boards based on what they think is important to discuss within the online group. In order to create a supportive and nurturing environment, remember to set ground rules that encompass the boundaries of which topics should and can be covered, especially if the group is open to the public eye.

While maintaining the group, in addition to encouraging bottom-up topic development, have research assistants or workers who help welcome new members and continually create new content when activity levels are low. The initial enthusiasm is hard to recreate, and therefore hiring a few people to be the constant or stable source of enthusiasm is helpful in order to maintain the community. As previously mentioned, people join online groups seeking information, but become active members due to the socio-emotional support that they find in the process. Therefore, give opportunities for members to offer informational support for one another in order to encourage them to seek and provide socio-emotional support.

FUTURE RESEARCH DIRECTIONS

As evident from the research and the three examples above, online informational and socio-emotional seem to have a positive effect on people. Indeed, the authors suggest that as ICT becomes more ingrained in society and organizations, exchanging support online will be common place and widely accepted. In addition to the recommendations for best practices above, the authors would like to offer two areas for future research: informational support process in social networking sites and socio-emotional support process in e-commerce, online dating, news sites, and other sites that were originally created for the sake of disseminating information.

Previous research has found that socio-emotional support processes take place in social networking sites such as Facebook (Frison & Eggermont, 2015; Valkenburg, Peter, & Schouten, 2006) and Twitter (Shepherd et al., 2015). However, informational support processes are under-studied within this context. More specifically, future research should examine how social networking sites enable users to offer informational support to one another, especially when the sites were not created for that purpose.

Additionally, little research has been done on socio-emotional support processes on e-commerce, online dating, news sites, and other sites. Studies can examine how key characteristics of a site foster or discourage the process of offering socio-emotional support to other users. For example, if users can deem a review on Amazon as "helpful," does that send a message to lurkers that users of Amazon are supportive of each other by denoting whether or not the reviews match the product?

CONCLUSION

In conclusion, this chapter has shed some light on the positive impacts that virtual communications can have on society. In addition to the literature review on offline and online social support, empirical findings from three research programs were offered. For example, professionals can connect with others in their field and exchange helpful advice about how to handle certain hardships related specifically to their work environment. The authors believe that online groups and virtual communities can become a source of comfort for those in need by offering informational and socio-emotional support in ways that are unique from and sometimes superior to face-to-face social support. More specifically, by enabling members to asynchronously access the support whenever they need it, online support in virtual communities can reach a wider audience than offline support which has to be experienced in-person and in real-time. Thus, online communication can positively affect real-life outcomes by improving the mental and physical health of those who need social support from their virtual networks.

REFERENCES

Amin, A., & Roberts, J. (2008). Knowing in action: Beyond communities of practice. *Research Policy*, *37*(2), 353–369. doi:10.1016/j.respol.2007.11.003

Armstrong, A., & Hagel, J. (1996). The real value of on-line communities. *Harvard Business Review*, *74*(3), 134–141.

Blanchard, A. L. (2008). Testing a model of sense of virtual community. *Computers in Human Behavior*, *24*(5), 2107–2123. doi:10.1016/j.chb.2007.10.002

Blanchard, A. L., Askay, D., & Callas, K. (2010). Sense of Community in Professional Virtual Communities. In S. D. Long (Ed.), *Communication, relationships, and practices in virtual work*. IGI Global. doi:10.4018/978-1-61520-979-8.ch009

Blanchard, A. L., & Horan, T. (1998). Virtual Communities and Social Capital. *Social Science Computer Review*, *16*(3), 293–397. doi:10.1177/089443939801600306

Carpenter, G. J., Carpenter, T. P., Kimbrel, N. A., Flynn, E. J., Pennington, M. L., Cammarata, C., & Gulliver, S. B. (2015). Social support, stress, and suicidal ideation in professional firefighters. *American Journal of Health Behavior*, *39*(2), 191–196. doi:10.5993/AJHB.39.2.5 PMID:25564831

Cobb, S. (1976). Social support as a moderator of life stress. *Psychosomatic Medicine*, *38*(5), 300–314. doi:10.1097/00006842-197609000-00003 PMID:981490

Cohen, S., & Janicki-Deverts, D. (2009). Can we improve our physical health by altering our social networks? *Perspectives on Psychological Science*, *4*(4), 375–378. doi:10.1111/j.1745-6924.2009.01141.x PMID:20161087

Cohen, S., & Wills, T. A. (1985). Stress, social support, and the buffering hypothesis. *Psychological Bulletin*, *98*(2), 310–357. doi:10.1037/0033-2909.98.2.310 PMID:3901065

Crump, S. A., Hamilton, D. L., Sherman, S. J., Lickel, B., & Thakkar, V. (2010). Group entitativity and similarity : Their differing patterns in perceptions of groups. European *Journal of Social Psychology, 1230*(December), 1212–1230.

Cullen, D. L. (1995). Psychotherapy in cyberspace. *The Clinician*, *26*(1), 6–7.

Eisenberger, R., Fasolo, P., & Davis-LaMastro, V. (1990). Perceived organizational support and employee diligence, commitment, and innovation. *The Journal of Applied Psychology*, *75*(1), 51–59. doi:10.1037/0021-9010.75.1.51

Eisenberger, R., Huntington, R., Hutchison, S., & Sowa, D. (1986). Perceived organizational support. *The Journal of Applied Psychology*, *71*(3), 500–507. doi:10.1037/0021-9010.71.3.500

Ell, K., Nishimoto, R., Mediansky, L., Mantell, J., & Hamovitch, M. (1992). Social relations, social support and survival among patients with cancer. *Journal of Psychosomatic Research*, *36*(6), 531–541. doi:10.1016/0022-3999(92)90038-4 PMID:1640391

Ellington, T. N. (2014). Bloggers, vloggers, and virtual sorority: A means of support for african american women wearing natural hair. *Journalism and Mass Communication*, *4*(9), 552–564.

Faraj, S., Jarvenpaa, S. L., & Majchrzak, A. (2011). Knowledge Collaboration in Online Communities. *Organization Science*, *22*(5), 1224–1239. doi:10.1287/orsc.1100.0614

Finfgeld-Connett, D. (2005). Clarification of social support. *Journal of Nursing Scholarship*, *37*(1), 4–9. doi:10.1111/j.1547-5069.2005.00004.x PMID:15813580

Frison, E., & Eggermont, S. (2015). The impact of daily stress on adolescents' depressed mood: The role of social support seeking through Facebook. *Computers in Human Behavior*, *44*, 315–325. doi:10.1016/j.chb.2014.11.070

Helgeson, V. S. (2003). Social support and quality of life. *Quality of Life Research: An International Journal of Quality of Life Aspects of Treatment, Care and Rehabilitation*, *12*(1), 25–31. doi:10.1023/A:1023509117524 PMID:12803308

Helgeson, V. S., & Cohen, S. (1996). Social support and adjustment to cancer: Reconciling descriptive, correlational, and intervention research. *Health Psychology*, *15*(2), 135–148. doi:10.1037/0278-6133.15.2.135 PMID:8681922

House, J. S. (1981). *Work stress and social support*. Reading, MA: Addison-Wesley.

Johnson, C. M. (2001). A survey of current research on online communities of practice. *The Internet and Higher Education*, *4*(1), 45–60. doi:10.1016/S1096-7516(01)00047-1

Kairam, S. R., Wang, D. J., & Leskovec, J. (2012, February). The life and death of online groups: Predicting group growth and longevity. In *Proceedings of the fifth ACM international conference on Web search and data mining* (pp. 673-682). ACM. doi:10.1145/2124295.2124374

Koopman, C., Hermanson, K., Diamond, S., Angell, K., & Spiegel, D. (1998). Social support, life stress, pain and emotional adjustment to advanced breast cancer. *Psycho-Oncology*, *7*(2), 101–111. doi:10.1002/(SICI)1099-1611(199803/04)7:2<101::AID-PON299>3.0.CO;2-3 PMID:9589508

Krause, N. (1986). Social support, stress, and well-being. *Journal of Gerontology*, *41*(4), 512–519. doi:10.1093/geronj/41.4.512 PMID:3722737

Lampe, C., Wash, R., Velasquez, A., & Ozkaya, E. (2010, April). Motivations to participate in online communities. In *Proceedings of the SIGCHI conference on Human factors in computing systems* (pp. 1927-1936). ACM.

Langford, C. P. H., Bowsher, J., Maloney, J. P., & Lillis, P. P. (1997). Social support: A conceptual analysis. *Journal of Advanced Nursing*, 25(1), 95–100. doi:10.1046/j.1365-2648.1997.1997025095.x PMID:9004016

LaRose, R., Eastin, M. S., & Gregg, J. (2001). Reformulating the Internet paradox: Social cognitive explanations of Internet use and depression. *Journal of Online Behavior*, 1(2). Retrieved from http://d3ds4oy7g1wrqq.cloudfront.net/sinergiaymente/myfiles/Depression-Journal.htm

Lee, E., & Hahn, K. (2015). Tone of writing on fashion retail websites, social support, e-shopping satisfaction, and category knowledge. *Clothing & Textiles Research Journal*, 33(2), 143–159. doi:10.1177/0887302X15568915

Lee, K. T., Noh, M. J., & Koo, D. M. (2013). Lonely people are no longer lonely on social networking sites: The mediating role of self-disclosure and social support. *Cyberpsychology, Behavior, and Social Networking*, 16(6), 413–418. doi:10.1089/cyber.2012.0553 PMID:23621716

Lenhart, A., Madden, M., Smith, A., Purcell, K., Zickuhr, K., & Rainie, L. (2011). *Teens, kindness and cruelty on social network sites*. Retrieved April 5, 2015, from http://www.pewinternet.org/2011/11/09/teens-kindness-and-cruelty-on-social-network-sites/

Leung, L. (2006). Stressful life events, motives for Internet use, and social support among digital kids. *Cyberpsychology & Behavior*, 10(2), 204–214. doi:10.1089/cpb.2006.9967 PMID:17474837

Lin, H. F., & Lee, G. G. (2006). Determinants of success for online communities: An empirical study. *Behaviour & Information Technology*, 25(6), 479–488. doi:10.1080/01449290500330422

Ling, K., Beenen, G., Ludford, P., Wang, X., Chang, K., Li, X., … Kraut, R. (2005). Using social psychology to motivate contributions to online communities. *Journal of Computer-Mediated Communication*, 10(4).

Ma, M., & Agarwal, R. (2007). Through a glass darkly: Information technology design, identity verification, and knowledge contribution in online communities. *Information Systems Research*, 18(1), 42–67. doi:10.1287/isre.1070.0113

Melrose, K. L., Brown, G. D., & Wood, A. M. (2015). When is received social support related to perceived support and well-being? When it is needed. *Personality and Individual Differences*, 77, 97–105. doi:10.1016/j.paid.2014.12.047

Mesch, G. S. (2006). Online communities. Handbook of Community Movements and Local Organizations, 227.

Panzarasa, P., Opsahl, T., & Carley, K. M. (2009). Patterns and dynamics of users' behavior and interaction: Network analysis of an online community. *Journal of the American Society for Information Science and Technology*, 60(5), 911–932. doi:10.1002/asi.21015

Park, N. (2012). Social side of rural internet use: Online communication, social support, and community satisfaction in a rural area. *International Telecommunications Policy Review, 19*(1).

Peirce, R. S., Frone, M. R., Russell, M., & Cooper, M. L. (1996). Financial stress, social support, and alcohol involvement: A longitudinal test of the buffering hypothesis in a general population survey. *Health Psychology, 15*(1), 38–47. doi:10.1037/0278-6133.15.1.38 PMID:8788539

Plant, R. (2004). Online communities. *Technology in Society, 26*(1), 51–65. doi:10.1016/j.techsoc.2003.10.005

Preece, J., & Maloney-Krichmar, D. (2003). Online communities: Focusing on sociability and usability. In J. Jacko & A. Sears (Eds.), Handbook of Human-Computer Interaction (pp. 596-620). Academic Press.

Ren, Y., Harper, F. M., Drenner, S., Terveen, L., Kiesler, S. B., & Kraut, R. E. (2012). Building Member Attachment in Online Communities : Applying Theories of Group Identity and Interpersonal Bonds. *Management Information Systems Quarterly, 36*(3), 841–864.

Ren, Y., Kraut, R. E., & Kiesler, S. B. (2007). Applying common identity and bond theory to the design of online communities. *Organization Studies, 28*(3), 379–410.

Rheingold, H. (1993). *The Virtual Community: Homesteading on the Electronic Frontier.* Addison Wesley.

Rutchick, A. M., Hamilton, D. L., & Sack, J. D. (2008). Antecedents of entitativity in categorically and dynamically construed groups. *European Journal of Social Psychology, 921*(May), 905–921.

Shepherd, A., Sanders, C., Doyle, M., & Shaw, J. (2015). Using social media for support and feedback by mental health service users: Thematic analysis of a twitter conversation. *BMC Psychiatry, 15*(1), 29. doi:10.1186/s12888-015-0408-y PMID:25881089

Shirai, Y., Silverberg Koerner, S., & Baete Kenyon, D. Y. (2009). Reaping caregiver feelings of gain: The roles of socio-emotional support and mastery. *Aging & Mental Health, 13*(1), 106–117. doi:10.1080/13607860802591054 PMID:19197696

Stroebe, W., & Stroebe, M. (1996). *The social psychology of social support.* Academic Press.

Uchino, B. N., Cacioppo, J. T., & Kiecolt-Glaser, J. K. (1996). The relationship between social support and physiological processes: A review with emphasis on underlying mechanisms and implications for health. *Psychological Bulletin, 119*(3), 488–531. doi:10.1037/0033-2909.119.3.488 PMID:8668748

Valkenburg, P. M., Peter, J., & Schouten, A. P. (2006). Friend networking sites and their relationship to adolescents' well-being and social self-esteem. *Cyberpsychology & Behavior, 9*(5), 584–590. doi:10.1089/cpb.2006.9.584 PMID:17034326

Verdugo, M. A., Schalock, R. L., Keith, K. D., & Stancliffe, R. J. (2005). Quality of life and its measurement: Important principles and guidelines. *Journal of Intellectual Disability Research, 49*(10), 707–717. doi:10.1111/j.1365-2788.2005.00739.x PMID:16162115

Walen, H. R., & Lachman, M. E. (2000). Social support and strain from partner, family, and friends: Costs and benefits for men and women in adulthood. *Journal of Social and Personal Relationships, 17*(1), 5–30. doi:10.1177/0265407500171001

Walther, J. B., & Bunz, U. (2005). The rules of virtual groups: Trust, liking, and performance in computer-mediated communication. *Journal of Communication*, *55*(4), 828–846. doi:10.1111/j.1460-2466.2005.tb03025.x

Weiser, E. B. (2001). The functions of Internet use and their social and psychological consequences. *Cyberpsychology & Behavior*, *4*(6), 723–743. doi:10.1089/109493101753376678 PMID:11800180

Welbourne, J. L., Blanchard, A. L., & Wadsworth, M. B. (2013). Motivations in virtual health communities and their relationship to community, connectedness and stress. *Computers in Human Behavior*, *29*(1), 129–139. doi:10.1016/j.chb.2012.07.024

Wellman, B., & Gulia, M. (1997). Net Surfers don't ride alone: Virtual communities as communities. In P. Kollock & M. Smith (Eds.), *Communities in Cyberspace*. Routledge.

Williams, M. (2007). Avatar watching: Participant observation in graphical online environments. *Qualitative Research*, *7*(1), 5–24. doi:10.1177/1468794107071408

Zimmer, B., & Alexander, G. (1996). The Rogerian Interface: For Open, Warm Empathy in Computer-mediated Collaborative Learning. *Innovations in Education and Training International*, *33*(1), 13–21. doi:10.1080/1355800960330103

KEY TERMS AND DEFINITIONS

Information and Communication Technologies (ICT): A term used to describe any type of device that enables the transfer of information between a sender and a receiver.

Informational Support: The process by which individuals share ideas or offer suggestions related to specific needs or problems.

Online Groups: A set of individuals who are connected through a shared belonging to an online site or forum.

Online Social Support: The process by which people comfort and uplift others in need via information and communication technologies.

Professional Virtual Communities: An online forum or site in which individuals can find information pertaining to their specific occupation.

Sense of Community: The extent to which a group feels like a community.

Socio-Emotional Support: The process by which people offer comforting words and gestures to those who are going through physical, mental, or emotional hardships.

Supportive Online Communities: Online communities that offer social support for users.

Virtual Communities: Online entities that exist on their own in which members generally focus on their attachment to and membership with the virtual community.

Chapter 11
Liquid Communication in Mobile Devices:
Affordances and Risks

Ana Serrano Tellería
Beira Interior University, Portugal

ABSTRACT

Mobile communication and devices have raised a series of challenges concerning the delimitation of public and private, intimate and personal spheres. Specifically, and because of its close connection to the nervous system and emotions, these devices allow a wide variety of affordances while, and in accordance to the broad scope of previous dimensions, a series of worrying risks – because of the same relationship and interdependence between users' rational and sensorial sides. Thus, an international state of the art review will be discussed and the results and conclusions of the 'Public and Private in Mobile Communications' European FEDER will be offered. A range of quantitative and qualitative methodologies were applied: surveys about general use and habits, personal data and images; focus groups; interviews in person and by telephone; content analysis with a special focus on social media and an observation ethnography and digital ethnography.

INTRODUCTION

Within the scope of the European FEDER project 'Public and Private in Mobile Communications' developed at LabCom.IFP at Beira Interior University (April 2013-15, Portugal), a range of both quantitative and qualitative methodologies have been applied. They were designed to, on the one hand, discover user attitudes, behaviors and performances and, on the other, delimit users' awareness and knowledge about this ecosystem. Specific research questions were focused on the ever-changing delimitations of the public and private spheres.

Therefore, the purpose of this chapter is to reflect on the international state of the art review as well as on the results obtained from the project. Core issues faced concerning the appropriateness of the methodology were the hypothesis posited on whether linear perspectives would be suitable to the perceived

DOI: 10.4018/978-1-4666-9899-4.ch011

non-linear modus operandi in the virtual media ecology. Apart from this reflection on the process itself, the intention is to offer a step forward in Portuguese research due to the fact that few initiatives have been carried out in this country on this issue.

This chapter will begin with the different approaches and concepts that framed and continue to attempt to explain the dichotomies between the public and private spheres in virtual communication. Bearing in mind that an international perspective agreement may be established, identifying some common user patterns, those shared conclusions will be addressed accordingly. Moreover, the specific features concerning Portuguese population and its specific technological appropriation will also be described. At the end of the chapter, the conclusions obtained will be given and compared with the overall tendencies identified.

BACKGROUND

Mobile devices and their media environment have produced a series of fluid parameters to configure online virtual communication, mainly altering space and time dimensions. In this sense, the research fields involved have indicated a variety of concepts that underline a main area of tension to deal with: the state of *perpetual contact* (Katz & Aakhus, 2002) and the *liquid environment* (Serrano Tellería & Oliveira, 2015).

From the creation of the profile and the digital identity to the emergence and maintenance of different kinds of networks off/online consciously and unconsciously, academics have delved into aspects and/ or dimensions of *identity*, *big data*, *social media*, *digital literacy* and *interface design* that reflect core problematics about how we deal with and understand this ecosystem.

These types of technologies were previously described as "extensions of the nervous system" by Vilém Flusser (1988) when he defined them as a revolution. Paraphrasing him (1990), the human being is seen here as a media user not just as someone who 'works' with information (*Homo Faber*), but one who 'plays' with information (*Homo Ludens*).

Media is everywhere and we live immersed "in" it (Deuze, 2012). Thus, it can be seen how interface design works to dilute the boundaries between human and machines (HCI), incorporating these mobile devices into our daily life by fulfilling our motivations and, at the same time, generating interactions to produce them (Serrano Tellería, 2015c).

Wonder, Love, Hate, Desire, Joy, and Sadness: The six primary passions of the soul described by Descartes (1649) are increasingly incorporated into mobile interface design and the construction of messages, altering the way our brain, and specifically our memory, deals with general content and personal data (Serrano Tellería, 2015c).

The connection between emotions and health has already been proved, with our brain as the technology that links them (MIT). Also, the relationship between memories and place has also been recently demonstrated – the process of episodic memory formation (Meyer, 2014). Furthermore, we have wearable technologies and *media life*, offering constant motivations for our desires and feelings. Therefore, as much as they may fulfill them, we can incorporate them too into our routine. Thus, emotion and motivation seem to be key elements and technologies must work like our brain to establish the proper connection between users and interfaces (Serrano Tellería, 2015c).

At the start (Fidalgo, Serrano, Carvalheiro *et al.*, 2013) of this research within the European FEDER project 'Public and Private in Mobile Communications' (LabCom.IFP, Beira Interior University, April 2013-2015), a core definition was identified: "It was I-alone that was reachable wherever I was: at a house, hotel, office, freeway or mail. Place did not matter, person did. The person has become the portal" (Wellman, 2001). Then, it was further investigated and developed as the research process advanced.

In the creation of a common world, reality is not guaranteed by the "common nature" of men, but because all are interested in the same subject (Arendt, 1997). The perspective of 'Human Being as a Communication Portal' (Fidalgo, Serrano, Carvalheiro *et al.*, 2013), in which the human condition is defined by attitude and ways of dealing with the human ecosystem (see for example Bateson 1979, 1991), has been a constant presence. This notion of relationship and interdependence had been, in fact, addressed by authors such as Elias (1980, pp.134): "The image of man in relationships has to be before the people in the plural. Obviously, we have to start with the image of a crowd of people, each one establishing an open and interdependent process."

Thus, a definition, hypothesis and questions were proposed, which shall be presented here. 'The Human Being as a Communication Portal' is defined at every moment by their attitude and the way of dealing with the surrounding environment, the public and private spheres and their participation in the common space. In altered dimensional coordinates of time and space, the Human Being becomes the manager of these spheres. The same action can be considered to be public or private in the same physical space depending on the specific situation. Heidegger's "dasein", in Castells' "space of flows" and "timeless time", leads to a relationship of existing by producing an appropriation of the space that flows and in a time constrained by Aakhus and Katz's *perpetual contact* (Fidalgo, Serrano, Carvalheiro *et al.*, 2013).

The main research questions were: Does the amplification of human abilities, which are diluted in space-time dimensions, and a continuous flow of data alter the implementation of part of the identity in possible online profiles? Are we aware of these changes and are they voluntary? How can we control technology that allows us to flow in this way?

Would new coordinates and dimensions in the definition of communication emerge? Would aspects of its analysis and the modes and models of communication also emerge? Is it possible to achieve a deep level of interaction with people we never meet?

Will the balance between authenticity and anonymity, privacy and functionality delimit the public and private spheres? Or are we dealing with a struggle between obscurity and hypervisibility that enables us to reach the spotlight of attention? What will the scope of the common space be?

In this sense, and taking into account the importance of time priority as a variable, an analysis of the concepts of space appropriation, profile and willfulness are proposed from a perspective that places the Human Being at the center, that is, as a communication portal (Fidalgo, Serrano, Carvalheiro *et al.*, 2013).

To highlight main concepts identified at that first stage of the research process and in the following steps up to its conclusion, eight lines of research are particularly relevant.

The first one is focused on *identity*: *cellular and nomadic intimacy* (Fortunati, 2002), the *modulations of intimacy* (Lasén, 2015*)* and the *fluidity of identity* (Stald, 2008) are key configurations. Then, social media have mostly defined a *network and social privatism* (Campbell, 2015) describing *core, diverse, weak and new ties*. Following *Big Data* and *Dataism* (van Dick, 2014), awareness and critiques of the *quantified self* (Walker Rettberg, 2014) and the *algorithmic self* (Pasquale, 2015) are outlined.

On the ethnography of social media developers in Silicon Valley, Marwick's argument and main critique (2013) is based on the fact that people who are not effective neoliberal subjects (entrepreneurs) are filtered out of these devices and platforms. Fuchs (2014) has also critiqued its neoliberalism but also offers a counterpart description of its potential to generate a new type of communism.

On these cognitive processes, *continuous partial attention* (Stone, 2002-...) is melted into *multitasking* and *multiplexing* practice (Starner, 2011), concerning technological appropriation. A *tutored self* was previously identified (Geser and Fidalgo in Fidalgo, Serrano, Carvalheiro *et al.,* 2013) when referring to the state of *perpetual contact* (Katz & Aakhus; 2002) and the users' emancipation from the off/online virtual crowd. *The tethered self* was also linked to the state of *always on* (Turkle, 2008, 2011) in which *the fear of missing out* appeared (Turkle, 2011; Rosen, 2013). Mobile communication and devices may improve several dimensions of freedom and increase our choices in life, while invading personal privacy and causing emotional, political and technological distress (Katz, 2008).

Therefore, *invisible audiences* (Rheingold, 2012; Boyd, 2014) play a determining role as the lack of awareness of its existence is one of the results of the *architecture of intimacy* (Turkle, 2011) or *disclosure* (Marichal, 2012) or *exposure* (Serrano Tellería, 2014) designed for social media (*The Desire for More*, Facebook; Grosser, 2014) and for the mobile user interface (Serrano Tellería, 2014).

Here, *mediated memories, normative discursive strategies* (Van Dijck, 2007), *terministic screens* (Markham, 2013), *normative behaviour* (LinkedIn & Facebook: Van Dijck, 2013) in which social media profiles are not a reflection of one's identity or neutral stages of self-performance, nor are they a means of self-expression (Horning, 2014); they are instead the very tools for shaping identities (Van Dijck, 2013) through *the filtered reality, the filtered world* (Walker Rettberg, 2014).

The *social self* – Marcel Proust – was remembered to describe how influential ICTs are becoming in shaping our personal identities. Never before in the history of humanity have so many people monitored, recorded, and reported so many details about themselves to such a large audience. The impact of all these micro-narratives on everyone and on all subjects is also changing our social selves and hence how we see ourselves, representing an immense, externalized stream of consciousness (Floridi, 2014).

The freedom to construct our personal identities online is no longer the freedom of anonymity; instead, it is the freedom associated with self-determination and autonomy insofar as users can manage it, as well as the uncontrolled searching of huge amounts of data. The online experience is a bit like Proust's account-book, but with us as co-authors (Floridi, 2014; Fidalgo, Serrano, Carvalheiro *et al.,* 2013; Serrano Tellería & Oliveira, 2015). "Privacy, precisely because it ensures we're never fully known to others or to ourselves, provides a shelter for imaginative freedom, curiosity and self-reflection. So to defend the private self is to defend the very possibility of creative and meaningful life" (Preston, 2014).

Thus, the dimensions of digital literacy highlighted were: attention; the capability of detecting trash; participation; collaboration and the clever use of networks. Also, the properties of any social network have been identified as: persistence, replicability, scalability and the ability to be searched, including the importance of being aware of what we share and with whom we share it (to the extent that behind networks there are invisible and potential audiences that lie, unsuspected, between the public and the private) (Rheingold, 2012; Boyd, 2014; who also alerted about *digital naïves*, youths). These are joined by the relevance of time and memory in social media, in which accessibility, durability, comprehensiveness, inequality and evolution are the main features to bear in mind (Brake, 2014), and the natural and inner disposition of humans to share (Hermida, 2014).

Finally, we find the proper characteristics of digital media: constant negotiation of rules in which norms and values are not clear; a decentralized model with a multimedia, flexible format, constantly changing, being updated, corrected and being revised; nonlinear content that is indifferent to distance; diverse resource sources with fragmented audiences whose feedback is extremely important (Kawamoto, 2003). It is further characterized by *spreadability* and the tension between *mass* and *collaborative culture* within itself (Jenkins, Ford & Green, 2013).

Those features are intertwined with Bauman's metaphor of modern life, so liquid life: fluidity, transience, reticula and the dissolution of defined borders and boundaries (Bauman, 2005; Aguado, Feijóo

& Martínez, 2013; Serrano Tellería & Oliveira, 2015). This, in a society where a "curious reversal" has redefined the private sphere characterized by the right to confidentiality as a sphere that has become prey to the right to publicity (Bauman, 2008).

Beyond the correlation between the impact of digital technology and digital features of the liquid society (which refers to reflections on the acceleration, dislocation, consumption and role of identity), the mobile medium particularly fits the fluidization parameters of the technological, institutional and cultural dimensions of the medium previously described by McQuail, 2006 (Aguado, Feijóo & Martínez, 2013; Serrano Tellería & Oliveira, 2015).

The Fluidity of Communication and Emotions: Between Liquid and Constellations of Spheres

The preliminary conclusions from the international perspective and our project (Serrano Tellería, 2015b,c): sociability, coordination and maintenance thereof as the most notable activities; the different perceptions about what *privacy* is; strong circumstantial pattern behavior, constant negotiation of rules, lack of rationality in some attitudes and performances, awareness of some risks but not delving into them properly, lack of awareness about invisible audiences and awareness about the digital footprint and 'Dataism'; users seemed to deal not 'with' liquid spheres, but 'in' a liquid environment and media ecology, configuring a *constellation of spheres* delimited by their *autonomy* (rather than by their *mobility*) and framed by *perpetual contact* and *timeless time*. It ought to be highlighted that until another definition of 'online time' emerges, the scope of this research adheres to it, although inconsistency may be found as a defined time is required to form a sphere and therefore to configure the constellations

The reason to propose the *constellations of spheres* concept rather than the *liquid spheres* concept to describe how users manage their *public and private spheres* and the range of dimensions considered (e.g. public and semi-public ones) is based on the core consideration that users still have and demonstrate a clear notion about what *privacy* is. Despite the different user concepts and perceptions found, what is revealed suggests that, depending on specific situations and media contexts, users constantly configure and reconfigure their spheres from an individual perspective and from a common scope perspective. The liquidity observed is rather linked to the inner environment (referring to the technological aspects), media ecology and environment (meaning society) that incentivize some interrelationships or dependency between the formation and elimination of the same spheres within the overall constellation(s). Each user may have his/her own different constellation(s) of spheres, some of which are shared with (a) user(s), other(s) with other(s) and so on. It may also be applied to *intimacy* and *personal* spheres.

Therefore, 'Human Being as a Communication Portal' handles the management of the public and private, intimate and personal spheres through a mobile device that amplifies the possibilities in a liquid environment, media ecology and environment. Challenges seem focus on the scope of the actions that may be recorded for ever and that may escape user control. Thus, the grades of *autonomy* and *authenticity* seem to also play a key role in a device closely linked to user emotions.

Focusing on an analysis of the technological environment of mobile devices – main operating systems, applications and platforms employed by users and their privacy policies and the terms and conditions – the notable conclusions found were: a lack of user awareness about immediate risks, a lack of rationality of users when providing personal data (e.g. the potential hazards of sharing, from concrete risks to more esoteric risks like surveillance, were too remote to influence user decisions, especially when compared with the immediate and tangible benefits of that same sharing process); the relevance of temporal priority in literacy as well as the limitations of the impact of users' knowledge on their actions (experiences intimately related to memory); the *liquid spheres* from a technical perspective and from the perspective of users' behavior. All this leads to a worrying environment if we also bear in mind that privacy policies and terms and conditions have long been described as ambiguous and confusing. Moreover, the relevance of language in the cognition process must be notable (Serrano Tellería & Oliveira; 2015).

Therefore, users manage a constant negotiation of circumstances based on the evaluation of each scenario framed by ambiguity and immediacy, which also determine reflection (the time required to analyze) and perception of the risk involved in each action. Moreover, the possibility of receiving stimuli of all types constantly influences how priority levels are established and how users' privacy is protected in the different layers and stages, according to their possibilities (Serrano Tellería & Oliveira; 2015).

PUBLIC AND PRIVATE IN MOBILE COMMUNIACATIONS

Methodology

Now that the state of the art both in the national and international scope (with awareness of the cultural differences) has been outlined, the results obtained in the 'P&P' project (Serrano Tellería, 2015d; Serrano Tellería, 2015e, Serrano Tellería, Branco, 2015; Serrano Tellería, Pereira, 2015; Serrano Tellería, Portovedo, Albuquerque, 2015) will be given. A broad view about general uses and habits will be introduced mainly using the quantitative approach offered by surveys (three online and about general users and perceptions, personal data and images).

Then, the variety of user actions, behaviors, knowledge, perceptions and performances will be discussed by analyzing the qualitative approach through focus groups as well as interviews in person and by phone. Content analysis has been accomplished by comparing the privacy terms and conditions of the mobile applications and platforms most employed by users. Another one was focused on user debates and image sharing through Twitter, Reddit and Instagram. The results will follow.

Both digital ethnography and observation ethnography were carried out as well. The former was mostly focused on describing the different strategies developed among the members of a Facebook group (carpooling), to which the researcher belonged, concerning types of conversations, levels of privacy, selection of contacts, etc. Meanwhile, the latter was focused on user actions, behaviors, and performances with mobile devices in an open public space, the main shopping center in the city.

The methodologies mentioned were complemented by a hybrid and experimental method developed during a workshop with BA students in Communication. It consisted of writing an essay at the end of the workshop, preceded by an enquiry using open questions. It was based on the consideration of writing as a suitable procedure to discover the participants' internalization and understanding of their cognitive and behavioral processes. The main results of all these qualitative methodologies will be further exposed.

In the first stage of this research (Fidalgo, Serrano Tellería, Carvalheiro *et al.*, 2013), the concept of *technology of intimacy* (Bennett, 2011; Carnegie, 2002; Boyce & Hancock, 2012) was followed to divide the state of the art review into different dimensions: *internal perspective, external extension, interpersonal interactions* and *societal reflection*. However, liquidity was perceived as covering different concepts, and conclusions may be included in the various dimensions, which were interrelated.

In the second stage, this liquidity was reinforced by an analysis of the technological environment and the societal environment as well as by the preliminary results and conclusions of the 'P&P' project.

Thus, other dimensions were proposed to better suit the dichotomy between the *liquid spheres* and the *constellations of spheres* hypothesis: overall users' habits and privacy, managing accounts and privacy, and managing media and privacy. This was strengthened in this last stage and the results will be displayed accordingly.

Overall Users' Habits and Privacy

Users worldwide showed an awareness of *Big Data* and were consequently concerned with personal information and Internet safety; however, most of them lacked the proper attitudes and knowledge to manage their accounts in this ever-changing, and hence challenging, online mobile ecosystem (Serrano Tellería, 2015b). As for the users' perceptions and understanding of *privacy*, the results are in line with those from Pew Research (Raine, Kiesler, & Madden, 2013; Madden, 2014). A constellation of concepts has emerged among users.

Despite differences between countries due to technological development and market implementation, which in most cases seem to be in accordance with the users' habits and mobile incorporation into their daily lives, some overall tendencies have been identified, such as the overall increase in its use.

Users recognized some of the existing and potential risks of surfing the web, but there was nonetheless a gap between their ideas and their final actions. In this respect, it was striking to discover that half of these users allowed their personal information to be used in order to access different kinds of services for free, even if they acknowledged the information they shared was personal. Also surprising was the fact that half of Internet users had concerns about apps' terms and conditions and data policies, which were difficult to understand properly, but, at the same time, they admitted to not reading them. In the specific case of our project, the results showed that half the users agreed to install an app firstly because others had done it before, and secondly because they trusted the companies or simply did not read the T&Cs or data policies. Clearer, user-centered policies and terms and conditions should therefore be developed.

According to the differences between countries regarding mobile appropriation-uses and performances, from the results of our project, basic functions like making calls and sending/receiving messages were still the main functions, while surfing the web was for secondary purposes within the Portuguese population. Other world tendencies showed that most mobile uses were "non-voice activities". However, the Portuguese exceed the European average in terms of accessing and using SNS. Overall and worldwide, there was also a manifest tendency toward the increased use of SNS, in which young people played a leading role. Internet users shared a concern about who had access to their content and the related lack of control.

In the 'P&P' project, they have been shown to be unaware about potential invisible audiences to be dealt with and revealed a possible misunderstanding of the complexity and subjective interpretations of *Big Data* and *Dataism*. They took preliminary steps to avoid data synchronization between accounts and contacts but mixed up the concepts of profile and digital identity, as described from a technological perspective. In addition, most users were not fully aware of the digital paths and footprints they made.

Delving into concrete data results from our project and about Portuguese population, based on an exploratory survey (ES), users mainly 'make calls' and 'send and receive text messages', and surf the Web ('visiting sites, browsing the Internet, searching for information' and also 'visiting social networking sites') several times a day. Based on interviews by telephone (IT); smartphones were used every day or almost every day: to make voice calls, to send and receive text messages, for entertainment (games, listening to music, watching videos), to look up information, to use social networks and to take photos/

make videos. Less frequently, smartphones were used to: send and receive emails, use location services, and for downloads.

Half could live without mobile phones, 32% acknowledged that they would miss the devices and 18% considered that they did not have such a powerful role in their lives. Most female adolescents from the focus group (FG) stated that "we cannot live without them", and not "having access to" smartphones was their greatest concern, rather than worrying much about losing the content/data on it. They explained that they trusted codes, companies, etc. On the other side, older users demonstrated a concern about losing their phones, mainly regarding codes (their children's homes, files, ID number, etc.) stored on the mobile devices.

Mobile phones were an integral part of the lives of Portuguese users (IT): it was rare for them to "turn off the phone" – 72% never did – they "sleep with the phone next to the bed" – 46% did so every day – and are "dependent" on the mobile phone, which made 42% of respondents check if they had messages, alerts, or missed calls every day even when it was not ringing or vibrating. These feelings were in line with those identified as a worldwide trend (Mashable, 2014; Serrano Tellería, 2015b).

It is widely thought that mobile phones benefits users' lives. The three strongest points were: being in touch with the people you "care about", enabling people to "manage everyday tasks" and helping to "participate and share collective issues". Telephone conversations were the preferred contact method (IT). However, while in the "public contact" this was almost unanimous, in "private contact" some people preferred to speak personally.

Mobile phone use was deemed to be strongly circumstantial, since there were no general rules stipulated by the actors depending on different situations – different contexts elicited different behaviors. They highly valued the potential of mobile phones in general for sociability, work and, in the specific case of older people, for security – an older person related how his mobile phone had helped him when he fell down in an elevator. At the same time, however, they criticized how these devices, apps and platforms favored the mixing of the public and private, intimate and personal spheres, for example, receiving calls and emails out of the working timetable (FG). Previously, sociability, coordination and the maintenance thereof (exploratory focus group – EFG) stood out the most in the case of mobile communication while issues related to personal and working life were also considered to be very important, in some cases essential.

They recognized (FG) "anxiety" when "having to be always available". Adolescents showed a preference to use SMS rather than calling when parents were around – e.g. common rooms at home and even in their rooms alone. Meanwhile, parents said that their children "spent hours talking" and recognized that they became concerned when they did not answer the phone. Retired people specifically criticized the "abusive" use of mobile devices and online communication by young people.

Participants tended to consider that data was always private, but in some cases (images) this did not stop them sharing/publishing it (EFG). There was great similarity between motivations and uses (content analysis, workshop with 44 BA students in Communication – CA), with only one respondent mentioning the privacy settings. Thirty-four considered that private life was at risk, only one said "no" and the rest explained that it would depend on their attitude: the value of a person's responsibility and willingness to decide was thought to be the determining feature. Worries about what could be published by others without their consent were also highlighted. Hence, there is a relationship between losing privacy and social media and awareness that everything published ceases to be private.

The issue of privacy appeared in terms of content/data and interaction contexts (FG). Moreover, the risks were not so evident because they continued to act as if they had privacy. Reluctance to speak in public near people they did not know, to constrain sociability or to interrupt mobile phone conversations and the strategy to minimize nuisance risks (silent mode/vibration) were pointed out as well. The main strategies employed were: vibration, mute, time off from the group to politely answer a call, not providing much information on social networks and filtering/selecting by closed circles or groups the contacts with which to share content, preventing the exposure of children's faces and habits/routines that could make it possible to draw a profile of the child, not enabling the location function on sites by limiting the GPS action and avoiding identification. Among adult graduates, refusing identification may be motivated by the justifiable and practical aspects of being exposed to their working group and, for example, being the target of comments, if they are in a position deemed inappropriate.

They believed that privacy depended on the ability to control the use made of the equipment, the content saved on their mobile devices and how it is shared on the Internet, especially on social networks (in-person interviews, I). They talked about the potential of smartphones as a means of intruding into private life, including the existence of some features that can record private situations, such as location – e.g. a company application that was 'recommended' to its workers that, apart from its main function, reveals where the person is. However, they seemed aware that if they have some control over smartphone applications, they can safeguard themselves. They also mentioned that there was a commitment to privacy. In this way, the people interviewed "let us know" that they employed safeguard strategies. They "confided in us" what was shared and how to control who had access to this information. Thus, it can be concluded that with knowledge of the tools available on the equipment and social networks, such as the privacy settings, some confidence is provided to users. Users revealed that they "feel secure" when those types of 'settings' were available to them and that by using them, they felt that their privacy was safe.

Mobile phone users seemed to have different behaviors receiving or making calls when among strangers, "feeling at ease" when receiving calls, but "looking away" when they made calls. Among the various locations/times considered to assess the degree of discomfort when receiving phone calls or making other uses of the mobile phone, two groups can be observed: (a) a group of places/occasions where it causes (some) discomfort, encompassing 'religious spaces', 'mealtimes', 'waiting rooms of hospitals and institutions' and 'the workplace'; (b) a group of places/occasions where it does not cause (particular) discomfort, encompassing 'restaurants, bars or cafes, etc.', 'social events', 'being at home' with other people or a group of friends. It should be noted that for all locations/times, receiving a phone call was more annoying than any other use given to their mobile phone (IT). Older people (FG) specifically referred to "talking loudly" in public spaces as impolite behavior.

Exposure of privacy through mobile phone conversations in public was not such an important feature. No one felt inhibited to answer a call or talk on the phone, but often resorted to 'background' privacy protection strategies, keeping voice volume low, which made the speech almost incomprehensible to the audience, and body strategies, like putting a hand in front of the mouth to stop anyone realizing what is being said (I and Ethnography-Observation, E-O).

Specifically in in-person interviews (I), this device was a means of communication associated with the public space as an extension of a landline phone, or going beyond the domestic sphere. Mobile phones/smartphones were referred to as the favored means of solving some domestic issues and to supervise/monitor children.

When handling mobile phones, some were alone and turned to the smartphone to mark their private space; others were in small groups (2 or 3 people) actively handling their devices and often communicating with little eye contact. There were those in larger groups (normally younger people) who saw the machine as a means of interaction, used to share content or conversations about what they were doing or do on the device – an almost collective use of the device. The handling of smartphones in public was presented primarily as a strategy for defining space or more private time. It was recurrent in use by younger people, aged between 15 and 35. However, it must be noted that when alone or in smaller groups, usage essentially involved exchanging messages, unlike what happens in larger groups where users favored accessing social networks and sometimes shared some content together or spoke openly about the subject (E-O).

The main theme (thematic analysis) among adolescents (AFG) was *privacy in the digital space*. Owing to its complexity, this included several subtopics: (weak) *privacy control strategies*; *actor's ability to choose*; *negotiation of actors as to what is public and what is private*; *invasion of privacy*; *violation of privacy*; *alienation of control* and *surveillance*. From the views expressed by participants, there seemed to be a false sense of control over their privacy. They revealed the danger of social networks, including some serious situations that result in violations of privacy, which depend largely on the choices made by the subjects. This meant that they could be classified as *digitally naïve*, as previously stated by Boyd (2014). They also showed a lack of awareness about invisible or imagined audiences and about the characteristics and features of social media.

Managing Accounts and Privacy

There was a wide range of definitions for *profile* (CA). In connection with the different accounts on digital services and/or social media, Hotmail was considered to be and not to be a *profile*: "Account, personal page, platform, image, portrait, space, location, a description of oneself, a description of us, an identification, a method, a way to quickly systematize basic information, place where I expose moments and events of my life". Most configurations of *profiles* were presented as voluntary and without risks and only one answer showed awareness of their commercial purposes. They included the results of their actions with the 'profile' as a part of it and did not specifically mention the digital footprint. Participants had between one and fifteen *profiles*, with an average of four profiles. Furthermore, there was a considerable variation in time and perceptions about the time spent on construction and maintenance: eleven chose the definition "short amount" and one emphasized "the required time". The ratings ranged from 15 minutes to 3 or 4 hours per day. It seemed that daily publications were not taken into account. All students used a real photograph of themselves on their *profiles*, stressing the importance of remaining visible and recognizable to their friends in order to achieve proper interaction with them.

Fifty-five percent (ES) did not allow apps to access their contacts or information and 57.7% (S) did not synchronize data with apps; 41.3% did so, and a mere 1% chose "do not know / no answer". Twenty-six synchronized their accounts (CA), nine did not answer, four specified the connection to a Hotmail account, which is required, but only one was aware of it and actually gave an explanation. Six said it was between Facebook and Instagram, and one specifically referred to "instant uploads". Among these answers, a couple responded with a general "yes" and another couple "no", four reported synchronizing all their accounts, two "most of them", three "some", one did so "rarely" and one responded "not necessarily".

One of the curious cases of using networks was reported during an AFG, regarding Facebook. The number of friends he had at the time was 130, in contrast with his peers, whose friend lists ranged between 300 and 1000. It was his third account, and he wanted to make a more refined selection based on what most interested him and what he wanted to see happen on his wall and was interested in following. He intended to dispense with the so-called "wall plague", that is, discard the things that "clogged" up his wall with things he did not want to see, such as "belly[ies] out" or " showing off", because "the people I'm friends with have something in common with me and have things I am interested in."

The selection of people they wanted to share information /content with, and before that, the reflection/ decision on what they wanted to/should publish, and allowing or refusing identification were aspects close to the ability to assume responsibilities (FG). As for selection, there were two management methods: monitoring the acceptance of friend requests and restricting the circle of people who were allowed to view the profile, through, for example, limiting friends of friends to friends, asking if they want to be photographed or not; and at a later stage, if they see any problem in publishing/sharing image on platforms such as social networking.

According to respondents (I), they resorted to strategies like: only sharing with some circles of friends or family; filtering when some publications appeared that they did not want to all people to see, including some minors; asking for notifications before accepting identification in photos; just putting up photos in which they felt less exposed – e.g. rejecting photos in swimwear; not sharing addresses and other more personal data on the network.

A respondent (I), a single 38 old civil engineer, concretely mentioned that there is "a fine line between what is private and what is not" (...) "It depends on the good judgment of each one of us, but it is a line that is very difficult to define, what is in the private sphere and what is in the public sphere. There are certain specific things that I do that I will not share on social networks or any other media whatever, and I've seen people sharing those same certain situations on social networks".

They were also very careful about exposing others, friends and acquaintances, and avoided sharing photos of them without authorization (I). They were also careful when sharing content when it comes to children or family situations. One interviewee, a 39-year old divorced man, a salesman at NOS[1], told us that he advised his children to only share what was essential and only accept friendship requests from people they knew (he has a son aged 11 and a daughter aged 16, both of whom have Facebook). However, there were some things that they had no problem with publishing, such as news or the songs they hear. Another interviewee, a chemistry researcher, acknowledged that she had no problem sharing photos of children in trunks in a group just for family members or close friends; although she clarified that she would never share scantily clad photos.

From another, complementary perspective, a female interviewee, 42 old cleaner, recommended against revealing 'true data' on Facebook and stated that "It was created almost exclusively for my kids to play with, nothing else (laughs) ... To play with each other, and then play there. It was my little one who created and to made all the changes on Facebook. He changed the addresses, changed his name, changed everything, you know ..." And she answered the question 'why was it changed?': "He was at school. Although we had already said so at home, the teacher at school taught them not to put the right data and their own photographs online, so that's what he did, he changed everything. I only noticed that everything was changed a few days later (laughs)".

When debating exposure, identity, intimacy, privacy, an adolescent (AFG) noted that the profile created on Facebook is not about a "faithful representation of the user, but a part, a segment of choices that can be more or less representative and more or less faithful to what the person really is." This aspect becomes particularly relevant when, under the guard of privacy, the information displayed is not real or fully real and, therefore, does not provide all the information that could immediately identify the individual. The teenager also considered the "status" description to be excessive, using pre-defined staging system expressions, such as "feeling happy," and exposing what people are doing, what they eat, or what time they do certain activities. Too much exhibition and dramatization are the result.

With more or less direct intervention (FG), the audience seemed to have effect on the user or, in other words, the user was influenced by the audience which will affect the type of content to publish and its purpose: considering the critical importance, value, need for acceptance and, following this, the need to show/say "I'm here, look at me". This aspect may lead to embarrassment or declared exposure.

As for the information available on social networks, Facebook and LinkedIn, and Facebook and Twitter were compared (FG). Facebook has a more informal and relaxed language to "play with" or to make some information fictional/to simulate fiction as if they were alter egos; conversely, LinkedIn has a format almost like a CV, with accurate and updated information – a dichotomy addressed in the FG of adult graduates. Adolescents focused on the Facebook and Twitter pair, noting that Facebook asked for more information than the latter; Twitter was satisfied with a user name and a sentence, while on Facebook "even the family is on there".

There was similar concern for the devices and locations from where users accessed the content they want (AFG), giving the example of the mistrust of the school computers, which do not allow history to be erased. In the private space of the home, one teenager admitted to using a code to lock the phone as a safeguard in case her mother tried to see it.

More than half (60%) used different passwords for different accounts (from data survey: DS), while 23.1% reported not having a differing set of passwords, using the same one to access the various accounts. Fifty-one point nine percent changed them, and 48.1% did not. As for altering the privacy settings, 51.9% did so, 31.3% had different settings for different parts, 13.5% had never changed the default settings and 1.9% did not know about the existence of privacy settings. When inquired (CA, 44) if different levels of privacy settings for the several 'accounts-profiles' were established, why and in which ones the settings varied, 28 answered affirmatively, 5 did not reply and 4 stated "the same". It ought to be highlighted that twelve mentioned their Facebook profile was only visible to "friends". They defined the different levels in accordance with the *accounts-profiles* and their functionalities. They equate "having privacy" with content that only your "friends" can see and setting one's own privacy levels. Forty-two altered privacy settings, and the 26 who changed the content did so in the following order: photographs, other content, location and comments – from the status of "public" to the status of only visible to "friends".

Privacy control strategies (AFG): most also changed the privacy rules, revealing minimal knowledge of them, in order to control who had access to their data. Some explicitly mentioned changing "friends of friends" to "friends". The use of access codes for mobile phones was cited by some, motivated partly by curiosity and partly to evade parental surveillance. *Alienation of control*: also regarding the use of access codes, although aware of their importance (the participants had used them in the past), many admitted they ignored them because of the work involved. Nearly 40% read privacy policies (DS), terms and conditions, 58.7% did not and 1.4% chose "do not know / no answer". They "were aware" (CA, 44 students) that once something is published, it is difficult to erase it forever. Eight directly related it to the Internet and 12 specifically to the social media. Eleven "were aware" that, despite the privacy policies, data can be held by others. These "others" could be "friends of friends" and not necessarily our direct friends, hackers, "malicious persons", "third parties" (i.e. business) and Facebook. Only one stated that "it is not as protected as it should be" (alienation, accustomed to this situation as normal).

Only a couple read the terms and conditions, four did not answer, one did not own a smartphone, twelve argued that these statements were too long and required much time, a couple checked them in case of additional costs, another couple justified themselves by explaining that reading them will imply spending more time on installation, five recognized "impatience" and "laziness", and the rest answered "no". Some situations could be plausibly described as *alienation of control* (AFG), particularly with regard to reading privacy policies before installing a new app. All respondents admitted to not reading them, merely clicking "accept". Simultaneously there was awareness that this behavior may carry risks and result in manipulation. *Privacy control strategies* (AFG): the concept of friendship was very broad, including all acquaintances. It also referred to other conclusions that indicated that adolescents perceive social media as an extension of their social relationships (Boyd, 2014). In terms of *negotiation of the actors* as to what is public and what is private, the idea prevailed that the availability of content was based on an agreement between the people involved, and care was taken not to offend sensibilities.

According to IT, less than a third of respondents read the application permissions; an equal number (31%) said they did it "sometimes" and 38% said they never read them. About 70% of respondents installed applications on their mobile phones. Those who did not (31%) claimed, above all, that they did not want to give access to their contacts and did not want to be found – location. Only 10% were willing to indicate their location in order to receive personalized adverts. The majority (61%) did not allow this kind of action. In some occasional cases (I), one warned "you just have Internet on your phone to stop having a private life and showing it to others, so others can access it" while another said "It depends (…) but I don't always read everything... Because I look... I have an idea, because if it is something I do not know and they start asking some questions, I uninstall it or maybe don't install it at all".

As regards the type of information that was stored on mobile phones, three groups can be established (IT): Almost all respondents (+ 70%) had 'contact information', 'pictures and videos', 'text messages' and 'applications'. Between 70% and 40% had the 'e-mail messages', 'notes /voice memos' and 'documents in PDF, Word, etc.'. Less than a third had: 'websites visited,' 'location information', 'password' and 'voice mail'. In general, the content stored on the phone was not considered "very private", with the majority of responses falling into the "private" category. The exceptions were 'passwords', considered 'very private' and applications assessed as 'not at all private'.

Managing Media and Privacy

71% of respondents used their phones for taking photos or videos between one and three times per week (ES). Forty (CA) used their mobile phones to take pictures, one did not, one did not have a camera phone and, finally, five only made use of it when they did not have a camera. The moments selected for pictures were in the company of family, friends, "moments to remember", "important dates", culture, travel. According to IT, 'family' and 'travel/holiday' were the most photographed subjects/shot with smartphones; more than 85% of respondents said that they did it. There were values of around 60%/70% for photographing/filming 'unexpected situations of everyday life', 'events' and 'meeting friends'. Below 50% were 'self-portraits', photos/filming of 'work' and 'mood'.

Regarding taking pictures of public events (survey of images: IS): 33% said that cultural events were a major time for recording video; 10% said the same about unusual events (20% and 5% for taking pictures respectively). 56% had already shared cultural events pictures on social networks; 24% did so with unusual events pictures. Only 9% ever captured images to send to newspapers.

Thirty-one did not take pictures or films of strangers; two did so rarely, upon finding a ridiculous or interesting situation; one did so depending on relevant; finally, six took into account the rights of/respect for others. According to IS, 81% did not shoot other people in public places (only 2% said do it without any warning or authorization); 77% said they would not do so if they found a public figure (but only a minority based this approach on the assessment of risk to privacy); 30% identified – tagged – people in the photos, when they are 'close' (family, friends, colleagues).

In the specific case of taking pictures of celebrities or publicly known people, two main positions were observed: Yes, without concern and no, on a scale of perceptions (FG). An interesting quote from one adolescent male was: "If he/she realized, yes, because he/she would probably know it will be published on some kind of social media" (…) If he/she agreed to the picture, he/she would probably also agree to it being uploaded on social media (…) no matter whether it would be seen by 10 or by 10,000, it is part of their job".

Seventeen (out of 44 students, CA) saved images taken both for personal purposes and/or to share on social media, and two preferred to take pictures for personal reasons. Concern about the dissemination of pictures of themselves (EFG) had to do with embarrassing situations and aesthetics of the images. Their publication in open or closed circles was based on common sense. *Privacy control strategies* (AFG): the strategy of not posting photos and pictures was suggested and remembered by parents.

A variation in the range of personal information published (AFG) not exceeding basic data like date of birth or high school, was given as one strategy; not including parents in social networks because of the possible tensions with friends and showing certain images in closed groups was another strategy.

The perceived risks (IS) with respect to pictures placed on the network itself mainly had to do with the possibility of revealing intimate situations, the body or compromising visibility (61% were concerned with it) and with the possibility of handling and decontextualization of images (63%). On the contrary, recognition itself was not a major concern (24%) nor was the identification of others/groups (27%) or habits (38%). Some female adolescents (FG) specifically highlighted not tagging or asking for permission as a way of respecting others and showed awareness of the vulnerability and security of social media. When referring to the way of taking pictures, "place" did not matter a lot, they did not even think about it.

One concern was the possibility of losing control over the 'image' (representation) that individuals wish to build themselves, and in extreme cases the possibility of blackmail/bullying. Losing rights to the images concerned 47%, but the vast majority gave up this right when uploading/putting pictures online.

A relationship can be seen (IT) between what was photographed and with whom it was shared in the formation of two groups: one more "private", which included photos/movies with the 'family', 'groups of friends', 'self-portraits' and 'holiday/travel' that were shared with those with whom they had a closer relationship (family and friends); and a more "public" group, with photos/movies of 'events', 'everyday situations', 'work' and 'mood' that were shared with those who were not so close (acquaintances, co-workers, closed circles, users in general).

Almost half (IS) considered that images involved greater risks to privacy (48%) than textual information (2%). Some answers did not indicate corresponding protection practices with the perception of this risk: only 11% did not use pictures of themselves on social networking profiles; those that only used it in a professional context were 7%; those who abstained from sharing photos on social networks constituted 22%. The motivations for sharing suggested that the impetus for interaction was greater than concerns about the risk.

68% (ES) checked if the app offered "app permission" but 61% did not read those "permissions" before installing; only 32% did that. 65.4% (DS) have abandoned apps due to a detected misuse of data, 21.2% chose "I will consider this possibility in the future", 12.5% did not, and 1% chose "do not know, no answer". *Privacy control strategies* (AGF): participants developed a set of weak strategies. Most discarded the use of apps in social media that show where people are at any given time. Also, the choice to download an app depended on knowing others who had already done so. The importance of peer behavior at this stage of the life cycle is also reflected in behavior when entering the digital world, as Boyd has said (2014).

92.3% (DS) were registered on a SNS, with the following data sharing distributions: 73.6% basic information; 13.9% contact information; 43.8% personal interests; 58.7% education and training; 36.1% work/job and 34.6% travels. 66.3% set data visibility and sharing on SNS to be visible only to friends, 15.4% had different data visibility settings for different people, 8.7% were not sure who could see their data, and 8.2% allowed everyone to see it. Thirty (out of 44, CA) felt that the information they shared was not secure, three felt that it was and the rest said that it depended. A gradation of awareness and knowledge was noted – users were aware of some risks but did not delve into the reasons or even know them.

Privacy Control Strategies (AFG): The interviewees were aware that access to SNS should be made on trusted devices, taking care to log out when they did. They also showed concern for what they published, preferring trivial things and things that do not compromise them. Some of them only did it for a very restricted circle of friends. Sending/accepting invitations was addressed to people they knew, at least by sight. The existence of awareness was a prevailing idea, but it was not linked to the risks inherent in the use of social media. Thus, this awareness did not lead to the mobilization of all the appropriate behaviors. The verbs and nouns used and the syntax employed are indicative of normalization and an acquired routine in the process of exposing personal information (CA).

There was an idea of risk in exposing personal aspects that may stay online indefinitely, but the practices seemed to reflect little concern (EFG). When asked if they regretted disclosing personal data (DS), 65.9% answered no, 15.4% yes on SNS and 17.8% said yes when online shopping. Regarding the use of tools for data protection, 85.1% answered no, 13.9% yes and 1% "do not know, no answer". *Invasion of privacy* (AFG): the majority referred to photos posted by parents and in which they were tagged.

Concerning the level of preoccupation with the lack of control about data (DS), people were rather concerned (31.3%), worried (30.3%), a little worried (28.2%) and not worried (9.19%). The reasons for this were: 54.8% believed the inner SNS structure hinders control over personal data, 16.3% had difficulty setting up the privacy of their personal data, 16.3% did not have time to set up privacy of their personal data and 12% gave other reasons. Asked if companies should store data and for how long, 66.3% said they should not save data, 24% answered for one year, and 18% indefinitely. 24% made bank transactions online, 75.5% did not, and 0.5% chose "do not know, no answer". On access to data by security agencies, 54.3% agreed only with a legal foundation, 38% did not, 7.2% agreed on a case-by-case basis, 0.5% chose "do not know, no answer". Most respondents (IT) considered that search engines, telephone operators and secret services must store the information for only one year. However, the secret service was given some more time; 35 and two respondents indicated periods of three and five years respectively.

Twenty-two (CA) felt they did not control the information available about them, whereas eight did. They showed concern about who controls the information – themselves or others – and especially about what others can publish about them and about the appropriation of information without their permission.

About transparency with regard to storage policies and disclosure to third parties of the data stored on social networks or email accounts (I), some interviewees were aware of this and found that these procedures were an invasion/violation of their privacy; others found that, in some cases, it can be useful and even consider that there should be such monitoring by the authorities, especially when there a crime is suspected, or that they were important for resolving (il)legal cases, for example. One interviewee (I), a single, 33-year-old male, who is a telecommunications technician, specifically mentioned that this "surveillance" – 'Big Brother' came from the beginning of the century, "it is not new (…) smartphones only spread it"; and even if you take care or restricted your online connection ("keeping a low profile"), "you are always potentially going to be observed".

Facebook (CA) was mentioned several times as the "profile" that displays the most data, because it requests users to provide it or because of its interaction-oriented nature. One respondent thought Facebook was more secure since it had more privacy settings. Only one person established a relationship between publications and personal data. They showed (EFG) high tolerance to invasion/harassment and unauthorized commercial use of personal data. At this point, they showed an initial awareness of the different sources that collected their personal data. However, the possibilities are wider than they may seem, concerning the profile and the digital identity technical settings. Therefore, is it important to circulate the required knowledge in this area.

In the specific case of a Facebook group, (Digital Ethnography, carpools, DEF), the following strategies were observed: public view but publications only from members accepted by administrators, members receive notifications on their profile page and may change this option and block them; it favors arranging travel by private message and not revealing phone numbers although some people did not care about it and disclosed their personal contacts in the group. Some group members were not embarrassed to talk in comments in the group, and did not worry about the fact that other members were reading. For the journeys, the observer-researcher realized that the publication of offers and requests was a last resort, and people first calling nearby contacts by phone.

Some people (DEF) become friends after contact with each other through the Facebook group, others do not. During the trips, people get to know each other and share some more personal issues such as goals for the future, what they did at the weekend, some amusing stories about themselves or people they know. When people were on the same course, they speak about it, perhaps talking more with each other, putting other occupants of the vehicle to the sidelines. Close relationships or continuous contact between people were only established with similar characteristics: age and course. The others greet each other only in specific situations, e.g. when pass each other in the city.

Moving onto the analysis of Twitter, Reddit and Instagram; by classifying the tweets by *Netlytic* and subsequent confirmation by reading them, it may be concluded that the hashtags *privacy, digital identity* and *username* had a more technological content, while the ones collected for *profile* and *anonymity* were more personal. It was noted that large amounts of the technological content of messages associated with *anonymity* were directly or indirectly related to the *Tor project*.

After the tweets collected for *mobile, socialmedia* and *self*, it was concluded that the content shared in *mobile* were essentially articles, news or applications in order to provide warnings or to help to protect data on mobile devices. In *socialmedia,* it was observed that most served to share articles and pages on how to improve presence on social networks, both in a marketing context and for "personal promotion" or, in the case of *privacy*, about controlling the levels of privacy settings on social networks. Finally, for *self*, most tweets were photographs (selfies) shared by users on the network through applications like Instagram (78%) or social networks (22%). It ought to be highlighted that, in the case of Instagram, viral, commonly used hashtags were in many cases employed to 'promote' images rather than because they were linked to the topic itself.

The messages of a more personal nature, e.g. that discuss actual cases of day-to-day life of users instead of simply sharing content such as articles or news were those on Reddit, which gets more interaction. Topics that created more controversy among users were those related to privacy and anonymity, where it was possible to make a clear division of users into two groups with opposing views. Conversations that generated particular controversy addressed the improper use of individuals' images, or discussing Facebook as an attack on the privacy of users. The analysis of the user accounts on Instagram revealed a 'diary' of their lives – e.g. one user employed it to follow a diet and check its results with the audience – mixing moments with friends, family and professional goals.

FUTURE RESEARCH DIRECTIONS

Thus, and as hinted at with the need to develop further research lines, academic work should thoroughly analyze users' perceptions and performances and raise awareness about *Dataism* and the consequences of apps, media, platforms and technologies as tools that shape our behaviors and online identities (even offline, as a consequence) to best suit their (mainly commercial) interests (Serrano Tellería, 2015b).

'Privacy education' and 'digital literacy' focused on managing identity on the Internet are research fields that will require an in-depth analysis. As well as developing clearer and user-centered policies and terms and conditions – which ought to involve app and platform developers, governments, citizenships, etc. – a concrete syllabus incorporating digital abilities, attitudes, capabilities and knowledge should be implemented in all stages of state education curriculums (Serrano Tellería & Branco; 2015).

Combined with interesting and notable areas in 'child protection and safety' and 'digital literacy', the proposed new lines would cover identity construction and management – meaning an overall scope of its design and definition, as mentioned previously, from technological and communicational perspectives. This would require an interdisciplinary approach mainly within Education, Communication, Psychology and Sociology, as well as an intersectional collaboration with technology (Serrano Tellería & Branco; 2015).

Aspects to investigate further would include raising awareness about the ever-changing and liquid characteristics of the online mobile ecosystem, about social media and technologies as tools that shape behaviors and identities, as well as the potential dimensions of identity to manage within this ecosystem: on the one hand, personal, professional, etc. and their spheres; on the other, technological differences between the 'profile' and the 'digital identity' in relation to the digital path and footprint and invisible audiences.

As for liquid communication management, it should raise awareness about how to handle and manage the constant negotiation of rules and the consequent formation of the constellations of spheres in relation to known and unknown-invisible audiences, raise awareness about the different users' notions and perceptions about what *privacy* is and the consequent repercussions it may have in their daily lives and warn about how both the user profile and the digital identity constantly offer both conscious and unconscious, consented and unconsented data and information about people. Moreover, it should delve into the analysis of these technologies as devices and tools intimately related to the nervous systems and emotions. Therefore, it should investigate the perspective of considering them as potential amplifiers of 'the Six Primary Passions of the Soul', leading to an interesting but at the same time dangerous flow of behavior that may be related to the lack of rationality in some users' patterns. In this sense, it ought to be highlighted how access to the list of contacts and location were the main aspects users took care about if remembering that, in our brain, memories are intrinsically tied to a specific location in the brain.

CONCLUSION

To introduce some conclusions reached, emotion could be considered a key element when configuring the user interface design and content on online mobile devices. The defining features of smartphones, like instantaneity, ubiquity and, concerning literacy, continuous partial attention, the relationship between memories and place, the lack of rationality in some user attitudes and performances, the limitation of the impact of users' knowledge on their actions, the strong circumstantial user pattern behavior, the ambiguity and volatility of terms and conditions' (Serrano Tellería & Oliveira; 2015), are added to the liquidity and mobility of our society and technology itself; they are intimately related to how users express their *Six Primary Passions of the Soul*.

Moreover, they have to deal with the constellations of and/or liquid spheres in a constant data flow that escapes clear awareness and a notion of the deeply involved risks.

Users' motivation to fulfil those six passions overruled their ability to clearly understand either the reflectivity (required time to analyze) or the management of the user interface design in every action, further influenced by the ambiguity of the required knowledge. Moreover, the possibility of receiving stimuli of all types constantly influences how priority levels are established in their management and performances (Serrano Tellería & Oliveira, 2015; Serrano Tellería, 2015b, 2015c).

Conclusions reached from the different perspectives lead to the paradox of dealing with former "solidity" and current "liquidity". It is reflected both in the user interface design and the content management and performance with mobile devices. This relationship of mutual influence between "old" and "new" media was previously stated by McLuhan in the laws describing the ecological approach method (Serrano Tellería & Oliveira, 2015; Serrano Tellería, 2015b, 2015c).

In this process of technological appropriation, an increased awareness and idea of the risks that the Internet and mobile communication involve can be observed. However, the same steps forward found a counterpart when consulting users about their trust in companies and devices and their proved knowledge and subsequent actions when surfing the web and performing online. In other words, users generally continued to lack the proper abilities and capacities to manage themselves online and showed a lack of rationality in some attitudes and behaviors and a gap between their ideas and knowledge and their final actions. Although they deployed a series of strategies to manage and control their privacy – mainly associated with the 'privacy settings' of the applications, devices and platforms themselves, like avoiding synchronization, access to contacts, location, identification tagging in images, controlling member and/or friend requests, and establishing circles and groups to share the information with – they are insufficient. Also, it ought to be stressed that they "felt secure" just knowing that these 'settings' are available, even though they are not enough to protect users' privacy, as experts have stated.

A remarkable observation was that general users seemed not to be aware enough about the implications of these applications, devices, platforms, tools and the liquid media ecology, technological environment and societal environment as features and parameters that shape their online and offline identities. Users showed an overall deep ignorance about the differences between the 'profile' and the 'digital identity'. Greater awareness about the digital path and invisible audiences should be encouraged.

Privacy seemed to flow in a gradation, like waves – following the metaphor of the liquid media ecology and environment – in an interdependent process of managing 'awareness' about privacy that appears to be highly determined by context. That is to say, it was considered that the delimitation of the public and private, intimate and personal spheres – the constellations of and/or liquid spheres – may not last much time online because the same context can change or be valued differently.

Here, it ought to be highlighted that there are different notions and perceptions about what privacy is, also bearing in mind that most users' worries are who and how their content and data are accessed. Then, a constant negotiation of rules – characteristics also defined for the digital content that showed no clear norms or rules – is managed in an ever-changing delimitation of the virtual space and time, to add to the various possible considerations about the scope of its context(s) by each user.

Therefore, the configuration of the public and private, intimate and personal constellations of and/ or liquid spheres within this liquid media ecology and environment seemed to be constantly changing, also since the main coordinates and dimensions, time and space, seemed similarly to change. Moreover, the added and supported sub-coordinates and dimensions, such as the context and the audience, seemed to follow the same pattern; this is the reason for describing this process as liquid and for the comparison with the ebb and flow of the waves. In this sense, core challenges may manage that unlimited flow on user data and content as well as the repercussion of the same flow in relation to invisible and potential future audiences. These main conclusions lead to the 'between constellations and liquid spheres' hypothesis. They appear to be liquid when they are changing 'state' and transform themselves into constellations when they have been conformed within a specific context and time. Their state and process of configuration and reconfiguration may change as quickly as small modifications in one of its core coordinates and dimensions – time and space – and sub-secondary ones are introduced: context, audience, etc.

REFERENCES

Aguado, J. M., Feijóo, C., & Martínez, I. J. (Eds.). (2013). La comunicación móvil. Hacia un Nuevo ecosistema digital. Barcelona: Gedisa.

Arendt, H. (1997). *A Condição Humana*. Rio de Janeiro: Forense Universitária.

Bateson, G. (1979). *Espíritu y naturaleza: una unidad necesaria (avances en teoría de sistemas, complejidad y ciencias humanas)*. Bantam Books.

Bateson, G. (1991). *Una unidad sagrada: nuevos pasos hacia una ecología de la mente*. Harper Collins Pub.

Bauman, Z. (2005). *Liquid Life*. Cambridge, MA: Polity.

Bauman, Z. (2008). Em busca da política. Rio de Janeiro: Zahar.

Bennett, P. N. (2011). Technological intimacy in haemodialysis nursing. *Nursing Inquiry*, *18*(3), 247–252. doi:10.1111/j.1440-1800.2011.00537.x PMID:21790875

Boyce, M. W., & Hancock, P. A. (2012). The Interpenetration of Mind and Machine. *Proceedings of the Human Factors and Ergonomics Society Annual Meeting*, *56*(1), 178-182.

Boyd, D. (2014). *It's Complicated. The Social Lifes of Networked Teens*. Yale University Press.

Brake, D. R. (2014). *Sharing our Lives Online. Risks and Exposure in Social Media*. Palgrave Macmillan.

Campbell, S. W. (2015). Mobile Communication and Network Privatism: A Literature Review of The Implications For Diverse, Weak, and New Ties. *Communication Research*, *3*(1), 1–21. Retrieved from http://www.rcommunicationr.org/index.php/component/jdownloads/finish/16/55?Itemid=0

Carnegie, T. A. M., & Fels, S. S. (2002). Beyond use: Toward a rhetoric of technological intimacy. *Technical Communication Quarterly, 11*(2), 214–216. doi:10.1207/s15427625tcq1102_8

Castells, M. (2008). Afterword. In C. Katz (Ed.), *Handbook of Mobile Communication Studies*. Cambridge, MA: MIT Press. doi:10.7551/mitpress/9780262113120.003.0033

Castells, M., Fernandez-Ardevol, M., Linchuan Qiu, J., & Araba, S. (2007). *Mobile Communication and Society: A Global Perspective*. Cambridge, MA: MIT Press.

Deuze, M. (2012). *Media Life*. Polity Press.

Elias, N. (1980). *Introdução à sociología*. Edições 70.

Fidalgo, A., Serrano Tellería, A., Carvalheiro, J. R., Canavilhas, J., & Correia, J. C. (2013). Human Being as a Communication Portal: The construction of the Profile on Mobile Phones. *Revista Latina de Comunicación Social 68*. Retrieved November, 8, 2014, from http://www.revistalatinacs.org/068/paper/989_Covilha /23_Telleriaen.html

Flusser, V. (1988). *"On writing, complexity and the technical revolutions"*. Interview in Onasbrück, European Media Art Festival. Retrieved November, 18, 2014, from https://www.youtube.com/watch?v=lyfOcAAcoH8&app=desktop

Foridi, L. (2014). The Facebook-ification of everything! Sex, authenticity and reality for the status update era. *Salon*. Sunday, Aug 31. Retrieved November, 8, 2014, from http://www.salon.com/2014/08/31/the_facebook_ification_of_everything_sex_authenticity_and_reality_for_the_status_update_era/?utm_source=twitter&utm_medium=socialflow

Fortunati, L. (2002). The Mobile Phone: Towards New Categories and Social Relations. In Information, Communication, and Society, (pp. 514-528). Academic Press.

Fuchs, C. (2014). *Social Media: A Critical Introduction*. London: Sage. doi:10.4135/9781446270066.n2

Grosser, B. (2014). What Do Metrics Want? How Quantification Prescribes Social Interaction on Facebook. *Computational Culture: A Journal of Software Studies*. Retrieved November, 17, 2014, from http://computationalculture.net/article/what-do-metrics-want

Hermida, A. (2014). *Tell Everyone: Why We Share and Why it Matters*. Doubleday Canada.

Horning, R. (2014). Social Media Is Not Self-Expression. *The New Inquiry*. Retrieved November, 17, 2014, from http://thenewinquiry.com/blogs/marginal-utility/social-media-is-not-self-expression/

Jenkins, H., Ford, S., & Green, J. (2013). *Spreadable Media. Creating Value and Meaning in a Networked Culture*. New York University Press.

Katz, J. E. (2008). *Mainstreamed Mobiles in Daily Life: Perspectives and Prospects. Katz, Castells. Handbook of Mobile Communication Studies*. Cambridge, MA: MIT Press.

Katz, J. E., & Aakhus, M. (Eds.). (2002). *Perpetual Contact. Mobile Communication, Private Talk, Public Performance*. Cambridge, UK: Cambridge University Press. doi:10.1017/CBO9780511489471

Kawamoto, K. (2003). *Media and Society In the Digital Age*. New York: University of Washington.

Lasén, A. (2015). Digital self-portraits, exposure and the modulation of intimacy. In Mobile and Digital Communication: Approaches to Public and Private. Covilhã, Portugal: LabCom Books.

Madden, M. (2014). Public Perceptions of Privacy and Security in the Post-Snowden Era. *Pew Research.* Retrieved November, 18, 2014, from http://www.pewinternet.org/2014/11/12/public-privacy-perceptions/

Marichal, J. (2012). *Facebook Democracy. The Architecture of Disclosure and the Threat to Public Life.* Ashgate.

Markham, A. (2013). Undermining "Data": A Critical Examination of a Core Term in Scientific Inquiry. *First Monday*, *18*(10). Retrieved November, 8, 2014, from http:// uncommonculture.org/ojs/index.php/ fm/article/view/4868/3749

Marwick, A. (2013). *Status Update: Celebrity, Publicity, and Branding in the Social Media Age.* New Haven, CT: Yale University Press.

Mashable. (2014). *Mobile-Minded.* Retrieved November, 18, 2014, from http://mashable.com/2014/11/17/ human-smartphone-relationship/#share-action:eyJzIjoidCIsImkiOiJfejQ5OXB4eDY0bnExZ3kwMyJ9

Meyer, R. (2014). In the Brain, Memories Are Inextricably Tied to Place. *The Atlantic.* Retrieved 14 September, 2014, from http://www.theatlantic.com/technology/archive/2014/08/in-the-brain-memories-are-inextricably-tied-to-place/375969/

Pasquale, F. (2015). The Algorithmic Self. *The Hedgehog Review, 17*(1). Retrieved March 14, 2015, from http://www.iasc-culture.org/THR/THR_article_2015_Spring_Pasquale.php

Preston, A. (2014). The Death of Privacy. *The Guardian.* Retrieved September, 11, 2014, from http://www. theguardian.com/world/2014/aug/03/internet-death-privacy-google-facebook-alex-preston?CMP=twt_gu

Raine, L., Kiesler, S., & Madden, M. (2013). Anonymity, Privacy, and Security Online. *Pew Research.* Retrieved 14 April, 2014, from http://www.pewinternet.org/2013/09/05/anonymity-privacy-and-security-online/

Rheingold, H. (2012). *Net smart. How to thrive online.* Cambridge, MA: The MIT Press.

Rosen, L. (2013). Always On, All the Time: Are We Suffering From FoMO? *Psychologytoday.* Retrieved November, 17, 2014, from http://www.psychologytoday.com/blog/rewired-the-psychology-technolo-gy/201305/always-all-the-time-are-we-suffering-fomo

Serrano Tellería, A. (2014). Interface Design on Mobile Phones: The Delimitation of the Public and Private Spheres. In *Proceedings of Designa: Interface International Conference on Design Research.* LabCom, Beira Interior University.

Serrano Tellería, A. (2015a). The Role of the Profile and The Digital Identity on the Mobile Content. In J. M. Aguado, C. Feijóo, & I. J. Martínez (Eds.), *Emerging Perspectives on the Mobile Content Evolution. IGI Global.*

Serrano Tellería, A. (2015b). Liquid Spheres or Constellations: Reflections Towards Mobile Devices. In Mobile and Digital Communication: Approaches to Public and Private (pp. 173-198). Covilhã, Portugal: LabCom Books, University of Beira Interior.

Serrano Tellería, A. (2015c). Emotion and Mobile Devices. In *Designa 'Desire', International Conference on Design Research.* Portugal: LabCom.

Serrano Tellería, A. (2015d). Twitter e a privacidade: a partilha de estratégias e ferramentas. In *IX Congresso SOPCOM: Associação Portuguesa de Ciências da Comunicação: Comunicação e Transformações Sociais.* University of Coimbra.

Serrano Tellería, A. (2015e). Reddit e a privacidade: uma análise das interacções e conversas. In: *IX Congresso SOPCOM: Associação Portuguesa de Ciências da Comunicação: Comunicação e Transformações Sociais.* University of Coimbra.

Serrano Tellería, A., & Branco, M. L. (2015) Educação para a privacidade no espaço digital: de subsídios para uma proposta curricular. In A Nova Fluidez de Uma Velha Dicotomia: Publico e Privado nas Comunicações Móveis. Covilhã, Portugal: Labcom books, University of Beira Interior.

Serrano Tellería, A., & Oliveira, M. (2015). Liquid Spheres on Smartphones: The Personal Information Policies. *International Journal of Interactive Mobile Technologies*, *9*(1). Retrieved from http://online-journals.org/index.php/i-jim/article/view/4065

Serrano Tellería, A., & Pereira, P. (2015). Instagram e a visibilidade das imagens dos utilizadores. In J. R. Carvalheiro (Ed.), *Público e privado nas comunicações móveis* (pp. 297–316). Coimbra, Portugal: Minerva Coimbra.

Serrano Tellería, A., Portovedo, S., & Albuquerque, A. I. (2015). Negociações da privacidade nos dispositivos móveis. In J. R. Carvalheiro (Ed.), *Público e privado nas comunicações móveis* (pp. 119–158). Coimbra, Portugal: Minerva Coimbra.

Stald, G. (2008). Mobile Identity: Youth, Identity, and Mobile Communication Media. In Youth, Identity, and Digital Media (pp. 143–164). Cambridge, MA: The MIT Press.

Starner, T. (2011). Multiplexing versus multitasking. *The Technium.* Retrieved 11 February 2014 from http://kk.org/thetechnium/2011/03/multiplexing-vs/

Stone, L. (2002-2014). *Continuous Partial Attention.* Retrieved November 8, 2014, from http://lindastone.net/qa/continuous-partial-attention/

Turkle, S. (2008). Always-On / Always-on-You": The Tethered Self. In J. E. Katz (Ed.), *Handbook of Mobile Communications Studies* (pp. 121–138). Cambridge, MA: MIT Press. doi:10.7551/mitpress/9780262113120.003.0010

Turkle, S. (2011). *Alone Together: Why We expect More from Technology and Less From Each Other?* New York: Basic Books.

Van Dijck, J. (2007). *Mediated Memories in the Digital Age.* Stanford, CA: Stanford UP.

Van Dijck, J. (2013). 'You have one identity': Performing the self on Facebook and LinkedIn. *Media, Culture & Society*, *35*, 199. Retrieved November, 14, 2014, from http://mcs.sagepub.com/content/35/2/199

Van Dijck, J. (2014). Datafication, Dataism and Dataveillance: Big Data between Scientific Paradigm and Ideology. *Surveillance & Society*, *2*(2), 197–208.

Walker Rettberg, J. (2014). *Seeing Ourselves Through Technology: How We Use Selfies, Blogs and Wearable Devices to See and Shape Ourselves*. Palgrave Macmillan. Retrieved November, 8, 2014, from http://www.academia.edu/8482366/Seeing_Ourselves_Through_Technology_How_We_Use_Selfies_Blogs_and_Wearable_Devices_to_See_and_Shape_Ourselves

Wellman, B. (2001). Physical Place and Cyberplace: The Rise of Personalized Networking. *International Journal of Urban and Regional Research*, 25(2), 227–252. doi:10.1111/1468-2427.00309

KEY TERMS AND DEFINITIONS

Architecture of Exposure: Reflects both the interface design and the inner information architecture of content and users performance, including interactivity and usability dimensions, observed mainly in Social Media and in mobile devices (see more at Serrano Tellería, 2014).

Constellations of Spheres: Describes how users manage their public, private, personal and intimate spheres within the online and mobile media ecologies as well as technological ambient/environments (see more at Serrano Tellería, 2015b, pp.190-191).

Digital Identity: The data employed to represent entities (persons, organizations, machines or software processes) in information systems and it may have three dimensions: social, legal, and computational.

Liquid Media Ecology: The hypothesis that relates the online and mobile media ecology as well as its technological ambient/ environments with Bauman's liquidity and the fluidization parameters of the technological, institutional and cultural media dimensions described by McQuail (2006. See more at Aguado, Feijóo & Martínez, 2013; Serrano Tellería & Oliveira, 2015; Serrano Tellería, 2015b).

Liquid Spheres: Describes de blurring boundaries between the public, private, personal and intimate spheres within the online and mobile media ecologies as well as technological ambient/environments (see more at Serrano Tellería & Oliveira, 2015; Serrano Tellería, 2015b, pp.190-191).

Liquid Technological Ambient/Environment: The hypothesis that relates the online and mobile media ecology as well as its technological ambient/environments with Bauman's liquidity and the fluidization parameters of the technological, institutional and cultural media dimensions described by McQuail (2006. See more at Aguado, Feijóo & Martínez, 2013; Serrano Tellería & Oliveira, 2015; Serrano Tellería, 2015b).

Online Profile: Structured information about the users of digital services. Its structure depends on the way the information has been gathered, the technology involved, the types of data or what the law allows.

ENDNOTE

[1]   "I usually say that they should only share the essential. But first of all they should only accept friends that are really their friends, that is ... Social networks have this "audience", there are many people who have four thousand friends, and, oh, I think that is very strange. Maybe they have these thirty-five hundred Facebook friends but do not actually know them at all, and I think it makes no sense. These are things I say to my children, who can accept yes, but friends, publications up to a certain level ... I've seen poses, etc., certain things I do not agree with on other very young girls' profiles... And you need to educate children, that is what I am doing, I think you need to educate

them about that. That is to say, I do not see any harm in publishing things if it is for her group of friends, but there should be a limit because there are things that seem excessive for very young girls, even for very old people I think certain photographs are too much (laughs), so ... imagine for girls!"

Chapter 12
Analyzing Multi–Modal Digital Discourses during MMORPG Gameplay through an Experiential Rhetorical Approach

Yowei Kang
Kainan University, Taiwan

Kenneth C. C. Yang
The University of Texas at El Paso, USA

ABSTRACT

The digital game industry has contributed disproportionally to the overall U.S. economy and GDP in spite of recent economic recession. The rapid ascent of MMORPGs as an increasingly popular digital game genre has affected the manners that gamers interact with each other to generate a new type of digital discourses and human experiences that are multimodal, synchronous, interactive, and engaging. Despite the existence of ample digital game research in user experience (UX) in the human-computer interaction (HCI) literature, there is a lack of programmatic exploration from a rhetorical perspective to examine the process and outcome of these digital interactions and co-generated discourses. Derived from the concept of "the rhetoric of experience," this book chapter analyzed a representative gaming session captured in real time to study digital discourses that represent various aspects of gameplay experiences in World of Warcraft. The chapter discusses the methodological and theoretical implications of this approach to analyze and study MMORPGs and other digital game genres.

DOI: 10.4018/978-1-4666-9899-4.ch012

INTRODUCTION

Emerging Digital Game as a Research Phenomenon

The Entertainment Software Association (henceforth, ESA) (2014) reports that U.S. consumers have spent $21.53 billion on digital game content, accessory, and hardware purchases. In 2014, the expenditure has increased to $22.41 billion (Entertainment Software Association [ESA], 2015a). Over 45% of users who subscribe to multi-player digital games report that they spent a monthly average of $11 dollars on virtual goods (McKinsey & Company, 2011). Latest usage behavior statistics also estimate that more than 150 million Americans are gamers and 42% of them play digital games at least three hours per week (ESA, 2015a, 2015b). Four out of five households (80%) own a device to play digital games, while 51% of the U.S. households own a dedicated game console (ESA, 2015b).

Despite the growing role of digital games in shaping contemporary human experiences, game-related research has often been marginalized and ignored as a serious academic research because of its content (Bogost, 2007; Humphreys, 2003). However, in recent years, scholars are compelled to examine this emerging field due to the increasing importance of the digital game industry, as well as the exponential growth of their users that span various demographics (ESA, 2015a, 2015b; Wolf, 2005). For example, in terms of gamers' age distribution, 56% of the gamers are under 35years old, while 27% of them are above 50 years old (ESA, 2015a, 2015b). In a global survey of 100,000 consumers (aged between 13 and 64+) in China, Europe, and North America, McKinsey & Company (2011) found an emerging *Gamer* segment who obtains their digital experiences through gaming console platforms in single- and multi-player gaming situations. Compared with other digital consumer segments, the *Gamer* segment is reported to spend 2.2 times more on playing digital games per day (McKinsey & Company, 2011).

With the growing presence of digital games in shaping human experiences, in the past decade, scholars from various disciplines have rushed to study digital games. For many gamers, playing digital games has become an important part of social life when 56% of the most frequent gamers interact with others (ESA, 2015b). The trend to interact with other gamers grows with the popularity of Massively Multiplayer Online Role-Playing Games (henceforth, MMORPGs) that digital game researchers found "intensely social" (Humphreys, 2003, p.2). Role-playing and interactions with other gamers in the virtual space have generated new research topics to examine, such as notions of self, identity, representation, collaboration, and social interaction (Raessens & Goldstein, 2005).

The rapid rise of MMORPGs as an increasingly popular digital game genre has affected the manners that gamers interact with each other to generate a new type of digital discourses and human experiences that are interactive, multimodal, synchronous, and engaging (Kang, 2011). MMORPGs refer to any network-mediated digital games where thousands of gamers are role-playing simultaneously in a graphical and 3-D environment (Filiciak, 2003; Hussain & Griffiths, 2008 ; Kang, 2011). Examples of popular MMORPGs include *Ultima Online, EverQuest, World of Warcarft*, and *Second Life* (Kang, 2011). MMORPGs, MMOs, and MMOGs have rapidly attracted much attention from digital game researchers (Chuang, 2006; Steinkuehler & Williams, 2006). However, there is a lack of exploration from a rhetorical perspective to examine the process and the outcome of digital interactions and discourses during gameplay. Extended from Kang (2011), the digital game environment is arguably equivalent to a virtual rhetorical situation from all gamers when they generate digital discourse in responding to the rhetorical situation created in MMORPGs. In other words, MMORPGs are designed to create a fantasied gaming space where gamers can collaborate and negotiate with other players to co-create an engaging user experience in a mythical world with chosen identities (Kang, 2011).

Objectives of this Chapter

This book chapter aims to analyze the multi-modal digital discourses during MMORPG gameplay from an experiential rhetorical approach. This approach and analytical technique are based on Kang's (2011) concept, "the rhetoric of experience," to study experiential representations and persuasive effects from the structural, procedural, locational, behavioral, and cognitive aspects of these gameplay experiences as a rhetorical phenomenon that involves the persuasive interactions among participants through their manipulation of symbols and actions. To analyze gameplayer experiences from a rhetorical perspective, this book chapter proposes to use Kang's (2011) concept, *hybrid interactive rhetorical engagements* (H.I.R.E.), as the analytical unit, to explore these multimodal digital discourses during MMORPG gameplay.

BACKGROUND

Studying Digital Game as Contemporary Human Experience

With the ubiquity of digital devices and platforms (McKinsey & Company, 2011), the concept of *digital human experience, digital consumer experience, digital customer experience,* or *digital experience* has increasingly appeared in the discourses of the literature and industry practices (Aponovich & Grannan, 2013; Digital Experiences, n.d.; Ihamäki, 2015). The business communities tend to approach this concept as the paramount goal to accomplish business success by generating consumer engagement and brand differentiation through technology-based solutions (Aponovich & Grannan, 2013; *Digital Experiences*, n.d.). For example, *Digital Experiences* (n.d.) develops the components of digital experiences which are composed of on-site experience technologies, off-site experience technologies, enterprise marketing and technologies, customer service and support technologies, and customer relationship management. Similarly, Forrester Research, Inc. conceptualizes that consumer experiences on a site are based on technology-based capabilities such as "an organization's web and mobile experiences, such as traditional and mobile websites, customer transactions, and mobile applications" (cited in Aponovich & Grannan, 2013, p. 5).

In human-computer interaction (HCI) and interface design literature, *user experience* (UX) has often been used as a design feature in any content delivery platform. Buxton (2007) stated *user experience* depends on whether a computer application design takes into consideration the context, the user, and the task (cited in Calvillo-Gámez, Cairns, & Cox, 2010). For example, Ihamäki (2015) employed this concept to study how to improve user experiences with mobile augmented reality devices. Mayhew and Follansbee (2012) also identified five qualities of a website to ensure positive *user experience*: functional integrity, graphic design, persuasiveness, usability, and utility. With the popularity of digital games and their design implications, scholars have extended UX research to study gaming experience (Calvillo-Gámez, Cairns, & Cox, 2010; Poels, IJsselsteijn, de Kort, & Van Iersel, 2010). In the context of digital games, the concept of user experience is defined as "the subjective relationship between user and application" as the result of the outcome and process of the interaction (McCarthy & Wright, 2004, cited in Calvillo-Gámez, Cairns, & Cox, 2010, p. 48). Conceptualizing *user experience* as the process and outcome of a series of interactions between gamers and game designers allows digital game scholars to examine how these interactions lead to different *user experience* during gameplay.

MAIN FOCUS OF THE CHAPTER

Issues, Controversies, Problems

This chapter proposes to study *user experience* (of digital games) by examining digital discourses produced during gameplay. The authors argue that these digital discourses can be viewed as the process and outcome of online multimodal persuasive interactions and can be studied as users' experiential representations. The authors thus apply a newly-developed theoretical concept, *hybrid interactive rhetorical engagements* (henceforth, H.I.R.E.) (Kang, 2011) to analyze these experiential digital discourses generated from multimodal persuasive interactions during gameplay. Although digital discourses are often studied from a sociolinguistic or communication perspective (such as Thurlow & Mroczek, 2011), the authors argue that there is a need to study digital games from a rhetorical perspective because current digital game studies have often limited to the following areas: 1) game design (Prensky, 2005; Raynauld, 2005; Salen & Zimmerman, 2005); 2) aesthetic and reception of gamers (Calvert, 2005; Gunter, 2005; Griffiths, 2000; Holmes & Pellegrini, 2005); 3) cultural (Bryce & Rutter, 2005; Edwards, 2004; Klabbers, 2003; Richard & Zaremba, 2005; Turkle, 2011) and social issues (Goldstein, 2005; Griffiths & Davies, 2005; Rushkoff, 2005; Schleiner, 2001). Despite the comprehensive coverage of these research areas, failure to address the rhetorical perspective of digital games left a void in the current digital game literature (See Figure 1).

Studying digital games from a rhetorical perspective by focusing on the persuasive digital discourses during gameplay is important to the understanding of this emerging phenomenon that has evidently shaped contemporary human experiences. First, unlike traditional stand-alone digital games, gamers' multimodal interactions constitute a major portion of their user experience when playing digital games. Collaborations among gamers rely on whether they are able to effectively persuade each player to complete a task to advance to another game hierarchy of accomplishment and status. Failure to communicate and persuade

Figure 1. Dimensions of digital game research
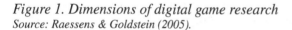
Source: Raessens & Goldstein (2005).

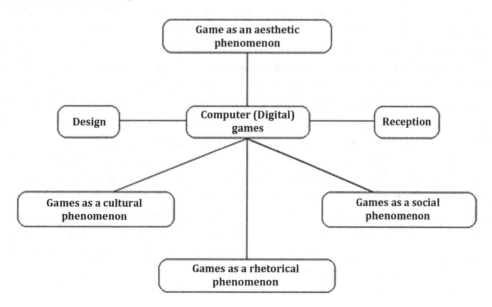

other gamers from the same guild to collaborate is bound to generate incoherent, frustrating, and often dissatisfied user experiences as a result of failed tasks resulting in eliminating from the game. Secondly, a compartmented approach to study digital games, while generating useful piecemeal insights into game design, users' reception, or even macro-level social and cultural issues, are likely to only provide limited understanding of how gamers interact and persuade each other online. Such an approach also does not lead to a holistic understanding of gamers' persuasive digital discourses generated during gameplay.

Therefore, the authors propose to study digital games as a rhetorical phenomenon to address the essential role of multimodal persuasive interactions to better understand gamers' behaviors. Playing digital games is a rhetorical act that involves the manipulations of symbols to persuade game participants during gameplay. The shift to conceptualize and analysis digital game discourses as experiential representations of user experiences during gameplay allows digital game scholars to understand the persuasive manipulations that digital games generate during gaming sessions. Similar to traditional and classical rhetoric that seeks to delight, entertain, educate, and persuade (Kang, 2011), the study of digital games as an experiential rhetorical phenomenon will enable game scholars to uncover what creates positive gamer/user experience, which can be used to design better game systems, to understand the aesthetic experience that gamers feel, and to examine the social and cultural consequences associated with digital games and gameplay.

The main purpose of this book chapter is to introduce the concept of H.I.R.E. as the analytical framework to study digital discourses during gameplay through its application in investigating one representative MMORPG gaming session of *World of Warcraft*. The book chapter attempts to demonstrate the theoretical and methodological implications of H.I.R.E. for digital game researchers and practitioners.

Hybrid Interactive Rhetorical Engagement (H.I.R.E.)

The study of persuasive digital discourses in MMORPGs as the experiential representations of gamers' interactions during gameplay has generated both methodological and theoretical implications. In terms of its methodological implications, the dominant approaches to study digital games and discourses have been mainly focusing on structure, design, reception, and aesthetic of the games (Raessens & Goldstein, 2005). Past studies of digital games have often centered on the classification and explanation of game genres (Consalvo & Dutton, 2006; Frasca, 2003; Herz, 1997; Kafai, 1998, 2006; Kerr, 2006; Subrahmanyam & Greenfield, 1998). However, normative and descriptive approaches have their limitations and often fail to capture the complexity of experiential digital discourses during gameplay. For example, Kerr (2006) categorizes games by examining characters, plots, and action created or action, simulation, and strategy required for gameplay. Other game scholars (e.g., Herz, 1997; Kerr, 2006; Lindley, 2002) also developed similar typologies for analyzing game genres. These typologies provide digital game researchers with a set of useful parameters to compare different digital games. Despite these attempts to categorize digital games, problems and criticism often arise because of many difficulties in accurately categorizing games (Kerr, 2006). Scholars have nevertheless continued to develop a typology for game genres to guide their study of a variety of digital games. To respond to criticisms, digital game scholars have introduced elaborate and non-game-related parameters to characterize and categorize games. For example, Elverdam and Aarseth (2007) developed an elaborate typology as an analytical framework to study all digital games (See Figure 2). Their typology is derived from a set of parameters such as time-space, virtual-physical, player composition-relation, struggle-game state parameters to categorize all digital games into eight broad dimensions to characterize digital games (Elverdam & Aarseth, 2007).

Figure 2. Overview of game typology model
Source: Elverdam & Aarseth (2007, January), p. 21.

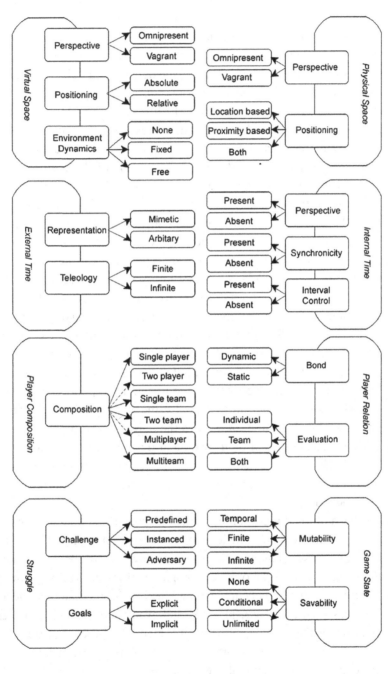

However, these fragmentary approaches to study digital games, while justifiable when digital games first become a worthy academic topic, have left much to be desired because they do not address a far more important question: What is the relationship between persuasive multimodal digital discourses during gameplay and gamers' experiences? The authors thus argue that, in order to properly study these experiential digital discourses, digital game researchers need to capture and examine real-time gaming sessions that will provide more comprehensive and realistic data to shed lights into gamers' experiences. This book chapter is based on a newly-developed rhetorical concept, *hybrid interactive rhetorical engagements* (H.I.R.E.) (Kang, 2011). The authors argue that H.I.R.E. is a useful concept and analytical unit to examine digital discourses as experienced by the gamers. These experiential digital discourses demonstrate both the process and outcome of their persuasive interactions and manipulations during gameplay.

As a theoretical concept developed from rhetorical theories, H.I.R.E. attempts to understand gamers' persuasive interactions in digital games as the focus of exploration into digital discourses. H.I.R.E. is situated within the rhetorical tradition that examines various rhetorical elements (e.g., aural, visual, textual, and kinetic) and their influence in entertaining, educating, informing, and persuading gamers. However, it goes one step further to link these structural elements into an organizing upper-level concept; that is, how gamer experiences during gameplay are represented as digital discourses. H.I.R.E. is particularly useful because the MMORPGs is full of fluidity and exchangeability of persuasive roles among game designers (rhetors) and gamers (audiences) in creating persuasive interactions in the gaming space where rhetorical actions and events are situated. Rhetorically, playing digital games can be equated with the involvement in creation, delivery, and comprehension of symbolic acts (Klabbers, 2003) that contribute to the formation of digital discourses. During gameplay, gamers try to make sense of symbols, icons, characters, scenes created by game designers, but at the same time they also want to understand what other gamers say and act to exert their persuasive intent. To explain gamer experiences further, the authors thus reason when gamers enter into a digital game by adapting themselves to structural and aesthetic design elements within the game, they learn the narratives from game designers, as well as other gamers, and transform and construct their own identities through the adoption of online avatars. Such experience is what Klabbers (2003) characterizes as, "engaging in embodied experience" (p.1). To better understand what gamers have experienced during gameplay, the analysis of generated digital discourses will be instrumental.

"Hybrid" refers to the multimedia capacities which advanced game technologies can provide by offering their users aural, visual, textual, kinetic elements during gameplay. These attributes form the characteristics of digital discourses generated during gameplay. In MMORPGs, gamers constantly exchange textual and aural messages to collaborate on completing their tasks during gameplay (Juul, 2005; Vorderer & Bryant, 2006). Visual elements are also enriched with broadband connection and blue-ray PS3 game devices. Devices such as mouse, joystick, and even virtual reality glove enable gamers to physically move their avatars in the virtual gaming environment. Real-time voice chat/communication is also possible through utilities such as *Ventrilo*, *MorphVox*, and *Xfire*. These technological advancements provide players enriched and intensive gameplay experiences.

"Interactivity" in H.I.R.E. refers to another key attribute of digital discourses and is viewed as an important part of the gamer experience (O'Brien & Toms, 2007). Although interactivity is a term with several different meanings (Kiousis, 2002), in the context of digital games, it refers to the process that a gamer can modify, based on the context and characters involved, the state and happening in a digital game by some action through an interface (Grodal, 2003). Interactivity embedded in digital game devices and gaming environments allow gamers to conduct real-time communication, modify gaming spaces, and navigate the digital game environment (Ryan, 1999). For example, a gamer can explore and respond to the gaming environment by interacting with the game interface, type in chats to converse with other gamers, and enjoy the pleasure of terminating an enemy by similar motor actions.

"Engagements" with digital games are both the reason and the result that gamers want to play MMOR-PGs. The level of engagement that gamers can experience in these environments cannot be understated because it constitutes an important part of their rhetorical experience. Many digital game researchers have often characterized a gaming environment as engaging (Humphreys, 2003; Pickering, 1995). For example, Sony's *EverQuest* was also called "EverCrack" in the gaming community because of its addictive qualities (Burrill, 2005). Despite several initial approaches to characterizing and conceptualizing gamer interactions in a digital game environment, the term, "engagement," is more appropriate and comprehensive in describing the process and the result of gamer experiences in MMORPGs.

Engagement is a psychological concept that refers to how and whether gamers are satisfied with their gameplay experiences (O'Brien & Toms, 2007). As such, rhetorical engagement can be defined as the interpretive, sympathetic, and interactive engagement with all game design elements that gamers are exposed to that have the purposes of educating, informing, entertaining, and persuading them (Tavinor, 2005). Furthermore, this concept can be extended to examine interactive rhetorical engagements with other gamers during gameplay. Such an experience can be said to be similar to hearing a speech, reading a novel, or watching a movie that can persuade, excite, or inspire the audience. Unlike the latter conventional rhetorical discourses, gamers (in particular those in MMORPGs) can take the role of the characters and have a more embodied hybrid interactive rhetorical experience. In other words, MMOR-PGs enable gamers to become an active rhetor to create rhetorical discourses to persuade other gamers to follow a strategy, to create plots unique to each gameplay session, and to experience the twists and turns as gamers co-write an adventure and fantasy novel similar to J.R.R. Tolkiens' *The Lord of the Rings*.

On the basis of discussions above, H.I.R.E. is a useful theoretical concept to describe the digital discourses of what gamers are likely to experience when playing MMORPGs. H.I.R.E. is also beneficial to study online persuasive interactions that are vital to gamers' satisfying gameplay experiences. Furthermore, because the concept of H.I.R.E. helps investigate MMORPG gamer experiences beyond the persuasive intents of game designers (rhetors), H.I.R.E. aims to capture the multiplicity of gameplay experiences by examining the role of participating gamers (audiences) and their fluid role as rhetors during gameplay.

H.I.R.E. refers to a state of engaging and interactive gameplay experiences when collaborating with other gamers in MMORPGs. Gamers interact with each other in the rhetorical space of digital games where rhetorical acts are performed to respond to the persuasive interactions of all game participants during gameplay. When gamers assume their roles in the gameplay acts during their gaming sessions, they utilize multimodal rhetorical discourses to persuade each other to perform the tasks leading to more a pleasurable and engaging experience they seek for when taking part in a game. H.I.R.E. properly characterizes gamer experiences and is produced by a combination of multimodal rhetorical interactions such as textual, aural, visual, and even kinetic interactivities. To sum up, H.I.R.E. is useful to research and analyze what gamers are likely to experience and feel from a sequence of persuasive interactions and interplays of textual, aural, visual, and kinetic rhetorical elements when playing digital games. Rhetorical engagements of the gamers are also derived from a series of rhetorical events made possible by the interactivity, immersion, interconnectivity, and role-playing functions abundant in MMORPGs. Furthermore, engagements with the digital game and other gamers are also the results of continuous persuasive exchanges during gameplay.

Research Questions

This book chapter analyzes one representative gaming session to answer the following research questions:

Question 1: How do digital game scholars describe and conceptualize digital gameplay experiences as a rhetorical phenomenon?

Question 2: How will the rhetoric of experience help analyze experiential representations of digital discourses during gameplay?

Solutions and Recommendations

Research Method

The concept of H.I.R.E. will be used to analyze multimodal digital discourses experienced by gamers when playing MMORPGs. The experience is designed and predetermined by MMORPG game developers (Humphreys, 2003). The emphasis on H.I.R.E. as gamers' ultimate digital discourses will be able to address the constraints of narratologist's approach by expanding the domain of study to cover "interactive texts" that encompass not only the text, but the role of audience/ gamers, and medium itself (Kerr, 2006).

One representative gaming session was chosen from the collected 120 gaming sessions when one of the authors participated in three guilds as a player in *World of Warcraft (WoW)* game over the past three years. The guilds included *Adult Swim*, *Legends of Velen*, and *Big Dogs*. *Adult Swim* is located in the realm of *Velen*. There are a total of 83 guild members (as of September 17, 2010). The character gender ratio is 63% male and 37% female, distributed among the following roles (with total number of guild members in the parentheses): *Death Knights* (11), *Druids* (10), *Hunters* (11), *Mages* (5), *Paladins* (9), *Priests* (7), *Rogues* (9), *Shamans* (5), *Warlocks* (7), and *Warriors* (9).

The selection of *World of Warcraft* (*WoW*) is based on its popularity among MMOPRG communities. Furthermore, MMORPGs, such as *World of Warcraft*, from traditional digital games, is enriched, real-time, character-playing, immersive (McMahan, 2003, p.67) and engaging experience that many gamers encounter. Right after its first launch by Blizzard Entertainment in November 2004, *World of Warcraft* has surpassed other MMORPGs in the digital game market (Ducheneaut, Yee, Nickell, & Moore, 2006). In 2005, *World of Warcraft* became one of the most popular and successful massively multiplayer role-playing games, with more than 6 million subscribers in the world (Ducheneaut et al., 2006). This widely popular MMORPG game is designed to create a virtual gaming space where gamers can collaborate and negotiate with other players to co-create an engaging gameplay experience in a mythical world with chosen identities. The game is designed to enable gamers to interact with other players using avatars, metaphors, concepts, and tools from the virtual medieval period. What is created in the virtual world is equivalent to the concept of game as "designed experience" (Squire, 2006) in which a wide range of human practices is conducted by gamers to "actively inhabit those worlds of rules and texts and render them meaningful" (Steinkuehler, 2006, p.97). Its gamers are required to select or create their own avatar characters designed by game developers. Interactions among gamers, though dependent on tasks, missions, and circumstances, are still scripted and pre-determined.

Description of the Gaming Session

The representative gaming session was used to demonstrate the theoretical and methodological benefits in analyzing MMORPG gaming sessions as rhetorical entities is a battle with *Lady Deathwhisper*, who is the second in command in the *Icecrown Citadel*. In this gaming session, the raid leader began by arranging each raid member in different strategic positions, so the raid can be ready for the upcoming battle with the arch-enemy, *Lady Deathwhisper*. The raid leader used aural commands to assign each guild member to either the right, left, or back positions. For example, aural interactivity was done by saying "Bodi going on the left," "Xander going on the back with RhhockeyBoy," "Character A is assigned to the right flank….. are assigned to the left flank. …… are assigned to the back of the room." Other gamers immediately provided aural feedback to clarify what to do after hearing the commands. These exchanges of aural interactivities demonstrated a sequence of persuasive expressions initiated by the raid leader. Even though the voice commands tended to be brief and succinct, they were persuasive because all identified raid members (such as *Bodi*, *Xander*, or *RhhockeyBoy*) all acted accordingly. These gamers demonstrated their kinetic responses after being persuaded by the raid leader. In other words, the aural interactivity initiated by the raid leader led to the persuasion of the raid members to respond by using kinetic interactivities (as demonstrated by the movement of avatars). The strategic positioning of each raid member was an important step because the leader needs to prepare every player by counting down before the raid began.

Discussions

Using H.I.R.E. to Analyze Persuasive Digital Discourses in this Gaming Session

The multimodal interactivities were not merely employed by interactions between the raid leader and gamers. Other raid members were found to generate digital discourses with ample textual and aural interactivities to communicate with each other, which ultimately show their gameplay experience. These multimodal digital discourses during gameplay were noteworthy persuasive interactions as seen in any MMORPG gaming session. For the fight with *Lady Deathwhisper*, the raid members had to kill the allies showing up on the left flank, right flank, and in the back close to the gate quickly and efficiently during the phase one. After the allies were terminated successfully, all *DPS* raid members needed to switch back to *Lady Deathwhisper* as soon as possible, so her *mana* shield was going to disappear and then went into the next phase of the fight. Also, *Damage per Second* (*DPS*) of the raid members played an important role during the complete period of the fight. The game was designed to contain the gameplay rule that, the higher amount of *DPS* a raid group had, the sooner a task can be done. The raid leader arranged the positions according to their classes and *DPS* attributes (melee and ranged) evenly to the left and right to make sure the time limitation was met.

Lady Deathwhisper is a Non-Player Character (NPC) and a virtual representation of various in-game design elements created by the designers of *World of Warcraft* to make the *Icecrown Citadel* raid dungeon persuasive. *Lady Deathwhisper* is an in-game character equipped with multimodal interactive capabilities to make the raid in the game convincing and entertaining. For example, *Lady Deathwhisper* often threatens the gamers with her aural and textual interactivities during the raid. She voices her anger by saying "What is this disturbance? You dare trespass on this hallowed ground. This shall be your final resting place…." In addition, her threats are presented in the textual area in red fonts at the left bottom of the screen. The use of the term, "hallowed ground", intends to present a sense of medieval atmosphere and carries the same meaning as a sacred ground blessed by priests, druids, and shamans. *Lady Deathwhisper* is programmed to cast *Death and Decay* spell, which is a green puddle on the ground and deals damage to players who stand in it. When *Lady Deathwhisper* continues to present her rhetorical manipulations either through aural, visual, or kinetic interactivities by voicing her threats, waving her magic power, and casting her green puddle spell visually, all gamers have to respond by either moving their avatars (i.e., kinetic interactivity), and discussing their strategies that will lead to more kinetic interactivities among these gamers, so they can avoid being terminated. In response, these gamers reacted promptly to make the gameplay enjoyable and engaging. At the beginning of this gaming session, the raid leader rearranged the gamers to a new strategic position. The raid leader also used aural commands to persuade selected gamers to respond by moving their avatars. Once this was done, *Lady Deathwhisper* voices another rounds of embedded aural interactivity. In response, the raid leader solicited the help of a caster, so the raid can be successful. During this raid, numerous interactivities were observed on the screen near the end of the session. Visually engaging images were shown when the gamers attack *Lady Deathwhisper*. Textual interactivities (such as "Out of Range" and "Dominate the Mind of Nugemage") that recorded spontaneous gamer actions were also presented to let the gamers know their status in the game.

Applying the concept of H.I.R.E. to analyze digital discourses during *WoW* gameplay enables digital game scholars to explore the embedded in-game design elements as persuasive manipulations by game designers (as rhetors) to make *Lady Deathwhisper* a persuasive character with her magical power. Her programmed behaviors are rhetorical in nature because they intend to persuade and invite multimodal interactivities from these gamers. Adding these visual effects (or visual interactivities) is game designers' persuasive tool to make *World of Warcraft* more engaging and entertaining. The battle with *Lady Deathwhisper* involves textual, aural, visual, and kinetic interactivities used by the gamers to interact with each other, game characters, and in-game interface. All these rhetorical manipulations also enable the gamers to fully immerse with the game environment and the characters in their pursuit of highly engaging intensive gameplay experiences. The experience of playing *WoW* is rhetorical in nature, in that all gamers constantly employ multimodal interactive expressions and practices to persuade other gamers and the in-game design elements. For example, *Lady Deathwhisper's* voice was heard by all raid members along with the textual representations of what she says. The raid leader coordinated through aural and textual commands to persuade all members and ensure all raid members work synergistically to defeat *Lady Deathwhisper*. The leader's persuasion was effective because he clearly recommended what should be done to make a successful raid.

The concept of H.I.R.E. enables researchers to examine digital discourses during gameplay as the experiential representations of persuasive digital discourses that occurred during gameplay among gamers and game designers. Although a thorough analysis of aural, visual, textual, and kinetic interactive components of these digital discourses might help researchers to understand what constitutes gamers' gameplay experiences, it does not address why gamers are persuaded during gameplay. In other word, this captured gaming session helps account for the persuasive interactions by which gamers rely on multimodal interactivities to be immersed in the game, so optimal engagements can be achieved. However, without effective persuasion, a MMORPG is not likely to maintain a high level of interest among many gamers. Furthermore, because playing *WoW* is made up of constant collaborations among gamers, the authors argue that the collaborative process in itself demonstrates how gamers have experienced through a series of persuasive interactions that prompt other players to adapt their motoric, cognitive, and emotional states to different gaming sessions.

These structural features of digital games demonstrate game designers' rhetorical manipulation to persuade gamers. Despite being fully aware of the make-believe world experienced in *WoW* gamers are persuaded to take part in these gameplay sessions with other players to seek entertainment and gratifications. Bogost (2007) refer to these types of embedded rhetorical expressions, executions, and practices as "procedural rhetoric" in which rules of gameplay constitute an important part of gamer experience. For example, when gamers adopt the avatar of a healer (class), they are given the capabilities to cast spells, heal other wounded gamers, and bolster the spirits of other gamers, according to the embedded gameplay rules for this avatar class.

The concept of H.I.R.E. provides digital game researchers to better understand gameplay as a process of persuasive interactions and to offer an analytical tool to evaluate why one MMORPG is more engaging and entertaining than the other. Theoretically, H.I.R.E. provides a close theoretical linkage to dominant rhetorical scholars like Kenneth Burke (1966) in explaining the persuasive process and outcome. According to Burke (1966) in *The Language as Symbolic Action*, any purposeful use of symbols can be considered as one type of symbolic action. The symbolic action is not limited to language and literature, but also includes magic, ritual, religion, and history as stated in Burke's (1965) another book, *Permanence and Change* and *Attitudes toward History*. As such, Walz (2004) contends gameplay is also a symbolic action among participating agents because persuasive manipulations exist in that rhetorical situation. The study of gameplay experience is thus appropriate to be examined by H.I.R.E., a theoretical concept from rhetorical theories.

During *WoW* gameplay, the gamers are required to produce their own multimodal symbolic activities pertinent to that situation, so their gameplay experience can be obtained. Textual, aural, visual, and kinetic interactivities are the commonly used symbols that game designers and gamers employ to respond to many persuasive acts during gameplay. The rhetorical manipulations during *WoW* gameplay are even more substantial and noticeable when compared with other conventional game platforms. For example, in *the Icecrown Citadel* raid dungeon to defeat *Lady Deathwhisper*, her ghoulish image is intentionally created by game designers to represent persuasively her role as *the Supreme Overseer of the Cult of the Damned*. This in-game design element is also equipped with many abilities to create different rhetorical situations for the gamers to respond. For example, *Lady Deathwhisper* is able to cast a *Death and Decay* spell on attacking gamers by inflicting 4,500 Shadow damage per second on all targets. She is also programmed to cast the *Dominate Mind* spell on one attacker within 50,000 yard range to charm them for 20 seconds. *Lady Deathwhisper* is designed by a carefully planned combination of visual, kinetic, aural, and textual interactive symbols that make her a convincing manipulative tool to persuade the gamers to fully engage with the boss during this raid. Such a full engagement often leads to the production of multimodal interactions from the gamers. Furthermore, different rhetorical manipulations are presented during gameplay such as when the *Dominate Mind* spell is cast on two players, *Duhagoeszap* and *Squirrelnut*. Any gamer, affected or not, will need to respond to the new rhetorical situation with two of their members under the spell. As such, casting a spell can be argued as a symbolic action by *Lady Deathwhisper* to manipulate these gamers to respond through using similar interactive symbols embedded in *WoW*. When a gamer is charmed by the *Dominate Mind* spell, the charmed gamer will be mind-controlled for 20 seconds and during the period their damage will be increased by 200% while healing increased by 500%.The spell will alter kinetic interactivity of the gamers during subsequent gameplays. This example shows the manipulative effects of an in-game design element on gamers and their gameplay experiences. How will the gamers respond to this situation? What will happen to those who are hit by the *Dominate Mind* spell? The decisions to initiate multimodal symbol-using activities for the situation demonstrate gamer reactions to the designer-initiated rhetorical manipulations.

Walz (2004) maintains gameplay is "a rhetorical performance between player(s) and game design, a symbolic action that takes place amongst agents" (p. 186). The above description clearly demonstrates the persuasive manifestation of *WoW* gameplay as observed in the persuasive use of in-game design elements to manipulate the multimodal responses of the gamers. Aural, visual, textual, and kinetic inter-activities constitute an essential part of gamers' experiences. The discussion above shows that a skillful manipulation of these in-game elements can lead to most gratifying gameplay experience among gamers. The analysis above also demonstrates how H.I.R.E. can provide an analytic tool to examine a gaming session by focusing on the key components in the concept of H.I.R.E.; that is, hybridity, interactivity, rhetoric, and engagement.

The Rhetoric of Experience

To argue that gamer experience in gaming sessions justify the proposition of "rhetoric of experience" (or "experiential rhetoric"), which requires the need to conceptualize gameplay experiences by game rhetorical scholars. Extending from Ermi and Mäyrä's model (2005) (See Figure 3), H.I.R.E. can be argued as a theoretical concept to study intensive and immersive experience that gamers enjoy when playing *WoW*. The unique game design features (such as narratives, role-playing capabilities, and global interconnectivity with other players) contribute to gamer experience with *WoW*.

Figure 3. Ermi and Mäyrä's SCI model

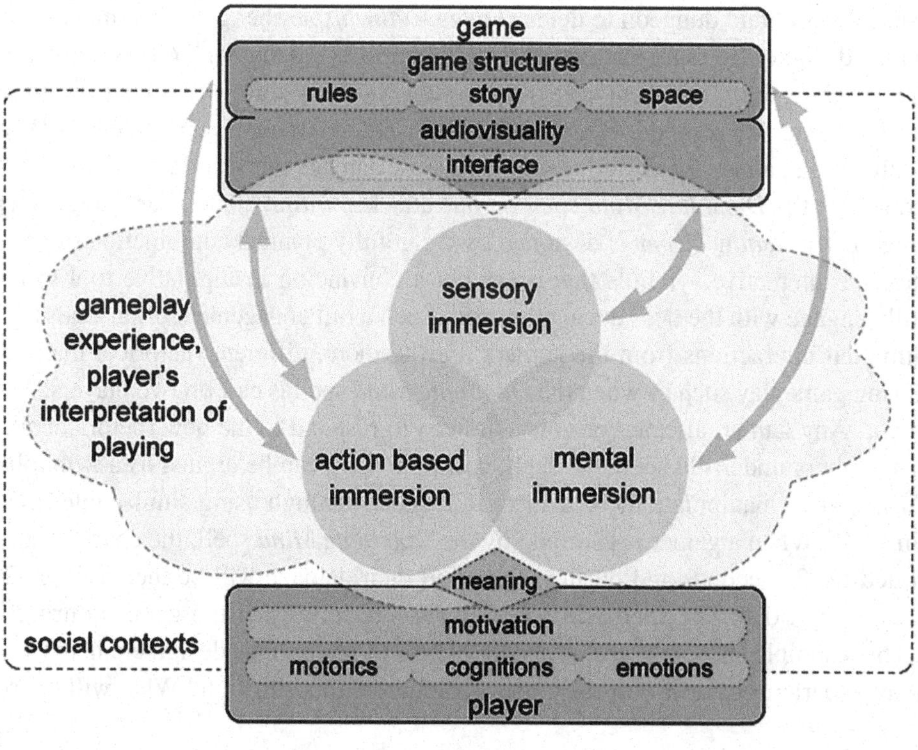

The design of *WoW* (including the writing of the game narratives, interface design, audio-visual discourses in cyberspace) is rhetorical because game designers aim to create the best possible games through their manipulations of these devices, so gamers will purchase or subscribe to these digital games. The process and outcome of employing digital discourses to persuade gamers to purchase the game or to take part in the gameplay are rhetorical in nature. Like rhetors in classical Greece, these game designers want to persuade gamers to take some actions that can lead to playful and pleasurable experience with the game (Korhonen, Montola, & Arrasvuori, 2009). However, what gamers really experience depends on their interpretation of the ample rhetorical expressions and practices manifested in the forms of online chats, discourses, collaboration, interaction made possible by the fictitious in-game design elements in *WoW*. The process of experiencing *WoW* gaming sessions is affected by other players' actions, their involvement with the gameplay, and exposure to audio-visual game design elements. All of these in the end contribute to the H.I.R.E. many *WoW* players are likely to feel. In any rhetorical situation, how gamers are persuaded is surely dependent on individual characteristics (such as cognition, emotion, and motorics).

Therefore, the authors call for "the rhetoric of experience" as a term to study experiential representations and effects from the structural, procedural, locational, behavioral, and cognitive aspects of the hybrid interactive rhetorical engagement (H.I.R.E.) experienced by the gamers. Through the analysis of one representative gaming session, this chapter situates the study of user experience within "the rhetoric of experience." In game research, the concept of "experience" has been widely studied and referred to as "user experience" (Korhonen et al., 2009), "flow" (Csikszentmihalyi, 1990), or "player experience" (Mäyrä, 2007). Some scholars have used the term, "gameplay," to refer to what gamers feel during the game (Tavinor, 2005). However, this term may encompass different activities that lead to variations in their experience. Scholars like Peña and Hancock (2006) also focus on types of interactions leading to the gameplay experiences felt by the players. Among these scholars, experience during gameplay is often treated as multi-dimensional (Mäyrä, 2007), contextualized (Mäyrä, 2007), and measurable (Korhonen et al., 2009). These conceptualizations provide an abundant foundation for game rhetoricians to understand how to define experience from the rhetoric of experience perspective.

The study of the experiential aspect of digital games, digital discourses, and gameplay has grabbed the attention of game scholars in recent years (Banks, 2002; Consalvo, 2006; Murray, 2006). On the basis of the close relationship between digital discourses and gamer experience, this chapter therefore argues that H.I.R.E. is a useful tool to analyze digital discourses as gamer experience representations during *WoW* gameplay. Other game scholars also agree gameplay experiences are designed and predetermined (Humphreys, 2005), because the *WoW* game developers need to utilize available programming devices to create a fictitious, yet believable, gaming space where the players participate in the creation and enjoyment of this unique experience. The concept of H.I.R.E. thus enables digital game scholars to examine what the gamers will experience as a result of participants' persuasive manipulations during gameplay. Therefore, the name, "rhetoric of experience," will be an appropriate nomenclature to describe any rhetorical research in digital games in general, and in *WoW* in particular.

This chapter claims that gamer experiences derive from the engagements with the multimodal persuasive discourses created by the game developers and co-generated players in a particular rhetorical situation. Rhetorical scholars like Kenneth Burke have also argued the link between symbol (symbolic action), audience's experience, and persuasion. In *Counter-Statement*, Burke (1968) equates the symbol as "the verbal parallel to a pattern of experience" (p. 152). For the symbol to be appealing to the audience, the patterns of experience of both the rhetors and the audiences need to "closely coincide" (Burke, 1968, p. 153). As stated above, *WoW* is the sophisticated creation of a fantasy game world when the game developers rhetorically manipulate the multimodal interactivities, in-game design elements, and procedural rules that are made available to them. In other words, the symbol-using activities of the designers represent the sharing and creation of their own experience in envisioning a fantasy world infested with dragons, mobs, undeads, and mythical characters.

To conclude, this book chapter attempts to demonstrate a rhetorical concept, H.I.R.E., is useful to analyze digital discourses during gameplay as gamers' experiential representations. The authors explain the concept of the rhetoric of experience. For the purposes of the discussions, H.I.R.E. is situated within *WoW* because of its popularity in MMORPGs. The concept, however, can be applied to any digital game platforms in the future, as long as there are persuasive acts involved during gameplay.

FUTURE RESEARCH DIRECTIONS

The preliminary analysis of one representative gaming session aims to provide a glimpse into the application of H.I.R.E. to analyzing digital discourses during gameplay as experiential representations of users' overall experiences. The analysis presented in this chapter discusses these characteristics of emerging digital persuasive digital discourses and their implications for understanding gamers' experiences in MMORPGs. In this chapter, the authors argue that user experiences with digital games (in general) and MMORPGs (in particular) should be studied as a rhetorical phenomenon to address the critical role of rhetorical theories to better study digital games. MMORPGs demand their players to coordinate their actions to successful complete a task—a rhetorical situation that entails numerous persuasive acts among gamers to reach a consensus for concerted efforts within their guild.

This book chapter analyzes digital discourses as part of the rhetoric of experience, yet this approach has generated more research directions for digital game researchers to study in the future. First, an important part in studying H.I.R.E. as the rhetoric of experience needs to examine the meaning-making process that gamers go through in comprehending and agreeing with multimodal rhetorical expressions and practices when playing *WoW*. Because gamer experience is conceptualized as both subjective and personal responses, the roles of motivation, motorics, cognitions, and emotions in assisting gamers with the meaning-making process should also be examined.

In "The Question Concerning Technology," Martin Heidegger proposes a term, "Enframing," to argue that revealing "is indeed the essence of technology" (Heidegger, 1977, p.30). As Heidegger (1977) continues to argue, "We are questioning concerning technology in order to bring to light our relationship to its essence. The essence of modern technology shows itself in what we call Enframing" (p. 23). Heidegger's position of equating technology with revealing (the truth) is similar to Plato's stance that rhetoric. Deriving from Heidegger's (1997) approach to technology, digital game scholars may study digital game technology by maintaining that rhetorical discourses are not just read or interpreted to understand what author/designer wants to say. Instead, scholars should study digital discourses as co-created by author/designer as well as audience/viewers/readers/players allows rhetoric and composition scholars to uncover the rhetoricity of technology as an area of study. In other words, while the writing (discourse creation) process is often completed when scholars study rhetorical discourses in traditional technologies, the writing (discourse creation) process is never finished and generative. As such, the study of digital game technology as a rhetorical process may cast doubt to the fundamental assumptions about rhetoric as an author/rhetor based enterprise by emphasizing the discourse creation process.

Unlike traditional digital games, MMORPGs allow users to take part in digital gameplay by creating their own characters (Feliciak, 2003). The computer-generated "electronic contact zone" (Selfe & Selfe, 1994) will enable users to "play an active role in modulating the transmissions that reach him, and has control over them" (Feliciak, 2003, p.91). The fluidity of users and game designers has led to a unique rhetorical domain that deserves further study. The emerging Massively Multiplayer Online Role-Playing Games (MMORPGs) is likely to challenge existing rhetorical traditions. Future digital game research can develop an activity-based rhetorical perspective that integrates Vygotsky's theory into the conceptualization of human rhetorical activity and the examination of rhetorical discourses facilitated by MMORPG players. As digital discourses during gameplay are also generated from human activities to respond to various rhetorical situations (Bitzer, 1968), the authors reason that, as a technology, MMORPGs have fundamentally transformed the process of rhetorical discourse generation, thus warranting a study of this emerging rhetorical tradition.

Theoretical Implications

Previous game researchers often focus on digital games as narratives by examining the structure and interpretation of game narratives. For example, Kerr (2006) summarizes contemporary game scholars often adopt one of the three approaches to study game narratives:

1. A classical, formalist, and narrow approach;
2. A historically-located and cultural post-structuralist approach;
3. Rejection of the narrative theories.

The limitations of these approaches are clear because gameplay experiences as a manifestation of persuasive interactions goes far beyond texts and narratives. The authors therefore argue if digital game scholars study H.I.R.E., in which texts and narratives make up an important part of gameplay experiences, the debates on how game narratives should be studied and if traditional narrative theories can be applied to dynamic interactive narratives will carry less theoretical significance. Furthermore, the long-lasting debates between narratologist (a text-centric approach to studying games) and ludologist (a gameplay-centric approach to studying games) can be resolved by studying H.I.R.E when game scholars begin to examine narratives and the process of using narratives leading to persuasive interactions during gameplay. This perspective has already been echoed by many game scholars who began to examine other non-textual components of gameplay experiences (such as visual, aural, kinetic, or procedural dimensions that make up of their experience) (Bogost, 2007; Bolter & Grusin, 2000; Darley, 2000; Kerr, 2006; Poole, 2000).

Secondly, the authors would argue the process of playing *WoW,* if conceptualized as a rhetorical process, cannot be fully understood by examining merely structural in-game design components (no matter whether they are audio, visual, kinetic, or textual) as stand-alone structural components (Humphreys, 2005). Connections between these elements should be examined to see how their synergetic integration leads to positive gameplay experiences. As such, H.I.R.E. offers a useful analytical tool to uncover the interconnectivity among these persuasive interactions demonstrated in the generated digital discourses. What gamers experience from playing *WoW* is influenced not only by these rhetor-centric in-game design components, but also by social, economic, cultural, and psychological aspects of gamers that become parts of gamer experience during gameplay (Humphreys, 2005; Yee, 2006). Humphreys (2005) claims gamer experience is derived from "a complex interplay between the rules and affordances of a game, the user's offline context, and the online social world created with other players" (p. 79). In this chapter, the authors reason that gamers create their own rhetorical experience once they are given the rhetorical tools embedded in any digital game to respond to numerous rhetorical manipulations during gameplay. To further extend this line of thinking, the generation and maintenance of rhetorical engagement with the game are not completely controlled by game designers; instead, interactions with existing game designers' rhetorical devices, and mostly importantly with other gamers during gameplay lead to these processes to create effective persuasive interactions and ultimately gratifying gameplay experiences as felt by many gamers during a gaming session.

Third, the experiential characteristics of digital discourses in MMORPGs will certainly pose challenges to rhetorical scholars in terms of what to study and how things work to create gameplay experiences. For example, van den Hoogen, IJsselsteijn, and de Kort (2008) observes game researchers are faced with developing "a coherent and fine-grained set of methods and tools that enable the measurement of entertainment experience in a sensitive, reliable and valid manner" (p.11). These problems are likely to attribute to the difficulty in defining what gamer experience is and what theoretical approaches are to be taken to study them. Psychologists like Csikszentmihalyi (1990) propose the concept of flow to capture how gamers feel when engaging in pleasurable activities. Nevertheless, because of its emphasis on intrinsic motivation of the gamers to seek entertainment as a psychological phenomenon, Csikszent-mihalyi's (1990) flow model does not take into consideration contextual (such as socio-cultural factors) influencing gamer experience.

To further describe what should be examined in digital game research, Aarseth (1997) argues gamer experience should be studied, but he does not elaborate how to study it. Kerr (2006) expands Aarseth's stance and states that gamer experience in a digital game are "influenced as much by the randomness built into the medium, as the choices made by the user and the organisation of the surface elements by the designer" (Kerr, 2006, p.21). Aaseth's (1997) proposition clearly indicates gamer actions play a vital role in constituting gamer experience during gameplay. The creation of their gameplay experiences often goes beyond what game designers have determined when a game is first conceptualized and designed.

Methodological Implications

Methods in current digital game research can be broadly divided into empirical-quantitative and human-istic-qualitative approaches that examine this important area of study with diverse ontological, episte-mological, and philosophical assumptions (Williams, 2006). Consalvo and Dutton (2006) observe game scholars who use empirical research methods often examined either gamers or the games themselves. Empirical research methods on behaviors of the gamers often use experiment (Cai, 2006; Smyth, 2007; Williams, 2006), questionnaire survey (Jansz & Martens, 2005; Williams, 2006), and in-depth interview (Schott & Horrell, 2005; Yates & Littleton, 1999). On the other hand, researchers who are interested in digital games themselves often content analyzed different types of games (Elverdam & Aarseth, 2007), game violence and its effects on aggression (Kinder, 2003), portrayals of woman or minority characters (Okorafor & Davenport, 2001; Ow, 2000), socio-emotional and task communication (Peña & Hancock, 2006), or the presence of avatars (Okorafor & Davenport, 2001).

Although scholars have identified potential areas of research in digital games, many have criticized the lack of theories in digital game study. Most game theories are borrowed from media research, which is criticized as "theoretical imperialism" (Mallon & Webb, 2006, p.209). As a result, Mallon and Webb (2006) point out there is a lack of analytical tools, methods, and interpretative approaches that have further hindered the development of game research as a distinctive discipline. The lack of methodology is an area that concerns many digital game researchers. Aarseth (1997) laments the lack of methodology and theory of game studies and notes that games "are analyzed willy-nilly, with tools that happen to be at hand, such as film theory or narratology" (p.1). Kücklich (2002) also criticizes narratological theoretical approaches to study games by stating that these approaches have "failed to yield valid results because they could not 'read' the games they were studying. Literary scholars were simply too absorbed in these fantastic worlds to pay attention to the rules governing that (game) universe" (p. 1). Communication scholars are often attracted to study how game contents can influence players and the manifestation of game contents to reflect existing problems in our world. Gamers' real experiences are often ignored as a viable research object as a result of the difficulty in data collection and the lack of a useful analytic tool.

CONCLUSION

H.I.R.E. is developed from the line of rhetorical research and this concept offers a potentially powerful analytical tool to examine the persuasive interactions during gameplay. The concept is comprehensive to cover all key characteristics of MMORPGs and future game genres. At the same time, the concept examines one important aspect of gameplay experiences; that is, being persuaded to interact with the in-design elements and with other gamers' symbolic action. Because of games constantly change due to the interactions and manipulations of players using symbols to persuade and convince other players, the rhetorical approach of digital games as H.I.R.E. intends to investigate will help advance digital game theories by examining the persuasive manipulations during gameplay.

In conclusion, the emergence of MMORPGs has created a new situation where "rhetorical events" not only occur between game designers and gamers, but among gamers themselves when they form a team to complete a raid or a mission. These interwoven "rhetorical events" continuously "write" or "re-write" game designer's rhetoric as a result of intense gamer interactions during gameplay (Kang, 2011). Therefore, the emergence of MMORPGs is important to digital game scholars because of the intense gameplay experiences felt by gamers in such an immersive environment, characterized by constant interactions with other gamers, with the game design elements, and with the overall socio-cultural milieu created in MMORPGs. Such intensive multimodal engagements with digital games are significant at individual, social, economic and political levels (Yee, 2006). The challenges to digital game research, both theoretically and methodologically, need to be addressed to advance the knowledge in this important phenomenon.

REFERENCES

Aarseth, E. J. (1997). Cybertext: Perspectives on ergodic literature. Baltimore, MD: Johns Hopkins University Press.

Aponovich, D., & Grannan, M. (2013, November 26). *Market overview: Digital customer experience delivery platforms*. Cambridge, MA: Forrester Research, Inc.

Banks, J. (2002). Gamers as co-creators: Enlisting the virtual audiences-a report from the net face. In M. Balnaves, T. O'Regan, & J. Sternberg (Eds.), *Mobilising the audience* (pp. 188–212). St. Lucia, Queensland: University of Queensland Press.

Bitzer, L. F. (1968, January). The rhetorical situation. *Philosophy & Rhetoric*, 1–14.

Bogost, I. (2007, July). *Persuasive games: The expressive power of videogames*. Cambridge, MA: The MIT Press.

Bolter, J. D., & Grusin, R. (2000). Remediation: Understanding new media. Cambridge, MA: The MIT Press.

Bryce, J., & Rutter, J. (2005). Gendered gaming in gendered space. In J. Raessens & J. Goldstein (Eds.), Handbook of computer game studies (pp. 301-310). Cambridge, MA: The MIT Press.

Burke, K. (1965). Permanence and change: An anatomy of purpose (2nd ed.). Indianapolis, IN: The Bobbs-Merrill Company, Inc.

Burke, K. (1966). Language as symbolic action: Essays on life, literature, and method. Berkeley, CA: The University of California Press.

Burke, K. (1968). Counter-statement. Los Angles, CA: University of California Press.

Burrill, D. A. (2005). Out of the box: Performance, drama, and interactive software. *Modern Drama*, *48*(3), 492–512. doi:10.3138/md.48.3.492

Cai, X. (2005, February). An experimental examination of the computer's time displacement effects. *New Media & Society*, *7*(1), 8–21. doi:10.1177/1461444805049139

Calvillo-Gámez, E. H., Cairns, P., & Cox, A. L. (2010). *Assessing the core elements of the gaming experience*. London: Springer. doi:10.1007/978-1-84882-963-3_4

Consalvo, M., & Dutton, N. (2006, December). Game analysis: Developing a methodological toolkit for the qualitative study of games. *Game Studies, 6*(1). Retrieved from http://gamestudies.org/0601/articles/consalvo_dutton

Csikszentmihalyi, M. (1990). *Flow: The psychology of optimal experience*. New York, NY: Harper.

Darley, A. (2000). *Visual digital culture. Surface play and spectacle in new media genres*. London: Routledge.

Digital Experiences. (n.d.). *Digital experiences ecosystem*. Retrieved April 26, 2015 from http://digitalexperiences.com.au/interactive/

Ducheneaut, N., Yee, N., Nickell, E., & Moore, R. J. (2006, October). Building an mmo with mass appeal: A look at gameplay in world of warcraft. *Games and Culture*, *1*(4), 281–317. doi:10.1177/1555412006292613

Elverdam, C., & Aarseth, E. (2007, January). Game classification and game design: Construction through critical analysis. *Games and Culture*, *2*(1), 3–22. doi:10.1177/1555412006286892

Entertainment Software Association. (2011). *Video game and the economy.* Washington, DC: Entertainment Software Association. Retrieved October 31, 2014, from http://www.theesa.com/gamesindailylife/economy.pdf

Entertainment Software Association. (2014). *Industry facts: Sales and genre data.* Washington, DC: The Entertainment Software Association. Retrieved November 10, 2014, from http://www.theesa.com/facts/salesandgenre.asp

Entertainment Software Association. (2015a, April 14). *Press release: More than 150 million Americans play video games.* Retrieved April 23, 2015, from http://www.theesa.com/article/150-million-americans-play-video-games/

Entertainment Software Association. (2015b). *Essential facts about the computer and video game industry.* Retrieved April 23, 2015, from http://www.theesa.com/wp-content/uploads/2015/04/ESA-Essential-Facts-2015.pdf

Ermi, L., & Mäyrä, F. (2005). *Fundamental components of the gameplay experience: Analyzing immersion.* Paper presented at the DiGRA 2005 Conference: Changing View-Worldds in Play, Vancouver, Canada.

Filiciak, M. (2003). Hyperidentities: Postmodern identity patterns in massively multiplayer online role-playing games. In M. J. P. Wolf & B. Perron (Eds.), *The video game theory reader* (pp. 87–102). New York, NY: Routledge.

Frasca, G. (2003). Simulation versus narrative: Introduction to ludology. In M. J. P. Wolf & B. Perron (Eds.), *The video game theory reader* (pp. 221–235). New York, NY: Routledge.

Grodal, T. (2003). Stories for eye, ear, and muscles: Video games, media, and embodied experiences. In M. J. P. Wolf & B. Perron (Eds.), *The video game theory reader* (pp. 129–155). New York, NY: Routledge.

Heidegger, M. (1977). *The question concerning technology, and other essays* (W. Lovitt, Trans.). New York, NY: Harper & Row, Publishers, Inc.

Herz, J. C. (1997). Joystick nation: How video game ate our quarters, won our hearts, and rewired our minds. Boston, MA: Little, Brown.

Humphreys, S. (2003). Online multiuser games: Playing for real. *Australian Journal of Communication, 30*(1), 79–91.

Humphreys, S. (2005, March). Productive players: Online computer games' challenge to conventional media forms. *Communication & Critical Cultural Studies, 2*(1), 37–51.

Ihamäki, P. (2015). Digital human experience models for augmented reality mobile wellness devices. *International Journal of Digital Human, 1*(1), 44–71. doi:10.1504/IJDH.2015.067134

Jansz, J., & Martens, L. (2005). Gaming at a lan event: The social context of playing video games. *New Media & Society, 7*(3), 333–355. doi:10.1177/1461444805052280

Juul, J. (2005). Games telling stories? In J. Raessens & J. Goldstein (Eds.), Handbook of computer game studies (pp. 219-226). Cambridge, MA: The MIT Press.

Kafai, Y. B. (1998). Video game designs by girls and boys: Variability and consistency of gender differences. In J. Cassell & H. Jenkins (Eds.), From barbie to mortal combat: Gender and computer games. Cambridge, MA: MIT Press.

Kafai, Y. B. (2006, January). Playing and making games for learning: Instructionist and constructionist perspectives for game studies. *Games and Culture*, *1*(1), 36–40. doi:10.1177/1555412005281767

Kang, Y. W. (2011). *Hybrid interactive rhetoric engagements in Massively Multiplayer Online Role-Playing Games (MMORPGs): Examining the role of rhetors and audiences in generative rhetorical discourses* (Diss. The University of Texas at El Paso). Ann Arbor, MI: UMI.

Kerr, A. (2006). *The business and culture of digital games: Gamework/gameplay*. London, UK: Sage Publications.

Kinder, M. (2003, Spring). Honoring the past and creating the future in hyperspace: New technologies and cultural specificity. *The Contemporary Pacific*, *15*(1), 93–115. doi:10.1353/cp.2003.0017

Kiousis, S. (2002). Interactivity: A concept explication. *New Media & Society*, *4*(3), 355–383. doi:10.1177/146144480200400303

Klabbers, J. H. G. (2003). *The gaming landscape: A taxonomy for classifying games and simulations*. Paper presented at the LEVEL UP: Digital Games Research Conference, Utrecht, The Netherlands.

Korhonen, H., Montola, M., & Arrasvuori, J. (2009). *Understanding playful user experience through digital games*. Paper presented at the International Conference on Designing Pleasurable of Products and Interface, Compiegne, France.

Kücklich, J. (2002). The study of computer games as a second-order cybernetic system. In F. Mäyrä (Ed.), *Computer games and digital cultures*. Tampere: Tampere University Press.

Lindley, C. (2002, June). The gameplay gestalt, narrative, and interactive storytelling. *Computer Games and Digital Culture Conference*, Tampere, Finland.

Mallon, B., & Webb, B. (2006, June). Applying a phenomenological approach to games analysis: A case study. *Simulation & Gaming*, *37*(2), 209–225.

Mayhew, D. J., & Follansbee, T. J. (2012). User experience requirements analysis within the usability engineering lifecycle. In J. A. Jacko (Ed.), *The human-computer interaction handbook: Fundamentals, evolving technologies, and emerging applications* (3rd ed., pp. 945–953). Boca Raton, FL: CRC Press.

Mäyrä, F. (2007). *The contextual game experience: On the socio-cultural contexts for meaning in digital play*. Paper presented at the 2007 Authors & Digital Games Research Association (DiGRA).

McKinsey & Company. (2011, May). *The world gone digital: Insights from McKinsey's global iconsumer research*. McKinsey & Company. Retrieved April 26, 2015, from https://www.mckinsey.com/~/media/McKinsey/dotcom/client_service/High%20Tech/PDFs/The_world_gone_digital.ashx

McMahan, A. (2003). Immersion, engagement, and presence: A method for analyzing 3-d video games. In M. J. P. Wolf & B. Perron (Eds.), *The video game theory reader* (pp. 67–86). New York, NY: Routledge.

Murray, J. H. (2006). Toward a cultural theory of gaming: Digital games and the co-evolution of media, mind, and culture. *Popular Communication, 4*(3), 185–202. doi:10.1207/s15405710pc0403_3

O'Brien, H. L., & Toms, E. G. (2007). What is user engagement? A conceptual framework for defining user engagement with technology. *Journal of the American Society for Information Science and Technology, 59*(6), 938–955. doi:10.1002/asi.20801

Okorafor, N., & Davenport, L. (2001, August). *Virtual women: Replacing the real.* The Association for Education in Journalism and Mass Communication.

Ow, J. (2000). The revenge of the yellowfaced cyborg: The rape of digital geishas and the colonization of cyber-coolies in 3d realms' shadow warrior. In B. Kolko, L. Nakamura, & G. Rodman (Eds.), *Race in cyberspace* (pp. 51–68). New York: Routledge.

Peña, J., & Hancock, J. T. (2006, February). An analysis of socio-emotional and task communication in online multimedia video games. *Communication Research, 33*(1), 92–109. doi:10.1177/0093650205283103

Pickering, A. (1995). The mangle of practice: Time, agency, & science. Chicago, IL: The University of Chicago Press.

Poels, K., IJsselsteijn, W., de Kort, Y., & Van Iersel, B. (2010). *Digital games, the aftermath: Qualitative insights into postgame experiences.* London: Springer.

Poole, S. (2000). *Trigger happy: Videogames and the entertainment revolution.* New York: Arcade.

Raessens, J., & Goldstein, J. (2005). Introduction. In J. Raessens & J. Goldstein (Eds.), Handbook of computer game studies (pp. xi-xvii). Cambridge, MA: The MIT Press.

Ryan, M.-L. (1999). Immersion vs. Interactivity: Virtual reality and literary theory. *SubStance, 28*(2), 110–137. doi:10.1353/sub.1999.0015

Schott, G., & Horrell, K. (2000). Girl gamers and their relationship with the gaming culture. *Convergence, 6*(4), 36–53.

Smyth, J. M. (2007). Beyond self-selection in video game play: An experimental examination of the consequences of massively multiplayer online role-playing game play. *Cyberpsychology & Behavior, 10*(5), 717–721. doi:10.1089/cpb.2007.9963 PMID:17927543

Squire, K. (2006). From content to context: Videogames as designed experience. *Educational Research, 35*(8), 19–29. doi:10.3102/0013189X035008019

Steinkuehler, C. A. (2006, January). Why game (culture) studies now? *Games and Culture, 1*(1), 97–102. doi:10.1177/1555412005281911

Subrahmanyam, K., & Greenfield, P. M. (1998). Computer games for girls: What makes them play. In J. Cassell & H. Jenkins (Eds.), From barbie to mrotal kombat: Gender and computer games. Cambridge, MA: The M.I.T. Press.

Tavinor, G. (2005, April). Videogames and interactive fiction. *Philosophy and Literature, 29*(1), 24–40. doi:10.1353/phl.2005.0015

Thurlow, C., & Mroczek, K. (Eds.). (2011, October 26). Digital discourse: Language in the new media. Cambridge, MA: Oxford University Press. doi:10.1093/acprof:oso/9780199795437.001.0001

van den Hoogen, W., IJsselsteijn, W., & de Kort, Y. (2008). *Exploring behavioral expressions of player experience in digital games.* Paper presented at the Workshop on Facial and Bodily Expression for Control and Adaptation of Games ECAG 2008, Amsterdam, The Netherlands.

Vorderer, P., & Bryant, J. (2006). *Playing video games: Motives, responses, and consequences.* Mahwah, NJ: Lawrence Erlbaum Associates.

Walz, S. P. (2004). Delightful identification & persuasion: Toward an analytical and applied rhetoric of digital games. *Works and Days, 22*(1&2), 185–200.

Williams, D. (2006, March). Virtual cultivation: Online worlds, offline perceptions. *Journal of Communication, 56*(1), 69–87. doi:10.1111/j.1460-2466.2006.00004.x

Williams, D., & Xiong, S. C. L. (2007). Can you hear me now? The impact of voice in an online gaming community. *Human Communication Research, 33*(4), 427–449. doi:10.1111/j.1468-2958.2007.00306.x

Wolf, M. J. P. (2005). Genre and the video game. In J. Raessens & J. Goldstein (Eds.), Handbook of computer game studies (pp. 193-204). Cambridge, MA: The MIT Press.

Yates, S. J., & Littleton, K. (1999, December). Understanding computer game cultures: A situated approach. *Information Communication and Society, 2*(4), 566–583. doi:10.1080/136911899359556

Yee, N. (2006, January). The labor of fun: How video games blur the boundaries of work and play. *Games and Culture, 1*(1), 68–71. doi:10.1177/1555412005281819

ADDITIONAL READING

Parnell, M. J. (2009). *Playing with scales: Creating a measurement scale to assess the experience of video games.* London: University College London.

Raessens, J. (2005). Computer games as participatory media culture. In J. Raessens & J. Goldstein (Eds.), Handbook of computer game studies (pp. 373-388). Cambridge, MA: The MIT Press.

Sherry, J., Lucas, K., Greenberg, B. S., & Lachlan, K. (2006). Video game uses and gratifications as predictors of use and game preferences. In P. Vorderer & J. Bryant (Eds.), *Playing computer games: Motives, responses, and consequences* (pp. 213–224). Mahwah, NJ: LEA Publishers.

Siwek, S. E. (2014). *Video games in the 21st century: The 2014 report.* Washington, DC: The Entertainment Software Association.

Yang, M., Roskos-Ewoldsen, D. R., Dinu, L., & Arpan, L. M. (2006, Winter). The effectiveness of "ingame" advertising: Comparing college students' explicit and implicit memory for brand names. *Journal of Advertising, 35*(4), 143–152. doi:10.2753/JOA0091-3367350410

KEY TERMS AND DEFINITIONS

Digital Discourse: Traditionally, the term refers to written and spoken messages. With the rise of new communication technologies, other forms of discourses also emerge ranging from interactive and multi-modal discourses.

Digital Game: Also known as video games or computer games.

Engagement: Engagement is a psychological concept that refers to how and whether gamers are satisfied with their gameplay experiences.

Entertainment Software Association (ESA): ESA is an U.S. association that represents companies and organizations that publish computer and video games.

Experiential Rhetoric: A term to study experiential representations and persuasive effects from the structural, procedural, locational, behavioral, and cognitive aspects of the hybrid interactive rhetorical engagement (H.I.R.E.) experienced by the gamers.

Game Genre: A term that refers to how digital games can be categorized by examining gameplay interaction, instead of narrative and visual differences. The classification of game genre is often based on challenges, plot, characters, etc in a digital game.

Gameplay: This term refers to how players interact with digital games. Gameplay refers to a set of behavioral patterns as programmed by the embedded rules that allow players to interact with each other and with the game through audio, visual, textual, and kinetic in-game design elements.

H.I.R.E: The term is abbreviated from *hybrid interactive rhetorical engagements* which is a concept and analytical unit to examine digital discourses as experienced by the gamers.

Hybrid: A term describing a variety of in-game design elements such as audio, visual, textual, and kinetic messages. Also known as multimodal.

Interactivity: A term commonly used in information science, computer science, human-computer interaction, communication, and digital humanity research. The concept of interactivity refers to the capability of the technology to allow two-way interaction among participants in a communication process.

MMORPGs: Abbreviated from Massively multiplayer online role-playing games that encompass role-playing functions and enable multiple players in various locations to compete in a virtual world.

User Experience (UX): The concept refers to how an individual's attitudes, behaviors, and emotions are influenced through interaction with a particular product, system, or service. A term commonly used in the human-computer interface (HCI) literature to describe the affective, meaningful, experiential, and practical aspects of human experiences.

World of Warcraft (*WoW*): A popular MMORPG product that was created in 2004 by Blizzard Entertainment. Various versions have been developed as part of the *WoW* franchise.

Related References

Aas, B. G. (2012). What's real? Presence, personality and identity in the real and online virtual world. In N. Zagalo, L. Morgado, & A. Boa-Ventura (Eds.), *Virtual worlds and metaverse platforms: New communication and identity paradigms* (pp. 88–99). Hershey, PA: Information Science Reference; doi:10.4018/978-1-60960-854-5.ch006

Aceti, V., & Luppicini, R. (2013). Exploring the effect of mhealth technologies on communication and information sharing in a pediatric critical care unit: A case study. In J. Tan (Ed.), *Healthcare information technology innovation and sustainability: Frontiers and adoption* (pp. 88–108). Hershey, PA: Medical Information Science Reference; doi:10.4018/978-1-4666-2797-0.ch006

Acilar, A. (2013). Factors affecting mobile phone use among undergraduate students in Turkey: An exploratory analysis. In I. Lee (Ed.), *Strategy, adoption, and competitive advantage of mobile services in the global economy* (pp. 234–246). Hershey, PA: Information Science Reference; doi:10.4018/978-1-4666-1939-5.ch013

Adams, A. (2013). Situated e-learning: Empowerment and barriers to identity changes. In S. Warburton & S. Hatzipanagos (Eds.), *Digital identity and social media* (pp. 159–175). Hershey, PA: Information Science Reference; doi:10.4018/978-1-4666-1915-9.ch012

Adeoye, B. F. (2013). Culturally different learning styles in online learning environments: A case of Nigerian university students. In L. Tomei (Ed.), *Learning tools and teaching approaches through ICT advancements* (pp. 228–240). Hershey, PA: Information Science Reference; doi:10.4018/978-1-4666-2017-9.ch020

Agarwal, N., & Mahata, D. (2013). Grouping the similar among the disconnected bloggers. In G. Xu & L. Li (Eds.), *Social media mining and social network analysis: Emerging research* (pp. 54–71). Hershey, PA: Information Science Reference; doi:10.4018/978-1-4666-2806-9.ch004

Aiken, M., Wang, J., Gu, L., & Paolillo, J. (2013). An exploratory study of how technology supports communication in multilingual groups. In N. Kock (Ed.), *Interdisciplinary applications of electronic collaboration approaches and technologies* (pp. 17–29). Hershey, PA: Information Science Reference; doi:10.4018/978-1-4666-2020-9.ch002

Aikins, S. K., & Chary, M. (2013). Online participation and digital divide: An empirical evaluation of U.S. midwestern municipalities. In *Digital literacy: Concepts, methodologies, tools, and applications* (pp. 63–85). Hershey, PA: Information Science Reference; doi:10.4018/978-1-4666-1852-7.ch004

Al Disi, Z. A., & Albadri, F. (2013). Arab youth and the internet: Educational perspective. In F. Albadri (Ed.), *Information systems applications in the Arab education sector* (pp. 163–178). Hershey, PA: Information Science Reference; doi:10.4018/978-1-4666-1984-5.ch012

Al-Dossary, S., Al-Dulaijan, N., Al-Mansour, S., Al-Zahrani, S., Al-Fridan, M., & Househ, M. (2013). Organ donation and transplantation: Processes, registries, consent, and restrictions in Saudi Arabia. In M. Cruz-Cunha, I. Miranda, & P. Gonçalves (Eds.), *Handbook of research on ICTs for human-centered healthcare and social care services* (pp. 511–528). Hershey, PA: Medical Information Science Reference; doi:10.4018/978-1-4666-3986-7.ch027

Al-Khaffaf, M. M., & Abdellatif, H. J. (2013). The effect of information and communication technology on customer relationship management: Jordan public shareholding companies. In R. Eid (Ed.), *Managing customer trust, satisfaction, and loyalty through information communication technologies* (pp. 342–350). Hershey, PA: Business Science Reference; doi:10.4018/978-1-4666-3631-6.ch020

Al-Nuaim, H. A. (2012). Evaluation of Arab municipal websites. In *Wireless technologies: Concepts, methodologies, tools and applications* (pp. 1170–1185). Hershey, PA: Information Science Reference; doi:10.4018/978-1-61350-101-6.ch505

Al-Nuaim, H. A. (2013). Developing user profiles for interactive online products in practice. In M. Garcia-Ruiz (Ed.), *Cases on usability engineering: Design and development of digital products* (pp. 57–79). Hershey, PA: Information Science Reference; doi:10.4018/978-1-4666-4046-7.ch003

Al Omoush, K. S., Alqirem, R. M., & Shaqrah, A. A. (2013). The driving internal beliefs of household internet adoption among Jordanians and the role of cultural values. In A. Zolait (Ed.), *Technology diffusion and adoption: global complexity, global innovation* (pp. 130–151). Hershey, PA: Information Science Reference; doi:10.4018/978-1-4666-2791-8.ch009

Al-Shqairat, Z. I., & Altarawneh, I. I. (2013). The role of partnership in e-government readiness: The knowledge stations (KSs) initiative in Jordan. In A. Mesquita (Ed.), *User perception and influencing factors of technology in everyday life* (pp. 192–210). Hershey, PA: Information Science Reference; doi:10.4018/978-1-4666-1954-8.ch014

AlBalawi, M. S. (2013). Web-based instructions: An assessment of preparedness of conventional universities in Saudi Arabia. In M. Khosrow-Pour (Ed.), *Cases on assessment and evaluation in education* (pp. 417–451). Hershey, PA: Information Science Reference; doi:10.4018/978-1-4666-2621-8.ch018

Alejos, A. V., Cuiñas, I., Expósito, I., & Sánchez, M. G. (2013). From the farm to fork: Information security accomplishment in a RFID based tracking chain for food sector. In P. Lopez, J. Hernandez-Castro, & T. Li (Eds.), *Security and trends in wireless identification and sensing platform tags: Advancements in RFID* (pp. 237–270). Hershey, PA: Information Science Reference; doi:10.4018/978-1-4666-1990-6.ch010

Alkazemi, M. F., Bowe, B. J., & Blom, R. (2013). Facilitating the Egyptian uprising: A case study of Facebook and Egypt's April 6th youth movement. In N. Azab (Ed.), *Cases on web 2.0 in developing countries: Studies on implementation, application, and use* (pp. 256–282). Hershey, PA: Information Science Reference; doi:10.4018/978-1-4666-2515-0.ch010

Almutairi, M. S. (2012). M-government: Challenges and key success factors – Saudi Arabia case study. In Wireless technologies: Concepts, methodologies, tools and applications (pp. 1698-1717). Hershey, PA: Information Science Reference. doi:10.4018/978-1-61350-101-6.ch611

Alyagout, F., & Siti-Nabiha, A. K. (2013). Public sector transformation: Privatization in Saudi Arabia. In N. Pomazalová (Ed.), *Public sector transformation processes and internet public procurement: Decision support systems* (pp. 17–31). Hershey, PA: Engineering Science Reference; doi:10.4018/978-1-4666-2665-2.ch002

Amirante, A., Castaldi, T., Miniero, L., & Romano, S. P. (2013). Protocol interactions among user agents, application servers, and media servers: Standardization efforts and open issues. In D. Kanellopoulos (Ed.), *Intelligent multimedia technologies for networking applications: Techniques and tools* (pp. 48–63). Hershey, PA: Information Science Reference; doi:10.4018/978-1-4666-2833-5.ch003

Andres, H. P. (2013). Shared mental model development during technology-mediated collaboration. In N. Kock (Ed.), *Interdisciplinary applications of electronic collaboration approaches and technologies* (pp. 125–142). Hershey, PA: Information Science Reference; doi:10.4018/978-1-4666-2020-9.ch009

Andrus, C. H., & Gaynor, M. (2013). Good IT requires good communication. In S. Sarnikar, D. Bennett, & M. Gaynor (Eds.), *Cases on healthcare information technology for patient care management* (pp. 122–125). Hershey, PA: Medical Information Science Reference; doi:10.4018/978-1-4666-2671-3.ch007

Annafari, M. T., & Bohlin, E. (2013). Why is the diffusion of mobile service not an evolutionary process? In I. Lee (Ed.), *Mobile services industries, technologies, and applications in the global economy* (pp. 25–38). Hershey, PA: Information Science Reference; doi:10.4018/978-1-4666-1981-4.ch002

Anupama, S. (2013). Gender evaluation of rural e-governance in India: A case study of E-Gram Suraj (e-rural good governance) scheme1. In *Digital literacy: Concepts, methodologies, tools, and applications* (pp. 1059–1074). Hershey, PA: Information Science Reference; doi:10.4018/978-1-4666-1852-7.ch055

Ariely, G. (2013). Boundaries of socio-technical systems and IT for knowledge development in military environments. In J. Abdelnour-Nocera (Ed.), *Knowledge and technological development effects on organizational and social structures* (pp. 224–238). Hershey, PA: Information Science Reference; doi:10.4018/978-1-4666-2151-0.ch014

Arsenio, A. M. (2013). Intelligent approaches for adaptation and distribution of personalized multimedia content. In D. Kanellopoulos (Ed.), *Intelligent multimedia technologies for networking applications: Techniques and tools* (pp. 197–224). Hershey, PA: Information Science Reference; doi:10.4018/978-1-4666-2833-5.ch008

Artail, H., & Tarhini, T. (2013). Runtime discovery and access of web services in mobile environments. In I. Lee (Ed.), *Mobile services industries, technologies, and applications in the global economy* (pp. 193–213). Hershey, PA: Information Science Reference; doi:10.4018/978-1-4666-1981-4.ch012

Asino, T. I., Wilder, H., & Ferris, S. P. (2013). Innovative use of ICT in Namibia for nationhood: Special emphasis on the Namibian newspaper. In H. Rahman (Ed.), *Cases on progressions and challenges in ICT utilization for citizen-centric governance* (pp. 205–216). Hershey, PA: Information Science Reference; doi:10.4018/978-1-4666-2071-1.ch009

Atici, B., & Bati, U. (2013). Identity of virtual supporters: Constructing identity of Turkish football fans on digital media. In S. Warburton & S. Hatzipanagos (Eds.), *Digital identity and social media* (pp. 256–274). Hershey, PA: Information Science Reference; doi:10.4018/978-1-4666-1915-9.ch018

Azab, N., & Khalifa, N. (2013). Web 2.0 and opportunities for entrepreneurs: How Egyptian entrepreneurs perceive and exploit web 2.0 technologies. In N. Azab (Ed.), *Cases on web 2.0 in developing countries: Studies on implementation, application, and use* (pp. 1–32). Hershey, PA: Information Science Reference; doi:10.4018/978-1-4666-2515-0.ch001

Bainbridge, W. S. (2013). Ancestor veneration avatars. In R. Luppicini (Ed.), *Handbook of research on technoself: Identity in a technological society* (pp. 308–321). Hershey, PA: Information Science Reference; doi:10.4018/978-1-4666-2211-1.ch017

Baporikar, N. (2013). Critical review of academic entrepreneurship in India. In A. Szopa, W. Karwowski, & P. Ordóñez de Pablos (Eds.), *Academic entrepreneurship and technological innovation: A business management perspective* (pp. 29–52). Hershey, PA: Information Science Reference; doi:10.4018/978-1-4666-2116-9.ch002

Barroca, L., & Gimenes, I. M. (2013). Computing postgraduate programmes in the UK and Brazil: Learning from experience in distance education with web 2.0 support. In N. Azab (Ed.), *Cases on web 2.0 in developing countries: Studies on implementation, application, and use* (pp. 147–171). Hershey, PA: Information Science Reference; doi:10.4018/978-1-4666-2515-0.ch006

Barton, S. M. (2013). Facilitating learning by going online: Modernising Islamic teaching and learning in Indonesia. In E. McKay (Ed.), *ePedagogy in online learning: New developments in web mediated human computer interaction* (pp. 74–92). Hershey, PA: Information Science Reference; doi:10.4018/978-1-4666-3649-1.ch005

Barzilai-Nahon, K., Gomez, R., & Ambikar, R. (2013). Conceptualizing a contextual measurement for digital divide/s: Using an integrated narrative. In *Digital literacy: Concepts, methodologies, tools, and applications* (pp. 279–293). Hershey, PA: Information Science Reference; doi:10.4018/978-1-4666-1852-7.ch015

Bénel, A., & Lacour, P. (2012). Towards a participative platform for cultural texts translators. In C. El Morr & P. Maret (Eds.), *Virtual community building and the information society: Current and future directions* (pp. 153–162). Hershey, PA: Information Science Reference; doi:10.4018/978-1-60960-869-9.ch008

Bentley, C. M. (2013). Designing and implementing online collaboration tools in West Africa. In N. Azab (Ed.), *Cases on web 2.0 in developing countries: Studies on implementation, application, and use* (pp. 33–60). Hershey, PA: Information Science Reference; doi:10.4018/978-1-4666-2515-0.ch002

Berg, M. (2012). Checking in at the urban playground: Digital geographies and electronic flâneurs. In F. Comunello (Ed.), *Networked sociability and individualism: Technology for personal and professional relationships* (pp. 169–194). Hershey, PA: Information Science Reference; doi:10.4018/978-1-61350-338-6.ch009

Bers, M. U., & Ettinger, A. B. (2013). Programming robots in kindergarten to express identity: An ethnographic analysis. In *Industrial engineering: Concepts, methodologies, tools, and applications* (pp. 1952–1968). Hershey, PA: Engineering Science Reference; doi:10.4018/978-1-4666-1945-6.ch105

Binsaleh, M., & Hassan, S. (2013). Systems development methodology for mobile commerce applications. In I. Khalil & E. Weippl (Eds.), *Contemporary challenges and solutions for mobile and multimedia technologies* (pp. 146–162). Hershey, PA: Information Science Reference; doi:10.4018/978-1-4666-2163-3.ch009

Bishop, J. (2013). Cooperative e-learning in the multilingual and multicultural school: The role of "classroom 2.0" for increasing participation in education. In P. Pumilia-Gnarini, E. Favaron, E. Pacetti, J. Bishop, & L. Guerra (Eds.), *Handbook of research on didactic strategies and technologies for education: Incorporating advancements* (pp. 137–150). Hershey, PA: Information Science Reference; doi:10.4018/978-1-4666-2122-0.ch013

Bishop, J. (2013). Increasing capital revenue in social networking communities: Building social and economic relationships through avatars and characters. In J. Bishop (Ed.), *Examining the concepts, issues, and implications of internet trolling* (pp. 44–61). Hershey, PA: Information Science Reference; doi:10.4018/978-1-4666-2803-8.ch005

Bishop, J. (2013). Lessons from the emotive project for increasing take-up of big society and responsible capitalism initiatives. In P. Pumilia-Gnarini, E. Favaron, E. Pacetti, J. Bishop, & L. Guerra (Eds.), *Handbook of research on didactic strategies and technologies for education: Incorporating advancements* (pp. 208–217). Hershey, PA: Information Science Reference; doi:10.4018/978-1-4666-2122-0.ch019

Blau, I. (2013). E-collaboration within, between, and without institutions: Towards better functioning of online groups through networks. In N. Kock (Ed.), *Interdisciplinary applications of electronic collaboration approaches and technologies* (pp. 188–203). Hershey, PA: Information Science Reference; doi:10.4018/978-1-4666-2020-9.ch013

Boskic, N., & Hu, S. (2013). Blended learning: The road to inclusive and global education. In E. Jean Francois (Ed.), *Transcultural blended learning and teaching in postsecondary education* (pp. 283–301). Hershey, PA: Information Science Reference; doi:10.4018/978-1-4666-2014-8.ch015

Botero, A., Karhu, K., & Vihavainen, S. (2012). Exploring the ecosystems and principles of community innovation. In A. Lugmayr, H. Franssila, P. Näränen, O. Sotamaa, J. Vanhala, & Z. Yu (Eds.), *Media in the ubiquitous era: Ambient, social and gaming media* (pp. 216–234). Hershey, PA: Information Science Reference; doi:10.4018/978-1-60960-774-6.ch012

Bowe, B. J., Blom, R., & Freedman, E. (2013). Negotiating boundaries between control and dissent: Free speech, business, and repressitarian governments. In J. Lannon & E. Halpin (Eds.), *Human rights and information communication technologies: Trends and consequences of use* (pp. 36–55). Hershey, PA: Information Science Reference; doi:10.4018/978-1-4666-1918-0.ch003

Brandão, J., Ferreira, T., & Carvalho, V. (2012). An overview on the use of serious games in the military industry and health. In M. Cruz-Cunha (Ed.), *Handbook of research on serious games as educational, business and research tools* (pp. 182–201). Hershey, PA: Information Science Reference; doi:10.4018/978-1-4666-0149-9.ch009

Brost, L. F., & McGinnis, C. (2012). The status of blogging in the republic of Ireland: A case study. In T. Dumova & R. Fiordo (Eds.), *Blogging in the global society: Cultural, political and geographical aspects* (pp. 128–147). Hershey, PA: Information Science Reference; doi:10.4018/978-1-60960-744-9.ch008

Burns, J., Blanchard, M., & Metcalf, A. (2013). Bridging the digital divide in Australia: The potential implications for the mental health of young people experiencing marginalisation. In *Digital literacy: Concepts, methodologies, tools, and applications* (pp. 772–793). Hershey, PA: Information Science Reference; doi:10.4018/978-1-4666-1852-7.ch040

Cagliero, L., & Fiori, A. (2013). News document summarization driven by user-generated content. In G. Xu & L. Li (Eds.), *Social media mining and social network analysis: Emerging research* (pp. 105–126). Hershey, PA: Information Science Reference; doi:10.4018/978-1-4666-2806-9.ch007

Camillo, A., & Di Pietro, L. (2013). Managerial communication in the global cross-cultural context. In B. Christiansen, E. Turkina, & N. Williams (Eds.), *Cultural and technological influences on global business* (pp. 397–419). Hershey, PA: Business Science Reference; doi:10.4018/978-1-4666-3966-9.ch021

Canazza, S., De Poli, G., Rodà, A., & Vidolin, A. (2013). Expressiveness in music performance: Analysis, models, mapping, encoding. In J. Steyn (Ed.), *Structuring music through markup language: Designs and architectures* (pp. 156–186). Hershey, PA: Information Science Reference; doi:10.4018/978-1-4666-2497-9.ch008

Carrasco, J. G., Ovide, E., & Puyal, M. B. (2013). Closing and opening of cultures. In F. García-Peñalvo (Ed.), *Multiculturalism in technology-based education: Case studies on ICT-supported approaches* (pp. 125–142). Hershey, PA: Information Science Reference; doi:10.4018/978-1-4666-2101-5.ch008

Carreras, I., Zanardi, A., Salvadori, E., & Miorandi, D. (2013). A distributed monitoring framework for opportunistic communication systems: An experimental approach. In V. De Florio (Ed.), *Innovations and approaches for resilient and adaptive systems* (pp. 220–236). Hershey, PA: Information Science Reference; doi:10.4018/978-1-4666-2056-8.ch013

Carter, M., Grover, V., & Thatcher, J. B. (2013). Mobile devices and the self: developing the concept of mobile phone identity. In I. Lee (Ed.), *Strategy, adoption, and competitive advantage of mobile services in the global economy* (pp. 150–164). Hershey, PA: Information Science Reference; doi:10.4018/978-1-4666-1939-5.ch008

Caruso, F., Giuffrida, G., Reforgiato, D., & Zarba, C. (2013). Recommendation systems for mobile devices. In I. Lee (Ed.), *Mobile services industries, technologies, and applications in the global economy* (pp. 221–242). Hershey, PA: Information Science Reference; doi:10.4018/978-1-4666-1981-4.ch014

Casamassima, L. (2013). eTwinning project: A virtual orchestra. In P. Pumilia-Gnarini, E. Favaron, E. Pacetti, J. Bishop, & L. Guerra (Eds.) Handbook of research on didactic strategies and technologies for education: Incorporating advancements (pp. 703-709). Hershey, PA: Information Science Reference. doi:10.4018/978-1-4666-2122-0.ch061

Caschera, M. C., D'Ulizia, A., Ferri, F., & Grifoni, P. (2012). Multiculturality and multimodal languages. In G. Ghinea, F. Andres, & S. Gulliver (Eds.), *Multiple sensorial media advances and applications: New developments in MulSeMedia* (pp. 99–114). Hershey, PA: Information Science Reference; doi:10.4018/978-1-60960-821-7.ch005

Catagnus, R. M., & Hantula, D. A. (2013). The virtual individual education plan (IEP) team: Using online collaboration to develop a behavior intervention plan. In N. Kock (Ed.), *Interdisciplinary applications of electronic collaboration approaches and technologies* (pp. 30–45). Hershey, PA: Information Science Reference; doi:10.4018/978-1-4666-2020-9.ch003

Ch'ng, E. (2013). The mirror between two worlds: 3D surface computing for objects and environments. In D. Harrison (Ed.), *Digital media and technologies for virtual artistic spaces* (pp. 166–185). Hershey, PA: Information Science Reference; doi:10.4018/978-1-4666-2961-5.ch013

Chand, A. (2013). Reducing digital divide: The case of the 'people first network' (PFNet) in the Solomon Islands. In *Digital literacy: Concepts, methodologies, tools, and applications* (pp. 1571–1605). Hershey, PA: Information Science Reference; doi:10.4018/978-1-4666-1852-7.ch083

Chatterjee, S. (2013). Ethical behaviour in technology-mediated communication. In J. Bishop (Ed.), *Examining the concepts, issues, and implications of internet trolling* (pp. 1–9). Hershey, PA: Information Science Reference; doi:10.4018/978-1-4666-2803-8.ch001

Chen, C., Chao, H., Wu, T., Fan, C., Chen, J., Chen, Y., & Hsu, J. (2013). IoT-IMS communication platform for future internet. In V. De Florio (Ed.), *Innovations and approaches for resilient and adaptive systems* (pp. 68–86). Hershey, PA: Information Science Reference; doi:10.4018/978-1-4666-2056-8.ch004

Chen, J., & Hu, X. (2013). Smartphone market in China: Challenges, opportunities, and promises. In I. Lee (Ed.), *Mobile services industries, technologies, and applications in the global economy* (pp. 120–132). Hershey, PA: Information Science Reference; doi:10.4018/978-1-4666-1981-4.ch008

Chen, Y., Lee, B., & Kirk, R. M. (2013). Internet use among older adults: Constraints and opportunities. In R. Zheng, R. Hill, & M. Gardner (Eds.), *Engaging older adults with modern technology: Internet use and information access needs* (pp. 124–141). Hershey, PA: Information Science Reference; doi:10.4018/978-1-4666-1966-1.ch007

Cheong, P. H., & Martin, J. N. (2013). Cultural implications of e-learning access (and divides): Teaching an intercultural communication course online. In A. Edmundson (Ed.), *Cases on cultural implications and considerations in online learning* (pp. 82–100). Hershey, PA: Information Science Reference; doi:10.4018/978-1-4666-1885-5.ch005

Chhanabhai, P., & Holt, A. (2013). The changing world of ICT and health: Crossing the digital divide. In *Digital literacy: Concepts, methodologies, tools, and applications* (pp. 794–811). Hershey, PA: Information Science Reference; doi:10.4018/978-1-4666-1852-7.ch041

Chuling, W., Hua, C. M., & Chee, C. J. (2012). Investigating the demise of radio and television broadcasting. In R. Sharma, M. Tan, & F. Pereira (Eds.), *Understanding the interactive digital media marketplace: Frameworks, platforms, communities and issues* (pp. 392–405). Hershey, PA: Information Science Reference; doi:10.4018/978-1-61350-147-4.ch031

Ciaramitaro, B. L. (2012). Introduction to mobile technologies. In B. Ciaramitaro (Ed.), *Mobile technology consumption: Opportunities and challenges* (pp. 1–15). Hershey, PA: Information Science Reference; doi:10.4018/978-1-61350-150-4.ch001

Cicconetti, C., Mambrini, R., & Rossi, A. (2013). A survey of wireless backhauling solutions for ITS. In R. Daher & A. Vinel (Eds.), *Roadside networks for vehicular communications: Architectures, applications, and test fields* (pp. 57–70). Hershey, PA: Information Science Reference; doi:10.4018/978-1-4666-2223-4.ch003

Ciptasari, R. W., & Sakurai, K. (2013). Multimedia copyright protection scheme based on the direct feature-based method. In K. Kondo (Ed.), *Multimedia information hiding technologies and methodologies for controlling data* (pp. 412–439). Hershey, PA: Information Science Reference; doi:10.4018/978-1-4666-2217-3.ch019

Code, J. (2013). Agency and identity in social media. In S. Warburton & S. Hatzipanagos (Eds.), *Digital identity and social media* (pp. 37–57). Hershey, PA: Information Science Reference; doi:10.4018/978-1-4666-1915-9.ch004

Comunello, F. (2013). From the digital divide to multiple divides: Technology, society, and new media skills. In *Digital literacy: Concepts, methodologies, tools, and applications* (pp. 1622–1639). Hershey, PA: Information Science Reference; doi:10.4018/978-1-4666-1852-7.ch085

Consonni, A. (2013). About the use of the DMs in CLIL classes. In F. García-Peñalvo (Ed.), *Multiculturalism in technology-based education: Case studies on ICT-supported approaches* (pp. 9–27). Hershey, PA: Information Science Reference; doi:10.4018/978-1-4666-2101-5.ch002

Constant, J. (2012). Digital approaches to visualization of geometric problems in wooden sangaku tablets. In A. Ursyn (Ed.), *Biologically-inspired computing for the arts: Scientific data through graphics* (pp. 240–253). Hershey, PA: Information Science Reference; doi:10.4018/978-1-4666-0942-6.ch013

Cossiavelou, V., Bantimaroudis, P., Kavakli, E., & Illia, L. (2013). The media gatekeeping model updated by R and I in ICTs: The case of wireless communications in media coverage of the olympic games. In M. Bartolacci & S. Powell (Eds.), *Advancements and innovations in wireless communications and network technologies* (pp. 262–288). Hershey, PA: Information Science Reference; doi:10.4018/978-1-4666-2154-1.ch019

Cropf, R. A., Benmamoun, M., & Kalliny, M. (2013). The role of web 2.0 in the Arab Spring. In N. Azab (Ed.), *Cases on web 2.0 in developing countries: Studies on implementation, application, and use* (pp. 76–108). Hershey, PA: Information Science Reference; doi:10.4018/978-1-4666-2515-0.ch004

Cucinotta, A., Minnolo, A. L., & Puliafito, A. (2013). Design and implementation of an event-based RFID middleware. In N. Karmakar (Ed.), *Advanced RFID systems, security, and applications* (pp. 110–131). Hershey, PA: Information Science Reference; doi:10.4018/978-1-4666-2080-3.ch006

D'Andrea, A., Ferri, F., & Grifoni, P. (2013). Assessing e-health in Africa: Web 2.0 applications. In N. Azab (Ed.), *Cases on web 2.0 in developing countries: Studies on implementation, application, and use* (pp. 442–467). Hershey, PA: Information Science Reference; doi:10.4018/978-1-4666-2515-0.ch016

de Guinea, A. O. (2013). The level paradox of e-collaboration: Dangers and solutions. In N. Kock (Ed.), *Interdisciplinary applications of electronic collaboration approaches and technologies* (pp. 166–187). Hershey, PA: Information Science Reference; doi:10.4018/978-1-4666-2020-9.ch012

Dhar-Bhattacharjee, S., & Takruri-Rizk, H. (2012). An Indo-British comparison. In C. Romm Livermore (Ed.), *Gender and social computing: Interactions, differences and relationships* (pp. 50–71). Hershey, PA: Information Science Publishing; doi:10.4018/978-1-60960-759-3.ch004

Díaz-Foncea, M., & Marcuello, C. (2013). ANOBIUM, SL: The use of the ICT as niche of employment and as tool for developing the social market. In T. Torres-Coronas & M. Vidal-Blasco (Eds.), *Social e-enterprise: Value creation through ICT* (pp. 221–242). Hershey, PA: Information Science Reference; doi:10.4018/978-1-4666-2667-6.ch013

Díaz-González, M., Froufe, N. Q., Brena, A. G., & Pumarola, F. (2013). Uses and implementation of social media at university: The case of schools of communication in Spain. In B. Pătruţ, M. Pătruţ, & C. Cmeciu (Eds.), *Social media and the new academic environment: Pedagogical challenges* (pp. 204–222). Hershey, PA: Information Science Reference; doi:10.4018/978-1-4666-2851-9.ch010

Ditsa, G., Alwahaishi, S., Al-Kobaisi, S., & Snášel, V. (2013). A comparative study of the effects of culture on the deployment of information technology. In A. Zolait (Ed.), *Technology diffusion and adoption: Global complexity, global innovation* (pp. 77–90). Hershey, PA: Information Science Reference; doi:10.4018/978-1-4666-2791-8.ch006

Donaldson, O., & Duggan, E. W. (2013). Assessing mobile value-added preference structures: The case of a developing country. In I. Lee (Ed.), *Strategy, adoption, and competitive advantage of mobile services in the global economy* (pp. 349–370). Hershey, PA: Information Science Reference; doi:10.4018/978-1-4666-1939-5.ch019

Douai, A. (2013). "In YouTube we trust": Video exchange and Arab human rights. In J. Lannon & E. Halpin (Eds.), *Human rights and information communication technologies: Trends and consequences of use* (pp. 57–71). Hershey, PA: Information Science Reference; doi:10.4018/978-1-4666-1918-0.ch004

Dromzée, C., Laborie, S., & Roose, P. (2013). A semantic generic profile for multimedia document adaptation. In D. Kanellopoulos (Ed.), *Intelligent multimedia technologies for networking applications: Techniques and tools* (pp. 225–246). Hershey, PA: Information Science Reference; doi:10.4018/978-1-4666-2833-5.ch009

Drucker, S., & Gumpert, G. (2012). The urban communication infrastructure: Global connection and local detachment. In *Wireless technologies: Concepts, methodologies, tools and applications* (pp. 1150–1169). Hershey, PA: Information Science Reference; doi:10.4018/978-1-61350-101-6.ch504

Drula, G. (2013). Media and communication research facing social media. In M. Pătruţ & B. Pătruţ (Eds.), *Social media in higher education: Teaching in web 2.0* (pp. 371–392). Hershey, PA: Information Science Reference; doi:10.4018/978-1-4666-2970-7.ch019

Dueck, J., & Rempel, M. (2013). Human rights and technology: Lessons from Alice in Wonderland. In J. Lannon & E. Halpin (Eds.), *Human rights and information communication technologies: Trends and consequences of use* (pp. 1–20). Hershey, PA: Information Science Reference; doi:10.4018/978-1-4666-1918-0.ch001

Dumova, T. (2012). Social interaction technologies and the future of blogging. In T. Dumova & R. Fiordo (Eds.), *Blogging in the global society: Cultural, political and geographical aspects* (pp. 249–274). Hershey, PA: Information Science Reference; doi:10.4018/978-1-60960-744-9.ch015

Dunn, H. S. (2013). Information literacy and the digital divide: Challenging e-exclusion in the global south. In *Digital literacy: Concepts, methodologies, tools, and applications* (pp. 20–38). Hershey, PA: Information Science Reference; doi:10.4018/978-1-4666-1852-7.ch002

Elias, N. (2013). Immigrants' internet use and identity from an intergenerational perspective: Immigrant senior citizens and youngsters from the former Soviet Union in Israel. In R. Luppicini (Ed.), *Handbook of research on technoself: Identity in a technological society* (pp. 293–307). Hershey, PA: Information Science Reference; doi:10.4018/978-1-4666-2211-1.ch016

Elizabeth, L. S., Ismail, N., & Tun, M. S. (2012). The future of the printed book. In R. Sharma, M. Tan, & F. Pereira (Eds.), *Understanding the interactive digital media marketplace: Frameworks, platforms, communities and issues* (pp. 416–429). Hershey, PA: Information Science Reference; doi:10.4018/978-1-61350-147-4.ch033

Erne, R. (2012). Knowledge worker performance in a cross-industrial perspective. In S. Brüggemann & C. d'Amato (Eds.), *Collaboration and the semantic web: Social networks, knowledge networks, and knowledge resources* (pp. 297–321). Hershey, PA: Information Science Reference; doi:10.4018/978-1-4666-0894-8.ch015

Ertl, B., Helling, K., & Kikis-Papadakis, K. (2012). The impact of gender in ICT usage, education and career: Comparisons between Greece and Germany. In C. Romm Livermore (Ed.), *Gender and social computing: Interactions, differences and relationships* (pp. 98–119). Hershey, PA: Information Science Publishing; doi:10.4018/978-1-60960-759-3.ch007

Estapé-Dubreuil, G., & Torreguitart-Mirada, C. (2013). ICT adoption in the small and medium-size social enterprises in Spain: Opportunity or priority? In T. Torres-Coronas & M. Vidal-Blasco (Eds.), *Social e-enterprise: Value creation through ICT* (pp. 200–220). Hershey, PA: Information Science Reference; doi:10.4018/978-1-4666-2667-6.ch012

Eze, U. C., & Poong, Y. S. (2013). Consumers' intention to use mobile commerce and the moderating roles of gender and income. In I. Lee (Ed.), *Strategy, adoption, and competitive advantage of mobile services in the global economy* (pp. 127–148). Hershey, PA: Information Science Reference; doi:10.4018/978-1-4666-1939-5.ch007

Farrell, R., Danis, C., Erickson, T., Ellis, J., Christensen, J., Bailey, M., & Kellogg, W. A. (2012). A picture and a thousand words: Visual scaffolding for mobile communication in developing regions. In W. Hu (Ed.), *Emergent trends in personal, mobile, and handheld computing technologies* (pp. 341–354). Hershey, PA: Information Science Reference; doi:10.4018/978-1-4666-0921-1.ch020

Fidler, C. S., Kanaan, R. K., & Rogerson, S. (2013). Barriers to e-government implementation in Jordan: The role of wasta. In A. Mesquita (Ed.), *User perception and influencing factors of technology in everyday life* (pp. 179–191). Hershey, PA: Information Science Reference; doi:10.4018/978-1-4666-1954-8.ch013

Filho, J. R. (2013). ICT and human rights in Brazil: From military to digital dictatorship. In J. Lannon & E. Halpin (Eds.), *Human rights and information communication technologies: Trends and consequences of use* (pp. 86–99). Hershey, PA: Information Science Reference; doi:10.4018/978-1-4666-1918-0.ch006

Fiordo, R. (2012). Analyzing blogs: A hermeneutic perspective. In T. Dumova & R. Fiordo (Eds.), *Blogging in the global society: Cultural, political and geographical aspects* (pp. 231–248). Hershey, PA: Information Science Reference; doi:10.4018/978-1-60960-744-9.ch014

Fischer, G., & Herrmann, T. (2013). Socio-technical systems: A meta-design perspective. In J. Abdelnour-Nocera (Ed.), *Knowledge and technological development effects on organizational and social structures* (pp. 1–36). Hershey, PA: Information Science Reference; doi:10.4018/978-1-4666-2151-0.ch001

Fleury, M., & Al-Jobouri, L. (2013). Techniques and tools for adaptive video streaming. In D. Kanellopoulos (Ed.), *Intelligent multimedia technologies for networking applications: Techniques and tools* (pp. 65–101). Hershey, PA: Information Science Reference; doi:10.4018/978-1-4666-2833-5.ch004

Freeman, I., & Freeman, A. (2013). Capacity building for different abilities using ICT. In T. Torres-Coronas & M. Vidal-Blasco (Eds.), *Social e-enterprise: Value creation through ICT* (pp. 67–82). Hershey, PA: Information Science Reference; doi:10.4018/978-1-4666-2667-6.ch004

Gallon, R. (2013). Communication, culture, and technology: Learning strategies for the unteachable. In R. Lansiquot (Ed.), *Cases on interdisciplinary research trends in science, technology, engineering, and mathematics: Studies on urban classrooms* (pp. 91–106). Hershey, PA: Information Science Reference; doi:10.4018/978-1-4666-2214-2.ch005

García, M., Lloret, J., Bellver, I., & Tomás, J. (2013). Intelligent IPTV distribution for smart phones. In D. Kanellopoulos (Ed.), *Intelligent multimedia technologies for networking applications: Techniques and tools* (pp. 318–347). Hershey, PA: Information Science Reference; doi:10.4018/978-1-4666-2833-5.ch013

García-Plaza, A. P., Zubiaga, A., Fresno, V., & Martínez, R. (2013). Tag cloud reorganization: Finding groups of related tags on delicious. In G. Xu & L. Li (Eds.), *Social media mining and social network analysis: Emerging research* (pp. 140–155). Hershey, PA: Information Science Reference; doi:10.4018/978-1-4666-2806-9.ch009

Gerpott, T. J. (2013). Attribute perceptions as factors explaining mobile internet acceptance of cellular customers in Germany: An empirical study comparing actual and potential adopters with distinct categories of access appliances. In I. Lee (Ed.), *Strategy, adoption, and competitive advantage of mobile services in the global economy* (pp. 19–48). Hershey, PA: Information Science Reference; doi:10.4018/978-1-4666-1939-5.ch002

Giambona, G. J., & Birchall, D. W. (2012). Collaborative e-learning and ICT tools to develop SME managers: An Italian case. In *Wireless technologies: Concepts, methodologies, tools and applications* (pp. 1606–1617). Hershey, PA: Information Science Reference; doi:10.4018/978-1-61350-101-6.ch605

Giannakos, M. N., Pateli, A. G., & Pappas, I. O. (2013). Identifying the direct effect of experience and the moderating effect of satisfaction in the Greek online market. In A. Scupola (Ed.), *Mobile opportunities and applications for e-service innovations* (pp. 77–97). Hershey, PA: Information Science Reference; doi:10.4018/978-1-4666-2654-6.ch005

Giorda, M., & Guerrisi, M. (2013). Educating to democracy and social participation through a "history of religion" course. In P. Pumilia-Gnarini, E. Favaron, E. Pacetti, J. Bishop, & L. Guerra (Eds.), *Handbook of research on didactic strategies and technologies for education: Incorporating advancements* (pp. 152–161). Hershey, PA: Information Science Reference; doi:10.4018/978-1-4666-2122-0.ch014

Goggins, S., Schmidt, M., Guajardo, J., & Moore, J. L. (2013). 3D virtual worlds: Assessing the experience and informing design. In B. Medlin (Ed.), *Integrations of technology utilization and social dynamics in organizations* (pp. 194–213). Hershey, PA: Information Science Reference; doi:10.4018/978-1-4666-1948-7.ch012

Gold, N. (2012). Rebels, heretics, and exiles: Blogging among estranged and questioning American Hasidim. In T. Dumova & R. Fiordo (Eds.), *Blogging in the global society: Cultural, political and geographical aspects* (pp. 108–127). Hershey, PA: Information Science Reference; doi:10.4018/978-1-60960-744-9.ch007

Görgü, L., Wan, J., O'Hare, G. M., & O'Grady, M. J. (2013). Enabling mobile service provision with sensor networks. In I. Lee (Ed.), *Mobile services industries, technologies, and applications in the global economy* (pp. 175–192). Hershey, PA: Information Science Reference; doi:10.4018/978-1-4666-1981-4.ch011

Gregory, S. J. (2013). Evolution of mobile services: An analysis. In I. Lee (Ed.), *Mobile services industries, technologies, and applications in the global economy* (pp. 104–119). Hershey, PA: Information Science Reference; doi:10.4018/978-1-4666-1981-4.ch007

Grieve, G. P., & Heston, K. (2012). Finding liquid salvation: Using the Cardean ethnographic method to document second life residents and religious cloud communities. In N. Zagalo, L. Morgado, & A. Boa-Ventura (Eds.), *Virtual worlds and metaverse platforms: New communication and identity paradigms* (pp. 288–305). Hershey, PA: Information Science Reference; doi:10.4018/978-1-60960-854-5.ch019

Guha, S., Thakur, B., Konar, T. S., & Chakrabarty, S. (2013). Web enabled design collaboration in India. In N. Kock (Ed.), *Interdisciplinary applications of electronic collaboration approaches and technologies* (pp. 96–111). Hershey, PA: Information Science Reference; doi:10.4018/978-1-4666-2020-9.ch007

Gulati, G. J., Yates, D. J., & Tawileh, A. (2013). Explaining the global digital divide: The impact of public policy initiatives on e-government capacity and reach worldwide. In *Digital literacy: Concepts, methodologies, tools, and applications* (pp. 39–62). Hershey, PA: Information Science Reference; doi:10.4018/978-1-4666-1852-7.ch003

Gupta, J. (2013). Digital library initiatives in India. In T. Ashraf & P. Gulati (Eds.), *Design, development, and management of resources for digital library services* (pp. 80–93). Hershey, PA: Information Science Reference; doi:10.4018/978-1-4666-2500-6.ch008

Gururajan, R., Hafeez-Baig, A., Danaher, P. A., & De George-Walker, L. (2012). Student perceptions and uses of wireless handheld devices: Implications for implementing blended and mobile learning in an Australian university. In *Wireless technologies: Concepts, methodologies, tools and applications* (pp. 1323–1338). Hershey, PA: Information Science Reference; doi:10.4018/978-1-61350-101-6.ch512

Gwilt, I. (2013). Data-objects: Sharing the attributes and properties of digital and material culture to creatively interpret complex information. In D. Harrison (Ed.), *Digital media and technologies for virtual artistic spaces* (pp. 14–26). Hershey, PA: Information Science Reference; doi:10.4018/978-1-4666-2961-5.ch002

Hackley, D. C., & Leidman, M. B. (2013). Integrating learning management systems in K-12 supplemental religious education. In A. Ritzhaupt & S. Kumar (Eds.), *Cases on educational technology implementation for facilitating learning* (pp. 1–22). Hershey, PA: Information Science Reference; doi:10.4018/978-1-4666-3676-7.ch001

Hale, J. R., & Fields, D. (2013). A cross-cultural measure of servant leadership behaviors. In M. Bocarnea, R. Reynolds, & J. Baker (Eds.), *Online instruments, data collection, and electronic measurements: Organizational advancements* (pp. 152–163). Hershey, PA: Information Science Reference; doi:10.4018/978-1-4666-2172-5.ch009

Hanewald, R. (2012). Using mobile technologies as research tools: Pragmatics, possibilities and problems. In *Wireless technologies: Concepts, methodologies, tools and applications* (pp. 130–150). Hershey, PA: Information Science Reference; doi:10.4018/978-1-61350-101-6.ch108

Hanewald, R. (2013). Professional development with and for emerging technologies: A case study with Asian languages and cultural studies teachers in Australia. In J. Keengwe (Ed.), *Pedagogical applications and social effects of mobile technology integration* (pp. 175–192). Hershey, PA: Information Science Reference; doi:10.4018/978-1-4666-2985-1.ch010

Hayhoe, S. (2012). Non-visual programming, perceptual culture and mulsemedia: Case studies of five blind computer programmers. In G. Ghinea, F. Andres, & S. Gulliver (Eds.), *Multiple sensorial media advances and applications: New developments in MulSeMedia* (pp. 80–98). Hershey, PA: Information Science Reference; doi:10.4018/978-1-60960-821-7.ch004

Henschke, J. A. (2013). Nation building through andragogy and lifelong learning: On the cutting edge educationally, economically, and governmentally. In V. Wang (Ed.), *Handbook of research on technologies for improving the 21st century workforce: Tools for lifelong learning* (pp. 480–506). Hershey, PA: Information Science Publishing; doi:10.4018/978-1-4666-2181-7.ch030

Hermida, J. M., Meliá, S., Montoyo, A., & Gómez, J. (2013). Developing rich internet applications as social sites on the semantic web: A model-driven approach. In D. Chiu (Ed.), *Mobile and web innovations in systems and service-oriented engineering* (pp. 134–155). Hershey, PA: Information Science Reference; doi:10.4018/978-1-4666-2470-2.ch008

Hernández-García, Á., Agudo-Peregrina, Á. F., & Iglesias-Pradas, S. (2013). Adoption of mobile video-call service: An exploratory study. In I. Lee (Ed.), *Strategy, adoption, and competitive advantage of mobile services in the global economy* (pp. 49–72). Hershey, PA: Information Science Reference; doi:10.4018/978-1-4666-1939-5.ch003

Hesapci-Sanaktekin, O., & Somer, I. (2013). Mobile communication: A study on smart phone and mobile application use. In I. Lee (Ed.), *Strategy, adoption, and competitive advantage of mobile services in the global economy* (pp. 217–233). Hershey, PA: Information Science Reference; doi:10.4018/978-1-4666-1939-5.ch012

Hill, S. R., Troshani, I., & Freeman, S. (2013). An eclectic perspective on the internationalization of Australian mobile services SMEs. In I. Lee (Ed.), *Mobile services industries, technologies, and applications in the global economy* (pp. 55–73). Hershey, PA: Information Science Reference; doi:10.4018/978-1-4666-1981-4.ch004

Ho, V. (2013). The need for identity construction in computer-mediated professional communication: A Community of practice perspective. In R. Luppicini (Ed.), *Handbook of research on technoself: Identity in a technological society* (pp. 502–530). Hershey, PA: Information Science Reference; doi:10.4018/978-1-4666-2211-1.ch027

Hudson, H. E. (2013). Challenges facing municipal wireless: Case studies from San Francisco and Silicon Valley. In A. Abdelaal (Ed.), *Social and economic effects of community wireless networks and infrastructures* (pp. 12–26). Hershey, PA: Information Science Reference; doi:10.4018/978-1-4666-2997-4.ch002

Humphreys, S. (2012). Unravelling intellectual property in a specialist social networking site. In A. Lugmayr, H. Franssila, P. Näränen, O. Sotamaa, J. Vanhala, & Z. Yu (Eds.), *Media in the ubiquitous era: Ambient, social and gaming media* (pp. 248–266). Hershey, PA: Information Science Reference; doi:10.4018/978-1-60960-774-6.ch015

Iglesias, A., Ruiz-Mezcua, B., López, J. F., & Figueroa, D. C. (2013). New communication technologies for inclusive education in and outside the classroom. In D. Griol Barres, Z. Callejas Carrión, & R. Delgado (Eds.), *Technologies for inclusive education: Beyond traditional integration approaches* (pp. 271–284). Hershey, PA: Information Science Reference; doi:10.4018/978-1-4666-2530-3.ch013

Igun, S. E. (2013). Gender and national information and communication technology (ICT) policies in Africa. In B. Maumbe & J. Okello (Eds.), *Technology, sustainability, and rural development in Africa* (pp. 284–297). Hershey, PA: Information Science Reference; doi:10.4018/978-1-4666-3607-1.ch018

Ikolo, V. E. (2013). Gender digital divide and national ICT policies in Africa. In *Digital literacy: Concepts, methodologies, tools, and applications* (pp. 812–832). Hershey, PA: Information Science Reference; doi:10.4018/978-1-4666-1852-7.ch042

Imran, A., & Gregor, S. (2013). A process model for successful e-government adoption in the least developed countries: A case of Bangladesh. In *Digital literacy: Concepts, methodologies, tools, and applications* (pp. 213–241). Hershey, PA: Information Science Reference; doi:10.4018/978-1-4666-1852-7.ch012

Ionescu, A. (2013). ICTs and gender-based rights. In J. Lannon & E. Halpin (Eds.), *Human rights and information communication technologies: Trends and consequences of use* (pp. 214–234). Hershey, PA: Information Science Reference; doi:10.4018/978-1-4666-1918-0.ch013

Iyamu, T. (2013). The impact of organisational politics on the implementation of IT strategy: South African case in context. In J. Abdelnour-Nocera (Ed.), *Knowledge and technological development effects on organizational and social structures* (pp. 167–193). Hershey, PA: Information Science Reference; doi:10.4018/978-1-4666-2151-0.ch011

Jadhav, V. G. (2013). Integration of digital reference service for scholarly communication in digital libraries. In T. Ashraf & P. Gulati (Eds.), *Design, development, and management of resources for digital library services* (pp. 13–20). Hershey, PA: Information Science Reference; doi:10.4018/978-1-4666-2500-6.ch002

Jäkälä, M., & Berki, E. (2013). Communities, communication, and online identities. In S. Warburton & S. Hatzipanagos (Eds.), *Digital identity and social media* (pp. 1–13). Hershey, PA: Information Science Reference; doi:10.4018/978-1-4666-1915-9.ch001

Janneck, M., & Staar, H. (2013). Playing virtual power games: Micro-political processes in inter-organizational networks. In B. Medlin (Ed.), *Integrations of technology utilization and social dynamics in organizations* (pp. 171–192). Hershey, PA: Information Science Reference; doi:10.4018/978-1-4666-1948-7.ch011

Januska, I. M. (2013). Communication as a key factor in cooperation success and virtual enterprise paradigm support. In P. Renna (Ed.), *Production and manufacturing system management: Coordination approaches and multi-site planning* (pp. 145–161). Hershey, PA: Engineering Science Reference; doi:10.4018/978-1-4666-2098-8.ch008

Jayasingh, S., & Eze, U. C. (2013). Consumers' adoption of mobile coupons in Malaysia. In I. Lee (Ed.), *Strategy, adoption, and competitive advantage of mobile services in the global economy* (pp. 90–111). Hershey, PA: Information Science Reference; doi:10.4018/978-1-4666-1939-5.ch005

Jean Francois, E. (2013). Transculturality. In E. Jean Francois (Ed.), *Transcultural blended learning and teaching in postsecondary education* (pp. 1–14). Hershey, PA: Information Science Reference; doi:10.4018/978-1-4666-2014-8.ch001

Jensen, S. S. (2012). User-driven content creation in second life a source of innovation? Three case studies of business and public service. In N. Zagalo, L. Morgado, & A. Boa-Ventura (Eds.), *Virtual worlds and metaverse platforms: New communication and identity paradigms* (pp. 1–15). Hershey, PA: Information Science Reference; doi:10.4018/978-1-60960-854-5.ch001

Johnston, W. J., Komulainen, H., Ristola, A., & Ulkuniemi, P. (2013). Mobile advertising in small retailer firms: How to make the most of it. In I. Lee (Ed.), *Strategy, adoption, and competitive advantage of mobile services in the global economy* (pp. 283–298). Hershey, PA: Information Science Reference; doi:10.4018/978-1-4666-1939-5.ch016

Kadas, G., & Chatzimisios, P. (2013). The role of roadside assistance in vehicular communication networks: Security, quality of service, and routing issues. In R. Daher & A. Vinel (Eds.), *Roadside networks for vehicular communications: Architectures, applications, and test fields* (pp. 1–37). Hershey, PA: Information Science Reference; doi:10.4018/978-1-4666-2223-4.ch001

Kale, S. H., & Spence, M. T. (2012). A trination analysis of social exchange relationships in e-dating. In C. Romm Livermore (Ed.), *Gender and social computing: Interactions, differences and relationships* (pp. 257–271). Hershey, PA: Information Science Publishing; doi:10.4018/978-1-60960-759-3.ch015

Kamoun, F. (2013). Mobile NFC services: Adoption factors and a typology of business models. In I. Lee (Ed.), *Mobile services industries, technologies, and applications in the global economy* (pp. 254–272). Hershey, PA: Information Science Reference; doi:10.4018/978-1-4666-1981-4.ch016

Kaneda, K., & Iwamura, K. (2013). New proposals for data hiding in paper media. In K. Kondo (Ed.), *Multimedia information hiding technologies and methodologies for controlling data* (pp. 258–285). Hershey, PA: Information Science Reference; doi:10.4018/978-1-4666-2217-3.ch012

Kastell, K. (2013). Seamless communication to mobile devices in vehicular wireless networks. In O. Strobel (Ed.), *Communication in transportation systems* (pp. 324–342). Hershey, PA: Information Science Reference; doi:10.4018/978-1-4666-2976-9.ch012

Kaye, B. K., & Johnson, T. J. (2012). Net gain? Selective exposure and selective avoidance of social network sites. In F. Comunello (Ed.), *Networked sociability and individualism: Technology for personal and professional relationships* (pp. 218–237). Hershey, PA: Information Science Reference; doi:10.4018/978-1-61350-338-6.ch011

Kaye, B. K., Johnson, T. J., & Muhlberger, P. (2012). Blogs as a source of democratic deliberation. In T. Dumova & R. Fiordo (Eds.), *Blogging in the global society: Cultural, political and geographical aspects* (pp. 1–18). Hershey, PA: Information Science Reference; doi:10.4018/978-1-60960-744-9.ch001

Kefi, H., Mlaiki, A., & Peterson, R. L. (2013). IT offshoring: Trust views from client and vendor perspectives. In J. Wang (Ed.), *Perspectives and techniques for improving information technology project management* (pp. 113–130). Hershey, PA: Information Science Reference; doi:10.4018/978-1-4666-2800-7.ch009

Khan, N. A., & Batoo, M. F. (2013). Stone inscriptions of Srinagar: A digital panorama. In T. Ashraf & P. Gulati (Eds.), *Design, development, and management of resources for digital library services* (pp. 58–79). Hershey, PA: Information Science Reference; doi:10.4018/978-1-4666-2500-6.ch007

Kim, P. (2012). "Stay out of the way! My kid is video blogging through a phone!": A lesson learned from math tutoring social media for children in underserved communities. In *Wireless technologies: Concepts, methodologies, tools and applications* (pp. 1415–1428). Hershey, PA: Information Science Reference; doi:10.4018/978-1-61350-101-6.ch517

Kisubi, A. T. (2013). A critical perspective on the challenges for blended learning and teaching in Africa's higher education. In E. Jean Francois (Ed.), *Transcultural blended learning and teaching in postsecondary education* (pp. 145–168). Hershey, PA: Information Science Reference; doi:10.4018/978-1-4666-2014-8.ch009

Koole, M., & Parchoma, G. (2013). The web of identity: A model of digital identity formation in networked learning environments. In S. Warburton & S. Hatzipanagos (Eds.), *Digital identity and social media* (pp. 14–28). Hershey, PA: Information Science Reference; doi:10.4018/978-1-4666-1915-9.ch002

Kordaki, M., Gorghiu, G., Bîzoi, M., & Glava, A. (2012). Collaboration within multinational learning communities: The case of the virtual community collaborative space for sciences education European project. In A. Juan, T. Daradoumis, M. Roca, S. Grasman, & J. Faulin (Eds.), *Collaborative and distributed e-research: Innovations in technologies, strategies and applications* (pp. 206–226). Hershey, PA: Information Science Reference; doi:10.4018/978-1-4666-0125-3.ch010

Kovács, J., Bokor, L., Kanizsai, Z., & Imre, S. (2013). Review of advanced mobility solutions for multimedia networking in IPv6. In D. Kanellopoulos (Ed.), *Intelligent multimedia technologies for networking applications: Techniques and tools* (pp. 25–47). Hershey, PA: Information Science Reference; doi:10.4018/978-1-4666-2833-5.ch002

Kreps, D. (2013). Performing the discourse of sexuality online. In S. Warburton & S. Hatzipanagos (Eds.), *Digital identity and social media* (pp. 118–132). Hershey, PA: Information Science Reference; doi:10.4018/978-1-4666-1915-9.ch009

Ktoridou, D., Kaufmann, H., & Liassides, C. (2012). Factors affecting WiFi use intention: The context of Cyprus. In *Wireless technologies: Concepts, methodologies, tools and applications* (pp. 1760–1781). Hershey, PA: Information Science Reference; doi:10.4018/978-1-61350-101-6.ch703

Kumar, N., Nero Alves, L., & Aguiar, R. L. (2013). Employing traffic lights as road side units for road safety information broadcast. In R. Daher & A. Vinel (Eds.), *Roadside networks for vehicular communications: Architectures, applications, and test fields* (pp. 118–135). Hershey, PA: Information Science Reference; doi:10.4018/978-1-4666-2223-4.ch006

Kvasny, L., & Hales, K. D. (2013). The evolving discourse of the digital divide: The internet, black identity, and the evolving discourse of the digital divide. In *Digital literacy: Concepts, methodologies, tools, and applications* (pp. 1350–1366). Hershey, PA: Information Science Reference; doi:10.4018/978-1-4666-1852-7.ch071

L'Abate, L. (2013). Of paradigms, theories, and models: A conceptual hierarchical structure for communication science and technoself. In R. Luppicini (Ed.), *Handbook of research on technoself: Identity in a technological society* (pp. 84–104). Hershey, PA: Information Science Reference; doi:10.4018/978-1-4666-2211-1.ch005

Laghos, A. (2013). Multimedia social networks and e-learning. In D. Kanellopoulos (Ed.), *Intelligent multimedia technologies for networking applications: Techniques and tools* (pp. 365–379). Hershey, PA: Information Science Reference; doi:10.4018/978-1-4666-2833-5.ch015

Lappas, G. (2012). Social multimedia mining: Trends and opportunities in areas of social and communication studies. In I. Ting, T. Hong, & L. Wang (Eds.), *Social network mining, analysis, and research trends: Techniques and applications* (pp. 1–16). Hershey, PA: Information Science Reference; doi:10.4018/978-1-61350-513-7.ch001

Lawrence, J. E. (2013). Barriers hindering ecommerce adoption: A case study of Kurdistan region of Iraq. In A. Zolait (Ed.), *Technology diffusion and adoption: Global complexity, global innovation* (pp. 152–165). Hershey, PA: Information Science Reference; doi:10.4018/978-1-4666-2791-8.ch010

Lawrence, K. F. (2013). Identity and the online media fan community. In S. Warburton & S. Hatzipanagos (Eds.), *Digital identity and social media* (pp. 233–255). Hershey, PA: Information Science Reference; doi:10.4018/978-1-4666-1915-9.ch017

Lee, M. J., Dalgarno, B., Gregory, S., Carlson, L., & Tynan, B. (2013). How are Australian and New Zealand higher educators using 3D immersive virtual worlds in their teaching? In B. Tynan, J. Willems, & R. James (Eds.), *Outlooks and opportunities in blended and distance learning* (pp. 169–188). Hershey, PA: Information Science Reference; doi:10.4018/978-1-4666-4205-8.ch013

Lee, S., Alfano, C., & Carpenter, R. G. (2013). Invention in two parts: Multimodal communication and space design in the writing center. In R. Carpenter (Ed.), *Cases on higher education spaces: Innovation, collaboration, and technology* (pp. 41–63). Hershey, PA: Information Science Reference; doi:10.4018/978-1-4666-2673-7.ch003

Leichsenring, C., Tünnermann, R., & Hermann, T. (2013). Feelabuzz: Direct tactile communication with mobile phones. In J. Lumsden (Ed.), *Developments in technologies for human-centric mobile computing and applications* (pp. 145–154). Hershey, PA: Information Science Reference; doi:10.4018/978-1-4666-2068-1.ch009

Lemos, A., & Marques, F. P. (2013). A critical analysis of the limitations and effects of the Brazilian national broadband plan. In A. Abdelaal (Ed.), *Social and economic effects of community wireless networks and infrastructures* (pp. 255–274). Hershey, PA: Information Science Reference; doi:10.4018/978-1-4666-2997-4.ch014

Leung, C. K., Medina, I. J., & Tanbeer, S. K. (2013). Analyzing social networks to mine important friends. In G. Xu & L. Li (Eds.), *Social media mining and social network analysis: Emerging research* (pp. 90–104). Hershey, PA: Information Science Reference; doi:10.4018/978-1-4666-2806-9.ch006

Li, B. (2012). Toward an infrastructural approach to understanding participation in virtual communities. In H. Li (Ed.), *Virtual community participation and motivation: Cross-disciplinary theories* (pp. 103–123). Hershey, PA: Information Science Reference; doi:10.4018/978-1-4666-0312-7.ch007

Li, L., Xiao, H., & Xu, G. (2013). Recommending related microblogs. In G. Xu & L. Li (Eds.), *Social media mining and social network analysis: Emerging research* (pp. 202–210). Hershey, PA: Information Science Reference; doi:10.4018/978-1-4666-2806-9.ch013

Liddell, T. (2013). Historical evolution of adult education in America: The impact of institutions, change, and acculturation. In V. Wang (Ed.), *Handbook of research on technologies for improving the 21st century workforce: Tools for lifelong learning* (pp. 257–271). Hershey, PA: Information Science Publishing; doi:10.4018/978-1-4666-2181-7.ch017

Liljander, V., Gummerus, J., Pihlström, M., & Kiehelä, H. (2013). Mobile services as resources for consumer integration of value in a multi-channel environment. In I. Lee (Ed.), *Strategy, adoption, and competitive advantage of mobile services in the global economy* (pp. 259–282). Hershey, PA: Information Science Reference; doi:10.4018/978-1-4666-1939-5.ch015

Litaay, T., Prananingrum, D. H., & Krisanto, Y. A. (2013). Indonesian legal perspectives on biotechnology and intellectual property rights. In *Digital rights management: Concepts, methodologies, tools, and applications* (pp. 834–845). Hershey, PA: Information Science Reference; doi:10.4018/978-1-4666-2136-7.ch039

Little, G. (2013). Collection development for theological education. In S. Holder (Ed.), *Library collection development for professional programs: Trends and best practices* (pp. 112–127). Hershey, PA: Information Science Reference; doi:10.4018/978-1-4666-1897-8.ch007

Losh, S. C. (2013). American digital divides: Generation, education, gender, and ethnicity in American digital divides. In *Digital literacy: Concepts, methodologies, tools, and applications* (pp. 932–958). Hershey, PA: Information Science Reference; doi:10.4018/978-1-4666-1852-7.ch048

Lovari, A., & Parisi, L. (2012). Public administrations and citizens 2.0: Exploring digital public communication strategies and civic interaction within Italian municipality pages on Facebook. In F. Comunello (Ed.), *Networked sociability and individualism: Technology for personal and professional relationships* (pp. 238–263). Hershey, PA: Information Science Reference; doi:10.4018/978-1-61350-338-6.ch012

Maamar, Z., Faci, N., Mostéfaoui, S. K., & Akhter, F. (2013). Towards a framework for weaving social networks into mobile commerce. In D. Chiu (Ed.), *Mobile and web innovations in systems and service-oriented engineering* (pp. 333–347). Hershey, PA: Information Science Reference; doi:10.4018/978-1-4666-2470-2.ch018

Maia, I. F., & Valente, J. A. (2013). Digital identity built on a cooperative relationship. In S. Warburton & S. Hatzipanagos (Eds.), *Digital identity and social media* (pp. 58–73). Hershey, PA: Information Science Reference; doi:10.4018/978-1-4666-1915-9.ch005

Maity, M. (2013). Consumer information search and decision-making on m-commerce: The role of product type. In I. Lee (Ed.), *Strategy, adoption, and competitive advantage of mobile services in the global economy* (pp. 73–89). Hershey, PA: Information Science Reference; doi:10.4018/978-1-4666-1939-5.ch004

Malinen, S., Virjo, T., & Kujala, S. (2012). Supporting local connections with online communities. In A. Lugmayr, H. Franssila, P. Näränen, O. Sotamaa, J. Vanhala, & Z. Yu (Eds.), *Media in the ubiquitous era: Ambient, social and gaming media* (pp. 235–250). Hershey, PA: Information Science Reference; doi:10.4018/978-1-60960-774-6.ch013

Mantoro, T., Milišic, A., & Ayu, M. (2013). Online authentication using smart card technology in mobile phone infrastructure. In I. Khalil & E. Weippl (Eds.), *Contemporary challenges and solutions for mobile and multimedia technologies* (pp. 127–144). Hershey, PA: Information Science Reference; doi:10.4018/978-1-4666-2163-3.ch008

Marcato, E., & Scala, E. (2013). Moodle: A platform for a school. In P. Pumilia-Gnarini, E. Favaron, E. Pacetti, J. Bishop, & L. Guerra (Eds.), *Handbook of research on didactic strategies and technologies for education: Incorporating advancements* (pp. 107–116). Hershey, PA: Information Science Reference; doi:10.4018/978-1-4666-2122-0.ch010

Markaki, O. I., Charalabidis, Y., & Askounis, D. (2013). Measuring interoperability readiness in south eastern Europe and the Mediterranean: The interoperability observatory. In A. Scupola (Ed.), *Mobile opportunities and applications for e-service innovations* (pp. 210–230). Hershey, PA: Information Science Reference; doi:10.4018/978-1-4666-2654-6.ch012

Martin, J. D., & El-Toukhy, S. (2012). Blogging for sovereignty: An analysis of Palestinian blogs. In T. Dumova & R. Fiordo (Eds.), *Blogging in the global society: Cultural, political and geographical aspects* (pp. 148–160). Hershey, PA: Information Science Reference; doi:10.4018/978-1-60960-744-9.ch009

Matei, S. A., & Bruno, R. J. (2012). Individualist motivators and community functional constraints in social media: The case of Wikis and Wikipedia. In F. Comunello (Ed.), *Networked sociability and individualism: Technology for personal and professional relationships* (pp. 1–23). Hershey, PA: Information Science Reference; doi:10.4018/978-1-61350-338-6.ch001

Matsuoka, H. (2013). Acoustic OFDM technology and system. In K. Kondo (Ed.), *Multimedia information hiding technologies and methodologies for controlling data* (pp. 90–103). Hershey, PA: Information Science Reference; doi:10.4018/978-1-4666-2217-3.ch005

McCarthy, J. (2013). Online networking: Integrating international students into first year university through the strategic use of participatory media. In F. García-Peñalvo (Ed.), *Multiculturalism in technology-based education: Case studies on ICT-supported approaches* (pp. 189–210). Hershey, PA: Information Science Reference; doi:10.4018/978-1-4666-2101-5.ch012

McDonald, A., & Helmer, S. (2013). A comparative case study of Indonesian and UK organisational culture differences in IS project management. In A. Mesquita (Ed.), *User perception and influencing factors of technology in everyday life* (pp. 46–55). Hershey, PA: Information Science Reference; doi:10.4018/978-1-4666-1954-8.ch005

McDonough, C. (2013). Mobile broadband: Substituting for fixed broadband or providing value-added. In I. Lee (Ed.), *Mobile services industries, technologies, and applications in the global economy* (pp. 74–86). Hershey, PA: Information Science Reference; doi:10.4018/978-1-4666-1981-4.ch005

McKeown, A. (2013). Virtual communitas, "digital place-making," and the process of "becoming". In D. Harrison (Ed.), *Digital media and technologies for virtual artistic spaces* (pp. 218–236). Hershey, PA: Information Science Reference; doi:10.4018/978-1-4666-2961-5.ch016

Medeni, T. D., Medeni, I. T., & Balci, A. (2013). Proposing a knowledge amphora model for transition towards mobile government. In A. Scupola (Ed.), *Mobile opportunities and applications for e-service innovations* (pp. 170–192). Hershey, PA: Information Science Reference; doi:10.4018/978-1-4666-2654-6.ch010

Melo, A., Bezerra, P., Abelém, A. J., Neto, A., & Cerqueira, E. (2013). PriorityQoE: A tool for improving the QoE in video streaming. In D. Kanellopoulos (Ed.), *Intelligent multimedia technologies for networking applications: Techniques and tools* (pp. 270–290). Hershey, PA: Information Science Reference; doi:10.4018/978-1-4666-2833-5.ch011

Mendoza-González, R., Rodríguez, F. Á., & Arteaga, J. M. (2013). A usability study of mobile text based social applications: Towards a reliable strategy for design evaluation. In M. Garcia-Ruiz (Ed.), *Cases on usability engineering: Design and development of digital products* (pp. 195–219). Hershey, PA: Information Science Reference; doi:10.4018/978-1-4666-4046-7.ch009

Metzger, M. J., Wilson, C., Pure, R. A., & Zhao, B. Y. (2012). Invisible interactions: What latent social interaction can tell us about social relationships in social network sites. In F. Comunello (Ed.), *Networked sociability and individualism: Technology for personal and professional relationships* (pp. 79–102). Hershey, PA: Information Science Reference; doi:10.4018/978-1-61350-338-6.ch005

Millo, G., & Carmeci, G. (2013). Insurance in Italy: A spatial perspective. In G. Borruso, S. Bertazzon, A. Favretto, B. Murgante, & C. Torre (Eds.), *Geographic information analysis for sustainable development and economic planning: New technologies* (pp. 158–178). Hershey, PA: Information Science Reference; doi:10.4018/978-1-4666-1924-1.ch011

Mingqing, X., Wenjing, X., & Junming, Z. (2012). The future of television. In R. Sharma, M. Tan, & F. Pereira (Eds.), *Understanding the interactive digital media marketplace: Frameworks, platforms, communities and issues* (pp. 406–415). Hershey, PA: Information Science Reference; doi:10.4018/978-1-61350-147-4.ch032

Miscione, G. (2013). Telemedicine and development: Situating information technologies in the Amazon. In J. Abdelnour-Nocera (Ed.), *Knowledge and technological development effects on organizational and social structures* (pp. 132–145). Hershey, PA: Information Science Reference; doi:10.4018/978-1-4666-2151-0.ch009

Modegi, T. (2013). Spatial and temporal position information delivery to mobile terminals using audio watermarking techniques. In K. Kondo (Ed.), *Multimedia information hiding technologies and methodologies for controlling data* (pp. 182–207). Hershey, PA: Information Science Reference; doi:10.4018/978-1-4666-2217-3.ch009

Montes, J. A., Gutiérrez, A. C., Fernández, E. M., & Romeo, A. (2012). Reality mining, location based services and e-business opportunities: The case of city analytics. In *Wireless technologies: Concepts, methodologies, tools and applications* (pp. 1520–1532). Hershey, PA: Information Science Reference; doi:10.4018/978-1-61350-101-6.ch601

Moreno, A. (2012). The social construction of new cultural models through information and communication technologies. In M. Safar & K. Mahdi (Eds.), *Social networking and community behavior modeling: Qualitative and quantitative measures* (pp. 68–84). Hershey, PA: Information Science Reference; doi:10.4018/978-1-61350-444-4.ch004

Morris, J. Z., & Thomas, K. D. (2013). Implementing BioSand filters in rural Honduras: A case study of his hands mission international in Copán, Honduras. In H. Muga & K. Thomas (Eds.), *Cases on the diffusion and adoption of sustainable development practices* (pp. 468–496). Hershey, PA: Information Science Reference; doi:10.4018/978-1-4666-2842-7.ch017

Mura, G. (2012). The MultiPlasticity of new media. In G. Ghinea, F. Andres, & S. Gulliver (Eds.), *Multiple sensorial media advances and applications: New developments in MulSeMedia* (pp. 258–271). Hershey, PA: Information Science Reference; doi:10.4018/978-1-60960-821-7.ch013

Murray, C. (2012). Imagine mobile learning in your pocket. In *Wireless technologies: Concepts, methodologies, tools and applications* (pp. 2060–2088). Hershey, PA: Information Science Reference; doi:10.4018/978-1-61350-101-6.ch807

Mutohar, A., & Hughes, J. E. (2013). Toward web 2.0 integration in Indonesian education: Challenges and planning strategies. In N. Azab (Ed.), *Cases on web 2.0 in developing countries: Studies on implementation, application, and use* (pp. 198–221). Hershey, PA: Information Science Reference; doi:10.4018/978-1-4666-2515-0.ch008

Nandi, B., & Subramaniam, G. (2012). Evolution in broadband technology and future of wireless broadband. In *Wireless technologies: Concepts, methodologies, tools and applications* (pp. 1928–1957). Hershey, PA: Information Science Reference; doi:10.4018/978-1-61350-101-6.ch801

Naser, A., Jaber, I., Jaber, R., & Saeed, K. (2013). Information systems in UAE education sector: Security, cultural, and ethical issues. In F. Albadri (Ed.), *Information systems applications in the Arab education sector* (pp. 148–162). Hershey, PA: Information Science Reference; doi:10.4018/978-1-4666-1984-5.ch011

Nemoianu, I., & Pesquet-Popescu, B. (2013). Network coding for multimedia communications. In D. Kanellopoulos (Ed.), *Intelligent multimedia technologies for networking applications: Techniques and tools* (pp. 1–24). Hershey, PA: Information Science Reference; doi:10.4018/978-1-4666-2833-5.ch001

Nezlek, G., & DeHondt, G. (2013). Gender wage differentials in information systems: 1991 – 2008 a quantitative analysis. In B. Medlin (Ed.), *Integrations of technology utilization and social dynamics in organizations* (pp. 31–47). Hershey, PA: Information Science Reference; doi:10.4018/978-1-4666-1948-7.ch003

Nishimura, A., & Kondo, K. (2013). Information hiding for audio signals. In K. Kondo (Ed.), *Multimedia information hiding technologies and methodologies for controlling data* (pp. 1–18). Hershey, PA: Information Science Reference; doi:10.4018/978-1-4666-2217-3.ch001

Norder, J. W., & Carroll, J. W. (2013). Applied geospatial perspectives on the rock art of the lake of the woods region of Ontario, Canada. In D. Albert & G. Dobbs (Eds.), *Emerging methods and multidisciplinary applications in geospatial research* (pp. 77–93). Hershey, PA: Information Science Reference; doi:10.4018/978-1-4666-1951-7.ch005

O'Brien, M. A., & Rogers, W. A. (2013). Design for aging: Enhancing everyday technology use. In R. Zheng, R. Hill, & M. Gardner (Eds.), *Engaging older adults with modern technology: Internet use and information access needs* (pp. 105–123). Hershey, PA: Information Science Reference; doi:10.4018/978-1-4666-1966-1.ch006

O'Hanlon, S. (2013). Health information technology and human rights. In J. Lannon & E. Halpin (Eds.), *Human rights and information communication technologies: Trends and consequences of use* (pp. 235–246). Hershey, PA: Information Science Reference; doi:10.4018/978-1-4666-1918-0.ch014

Odella, F. (2012). Social networks and communities: From traditional society to the virtual sphere. In M. Safar & K. Mahdi (Eds.), *Social networking and community behavior modeling: Qualitative and quantitative measures* (pp. 1–25). Hershey, PA: Information Science Reference; doi:10.4018/978-1-61350-444-4.ch001

Okazaki, S., Romero, J., & Campo, S. (2012). Capturing market mavens among advergamers: A case of mobile-based social networking site in Japan. In I. Ting, T. Hong, & L. Wang (Eds.), *Social network mining, analysis, and research trends: Techniques and applications* (pp. 291–305). Hershey, PA: Information Science Reference; doi:10.4018/978-1-61350-513-7.ch017

Omojola, O. (2012). Exploring the impact of Google Igbo in South East Nigeria. In R. Lekoko & L. Semali (Eds.), *Cases on developing countries and ICT integration: Rural community development* (pp. 62–73). Hershey, PA: Information Science Reference; doi:10.4018/978-1-60960-117-1.ch007

Ovide, E. (2013). Intercultural education with indigenous peoples and the potential of digital technologies to make it happen. In F. García-Peñalvo (Ed.), *Multiculturalism in technology-based education: Case studies on ICT-supported approaches* (pp. 59–78). Hershey, PA: Information Science Reference; doi:10.4018/978-1-4666-2101-5.ch005

Owusu-Ansah, A. (2013). Exploring Hofstede's cultural dimension using Hollins' structured dialogue to attain a conduit for effective intercultural experiences. In E. Jean Francois (Ed.), *Transcultural blended learning and teaching in postsecondary education* (pp. 52–74). Hershey, PA: Information Science Reference; doi:10.4018/978-1-4666-2014-8.ch004

Özdemir, E. (2012). Gender and e-marketing: The role of gender differences in online purchasing behaviors. In C. Romm Livermore (Ed.), *Gender and social computing: Interactions, differences and relationships* (pp. 72–86). Hershey, PA: Information Science Publishing; doi:10.4018/978-1-60960-759-3.ch005

Palmer, M. H., & Hanney, J. (2012). Geographic information networks in American Indian governments and communities. In S. Dasgupta (Ed.), *Technical, social, and legal issues in virtual communities: Emerging environments: Emerging environments* (pp. 52–62). Hershey, PA: Information Science Reference; doi:10.4018/978-1-4666-1553-3.ch004

Pande, R. (2013). Gender gaps and information and communication technology: A case study of India. In *Digital literacy: Concepts, methodologies, tools, and applications* (pp. 1425–1439). Hershey, PA: Information Science Reference; doi:10.4018/978-1-4666-1852-7.ch075

Park, J., Chung, T., & Hur, W. (2013). The role of consumer innovativeness and trust for adopting internet phone services. In A. Scupola (Ed.), *Mobile opportunities and applications for e-service innovations* (pp. 22–36). Hershey, PA: Information Science Reference; doi:10.4018/978-1-4666-2654-6.ch002

Parke, A., & Griffiths, M. (2013). Poker gambling virtual communities: The use of computer-mediated communication to develop cognitive poker gambling skills. In R. Zheng (Ed.), *Evolving psychological and educational perspectives on cyber behavior* (pp. 190–204). Hershey, PA: Information Science Reference; doi:10.4018/978-1-4666-1858-9.ch012

Paschou, M., Sakkopoulos, E., Tsakalidis, A., Tzimas, G., & Viennas, E. (2013). An XML-based customizable model for multimedia applications for museums and exhibitions. In D. Kanellopoulos (Ed.), *Intelligent multimedia technologies for networking applications: Techniques and tools* (pp. 348–363). Hershey, PA: Information Science Reference; doi:10.4018/978-1-4666-2833-5.ch014

Pauwels, L. (2013). Images, self-images, and idealized identities in the digital networked world: Reconfigurations of family photography in a web-based mode. In S. Warburton & S. Hatzipanagos (Eds.), *Digital identity and social media* (pp. 133–147). Hershey, PA: Information Science Reference; doi:10.4018/978-1-4666-1915-9.ch010

Peachey, A., & Withnail, G. (2013). A sociocultural perspective on negotiating digital identities in a community of learners. In S. Warburton & S. Hatzipanagos (Eds.), *Digital identity and social media* (pp. 210–224). Hershey, PA: Information Science Reference; doi:10.4018/978-1-4666-1915-9.ch015

Peixoto, E., Martins, E., Anjo, A. B., & Silva, A. (2012). Geo@NET in the context of the platform of assisted learning from Aveiro University, Portugal. In M. Cruz-Cunha (Ed.), *Handbook of research on serious games as educational, business and research tools* (pp. 648–667). Hershey, PA: Information Science Reference; doi:10.4018/978-1-4666-0149-9.ch033

Pillay, N. (2013). The use of web 2.0 technologies by students from developed and developing countries: A New Zealand case study. In N. Azab (Ed.), *Cases on web 2.0 in developing countries: Studies on implementation, application, and use* (pp. 411–441). Hershey, PA: Information Science Reference; doi:10.4018/978-1-4666-2515-0.ch015

Pimenta, M. S., Miletto, E. M., Keller, D., Flores, L. V., & Testa, G. G. (2013). Technological support for online communities focusing on music creation: Adopting collaboration, flexibility, and multiculturality from Brazilian creativity styles. In N. Azab (Ed.), *Cases on web 2.0 in developing countries: Studies on implementation, application, and use* (pp. 283–312). Hershey, PA: Information Science Reference; doi:10.4018/978-1-4666-2515-0.ch011

Pina, P. (2013). Between scylla and charybdis: The balance between copyright, digital rights management and freedom of expression. In *Digital rights management: Concepts, methodologies, tools, and applications* (pp. 1355–1367). Hershey, PA: Information Science Reference; doi:10.4018/978-1-4666-2136-7.ch067

Pitsillides, S., Waller, M., & Fairfax, D. (2013). Digital death: What role does digital information play in the way we are (re)membered? In S. Warburton & S. Hatzipanagos (Eds.), *Digital identity and social media* (pp. 75–90). Hershey, PA: Information Science Reference; doi:10.4018/978-1-4666-1915-9.ch006

Polacek, P., & Huang, C. (2013). QoS scheduling with opportunistic spectrum access for multimedia. In M. Ku & J. Lin (Eds.), *Cognitive radio and interference management: Technology and strategy* (pp. 162–178). Hershey, PA: Information Science Reference; doi:10.4018/978-1-4666-2005-6.ch009

Potts, L. (2013). Balancing McLuhan with Williams: A sociotechnical view of technological determinism. In J. Abdelnour-Nocera (Ed.), *Knowledge and technological development effects on organizational and social structures* (pp. 109–114). Hershey, PA: Information Science Reference; doi:10.4018/978-1-4666-2151-0.ch007

Prescott, J., & Bogg, J. (2013). Stereotype, attitudes, and identity: Gendered expectations and behaviors. In *Gendered occupational differences in science, engineering, and technology careers* (pp. 112–135). Hershey, PA: Information Science Reference; doi:10.4018/978-1-4666-2107-7.ch005

Preussler, A., & Kerres, M. (2013). Managing social reputation in Twitter. In S. Warburton & S. Hatzipanagos (Eds.), *Digital identity and social media* (pp. 91–103). Hershey, PA: Information Science Reference; doi:10.4018/978-1-4666-1915-9.ch007

Prieger, J. E., & Church, T. V. (2013). Deployment of mobile broadband service in the United States. In I. Lee (Ed.), *Mobile services industries, technologies, and applications in the global economy* (pp. 1–24). Hershey, PA: Information Science Reference; doi:10.4018/978-1-4666-1981-4.ch001

Puumalainen, K., Frank, L., Sundqvist, S., & Tuppura, A. (2012). The critical mass of wireless communications: Differences between developing and developed economies. In *Wireless technologies: Concepts, methodologies, tools and applications* (pp. 1719–1736). Hershey, PA: Information Science Reference; doi:10.4018/978-1-61350-101-6.ch701

Rabino, S., Rafiee, D., Onufrey, S., & Moskowitz, H. (2013). Retention and customer share building: Formulating a communication strategy for a sports club. In H. Kaufmann & M. Panni (Eds.), *Customer-centric marketing strategies: Tools for building organizational performance* (pp. 511–529). Hershey, PA: Business Science Reference; doi:10.4018/978-1-4666-2524-2.ch025

Rahman, H., & Kumar, S. (2012). Mobile computing: An emerging issue in the digitized world. In A. Kumar & H. Rahman (Eds.), *Mobile computing techniques in emerging markets: Systems, applications and services* (pp. 1–22). Hershey, PA: Information Science Reference; doi:10.4018/978-1-4666-0080-5.ch001

Ratten, V. (2013). Adoption of mobile reading devices in the book industry. In I. Lee (Ed.), *Strategy, adoption, and competitive advantage of mobile services in the global economy* (pp. 203–216). Hershey, PA: Information Science Reference; doi:10.4018/978-1-4666-1939-5.ch011

Ratten, V. (2013). Mobile banking in the youth market: Implications from an entrepreneurial and learning perspective. In I. Lee (Ed.), *Strategy, adoption, and competitive advantage of mobile services in the global economy* (pp. 112–126). Hershey, PA: Information Science Reference; doi:10.4018/978-1-4666-1939-5.ch006

Ratten, V. (2013). Social e-enterprise through technological innovations and mobile social networks. In T. Torres-Coronas & M. Vidal-Blasco (Eds.), *Social e-enterprise: Value creation through ICT* (pp. 96–109). Hershey, PA: Information Science Reference; doi:10.4018/978-1-4666-2667-6.ch006

Rego, P. A., Moreira, P. M., & Reis, L. P. (2012). New forms of interaction in serious games for rehabilitation. In M. Cruz-Cunha (Ed.), *Handbook of research on serious games as educational, business and research tools* (pp. 1188–1211). Hershey, PA: Information Science Reference; doi:10.4018/978-1-4666-0149-9.ch062

Reinhard, C. D. (2012). Virtual worlds and reception studies: Comparing engagings. In N. Zagalo, L. Morgado, & A. Boa-Ventura (Eds.), *Virtual worlds and metaverse platforms: New communication and identity paradigms* (pp. 117–136). Hershey, PA: Information Science Reference; doi:10.4018/978-1-60960-854-5.ch008

Rieser, M. (2013). Mobility, liminality, and digital materiality. In D. Harrison (Ed.), *Digital media and technologies for virtual artistic spaces* (pp. 27–45). Hershey, PA: Information Science Reference; doi:10.4018/978-1-4666-2961-5.ch003

Rodrigues, R. G., Pinheiro, P. G., & Barbosa, J. (2012). Online playability: The social dimension to the virtual world. In M. Cruz-Cunha (Ed.), *Handbook of research on serious games as educational, business and research tools* (pp. 391–421). Hershey, PA: Information Science Reference; doi:10.4018/978-1-4666-0149-9.ch021

Romm-Livermore, C., Somers, T. M., Setzekorn, K., & King, A. L. (2012). How e-daters behave online: Theory and empirical observations. In C. Romm Livermore (Ed.), *Gender and social computing: Interactions, differences and relationships* (pp. 236–256). Hershey, PA: Information Science Publishing; doi:10.4018/978-1-60960-759-3.ch014

Rosaci, D., & Sarnè, G. M. (2012). An agent-based approach to adapt multimedia web content in ubiquitous environment. In S. Bagchi (Ed.), *Ubiquitous multimedia and mobile agents: Models and implementations* (pp. 60–84). Hershey, PA: Information Science Reference; doi:10.4018/978-1-61350-107-8.ch003

Rosas, O. V., & Dhen, G. (2012). One self to rule them all: A critical discourse analysis of French-speaking players' identity construction in World of Warcraft. In N. Zagalo, L. Morgado, & A. Boa-Ventura (Eds.), *Virtual worlds and metaverse platforms: New communication and identity paradigms* (pp. 337–366). Hershey, PA: Information Science Reference; doi:10.4018/978-1-60960-854-5.ch022

Rouibah, K., & Abbas, H. A. (2012). Effect of personal innovativeness, attachment motivation and social norms on the acceptance of camera mobile phones: An empirical study in an Arab country. In W. Hu (Ed.), *Emergent trends in personal, mobile, and handheld computing technologies* (pp. 302–323). Hershey, PA: Information Science Reference; doi:10.4018/978-1-4666-0921-1.ch018

Ruiz-Mafé, C., Sanz-Blas, S., & Martí-Parreño, J. (2013). Web 2.0 goes mobile: Motivations and barriers of mobile social networks use in Spain. In N. Azab (Ed.), *Cases on web 2.0 in developing countries: Studies on implementation, application, and use* (pp. 109–146). Hershey, PA: Information Science Reference; doi:10.4018/978-1-4666-2515-0.ch005

Rybas, S. (2012). Community embodied: Validating the subjective performance of an online class. In H. Li (Ed.), *Virtual community participation and motivation: Cross-disciplinary theories* (pp. 124–141). Hershey, PA: Information Science Reference; doi:10.4018/978-1-4666-0312-7.ch008

Sabelkin, M., & Gagnon, F. (2013). Data transmission oriented on the object, communication media, application, and state of communication systems. In M. Bartolacci & S. Powell (Eds.), *Advancements and innovations in wireless communications and network technologies* (pp. 117–132). Hershey, PA: Information Science Reference; doi:10.4018/978-1-4666-2154-1.ch009

Sajeva, S. (2013). Towards a conceptual knowledge management system based on systems thinking and sociotechnical thinking. In J. Abdelnour-Nocera (Ed.), *Knowledge and technological development effects on organizational and social structures* (pp. 115–130). Hershey, PA: Information Science Reference; doi:10.4018/978-1-4666-2151-0.ch008

Salo, M., Olsson, T., Makkonen, M., & Frank, L. (2013). User perspective on the adoption of mobile augmented reality based applications. In I. Lee (Ed.), *Strategy, adoption, and competitive advantage of mobile services in the global economy* (pp. 165–188). Hershey, PA: Information Science Reference; doi:10.4018/978-1-4666-1939-5.ch009

Samanta, S. K., Woods, J., & Ghanbari, M. (2013). Automatic language translation: An enhancement to the mobile messaging services. In A. Mesquita (Ed.), *User perception and influencing factors of technology in everyday life* (pp. 57–75). Hershey, PA: Information Science Reference; doi:10.4018/978-1-4666-1954-8.ch006

Santo, A. E., Rijo, R., Monteiro, J., Henriques, I., Matos, A., Rito, C., & Marcelino, L. et al. (2012). Games improving disorders of attention deficit and hyperactivity. In M. Cruz-Cunha (Ed.), *Handbook of research on serious games as educational, business and research tools* (pp. 1160–1174). Hershey, PA: Information Science Reference; doi:10.4018/978-1-4666-0149-9.ch060

Sarker, S., Campbell, D. E., Ondrus, J., & Valacich, J. S. (2012). Mapping the need for mobile collaboration technologies: A fit perspective. In N. Kock (Ed.), *Advancing collaborative knowledge environments: New trends in e-collaboration* (pp. 211–233). Hershey, PA: Information Science Reference; doi:10.4018/978-1-61350-459-8.ch013

Sasajima, M., Kitamura, Y., & Mizoguchi, R. (2013). Method for modeling user semantics and its application to service navigation on the web. In G. Xu & L. Li (Eds.), *Social media mining and social network analysis: Emerging research* (pp. 127–139). Hershey, PA: Information Science Reference; doi:10.4018/978-1-4666-2806-9.ch008

Scheel, C., & Pineda, L. (2013). Building industrial clusters in Latin America: Paddling upstream. In J. Abdelnour-Nocera (Ed.), *Knowledge and technological development effects on organizational and social structures* (pp. 146–166). Hershey, PA: Information Science Reference; doi:10.4018/978-1-4666-2151-0.ch010

Sell, A., Walden, P., & Carlsson, C. (2013). Segmentation matters: An exploratory study of mobile service users. In D. Chiu (Ed.), *Mobile and web innovations in systems and service-oriented engineering* (pp. 301–317). Hershey, PA: Information Science Reference; doi:10.4018/978-1-4666-2470-2.ch016

Sermon, P., & Gould, C. (2013). Site-specific performance, narrative, and social presence in multi-user virtual environments and the urban landscape. In D. Harrison (Ed.), *Digital media and technologies for virtual artistic spaces* (pp. 46–58). Hershey, PA: Information Science Reference; doi:10.4018/978-1-4666-2961-5.ch004

Servaes, J. (2012). The role of information communication technologies within the field of communication for social change. In *Wireless technologies: Concepts, methodologies, tools and applications* (pp. 1117–1135). Hershey, PA: Information Science Reference; doi:10.4018/978-1-61350-101-6.ch502

Seth, N., & Patnayakuni, R. (2012). Online matrimonial sites and the transformation of arranged marriage in India. In C. Romm Livermore (Ed.), *Gender and social computing: Interactions, differences and relationships* (pp. 272–295). Hershey, PA: Information Science Publishing; doi:10.4018/978-1-60960-759-3.ch016

Shaffer, G. (2013). Lessons learned from grassroots wireless networks in Europe. In A. Abdelaal (Ed.), *Social and economic effects of community wireless networks and infrastructures* (pp. 236–254). Hershey, PA: Information Science Reference; doi:10.4018/978-1-4666-2997-4.ch013

Shen, J., & Eder, L. B. (2013). An examination of factors associated with user acceptance of social shopping websites. In A. Mesquita (Ed.), *User perception and influencing factors of technology in everyday life* (pp. 28–45). Hershey, PA: Information Science Reference; doi:10.4018/978-1-4666-1954-8.ch004

Shen, K. N. (2012). Identification vs. self-verification in virtual communities (VC): Theoretical gaps and design implications. In C. El Morr & P. Maret (Eds.), *Virtual community building and the information society: Current and future directions* (pp. 208–236). Hershey, PA: Information Science Reference; doi:10.4018/978-1-60960-869-9.ch011

Shi, Y., & Liu, Z. (2013). Cultural models and variations. In *Industrial engineering: Concepts, methodologies, tools, and applications* (pp. 1560–1573). Hershey, PA: Engineering Science Reference; doi:10.4018/978-1-4666-1945-6.ch083

Shiferaw, A., Sehai, E., Hoekstra, D., & Getachew, A. (2013). Enhanced knowledge management: Knowledge centers for extension communication and agriculture development in Ethiopia. In B. Maumbe & C. Patrikakis (Eds.), *E-agriculture and rural development: Global innovations and future prospects* (pp. 103–116). Hershey, PA: Information Science Reference; doi:10.4018/978-1-4666-2655-3.ch010

Simão de Vasconcellos, M., & Soares de Araújo, I. (2013). Massively multiplayer online role playing games for health communication in Brazil. In K. Bredl & W. Bösche (Eds.), *Serious games and virtual worlds in education, professional development, and healthcare* (pp. 294–312). Hershey, PA: Information Science Reference; doi:10.4018/978-1-4666-3673-6.ch018

Simour, L. (2012). Networking identities: Geographies of interaction and computer mediated communication1. In S. Dasgupta (Ed.), *Technical, social, and legal issues in virtual communities: Emerging environments: Emerging environments* (pp. 235–246). Hershey, PA: Information Science Reference; doi:10.4018/978-1-4666-1553-3.ch016

Singh, G. R. (2013). Cyborg in the village: Culturally embedded resistances to blended teaching and learning. In E. Jean Francois (Ed.), *Transcultural blended learning and teaching in postsecondary education* (pp. 75–90). Hershey, PA: Information Science Reference; doi:10.4018/978-1-4666-2014-8.ch005

Singh, M., & Iding, M. K. (2013). Does credibility count?: Singaporean students' evaluation of social studies web sites. In R. Zheng (Ed.), *Evolving psychological and educational perspectives on cyber behavior* (pp. 230–245). Hershey, PA: Information Science Reference; doi:10.4018/978-1-4666-1858-9.ch014

Singh, S. (2013). Information and communication technology and its potential to transform Indian agriculture. In B. Maumbe & C. Patrikakis (Eds.), *E-agriculture and rural development: Global innovations and future prospects* (pp. 140–168). Hershey, PA: Information Science Reference; doi:10.4018/978-1-4666-2655-3.ch012

Siqueira, S. R., Rocha, E. C., & Nery, M. S. (2012). Brazilian occupational therapy perspective about digital games as an inclusive resource to disabled people in schools. In M. Cruz-Cunha (Ed.), *Handbook of research on serious games as educational, business and research tools* (pp. 730–749). Hershey, PA: Information Science Reference; doi:10.4018/978-1-4666-0149-9.ch037

Siti-Nabiha, A., & Salleh, D. (2013). Public sector transformation in Malaysia: Improving local governance and accountability. In N. Pomazalová (Ed.), *Public sector transformation processes and internet public procurement: Decision support systems* (pp. 276–290). Hershey, PA: Engineering Science Reference; doi:10.4018/978-1-4666-2665-2.ch013

Siwar, C., & Abdulai, A. (2013). Sustainable development and the digital divide among OIC countries: Towards a collaborative digital approach. In *Digital literacy: Concepts, methodologies, tools, and applications* (pp. 242–261). Hershey, PA: Information Science Reference; doi:10.4018/978-1-4666-1852-7.ch013

Smith, P. A. (2013). Strengthening and enriching audit practice: The socio-technical relevance of "decision leaders". In J. Abdelnour-Nocera (Ed.), *Knowledge and technological development effects on organizational and social structures* (pp. 97–108). Hershey, PA: Information Science Reference; doi:10.4018/978-1-4666-2151-0.ch006

Smith, P. A., & Cockburn, T. (2013). Generational demographics. In *Dynamic leadership models for global business: Enhancing digitally connected environments* (pp. 230–256). Hershey, PA: Business Science Reference; doi:10.4018/978-1-4666-2836-6.ch009

Smith, P. A., & Cockburn, T. (2013). Leadership, global business, and digitally connected environments. In *Dynamic leadership models for global business: Enhancing digitally connected environments* (pp. 257–296). Hershey, PA: Business Science Reference; doi:10.4018/978-1-4666-2836-6.ch010

Sohrabi, B., Gholipour, A., & Amiri, B. (2013). The influence of information technology on organizational behavior: Study of identity challenges in virtual teams. In N. Kock (Ed.), *Interdisciplinary applications of electronic collaboration approaches and technologies* (pp. 79–95). Hershey, PA: Information Science Reference; doi:10.4018/978-1-4666-2020-9.ch006

Soitu, L., & Paulet-Crainiceanu, L. (2013). Student-faculty communication on Facebook: Prospective learning enhancement and boundaries. In B. Pătruţ, M. Pătruţ, & C. Cmeciu (Eds.), *Social media and the new academic environment: Pedagogical challenges* (pp. 40–67). Hershey, PA: Information Science Reference; doi:10.4018/978-1-4666-2851-9.ch003

Solvoll, T. (2013). Mobile communication in hospitals: What is the problem? In C. Rückemann (Ed.), *Integrated information and computing systems for natural, spatial, and social sciences* (pp. 287–301). Hershey, PA: Information Science Reference; doi:10.4018/978-1-4666-2190-9.ch014

Somboonviwat, K. (2013). Topic modeling for web community discovery. In G. Xu & L. Li (Eds.), *Social media mining and social network analysis: Emerging research* (pp. 72–89). Hershey, PA: Information Science Reference; doi:10.4018/978-1-4666-2806-9.ch005

Speaker, R. B., Levitt, G., & Grubaugh, S. (2013). Professional development in a virtual world. In J. Keengwe & L. Kyei-Blankson (Eds.), *Virtual mentoring for teachers: Online professional development practices* (pp. 122–148). Hershey, PA: Information Science Reference; doi:10.4018/978-1-4666-1963-0.ch007

Stevenson, G., & Van Belle, J. (2013). Using social media technology to improve collaboration: A case study of micro-blogging adoption in a South African financial services company. In N. Azab (Ed.), *Cases on web 2.0 in developing countries: Studies on implementation, application, and use* (pp. 313–341). Hershey, PA: Information Science Reference; doi:10.4018/978-1-4666-2515-0.ch012

Strang, K. D. (2013). Balanced assessment of flexible e-learning vs. face-to-face campus delivery courses at an Australian university. In M. Khosrow-Pour (Ed.), *Cases on assessment and evaluation in education* (pp. 304–339). Hershey, PA: Information Science Reference; doi:10.4018/978-1-4666-2621-8.ch013

Strömberg-Jakka, M. (2013). Social assistance via the internet: The case of Finland in the European context. In J. Lannon & E. Halpin (Eds.), *Human rights and information communication technologies: Trends and consequences of use* (pp. 177–195). Hershey, PA: Information Science Reference; doi:10.4018/978-1-4666-1918-0.ch011

Sultanow, E., Weber, E., & Cox, S. (2013). A semantic e-collaboration approach to enable awareness in globally distributed organizations. In N. Kock (Ed.), *Interdisciplinary applications of electronic collaboration approaches and technologies* (pp. 1–16). Hershey, PA: Information Science Reference; doi:10.4018/978-1-4666-2020-9.ch001

Sun, H., Gui, N., & Blondia, C. (2013). A generic adaptation framework for mobile communication. In V. De Florio (Ed.), *Innovations and approaches for resilient and adaptive systems* (pp. 196–207). Hershey, PA: Information Science Reference; doi:10.4018/978-1-4666-2056-8.ch011

Surgevil, O., & Özbilgin, M. F. (2012). Women in information communication technologies. In C. Romm Livermore (Ed.), *Gender and social computing: Interactions, differences and relationships* (pp. 87–97). Hershey, PA: Information Science Publishing; doi:10.4018/978-1-60960-759-3.ch006

Sylaiou, S., White, M., & Liarokapis, F. (2013). Digital heritage systems: The ARCO evaluation. In M. Garcia-Ruiz (Ed.), *Cases on usability engineering: Design and development of digital products* (pp. 321–354). Hershey, PA: Information Science Reference; doi:10.4018/978-1-4666-4046-7.ch014

Sylvester, O. A. (2013). Impact of information and communication technology on livestock production: The experience of rural farmers in Nigeria. In B. Maumbe & C. Patrikakis (Eds.), *E-agriculture and rural development: Global innovations and future prospects* (pp. 68–75). Hershey, PA: Information Science Reference; doi:10.4018/978-1-4666-2655-3.ch007

Taha, K., & Elmasri, R. (2012). Social search and personalization through demographic filtering. In I. Ting, T. Hong, & L. Wang (Eds.), *Social network mining, analysis, and research trends: Techniques and applications* (pp. 183–203). Hershey, PA: Information Science Reference; doi:10.4018/978-1-61350-513-7.ch012

Tai, Z. (2012). Fame, fantasy, fanfare and fun: The blossoming of the Chinese culture of blogmongering. In T. Dumova & R. Fiordo (Eds.), *Blogging in the global society: Cultural, political and geographical aspects* (pp. 37–54). Hershey, PA: Information Science Reference; doi:10.4018/978-1-60960-744-9.ch003

Taifi, N., & Gharbi, K. (2013). Technology integration in strategic management: The case of a micro-financing institutions network. In T. Torres-Coronas & M. Vidal-Blasco (Eds.), *Social e-enterprise: Value creation through ICT* (pp. 263–279). Hershey, PA: Information Science Reference; doi:10.4018/978-1-4666-2667-6.ch015

Talib, S., Clarke, N. L., & Furnell, S. M. (2013). Establishing a personalized information security culture. In I. Khalil & E. Weippl (Eds.), *Contemporary challenges and solutions for mobile and multimedia technologies* (pp. 53–69). Hershey, PA: Information Science Reference; doi:10.4018/978-1-4666-2163-3.ch004

Tamura, H., Sugasaka, T., & Ueda, K. (2012). Lovely place to buy!: Enhancing grocery shopping experiences with a human-centric approach. In A. Lugmayr, H. Franssila, P. Näränen, O. Sotamaa, J. Vanhala, & Z. Yu (Eds.), *Media in the ubiquitous era: Ambient, social and gaming media* (pp. 53–65). Hershey, PA: Information Science Reference; doi:10.4018/978-1-60960-774-6.ch003

Tawileh, W., Bukvova, H., & Schoop, E. (2013). Virtual collaborative learning: Opportunities and challenges of web 2.0-based e-learning arrangements for developing countries. In N. Azab (Ed.), *Cases on web 2.0 in developing countries: Studies on implementation, application, and use* (pp. 380–410). Hershey, PA: Information Science Reference; doi:10.4018/978-1-4666-2515-0.ch014

Teixeira, P. M., Félix, M. J., & Tavares, P. (2012). Playing with design: The universality of design in game development. In M. Cruz-Cunha (Ed.), *Handbook of research on serious games as educational, business and research tools* (pp. 217–231). Hershey, PA: Information Science Reference; doi:10.4018/978-1-4666-0149-9.ch011

Teusner, P. E. (2012). Networked individualism, constructions of community and religious identity: The case of emerging church bloggers in Australia. In F. Comunello (Ed.), *Networked sociability and individualism: Technology for personal and professional relationships* (pp. 264–288). Hershey, PA: Information Science Reference; doi:10.4018/978-1-61350-338-6.ch013

Tezcan, M. (2013). Social e-entrepreneurship, employment, and e-learning. In T. Torres-Coronas & M. Vidal-Blasco (Eds.), *Social e-enterprise: Value creation through ICT* (pp. 133–147). Hershey, PA: Information Science Reference; doi:10.4018/978-1-4666-2667-6.ch008

Thatcher, B. (2012). Approaching intercultural rhetoric and professional communication. In *Intercultural rhetoric and professional communication: Technological advances and organizational behavior* (pp. 1–38). Hershey, PA: Information Science Reference; doi:10.4018/978-1-61350-450-5.ch001

Thatcher, B. (2012). Borders and etics as units of analysis for intercultural rhetoric and professional communication. In *Intercultural rhetoric and professional communication: Technological advances and organizational behavior* (pp. 39–74). Hershey, PA: Information Science Reference; doi:10.4018/978-1-61350-450-5.ch002

Thatcher, B. (2012). Core competencies in intercultural teaching and research. In *Intercultural rhetoric and professional communication: Technological advances and organizational behavior* (pp. 318–342). Hershey, PA: Information Science Reference; doi:10.4018/978-1-61350-450-5.ch011

Thatcher, B. (2012). Distance education and e-learning across cultures. In *Intercultural rhetoric and professional communication: Technological advances and organizational behavior* (pp. 186–215). Hershey, PA: Information Science Reference; doi:10.4018/978-1-61350-450-5.ch007

Thatcher, B. (2012). Information and communication technologies and intercultural professional communication. In *Intercultural rhetoric and professional communication: Technological advances and organizational behavior* (pp. 97–123). Hershey, PA: Information Science Reference; doi:10.4018/978-1-61350-450-5.ch004

Thatcher, B. (2012). Intercultural rhetorical dimensions of health literacy and medicine. In *Intercultural rhetoric and professional communication: Technological advances and organizational behavior* (pp. 247–282). Hershey, PA: Information Science Reference; doi:10.4018/978-1-61350-450-5.ch009

Thatcher, B. (2012). Legal traditions, the universal declaration of human rights, and intercultural professional communication. In *Intercultural rhetoric and professional communication: Technological advances and organizational behavior* (pp. 216–246). Hershey, PA: Information Science Reference; doi:10.4018/978-1-61350-450-5.ch008

Thatcher, B. (2012). Organizational theory and communication across cultures. In *Intercultural rhetoric and professional communication: Technological advances and organizational behavior* (pp. 159–185). Hershey, PA: Information Science Reference; doi:10.4018/978-1-61350-450-5.ch006

Thatcher, B. (2012). Teaching intercultural rhetoric and professional communication. In *Intercultural rhetoric and professional communication: Technological advances and organizational behavior* (pp. 343–378). Hershey, PA: Information Science Reference; doi:10.4018/978-1-61350-450-5.ch012

Thatcher, B. (2012). Website designs as an indicator of globalization. In *Intercultural rhetoric and professional communication: Technological advances and organizational behavior* (pp. 124–158). Hershey, PA: Information Science Reference; doi:10.4018/978-1-61350-450-5.ch005

Thatcher, B. (2012). Writing instructions and how-to-do manuals across cultures. In *Intercultural rhetoric and professional communication: Technological advances and organizational behavior* (pp. 283–317). Hershey, PA: Information Science Reference; doi:10.4018/978-1-61350-450-5.ch010

Thirumal, P., & Tartakov, G. M. (2013). India's Dalits search for a democratic opening in the digital divide. In *Digital literacy: Concepts, methodologies, tools, and applications* (pp. 852–871). Hershey, PA: Information Science Reference; doi:10.4018/978-1-4666-1852-7.ch044

Thomas, G. E. (2013). Facilitating learning with adult students in the transcultural classroom. In E. Jean Francois (Ed.), *Transcultural blended learning and teaching in postsecondary education* (pp. 193–215). Hershey, PA: Information Science Reference; doi:10.4018/978-1-4666-2014-8.ch011

Tripathi, S. N., & Siddiqui, M. H. (2013). Designing effective mobile advertising with specific reference to developing markets. In I. Lee (Ed.), *Strategy, adoption, and competitive advantage of mobile services in the global economy* (pp. 299–324). Hershey, PA: Information Science Reference; doi:10.4018/978-1-4666-1939-5.ch017

Truong, Y. (2013). Antecedents of consumer acceptance of mobile television advertising. In A. Mesquita (Ed.), *User perception and influencing factors of technology in everyday life* (pp. 128–141). Hershey, PA: Information Science Reference; doi:10.4018/978-1-4666-1954-8.ch010

Tsuneizumi, I., Aikebaier, A., Ikeda, M., Enokido, T., & Takizawa, M. (2013). Design and implementation of hybrid time (HT) group communication protocol for homogeneous broadcast groups. In N. Bessis (Ed.), *Development of distributed systems from design to application and maintenance* (pp. 282–293). Hershey, PA: Information Science Reference; doi:10.4018/978-1-4666-2647-8.ch017

Tzoulia, E. (2013). Legal issues to be considered before setting in force consumer-centric marketing strategies within the European Union. In H. Kaufmann & M. Panni (Eds.), *Customer-centric marketing strategies: Tools for building organizational performance* (pp. 36–56). Hershey, PA: Business Science Reference; doi:10.4018/978-1-4666-2524-2.ch003

Underwood, J., & Okubayashi, T. (2013). Comparing the characteristics of text-speak used by English and Japanese students. In R. Zheng (Ed.), *Evolving psychological and educational perspectives on cyber behavior* (pp. 258–271). Hershey, PA: Information Science Reference; doi:10.4018/978-1-4666-1858-9. ch016

Unoki, M., & Miyauchi, R. (2013). Method of digital-audio watermarking based on cochlear delay characteristics. In K. Kondo (Ed.), *Multimedia information hiding technologies and methodologies for controlling data* (pp. 42–70). Hershey, PA: Information Science Reference; doi:10.4018/978-1-4666-2217-3.ch003

Usman, L. M. (2013). Adult education and sustainable learning outcome of rural widows of central northern Nigeria. In V. Wang (Ed.), *Technological applications in adult and vocational education advancement* (pp. 215–231). Hershey, PA: Information Science Reference; doi:10.4018/978-1-4666-2062-9.ch017

Usoro, A., & Khan, I. U. (2013). Trust as an aspect of organisational culture: Its effects on knowledge sharing in virtual communities. In R. Colomo-Palacios (Ed.), *Enhancing the modern organization through information technology professionals: Research, studies, and techniques* (pp. 182–199). Hershey, PA: Business Science Reference; doi:10.4018/978-1-4666-2648-5.ch013

Utz, S. (2012). Social network site use among Dutch students: Effects of time and platform. In F. Comunello (Ed.), *Networked sociability and individualism: Technology for personal and professional relationships* (pp. 103–125). Hershey, PA: Information Science Reference; doi:10.4018/978-1-61350-338-6.ch006

Vasilescu, R., Epure, M., & Florea, N. (2013). Digital literacy for effective communication in the new academic environment: The educational blogs. In B. Pătruţ, M. Pătruţ, & C. Cmeciu (Eds.), *Social media and the new academic environment: Pedagogical challenges* (pp. 368–390). Hershey, PA: Information Science Reference; doi:10.4018/978-1-4666-2851-9.ch018

Vladimirschi, V. (2013). An exploratory study of cross-cultural engagement in the community of inquiry: Instructor perspectives and challenges. In Z. Akyol & D. Garrison (Eds.), *Educational communities of inquiry: Theoretical framework, research and practice* (pp. 466–489). Hershey, PA: Information Science Reference; doi:10.4018/978-1-4666-2110-7.ch023

Vuokko, R. (2012). A practice perspective on transforming mobile work. In *Wireless technologies: Concepts, methodologies, tools and applications* (pp. 1104–1116). Hershey, PA: Information Science Reference; doi:10.4018/978-1-61350-101-6.ch501

Wall, M., & Kirdnark, T. (2012). The blogosphere in the "land of smiles": Citizen media and political conflict in Thailand. In T. Dumova & R. Fiordo (Eds.), *Blogging in the global society: Cultural, political and geographical aspects* (pp. 19–36). Hershey, PA: Information Science Reference; doi:10.4018/978-1-60960-744-9.ch002

Warburton, S. (2013). Space for lurking: A pattern for designing online social spaces. In S. Warburton & S. Hatzipanagos (Eds.), *Digital identity and social media* (pp. 149–158). Hershey, PA: Information Science Reference; doi:10.4018/978-1-4666-1915-9.ch011

Warren, S. J., & Lin, L. (2012). Ethical considerations for learning game, simulation, and virtual world design and development. In H. Yang & S. Yuen (Eds.), *Handbook of research on practices and outcomes in virtual worlds and environments* (pp. 1–18). Hershey, PA: Information Science Publishing; doi:10.4018/978-1-60960-762-3.ch001

Wasihun, T. A., & Maumbe, B. (2013). Information and communication technology uses in agriculture: Agribusiness industry opportunities and future challenges. In B. Maumbe & C. Patrikakis (Eds.), *E-agriculture and rural development: Global innovations and future prospects* (pp. 235–251). Hershey, PA: Information Science Reference; doi:10.4018/978-1-4666-2655-3.ch017

Webb, L. M., Fields, T. E., Boupha, S., & Stell, M. N. (2012). U.S. political blogs: What aspects of blog design correlate with popularity? In T. Dumova & R. Fiordo (Eds.), *Blogging in the global society: Cultural, political and geographical aspects* (pp. 179–199). Hershey, PA: Information Science Reference; doi:10.4018/978-1-60960-744-9.ch011

Weeks, M. R. (2012). Toward an understanding of online community participation through narrative network analysis. In H. Li (Ed.), *Virtual community participation and motivation: Cross-disciplinary theories* (pp. 90–102). Hershey, PA: Information Science Reference; doi:10.4018/978-1-4666-0312-7.ch006

White, J. R. (2013). Language economy in computer-mediated communication: Learner autonomy in a community of practice. In B. Zou, M. Xing, Y. Wang, M. Sun, & C. Xiang (Eds.), *Computer-assisted foreign language teaching and learning: Technological advances* (pp. 75–90). Hershey, PA: Information Science Reference; doi:10.4018/978-1-4666-2821-2.ch005

Whitworth, B., & Liu, T. (2013). Politeness as a social computing requirement. In J. Bishop (Ed.), *Examining the concepts, issues, and implications of internet trolling* (pp. 88–104). Hershey, PA: Information Science Reference; doi:10.4018/978-1-4666-2803-8.ch008

Wichowski, D. E., & Kohl, L. E. (2013). Establishing credibility in the information jungle: Blogs, microblogs, and the CRAAP test. In M. Folk & S. Apostel (Eds.), *Online credibility and digital ethos: Evaluating computer-mediated communication* (pp. 229–251). Hershey, PA: Information Science Reference; doi:10.4018/978-1-4666-2663-8.ch013

Williams, J. (2013). Social cohesion and free home internet in New Zealand. In A. Abdelaal (Ed.), *Social and economic effects of community wireless networks and infrastructures* (pp. 135–159). Hershey, PA: Information Science Reference; doi:10.4018/978-1-4666-2997-4.ch008

Williams, S., Fleming, S., Lundqvist, K., & Parslow, P. (2013). This is me: Digital identity and reputation on the internet. In S. Warburton & S. Hatzipanagos (Eds.), *Digital identity and social media* (pp. 104–117). Hershey, PA: Information Science Reference; doi:10.4018/978-1-4666-1915-9.ch008

Winning, R. (2013). Behind the sonic veil: Considering sound as the mediator of illusory life in variable and screen-based media. In D. Harrison (Ed.), Digital media and technologies for virtual artistic spaces (pp. 117-134). Hershey, PA: Information science reference. doi:10.4018/978-1-4666-2961-5.ch009

Wolfe, A. (2012). Network perspective on structures related to communities. In M. Safar & K. Mahdi (Eds.), *Social networking and community behavior modeling: Qualitative and quantitative measures* (pp. 26–50). Hershey, PA: Information Science Reference; doi:10.4018/978-1-61350-444-4.ch002

Worden, S. (2013). The earth sciences and creative practice: Exploring boundaries between digital and material culture. In D. Harrison (Ed.), *Digital media and technologies for virtual artistic spaces* (pp. 186–204). Hershey, PA: Information Science Reference; doi:10.4018/978-1-4666-2961-5.ch014

Xing, M., Zou, B., & Wang, D. (2013). A wiki platform for language and intercultural communication. In B. Zou, M. Xing, Y. Wang, M. Sun, & C. Xiang (Eds.), *Computer-assisted foreign language teaching and learning: Technological advances* (pp. 1–15). Hershey, PA: Information Science Reference; doi:10.4018/978-1-4666-2821-2.ch001

Xu, G., Gu, Y., & Yi, X. (2013). On group extraction and fusion for tag-based social recommendation. In G. Xu & L. Li (Eds.), *Social media mining and social network analysis: Emerging research* (pp. 211–223). Hershey, PA: Information Science Reference; doi:10.4018/978-1-4666-2806-9.ch014

Yakura, E. K., Soe, L., & Guthrie, R. (2012). Women in IT careers: Investigating support for women in the information technology workforce. In C. Romm Livermore (Ed.), *Gender and social computing: Interactions, differences and relationships* (pp. 35–49). Hershey, PA: Information Science Publishing; doi:10.4018/978-1-60960-759-3.ch003

Yang, Y., Rahim, A., & Karmakar, N. C. (2013). 5.8 GHz portable wireless monitoring system for sleep apnea diagnosis in wireless body sensor network (WBSN) using active RFID and MIMO technology. In N. Karmakar (Ed.), *Advanced RFID systems, security, and applications* (pp. 264–303). Hershey, PA: Information Science Reference; doi:10.4018/978-1-4666-2080-3.ch012

Yu, Z., Liang, Y., Yang, Y., & Guo, B. (2013). Supporting social interaction in campus-scale environments by embracing mobile social networking. In G. Xu & L. Li (Eds.), *Social media mining and social network analysis: Emerging research* (pp. 182–201). Hershey, PA: Information Science Reference; doi:10.4018/978-1-4666-2806-9.ch012

Zaman, M., Simmers, C. A., & Anandarajan, M. (2013). Using an ethical framework to examine linkages between "going green" in research practices and information and communication technologies. In B. Medlin (Ed.), *Integrations of technology utilization and social dynamics in organizations* (pp. 243–262). Hershey, PA: Information Science Reference; doi:10.4018/978-1-4666-1948-7.ch015

Zarmpou, T., Saprikis, V., & Vlachopoulou, M. (2013). Examining behavioral intention toward mobile services: An empirical investigation in Greece. In A. Scupola (Ed.), *Mobile opportunities and applications for e-service innovations* (pp. 37–56). Hershey, PA: Information Science Reference; doi:10.4018/978-1-4666-2654-6.ch003

Zavala Pérez, J. M. (2012). Registry culture and networked sociability: Building individual identity through information records. In F. Comunello (Ed.), *Networked sociability and individualism: Technology for personal and professional relationships* (pp. 41–62). Hershey, PA: Information Science Reference; doi:10.4018/978-1-61350-338-6.ch003

Zemliansky, P., & Goroshko, O. (2013). Social media and other web 2.0 technologies as communication channels in a cross-cultural, web-based professional communication project. In B. Pătruţ, M. Pătruţ, & C. Cmeciu (Eds.), *Social media and the new academic environment: Pedagogical challenges* (pp. 256–272). Hershey, PA: Information Science Reference; doi:10.4018/978-1-4666-2851-9.ch013

Zervas, P., & Alexandraki, C. (2013). The realisation of online music services through intelligent computing. In D. Kanellopoulos (Ed.), *Intelligent multimedia technologies for networking applications: Techniques and tools* (pp. 291–317). Hershey, PA: Information Science Reference; doi:10.4018/978-1-4666-2833-5.ch012

Zhang, J., & Mao, E. (2013). The effects of consumption values on the use of location-based services on smartphones. In I. Lee (Ed.), *Strategy, adoption, and competitive advantage of mobile services in the global economy* (pp. 1–18). Hershey, PA: Information Science Reference; doi:10.4018/978-1-4666-1939-5.ch001

Zhang, S., Köbler, F., Tremaine, M., & Milewski, A. (2012). Instant messaging in global software teams. In N. Kock (Ed.), *Advancing collaborative knowledge environments: New trends in e-collaboration* (pp. 158–179). Hershey, PA: Information Science Reference; doi:10.4018/978-1-61350-459-8.ch010

Zhang, T., Wang, C., Luo, Z., Han, S., & Dong, M. (2013). RFID enabled vehicular network for ubiquitous travel query. In D. Chiu (Ed.), *Mobile and web innovations in systems and service-oriented engineering* (pp. 348–363). Hershey, PA: Information Science Reference; doi:10.4018/978-1-4666-2470-2.ch019

Zhang, W. (2012). Virtual communities as subaltern public spheres: A theoretical development and an application to the Chinese internet. In H. Li (Ed.), *Virtual community participation and motivation: Cross-disciplinary theories* (pp. 143–159). Hershey, PA: Information Science Reference; doi:10.4018/978-1-4666-0312-7.ch009

Zhang, X., Wang, L., Li, Y., & Liang, W. (2013). Global community extraction in social network analysis. In G. Xu & L. Li (Eds.), *Social media mining and social network analysis: Emerging research* (pp. 156–171). Hershey, PA: Information Science Reference; doi:10.4018/978-1-4666-2806-9.ch010

Zhang, X., Wang, L., Li, Y., & Liang, W. (2013). Local community extraction in social network analysis. In G. Xu & L. Li (Eds.), *Social media mining and social network analysis: Emerging research* (pp. 172–181). Hershey, PA: Information Science Reference; doi:10.4018/978-1-4666-2806-9.ch011

Zulu, S. F. (2013). Emerging information and communication technology policy framework for Africa. In B. Maumbe & J. Okello (Eds.), *Technology, sustainability, and rural development in Africa* (pp. 236–256). Hershey, PA: Information Science Reference; doi:10.4018/978-1-4666-3607-1.ch016

Compilation of References

Aarseth, E. J. (1997). Cybertext: Perspectives on ergodic literature. Baltimore, MD: Johns Hopkins University Press.

Abram, S. (2007). At Second Life, info pros will find much to see, do, learn, play with, try out. *Information Outlook*, *11*(4), 34–36.

Adamic, L. (2012). Information propagation and filtering over social networks. *Collective Intelligence Proceedings*.

Adams, M. B., Kaplan, B., Sobko, H. J., Kuziemsky, C., Ravvaz, K., & Koppel, R. (2015). Learning from colleagues about healthcare IT implementation and optimization: Lessons from a medical informatics listserv. *Journal of Medical Systems*, *39*(1), 157. doi:10.1007/s10916-014-0157-3 PMID:25486893

Agency for Healthcare Research and Quality. (2013) Using Decision Aids in Shared Decisionmaking. *AHRQ Health Care Innovations Exchange*. Retrieved April, 29 2015 from https://innovations.ahrq.gov/issues/2013/08/28/using-decision-aids-shared-decisionmaking

Aguado, J. M., Feijóo, C., & Martínez, I. J. (Eds.). (2013). La comunicación móvil. Hacia un Nuevo ecosistema digital. Barcelona: Gedisa.

AHA Strategic Policy Planning Committee. (2001). *Workforce Supply for Hospitals and Health Systems: Issues and recommendations*. Retrieved on March 17, 2015 from http://www.aha.org/advocacy-issues/workforce/workforceB0123.shtml

Ajami, S., & Arab-Chadegani, R. (2013). Barriers to implement Electronic Health Records (EHRs). *Materia Socio-Medica*, *25*(3), 213–215. doi:10.5455/msm.2013.25.213-215 PMID:24167440

Ajami, S., Ketabi, S., Isfahani, S. S., & Heidari, A. (2011). Readiness Assessment of Electronic Health Records Implementation. *Acta Informatica Medica*, *19*(4), 224–227. doi:10.5455/aim.2011.19.224-227 PMID:23407861

Ajzen, I., & Fishbein, M. (1980). *Understanding Attitudes and Predicting Social Behavior*. Englewood Cliffs, NJ: Prentice Hall.

Alamantarioutou, K. (2014). Collective intelligence for knowledge building and research in community of practice and virtual learning environments. *International Journal of Health Research and Innovation*, *2*(1), 51–64.

Albors, J., Ramos, J., & Hervas, J. (2008). New learning network paradigms: Communications of objectives, crowdsourcing, wikis and open source. *International Journal of Information Management*, *28*(3), 194–202. doi:10.1016/j.ijinfomgt.2007.09.006

Algesheimer, R., Dholakia, U. M., & Gurău, C. (2011). Virtual Team Performance in a Highly Competitive Environment. *Group & Organization Management*, *36*(2), 161–190. doi:10.1177/1059601110391251

Alliance Library System. (2008). Retrieved March 11, 2008 from http://www.alliancelibrarysystem.com/about/mission.cfm

Alliance Second Life Google Group Members. (2008). Retrieved January 28, 2008, from http://groups.google.com/group/alliancesecondlife/members

Amabile, T. M. (1985). Motivation and creativity: Effects of motivational orientation on creative writers. *Journal of Personality and Social Psychology, 48*(2), 393–399. doi:10.1037/0022-3514.48.2.393

Amabile, T. M. (1997). Motivating creativity in organizations: On doing what you love and loving what you do. *California Management Review, 40*(1), 39–58. doi:10.2307/41165921

Amabile, T. M. (1998). How to kill creativity. *Harvard Business Review, 76*(5), 77–87. PMID:10185433

American Society for Training & Development Research. (2008). *State of the Industry*. ASTD Research: Connecting Research to Performance. Retrieved March 15, 2015 from https://www.td.org/Publications/Research-Reports/2008/2008-State-Of-The-Industry?mktcops=c.learning-and-development~c.lt~c.sr-leader

Amin, A., & Roberts, J. (2008). Knowing in action: Beyond communities of practice. *Research Policy, 37*(2), 353–369. doi:10.1016/j.respol.2007.11.003

Anantatmula, V., & Thomas, M. (2010). Managing global projects: A structured approach for better performance. *Project Management Journal, 41*(2), 60–72. doi:10.1002/pmj.20168

Andriessen, J., Baker, M., & Suthers, D. (2003). Argumentation, computer support, and the educational context of confronting cognitions. In J. Andriessen, M. Baker, & D. Suthers (Eds.), *Arguing to learn: Confronting cognitions in computer-supported collaborative learning environments* (pp. 1–25). Dordrecht, Germany: Kluwer. doi:10.1007/978-94-017-0781-7_1

Andriopoulos, C. (2001). Determinants of organisational creativity: A literature review. *Management Decision, 39*(10), 834–841. doi:10.1108/00251740110402328

Andriopoulos, C., & Dawson, P. (2009). *Managing Change, Creativity and Innovation*. London, UK: Sage Publications Ltd.

Aponovich, D., & Grannan, M. (2013, November 26). *Market overview: Digital customer experience delivery platforms*. Cambridge, MA: Forrester Research, Inc.

Arendt, H. (1997). *A Condição Humana*. Rio de Janeiro: Forense Universitária.

Armstrong, A., & Hagel, J. (1996). The real value of on-line communities. *Harvard Business Review, 74*(3), 134–141.

Association for Training Development. (2014). *State of the Industry*. ATD Research: Connecting Research to Performance. Retrieved March 19, 2015 from https://www.td.org/Publications/Research-Reports/2014/2014-State-of-the-Industry?mktcops=c.learning-and-development%7ec.lt%7ec.sr-leader%7ec.learning-and-development

Au, W. J. (2014, March 9). *Second Life turns 10: what it did wrong, and why it may have its own second life — Tech News and Analysis*. Retrieved from http://gigaom.com/2013/06/23/second-life-turns-10-what-it-did-wrong-and-why-it-will-have-its-own-second-life/

Avolio, B. J., Kahai, S., & Dodge, G. E. (2001). E-leadership: Implications for theory, research, and practice. *The Leadership Quarterly, 11*(4), 615–668. doi:10.1016/S1048-9843(00)00062-X

Ayoko, O. B., Konrad, A. M., & Boyle, M. V. (2011). Online work: Managing conflict and emotions for performance in virtual teams. *European Management Journal, 30*(2), 156–174. doi:10.1016/j.emj.2011.10.001

Baggio, B. (2005). *What impact are the main issues/concerns associated with learning objects having on training and education*. Unpublished manuscript, Department of Education, Capella University.

Baggio, B., & Beldarrain, Y. (2011). Anonymity and Learning in Digitally Mediated Communications: Authenticity and Trust in Cyber Education. Academic Press.

Baggio, B. (2012). *You, You Online, You When Nobody Knows It Is You Online. Michaels Allen's eLearning Annual 2012*. San Francisco, CA: John Wiley & Sons.

Bailenson, J. N., Beall, A. C., Loomis, J., Blascovich, J., & Turk, M. (2004). Transformed Social Interaction: Decoupling Representation from Behavior and Form in Collaborative Virtual Environments. *Presence (Cambridge, Mass.)*, *13*(4), 428–441. doi:10.1162/1054746041944803

Bailenson, J. N., Blascovich, J., Beall, A. C., & Loomis, J. M. (2003). Interpersonal Distance in Immersive Virtual Environments. *Personality and Social Psychology Bulletin*, *29*(7), 819–833. doi:10.1177/0146167203029007002 PMID:15018671

Bainbridge, W. S. (2007). The Scientific Research Potential of Virtual Worlds. *Science, 5837*(27), 472 – 476.

Baker, S. (1996). *Consumer cognitions: mapping personal benefits relating to perfume purchase in the UK and Germany* Paper presented at the 207th ESOMAR Seminar: Capturing the Elusive Appeal of Fragrance: Techniques, Experiences, Challenges, Amsterdam, The Netherlands.

Bandura, A. (1997). *Self-efficacy*. New York: Freeman.

Bandyopadhyay, K., & Fraccastoro, K. A. (2007). The Effect of culture on user acceptance of information technology. *Communications of the Association for Information Systems*, *19*, 23. Available at http://aisel.aisnet.org/cais/vol19/iss1/23

Banks, J. (2002). Gamers as co-creators: Enlisting the virtual audiences-a report from the net face. In M. Balnaves, T. O'Regan, & J. Sternberg (Eds.), *Mobilising the audience* (pp. 188–212). St. Lucia, Queensland: University of Queensland Press.

Bao, J. (2013). *Online social behavior reflects discrepant personality*. Retrieved October 13, 2015 from http://poseidon01.ssrn.com/

Barlow, J., & Dennis, A. (2014). Not as smart as we think. *Collective Intelligence*, *1*, 1–5.

Bartle, R. A. (2004). *Designing virtual worlds*. Indianapolis, IN: New Riders.

Bartunov, S., Korshunov, A., Park, S., Ryu, W., & Lee, H. (2012). *Joint link-attribute user identity resolution in online social networks*. The 6th SNA-KDD Workshop' 12, Beijing, China.

Bateman, P. J., Gray, P. H., & Butler, B. S. (2011). The impact of community commitment on participation in online communities. *Information Systems Research*, *22*(4), 841–854. doi:10.1287/isre.1090.0265

Bateson, G. (1979). *Espíritu y naturaleza: una unidad necesaria (avances en teoría de sistemas, complejidad y ciencias humanas)*. Bantam Books.

Bateson, G. (1991). *Una unidad sagrada: nuevos pasos hacia una ecología de la mente*. Harper Collins Pub.

Bateson, G., & Donaldson, R. E. (1991). *A sacred unity : further steps to an ecology of mind* (1st ed.). New York: Cornelia & Michael Bessie Book.

Bauman, Z. (2008). Em busca da política. Rio de Janeiro: Zahar.

Bauman, Z. (2005). *Liquid Life*. Cambridge, MA: Polity.

Baumeister, R. F., & Leary, M. R. (1995). The need to belong: Desire for interpersonal attachments as a fundamental human motivation. *Psychological Bulletin*, *117*(3), 497–529. doi:10.1037/0033-2909.117.3.497 PMID:7777651

Beall, A. C., Bailenson, J. N., Loomis, J., Blascovich, J., & Rex, C. S. (2008). *Non-Zero-Sum Gaze in Immersive Virtual Environments*. Retrieved from vhil.stanford.edu/pubs/2003/beall-non-zero.pdf

Beidas, R. S., Koerner, K., Weingardt, K. R., & Kendall, P. C. (2011). Training Research: Practical recommendations for maximum impact. *Administration and Policy in Mental Health*, *38*(4), 223–237. doi:10.1007/s10488-011-0338-z PMID:21380792

Bell, L., Peters, T., & Pope, K. (2008). *Enjoying your first life? Why not add a second? Developing library services in Second Life*. Retrieved August 25, 2008, from http://seriousgamessource.com/features/feature_063006_second_life_library.php

Bellamy, A., & Becker, J. (2015). *An exploratory analysis of the relationship between personality characteristics and the perceptions of virtual merchandising*. Retrieved October 13, 2015 from http://www.scirp.org/journal/PaperInformation.aspx?PaperID=54664

Bell, B. S., & Kozlowski, S. W. J. (2002). A typology of virtual teams: Implications for effective leadership. *Group & Organization Management*, *27*(1), 14–49. doi:10.1177/1059601102027001003

Bell, L., Lindbloom, M.-C., Peters, T., & Pope, K. (2008). Virtual libraries and education in virtual worlds: Twenty-first century library services. *Policy Futures in Education*, *6*(1), 49–58. doi:10.2304/pfie.2008.6.1.49

Benkler, Y. (2005). Coase's Penguin, or, Linux and the Nature of the Firm. In R. A. Ghosh (Ed.), *CODE : collaborative ownership and the digital economy* (pp. 169–206). Cambridge, MA: MIT.

Bennett, S., Agostinho, S., Lockyer, L., Harper, B., & Lukasiak, J. (2006). Support university teachers create pedagogically sound learning environment using learning designs and learning objects. *IADIS International Journal*, *4*(1), 16-26. Retrieved from http://ro.uow.edu.au/cgi/viewcontent.cgi?article=2511&context=edupapers

Bennett, P. N. (2011). Technological intimacy in haemodialysis nursing. *Nursing Inquiry*, *18*(3), 247–252. doi:10.1111/j.1440-1800.2011.00537.x PMID:21790875

Bennett, W. L., & Segerberg, A. (2012). The logic of connective action: Digital media and the personalization of contentious politics. *Information Communication and Society*, *15*(5), 739–768. doi:10.1080/1369118X.2012.670661

Bennis, W., & Sample, S. B. (2015). *The art and adventure of leadership: Understanding failure, resilience, and success*. Hoboken, NJ: John Wiley & Sons.

Beranek, P., & Clairborne, M. (2012). The impact of training on virtual project teams: A TIP investigation. *International Journal of Information Technology Project Management*, *3*(1), 36–48. doi:10.4018/jitpm.2012010103

Bernard, R. M., Abrami, P. C., Lou, Y., Borokhovski, E., Wade, A., Wozney, L., & Huang, B. et al. (2004). How does distance education compare with classroom instruction? A meta-analysis of the empirical literature. *Review of Educational Research*, *74*(3), 379–439. doi:10.3102/00346543074003379

Berry, G. R. (2011). Enhancing Effectiveness on Virtual Teams. *Journal of Business Communication*, *48*(2), 186–206. doi:10.1177/0021943610397270

Bichelmeyer, B., Boling, E., & Gibbons, A. (2006). Reflections on instructional design and technology models: Their impact on research, practice and teaching in IDT. In M. Orey, J. McLendon, & R. Branch (Eds.), *Educational media and technology yearbook 2006* (pp. 33–50). Westport, CT: Libraries Unlimited.

Bierly, P. E. III, Stark, E. M., & Kessler, E. H. (2009). The moderating effects of virtuality on the antecedents and outcome of NPD team trust. *Journal of Product Innovation Management*, *26*(5), 551–565. doi:10.1111/j.1540-5885.2009.00680.x

Bitzer, L. F. (1968, January). The rhetorical situation. *Philosophy & Rhetoric*, 1–14.

Blackmore, S. J. (1999). *The meme machine*. New York: Oxford University Press.

Blanchard, A. L. (2008). Testing a model of sense of virtual community. *Computers in Human Behavior, 24*(5), 2107–2123. doi:10.1016/j.chb.2007.10.002

Blanchard, A. L., Askay, D., & Callas, K. (2010). Sense of Community in Professional Virtual Communities. In S. D. Long (Ed.), *Communication, relationships, and practices in virtual work*. IGI Global. doi:10.4018/978-1-61520-979-8.ch009

Blanchard, A. L., & Horan, T. (1998). Virtual Communities and Social Capital. *Social Science Computer Review, 16*(3), 293–397. doi:10.1177/089443939801600306

Blau, I., & Barak, A. (2012). How do personality synchronous media, and discussion topic affect participation? *Journal of Educational Technology & Society, 15*(2), 12–24.

Blumer, T., & Doering, N. (2012). Are we the same online? The expression of the five factor personality traits on the computer and the Internet. *Cyberpsychology: Journal of Psychosocial Research on Cyberspace, 6*(3), article 1. Retrieved October 11, 2015 from http://www.cyberpsychology.eu/view.php?cisloclanku=2012121201

Boder, A. (2006). Collective intelligence: A keystone in knowledge management. *Journal of Knowledge Management, 10*(1), 81–93. doi:10.1108/13673270610650120

Boellstorff, T. (2008). *Coming of age in Second Life: An anthropologist explores the virtually human*. Princeton Univ Pr.

Boellstorff, T. (2008). *Coming of age in second life: an anthropologist explores the virtually human*. Princeton, NJ: Princeton University Press.

Bogost, I. (2007, July). *Persuasive games: The expressive power of videogames*. Cambridge, MA: The MIT Press.

Bolter, J. D., & Grusin, R. (2000). Remediation: Understanding new media. Cambridge, MA: The MIT Press.

Bonabeau, E. (2009). Decisions 2.0: The power of collective intelligence. *Sloan Management Review, 50*(2), 45–52.

Book, B. (2004). *Moving Beyond the Game: Social Virtual Worlds*. Academic Press.

Bostrom, N. (2003). Are We Living in a Computer Simulation? *The Philosophical Quarterly, 53*(211), 243–255. doi:10.1111/1467-9213.00309

Boule, M. (2008). Changing the way we work. *Library Technology Reports, 44*(1), 6–9.

Bourdieu, P. (1977). *Outline of a theory of practice*. Cambridge, UK: Cambridge University Press. doi:10.1017/CBO9780511812507

Bourne, H., & Jenkins, M. (2005). Eliciting managers' personal values: An adaptation of the laddering interview method. *Organizational Research Methods, 8*(4), 410–428. doi:10.1177/1094428105280118

Boyce, M. W., & Hancock, P. A. (2012). The Interpenetration of Mind and Machine.*Proceedings of the Human Factors and Ergonomics Society Annual Meeting, 56*(1), 178-182.

Boyd, D. (2014). *It's Complicated. The Social Lifes of Networked Teens*. Yale University Press.

Brabham, D. (2010). Moving the crowd at threadless. *Information Communication and Society, 13*(8), 1122–1145. doi:10.1080/13691181003624090

Brake, T. (2006). Leading global virtual teams. *Industrial and Commercial Training, 38*(3), 116-121.

Brake, D. R. (2014). *Sharing our Lives Online. Risks and Exposure in Social Media.* Palgrave Macmillan.

Brake, T. (2008). *Where in the world is my team? Making a success of your virtual global workplace.* John Wiley & Sons.

Brand, S. (1988). *The Media Lab : inventing the future at MIT.* New York: Penguin Books.

Braun, V., & Clarke, V. (2006). Using thematic analysis in psychology. *Qualitative Research in Psychology, 3*(2), 77–101. doi:10.1191/1478088706qp063oa

Brown, A., & Green, T. A. (2006). *The essentials of instructional design.* Boston, MA: Pearson Education, Inc.

Bryan, L. L., & Joyce, C. I. (2007). *Mobilizing minds : creating wealth from talent in the 21st-century organization.* New York: McGraw-Hill.

Bryce, J., & Rutter, J. (2005). Gendered gaming in gendered space. In J. Raessens & J. Goldstein (Eds.), Handbook of computer game studies (pp. 301-310). Cambridge, MA: The MIT Press.

Buchanan, J. (2008). Developing leadership capacity through organizational learning. *Journal Of College Teaching & Learning, 5*(3), 17–24.

Buckland, A., & Godfrey, K. (2008, August). Gimmick or groundbreaking? Canadian academic libraries using chat reference in multi-user virtual environments. *Proceedings of the World Library and Information Congress, 74th IFLA General Council and Meeting.* Retrieved October 31, 2008, from http://www.ifla.org/IV/ ifla74/papers/158-Buckland_Godfrey-en.pdf

Buecheler, T., Sieg, J., Fuchslin, R., & Pfeifer, R. (2010). Crowdsourcing, open innovation and collective intelligence in the scientific method.*Proceedings of the ALIFE XII Conference.*

Burke, K. (1965). Permanence and change: An anatomy of purpose (2nd ed.). Indianapolis, IN: The Bobbs-Merrill Company, Inc.

Burke, K. (1966). Language as symbolic action: Essays on life, literature, and method. Berkeley, CA: The University of California Press.

Burke, K. (1968). Counter-statement. Los Angles, CA: University of California Press.

Burke, R., & Barron, S. (2014). *Project management leadership: Building creative teams.* Wiley.

Burrill, D. A. (2005). Out of the box: Performance, drama, and interactive software. *Modern Drama, 48*(3), 492–512. doi:10.3138/md.48.3.492

Cai, X. (2005, February). An experimental examination of the computer's time displacement effects. *New Media & Society, 7*(1), 8–21. doi:10.1177/1461444805049139

California. (2009). *State Health Care Workforce Development Planning Grant.* Retrieved March 17, 2015 from http://www.cwib.ca.gov/res/docs/special_committees/hwdc/meeting_materials/2013/California%20State%20Healthcare%20Workforce%20Development%20Planning%20Grant%20-%202012.pdf

Calvillo-Gámez, E. H., Cairns, P., & Cox, A. L. (2010). *Assessing the core elements of the gaming experience.* London: Springer. doi:10.1007/978-1-84882-963-3_4

Campbell, S. W. (2015). Mobile Communication and Network Privatism: A Literature Review of The Implications For Diverse, Weak, and New Ties. *Communication Research, 3*(1), 1–21. Retrieved from http://www.rcommunicationr.org/index.php/component/jdownloads/finish/16/55?Itemid=0

Capra, F. (1983a). The Tao of physics: an exploration of the parallels between modern physics and Eastern mysticism (2nd ed.). Boulder, CO: Shambhala.

Capra, F. (1983b). *The turning point : science, society, and the rising culture*. Toronto: Bantam Books.

Carnegie, T. A. M., & Fels, S. S. (2002). Beyond use: Toward a rhetoric of technological intimacy. *Technical Communication Quarterly, 11*(2), 214–216. doi:10.1207/s15427625tcq1102_8

Carpenter, G. J., Carpenter, T. P., Kimbrel, N. A., Flynn, E. J., Pennington, M. L., Cammarata, C., & Gulliver, S. B. (2015). Social support, stress, and suicidal ideation in professional firefighters. *American Journal of Health Behavior, 39*(2), 191–196. doi:10.5993/AJHB.39.2.5 PMID:25564831

Carte, T. A., Chidambaram, L., & Becker, A. (2006). Emergent leadership in self-managed virtual teams. *Group Decision and Negotiation, 15*(4), 323–343. doi:10.1007/s10726-006-9045-7

Cascio, W. F. (2000). Managing a virtual workplace. *The Academy of Management Executive, 14*(3), 81-90.

Cascio, W. F., & Shurygailo, S. (2003). E-leadership and virtual teams. *Organizational Dynamics, 31*(4), 362–376. doi:10.1016/S0090-2616(02)00130-4

Castells, M. (2000). *The rise of the network society* (2nd ed.). Malden, MA: Blackwell Publishers.

Castells, M. (2008). Afterword. In C. Katz (Ed.), *Handbook of Mobile Communication Studies*. Cambridge, MA: MIT Press. doi:10.7551/mitpress/9780262113120.003.0033

Castells, M., Fernandez-Ardevol, M., Linchuan Qiu, J., & Araba, S. (2007). *Mobile Communication and Society: A Global Perspective*. Cambridge, MA: MIT Press.

Castronova, E. (2005). Synthetic worlds : the business and culture of online games. Chicago: University of Chicago Press. Retrieved from http://www.loc.gov/catdir/toc/ecip059/2005007796.html

Castronova, E. (2007). *Exodus to the virtual world : how online fun is changing reality*. New York: Palgrave Macmillan. Retrieved from http://www.loc.gov/catdir/enhancements/fy0711/2007014272-b.htmlhttp://www.loc.gov/catdir/enhancements/fy0714/2007014272-d.htmlhttp://www.loc.gov/catdir/enhancements/fy0714/2007014272-t.html

Castronova, E. (2005). *Synthetic worlds: The business and culture of online games*. Chicago: University of Chicago Press.

Cavanaugh, C. (2001). The effectiveness of interactive distance education technologies in K-12 learning: A meta-analysis. *International Journal of Educational Telecommunications, 7*(1), 73–78.

Cavaye, A. L. M. (1996). Case Study Research: A Multi-Faceted Research Approach for IS. *Information Systems Journal, 6*(3), 227–242. doi:10.1111/j.1365-2575.1996.tb00015.x

Chamakiotis, P., Dekoninck, E. A., & Panteli, N. (2013). Factors Influencing Creativity in Virtual Design Teams: An Interplay between Technology, Teams and Individuals. *Creativity and Innovation Management, 22*(3), 265–279. doi:10.1111/caim.12039

Chamakiotis, P., & Panteli, N. (2010). E-Leadership Styles for Global Virtual Teams. In P. Yoong (Ed.), *Leadership in the Digital Enterprise: Issues and Challenges* (pp. 143–161). Hershey, PA: IGI Global. doi:10.4018/978-1-60566-958-8.ch011

Chang, C. M. (2011). New organizational designs for promoting creativity: A case study of virtual teams with anonymity and structured interactions. *Journal of Engineering and Technology Management, 28*(4), 268–282. doi:10.1016/j.jengtecman.2011.06.004

Charmaz, K. (2006). *Constructing grounded theory: A practical guide through qualitative analysis*. London: Sage.

Cheng, L., Farnham, S., & Stone, L. (2002). Lessons learned: Building and deploying shared virtual environments. In R. Schroeder (Ed.), *The social life of avatars: Presence and interaction in shared virtual environments* (pp. 90–111). New York: Springer-Verlag. doi:10.1007/978-1-4471-0277-9_6

Chen, H. L., Fan, H. L., & Tsai, C. C. (2014). The role of community trust and altruism in knowledge sharing: An investigation of a virtual community of teacher professionals. *Journal of Educational Technology & Society, 17*(3), 168–179.

Chen, M. H. (2006). Understanding the benefits and detriments of conflict on team creativity process. *Creativity and Innovation Management, 15*(1), 105–116. doi:10.1111/j.1467-8691.2006.00373.x

China Internet Network Information Center (CNNIC). (2015). *35ᵗʰ Statistical Report on China's Internet Development*. Retrieved on June 2, 2015, at http://www.cnnic.com.cn/hlwfzyj/hlwxzbg/hlwtjbg/201502/t20150203_51634.htm

Chinowsky, P., Robinson, B., & Robinson, S. (2013). *The use of personality assessment measures in social network analysis*. Presented at Engineering Project Organization Conference, Devil's Thumb Ranch, CO.

Chiu, C., Hsu, M., & Wang, E. (2006). Understanding knowledge sharing in virtual communities: An integration of social capital and social cognitive theories. *Decision Support Systems, 42*(3), 1872–1888. doi:10.1016/j.dss.2006.04.001

Chorley, M., Whitaker, R., & Allen, S. (2015). Personality and location-based social networks. *Computers in Human Behavior, 46*, 45–56. doi:10.1016/j.chb.2014.12.038

Chorpita, B. F., & Regan, J. (2009). Dissemination of effective mental health treatment procedures: Maximizing the return on a significant investment. *Behaviour Research and Therapy, 47*(11), 990–993. doi:10.1016/j.brat.2009.07.002 PMID:19632669

Chown, M. (2007). The never-ending days of being dead : dispatches from the frontline of science. London: Faber and Faber. Retrieved from http://www.loc.gov/catdir/toc/fy0712/2007390061.html

Chreim, S. (2015). The (non)distribution of leadership roles: Considering leadership practices and configurations. *Human Relations, 68*(4), 517–543. doi:10.1177/0018726714532148

Cobb, S. (1976). Social support as a moderator of life stress. *Psychosomatic Medicine, 38*(5), 300–314. doi:10.1097/00006842-197609000-00003 PMID:981490

Cohen, S., & Janicki-Deverts, D. (2009). Can we improve our physical health by altering our social networks? *Perspectives on Psychological Science, 4*(4), 375–378. doi:10.1111/j.1745-6924.2009.01141.x PMID:20161087

Cohen, S., & Wills, T. A. (1985). Stress, social support, and the buffering hypothesis. *Psychological Bulletin, 98*(2), 310–357. doi:10.1037/0033-2909.98.2.310 PMID:3901065

Consalvo, M., & Dutton, N. (2006, December). Game analysis: Developing a methodological toolkit for the qualitative study of games. *Game Studies, 6*(1). Retrieved from http://gamestudies.org/0601/articles/consalvo_dutton

Cook, K. S., & Rice, E. (2003). Social exchange theory. In J. Delamater (Ed.), *Handbook of social psychology* (pp. 53–76). New York: Kluwer Academic/Plenum Publishers.

Cormick, G., Kim, N., Rodgers, A., Gibbons, L., Buekens, P., Belizán, J., & Althabe, F. (2012). *Interest of pregnant women in the use of SMS (short message service) text messages for the improvement of perinatal and postnatal care.* Retrieved from http://www.reproductive-health-journal.com/content/9/1/9

Corrigan, R. W., Steiner, L., McCracken, S. G., Blaser, B., & Barr, M. (2001). Strategies for disseminating evidence-based practices to staff who treat people with serious mental illness. *Psychiatric Services (Washington, D.C.), 52*(12), 1598–1606. doi:10.1176/appi.ps.52.12.1598 PMID:11726749

Covey, S. R. (1996). Three roles of the leader in the new paradigm. In F. Hesselbein, M. Goldsmith, & R. Beckhard (Eds.), *The leader of the future* (pp. 149–159). San Francisco: Jossey-Bass.

Cramton, C. D., & Webber, S. S. (2005). Relationships among geographic dispersion, team processes, and effectiveness in software development work teams. *Journal of Business Research, 58*(6), 758–765. doi:10.1016/j.jbusres.2003.10.006

Creswell, J. W. (2007). *Qualitative inquiry and research design: Choosing among five approaches* (2nd ed.). Thousand Oaks, CA: Sage.

Crisp, C. B., & Jarvenpaa, S. L. (2013). Swift Trust in Global Virtual Teams. *Journal of Personnel Psychology, 12*(1), 45–56. doi:10.1027/1866-5888/a000075

Cropanzano, R., & Mitchell, M. S. (2005). Social exchange theory: An interdisciplinary review. *Journal of Management, 31*(6), 874–900. doi:10.1177/0149206305279602

Crump, S. A., Hamilton, D. L., Sherman, S. J., Lickel, B., & Thakkar, V. (2010). Group entitativity and similarity : Their differing patterns in perceptions of groups. European *Journal of Social Psychology, 1230*(December), 1212–1230.

CSI Solutions LLC. (2013). *The business case for behavioral health care*. Retrieved March 19, 2015 from http://www.integration.samhsa.gov/integrated-care-models/The_Business_Case_for_Behavioral_Health_Care_Monograph.pdf

Csikszentmihalyi, M. (1990). *Flow: The psychology of optimal experience*. New York, NY: Harper.

Cullen, D. L. (1995). Psychotherapy in cyberspace. *The Clinician, 26*(1), 6–7.

Curry, K. (2012). Increasing communication in the intensive care unit: Is blogging the answer? *Critical Care Nursing Quarterly, 35*(4), 328–334. doi:10.1097/CNQ.0b013e318266c010 PMID:22948365

Cutler, A. (2014). *Leadership psychology: How the best leaders inspire their people*. London: Kogan Page.

Darley, A. (2000). *Visual digital culture. Surface play and spectacle in new media genres*. London: Routledge.

Dartmouth-Hitchcock Medical Center. (n.d.). *Center for Shared Decision Making - About Shared Decision Making*. Retrieved April 29, 2015 from http://www.dartmouth-hitchcock.org/medical-information/decision_making_help.html

Davenport, T. H. (2011). Rethinking knowledge work: A strategic approach. *McKinsey Quarterly*. Retrieved from http://www.mckinsey.com/insights/organization/rethinking_knowledge_work_a_strategic_approach

Davis, F. D. (1989). Perceived usefulness, perceived ease of use, and user acceptance of information technology. *Management Information Systems Quarterly, 13*(3), 319. doi:10.2307/249008

Dawkins, R. (1976). *The selfish gene*. Oxford, UK: Oxford University Press.

Day, D. V. (2014). The future of leadership: Challenges and prospects. In D. V. Day (Ed.), *The Oxford handbook of leadership and organizations* (pp. 859–869). doi:10.1093/oxfordhb/9780199755615.013.041

De Nood, D., & Attema, J. (2006). *The Second Life of Virtual Reality*. Retrieved January 1, 2007, from http://www.epn.net

Deegan, P. E., Rapp, C., Holter, M., & Riefer, M. (2008). Best Practices: A Program to Support Shared Decision Making in an Outpatient Psychiatric Medication Clinic. *Psychiatric Services Journal, 59*(6), 603–605. doi:10.1176/ps.2008.59.6.603 PMID:18511580

Delaware Health and Social Services, Division of Public Health. (2014). *The First Delaware State Health Improvement Plan, Assessing and Improving Community Health in Delaware*. Retrieved March 17, 2015 from http://dhss.delaware.gov/dhss/dph/files/shaship.pdf

DeLuca, D., & Valacich, J. S. (2006). Virtual teams in and out of synchronicity. *Information Technology & People, 19*(4), 323–344. doi:10.1108/09593840610718027

Dennis, A. R., Fuller, R. M., & Valacich, J. S. (2008). Media, tasks, and communication processes: A theory of media synchronicity. *Management Information Systems Quarterly, 32*(3), 575–600.

Denzin, N. K. (1997). *Interpretive ethnography: ethnographic practices for the 21st century*. Thousand Oaks, CA: Sage Publications. doi:10.4135/9781452243672

DeSanctis, G., & Monge, P. (1999). Introduction to the special issue: Communication processes for virtual organizations. *Organization Science, 10*(6), 693–703. doi:10.1287/orsc.10.6.693

Deuze, M. (2012). *Media Life*. Polity Press.

DeVane, B., Durga, S., & Squire, K. (2010). Economists who think like ecologists: Reframing systems thinking in games for learning. *E-Learning and Digital Media, 7*(1), 3–20. doi:10.2304/elea.2010.7.1.3

Dewey, J. (1937). *Democracy and education: An introduction to the philosophy of education*. New York, NY: Macmillan.

Dich, L., McKee, H., & Porter, J. (2013). *Ethical issues in online course design: negotiating identity, privacy, and ownership*. Retrieved October 13, 2015 from http://spir.aoir.org/index.php/spir/article/view/866/pdf

Dieleman, C. & Duncan, E. A. (2013). Investigating the purpose of an online discussion group for health professionals: a case example from forensic occupational therapy. *BMC Health Services Research Journal, 13*, 253. doi: .10.1186/1472-6963-13-253

Digital Experiences. (n.d.). *Digital experiences ecosystem*. Retrieved April 26, 2015 from http://digitalexperiences.com.au/interactive/

Dishon, D., & O'Leary, P. (1994). *Guidebook of cooperative learning: A techniques for creting more effective schools*. Holmes Beach, FL: Learning Publications.

Dixon, N. M. (2000). Common knowledge: how companies thrive by sharing what they know. Boston: Harvard Business School.

Dixon, K. R., & Panteli, N. (2010). From virtual teams to virtuality in teams. *Human Relations, 63*(8), 1177–1197. doi:10.1177/0018726709354784

Diziol, D., Walker, E., Rummel, N., & Koedinger, K. (2010). Using intelligent tutor technology to implement adaptive support for student collaboration. *Educational Psychology Review, 22*(1), 89–102. doi:10.1007/s10648-009-9116-9

Dodds, P., & Fletcher, J. D. (2003, June). *Opportunities for new "smart" learning environments enabled by next generation web capabilities*. In Ed-Media World Conference on Educational Multimedia, Hypermedia & Telecommunications Symposium conducted at meeting of the Association for the Advancement of Computing in Education, Honolulu, HI.

Driscoll, M. P. (2005). *Psychology of learning for instruction* (3rd ed.). Boston, MA: Pearson Education, Inc.

Drucker, P. F. (1995). Not enough generals were killed. In F. Hesselbein, M. Goldsmith, & R. Beckhard (Eds.), *The leader of the future* (pp. xi–xv). San Francisco: Jossey-Bass.

Duarte, D. L., & Snyder, N. T. (2006). *Mastering virtual teams: Strategies, tools, and techniques that succeed*. San Francisco: Jossey-Bass.

Ducheneaut, N., Yee, N., Nickell, E., & Moore, R. J. (2006, October). Building an mmo with mass appeal: A look at gameplay in world of warcraft. *Games and Culture, 1*(4), 281–317. doi:10.1177/1555412006292613

Durkheim, E. (1984). *The division of labor in society* (W. D. Halls, Trans.). New York: Free Press. (Originally published in German in 1893) doi:10.1007/978-1-349-17729-5

Easterby-Smith, M., Thorpe, R., & Lowe, A. (2002). *Management research: An introduction.* London, UK: Sage Publications Ltd.

Ebrahim, N. A., Ahmed, S., & Taha, Z. (2009). Virtual Teams: A Literature Review. *Australian Journal of Basic and Applied Sciences, 3*(3), 2653–2669.

Eisenberger, R., Fasolo, P., & Davis-LaMastro, V. (1990). Perceived organizational support and employee diligence, commitment, and innovation. *The Journal of Applied Psychology, 75*(1), 51–59. doi:10.1037/0021-9010.75.1.51

Eisenberger, R., Huntington, R., Hutchison, S., & Sowa, D. (1986). Perceived organizational support. *The Journal of Applied Psychology, 71*(3), 500–507. doi:10.1037/0021-9010.71.3.500

Elias, N. (1980). *Introdução à sociología.* Edições 70.

Ellington, T. N. (2014). Bloggers, vloggers, and virtual sorority: A means of support for african american women wearing natural hair. *Journalism and Mass Communication, 4*(9), 552–564.

Ellis, D., Oldridge, R., & Vasconcelos, A. (2004). Community and virtual community. *Annual Review of Information Science & Technology, 38*(1), 145–186. doi:10.1002/aris.1440380104

Ell, K., Nishimoto, R., Mediansky, L., Mantell, J., & Hamovitch, M. (1992). Social relations, social support and survival among patients with cancer. *Journal of Psychosomatic Research, 36*(6), 531–541. doi:10.1016/0022-3999(92)90038-4 PMID:1640391

Elverdam, C., & Aarseth, E. (2007, January). Game classification and game design: Construction through critical analysis. *Games and Culture, 2*(1), 3–22. doi:10.1177/1555412006286892

Engeström, Y. (1987). *Learning by expanding: An activity-theoretical approach to developmental research.* Helsinki, Finland: Orienta-Konsultit.

Entertainment Software Association. (2011). *Video game and the economy.* Washington, DC: Entertainment Software Association. Retrieved October 31, 2014, from http://www.theesa.com/gamesindailylife/economy.pdf

Entertainment Software Association. (2014). *Industry facts: Sales and genre data.* Washington, DC: The Entertainment Software Association. Retrieved November 10, 2014, from http://www.theesa.com/facts/salesandgenre.asp

Entertainment Software Association. (2015a, April 14). *Press release: More than 150 million Americans play video games.* Retrieved April 23, 2015, from http://www.theesa.com/article/150-million-americans-play-video-games/

Entertainment Software Association. (2015b). *Essential facts about the computer and video game industry.* Retrieved April 23, 2015, from http://www.theesa.com/wp-content/uploads/2015/04/ESA-Essential-Facts-2015.pdf

Ermi, L., & Mäyrä, F. (2005). *Fundamental components of the gameplay experience: Analyzing immersion.* Paper presented at the DiGRA 2005 Conference: Changing View-Worldds in Play, Vancouver, Canada.

Ertmer, P. A., & Newby, T. J. (2013). Behaviorism, cognitivism, and constructivism: Comparing critical features from an instructional design perspective. *Performance Improvement Quarterly, 26*(2), 43–71. doi:10.1002/piq.21143

Evans, R. (1996). *The human side of school change: Reform, resistance, and the real-life problems of innovation.* San Francisco: Jossey-Bass.

Everson, K. (2014). *Special report: learning providers in the know, in the now*. Workforce®. Retrieved on February 26, 2015 from http://www.workforce.com/articles/print/21006-special-report-learning-providers-in-the-know

Faraj, S., Jarvenpaa, S. L., & Majchrzak, A. (2011). Knowledge Collaboration in Online Communities. *Organization Science, 22*(5), 1224–1239. doi:10.1287/orsc.1100.0614

Felipe, R., Feit, B., & Thomas, C. (2014, August 21). *Making Apps and Web-based Tools Part of Your Integrated Behavioral Health Team* [Webinar]. Retrieved from www.integration.samhsa.gov

Fidalgo, A., Serrano Tellería, A., Carvalheiro, J. R., Canavilhas, J., & Correia, J. C. (2013). Human Being as a Communication Portal: The construction of the Profile on Mobile Phones. *Revista Latina de Comunicación Social 68*. Retrieved November, 8, 2014, from http://www.revistalatinacs.org/068/paper/989_Covilha /23_Telleriaen.html

Filiciak, M. (2003). Hyperidentities: Postmodern identity patterns in massively multiplayer online role-playing games. In M. J. P. Wolf & B. Perron (Eds.), *The video game theory reader* (pp. 87–102). New York, NY: Routledge.

Finfgeld-Connett, D. (2005). Clarification of social support. *Journal of Nursing Scholarship, 37*(1), 4–9. doi:10.1111/j.1547-5069.2005.00004.x PMID:15813580

Fixsen, D. L., Naoom, S. F., Blase, K. A., Friedman, R. M., & Wallace, F. (2005). Implementation research: A synthesis of the literature. Tampa, FL: University of South Florida, Louis de la Parte Florida Mental Health Institute, National Implementation Research Network. (FMHI Publication No. 231).

Flusser, V. (1988). *"On writing, complexity and the technical revolutions"*. Interview in Onasbrück, European Media Art Festival. Retrieved November, 18, 2014, from https://www.youtube.com/watch?v=lyfOcAAcoH8&app=desktop

Foridi, L. (2014). The Facebook-ification of everything! Sex, authenticity and reality for the status update era. *Salon*. Sunday, Aug 31. Retrieved November, 8, 2014, from http://www.salon.com/2014/08/31/the_facebook_ification_of_everything_sex_authenticity_and_reality_for_the_status_update_era/?utm_source=twitter&utm_medium=socialflow

Fortunati, L. (2002). The Mobile Phone: Towards New Categories and Social Relations. In Information, Communication, and Society, (pp. 514-528). Academic Press.

Foster, A. L. (2005). The avatars of research. *The Chronicle of Higher Education, 52*(6), A35.

Frasca, G. (2003). Simulation versus narrative: Introduction to ludology. In M. J. P. Wolf & B. Perron (Eds.), *The video game theory reader* (pp. 221–235). New York, NY: Routledge.

Freeman, R. E. (1994). *Instructional design: Capturing the classroom for distance learning*. Chicago, IL: The Association of Christian Continuing Education Schools and Seminaries (ACCESS). Retrieved from http://p4mriunimed.files.wordpress.com/2009/09/instructional-design.pdf

Freiermuth, M. R. (2002). Internet chat: Collaborating and learning via e-conversations. *TESOL Journal, 11*(3), 36–40.

Freifeld, L. (2013, October). How-to: Use technology to reinforce training. *Training: The source for professional development*. Retrieved January 23, 2015, from http://www.trainingmag.com/content/how-use-technology-reinforce-training

Frison, E., & Eggermont, S. (2015). The impact of daily stress on adolescents' depressed mood: The role of social support seeking through Facebook. *Computers in Human Behavior, 44*, 315–325. doi:10.1016/j.chb.2014.11.070

Fuchs, C. (2014). *Social Media: A Critical Introduction*. London: Sage. doi:10.4135/9781446270066.n2

Garreau, J. (2005). *Radical evolution: the promise and peril of enhancing our minds, our bodies--and what it means to be human* (1st ed.). New York: Doubleday.

Gartner. (2007). *Gartner Says 80 Percent of Active Internet Users Will Have A "Second Life" in the Virtual World by the End of 2011*. Retrieved April 24, 2007, from http://www.gartner.com/it/page.jsp?id=503861

Gell-Mann, M. (1994). *The quark and the jaguar: adventures in the simple and the complex*. London: Little, Brown.

Gerbaudo, P. (2012). *Tweets and the streets: Social media and contemporary activism*. New York: Pluto Press.

Ghosh, R. A. (2005b). Cooking-Pot Markets and Balanced Value Flows. In R. A. Ghosh (Ed.), *CODE: collaborative ownership and the digital economy* (pp. 153–168). Cambridge, MA: MIT.

Ghosh, R. A. (Ed.). (2005a). *CODE: collaborative ownership and the digital economy*. Cambridge, MA: MIT.

Gibbons, A. S., Merrill, P. F., Swan, R., Campbell, J. O., Christensen, E., Insalaco, M., & Wilken, W. (2008). Reexamining the implied role of the designer. *The Quarterly Review of Distance Education*, *9*(2), 127–137.

Gibson, W. (1984). *Neuromancer*. New York: Ace Books.

Gilson, L. L., Maynard, M. T., Jones Young, N. C., Vartiainen, M., & Hakonen, M. (2015). Virtual Teams Research: 10 Years, 10 Themes, and 10 Opportunities. *Journal of Management*, *41*(3), 1313–1337. doi:10.1177/0149206314559946

Gittell, R., & Vidal, A. (1998). *Community organizing: Building social capital as a development strategy*. Thousand Oaks, CA: Sage Publications.

Gotham, H. J. (2004). Diffusion of Mental Health and Substance Abuse Treatments: Development, Dissemination, and Implementation. *Clinical Psychology: Science and Practice*, *11*(2), 160–176. doi:10.1093/clipsy.bph067

Grassian, E., & Trueman, R. B. (2006). Stumbling, bumbling, teleporting and flying . . . Librarian avatars in Second Life. *RSR. Reference Services Review*, *35*(1), 84–89. doi:10.1108/00907320710729373

Grasso, A., & Convertino, G. (2012). Collective intelligence in organizations: Tools and studies. *Computer Supported Cooperative Work*, *21*(4-5), 357–369. doi:10.1007/s10606-012-9165-3

Grau, O. (2003). *Virtual art: From illusion to immersion (Rev. and expanded)*. Cambridge, MA: MIT Press.

Greenberg, J., & Baron, R. (2002). *Behavior in organizations* (10th ed.). Englewood Cliffs, NJ: Prentice Hall.

Greene, B. (2005). The Fabric of the Cosmos: Space, Time and the Texture of Reality (New Ed.). Penguin.

Greene, B. (2011). *The Hidden Reality: Parallel Universes and the Deep Laws of the Cosmos*. Penguin.

Gregg, D. (2010). Designing for collective intelligence. *Communications of the ACM*, *53*(4), 134–138. doi:10.1145/1721654.1721691

Griffith, T. L., Sawyer, J. E., & Neale, M. A. (2003). Virtualness and knowledge in teams: Managing the love triangle of organizations, individuals, and information technology. *Management Information Systems Quarterly*, *27*(2), 265–287.

Grodal, T. (2003). Stories for eye, ear, and muscles: Video games, media, and embodied experiences. In M. J. P. Wolf & B. Perron (Eds.), *The video game theory reader* (pp. 129–155). New York, NY: Routledge.

Gronlund, N. E. (2009). *Writing Instructional Objectives* (8th ed.). Upper Saddle River, NJ: Peason Education, Inc.

Grosser, B. (2014). What Do Metrics Want? How Quantification Prescribes Social Interaction on Facebook. *Computational Culture: A Journal of Software Studies*. Retrieved November, 17, 2014, from http://computationalculture.net/article/what-do-metrics-want

Guimaraes, M. J. L. J. (2005). Doing anthropology in cyberspace: fieldwork boundaries and social environments. In C. Hine (Ed.), Virtual methods: issues in social research on the Internet (pp. 141–156). Oxford, UK: Berg. Retrieved from http://www.loc.gov/catdir/toc/ecip056/2005001815.html

Gusfield, J. R. (1975). *Community: A critical response.* New York: Harper & Row.

Haines, R. (2014). Group development in virtual teams: An experimental reexamination. *Computers in Human Behavior, 39,* 213–222. doi:10.1016/j.chb.2014.07.019

Halberstam, J. (2003). What's that smell? Queer temporalities and subcultural lives. *International Journal of Cultural Studies, 6*(3), 313–333. doi:10.1177/13678779030063005

Hamel, G. (2007). *The future of management.* Boston: Harvard Business School Press.

Hao, C. (2010). A comparative study of collaborative learning in "paper scribbles" and "group scribbles". *Australasian Journal of Educational Technology, 26*(5), 659–674.

Haraway, D. (1992). The Promises of Monsters. In L. Grossberg, C. Nelson, & P. A. Treichler (Eds.), *Cultural studies* (pp. 295–337). New York: Routledge.

Haraway, D. (1993). A cyborg manifesto. In S. During (Ed.), *The Cultural studies reader* (pp. 271–291). London: Routledge.

Harrysson, M., Metayer, E., & Sarrazin, H. (2012). How "social intelligence" can guide decisions. *The McKinsey Quarterly,* (November), 2012.

Harvey, B. (2005a). *Learning objects and instructional design* [Report R49/0503]. Retrieved from Athabasca University website: http://cde.athabascau.ca/softeval/reports/R490503.pdf

Heidegger, M. (1977). *The question concerning technology, and other essays* (W. Lovitt, Trans.). New York, NY: Harper & Row, Publishers, Inc.

Heider, D. (2009). Identity and reality: What does it mean to live virtually? In *Living Virtually: Researching New Worlds* (pp. 131–143). New York: Peter Lang.

Heifetz, R. A., & Laurie, D. L. (1997). The work of leadership. *Harvard Business Review, 75*(1), 124. PMID:10174450

Heim, M. (1993). *The metaphysics of virtual reality.* New York: Oxford University Press.

Heim, M. (1998). *Virtual realism.* New York: Oxford University Press.

Helgeson, V. S. (2003). Social support and quality of life. *Quality of Life Research: An International Journal of Quality of Life Aspects of Treatment, Care and Rehabilitation, 12*(1), 25–31. doi:10.1023/A:1023509117524 PMID:12803308

Helgeson, V. S., & Cohen, S. (1996). Social support and adjustment to cancer: Reconciling descriptive, correlational, and intervention research. *Health Psychology, 15*(2), 135–148. doi:10.1037/0278-6133.15.2.135 PMID:8681922

Hermida, A. (2014). *Tell Everyone: Why We Share and Why it Matters.* Doubleday Canada.

Herz, J. C. (1997). Joystick nation: How video game ate our quarters, won our hearts, and rewired our minds. Boston, MA: Little, Brown.

Hesse, B., O'Connell, M., Augustson, E., Chou, W., Shaikh, A., & Rutten, L. (2011). Realizing the promise of Web 2.0: Engaging community intelligence. *Journal of Health Communication, 16*(sup1), 10–31. doi:10.1080/10810730.2011.589882 PMID:21843093

Highsmith, J. A. (2004). *Agile project management : creating innovative products.* Boston: Addison-Wesley.

Higson, P., & Sturgess, A. (2014). *Uncommon leadership: How to build competitive advantage by thinking differently.* London: Kogan Page.

Hine, C. (2000). Virtual ethnography. London: SAGE. Retrieved from http://www.loc.gov/catdir/enhancements/fy0656/00269452-d.htmlhttp://www.loc.gov/catdir/enhancements/fy0656/00269452-t.html

Hine, C. (2005). *Virtual methods: issues in social research on the Internet.* Oxford, UK: Berg. Retrieved from http://www.loc.gov/catdir/toc/ecip056/2005001815.html

Hoch, J. E., & Kozlowski, S. W. J. (2014). Leading virtual teams: Hierarchical leadership, structural supports, and shared team leadership. *The Journal of Applied Psychology, 99*(3), 390–403. doi:10.1037/a0030264 PMID:23205494

Hofstede, B. (1997). *Cultures and organizations: software of the mind.* London: McGraw Hill.

Holmes, C., Kirwan, J., Bova, M., & Belcher, T. (2015, Spring). An investigation of personality traits in relation to job performance of online instructors. *Online Journal of Distance Learning Administration, XVIII,* 1.

Honebein, P. C., & Sink, D. L. (2012). The practice of eclectic instructional design. *Performance Improvement, 51*(10), 26–31. doi:10.1002/pfi.21312

Hong, L., & Page, S. (2008). Some microfoundations of collective wisdom. *Collective Wisdom,* 56-71.

Horning, R. (2014). Social Media Is Not Self-Expression. *The New Inquiry.* Retrieved November, 17, 2014, from http://thenewinquiry.com/blogs/marginal-utility/social-media-is-not-self-expression/

House, J. S. (1981). *Work stress and social support.* Reading, MA: Addison-Wesley.

Huang, S., & Shiu, S. (2012). A user-centric adaptive learning system for e-learning 2.0. *Journal of Educational Technology & Society, 15*(3), 214–225.

Hummon, D. M. (1992). Community attachment: Local sentiment and sense of place. In I. Altman & S. M. Low (Eds.), *Place attachment* (pp. 253–278). New York: Plenum. doi:10.1007/978-1-4684-8753-4_12

Humphreys, S. (2003). Online multiuser games: Playing for real. *Australian Journal of Communication, 30*(1), 79–91.

Humphreys, S. (2005, March). Productive players: Online computer games' challenge to conventional media forms. *Communication & Critical Cultural Studies, 2*(1), 37–51.

Hunter, I. (2008). *Imagine: what Wedgwood, Da Vinci, Mozart, Eiffel, Disney (and many others) can teach us about innovation.* North Shore, New Zealand: Penguin.

Hussi, T. (2003). *Reconfiguring knowledge management: Combining Intellectual Capital, Intangible Assets and Knowledge Creation.* The Research Institute of the Finnish Economy.

Iacono, A. (2010). OPAC, users, web. Future developments for online library catalogues. *Bollettino AIB, 50*(1/2), 69–88.

Ihamäki, P. (2015). Digital human experience models for augmented reality mobile wellness devices. *International Journal of Digital Human, 1*(1), 44–71. doi:10.1504/IJDH.2015.067134

Illinois Public Health Institute. (2006). *State Health Improvement Plan, forces of change assessment.* Retrieved March 17, 2015 from http://www.idph.state.il.us/ship/Assessments/ForcesofChangeExecutiveSummary.pdf

Institute for Healthcare Improvement. (2014). *IHI 90-day R&D Project Final Summary Report: Integrating behavioral health and primary care.* Retrieved March 19, 2015 from http://www.ihi.org/resources/Pages/Publications/BehavioralHealthIntegrationIHI90DayRDProject.aspx

Jalilvand, M., Esfahani, S., & Samiei, N. (2011). Electronic word-of-mouth: Challenges and opportunities. *Procedia Computer Science*, *3*, 42–46. doi:10.1016/j.procs.2010.12.008

Jansz, J., & Martens, L. (2005). Gaming at a lan event: The social context of playing video games. *New Media & Society*, *7*(3), 333–355. doi:10.1177/1461444805052280

Jeffreys, M. R. (2004). *Nursing student retention. Understanding the process and making a difference*. New York, NY: Springer Publishing Company.

Jenkins, H. (2006). *Convergence culture: Where old and new media collide*. New York: New York University Press.

Jenkins, H., Ford, S., & Green, J. (2013). *Spreadable Media. Creating Value and Meaning in a Networked Culture*. New York University Press.

Joffe, H. (2011). Thematic analysis. In D. Harper & A. R. Thompson (Eds.), *Qualitative research methods in mental health and psychotherapy: A guide for students and practitioners* (pp. 209–223). Malden, MA: Wiley & Blackwell. doi:10.1002/9781119973249.ch15

Johansson, F. (2004). The Medici effect: breakthrough insights at the intersection of ideas, concepts, and cultures. Boston: Harvard Business School Press. Retrieved from http://www.loc.gov/catdir/toc/ecip0415/2004003850.html

Johnson, C. M. (2001). A survey of current research on online communities of practice. *The Internet and Higher Education*, *4*(1), 45–60. doi:10.1016/S1096-7516(01)00047-1

Jonsen, K., Maznevski, M., & Davison, S. C. (2012). Global virtual team dynamics and effectiveness. In G. K. Stahl, I. Bjorkman, & S. Morris (Eds.), *Handbook of research in international human resource management* (pp. 363–392). London: Edward Elgar Publishing.

Joseph, C., Muthusamy, C., Michael, A., & Telajan, D. (2013). strategies applied in SMS: An analysis of SMS column in star newspaper. *Asian Social Science*, *9*(15), 8–13. doi:10.5539/ass.v9n15p8

Joshi, A., & Lazarova, M. B. (2005). Do global teams need global leaders? Identifying leadership competencies in multinational teams. In D. L. Shapiro (Ed.), *Managing multinational teams: Global perspectives* (pp. 281–301). Amsterdam: Elsevier. doi:10.1016/S0747-7929(05)18011-1

Jude-York, D., Davis, L. D., & Wise, S. L. (2000). *Virtual teaming: Breaking the boundaries of time and place*. Menlo Park, CA: Crisp Publications, Inc.

Jung, C.G. (1976). Psychological Types. *Collected Works, 6*, ¶ 757

Juul, J. (2005). Games telling stories? In J. Raessens & J. Goldstein (Eds.), Handbook of computer game studies (pp. 219-226). Cambridge, MA: The MIT Press.

Kafai, Y. B. (1998). Video game designs by girls and boys: Variability and consistency of gender differences. In J. Cassell & H. Jenkins (Eds.), From barbie to mortal combat: Gender and computer games. Cambridge, MA: MIT Press.

Kafai, Y. B. (2006, January). Playing and making games for learning: Instructionist and constructionist perspectives for game studies. *Games and Culture*, *1*(1), 36–40. doi:10.1177/1555412005281767

Kairam, S. R., Wang, D. J., & Leskovec, J. (2012, February). The life and death of online groups: Predicting group growth and longevity. In *Proceedings of the fifth ACM international conference on Web search and data mining* (pp. 673-682). ACM. doi:10.1145/2124295.2124374

Kamssu, A., Siekpe, J., & Ellzy, J. (2004). Shortcomings to globalization: Using Internet technology and electronic commerce in developing countries. *Journal of Developing Areas*, *38*(1), 151–169. doi:10.1353/jda.2005.0010

Kane, G. C., Alavi, M., Labianca, G. J., & Borgatti, S. P. (2014). What's different about social media networks? A framework and research agenda. *Management Information Systems Quarterly, 38*(1), 274–304.

Kang, Y. W. (2011). *Hybrid interactive rhetoric engagements in Massively Multiplayer Online Role-Playing Games (MMORPGs): Examining the role of rhetors and audiences in generative rhetorical discourses* (Diss. The University of Texas at El Paso). Ann Arbor, MI: UMI.

Katz, J. E. (2008). *Mainstreamed Mobiles in Daily Life: Perspectives and Prospects. Katz, Castells. Handbook of Mobile Communication Studies.* Cambridge, MA: MIT Press.

Katz, J. E., & Aakhus, M. (Eds.). (2002). *Perpetual Contact. Mobile Communication, Private Talk, Public Performance.* Cambridge, UK: Cambridge University Press. doi:10.1017/CBO9780511489471

Kawamoto, K. (2003). *Media and Society In the Digital Age.* New York: University of Washington.

Kayworth, T. R., & Leidner, D. E. (2000). The global virtual manager: A prescription for success. *European Management Journal, 18*(2), 183–194. doi:10.1016/S0263-2373(99)00090-0

Keller, J. M. (1984). The use of the ARCS model of motivation in teacher training. In K. Shaw & A. J. Trott (Eds.), Aspects of Educational Technology Volume XVII: Staff Development and Career Updating. London: Kogan Page.

Keller, J. M. (1988). Motivational design. In Encyclopaedia of Education Media Communications and Technology (2nd ed.; pp. 406-409). Westport, CT. Greenwood Press.

Keller, J. M. (1983). Motivational design of instruction. In C. M. Reigeluth (Ed.), *Instructional-design theories and models: An overview of their current status.* Hillsdale, NJ: Lawrence Erlbaum Associates.

Keller, J. M. (1987). Development and use of the ARCS model of motivational design. *Journal of Instructional Development, 10*(3), 2–10. doi:10.1007/BF02905780

Keller, J. M. (1999). Motivation in cyber learning environments. *Educational Technology International, 1*(1), 7–30.

Keller, J. M. (2010). *Motivational design for learning and performance: The ARCS model approach.* New York: Springer. doi:10.1007/978-1-4419-1250-3

Kellett, J., Humphrey, R., & Sleeth, R. (2009). Career development, collective efficacy, and individual task performance. *Career Development International, 14*(6), 534–546. doi:10.1108/13620430910997286

Kelly, K. (1994). *Out of control: the rise of neo-biological civilization.* Reading, MA: Addison-Wesley.

Kerr, A. (2006). *The business and culture of digital games: Gamework/gameplay.* London, UK: Sage Publications.

Kim, H. (2011). *Effects of SMS Text messaging on vocabulary learning.* Received October 10, 2015 from http://kmjournal.bada.cc/wp-content/uploads/2013/05/14-2-7HSKim.pdf

Kim, P., Hong, J., Bonk, C., & Lim, G. (2011). Effects of group reflection variations in project-based learning integrated in a Web 2.0 learning space. *Interactive Learning Environments, 19*(4), 333–349. doi:10.1080/10494820903210782

Kinder, M. (2003, Spring). Honoring the past and creating the future in hyperspace: New technologies and cultural specificity. *The Contemporary Pacific, 15*(1), 93–115. doi:10.1353/cp.2003.0017

Kiousis, S. (2002). Interactivity: A concept explication. *New Media & Society, 4*(3), 355–383. doi:10.1177/146144480200400303

Kitmoller, A., & Lauring, J. (2013). When global virtual teams share knowledge: Media richness, cultural difference, and language commonality. *Journal of World Business, 48*(3), 398–406. doi:10.1016/j.jwb.2012.07.023

Klabbers, J. H. G. (2003). *The gaming landscape: A taxonomy for classifying games and simulations.* Paper presented at the LEVEL UP: Digital Games Research Conference, Utrecht, The Netherlands.

Klein, M. (2012). Enabling large-scale deliberation using attention-mediation metrics. *Computer Supported Cooperative Work, 21*(4-5), 449–473. doi:10.1007/s10606-012-9156-4

Kluckhohn, F. R., & Strodtbeck, F. L. (1961). *Variations in value orientations.* Evanston, IL: Row, Peterson.

Koch, R., & Leitner, K.-H. (2008). The Dynamics and Functions of Self-Organization in the Fuzzy Front End: Empirical Evidence from the Austrian Semiconductor Industry. *Creativity and Innovation Management, 17*(3), 216–226. doi:10.1111/j.1467-8691.2008.00488.x

Kollock, P., & Smith, M. A. (1999). Communities in cyberspace. In M. A. Smith & P. Kollock (Eds.), *Communities in cyberspace* (pp. 3–25). New York: Routledge.

Koopman, C., Hermanson, K., Diamond, S., Angell, K., & Spiegel, D. (1998). Social support, life stress, pain and emotional adjustment to advanced breast cancer. *Psycho-Oncology, 7*(2), 101–111. doi:10.1002/(SICI)1099-1611(199803/04)7:2<101::AID-PON299>3.0.CO;2-3 PMID:9589508

Korhonen, H., Montola, M., & Arrasvuori, J. (2009). *Understanding playful user experience through digital games.* Paper presented at the International Conference on Designing Pleasurable of Products and Interface, Compiegne, France.

Kouzes, J., & Posner, B. (2002). *The leadership practices inventory: theory and evidence behind the five practices of exemplary leaders.* Retrieved from http://www.leadershipchallenge.com/UserFiles/lc_jb_appendix.pdf

Kouzes, J., & Posner, B. (2015). *The leadership challenge: Achieve the extraordinary.* Retrieved from http://www.leadershipchallenge.com/about-section-our-authors.aspx

Kouzes, J., & Posner, B. (1995). *The leadership challenge.* San Francisco: Jossey-Bass.

Kouzes, J., & Posner, B. (1997). *The leadership practices inventory facilitator's guide.* San Francisco: Jossey-Bass.

Kozinets, R. V. (2002). The Field behind the Screen: Using Netnography for Marketing Research in Online Communities. *JMR, Journal of Marketing Research, 39*(1), 61–72. doi:10.1509/jmkr.39.1.61.18935

Krause, N. (1986). Social support, stress, and well-being. *Journal of Gerontology, 41*(4), 512–519. doi:10.1093/geronj/41.4.512 PMID:3722737

Kucia, J. F., & Gravett, L. S. (2014). *Leadership in balance: New habits of the mind.* Palgrave Macmillan. doi:10.1057/9781137393449

Kücklich, J. (2002). The study of computer games as a second-order cybernetic system. In F. Mäyrä (Ed.), *Computer games and digital cultures.* Tampere: Tampere University Press.

Kurzweil, R. (2005). *The singularity is near: when humans transcend biology.* New York: Viking.

Kurzweil, R. (2012). *How to create a mind: the secret of human thought revealed.* New York: Viking.

Lake, J. (2014). *Integrative mental health care: A therapist's handbook.* New York, NY: W. W. Norton & Company, Inc.

Lampe, C., Wash, R., Velasquez, A., & Ozkaya, E. (2010, April). Motivations to participate in online communities. In *Proceedings of the SIGCHI conference on Human factors in computing systems* (pp. 1927-1936). ACM.

Langford, C. P. H., Bowsher, J., Maloney, J. P., & Lillis, P. P. (1997). Social support: A conceptual analysis. *Journal of Advanced Nursing, 25*(1), 95–100. doi:10.1046/j.1365-2648.1997.1997025095.x PMID:9004016

Lankes, R. D., Silverstein, J., Nicholson, S., & Marshall, T. (2007). Participatory networks: The library as conversation. Proceedings of the Sixth International Conference on Conceptions of Library and Information Science. *Information Research, 12*(4). Retrieved October 28, 2008, from http://informationr.net/ir/12-4/colis/colis05.html

Lankes, R. D., Silverstein, J., & Nicholson, S. (2007). Participatory networks: The library as conversation. *Information Technology & Libraries, 26*(4), 17–33.

LaRose, R., Eastin, M. S., & Gregg, J. (2001). Reformulating the Internet paradox: Social cognitive explanations of Internet use and depression. *Journal of Online Behavior, 1*(2). Retrieved from http://d3ds4oy7g1wrqq.cloudfront.net/sinergiaymente/myfiles/Depression-Journal.htm

Larson, M. (2007). *Understanding social networking: Online young people's construction and co-construction of identity online*. Retrieved October 11, 2015 from https://www.academia.edu/635848/Understanding_social_networking_On_young_peoples_construction_and_co-construction_of_identity_online

Lasén, A. (2015). Digital self-portraits, exposure and the modulation of intimacy. In Mobile and Digital Communication: Approaches to Public and Private. Covilhã, Portugal: LabCom Books.

Laszlo, E. (2007). Science and the akashic field: an integral theory of everything (2nd ed.). Rochester, VT: Inner Traditions. Retrieved from http://www.loc.gov/catdir/toc/ecip078/2007000623.htmlhttp://www.loc.gov/catdir/enhancements/fy0705/2007000623-b.htmlhttp://www.loc.gov/catdir/enhancements/fy0705/2007000623-d.htmlhttp://www.loc.gov/catdir/enhancements/fy0705/2007000623-s.html

Laszlo, E. (1987). *Evolution: the grand synthesis*. Boston: New Science Library.

Laszlo, E., & Loye, D. (1998). *The evolutionary outrider : the impact of the human agent on evolution: essays honoring Ervin Laszlo*. Westport, CT: Praeger.

Laudon, K. C., & Laudon, J. P. (2006). *Management Information Systems: Managing the Digital Firm*. Upper Saddle River, NJ: Pearson/Prentice Hall.

Laurillard, D. (2008). Technology enhanced learning as a tool for pedagogical innovation. *Journal of Philosophy of Education, 42*(3-4), 521–533. Retrieved from http://onlinelibrary.wiley.com/doi/10.1111/j.1467-9752.2008.00658.x/abstract

Lave, J., & Wenger, E. (1991). *Situated learning*. Cambridge, UK: Cambridge University Press. doi:10.1017/CBO9780511815355

Leadbetter, C., & Demos (Organization). (2002). *Innovate from within: An open letter to the new Cabinet Secretary.* London. *Demos (Mexico City, Mexico)*.

Lee, E., & Hahn, K. (2015). Tone of writing on fashion retail websites, social support, e-shopping satisfaction, and category knowledge. *Clothing & Textiles Research Journal, 33*(2), 143–159. doi:10.1177/0887302X15568915

Lee, K. T., Noh, M. J., & Koo, D. M. (2013). Lonely people are no longer lonely on social networking sites: The mediating role of self-disclosure and social support. *Cyberpsychology, Behavior, and Social Networking, 16*(6), 413–418. doi:10.1089/cyber.2012.0553 PMID:23621716

Lenhart, A., Madden, M., Smith, A., Purcell, K., Zickuhr, K., & Rainie, L. (2011). *Teens, kindness and cruelty on social network sites*. Retrieved April 5, 2015, from http://www.pewinternet.org/2011/11/09/teens-kindness-and-cruelty-on-social-network-sites/

Leonard, D., & Swap, W. (2004). Deep Smarts. *Harvard Business Review*, 13.

Lepsinger, R., & DeRosa, D. (2010). *Virtual team success: A practical guide for working and leading from a distance*. Hoboken, NJ: John Wiley & Sons.

Lessig, L. (2006). Code: Version 2.0 (2nd ed.). New York: Academic Press.

Lessig, L. (2008). Remix: making art and commerce thrive in the hybrid economy. New York: Penguin Press. Retrieved from http://www.loc.gov/catdir/enhancements/fy0906/2008032392-d.html doi:10.5040/9781849662505

Lessig, L. (2004). *Free culture: how big media uses technology and the law to lock down culture and control creativity*. New York: Penguin Press.

Letaief, R., Favier, M., & Coat, F. (2006). Creativity and the Creation Process in Global Virtual Teams: Case Study of the Intercultural Virtual Project. In F. Feltz, B. Otajacques, A. Oberweis, & N. Poussing (Eds.), *Information Systems and Collaboration: State of the Art and Perspective* (Vol. P-92, pp. 242–258). Bonn, Germany: GI-Edition.

Leung, L. (2006). Stressful life events, motives for Internet use, and social support among digital kids. *Cyberpsychology & Behavior, 10*(2), 204–214. doi:10.1089/cpb.2006.9967 PMID:17474837

Levenberg, A., & Caspi, A. (2010). Comparing perceived formal and informal learning in face-to-face versus online environments. *Interdisciplinary Journal of E-Learning and Learning Objects, 6*. Retrieved from http://www.ijello.org/Volume6?IJELLOv6p323-333Levenburg706.pdf

Levy, P. (1997). *Collective intelligence: Mankind's emerging world in cyberspace*. New York: Plenum Trade.

Linden Lab. (2008). *About us*. Retrieved January 2, 2008, from http://lindenlab.com/about

Lindley, C. (2002, June). The gameplay gestalt, narrative, and interactive storytelling.*Computer Games and Digital Culture Conference*, Tampere, Finland.

Ling, K., Beenen, G., Ludford, P., Wang, X., Chang, K., Li, X., … Kraut, R. (2005). Using social psychology to motivate contributions to online communities. *Journal of Computer-Mediated Communication, 10*(4).

Lin, H. F., & Lee, G. G. (2006). Determinants of success for online communities: An empirical study. *Behaviour & Information Technology, 25*(6), 479–488. doi:10.1080/01449290500330422

Lipnack, J., & Stamps, J. (2000). *Virtual Teams: People working across boundaries with technology*. New York, NY: John Wiley & Sons.

Loke, J. (2009). Identity and Gender in Second Life. In *Living virtually: researching new worlds* (pp. 145–161). New York: Peter Lang.

Lombard, M., & Ditton, T. (1997). At the heart of it all: The concept of presence. *Journal of Computer-Mediated Communication, 3*(2). Retrieved from http://jcmc.indiana.edu/vol3/issue2/lombard.html

Luo, L. (2008). Reference service in Second Life: An overview. *RSR. Reference Services Review, 36*(3), 289–300. doi:10.1108/00907320810895378

Lushniak, B. D. (2014). *Why should you care about mental health*. Mentalhealth.gov. Retrieved March 18, 2015 from http://www.mentalhealth.gov/blog/2014/10/why-you-should-care-about-mental-health.html

Madden, M. (2014). Public Perceptions of Privacy and Security in the Post-Snowden Era. *Pew Research*. Retrieved November, 18, 2014, from http://www.pewinternet.org/2014/11/12/public-privacy-perceptions/

Maier, P., & Warren, A. (2000). *Integrating technology in learning and teaching* (2nd ed.). New York, NY: Routledge.

Majchrzak, A., Faraj, S., Kane, G., & Azad, B. (2013). The contradictory influence of social media affordances on online communal knowledge sharing. *Journal of Computer-Mediated Communication*, *19*(1), 38–55. doi:10.1111/jcc4.12030

Malaby, T. M. (2009). *Making virtual worlds: Linden Lab and Second Life*. Ithaca, NY: Cornell University Press.

Malhotra, A., Majchrzak, A., & Rosen, B. (2007). Leading virtual teams. *The Academy of Management Perspectives*, *21*(1), 60–69. doi:10.5465/AMP.2007.24286164

Malkiel, Y. (1975). Etymology and modern linguistics. *Lingua*, *36*(2–3), 101–120. doi:10.1016/0024-3841(75)90009-1

Mallon, B., & Webb, B. (2006, June). Applying a phenomenological approach to games analysis: A case study. *Simulation & Gaming*, *37*(2), 209–225.

Malone, T. W., Laubacher, R., & Dellarocas, C. (2010). The collective intelligence genome. *Sloan Management Review*, *51*(3), 21–31.

Ma, M., & Agarwal, R. (2007). Through a glass darkly: Information technology design, identity verification, and knowledge contribution in online communities. *Information Systems Research*, *18*(1), 42–67. doi:10.1287/isre.1070.0113

Margulis, L. (1970). *Origin of eukaryotic cells; evidence and research implications for a theory of the origin and evolution of microbial, plant, and animal cells on the Precambrian earth*. New Haven, CT: Yale University Press.

Margulis, L., & Sagan, D. (1991). *Mystery dance: on the evolution of human sexuality*. New York: Summit Books.

Margulis, L., & Sagan, D. (1997). *Slanted truths: essays on Gaia, symbiosis, and evolution*. New York: Copernicus. doi:10.1007/978-1-4612-2284-2

Marichal, J. (2012). *Facebook Democracy. The Architecture of Disclosure and the Threat to Public Life*. Ashgate.

Marinova, D., & Phillimore, J. (2003). Models of Innovation. In L. V. Shavinina (Ed.), *The international handbook on innovation* (pp. 44–53). Amsterdam: Elsevier. doi:10.1016/B978-008044198-6/50005-X

Markham, A. (2013). Undermining "Data": A Critical Examination of a Core Term in Scientific Inquiry. *First Monday*, *18*(10). Retrieved November, 8, 2014, from http:// uncommonculture.org/ojs/index.php/fm/article/view/4868/3749

Markley, R. (1996). *Virtual realities and their discontents*. Baltimore, MD: Johns Hopkins University Press.

Marshall, D., Pyron, T., Jimenez, J., Coffman, J., Pearsol, J., & Koester, D. (2014). Improving public health through state health improvement planning: A framework for action. *Journal of Public Health Management and Practice*, *20*(1), 23–28. doi:10.1097/PHH.0b013e3182a5a4b8 PMID:24322682

Martins, L. L., & Shalley, C. E. (2011). Creativity in Virtual Work: Effects of Demographic Differences. *Small Group Research*, *42*(5), 536–561. doi:10.1177/1046496410397382

Marwick, A. (2013). *Status Update: Celebrity, Publicity, and Branding in the Social Media Age*. New Haven, CT: Yale University Press.

Mashable. (2014). *Mobile-Minded*. Retrieved November, 18, 2014, from http://mashable.com/2014/11/17/human-smartphone-relationship/#share-action:eyJzIjoidCIsImkiOiJfejQ5OXB4eDY0bnExZ3kwMyJ9

Masys, D. (2002). Effects of current and future information technologies on the health care workforce. *Health Affairs*, *21*(5), 33–41. doi:10.1377/hlthaff.21.5.33 PMID:12224907

Mather, C., & Cummings, E. (2014). Usability of a virtual community of practice for workforce development of clinical supervisors. In H. Grain, F. Martin-Sanchez, & L. Schaper (Eds.), Investing in E-Health: People, Knowledge and Technology for a Healthy Future (pp. 104-109). IOS Press.

Maturana, H. R., & Varela, F. J. (1992). The tree of knowledge: the biological roots of human understanding (Rev.). Boston: Shambhala.

Maturana, H. R., & Varela, F. J. (1980). *Autopoiesis and cognition: the realization of the living*. Springer. doi:10.1007/978-94-009-8947-4

Mau, B., Leonard, J., & Institute without Boundaries. (2004). *Massive change*. London: Phaidon.

Ma, W. W., & Yuen, A. H. (2011). Understanding online knowledge sharing: An interpersonal relationship perspective. *Computers & Education*, *56*(1), 210–219. doi:10.1016/j.compedu.2010.08.004

May, M. E. (2007). The elegant solution: Toyota's formula for mastering innovation. New York: Free Press. Retrieved from http://www.loc.gov/catdir/enhancements/fy0665/2006048411-d.htmlhttp://www.loc.gov/catdir/enhancements/fy0666/2006048411-s.htmlhttp://www.loc.gov/catdir/enhancements/fy0666/2006048411-t.html

Mayhew, D. J., & Follansbee, T. J. (2012). User experience requirements analysis within the usability engineering lifecycle. In J. A. Jacko (Ed.), *The human-computer interaction handbook: Fundamentals, evolving technologies, and emerging applications* (3rd ed., pp. 945–953). Boca Raton, FL: CRC Press.

Maynard, M. T., Mathieu, J. E., Rapp, T. L., & Gilson, L. L. (2012). Something(s) old and something(s) new: Modeling drivers of global virtual team effectiveness. *Journal of Organizational Behavior*, *33*, 342–365. doi:10.1002/job.1772

Mäyrä, F. (2007). *The contextual game experience: On the socio-cultural contexts for meaning in digital play*. Paper presented at the 2007 Authors & Digital Games Research Association (DiGRA).

McCaughey, M., & Ayers, M. D. (Eds.). (2003). *Cyberactivism: Online activism in theory and practice*. New York: Routledge.

McElroy, M. (2006). *The new knowledge management: Complexity, learning and sustainable innovation*. Boston, MA: Elsevier Science.

McGrath, J. (1991). Time, interaction, and performance (TIP): A theory of groups. *Small Group Research*, *22*(2), 147–174. doi:10.1177/1046496491222001

McKinsey & Company. (2011, May). *The world gone digital: Insights from McKinsey's global iconsumer research*. McKinsey & Company. Retrieved April 26, 2015, from https://www.mckinsey.com/~/media/McKinsey/dotcom/client_service/High%20Tech/PDFs/The_world_gone_digital.ashx

McLoughlin, D., & Mynard, J. (2009, May). An analysis of higher order thinking in online discussions. *Innovations in Education and Teaching International*, *46*(2), 147–160. doi:10.1080/14703290902843778

McLuhan, M. (1964). *Understanding media: The extensions of man*. New York: McGraw Hill.

McMahan, A. (2003). Immersion, engagement, and presence: A method for analyzing 3-d video games. In M. J. P. Wolf & B. Perron (Eds.), *The video game theory reader* (pp. 67–86). New York, NY: Routledge.

McMillan, D. W., & Chavis, D. M. (1986). Sense of community: A definition and theory. *Journal of Community Psychology*, *14*(1), 6–23. doi:10.1002/1520-6629(198601)14:1<6::AID-JCOP2290140103>3.0.CO;2-I

Means, B., Toyama, Y., Murphy, R., Bakia, M., & Jones, K. (2010). *Evaluation of Evidence-Based Practices in Online Learning: A Meta-Analysis and Review of Online Learning Studies*. U. S. Department of Education. Retrieved February 24, 2015 from http://eric.ed.gov/?id=ED505824

Mee, N. (2012). *Higgs Force: Cosmic Symmetry Shattered* (2nd ed.). Quantum Wave Publishing.

Melrose, K. L., Brown, G. D., & Wood, A. M. (2015). When is received social support related to perceived support and well-being? When it is needed. *Personality and Individual Differences*, *77*, 97–105. doi:10.1016/j.paid.2014.12.047

Melymuka, K. (1997). Virtual realities. *Computerworld*, *31*(17), 70–72.

Meng, M. (2005). *IT Design for sustaining virtual communities and identity based approach*. (Dissertation). University of Maryland, College Park, MD.

Merriam-Webster. (2015). *Definition of the word "virtual"*. Retrieved from http://www.merriam-webster.com/dictionary/virtual

Mesch, G. S. (2006). Online communities. Handbook of Community Movements and Local Organizations, 227.

Meyer, R. (2014). In the Brain, Memories Are Inextricably Tied to Place. *The Atlantic*. Retrieved 14 September, 2014, from http://www.theatlantic.com/technology/archive/2014/08/in-the-brain-memories-are-inextricably-tied-to-place/375969/

Mezirow, J. (1991). *Transformative dimensions of adult learning*. San Francisco, CA: Jossey-Bass.

Montague, R. (2007). Your brain is (almost) perfect: how we make decisions. New York: Plume.

Moore, M. (1994). Administrative barriers to adoption of distance education. *American Journal of Distance Education*, *8*(3), 1–4. doi:10.1080/08923649409526862

Moore, M., & Kearsley, G. (2005). *Distance education: A systems view* (2nd ed.). Belmont, CA: Wadsworth.

Morris, C. G., & Maisto, A. A. (2008). *Understanding Psychology* (8th ed.). Saddle River, NJ: Pearson.

Mowat, J. (2007, July). The instructional design of learning objects. *Learning Solutions Magazine*. Retrieved from https://www.learningsolutionsmag.com/articles/176/the-instructional-design-of-learning-objects

Mumford, M. D., Hunter, S. T., Eubanks, D. L., Bedell, K. E., & Murphy, S. T. (2007). Developing leaders for creative efforts: A domain-based approach to leadership development. *Human Resource Management Review*, *17*(4), 402–417. doi:10.1016/j.hrmr.2007.08.002

Murray, J. A. H., & Philological Society (Great Britain). (1971). *The compact edition of the Oxford English Dictionary: Complete text reproduced micrographically* (Vols. 1–2). Oxford, UK: Oxford University Press.

Murray, J. H. (2006). Toward a cultural theory of gaming: Digital games and the co-evolution of media, mind, and culture. *Popular Communication*, *4*(3), 185–202. doi:10.1207/s15405710pc0403_3

Muzio, J. A., Heins, T., & Mundell, R. (2002). Experiences with reusable e-learning objects: From theory to practice. *The Internet and Higher Education*, *5*(1), 21–34. doi:10.1016/S1096-7516(01)00078-1

Nandhakumar, J., & Baskerville, R. (2006). Durability of online teamworking: Patterns of trust. *Information Technology & People*, *19*(4), 371–389. doi:10.1108/09593840610718045

Nanus, B. (1992). *Visionary leadership: Creating a compelling sense of direction for your organization*. San Francisco: Jossey-Bass.

Nemiro, J. E. (2001). Connection in creative virtual teams. *Journal of Behavioral and Applied Management*, *2*(2), 92–112.

Nemiro, J. E. (2007). The Building Blocks for Creativity in Virtual Teams. In S. P. MacGregor & T. Torres-Coronas (Eds.), *Higher creativity for virtual teams: developing platforms for co-creation* (pp. 98–121). Hershey, PA: IGI Global. doi:10.4018/978-1-59904-129-2.ch005

Neufeld, D., Wan, Z., & Fang, Y. (2008). Remote leadership, communication effectiveness, and leader performance. *Journal of Group Decision and Negotiation, 19*(3), 227–246. doi:10.1007/s10726-008-9142-x

Nonnecke, B., Preece, J., & Andrews, D. (2004). What lurkers and posters think of each other. *Proceedings of the 37th Annual Hawaii International Conference on System Sciences* (HICSS'04). Retrieved September 30, 2008, from http://www2.computer.org/portal/web/ csdl/abs/proceedings/hicss/2004/2056/07/205670195aabs.htm

Norris, P. (2004). The bridging and bonding role of online communities. In P. N. Howard & S. Jones (Eds.), *Society online: The Internet in context* (pp. 31–41). Thousand Oaks, CA: Sage. doi:10.4135/9781452229560.n2

Norris, P. (2011). *Democratic deficit: Critical citizens revisited.* New York: Cambridge University Press. doi:10.1017/CBO9780511973383

O'Leary, R. (n.d.). Virtual Learning Environment. *ALT/LTSN Generic Centre Leaflet 2.* Retrieved from https://www.alt.ac.uk/sites/default/files/assets_editor_uploads/documents/eln002.pdf

O'Brien, H. L., & Toms, E. G. (2007). What is user engagement? A conceptual framework for defining user engagement with technology. *Journal of the American Society for Information Science and Technology, 59*(6), 938–955. doi:10.1002/asi.20801

Ocker, R. J. (2005). Influences on creativity in asynchronous virtual teams: A qualitative analysis of experimental teams. *IEEE Transactions on Professional Communication, 48*(1), 22–39. doi:10.1109/TPC.2004.843294

Ohio Department of Health. (2012). *Ohio 2012 – 2014 State Health Improvement Plan.* Retrieved March 17, 2015 from http://www.odh.ohio.gov/~/media/ODH/ASSETS/Files/lhd/Ohio%202012-14%20SHIP.ashx

Okorafor, N., & Davenport, L. (2001, August). *Virtual women: Replacing the real.* The Association for Education in Journalism and Mass Communication.

Oldenburg, R. (1999). *The great good place: Cafes, coffee shops, bookstores, bars, hair salons, and other hangouts at the heart of a community.* New York: Marlowe.

Ondrejka, C. R. (n.d.). *Escaping the Gilded Cage: User Created Content and Building the Metaverse.* SSRN. Retrieved from http://ssrn.com/paper=538362

Online Computer Library Center, Inc. (OCLC). (2005). *Perceptions of libraries and information resources.* Dublin, OH: OCLC Online Computer Library Center, Inc. Retrieved March 27, 2008 from http://www.oclc.org/reports/pdfs/Percept_all.pdf

Ow, J. (2000). The revenge of the yellowfaced cyborg: The rape of digital geishas and the colonization of cyber-coolies in 3d realms' shadow warrior. In B. Kolko, L. Nakamura, & G. Rodman (Eds.), *Race in cyberspace* (pp. 51–68). New York: Routledge.

Page, S. E. (2007). The difference: how the power of diversity creates better groups, firms, schools, and societies. Princeton, NJ: Princeton University Press. Retrieved from http://www.loc.gov/catdir/enhancements/fy0704/2006044678-d.htmlhttp://www.loc.gov/catdir/enhancements/fy0704/2006044678-t.htmlhttp://www.loc.gov/catdir/enhancements/fy0734/2006044678-b.html

Panteli, N. (2004). Situating Trust within Virtual Teams. In S. Reddy (Ed.), *Virtual Teams: Contemporary Insights* (pp. 20–40). Hyderabad, India: ICFAI University Press.

Panzarasa, P., Opsahl, T., & Carley, K. M. (2009). Patterns and dynamics of users' behavior and interaction: Network analysis of an online community. *Journal of the American Society for Information Science and Technology, 60*(5), 911–932. doi:10.1002/asi.21015

Park, N. (2012). Social side of rural internet use: Online communication, social support, and community satisfaction in a rural area. *International Telecommunications Policy Review, 19*(1).

Parsons, T. (1951). *The social system.* New York, NY: Free Press.

Parvanta, C., Roth, Y., & Keller, H. (2013). Crowdsourcing 101: A few basics to make you the leader of the pack. *Health Promotion Practice, 14*(2), 163–167. doi:10.1177/1524839912470654 PMID:23299912

Pasquale, F. (2015). The Algorithmic Sel*f*. *The Hedgehog Review, 17*(1). Retrieved March 14, 2015, from http://www.iasc-culture.org/THR/THR_article_2015_Spring_Pasquale.php

Pawlowski, J. M. (2002). Reusable models of pedagogical concepts - a framework for pedagogical and content design. In Proceedings of World Conference on Educational Multimedia, Hypermedia and Telecommunications. Chesapeake, VA: AACE. Retrieved from http://www.editlib.org/p/10229

Peirce, R. S., Frone, M. R., Russell, M., & Cooper, M. L. (1996). Financial stress, social support, and alcohol involvement: A longitudinal test of the buffering hypothesis in a general population survey. *Health Psychology, 15*(1), 38–47. doi:10.1037/0278-6133.15.1.38 PMID:8788539

Peña, J., & Hancock, J. T. (2006, February). An analysis of socio-emotional and task communication in online multimedia video games. *Communication Research, 33*(1), 92–109. doi:10.1177/0093650205283103

Pennsylvania Department of Health. (2004). *State Health Improvement Plan: White Paper: The nurse workforce in Pennsylvania.* Retrieved March 19, 2015 from http://www.dsf.health.state.pa.us/health/lib/health/ship/nursewhitepaper.pdf

Pentland, A. (2010). *Honest Signals: How They Shape Our World.* The MIT Press.

Pentland, A. (2014). *Social Physics: how good ideas spread - the lessons from a new science.* Scribe.

Penz, E. (2007). Paradoxical effects of the internet from a consumer behavior perspective. *Emerald Business, 3*(4), 364–380.

Peters, T. (2007). *A report on the first year of operation of the Alliance Second Life Library 2.0 Project also known as the Alliance Information Archipelago.* Unpublished report. TAP Information Services. Retrieved January 2, 2008, from http://www.alliancelibrarysystem.com/pdf/07sllreport.pdf

Peters, T. J. (1997). *The circle of innovation: you can't shrink your way to greatness* (1st ed.). New York: Knopf.

Peters, T. J. (2003). *Re-imagine!* [business excellence in a disruptive age]. London: Dorling Kindersley.

Pickering, A. (1995). The mangle of practice: Time, agency, & science. Chicago, IL: The University of Chicago Press.

Pinchot, J., Douglas, D., Paulette, K., & Rota, D. (2011). Talk to text: Changing communication patterns. *Consair Proceedings, V41830, Conference for Information Systems Applied Research.*

Pine, B. J., & Gilmore, J. H. (1999). *The experience economy: work is theatre & every business a stage.* Boston: Harvard Business School Press.

Pink, D. H. (2010). *Drive: The Surprising Truth About What Motivates Us.* Edinburgh, UK: Canongate Books.

Plant, R. (2004). Online communities. *Technology in Society, 26*(1), 51–65. doi:10.1016/j.techsoc.2003.10.005

Poels, K., IJsselsteijn, W., de Kort, Y., & Van Iersel, B. (2010). *Digital games, the aftermath: Qualitative insights into postgame experiences.* London: Springer.

Poole, S. (2000). *Trigger happy: Videogames and the entertainment revolution.* New York: Arcade.

Porter, M., & Miller, V. (1985). How information gives you a competitive Advantage. *Harvard Business Review*, (July-August), 149–160.

Portes, A. (1998). Social capital: Its origins and applications in modern sociology. *Annual Review of Sociology*, *24*(1), 1–24. doi:10.1146/annurev.soc.24.1.1

Powell, A., Piccoli, G., & Ives, B. (2004). Virtual teams: A review of current literature and directions for future research. *ACM SIGMIS Database*, *35*(1), 6–36. doi:10.1145/968464.968467

Prahalad, C. K., & Ramaswamy, V. (2004). *The Future of Competition: Co-Creating Unique Value With Customers*. Boston: Harvard Business Review Press.

Preece, J., & Maloney-Krichmar, D. (2003). Online communities: Focusing on sociability and usability. In J. Jacko & A. Sears (Eds.), Handbook of Human-Computer Interaction (pp. 596-620). Academic Press.

Preston, A. (2014). The Death of Privacy. *The Guardian*. Retrieved September, 11, 2014, from http://www.theguardian.com/world/2014/aug/03/internet-death-privacy-google-facebook-alex-preston?CMP=twt_gu

Puccio, G., Murdock, M., & Mance, M. (2011). *Creative leadership: Skills that drive change*. Thousand Oaks, CA: Sage Publications.

Putnam, R. D. (2000). *Bowling alone: The collapse and revival of American community*. New York: Simon & Schuster. doi:10.1145/358916.361990

Raessens, J., & Goldstein, J. (2005). Introduction. In J. Raessens & J. Goldstein (Eds.), Handbook of computer game studies (pp. xi-xvii). Cambridge, MA: The MIT Press.

Raine, L., Kiesler, S., & Madden, M. (2013). Anonymity, Privacy, and Security Online. *Pew Research*. Retrieved 14 April, 2014, from http://www.pewinternet.org/2013/09/05/anonymity-privacy-and-security-online/

Raney, L. (Ed.). (2015). *Integrated care: Working at the interface of primary care and behavioral health*. Arlington, VA: American Psychiatric Publishing.

Reeves, B., & Read, J. L. (2009). *Total engagement: using games and virtual worlds to change the way people work and businesses compete*. Boston: Harvard Business Press.

Reigeluth, C. M. (1999). *Instructional-design theories and models: A new paradigm of instructional theory* (Vol. 2). Mahwah, NJ: Lawrence Erlbaum Associates.

Ren, Y., Harper, F. M., Drenner, S., Terveen, L., Kiesler, S. B., & Kraut, R. E. (2012). Building Member Attachment in Online Communities : Applying Theories of Group Identity and Interpersonal Bonds. *Management Information Systems Quarterly*, *36*(3), 841–864.

Ren, Y., Kraut, R. E., & Kiesler, S. B. (2007). Applying common identity and bond theory to the design of online communities. *Organization Studies*, *28*(3), 379–410.

Reynolds, T. J., & Gutman, J. (1988). Laddering theory, method, analysis, and interpretation. *Journal of Advertising Research*, *28*(1), 11–31.

Rheingold, H. (1993). *The Virtual Community: Homesteading on the Electronic Frontier*. Addison Wesley.

Rheingold, H. (2012). *Net smart. How to thrive online*. Cambridge, MA: The MIT Press.

Richey, R. C., & Klein, J. D. (2007). *Design and development research*. New York, NY: Routledge.

Riva, G., & Ijsselsteijn, W. A. (2003). Being There: The experience of presence in mediated environments. In *Being there: Concepts, effects and measurements of user presence in synthetic environments* (pp. 4–16). Amsterdam: IOS Press.

Riva, G., & Waterworth, J. (2003). *Presence and the Self: a cognitive neuroscience approach*. Retrieved January 1, 2007, from http://presence.cs.ucl.ac.uk/presenceconnect/articles/Apr2003/jwworthApr72003114532/jwworthApr72003114532.html

Riva, G., Davide, F., & Ijsselsteijn, W. A. (2003). Being there: concepts, effects and measurements of user presence in synthetic environments. Amsterdam: IOS Press.

Rive, P. B. (2012). Design in a Virtual Innovation Ecology: A Cybernetic Systems Approach to Knowledge Creation and Design Collaboration in Second Life. Wellington, New Zealand: Victoria University of Wellington. Retrieved from http://researcharchive.vuw.ac.nz/handle/10063/2747

Rive, P. B., Thomassen, A., Lyons, M., & Billinghurst, M. (2008). *Face to Face with the White Rabbit: Sharing Ideas in Second Life*. Presented at the IEEE International Professional Communications Conference. doi:10.1109/IPCC.2008.4610236

Rive, P. B. (2008). Knowledge Transfer and Marketing in Second Life. In P. Zemliansky & K. St. Amant (Eds.), *Handbook of research on virtual workplaces and the new nature of business practices* (pp. 424–438). Hershey, PA: Information Science Reference. doi:10.4018/978-1-59904-893-2.ch030

Rive, P. B., & Thomassen, A. (2012). International Collaboration and Design Innovation in Virtual Worlds: Lessons from Second Life. In *Computer-Mediated Communication Across Cultures: International Interactions in Online Environments* (pp. 429–448). Hershey, PA: Information Science Reference - IGI Global.

Roberts, K. (2004). *Lovemarks: the future beyond brands*. Auckland, New Zealand: Reed.

Rogers, E. M. (2003). *Diffusion of Innovations* (5th ed.). Free Press.

Rosen, L. (2013). Always On, All the Time: Are We Suffering From FoMO? *Psychologytoday*. Retrieved November, 17, 2014, from http://www.psychologytoday.com/blog/rewired-the-psychology-technology/201305/always-all-the-time-are-we-suffering-fomo

Rosenberg, M. J. (2001). e-Learning: Strategies for delivering knowledge in the digital age. New York, NY: McGraw-Hill.

Rothwell, W. J., & Kazanas, H. C. (2008). *Mastering the instructional design process: A systematic approach* (4th ed.). San Francisco, CA: Pfeiffer.

Rutchick, A. M., Hamilton, D. L., & Sack, J. D. (2008). Antecedents of entitativity in categorically and dynamically construed groups. *European Journal of Social Psychology, 921*(May), 905–921.

Ryan, M.-L. (1999). Immersion vs. Interactivity: Virtual reality and literary theory. *SubStance, 28*(2), 110–137. doi:10.1353/sub.1999.0015

Rybas, N., & Gajjala, R. (2007). Developing Cyberethnographic Research Methods for Understanding Digitally Mediated Identities. *Forum Qualitative Sozial Forschung, 8*(3). Retrieved from http://www.qualitative-research.net/index.php/fqs/article/viewArticle/282/619

Ryder, M. (2010). *Instructional design models & theories*. Retrieved from http://www.instructionaldesigncentral.com/htm/IDC_instructionaldesignmodels.htm

Saade, R., Kira, D., & Nebeb, F. (2012). *Understanding the role of personality traits on beliefs in online learning*. Retrieved October 11, 2015 from http://proceedings.informingscience.org/InSITE2012/InSITE12p613-624Saade0155.pdf

SAMHSA. (2014, Fall). Building the behavioral health workforce. *SAMHSA News, 22*(4). Retrieved April 12, 2015 from http://www.samhsa.gov/samhsaNewsLetter/Volume_22_Number_4/building_the_behavioral_health_workforce/

Schott, G., & Horrell, K. (2000). Girl gamers and their relationship with the gaming culture. *Convergence, 6*(4), 36–53.

Schultze, U., & Orlikowski, W. J. (2010). Research Commentary---Virtual Worlds: A Performative Perspective on Globally Distributed, Immersive Work. *Information Systems Research, 21*(4), 810–821. doi:10.1287/isre.1100.0321

Schultz, M. F. (2006). Fear and norms and rock & roll: What jambands can teach us about persuading people to obey copyright law. *Berkeley Technology Law Journal, 21*(651), 651–728.

Schutz, A. (1946). The well informed citizen: An essay on the social distribution of knowledge. *Social Research, 1*(3), 463–478. PMID:20285192

Schwartz, S. H., & Bilsky, W. (1990). Toward a Theory of the Universal Content and Structure of Values: Extensions and Cross-Cultural Replications. *Journal of Personality and Social Psychology, 58*(5), 878–891. doi:10.1037/0022-3514.58.5.878

Schweitzer, L., & Duxbury, L. (2010). Conceptualizing and measuring the virtuality of teams. *Information Systems Journal, 20*(3), 267–295. doi:10.1111/j.1365-2575.2009.00326.x

Scott, M. E. (2013). Communicate through the roof: A case study analysis of the communicative rules and resources of an effective global virtual team. *Communication Quarterly, 61*(3), 301–318. doi:10.1080/01463373.2013.776987

Second Life Librarians: Community Search. (2008). Retrieved January 2, 2008, from http://secondlife.com/community/search.php?search_terms=second+life+librarians&search_type=all&commit=Search&all_mature=n&events_mature=n&events_date_from=&events_date_to=&parcels_mature=n&parcels_max_price=&classifieds_mature=n&groups_mature=n

Segerstad, Y., & Weilenmann, A. (2013). Methodological challenges for studying cross-platform conversations.Selected Papers of Internet Research, 14.

Senge, P. (1990). *The fifth discipline: The art and practice of the learning organization.* New York, NY: Doubleday.

Serrano Tellería, A. (2014). Interface Design on Mobile Phones: The Delimitation of the Public and Private Spheres. In *Proceedings of Designa: Interface International Conference on Design Research.* LabCom, Beira Interior University.

Serrano Tellería, A. (2015b). Liquid Spheres or Constellations: Reflections Towards Mobile Devices. In Mobile and Digital Communication: Approaches to Public and Private (pp. 173-198). Covilhã, Portugal: LabCom Books, University of Beira Interior.

Serrano Tellería, A. (2015c). Emotion and Mobile Devices. In *Designa 'Desire', International Conference on Design Research.* Portugal: LabCom.

Serrano Tellería, A., & Branco, M. L. (2015) Educação para a privacidade no espaço digital: de subsídios para uma proposta curricular. In A Nova Fluidez de Uma Velha Dicotomia: Publico e Privado nas Comunicações Móveis. Covilhã, Portugal: Labcom books, University of Beira Interior.

Serrano Tellería, A. (2015a). The Role of the Profile and The Digital Identity on the Mobile Content. In J. M. Aguado, C. Feijóo, & I. J. Martínez (Eds.), *Emerging Perspectives on the Mobile Content Evolution. IGI Global.*

Serrano Tellería, A. (2015d). Twitter e a privacidade: a partilha de estratégias e ferramentas. In *IX Congresso SOPCOM: Associação Portuguesa de Ciências da Comunicação: Comunicação e Transformações Sociais.* University of Coimbra.

Serrano Tellería, A. (2015e). Reddit e a privacidade: uma análise das interacções e conversas. In: *IX Congresso SOPCOM: Associação Portuguesa de Ciências da Comunicação: Comunicação e Transformações Sociais.*University of Coimbra.

Serrano Tellería, A., & Oliveira, M. (2015). Liquid Spheres on Smartphones: The Personal Information Policies. *International Journal of Interactive Mobile Technologies*, *9*(1). Retrieved from http://online-journals.org/index.php/i-jim/article/view/4065

Serrano Tellería, A., & Pereira, P. (2015). Instagram e a visibilidade das imagens dos utilizadores. In J. R. Carvalheiro (Ed.), *Público e privado nas comunicações móveis* (pp. 297–316). Coimbra, Portugal: Minerva Coimbra.

Serrano Tellería, A., Portovedo, S., & Albuquerque, A. I. (2015). Negociações da privacidade nos dispositivos móveis. In J. R. Carvalheiro (Ed.), *Público e privado nas comunicações móveis* (pp. 119–158). Coimbra, Portugal: Minerva Coimbra.

Shafran, R., Clark, D. M., Fairburn, C. G., Arntz, A., Barlow, D. H., Ehlers, A., & Wilson, G. T. (2009). Mind the gap: Improving the dissemination of CBT. *Behaviour Research and Therapy*, *47*, 902–909. doi:10.1016/j.brat.2009.07.003 PMID:19664756

Shepherd, A., Sanders, C., Doyle, M., & Shaw, J. (2015). Using social media for support and feedback by mental health service users: Thematic analysis of a twitter conversation. *BMC Psychiatry*, *15*(1), 29. doi:10.1186/s12888-015-0408-y PMID:25881089

Shields, R. (2003). *The virtual*. London: Routledge.

Shirai, Y., Silverberg Koerner, S., & Baete Kenyon, D. Y. (2009). Reaping caregiver feelings of gain: The roles of socioemotional support and mastery. *Aging & Mental Health*, *13*(1), 106–117. doi:10.1080/13607860802591054 PMID:19197696

Shirky, C. (2005, July). *Institutions vs. collaboration*. [Video file]. Retrieved October 31, 2008, from http://www.ted.com/index.php/talks/clay_shirky_on_institutions_ versus_collaboration.html

Sipek, S. (2015). *Health care reform creates problems, and jobs to solve them*. Workforce®. Retrieved February 18, 2015 from http://www.workforce.com/articles/21035

Skoyles, J. R., & Sagan, D. (2002). Up from dragons: the evolution of human intelligence. New York: McGraw-Hill. Retrieved from http://www.loc.gov/catdir/bios/mh041/2001007857.htmlhttp://www.loc.gov/catdir/description/mh021/2001007857.html

Smith, E. (n.d.). *Learning to learn online*. Retrieved from http://www.ascilite.org.au/conferences/brisbane99/papers/smith.pdf

Smith, P. L., & Ragan, T. J. (2005). *Instructional design* (3rd ed.). Hoboken, NJ: John Wiley & Sons, Inc.

Smyth, J. M. (2007). Beyond self-selection in video game play: An experimental examination of the consequences of massively multiplayer online role-playing game play. *Cyberpsychology & Behavior*, *10*(5), 717–721. doi:10.1089/cpb.2007.9963 PMID:17927543

Social Security Administration. (2015). *Social Security Announces Vision 2025, a Long-Range Service Delivery Vision* [News release]. Retrieved from http://www.ssa.gov/news/press/releases.html#!/post/4-2015-8

Sohmen, V. S. (2015). Reflections on creative leadership. *International Journal of Global Business*, *8*(1), 1–14.

Squire, K. (2006). From content to context: Videogames as designed experience. *Educational Research*, *35*(8), 19–29. doi:10.3102/0013189X035008019

Srite, M. (2006). Culture as an explanation of technology acceptance differences: An empirical investigation of Chinese and US users. *Australasian Journal of Information Systems*, *14*(1), 5–23. doi:10.3127/ajis.v14i1.4

Stake, R. E. (1995). *The art of case study research*. Thousand Oaks, CA: Sage.

Stald, G. (2008). Mobile Identity: Youth, Identity, and Mobile Communication Media. In Youth, Identity, and Digital Media (pp. 143–164). Cambridge, MA: The MIT Press.

Starner, T. (2011). Multiplexing versus multitasking. *The Technium*. Retrieved 11 February 2014 from http://kk.org/thetechnium/2011/03/multiplexing-vs/

Steinkuehler, C. A. (2006, January). Why game (culture) studies now? *Games and Culture*, *1*(1), 97–102. doi:10.1177/1555412005281911

Stewart, T. A. (2001). *The wealth of knowledge: intellectual capital and the twenty-first century organization* (1st ed.). New York: Currency.

Stokoe, E. (2014). From talk to text-Using the "Conversation analytic role play method" to engage (potential) mediation clients in spoken and written communications. *Research on Language and Social Interaction, 47*(3).

Stone, L. (2002-2014). *Continuous Partial Attention*. Retrieved November 8, 2014, from http://lindastone.net/qa/continuous-partial-attention/

Stroebe, W., & Stroebe, M. (1996). *The social psychology of social support*. Academic Press.

Strubel, J., Pookulangara, S., & Murray, A. (2013). Musical identity online. *International Jouranl of Costume and Fashion, 13*(2), 15–29.

Subrahmanyam, K., & Greenfield, P. M. (1998). Computer games for girls: What makes them play. In J. Cassell & H. Jenkins (Eds.), From barbie to mrotal kombat: Gender and computer games. Cambridge, MA: The M.I.T. Press.

Sude, M. (2013). Text messaging and private practice: Ethical Challenges and guidelines for developing personal best practices. *Journal of Mental Health Counseling, 3*(3), 211–227. doi:10.17744/mehc.35.3.q37l2236up62l713

Sunstein, C. R. (2006). Infotopia: how many minds produce knowledge. Oxford, UK: Oxford University Press. Retrieved from http://ezproxy.aut.ac.nz/login?url=http://www.loc.gov/catdir/toc/ecip065/2005036052.htmlhttp://ezproxy.aut.ac.nz/login?url=http://www.loc.gov/catdir/enhancements/fy0635/2005036052-d.html

Sunstein, C. (2006). *Infotopia: How many minds produce knowledge*. London: Oxford University Press.

Surowiecki, J. (2004). *The wisdom of crowds*. New York, NY: Doubleday.

Tai, Z. (2006). *The Internet in China: Cyberspace and civil society*. New York: Routledge.

Tai, Z. (2010). Casting the ubiquitous net of information control: Internet surveillance in China from Golden Shield to Green Dam. *International Journal of Advanced Pervasive and Ubiquitous Computing, 2*(1), 53–70. doi:10.4018/japuc.2010010104

Talbot, D. (2008). The fleecing of the avatars. *Technology Review, 111*(1), 58–62.

Tapscott, D., & Williams, A. (2006). *Wikinomics: How mass collaboration changes everying*. New York: Portfolio.

Tapscott, D., & Williams, A. D. (2006). *Wikinomics: how mass collaboration changes everything*. New York: Portfolio.

Tavinor, G. (2005, April). Videogames and interactive fiction. *Philosophy and Literature, 29*(1), 24–40. doi:10.1353/phl.2005.0015

Taylor, M. C. (1997). *Hiding*. Chicago: University of Chicago Press.

Teece, D. J. (2000). *Managing intellectual capital: organizational, strategic, and policy dimensions*. Oxford, UK: Oxford University Press.

Texas Department of State Health Service. (2014). *The mental health work shortage in Texas*. Retrieved March 19, 2015 from http://www.dshs.state.tx.us/legislative/2014/Attachment1-HB1023-MH-Workforce-Report-HHSC.pdf

Thatcher, S., & Brown, S. A. (2010). Individual creativity in teams: The importance of communication media mix. *Decision Support Systems*, *49*(3), 290–300. doi:10.1016/j.dss.2010.03.004

The Compact edition of the Oxford English dictionary: complete text reproduced micrographically. (1971). Oxford, UK: Clarendon Press.

Thomas, K. (2009, November/December). The four intrinsic rewards that drive employee engagement. *Ivey Business Journal: Improving the Practice of Management The Workplace*.

Thomas, S. (1994). Artifactual study in the analysis of culture: A defense of content analysis in a postmodern age. *Communication Research*, *21*(6), 683–697. doi:10.1177/009365094021006002

Thomassen, A. (2003). *In Control: Engendering a continuum of flow of a cyclic process within the context of potentially disruptive GUI interactions for web based applications*. Utrecht, The Netherlands: Hogeschool Voor De Kunsten Utrecht.

Thomassen, A., & Rive, P. (2010). How to enable knowledge exchange in Second Life in design education? *Learning, Media and Technology*, *35*(2), 155–169. doi:10.1080/17439884.2010.494427

Thomson, R., Ito, N., Suda, H., Lin, F., Liu, Y., Hayasaka, R., ... Wang, Z. (2012). *Trusting tweets: The Fukushima disaster and information source credibility on Twitter*. Presented at the 9th International ISCRAM Conference, Vancouver, Canada.

Thurlow, C., & Mroczek, K. (Eds.). (2011, October 26). Digital discourse: Language in the new media. Cambridge, MA: Oxford University Press. doi:10.1093/acprof:oso/9780199795437.001.0001

Tierney, P., Farmer, S. M., & Graen, G. B. (1999). An examination of leadership and employee creativity: The relevance of traits and relationships. *Personnel Psychology*, *52*(3), 591–620. doi:10.1111/j.1744-6570.1999.tb00173.x

Tiffin, J. (1995). *In Search of the Virtual Class: Education in an Information Society*. London: RoutledgeFalmer. doi:10.4324/9780203291184

Tiffin, J., & Rajasingham, L. (2003). *The Global Virtual University*. London: RoutledgeFalmer. doi:10.4324/9780203464670

Tobin, T. J. (2015). *Your leadership story: Use your story to energize, inspire, and motivate*. Oakland, CA: Berrett-Koehler.

Tong, Y., Yang, X., & Teo, H. H. (2013). Spontaneous virtual teams: Improving organizational performance through information and communication technology. *Business Horizons*, *56*(3), 361–375. doi:10.1016/j.bushor.2013.01.003

Townsend, A. M., DeMarie, S. M., & Hendrickson, A. R. (1998). Virtual teams: Technology and the workplace of the future. *The Academy of Management Executive*, *12*(3), 17-29.

Trueman, R. B., Peters, T., & Bell, L. (2007). Get a Second Life! Libraries in virtual worlds. In R. S. Gordon (Ed.), *Information tomorrow: Reflections on technology and the future of public and academic libraries* (pp. 159–171). Medford, NJ: Information Today.

Turkle, S. (2008). Always-On / Always-on-You": The Tethered Self. In J. E. Katz (Ed.), *Handbook of Mobile Communications Studies* (pp. 121–138). Cambridge, MA: MIT Press. doi:10.7551/mitpress/9780262113120.003.0010

Turkle, S. (2011). *Alone Together: Why We expect More from Technology and Less From Each Other?* New York: Basic Books.

Turner, F. (2006). *From counterculture to cyberculture: Stewart Brand, the Whole Earth Network, and the rise of digital utopianism*. Chicago: University of Chicago Press. doi:10.7208/chicago/9780226817439.001.0001

U.S. Census Bureau. (2013). *Computer and Internet Use Main*. Retrieved March 31, 2015 from http://www.census.gov/hhes/computer/

U.S. National Center for Educational Statistics Digest of Educational Statistics. (2011). *School enrollment with projections* (Table 219). Retrieved from http://www.census.gov/compendia/statab/cats/education.html

U.S. National Center for Educational Statistics. (2011). Programs and Plans of the National Center for Education Statistics 2005 Edition. *Education Statistics Quarterly, 7*(1), 1-11. Retrieved from http://nces.ed.gov/pubs2006/2006614_1.pdf

Uchino, B. N., Cacioppo, J. T., & Kiecolt-Glaser, J. K. (1996). The relationship between social support and physiological processes: A review with emphasis on underlying mechanisms and implications for health. *Psychological Bulletin, 119*(3), 488–531. doi:10.1037/0033-2909.119.3.488 PMID:8668748

Valkenburg, P. M., Peter, J., & Schouten, A. P. (2006). Friend networking sites and their relationship to adolescents' well-being and social self-esteem. *Cyberpsychology & Behavior, 9*(5), 584–590. doi:10.1089/cpb.2006.9.584 PMID:17034326

van den Hoogen, W., IJsselsteijn, W., & de Kort, Y. (2008). *Exploring behavioral expressions of player experience in digital games*. Paper presented at the Workshop on Facial and Bodily Expression for Control and Adaptation of Games ECAG 2008, Amsterdam, The Netherlands.

Van Dijck, J. (2013). 'You have one identity': Performing the self on Facebook and LinkedIn. *Media, Culture & Society, 35*, 199. Retrieved November, 14, 2014, from http://mcs.sagepub.com/content/35/2/199

Van Dijck, J. (2007). *Mediated Memories in the Digital Age*. Stanford, CA: Stanford UP.

Van Dijck, J. (2014). Datafication, Dataism and Dataveillance: Big Data between Scientific Paradigm and Ideology. *Surveillance & Society, 2*(2), 197–208.

van Gelder, S. (2005). The new imperatives for global branding: Strategy, creativity and leadership. *The Journal of Brand Management, 12*(5), 395–404. doi:10.1057/palgrave.bm.2540234

Verdugo, M. A., Schalock, R. L., Keith, K. D., & Stancliffe, R. J. (2005). Quality of life and its measurement: Important principles and guidelines. *Journal of Intellectual Disability Research, 49*(10), 707–717. doi:10.1111/j.1365-2788.2005.00739.x PMID:16162115

von Hippel, E. (2005). Democratizing innovation. Cambridge, MA: MIT Press. Retrieved from http://mit.edu/evhippel/www/books.htm

Von Krogh, G., Nonaka, I., & Ichijo, K. (2000). *Enabling knowledge creation: how to unlock the mystery of tacit knowledge and release the power of innovation*. Oxford, UK: Oxford University Press. doi:10.1093/acprof:oso/9780195126167.001.0001

Vorderer, P., & Bryant, J. (2006). *Playing video games: Motives, responses, and consequences*. Mahwah, NJ: Lawrence Erlbaum Associates.

Vygotsky, L., & Luria, A. (1994). Tool and symbol in child development. In R. van der Veer & J. Valsiner (Eds.), *The Vygotsky reader* (pp. 99–174). Oxford, UK: Oxford University Press.

Walen, H. R., & Lachman, M. E. (2000). Social support and strain from partner, family, and friends: Costs and benefits for men and women in adulthood. *Journal of Social and Personal Relationships, 17*(1), 5–30. doi:10.1177/0265407500171001

Walker Rettberg, J. (2014). *Seeing Ourselves Through Technology: How We Use Selfies, Blogs and Wearable Devices to See and Shape Ourselves*. Palgrave Macmillan. Retrieved November, 8, 2014, from http://www.academia.edu/8482366/ Seeing_Ourselves_Through_Technology_How_We_Use_Selfies_Blogs_and_Wearable_Devices_to_See_and_Shape_ Ourselves

Walther, J. B., & Bunz, U. (2005). The rules of virtual groups: Trust, liking, and performance in computer-mediated communication. *Journal of Communication, 55*(4), 828–846. doi:10.1111/j.1460-2466.2005.tb03025.x

Walz, S. P. (2004). Delightful identification & persuasion: Toward an analytical and applied rhetoric of digital games. *Works and Days, 22*(1&2), 185–200.

Way, K., Ottenbacher, M., & Harrington, R. (2011). Is crowdsourcing useful for enhancing innovation and learning outcomes in culinary and hospitality education? *Journal of Culinary Science & Technology, 9*(4), 261–281. doi:10.10 80/15428052.2011.627259

Weick, K. E. (1991). The nontraditional quality of organizational learning. *Organization Science, 2*(1), 116–124. [RE-MOVED HYPERLINK FIELD] doi:10.1287/orsc.2.1.116

Weiser, E. B. (2001). The functions of Internet use and their social and psychological consequences. *Cyberpsychology & Behavior, 4*(6), 723–743. doi:10.1089/109493101753376678 PMID:11800180

Welbourne, J. L., Blanchard, A. L., & Wadsworth, M. B. (2013). Motivations in virtual health communities and their relationship to community, connectedness and stress. *Computers in Human Behavior, 29*(1), 129–139. doi:10.1016/j. chb.2012.07.024

Wellman, B. (2001). Physical Place and Cyberplace: The Rise of Personalized Networking. *International Journal of Urban and Regional Research, 25*(2), 227–252. doi:10.1111/1468-2427.00309

Wellman, B., & Gulia, M. (1997). Net Surfers don't ride alone: Virtual communities as communities. In P. Kollock & M. Smith (Eds.), *Communities in Cyberspace*. Routledge.

Wellman, B., & Gulia, M. (1999). Virtual communities as communities: Net surfers don't ride alone. In M. A. Smith & P. Kollock (Eds.), *Communities in cyberspace* (pp. 167–194). New York: Routledge.

Wellman, B., Haase, A. Q., Witte, J., & Hampton, K. (2001). Does the Internet increase, decrease, or supplement social capital? Social networks, participation, and community commitment. *The American Behavioral Scientist, 45*(3), 436–455. doi:10.1177/00027640121957286

Wertheim, M. (1999). *The pearly gates of cyberspace: a history of space from Dante to the Internet*. New York: W.W. Norton.

Western Interstate Commission for Higher Education. (n.d.). *Behavioral Health Workforce Development*. Retrieved February 26, 2015 from http://www.wiche.edu/mentalHealth/10926

Wiener, N. (1954). *The human use of human beings: cybernetics and society* (2nd ed.). New York: Doubleday.

Wiener, N. (1961). *Cybernetics: or control and communication in the animal and the machine* (2nd ed.). Cambridge, MA: M.I.T. Press. doi:10.1037/13140-000

Williams, D. (2006, March). Virtual cultivation: Online worlds, offline perceptions. *Journal of Communication, 56*(1), 69–87. doi:10.1111/j.1460-2466.2006.00004.x

Williams, D. D. (2002). The instructional use of learning objects. In D. Wiley (Ed.), *Evaluation of learning objects and instruction using learning objects* (pp. 173–199). Bloomington, IN: Agency for Instructional Technology and Association for Education Communications & Technology.

Williams, D., & Xiong, S. C. L. (2007). Can you hear me now? The impact of voice in an online gaming community. *Human Communication Research*, *33*(4), 427–449. doi:10.1111/j.1468-2958.2007.00306.x

Williams, M. (2007). Avatar watching: Participant observation in graphical online environments. *Qualitative Research*, *7*(1), 5–24. doi:10.1177/1468794107071408

Wolf, M. J. P. (2005). Genre and the video game. In J. Raessens & J. Goldstein (Eds.), Handbook of computer game studies (pp. 193-204). Cambridge, MA: The MIT Press.

Wolf, A. W., & Goldfried, M. R. (2014). Clinical Experiences in Using Cognitive-Behavior Therapy to Treat Panic Disorder. *Behavior Therapy*, *45*(1), 36–46. doi:10.1016/j.beth.2013.10.002 PMID:24411112

Wong, L., & Looi, C. (2012). Swarm intelligence: New techniques for adaptive systems to provide learning support. *Interactive Learning Environments*, *20*(1), 19–40. doi:10.1080/10494821003714681

Woodman, R. W., Sawyer, J. E., & Griffin, R. W. (1993). Toward a theory of organizational creativity. *Academy of Management Review*, *18*(2), 293–321.

Woolfolk, A. (2011). *Educational psychology: Active learning edition* (11th ed.). Boston, MA: Pearson.

Yates, S. J., & Littleton, K. (1999, December). Understanding computer game cultures: A situated approach. *Information Communication and Society*, *2*(4), 566–583. doi:10.1080/136911899359556

Yee, N. (2006, January). The labor of fun: How video games blur the boundaries of work and play. *Games and Culture*, *1*(1), 68–71. doi:10.1177/1555412005281819

Ye, J., Xiong, X., & Wu, S. (2013). Dynamic model for anonymity measurement based on information entropy. *Journal of Internet Services and Information Security*, *4*(2), 27–37.

Yin, R. K. (2008). *Case study research: Design and methods*. Thousand Oaks, CA: Sage Publications, Inc.

Zaccaro, S. J. (2014). Leadership memes: From ancient history and literature to twenty-first century theory and research. In D. V. Day (Ed.), *The Oxford handbook of leadership and organizations* (pp. 13–39). doi:10.1093/oxfordhb/9780199755615.013.001

Zander, L., Mockaitis, A. I., & Butler, C. L. (2012). Leading global teams. *Journal of World Business*, *47*(4), 592–603. doi:10.1016/j.jwb.2012.01.012

Zhao, Y., Lei, J., Yan, B., Lai, C., & Tan, H. S. (2005). What Makes the Difference? A Practical Analysis of Research on the Effectiveness of Distance Education. *Teachers College Record*, *107*(8), 1836–1884. doi:10.1111/j.1467-9620.2005.00544.x

Zimmer, B., & Alexander, G. (1996). The Rogerian Interface: For Open, Warm Empathy in Computer-mediated Collaborative Learning. *Innovations in Education and Training International*, *33*(1), 13–21. doi:10.1080/1355800960330103

Zofi, Y. (2012). *A manager's guide to virtual teams*. Amacom.

About the Contributors

Bobbe Gaines Baggio (Ph.D.) is an accomplished author, speaker and educator. Her specific expertise is in how to use technologies to help people learn. She is currently the Associate Dean of Graduate Programs and online Learning at The American University in Washington, D.C. and former Director of the M.S. in Instructional Technology Management and B.A. in Organizational Leadership at La Salle University in Philadelphia, PA.

* * *

Latonia M. Ayscue, (Ph.D.) Instructional and Curriculum Designer, Professor, Human Resources Professional with experience in creating tools to inspire learners to reach their full potential. My passion for education kindled while young when my father emphatically pushed me to move on to pursue higher education. My understanding of how powerful education is the drive that inspires me to pursue provocative methods to reach learners. Experienced in designing and create learning environments where communication is deliberate and receptive, conducive to learning, engaging, challenging and stimulating but not frustrating and intimidating.

Anita Lynn Blanchard (Ph.D.) is an associate professor of Psychology and Organization Science at UNC Charlotte. She is the co-director of the VICE Research Group at UNC Charlotte. Her research focuses on professional and social virtual communities, online feelings of entitativity, and understanding the role of identity in groups and organizations for employee health and group functioning.

Petros Chamakiotis (Ph.D.) is a Lecturer in Information Systems in the School of Business, Management and Economics at the University of Sussex, UK, and the Secretary of the IFIP Working Group 9.5 on Virtuality & Society. His research interests include virtual teams, leadership, creativity, connectivity, and work-life boundaries. Until recently, he worked on an EPSRC-funded project, entitled Digital Brain Switch, exploring the implications of information and communication technologies (ICTs) for transitions across work-life boundaries. He earned his PhD from the University of Bath, UK, with the support of an EPSRC scholarship, and was previously with Royal Holloway and Birkbeck, both Colleges of the University of London, UK. Prior to becoming an academic, Petros worked in junior management positions in Madrid, Spain. He is fluent in English, Greek and Spanish.

Lesley Farmer (Ed.D.) is a Professor at California State University Long Beach, coordinates the Librarianship program and is the ASEC Department Chair. Dr. Farmer has worked as a library media teacher in K-12 school settings as well as in public, special and academic libraries. She served as International Association for School Librarianship VP Association Relations, chairs the IFLA School Libraries section, and coordinates the Education Section of Special Libraries Association professional development. Dr. Farmer recieved the 2011 ALA Beta Phi Mu Award for contribution to education, the 2015 SLA Anna Galler Award, and the ALA LIRT Library Recognition Award. Dr. Farmer is a frequent presenter and writer for the profession. Her latest books include *Information and Digital Literacies: A Curricular Guide for Middle and High School Librarians* (Rowman & Littlefield, 2015) and *Library Services for Youth with Autism Spectrum Disorders* (ALA, 2013).

Shahar Gur is a PhD student in the Organizational Science program at UNC Charlotte. She holds a bachelor's degree in Psychology from UNC Chapel Hill. Her research focuses on groups and prosocial workplace issues. She is a member of the VICE Research Group at UNC Charlotte.

Susanne Ingle, MSIS, MLIS, is a Corporate Digital Librarian and has eight years of experience researching and writing on various topics, to include behavioral health and education. She has supported a state-run Medical Library for substance abuse and mental health staff and has observed the challenges and opportunities in the behavioral health field, especially with regard to technology. She has also taught information systems courses at the college-level for a number of years to adult learners, developing first hand knowledge of learning styles and cultural barriers to technology adoption.

Yowei Kang (Ph.D.) is Assistant Professor at Degree Program of Creative Industries and Digital Film, Kainan University, Taiwan. His research interests focus on digital game research, technology and rhetoric, composition pedagogy using digital game technology, and teaching English as a second language (ESL).

Michelle Kowalsky is a Learning Design Librarian at Rowan University who assists undergraduates, graduate students, and their faculty in learning the art and science of research. She has been a teacher and librarian for 20 years, also at the K-12 level, and is a National Board Certified Teacher of Library Media. She has worked in college libraries, school libraries, corporate libraries, and public libraries throughout her career, and contributes to the profession as an Education and LIS professor. Her interests focus on the intersections between libraries and technologies, and also between learning and technologies. The communication of librarians and teachers, their work in information literacy and lesson design, and the results which these efforts have on student learning are her current areas of investigation.

Carol L. Kuprevich (Ed.D.) is an independent consultant in behavioral healthcare and is the Director of Community Planning, Program Development, and Training with the Delaware Department of Health and Social Services. She is on the advisory board of several university programs, on the board of directors for the National Association of Case Management and several non-profit service providers. She has degrees from the Pennsylvania State University, University of Detroit, and Wilmington University. Dr. Kuprevich has worked throughout the United States in consulting roles as well as in management and direct service within behavioral healthcare over the last few decades.

Xiaolong Liu, (Ph.D.) candidate in political science at Sun Yat-Sen University, is an associate professor in the Department of Humanities and Social Sciences at Guangdong Pharmaceutical University, China. His research focuses on the social and political effects of social media in China. He has published several articles exploring the changes of the political landscape in China with various Chinese academic journals. He is currently conducting a research project examining state regulations of social media in China. He is a visiting scholar in the College of Communication and Information at the University of Kentucky for a 2014-2015 academic year.

Niki Panteli (Ph.D.) is a Professor of Information Systems at the School of Management, Royal Holloway University of London, UK. She has done extensive research in the field of virtuality, virtual teams, online communities and computer-mediated communication systems. Within this field, she has studied issues of trust, creativity, conflict and collaborations in virtual, geographically dispersed environments. Her research has appeared in numerous management and Information Systems journals, such as Human Relations, Information Systems Journal, Communications of the ACM, Decision Support Systems, Information and Management and IEEE Transactions on Professional Communication, among others.

Pete Rive (Ph.D.) has researched and developed virtual reality, and virtual world solutions for education and business for the past fifteen years. He has also worked in the screen and digital content industry for thirty years and has chaired Film Auckland; the Auckland Screen and Digital Content Strategy; and Colab Advisory Board at Auckland University of Technology. He specialises in creative collaboration and design innovation in virtual worlds and has taught, presented, and be published on these topics.

Zixue Tai (Ph.D.) is Associate Professor in the College of Communication and Information at the University of Kentucky. He teaches undergraduate and graduate courses in media effects, world media systems, advanced multimedia, video game studies, and social media theory and practice. His research interests pertain to a multitude of issues in the new media landscape of China. He is the author of The Internet in China: Cyberspace and Civil Society (Routledge, hardback in 2006; paperback released in 2013), and is completing a book on gold farming in China. Besides contributions to about two dozen edited volumes, his numerous publications can also be found in journals such as International Communication Gazette, Journalism & Mass Communication Quarterly, New Media & Society, Journal of Communication, Sociology of Health & Illness, and Psychology & Marketing.

Ana Serrano Tellería, (Ph.D.) Beira Interior University, Faculty of Arts and Letters, is an Assistant Professor (Accredited by ANECA, Spanish National Official Agency). Posdoc, coordinator of 5 Ph.D candidates in the European FEDER project 'Public and Private in Mobile Communications' at LabCom, Beira Interior University, Portugal (April 2013 - 2015), European Union and MAIS CENTRO - Portuguese Government. Lecturer of Cyberculture (2013-14). Full grant (EEUU Embassy in Spain) for Seminar 'Entrepreneurial Journalism: A Renewed Hope' (2014), University of Cuenca, Spain. Extraordinary Ph.D Award (Creativity, innovation, impact and relevance; 2012), Ph.D. ('Initial Node Design on Cybermedia: A Comparative Study', 2010) and Bachelor in Journalism (2002) by the University of The Basque Country, Spain. Full grant (2006-08) and research contract (2008-10) to develop Ph.D by University of the Basque Country. First cycle of English Translation and Interpretation, University of Alicante, Spain (2000). Management of European projects and International Cooperation ones in Documenta (2012-13). Responsible of the Communication Department in the Territorial Development Agency "Campoo Los Valles" (2011).

Jamie S. Switzer (Ed.D.) received her doctorate in Educational Technology from Pepperdine University, and also holds degrees in Technical Communication from Colorado State University and Radio/TV/Film from Texas Christian University. She has over 26 years of research experience with virtual communication and new media technologies. Dr. Switzer conducts research on virtual environments, computer-mediated communication, new media technologies, and online mentoring. She has published several book chapters, such as in the The Handbook of Research on Virtual Workplaces and in the forthcoming Handbook on 3D3C Virtual Worlds, and in several different journals, including the Journal of Virtual Worlds Research.

Ralph V. Switzer (J.D., CPA) received his doctorate from the University of Illinois. Dr. Switzer was the University Mediation Officer at Colorado State University for five years, and also served as counsel to the U.S. Department of Justice. He has published several books, including the Research and Report Handbook. He has published a book chapter in the Handbook on 3D3C Virtual Worlds. He has published extensively in journals, including Journal of Virtual Worlds Research and the Journal of Business and Economic Perspectives. He has also been quoted in publications such as Smart Money Magazine, published by The Wall Street Journal.

Kenneth C. C. Yang (Ph.D.) is Professor in the Department of Communication at the University of Texas at El Paso, USA. His research focuses on new media, consumer behavior, and international advertising. Some of his many works have been published in Far Eastern University Communication Journal, International Journal of Consumer Marketing, Journal of Intercultural Communication Studies, and Telematics and Informatics.

Lisa Slattery Walker (Ph.D.) (formerly known as Rashotte) received her PhD in Sociology from the University of Arizona in 1998. She joined the UNC Charlotte faculty in 1998 and was promoted to Professor of Sociology and Organizational Science in 2010. Her research focuses on small group interaction, nonverbal behaviors, identity, emotions, gender, and expectations. She is the co-director of the VICE Research Group at UNC Charlotte.

Index

Printed in the United States
By Bookmasters